STUDY TEX

ACCA

Published by

Get Through Guides
Unit 2, 308A Melton Road
Leicester LE47SL
United Kingdom

Website: www.GetThroughGuides.co.uk

Email: enquiries@GetThroughGuides.co.uk

Student Support Forum: http://GetThroughGuides.co.uk/forum

Contents

About the paper

The syllabus is assessed by a three-hour paper-based examination.

The examination consists of seven 10 mark questions assessing knowledge of the law, and three 10 mark application questions.

New amendments

Knowledge of new examinable regulations will not be assessed until at least six calendar months after the last day of the month in which documents are issued or legislation is passed. The relevant cut-off date for the June examinations is 30 November of the previous year, and for the December examinations, it is 31 May of the same year.

GTG - Products

Study Text	Covers all learning outcomes in an informative and interactive way. Has plenty of test questions and examples to bring the theory alive. Where needed, our texts also have glossaries and extensive indexes.	
Question Bank	Exam standard questions have been put together, based on pilot papers, past exam questions and others that we believe are likely to come up. Detailed explanations have been given for the right and wrong answers, to enhance your understanding	
Key Notes	These pocket size revision aids help ensure you have understood the most important parts of the syllabus. They are diagrammatic, concise and memorable!	
Trial exams	These practice exams are for you to gauge whether your understanding is correct.	

For colleges/tuition providers adopting our materials, GTG also produces:

Student Notes	These notes cover the core areas of the syllabus in an enlightening and interactive manner. They include lots of diagrams and mnemonics to make it a more interesting experience for the student (and the tutor!)	
Powerpoint slides	These slides make the material come to life, by including more case studies and step by step ways to solving problems.	

Syllabus

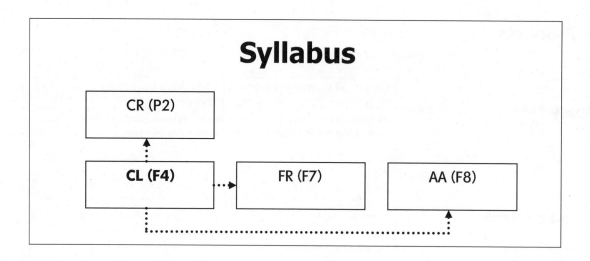

AIM

To develop knowledge and skills in the understanding of the general legal framework, and of specific legal areas relating to business, recognising the need to seek further specialist legal advice where necessary.

MAIN CAPABILITIES

On successful completion of this paper candidates should be able to:

A   Identify the essential elements of the legal system, including the main sources of law

B   Recognise and apply the appropriate legal rules relating to the law of obligations

C   Explain and apply the law relating to employment relationships

D   Distinguish between alternative forms and constitutions of business organisations

E   Recognise and compare types of capital and the financing of companies

F   Describe and explain how companies are managed, administered and regulated

G   Recognise the legal implications relating to companies in difficulty or in crisis

H   Demonstrate an understanding of governance and ethical issues relating to business.

RELATIONAL DIAGRAM OF MAIN CAPABILITIES

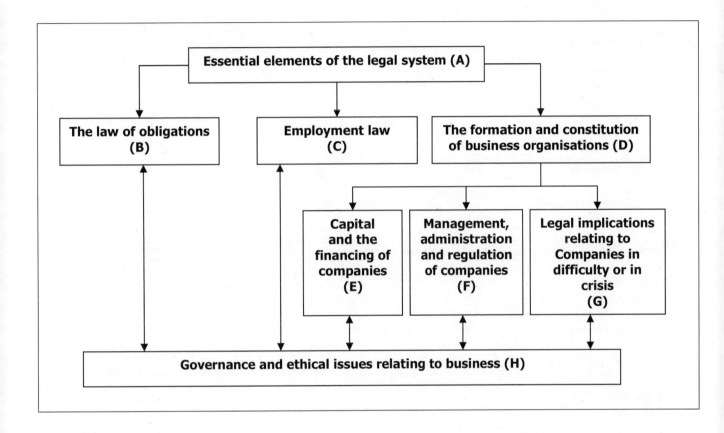

RATIONALE

Corporate and Business Law is divided into eight areas. The syllabus starts with an introduction to the overall English legal system such as the court system and sources of law – including – human rights legislation. It then leads into the area of the law of obligations including contract and tort, which underpin business transactions generally.

The syllabus then covers a range of specific legal areas relating to various aspects of business of most concern to finance professionals. These are the law relating to employment and the law relating to companies. These laws include the formation and constitution of companies, the financing of companies and types of capital, and the day-to-day management, the administration and regulation of companies and legal aspects of companies facing difficulty or in crisis.

The final section links back to all the previous areas. This section deals with corporate governance, ethics and ethical behaviour relating to business including criminal law.

DETAILED SYLLABUS

A   Essential elements of the legal system

1. Court structure
2. Sources of law
3. Human rights

B   The law of obligations

1. Formation of contract
2. Content of contracts
3. Breach of contract and remedies
4. The law of torts
5. Professional negligence

C   Employment law

1. Contract of employment
2. Dismissal and redundancy

D   The formation and constitution of business organisations

1. Agency law
2. Partnerships
3. Corporations and legal personality
4. Company formations

E   Capital and the financing of companies

1. Share capital
2. Loan capital
3. Capital maintenance and dividend law

F   Management, administration and regulation of companies

1. Company directors
2. Other company officers
3. Company meetings and resolutions

G   Legal implications relating to companies in difficulty or in crisis

1. Insolvency

H   Governance and ethical issues relating to business

1. Corporate governance
2. Fraudulent behaviour

SECTION A - ESSENTIAL ELEMENTS OF THE LEGAL SYSTEM

COURT STRUCTURE

Before studying the court structure we have to understand why the court structure came into existence. As civilisations grew, and people began to live together in large communities, conflicts were inevitable. In order to settle disputes, shared values and customs eventually became formal laws. In time, courts were established to enforce these laws.

The development of laws, with courts to enforce them, meant that similar actions were then treated in a similar way. People could understand, ahead of time, what the consequences of their actions would be.

The United Kingdom of Great Britain and Northern Ireland consists of four countries forming three distinct jurisdictions each having its own legal and judicial system: England & Wales, Scotland, and Northern Ireland. However, many Parliament Acts also apply to all these jurisdictions.

As an accountant you will be working for an organisation that operates within a national legal system. Basic awareness of the English legal system will help you as a professional to understand the legal framework within which you generally have to operate, not matter where you are in the world. This Study Guide gives you an outline of the court structure existing in UK.

This topic is mainly covered as a straightforward section A question in your examination.

LEARNING OUTCOMES

a) Define law and distinguish types of law
b) Explain the structure and operation of the courts and tribunals systems

Introduction

Why does it matter whether an offence is civil or criminal?

If you are involved in the judicial process, or if you are thinking of taking your case to court, it's important to understand whether civil or criminal law applies because the procedure for each is different. Lots of people think that you only go to court if you are being charged with a crime but that is not true. You can go to court with a variety of different problems and not all of them are about crime.

Most housing problems will be dealt with by civil law but there might be situations in which criminal law is relevant. For example, if you are being accused of behaving in an antisocial way in your neighbourhood, it could cause problems with your landlord but you might also be charged with breach of the peace or a more serious criminal offence.

1. Define law and distinguish types of law

[Learning outcome a]

Meaning of law

> **Definition**
>
> Law is defined as a rule or body of rules of conduct inherent in human nature and essential and binding upon human society.

> **Definition**
>
> Law means the rules established by a governing authority to institute and maintain orderly co-existence.

These are the rules required to regulate the actions of the people and they are an essential element of any community. If any of the rules are broken then penalty and punishments can be imposed.

Types of law

The law is broadly divided in two types: Civil Law and Criminal Law.

Diagram 1: Types of law

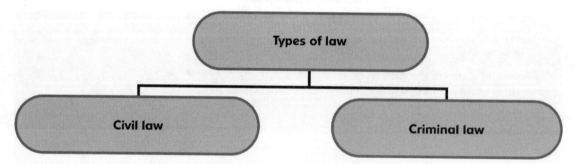

1. Civil law

Civil law is about the rights and obligations of individuals and organisations. It governs the relationship between private individuals. **This law is mainly concerned with arguments between individuals and organisations.** Civil law affects almost every aspect of one's daily life.

Example

It resolves disputes related to:
- ➤ our personal relationships within families
- ➤ neighbours
- ➤ members of communities
- ➤ our work (whether as employees, employer or entrepreneurs),
- ➤ our leisure time (as shoppers and consumers)

Civil law is not concerned with punishment as such but mainly tries to compensate the victims for the damage they suffered. The result of any civil law case is normally financial compensation.

Civil law affects a wider range of activities. Yet, it produces fewer cases in court because most are settled before they reach court.

Civil law disputes includes

a) The law of contract

Example

Buying a bus ticket or a CD involves entering into a contract. Any disputes among the parties to contract are dealt with under civil law.

---

b) A major part of commercial law including specialised areas such as banking, bankruptcy, insurance, shipping etc.

c) The law of torts (damage or injury – see later chapter).

Example

Torts of trespass to land or defamatory statements are actionable under civil law.

---

d) Family law deals with issues of marriage and children.

e) The law of property : this deals with
➢ Ownership of land
➢ Property transactions - boundary disputes, trespass
➢ Establishment of trusts (property held on behalf of others)
➢ Distribution of property of deceased persons

f) Work-related disputes

Example

Disputes relating to unfair dismissal, personal injury etc

---

g) Consumer disputes

Example

Disputes relating to supply of faulty goods

---

h) Copyright or intellectual property disputes

Example

Music sampling, plagiarism (copying someone else's material and passing it off as your own)

Civil cases are brought before civil courts by claimants, who are usually private individuals or companies. The claimant sues the defendant; therefore, a civil case is referred to as, for example, **James v John.**

Civil cases are first dealt with by County Courts and the High Court. If the parties to the suit are not satisfied with the decision of these first courts, they may appeal to Appellate Courts. These are the Divisional Court (part of the High Court), the Court of Appeal, the House of Lords and the Judicial Committee of the Privy Council. The hierarchy of courts is discussed in detail later in this Study Guide.

The degree of proof in civil law cases is lower. The cases are primarily judged on the basis of balance of probabilities

If the case is proven, the defendant normally compensates the claimant by payment of monetary damages. Sometimes, the claimant may be able to obtain a court order to stop the defendant from committing further intrusions or attacks - this is called an injunction.

2. Criminal law

Criminal law, on the other hand, punishes people for wrongful acts done by them. **The criminal process focuses on punishing the accused, not compensating the victims of the crime.**

Example

If someone attacks another person with a knife, they will be dealt with under criminal law.

Criminal law deals with crime. A crime is an act or omission prohibited and punishable by law. A 'criminal offence' includes any infringement of the criminal law i.e. breaking of the rules administering the society. Criminal offences range from small offences to severe offences.

Example

Severe crimes like murder and rape are dealt with by criminal law as are some minor crimes like speeding or causing a disturbance in the street.

In criminal law, the suit is initiated by the state or federal government through a prosecutor unlike civil law, where the suit is initiated by the victim. In criminal cases, the parties are referred to as, for example, the Crown against Peter **not versus** and will be cited R. v. Peter. Most case indexes use the initial letter "R' ('R' signifying the Regina, the Queen).

In a criminal case, the defendant must be proven guilty "beyond reasonable doubt."

Example O.J. Simpson trial

It was not proven "beyond reasonable doubt" that he murdered his wife. So he was not punished under criminal law. In the subsequent civil trial on the basis of "balance of probabilities' it was proven that he was responsible for her death. This led to financial compensation to the victim's family.

The person guilty of criminal offences may be punished by way of fines or imprisonment or both.

It is important to note that one incident can give rise to both a civil as well as a criminal action.

Example

If a drunken driver accidentally kills someone, the police, acting for the state, may arrest and charge the driver under the Criminal Code. This is because the driver's action is regarded as a wrong against society as a whole, and accordingly should be punished through the criminal law process. If found guilty, the driver could be sentenced to serve a jail term and / or pay a fine (which would go to the state, not to the victim's family).

The victim's family, on the other hand, have the right to file a civil law suit for damages. If the court finds that the driver (the defendant) committed a serious wrong against the family (the claimant), it can order the driver to pay compensation to the family for any suffering or economic loss they have suffered.

Test yourself 1

Distinguish between civil law and criminal law.

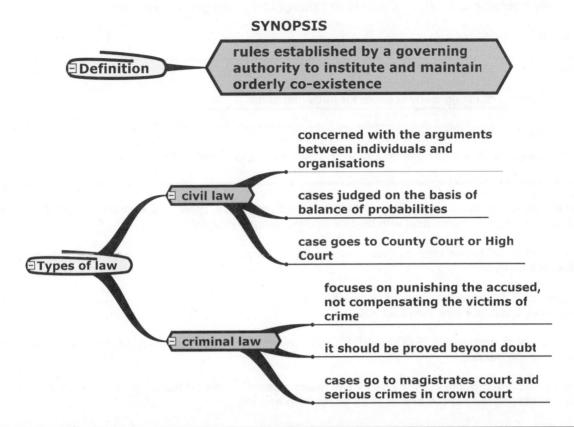

SYNOPSIS

⊟ Definition — rules established by a governing authority to institute and maintain orderly co-existence

⊟ Types of law
- ⊟ civil law
  - concerned with the arguments between individuals and organisations
  - cases judged on the basis of balance of probabilities
  - case goes to County Court or High Court
- ⊟ criminal law
  - focuses on punishing the accused, not compensating the victims of crime
  - it should be proved beyond doubt
  - cases go to magistrates court and serious crimes in crown court

2. Explain the structure and operation of the courts and tribunals systems
[Learning outcome b]

The two important civil courts are the County Court and High Court. All civil cases are filed to these courts first.

The High Court is divided into three parts:
a) Chancery Division
b) Family Division and
c) Queen's Bench Division.

If the claimant is not satisfied with the result in the above courts, he may appeal further. Depending upon the subject matter of the case, appeals can be filed with:

➢ The Divisional Court which is a part of the High Court,
➢ Employment Appeal Tribunal,
➢ Court of Appeal and
➢ Judicial Committee of the House of Lords,

2.1 Civil court structure in the UK

The civil court structure comprises the following:

1. Magistrates' courts: Magistrates' courts have a **significant, although limited, civil jurisdiction**. They mainly deal with:

➢ Family proceedings under the Domestic Proceedings and Magistrates' Courts Act (DPMCA) 1978 and the Children Act (CA) 1989. In such cases the court is termed a 'family proceedings court'.

➢ Adoption proceedings

➢ Maintenance relating to spouses and children

➢ Under the DPMCA 1978, the court also has the power to make personal protection orders and exclusion orders in cases of matrimonial violence

➢ Applications for residence and contact orders (CA 1989)

➤ Recovery in relation to council tax arrears and charges for water, gas and electricity

➤ Licences

Example

Granting, renewing or taking away licences for pubs and clubs

---

Tips

Magistrates' courts have no jurisdiction over claims in contract or tort.

---

2. County Court: Claims of small value are filed in a County Court. There is a network of 250 County Courts around the country which also deal with divorce and bankruptcy matters.

Before the 1999 civil justice reforms, jurisdiction of the County Courts and the High Court was **split on a strict financial limit basis** as:

➤ County court cases with a value of less than £25,000
➤ High court cases of more than £50,000

Cases of a value between £25,000 and £50,000 were allocated according to the complexity and the importance of the matter.

The new civil system brought in by the 1999 civil justice reforms works on the basis of the court, upon receipt of the claim, allocating the case to one of three tracks for a hearing.

These tracks are: the small claims track, the fast track and the multi-track

a) Small claims track: The small claims track provides a simple and informal way of resolving disputes. A claimant is allowed to file a suit without a solicitor.

The amount in dispute should be less than £5,000.
With court approval, this track can also be used for cases involving claims exceeding £5,000.

The types of claim are usually:

➤ consumer claims (e.g. goods sold, faulty goods or workmanship).
➤ accident claims.
➤ disputes about ownership of goods.
➤ disputes between landlords and tenants about repairs, deposits, rent arrears. **But disputes about possession of property are not dealt with by the small claims track.**

The proceedings of the small claims track are very informal. There are limited grounds of appeals. The small claims are dealt with by a single district judge.

b) Fast track: Cases most commonly dealt with are routine personal injury cases and consumer cases.

The amount in dispute would normally be more than £5,000 but less than £15,000.

Timetable and evidence needed: The cases allocated to the fast track will generally require only limited 'disclosure'. A period of 30 weeks is allowed to prepare for the trial and for written expert evidence (if needed). The fast track trial lasts for no more than one day (five hours).

The fast track claims are dealt with by a single Circuit Judge.

c) Multi-track: The multi-track deals with complex cases under £15,000 and any cases more than £15,000.

Tips

Quick revision

1. The **Small claims track** - £5,000 or less
2. The **Fast track** - £5,000 to £15,000
3. The **Multi-track** - £15,000 plus

Example

1) Suit for compensation for faulty services provided by dry-cleaners. The amount claimed was £3,000.
   As the amount of the **claim is less than £5,000**, it will be dealt with by the **small claims track.**
2) Suit for compensation against the seller for selling faulty televisions. The amount claimed was £8,100.
   As the amount of the **claim is more than £5, 000 but less than £15, 000**, it will be dealt with by the **fast track.**
3) Disputes between landlords and tenants for rent arrears. The amount claimed was £20,000.
   As the amount of the **claim is more than £15, 000**, it will be dealt with by the **Multi-track.**

Test yourself 2

Identify which track will deal with the cases given below:

1) Suit for compensation for faulty services provided by a garage. The amount claimed was £5,000.
2) Suit for compensation against the seller for selling faulty washing machines. The amount claimed was £38,000.
3) Suit for compensation against landlord for not making repairs to the rented property. The amount claimed was £9,900.
4) Dispute relating to possession of property. The amount claimed was £1,700

3. High Court: More substantial civil claims (over around £25,000) are heard in the High Court. The High Court is organised into three divisions according to **case type**. The administrative divisions of High Court are: the Chancery Division, the Queen's Bench Division and the Family Division.

a) Chancery Division: The work of the Chancery Division covers a broad spectrum. It deals with many different matters including:

➢ Disputes between landlord and tenant relating to property
➢ Disputes relating to intellectual property
➢ Disputes relating to patents
➢ Disputes relating to trademarks
➢ Disputes relating to copyright and
➢ Disputes relating to passing-off
➢ Matters relating to insolvency
➢ Commercial frauds and business disputes
➢ Matters relating to the management of companies.
➢ This division also deals with the trusts, tax, partnerships, bankruptcy, sale of land etc.

b) Family Division: The Family Division mainly deals with:

➢ Family proceedings including divorce. Divorce is mainly dealt with through County Courts but the High Court hears a number of small but contested cases.
➢ Children's cases including abuse, domestic violence, and adoption
➢ Child welfare matters involving
✓ Cases brought by child protection agencies
✓ Cases brought by local authorities
✓ Cases brought by parents and guardians regarding custody and access
➢ Administration of wills

c) Queen's Bench Division: This deals with all the remaining business of the High Court – disputes over contracts or torts or land. The Queen's Bench also has some specialist sub-divisions including:

i.   A Commercial Court
ii. A Crown Office List that deals with actions against public authorities and
iii. An admiralty court that deals with shipping matters.

The Commercial and Admiralty courts cover issues and claims relating to:

➢ business documents or contracts
➢ export or import of goods
➢ carriage of goods by land, sea, air or pipeline
➢ exploitation of oil and gas reserves or other natural resources
➢ insurance and re-insurance
➢ banking and financial services

> operation of markets and exchanges
> purchase and sale of commodities
> construction of ships
> business agencies
> arbitration

4.The Court of Appeal (Civil division)

The Court of Appeal was established by the Judicature Act 1873. The court hears appeals from

a) The three divisions of the High Court i.e.
   > Divisional Court of the Queens Bench
   > Divisional Court of the Chancery Division
   > Divisional Court of the Family Division
b) The County Courts
c) The Employment Appeal Tribunal
d) The Lands Tribunal and
e) The Transport Tribunal.

The most senior judge is the Master of the Rolls. Usually, three judges hear an appeal. But for very important cases there could be five judges to hear an appeal.

5. The House of Lords

The House of Lords is the final court of appeal in civil as well as criminal law. Most appeals reaching the House of Lords come from the Court of Appeal. There is also a 'leapfrog' procedure whereby an appeal may go to the Lords directly from the High court. This happens when the High Court judge certifies the case as being suitable for the Lords to hear and the House of Lords allows this.

Usually, five Lords hear an appeal but seven Lords sometimes hear very important cases on fact of law.

Tips	Summary: the system of appeal in civil cases

> From a County Court or the High Court, there is an appeal to the civil division of the Court of Appeal.
> From the High Court, there may be an appeal to the House of Lords on a matter of legal importance.
> From the Court of Appeal, there can be an appeal to the House of Lords on fact or law, but usually an appeal is only allowed on matters of legal importance.

6. The European court of Justice

The function of the ECJ, which is at Luxembourg, is to ensure that in the interpretation and application of the EEC Treaty (1957) the law is observed.

The court is the ultimate authority on European Community law. By virtue of the European Communities Act 1972, European law has been enacted into English law. So the decisions of the court have a direct impact upon the English jurisdiction.

7.The European Court of Human Rights

The ECHR, which is at Strasbourg, is the final court of appeal in relation to matters concerning the 1950 European Convention on Human Rights. The United Kingdom has now made the 1950 European Convention on Human Rights a part of its domestic law through the enactment of the Human Rights Act 1998.

Diagram 2: Civil court structure

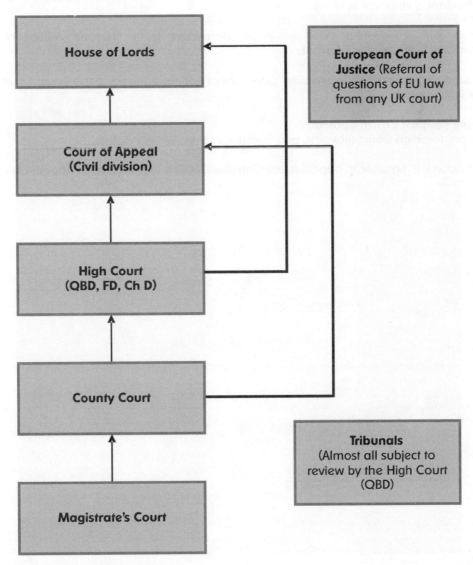

2.2 The criminal court structure in the UK

The criminal court structure comprises the following:

1. Magistrates' court:: Most criminal cases which come to the Magistrates' court are of a less serious nature

---

Example

Cases involving minor theft or shoplifting are normally dealt with by the magistrates' courts.

These are sent for summary trial in one of about 400 Magistrates' courts. A summary trial is before a bench of magistrates. In most cases, there are three magistrates who are lay people – they are not professional judges. Like the jury they come from the local community.

Some cases are presided over by a district judge or a stipendiary magistrate. These are legally qualified and salaried people.

Magistrates cannot normally order sentences of imprisonment which exceed six months or fines exceeding £5,000. Offenders may be sent by the magistrates to the Crown Court if a more severe sentence is thought necessary.

From the Magistrate's Court, appeals go to the Crown Court on matters of fact or law.

2. Crown Court: Verdicts on the more serious criminal offences, including murder, rape and robbery, are given by the Crown Court. It also hears appeals against the decisions of the Magistrates' Courts. There is only one Crown Court. However, it has 78 centres across England and Wales.

A judge and jury must be present at a Crown Court trial. The judge presides over the trial process and decides on legal issues such as whether evidence is admissible. The jury decides whose version of events is more believable, what the facts of the case are and how the law applies to these facts. In doing so, the jury decides whether the defendant is innocent or guilty.

In criminal cases, the prosecution must prove the defendant guilty "beyond reasonable doubt." This requirement is known as the burden of proof.

3. Criminal Division of the Court of Appeal: The Court of Appeal normally sits at the Royal Courts of Justice in London. It deals with appeals in

➢ Criminal cases from the Crown Court and
➢ Civil cases from the High Court, tribunals, and in certain cases, County Courts.

From the Crown Court it is possible to appeal to the Criminal Division of the Court of Appeal on matters of fact of law.

Diagram 3: Court Structure in England and Wales

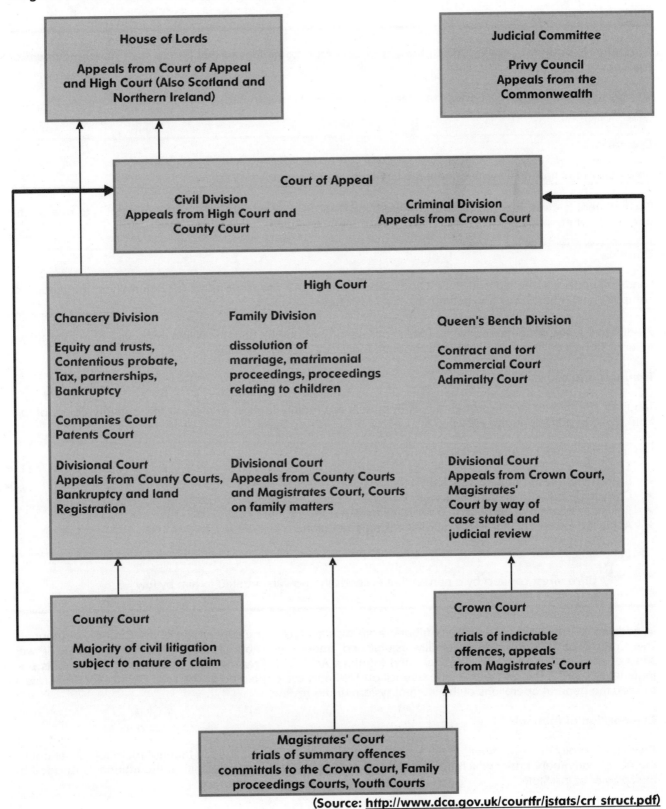

(Source: http://www.dca.gov.uk/courtfr/jstats/crt struct.pdf)

2.3 Tribunal system

A large number of tribunals have been established in Britain since 1945. The basic intention behind the establishment and growth of tribunals was to provide a specialist forum to resolve the conflicts between the welfare state functionaries and private citizens. Tribunals mainly deal with conflicts between the general public and government departments.

> **Definition**
>
> A tribunal is an assembly to conduct judicial business.

A tribunal is an independent judicial body that acts as a court for specific issues such as employment or transport.

Various tribunals are set up **under the various Acts of Parliament** which work as an alternative to the court system.

Example

An employment tribunal is set up under the Employment Tribunals Act 1996

Each tribunal is given a particular area of operation. The primary responsibility of the tribunal is to rule on the operations of the particular scheme established under those Acts.

Example

Lands tribunals established under the Lands Tribunal Act 1949 are responsible for determining the legality of compulsory purchase orders over land, the level of compensation etc.

---

70 different types of administrative tribunals operate throughout the country. Within each type of administrative tribunal, hundreds of individual tribunals operate locally all over the country.

Tribunals and courts

Tribunals are inferior to the normal courts. Tribunals are mainly formed to prevent the ordinary courts of law from being overburdened by cases.

Tribunals are subject to judicial review if: they

➢ Breach the rules of natural justice or
➢ Carry their duties in an ultra vires way or
➢ Refuse to hear an application in a wrongful manner or
➢ Apply the law in an improper way while taking a decision.

> **Tips**
>
> **Ultra-vires:** conduct by a person that exceeds the powers granted to him by law

In addition to the control of the courts, tribunals are also subject to the supervision of the Council on Tribunals. The Council of Tribunals was originally established under the Tribunals and Inquiries Act 1958. It was subsequently amended by the Tribunals and Inquiries Act 1971. Presently it is subject to the Tribunals and Inquiries Act 1992. The members of the Council on Tribunals are appointed by the Lord Chancellor. Their role is to keep the general operations of the tribunal system under review.

Composition of tribunals

There are usually three members in the tribunal. The procedure for nominating tribunal members is set out by the Act of Parliament under which the tribunal is set up. Usually, the membership of the tribunal is decided by the Minister of the State.

The chairman of the tribunal is expected to be a legally qualified person. The other two members are representatives from the society with specialist knowledge of the issues which the tribunal was set up to deal with. They possess administrative and technical knowledge of the issues to be dealt with by the tribunal. This helps the tribunal to base its decisions on actual practice.

> **Example**
>
> An employment tribunal's responsibility is to deal with employment-related issues. The panel of this tribunal usually includes a trade union representative and an employer's representative. As they possess experience and knowledge of the issues related to an employment relationship, they can analyse the situation in a better manner than a person with legal training but no first hand experience of the administrative aspects of an employment relationship.

Types of tribunal

Tribunals are of two types:
1) Administrative tribunals
2) Domestic tribunals

1. Administrative tribunals are set up under particular legislative provisions to deal with matters of public relevance. There are various tribunals working in various areas of operations.

Some of these tribunals are as follows:

a) Employment tribunals

Employment tribunals are formed to solve the disputes between employer and employee.

These are governed by the Employment Tribunals Act 1996. The composition of the tribunal, the major areas of competence of the members of the tribunal and the procedure for nominating tribunal members are set out by this Act.

Usually, an employment tribunal is made up of:

➢ A legally qualified chairman,
➢ A representative chosen from a panel representing employers and
➢ Another representative chosen from panel representing employees.

Employments tribunals have jurisdiction over various statutory provisions relating to employment issues and look into the matters including:

➢ Issues arising in relation to unfair dismissal
➢ Disputes in relation to redundancy
➢ Disputes in relation to race discrimination
➢ Claims against disability
➢ Disputes relating to the provision of maternity pay
➢ Various ancillary matters relating to trade union membership and activities.

The hearing at the tribunal is relatively informal. The parties at the hearing can represent themselves or are represented by:

➢ Solicitors or barristers or
➢ Trade union officials or
➢ Any other person they wish to represent them.

From the employment tribunal it is possible to appeal to the employment appeal tribunal on matters of fact of law.

b) Social security appeals tribunals

The function entrusted to the social security appeal tribunal is to **ensure** that the **discretionary powers delegated to the State functionaries** to implement the safety provisions **are not abused by these functionaries.**

A number of safety provisions are provided by various Social Security Acts with the objective of ensuring a basic standard of living in the society. To facilitate the achievement of this objective, the task of implementation of the related provisions of the Act is entrusted to various state functionaries. Considerable discretionary powers have been granted to these functionaries to enable them to implement the various complex provisions of the legislation. The tribunal has to ensure that the discretionary powers are used by the functionaries to meet the objective of the legislation.

These tribunals are responsible for hearing and deciding the correctness of the decisions made by adjudication officers. Adjudication officers are the people who actually determine the level of benefit that individuals are entitled to receive.

c) Immigration appeal tribunal

This tribunal's area is to hear appeals from individuals who have been refused entry into the UK or who have been refused permission to extend their stay in the UK.

d) Rents assessment committee

This committee deals with:
➢ Matters relating to rent charged for property
➢ Disputes between landlords and tenants

This committee has **powers to determine rent** for furnished and unfurnished tenancies.

This committee also hears appeals from decisions of rent officers.

2. Domestic tribunals: The internal disciplinary procedures of particular institutions are also termed 'tribunals". The institutions need not be necessarily those which are created under legislation. As opposed to administrative tribunals, domestic tribunals are mainly concerned with private matters.

Example

The disciplinary committees of professional institutions such as the Bar of Council, the Law Society or the British Medical Association are all termed tribunals. Their concern is limited to matters relating to these institutions only and not to the general public.

Various powers have been granted to domestic tribunals to ensure that they function smoothly.

The ordinary courts control the powers delegated to domestic tribunals to ensure that they do not breach the rules of natural justice and do not carry out their duties in an ultra vires way.

Advantages of tribunals:

➢ **Speed of operation:** Compared to ordinary courts, tribunals are much quicker to hear cases. The issues are discussed and finalised in a short span of time.

➢ **Law cost:** The tribunal procedure is much less expensive than using the ordinary courts to decide cases. There is no court fee involved in tribunal proceedings. Also, normally, no costs are awarded against the loser.

➢ **Informality in proceedings**: The strict rules relating to evidence, pleading and procedures which apply in courts are not binding in tribunal proceedings. The complainants need not be represented by a lawyer. The participants may express their views themselves or be represented by any other person.

➢ **Flexibility:** Tribunals are inferior and subject to the ordinary courts. Owing to this, they are governed by precedents in the courts. Still, they are not bound by the strict rules of precedents and can implement flexibility in their decision-making.

Tips

A precedent is a legal case establishing a principle or rule. It is studied in detail in SG A 2

➢ **Expertise:** Two out of the three members of a tribunal are common representatives with expert knowledge in the area of operation of the tribunal. Tribunals gain the advantage of their expert knowledge as against the more general legal expertise of the chairman.

➢ **Accessibility**: Tribunals provide an easily-accessible forum for individuals to seek redressal of their grievances.

Disadvantages of tribunals: Some of the weaknesses of the tribunal system are outlined below:

➤ There is no uniformity in relation to appeals against the decisions of the tribunal. To whom the appeal can be made against the decision of the tribunal depends on the provisions of the statute under which a particular tribunal operates.

➤ Issues of general public importance might not get due recognition and consideration.

➤ As the parties at the hearing can represent themselves or be represented by any other person, who need not be a lawyer, the representative may fail to represent himself effectively.

SYNOPSIS

- Court structure
  - civil court structure
    - Magistrates' Court
    - County Court
    - High Court
    - Court of Appeal (civil division)
    - House of Lords
    - European Court of Justice
    - European Court of Human Rights
  - criminal court structure
    - Magistrates' Court
    - Crown Court
    - Court of Appeal (criminal division)
- Tribunal
  - assembly to conduct judicial business
  - three members

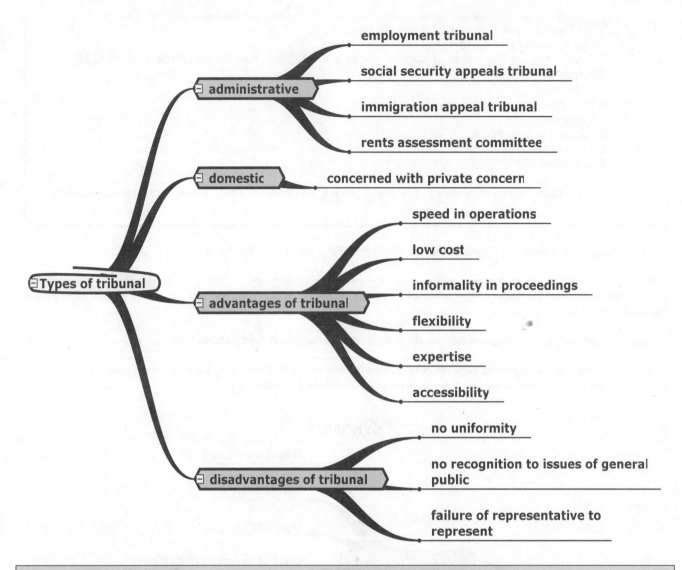

Answer to Test Yourself

Answer 1

Basis of distinction	Civil law	Criminal law
Meaning	It deals with the rights and duties of one individual to another. For example, if a person is not paid the agreed salary for the work done by him, it would be a civil matter.	It is concerned with establishing social order and protecting the community as a whole. It gives a set of rules for peaceful, safe and orderly living. For example, if someone attacks another person with knife this would be dealt by criminal law.
Who files the suit	The victim files the suit	The suit is filed by the state or federal government through a prosecutor.
Terminology used	A civil case is referred to as claimant and defendant e.g. James v John	A criminal prosecution is brought in the name of the Crown. A criminal case is referred to as R against defendant e.g. R v James
Burden of proof	A civil case is decided on the **balance of probabilities** (i.e. whether it is "likely" that the defendant has committed a wrong.	The prosecutor in a criminal law case has to prove to the judge or jury "**beyond reasonable doubt**" that the defendant is guilty of the crime charged.

Compensation	The party found guilty normally compensates the other party by the paying of damages	The guilty can be fined or sent to prison, or both.
Courts	A civil case goes to: ➢ **County Court** if the claim is less than £25,000 ➢ **High Court** if the claim is more than £50,000. ➢ Cases of a value between £25,000 and £50,000 are allocated according to the complexity and the importance of the matter. ➢ Court of Appeal ➢ House of Lords	A criminal case goes to: ➢ Magistrates' Court ➢ Youth Court in case of young people ➢ Crown Court (for serious crimes)

Answer 2

1) As the amount of the claim is **£5,000**, it will be dealt with by the **Small Claims Track.**
2) As the amount of the **claim is more than £15,000**, it will be dealt with by the **Multi-Track.**
3) As the amount of the **claim is more than £5,000 but less than £15,000**, it will be dealt via **Fast Track.**
4) Disputes about **possession of property** are **not dealt with by the Small Claims track** even though the amount claimed is **less than £5,000.**

Quick Quiz

State true or false

1) Multi-track deals only with cases involving claims of more than £15,000 in amount.

2) At a tribunal, the parties to the hearing can only be represented by solicitors.

3) An action for civil wrongs is brought by a claimant against the defendant whereas a suit for criminal offence is initiated by the state or federal government against the defendant.

4) Administrative tribunals are set up under the Acts of Parliament

5) Criminal cases are decided On the balance of probabilities

Answers to Quick Quiz

1) **False**, multi-track also deals with complex cases even if the claim is under £15,000.

2) **False**, the parties to the hearing can represent themselves or are represented by solicitors, barristers, trade union officials or any other person they wish to represent them.

3) **True**

4) **True**

5) **False**, in a criminal case, the defendant must be proven guilty "beyond reasonable doubt.

Self Examination Questions

Question 1

Explain the three track system for allocating cases between courts.

Answer to Self Examination Question

Answer 1

The 1999 civil justice reforms split the jurisdiction of the country courts from that of the High Courts on a strict financial limits basis as follows.

➢ Cases with a value of less than £25,000 are heard by country court.

➢ Cases with a value more than £50,000 are heard by the High Court.

➢ Cases of value between £25,000 and £50,000 are allocated to country courts or High Courts on the basis of complexities and the importance of the issues concerned.

According to the Civil Procedure Rules Part 26, cases in the county courts are assigned to one of three tracks: the multi-track, the fast track or the small claims track.

1) Small claims track (Civil Procedure Rules Part 27): The small claims track provides a simple and informal way of resolving disputes. The proceedings at small claim track are very informal. A claimant is not required to be represented by a solicitor.

The small claims track deals with cases where the amount in dispute is £5,000 or less. However, with the court's approval, this track can also be used for cases involving claims exceeding £5,000.

The **small claims track** usually deals with the following type of cases:

➢ Consumer claims (e.g. goods sold, faulty goods or workmanship),
➢ Accident claims
➢ Disputes about ownership of goods
➢ Disputes between landlords and tenants about repairs, deposits, rent arrears etc. However, disputes regarding the possession of the property are not dealt with by the small claims track.

The small claims are dealt by a single District Judge sitting alone.

2) Fast track (Civil Procedure Rules Part 28): This track mostly deals with routine personal injury and consumer cases.

The cases where the amount in dispute is more than £5,000 but less than £15,000 are normally allocated to the fast track.

The fast track trial lasts no more than one day (five hours).

The fast track claims are heard by a single circuit judge sitting alone.

3) Multi-track (Civil Procedure Rules Part 29): Multi-track deals with complex cases under £15, 000 and any cases in excess of £15,000.

SECTION A - ESSENTIAL ELEMENTS OF THE LEGAL SYSTEM

SOURCES OF LAW

Get through intro

Sources of law are recognised by a legal system as embodying rules and principles which have the force of law. The law is mainly derived from three sources: case law, legislation and the European community.

In common law systems, where law developed in the courts, most law and principles are found within decisions of the courts.

This Study Guide deals with the framework of the law which includes how the law is created, what is the procedure to be followed for applying the law, how the law is to be interpreted etc.

A working knowledge of the English legal system will help you in your professional life to tackle any legal issues you come across.

This Study Guide is very important from an examination point of view. Questions from this chapter are frequently asked in the ACCA examinations. You must devote considerable time and attention to studying this Study Guide.

LEARNING OUTCOMES

a) Explain what is meant by case law and precedent within the context of the hierarchy of the courts
b) Explain legislation and evaluate delegated legislation
c) Illustrate the rules and presumptions used by the courts in interpreting statutes

Introduction

Precedent means judges are required to follow the rule of law established in the previous decided cases of the court of equal status or higher, if the legal principle involved is the same and the facts are similar.

Judicial precedent is a system of law-making by judges rather than by parliament. The general applicable decisions made by the judges, referred to as precedents, are used as models for future cases.

In Donoghue v Stevenson (1932), the principle of law set out by House of Lords was that the manufacturer owes a duty of care to the ultimate consumers of his products. (The claimant had stomach pain after drinking some ginger beer from a bottle containing a decomposed snail, Refer to SG B4 for the detailed case study)

The House of Lords occupies the highest position in the English court structure. All decisions taken in this court are obligatory on all courts below it in the hierarchy.

Suppose a similar case comes up before the court e.g. a lady buys a tin of fruit juice and finds a cockroach in the tin. She then sues the juice manufacturer. In this case, the principle set by the House of Lords in the Donoghue v Stevenson (1932) case that the manufacturer owes a duty of care to a consumer will be applied.

This Study Guide discusses the precedent concept in detail.

1. Explain what is meant by case law and precedent within the context of the hierarchy of the courts

[Learning outcome a]

1.1 Judicial precedent

Common law is judge made law and is law based on judicial decisions rather than on statutes.

It is based on the system of precedent. The legal decisions applied in previous cases are applied to current cases by judges and decisions are made on this basis.

Definition

In law, a precedent is a legal case establishing a principle or rule which a court may need to adopt when deciding subsequent cases with similar issues or facts.

Binding precedent

The doctrine of binding precedent or stare decisis is central to the English legal system. A precedent is a statement of the law made by a judge when deciding a case.

The doctrine, states that **within the hierarchy of the English courts a decision by a higher court will be binding on those lower than it.**

This means that when judges try a case they will check to see if a similar case has come before a court previously, and if there was a precedent set by **higher court, then the judge should follow that precedent.**

Example

A principle was set out by the House of Lords in one of its cases. If any case which contains similar facts comes up before the Court of Appeal, it will be binding for the Court of Appeal to base its decision on the precedent set out by the House of Lords. This is because the House of Lords is higher in the hierarchy of courts than the Court of Appeal.

The House of Lords however does not have to follow its own precedents.

Tips

Stare Decisis is a term used with binding precedent. It means to stand by a decision.

Persuasive precedents

Persuasive precedents are those that have been **set by courts lower in the hierarchy**, they may be persuasive but are not binding

If there is a precedent set in a lower court, the judge does not have to follow it, but may consider it and will not overrule it without due consideration.

Example

The Court of Appeal is not bound by decisions of the High Court as the High court is lower than the Court of Appeal in the judicial hierarchy.

Diagram 1: Types of precedent

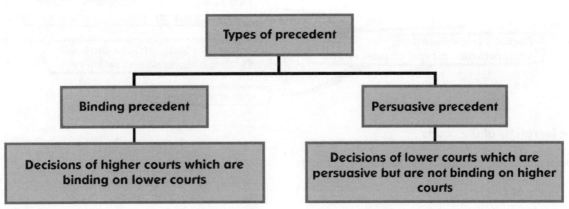

It is, however, important to note that not every part of the case is a binding precedent. There are three main factors that need to be considered in order to understand which part of a precedent is binding and which is persuasive.

1. Ratio decidendi literally mans the reason for the decision.

These refer to the **principles of law applied by a court** upon which a judicial decision is based. Therefore, the principle of law on **which a particular case is decided creates the precedent** and not the actual decision itself.

Ratio decidendi does not take the facts of the case into consideration but refers to the principle of law applied in that case to make a decision.

Example

In Donoghue v Stevenson (1932), the principle of law applied was that a person owes a duty of care to avoid acts or omissions that he could reasonably foresee might injure his neighbour. It was held that the manufacturer of ginger beer owed a duty of care to the ultimate consumers of his products. Therefore **this principle is the ratio decidendi** and the other facts, such as the consumer swallowed a decomposed snail do not form part of the precedent.

Whether the claimant won or lost is not material for setting the precedent.

---

2. Obiter dicta literally means things said in passing.

These are words said by a judge in relation to a legal point but which does not form the basis of the decision. Obiter Dictum is not binding on future judges and is therefore persuasive in nature.

Example

Where the judge, in explaining his ruling, provides a hypothetical set of facts and explains how he or she believes the law would apply to those facts.

---

3. Material facts

For a precedent to be binding on a judge in a later case, it is important that the material facts of the case which has come before the court previously and the new case must be similar.

SYNOPSIS

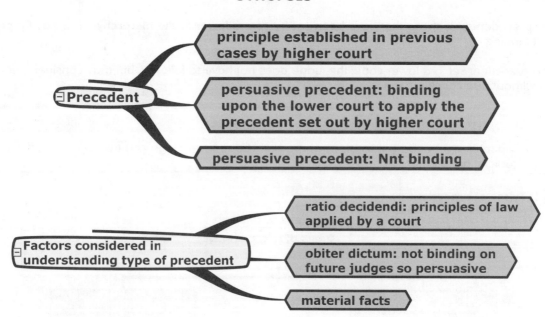

1.2 The hierarchy of the courts

Precedent within the context of the hierarchy of courts

1. The House of Lords

The House of Lords **occupies the highest position** in the English court structure. All decisions taken in this court are obligatory for all courts below it in the hierarchy.

Up to 1966 the House of Lords regarded itself as bound by its previous decisions. In the year 1966 however, a Practice Statement made by Lord Gardiner declared that, in future, the House of Lords would have the power to depart from its previous decisions, in cases where this was thought appropriate.

Since then, there have been several cases in which the House of Lords has overruled or amended its own earlier decisions. However, the House of Lords exercises this power with a significant degree of caution.

Another point which is important to realise is that the House of Lords is no longer the Supreme Court. In fact, its decisions are subject to the decisions of the European Court of Justice in terms of European Community law, and the European Court of Human Rights in matters relating to human rights.

2. The Court of Appeal

All decisions taken in this court are mandatory on all courts **except for the House of Lords**. In civil cases the Court of Appeal is generally bound by:
➢ Previous decisions of the House of Lords and
➢ Its own previous decisions.

There are, however, a number of **exceptions to this general rule**. These exceptions arise when

a) Two previous decisions of the Court of Appeal are conflicting.

b) The House of Lords has overruled a previous decision of the Court of Appeal. Previous decisions of The Court of Appeal which are inconsistent with European Community law or with a later decision of the European Court of Justice can also be ignored.

c) The previous decision was made in the ignorance of an authority which would have reached a different conclusion. – per incuriam

---

Example

Where a statute or an important case was not brought to the attention of the court or was ignored

If a court in the criminal division of the Court of Appeal considers one of its previous decisions to have been based on either a misunderstanding, or a misapplication, of the law then it is also not bound by this decision.

3. Divisions of High Court

A Divisional Court of the High Court is bound by the doctrine of stare decisis in the normal way and must follow the decisions of:

➢ The House of Lords and
➢ The Court of Appeal.

It is also normally bound by previous decisions at its own level.

Also, in criminal appeal cases, the Queen's Bench Divisional Court may refuse to follow its own earlier decisions where it feels the earlier decision to have been wrongly made.

Tips

Stare decisis: the doctrine of binding precedent.

4. The High Court:

The High Court is **bound by the decisions of superior courts**. Decisions by individual High Court judges are binding on courts inferior in the hierarchy. However, such decisions are not binding on other High Court judges, although they are of strong persuasive authority and tend to be followed in practice.

5. Other courts

Other Courts such as County Courts, the Crown Court and Magistrates' Courts **cannot create precedent** as their decisions are not usually reported so they are not part of the system of precedent.

SYNOPSIS

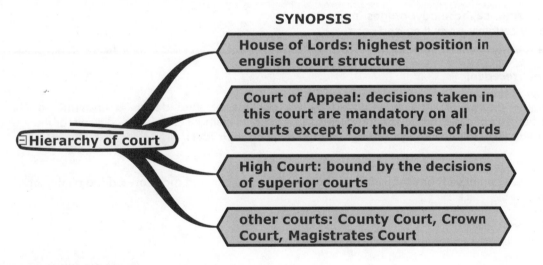

Hierarchy of court

House of Lords: highest position in english court structure

Court of Appeal: decisions taken in this court are mandatory on all courts except for the house of lords

High Court: bound by the decisions of superior courts

other courts: County Court, Crown Court, Magistrates Court

The nature of precedent

The main mechanisms through which judges alter or avoid precedents are:

➢ **Overruling:** This is the procedure which allows a decision made by a judge in a previous case to be disregarded by a court higher up in the hierarchy of courts.

➢ **Distinguishing**: This happens when a judge considers the facts of a previous case to be substantially different from the facts of the current case. As a result, the court will not be bound by the ruling on the previous case.

Basis of precedent

The operation of the doctrine of binding precedent depends on the existence of an extensive reporting service to provide access to previous judicial decisions. Hence, the following are the pre-requisites for using a precedent system:

> **Reports:** Adequate and reliable reports of earlier decisions must be available.

> **Rules:** Rules for extracting legal principles from previous sets of facts and applying them to current facts should be clearly defined.

Test yourself 1

Which of the following decisions binds a Country Court?
1) Decisions of the High Court
2) Decisions of the Crown Court
3) Decisions of the Court of Appeal
4) Decisions of House of Lords

Advantages of precedent

There are numerous perceived advantages of the doctrine of stare decisis; amongst which are:

a) **Time and cost saving**: Precedents save the time of the judiciary, lawyers and their clients for the reason that cases do not have to be re-argued. In respect of potential litigants it saves them money in court expenses because they can apply to their solicitor / barrister for guidance as to how their particular case is likely to be decided in the light of previous cases on the same or similar points.

b) **Certainty**: Once the legal rule has been established in one case, individuals can act with regard to that rule relatively secure in the knowledge that it will not be changed by some later court.

c) **Flexibility**: Precedents provide flexibility in operations. This refers to the fact that the various mechanisms, by means of which judges can manipulate the common law, provide them with an opportunity to develop law in particular areas without waiting for Parliament to enact legislation.

Tips
Tip to memorise these advantages (mnemonic)
Flexibility certainly saves time and costs.

Disadvantages of precedent

a) **Uncertainty**: The degree of certainty provided by the doctrine of stare decisis is undermined. This is because a large number of cases are reported which can be cited as authorities. It is very difficult for the judges to select which authority to follow through **distinguishing cases on their facts**.

b) **Voluminous:**
> The decided cases comprise many thousands of pages of law reports and more are added all the time.
> Judgments are
  ✓ very long
  ✓ not easily readable
  ✓ The ratio decidendi are sometimes difficult to ascertain.

c) **Complexities:** It is difficult to pinpoint clearly the appropriate principles laid down by judges for each decision of each case.

d) **Rigidity:** This refers to possibility that the law in relation to any particular area may become set on the basis of an unjust precedent with the consequence that previous injustices are continued.

Example

An example of this is the long delay in the recognition of the possibility of rape within marriage, which has only been recognised relatively recently. Cite relevant authority

---

e) **Unconstitutionality:** This is a fundamental question that refers to the fact that, in actually making law rather simply applying it, the judiciary are, in fact, acting outside their theoretical constitutional role.

Diagram 2: Advantages and disadvantages of precedent

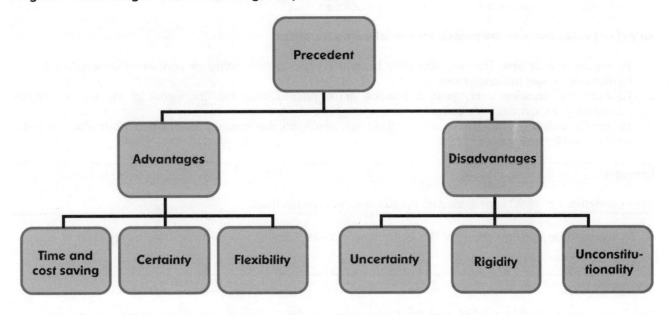

SYNOPSIS

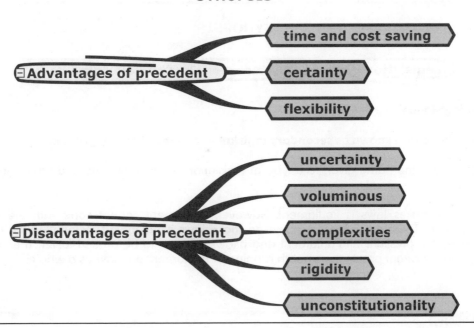

Test Yourself 2

State in brief, the advantages and disadvantages of precedent.

2. Explain legislation and evaluate delegated legislation

[Learning outcome b]

2.1 Legislation

Definition

Legislation is law which has been enacted by a legislature or other governing body.

In the United Kingdom, there are two ways to pass legislation:
➢ As Acts of Parliament and
➢ As delegated legislation

Acts of Parliament are prepared by the Parliament itself. An Act of Parliament is treated as the main source of law. It is binding on everyone falling within that jurisdiction.

An Act of Parliament may be passed for the following purposes:

1. **To create a new law:** The new law may have the effect of amending or cancelling an existing law or formulating a new law altogether.
2. To authorise **taxation** every year, a Finance Act is passed after the Chancellor of the Exchequer has published the Government's budget.
3. **To codify existing law:** This is the method by which all the existing laws on a particular issue are superseded by one statute.

Example

The Partnership Act 1890 superseded all the existing partnership laws

---

4. **To consolidate existing statutes:** This is the way of consolidating two or more statutes together in a single statute.

Example

The Employment Rights Act 1996 and the Companies Act 1985 consolidate all the provisions contained in various statutes on a particular topic in one statute.

SYNOPSIS

Legislation — law enacted by the governing body

2.2 Delegated legislation

Delegated legislation is also known as **secondary legislation or subordinate legislation**.

Delegated legislation is the name given to a type of legislation or law that is passed other than a statute (an Act).

The authority which makes laws is Parliament. However, Parliament cannot cope with the ever-increasing demand for new laws. Therefore, often the power to make laws is delegated. Delegating the responsibility to another body takes the pressure off Parliament and allows the acts to be passed faster. Therefore, delegated legislation plays an important part in the smooth running of Parliament and law as a whole.

Meaning

Definition
Delegated legislation is the law made by executive authority acting under powers given to them by the primary legislation in order to implement and administer the requirements of various acts.

In this way the legislation does not go through the two Houses of Parliament. Delegated legislation is mainly **concerned with relatively narrow, technical matters.**

Power to make laws is delegated to an authority by Parliament to create the rules and regulations that give substance to statutes. Usually a Minister of the Crown is delegated this power. However, it may sometimes be a public corporation such as British Rail, or a local authority, or even the Privy Council.

The delegation enables these bodies to pass:

1. Rules
2. Regulations
3. Orders (including commencement orders and orders in council) or
4. Bye-laws without the need for parliamentary approval

Once made a piece of delegated legislation is usually presented to Parliament to be reviewed by a standing committee and sometimes a joint committee (of both houses).

Parliament must ensure that the delegated legislation adheres to the scope of the primary legislation that enabled it and does not exceed the powers granted to that body.

It is worth noting that **unlike primary legislation, delegated legislation may be questioned by the courts.**

2.3 Types of delegated legislation

There are various types of delegated legislation as follows:

1. **Orders in council:** This is a method of introducing legislation whereby orders are prepared by the Government but, instead of going through Parliament, they are approved by the Privy Council (a non party political group of accomplished parliamentarians). .

These orders are used only in case of national emergency.

2. **Statutory instruments:** These refer to rules, regulations and orders. In order to legitimise delegation, an Act of Parliament (referred to as an enabling Act) is passed which allows an alternative authority (usually the Minister of the Crown) to make these laws, within certain limits.

3. **Bye-laws:** The power to make these laws is delegated to local bodies through enabling Acts passed by Parliament. These laws are binding on all persons coming within their areas.

4. **Rules:** Under Acts such as the County Courts Act 1984, Court Rule Committees are delegated authority over certain courts and the power to make the rules governing procedure in these courts.

5. **Regulations:** Power may be delegated to a professional body to allow it to turn its regulations governing a particular profession into laws.

Example

Under the Solicitors' Act 1974, the Law Society now has the power to control the conduct of practising solicitors.

Diagram 3: Types of legislation

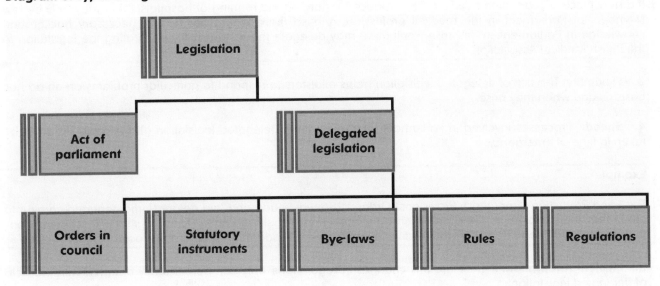

SYNOPSIS

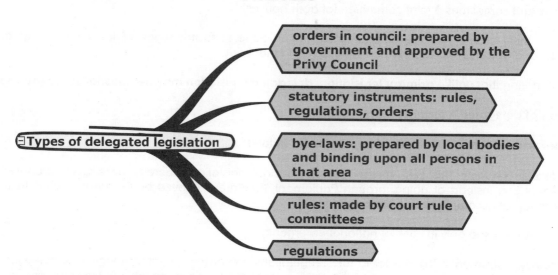

Types of delegated legislation

- **orders in council:** prepared by government and approved by the Privy Council
- **statutory instruments:** rules, regulations, orders
- **bye-laws:** prepared by local bodies and binding upon all persons in that area
- **rules:** made by court rule committees
- **regulations**

2.4 Advantages of delegated legislation

1. Time saving: With the help of delegated legislation, parliamentary time is saved. It allows Parliament to concentrate on broad issues of policy rather than masses of detail.

> **Example**
>
> The Road Traffic Act 1972 included a general requirement for motor-cyclists to wear protective helmets, but left the Secretary of State to draw up detailed regulations as to the type of helmet required. The Motor Cycles (Protective Helmets) Regulations 1980 contain further details about the requirements.

2. Expert knowledge: It allows technical matters to be determined by those competent to do so. It enables the use of expert knowledge which is not available within the civil service. On technical matters, for e.g., it may possible that there are very few persons in Parliament with technical knowledge of the subject.

> **Example**
>
> If a new piece of legislation needs to be introduced regarding the running of hospitals, there may only be few Members of Parliament in the medical profession, and so there would not be the necessary background knowledge in Parliament. In this case, Parliament may delegate the responsibility of creating the legislation to the British Medical Association.

3. Flexibility: The use of delegated legislation helps ministers to respond to particular problems on an ad hoc basis as and when they arise.

4. Speed: Processes involved in Parliament take much time. Delegated legislation allows rapid action to be taken in time of emergency.

> **Example**
>
> The Food Protection (Emergency Provisions) Order 1986 was made and laid before Parliament and came into effect less than two hours later, prohibiting the movement or slaughter for food of sheep in certain areas thought to have been affected by radioactive fallout from the incident at the Chernobyl power station.

5. Efficient Adaptation: If there are any changes in regulations, they can be efficiently adapted with the help of delegated legislation.

SYNOPSIS

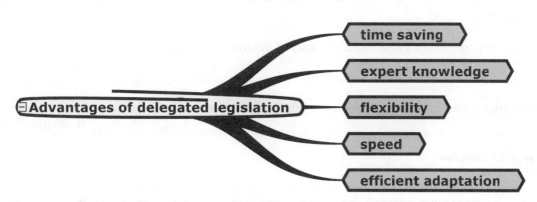

2.5 Disadvantages of delegated legislation

1. Unconstitutional: Delegated legislation is unconstitutional in the sense that key issues and regulations are prepared without the sanction of the proper person who has the authority i.e. the proper elected authority, the House of Commons.

2. Loss of Accountability and Control: The question of accountability is an important issue concerning the use of delegated legislation

Although Parliament is presumed to be the source of statute law, delegated legislation allows the details of these laws to be decided elsewhere (i.e. by the Government ministers and the civil servants who work under them). This raises the question of whether it is appropriate to give so much power to un-elected individuals.

3. Lack of publicity: Usually, these laws are published in large volume, so there is lack of publicity and knowledge about the laws.

4. Bulk: There is so much delegated legislation that Members of Parliament, let alone the general public, may find it difficult to keep on top of it.

Diagram 4: Advantages and disadvantages of delegated legislation

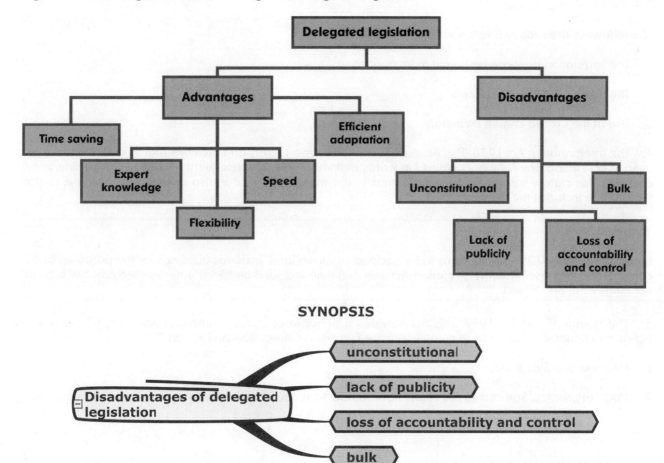

SYNOPSIS

Test Yourself 3

State in brief, the advantages and disadvantages of delegated legislation.

---

3. Illustrate the rules and presumptions used by the courts in interpreting statutes
[Learning outcome c]

Interpretation of Statutes

There are various aids to assist the judge in how to interpret statutes. The interpretation of statutes is not an easy task. The legislation will originally have been written by experts (Parliamentary draftsmen) who write in precise and technical language. Circumstances may be encountered which were not considered by the draftsmen. Owing to this, there is often ambiguity or vagueness in the words and phrases used in the Statutes. So judges assign meanings to ambiguous words in the statute. This process is called Interpretation of statutes.

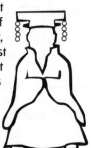

Lord Denning in Seaford Court Estates Ltd v Asher (1949) observed, "English language is not an instrument of mathematical precision... It would certainly save the judges from the trouble if the Acts of Parliament were drafted with divine precision and perfect clarity. In the absence of it, when a defect appears, a judge cannot simply fold hands and blame the draftsman... He must set to work on the constructive task of finding the intention of Parliament and he must do this not only from the language of the statute, but also from a consideration of the social conditions which gave rise to it, and of the mischief which it was passed to remedy. Then, he must supplement the written word so as to give 'force and life' to the intention of the legislature... A judge should ask himself the question, how, if the Makers of the Act had themselves come across the ruck in the context of it, they would have straightened it out? He must do what they could have done. A judge must not alter the material of which Act is woven but he can and should iron out the crease."

As is clear from the words of Lord Denning, where the words used in a Statute are not clear, the judges must apply the rules of interpretation and give effect to the intention of the legislature.

3.1 Aids to interpretation

The following are aids to interpretation:

1. The Legislation itself can be an aid to interpretation.

2. The existing judicial precedents

3. Use of the Oxford English Dictionary

4. The Interpretation Act 1978. This Act defines many common terms and provides that its definitions are to be used in construing any Act that contains the words defined (unless a subsequent Act defines them differently). It also includes certain assumptions such as terms in the masculine gender also include the feminine, and that the singular includes the plural.

Example

In **Hutton v. Esher UDC (1973)** it was to be decided whether "land" includes buildings for the purposes of compulsory purchase? **The Interpretation Act** said that land included buildings unless stated otherwise, so the buildings were purchased.

---

5. The Human Rights Act 1997. This Act provides a principle of statutory interpretation that, where possible, Acts are to be interpreted so as to comply with the European Convention on Human Rights.

6. Heading and Side notes

7. Code of practice. Sometimes the courts have to refer to a code of practice for interpretation of a statute.

Example

The Trade Union and Labour Relations (Consolidation) Act 1992 provides that if the employee is the member of a trade union, an employer is required to provide him a 'reasonable' time off for union activities. It further states that in order to decide what is 'reasonable time', the relevant provisions of the code of practice issued by the Advisory, Conciliation and Arbitration Service (ACAS) should be applied.

---

8.   The long title and preamble (all Acts have preambles, and all Private Acts and all old Public Acts have long titles), but they cannot prevail over clear enacting words.

Example

In **Fisher v. Raven (1964),** the long title was used to decide that debtors for the purposes of Act were ordinary debtors

---

3.2 Rules used by the courts for interpreting statutes.

The following are the rules used by judges in interpreting statutes:

1. The Literal rule
This indicates following the literal, ordinary or natural meaning of words.

Under this rule, the judge is required to consider what the legislation actually says rather than considering what it might mean. According to this rule, the words of the statutes should be taken in their ordinary and grammatical meanings.

However, this rule is applicable where:

➢   The words are clear
➢   The language is plain and
➢   Only one meaning can be derived from the wording of the statute

Jervis CJ in Abley v. Dale (1851) observed "if the precise words used are plain and unambiguous, in our judgment we are bound to construe them in their ordinary sense, even though it does lead to an absurdity or manifest injustice".

Example

In **Fisher v. Bell (1961),** the court followed the contract law interpretation of the meaning of 'offer' in the Act in question. In this case, the accused was charged for displaying, for the purposes of sale, a flick-knife in a shop window. This was held not to be an 'offer for sale' for the purposes of the Act but merely an invitation to treat, inviting members of the public to make an offer for sale.

However, the irony of this rule is that its use may defeat the intention of Parliament.

Example

In the case of **Whiteley v. Chapel (1868)**, the court came to the reluctant conclusion that Whiteley could not be convicted of impersonating any **person entitled to vote** at an election, because the person he impersonated was dead, and on a literal construction of the relevant statutory provision, the deceased was not a person entitled to vote. This surely cannot have been the intention of Parliament.

---

2. The Golden Rule
This rule is applied if

➢   There is ambiguity or vagueness in the words or phrases of the statute, or
➢   Where there are two apparently contradictory meanings to a particular word used in the statute

The Court will take the least absurd meaning. The ordinary sense of the words is to be adhered to, unless it would lead to absurdity. However, when the ordinary sense leads to absurdity, it may be modified to avoid the absurdity **but no further.**

Example

In **Adler v. George,** it was an offence to obstruct the Forces "in the vicinity of".......... This was modified to avoid the absurdity of it not including "in", hence the Act was changed to "in' or 'in the vicinity of'...

---

3. The Mischief Rule

If the literal rule does not give any result, then this rule should be applied. This rule considers the 'mischief' which the statute is aimed to address, so it is called the **Mischief Rule.**

This principle of this rule was laid down in the Heydon's case (1584)

This rule operates to enable judges to interpret a statute in such a way as to punish the mischief the statute was enacted to prevent. Present practice is to go beyond the actual body of the legislation to determine what mischief a particular Act was aimed at redressing.

Heydon's Case 1584: the criteria for the Mischief Rule:

a) What was common law before the Act?
b) What was the mischief for which the existing law did not provide?
c) What punishment has Parliament decided upon?
d) Judge should make such constructions on the Act to suppress the mischief and subtle inventions and evasions for continuance of the mischief, according to the true intent of the makers of the Act.

Example

The mischief rule was applied in **Corkery v. Carpenter (1951)**. In that case, a person was arrested for being drunk in charge of a bicycle. He was subsequently charged under the Licensing Act with being drunk in charge of a carriage. However, specific reference was not made to a bicycle in the legislation.

The court decided that, as the purpose of the Act was to prevent people from using any form of transport on the public highways whilst in a state of intoxication, the cyclist was charged.

---

4. The Eiusdem Generis Rule

Eiusdem Generis means 'of the same kind'. The rule states that **general words following specific words are to be construed with reference to the words preceding them.**

This rule is used when a statute includes a list of items and an 'and similar items' clause.

Example

Where a statute uses the words 'such as oxen, bulls, goat, cows, buffaloes, sheep, horses, etc.', the word 'etc.' cannot include wild animals such as a lion or tiger. Also, not all domestic animals would be covered.

The illustration given relates to all four-legged animals and hence other domestic animals such as dogs, cats etc. can be included but not a cockerel or a hen since a cockerel or hen has no similarity with the illustrations of the other domestic animals given.

---

5. The 'expressio unius est exclusio alterius' rule

The meaning of this expression is **'specifying one thing implies exclusion of others'** i.e. if a particular thing is expressed in the legislation then it totally excludes anything else.

Example

In **R. v. Inhabitant of Sedgley** it was held that "lands and coalmines" implicitly excluded other types of mines from the scope of 'lands'.
In **Tempet v. Kilner (1846)** it was held that "goods, wares and merchandise" did not include stocks and shares.

---

6. The Contextual Rule

This requires that the meaning of the word should be in the context of the statute.

Example

In **Muir v. Keay,** it was held that entertainment need not be celebration, but by the context of the Act could be just the consumption of food and drink

Diagram 5: Rules in interpreting statute

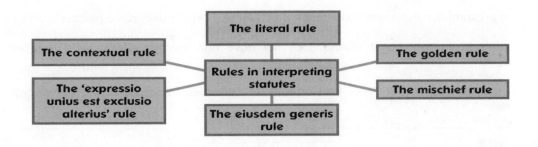

SYNOPSIS
Rules and presumptions used by the courts in interpreting statutes

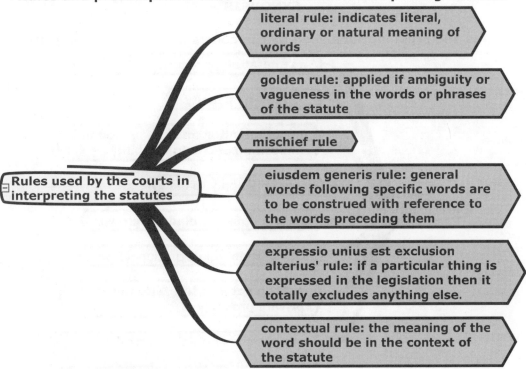

3.3 Presumptions of statute interpretation

1. There is a presumption against altering the common law (even though many statutes have that express intention) or statute law unless:
   a. Express provision is made, or
   b. The new law is irreconcilable with the statute or common law.

2. There is a presumption that judges have no power to decide that a law is illegal or unconstitutional

Example

Chenny v. Conn: the production of nuclear weapons under an Act allegedly contravened a treaty prohibiting their manufacture. This did not matter, since judges have no power to determine the legality of an Act.

3. There is a presumption that if there is no fault no penalty will be imposed.

4. There is a presumption that criminal liability will be imposed only if **mens rea (guilty intention)** is proved.

5. There is a presumption that Acts **only apply to the UK** unless contrary intention is expressed.

6. There is a presumption that a statute does not bind the Crown.

7. There is a presumption against violating international law.

8. There is a presumption that statutes do not apply to offences committed abroad.

9. There is a presumption that Acts do not interfere with rights to private property.

10. There is a presumption that compensation be paid where a statute deprives a person of property.

11. There is a presumption that a statute does not have retrospective effects on a date earlier than its becoming law.

12. There is a presumption that Penal laws should be construed in favour of the person whose liberty is threatened.

Test Yourself 4

Explain the Eiusdem Generis Rule of statute interpretation.

SYNOPSIS

Rules and presumptions used by the courts in interpreting statutes

Presumptions
- no alteration in common law
- no fault no penalty
- guilty intention must be proved for imposition of criminal liability
- acts only apply to uk
- statute does not bind the crown
- no violation of international law
- acts do not interfere with rights to private property
- statute does not have retrospective effect

Answers to Test Yourself

Answer 1

Decisions of the High Court, the Court of Appeal **and House of Lords bind the** County Court. The Crown Court cannot create any binding precedent.

Answer 2

Advantages of precedent

There are numerous perceived advantages of the doctrine of stare decisis; including:

a) Time and cost saving.
➤ It saves the time of the judiciary, lawyers and their clients
➤ The cases do not have to be re-argued.
➤ It saves money in court expenses because the parties in the case can apply to their solicitor / barrister for guidance as to how their particular case is likely to be decided in the light of previous cases on the same or similar points.

b) Certainty: Once the legal rule has been established in one case, it will not be changed by some later court. Similar cases will be treated alike and are not subjected to the whims and fancies of individual judges.

c) Flexibility: Law needs to be flexible to meet the needs of an ever-changing society and case laws can make changes faster than Parliament. If some mechanism is available to the judges by means of which they can manipulate the common law, this provides them with an opportunity to develop law in particular areas without waiting for Parliament to enact legislation.

For e.g., in **Re: A (2000),** it dealt with the question of whether Siamese twins would be separated by an operation when the hospital recommended this, but the parents had clearly expressed their objection. In this case, the House of Lords allowed the operation to proceed without waiting for Parliament to enact legislation.

Disadvantages of precedent

a) Voluminous: Hundreds of thousands of decided cases comprise many thousands of pages of law reports and more are added all the time. Judgements are very long and not readable and the ratio decidendi are difficult to find.

b) Complexities: It is also difficult to pinpoint clearly the appropriate principles laid by judges for each of each case.

c) Uncertainty: A large number of cases are decided by each court every year. Hence it is difficult for judges to select which authority to follow through distinguishing cases on their facts.

d) Rigidity: Judges have to follow a binding precedent even though they think it is bad law or inappropriate. The law in relation to any particular area may become set on the basis of an unjust precedent. As a result, the previous injustices continued.

e) Unconstitutionality: Delegated legislation is unconstitutional in the sense that key issues and regulations are prepared without the sanction of the proper person who has the authority i.e. a Member of the House of Commons.

Answer 3

Advantages of delegated legislation are as follows:

a) **Time saving:** Delegated legislation saves the precious time of the Parliament. It allows Parliament to concentrate on more important issues of policy rather than masses of detail.

For e.g., the Road Traffic Act 1972 included a general requirement for motor-cyclists to wear protective helmets. But the work of drawing the detailed regulations as to the type of helmet required was left to the Secretary of State.

b) **Expert knowledge:** Members of Parliament cannot be expected to possess technical knowledge of all matters for which law is to be formed. So the delegation enables taking advantage of experts' knowledge from various fields. For e.g., if a new piece of legislation needs to be introduced regarding the running of hospitals, there may only be few Members of Parliament in the medical profession, and so there would not be the necessary background knowledge in Parliament. In this case, Parliament may delegate the responsibility of creating the legislation to the British Medical Association.

c) **Flexibility:** The use of delegated legislation permits ministers to respond on an ad hoc basis to particular problems as and when they arise.

d) **Speed:** Processes involved in the Parliament take much time. Delegated legislation allows rapid action to be taken in times of emergency.

For e.g., The Food Protection (Emergency Provisions) Order 1986 was made and laid before Parliament and came into effect less than two hours later, prohibiting the movement or slaughter for food of sheep in certain areas thought to have been affected by radioactive fallout from the incident at the Chernobyl power station

e) **Efficient adaptation:** If there are any changes in regulations, they can be efficiently adapted with the help of delegated legislation.

Disadvantages of delegated legislation are as follows:

a) **Unconstitutional:** Regulations are meant to be prepared by elected representatives i.e. the House of Commons. However, for delegated legislation, this power is delegated to civil servants who are not elected democratically.

b) **Loss of accountability and control:** The question of accountability is an important issue concerning the use of delegated legislation

Although Parliament is presumed to be the source of statute law, delegated legislation allows the details of these laws to be decided elsewhere (i.e. by the Government ministers and the civil servants who work under them). This raises the question of whether it is appropriate to give so much power to un-elected individuals.

c) **Lack of publicity:** Usually, these laws are published in large volume, so there is lack of publicity and knowledge about the laws.

d) **Bulk:** There is so much delegated legislation that Members of Parliament, let alone the general public, may find it difficult to keep on top of it.

Answer 4

The meaning of the word Eiusdem Geners is 'of the same kind'. The rule states that general words following specific words are to be construed with reference to the words preceding them. This rule is used when a statute includes a list of items and an 'and similar items' clause. For e.g., where a statute uses the words 'such as oxen, bulls, goat, cows, buffaloes, sheep, horses, etc', the word 'etc' cannot include wild animals such as a lion or tiger. In addition, not all domestic animals would be covered. The illustration given relates to four-legged animals and hence other domestic animals such as dogs, cats etc. can be included but not a cockerel or a hen since a cockerel or hen has no similarity with the illustrations of other domestic animals given.

Quick Quiz

State true or false

1) Decisions of higher courts are binding on the courts lower to them in the hierarchy.

2) The House of Lords is the supreme court in the UK

3) All decisions taken by the Court of Appeal are binding on all other courts.

4) The authority of Parliament to create rules and regulations is usually delegated to the Minister of the Crown.

5) Ratio decidendi and Obiter dicta are both binding.

6) The House of Lords does not have to follow its own precedents

Answers to Quick Quiz

1. **True,** the decisions of higher courts in the hierarchy are binding precedents and have to be followed by the lower courts if the facts of the two cases are similar.

2. **False,** decisions of the House of Lords are subject to decisions of the European Court of Justice in matters relating to European Community law.

3. **False,** only the decisions of higher courts are binding. Therefore, decisions taken by the Court of Appeal are binding only on courts lower to it in hierarchy. They are not binding on the House of Lords as it is superior to the Court of Appeal in the hierarchy.

4. **True,** however, it may sometimes be a public corporation such as British Rail, or a local authority, or even the Privy Council.

5. **False,** only ratio decidendi is binding

6. **True**

Self-Examination Questions

Question 1

Explain the concept of 'Binding precedent' in relation to English legal system.

Question 2

What are the various presumptions of statute interpretation?

Question 3

When is the precedent not binding?

Answers to Self Examination Questions

Answer 1

A precedent is a principle of law made set out by a judge in deciding a case. The doctrine, states that within the hierarchy of the English courts a decision made by a higher court will be binding on those lower than it in that hierarchy.

When judges try a case they will check to see if a similar case has come before a court previously. If there was a precedent set by **a higher court, then the judge in the present case should follow the rule of law established in the earlier case.**

Where the precedent is from a lower court in the hierarchy, it is only a persuasive precedent. The judge in the new case is not bound to follow it. However, he will certainly consider it and judge its applicability in the present case.

Answer 2

Presumptions of statute interpretation

1)   The common law or statute law will not be altered unless express provision is made, or the new law is irreconcilable with the statute or common law.

2)   The judges may not decide that a law is illegal or unconstitutional.

3)   Penalty will not be imposed unless there is some fault.

4)   Guilty intention is required for criminal offences.

5)   Acts only apply to the UK unless contrary intention is expressed.

6)   A statute does not bind the Crown.

7)   International law will not be violated while making the law.

8)   Statutes do not apply to offences committed abroad.

9)   Acts do not interfere with rights to private property and compensation will be paid where a statute deprives a person of his property.

10)   No arbitrary discretion will be granted to the officials.

11)   The legislation will not be made effective retrospectively.

12)   Penal laws will be construed in favour of the person whose liberty is threatened.

Answer 3

A precedent will not be binding if:

➢ It has been overruled by a higher court
For example, a principle of law was set out by the Court of Appeal. The House of Lords overruled that principle in a later case which came up before it. As a result, the principle is no longer binding for the lower courts to follow. It is important to note, however, that the overruling of some principle by a higher court will not reverse the actual decision in the case, given by the lower court.

➢ It has been overruled by the statute

➢ If it was found there was a lack of care in the decision setting the precedent. For example if a statutory provision or precedent had not been brought to the court's decision. The precedent set out by such decision will not be binding.

➢ If a court finds a material difference between cases then it can choose not to be bound by the precedent

SECTION A - ESSENTIAL ELEMENTS OF THE LEGAL SYSTEM

HUMAN RIGHTS

Get through intro

The Human Rights Act 1998 is considered to be the most important piece of constitutional legislation passed in the United Kingdom. Previously people had to take submit complaints about their human rights to the European Court of Human Rights in Strasbourg, France.

In October 2000, the Human Rights Act came into effect in the UK.

This Study Guide tells you what rights are contained in the Human Rights Act. Awareness and knowledge of human rights will surely be very useful for you in your professional life. Along with that, as an individual, it will be very useful for you to be aware of your fundamental rights.

Understanding this Study Guide is also important from an examination point of view as there may be a straightforward question on this topic in the exam paper.

LEARNING OUTCOMES

a) Identify the concept of human rights as expressed in the Human Rights Act, 1998
b) Explain the impact of human rights law on statutory interpretation
c) Explain the impact of human rights law on the common law

Introduction

What does the Human Rights Act do?

Through the Human Rights Act, the human rights contained in the European Court of Human Rights (ECHR) became enforceable in UK law. As a result, it is illegal for a public authority to act in a way that is incompatible with a convention. Anyone who feels that their human rights have been breached by the action of a public authority may raise the matter in an appropriate court or tribunal. If they have pursued the case as far as they can in the UK, but are still unsatisfied with the verdict, they may take their complaint to the European Court of Human Rights (ECHR).

The House of Lords is the topmost authority in the hierarchy of UK legal authorities. However, the decisions of the European Court of Justice in terms of European Community law, and, due to the Human Rights Act 1998, the decisions of the European Court of Human Rights in matters relating to human rights, are binding on the decisions of the House of Lords.

The Human Rights are conventions are discussed in this Study Guide.

1. Identify the concept of human rights as expressed in the Human Rights Act, 1998
[Learning outcome a]

Human rights are the rights of human beings. All citizens have equal human rights. Cultural or economic differences, nationality and ethnicity do not affect them.

The main characteristic of human rights is that they are **universal** and **inherent**. They are the inbuilt rights of every individual and **include the basic and fundamental right to life.**

The Human Rights Act 1998 is an United Kingdom Act of Parliament which received Royal Assent on November 9, 1998, and came into force on October 2, 2000. Its aim is to "give further effect" in UK law to the rights contained in the European Convention on Human Rights.

The Human Rights Act 1998 has incorporated the following Convention rights into UK law:

1. Right to life (Article 2 of Convention)

a) Everyone's right to life shall be protected by law.

b) No one shall be deprived of his life intentionally except in the execution of a criminal following his conviction for a crime for which this penalty is provided by law.

c) Article 2 set out in the Convention states that deprivation of life shall not be regarded as a contravention of the right to life when it results from the use of force.

  i. In defense of any person from unlawful violence
  ii. In order to effect a lawful arrest
  iii. To prevent the escape of a person lawfully detained
  iv. In action lawfully taken for the purpose of suppressing a riot or civil disobedience

2. Prohibition on torture (Article 3 of Convention)

No one shall be subjected to torture or inhuman or degrading treatment or punishment.

3. Prohibition on slavery and forced labour (Article 4 of Convention)

a) No one shall be required to perform forced or compulsory labour.

b) Article 4 set out in the Convention states that the term 'forced or compulsory labour' shall not include:

  i. Any service of a military character
  ii. Any service exacted in the case of an emergency or calamity threatening the life or well-being of the community
  iii. Any work or service which forms part of normal civic obligations

4. Right to liberty and security (Article 5 of Convention)

a) Everyone has the right to liberty and security..

b) No one shall be deprived of his liberty except in the following cases and in accordance with a procedure prescribed by law:

    i.   The lawful detention of a person after conviction by a competent court

    ii.   The lawful arrest or detention of a person for non-compliance with the lawful order of a court or in order to secure the fulfillment of any obligation prescribed by law

    iii.   The lawful arrest or detention of a person effected for the purpose of bringing him before the competent legal authority on reasonable suspicion of having committed an offence or when it is reasonably considered necessary to prevent his committing an offence

    iv.   The detention of a minor by lawful order for the purpose of educational supervision or his lawful detention for the purpose of bringing him before the competent legal authority

    v.   The lawful detention of persons for the prevention of the spreading of infectious diseases, of persons of unsound mind, alcoholics or drug addicts

    vi.   The lawful arrest or detention of a person to prevent his affecting an unauthorised entry into the country

c) Everyone who is arrested shall be informed promptly, in a language which he understands, of the reason for his arrest and of any charge against him.

d) Everyone arrested or detained shall be brought promptly before a judge or other officer authorised by law to exercise judicial power and shall be entitled to trial within a reasonable time or to release pending trial. Release may be conditioned by guarantees to appear for trial.

e) Everyone who is deprived of his liberty by arrest or detention shall be entitled to take proceedings by which the lawfulness of his detention shall be decided speedily by a court and his release ordered if the detention is not lawful.

f) Everyone who has been the victim of arrest or detention in contravention of the provisions of this Article shall have an enforceable right to compensation.

5. Right to a fair trial (Article 6 of Convention)

a) In the determination of his civil rights and obligations or of any criminal charge against him, everyone is entitled to a fair and public hearing within a reasonable time by an independent and impartial tribunal established by law.

b) Judgement shall be pronounced publicly, but the press and public may be excluded from all or part of the trial in special circumstances where publicity would prejudice the interests of justice.

c) Everyone charged with a criminal offence shall be presumed innocent until proven guilty according to law.

d) Everyone charged with a criminal offence has the following minimum rights:

    i.   To be informed promptly, in a language which he understands and in detail, of the nature and cause of the accusation against him

    ii.   To have adequate time and facilities for the preparation of his defence

    iii.   To defend himself in person or through legal assistance of his own choice. If he has not sufficient means to pay for legal assistance, legal assistance to be given free when the interests of justice so require.

    iv.   To examine or have examined witnesses against him and to obtain the attendance and examination of witnesses on his behalf.

    v.   To have the free assistance of an interpreter if he cannot understand or speak the language used in court.

6. **No punishment without law** (Article 7 of Convention)

a) No one shall be held guilty of any criminal offence on account of any act or omission which did not constitute a criminal offence under national or international law at the time when it was committed.

b) Heavier penalty than that was applicable at the time the criminal offence was committed will not be charged.

7. **Right to respect for private and family life** (Article 8 of Convention)

a) Everyone has the right to respect for his private and family life, his home and his correspondence.

b) There shall be no interference by a public authority with the exercise of this right except if necessary for:

   i.   Interests of security
   ii. Public safety
   iii. The economic well-being of the country
   iv. The prevention of disorder or crime
   v.   The protection of health or morals
   vi. The protection of the rights and freedoms others

Article 8 set out in the Convention guarantees respect for four things: a person's private life, family life, home and correspondence.

8. **Freedom of thought, conscience and religion** (Article 9 of Convention)

a) Everyone has the right to freedom of thought, conscience and religion.

b) Everyone has the freedom to change his religion or belief.

c) Everyone has the freedom to manifest his religion or belief, in worship, teaching, practice and observance. This freedom shall be subject only to such limitations as are prescribed by law and are necessary :

   i.   In the interests of public safety
   ii. For the protection of public order, health or morals
   iii. For the protection of the rights and freedoms of others

9. **Freedom of expression** (Article 10 of Convention)

a) Everyone has the right to freedom of expression.

b) Everyone has the freedom to hold opinions and to receive and impart information and ideas without interference by public authority. However, this freedom shall not prevent States from requiring the licensing of broadcasting, television or cinema enterprises.

10. **Freedom of assembly and association** (Article 11 of Convention)

a) Everyone has the right to freedom of peaceful assembly and to freedom of association with others.

b) Everyone has the right to form and to join trade unions for the protection of his interests.

c) No restrictions shall be placed on the exercise of these rights other than those which are necessary:

   i.   In the interests of national security or public safety
   ii. For the prevention of disorder or crime
   iii. For the protection of health or morals
   iv. For the protection of the rights and freedoms of others

However, this right shall not prevent the imposition of lawful restrictions on the exercise of these rights by :

i.   Members of the armed forces
ii.   Members of the police
iii. Members of the administration of the state

11. Right to marry and found a family (Article 12 of Convention)

Men and women of marriageable age have the right to marry and to found a family.

12. Prohibition on discrimination (Article 14 of Convention)

The enjoyment of the rights and freedoms set forth in the Convention shall be secured without discrimination on any ground such as:

➢   sex
➢   race
➢   color
➢   language
➢   religion
➢   political or other opinion
➢   national or social origin

Diagram 1: Human rights in UK

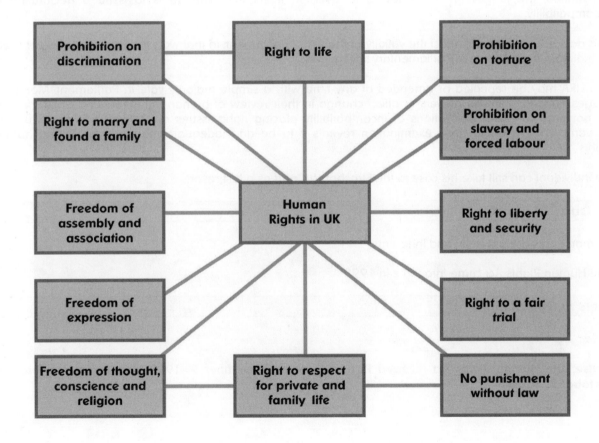

2. Explain the impact of human rights law on statutory interpretation
Explain the impact of human rights law on the common law

[Learning outcome b & c]

Judges must interpret legislation as far as possible in a way that is compatible with the Convention Rights. If this is not possible, courts can strike down incompatible delegated legislation, or can make a declaration of incompatibility in relation to primary legislation (Acts of Parliament). The judges, however, cannot strike down primary legislation.

Tips

Delegated legislation: law made by ministers under powers granted to them in Acts of Parliament.

In particular,

1. The Act makes it unlawful for any public body to act in a way which is incompatible with the convention, unless the wording of an Act of Parliament means they have no other choice.

2. It also requires UK judges take account of decisions of the Strasbourg court, and to interpret legislation, as far as possible, in a way which is compatible with the convention.

3. However, if it is not possible to interpret an Act of Parliament so as to make it compatible with the convention, the judges are not allowed to override it. All they can do is to issue a declaration of incompatibility.

4. This declaration does not affect the validity of the Act of Parliament: in that way, the Human Rights Act seeks to maintain the principle of Parliamentary sovereignty.

5. The HRA may be repealed or amended at any time with a simple majority vote in Parliament. Moreover, judges have very limited powers to affect change in their review of human rights matters. While they are empowered to issue declarations of incompatibility placing rights issues on a fast track procedure for Governmental change, close examination reveals it to be an inadequate means of protecting human rights

6. An individual can still take his case to the Strasbourg Court as a last resort.

Quick Quiz

1. Human rights are universal and inherent

2. The Human Rights Act came into force in 1998

Answers to Quick Quiz

1. **True**

2. **False,** The Human Rights Act received Royal Assent on November 9, 1998, and came into force **on October 2, 2000.**

Self Examination Question

Question 1

Explain the right to liberty and security.

Answer to Self Examination Question

Answer 1

Right to liberty and security

1. Everyone has the right to liberty and security. No one shall be deprived of his liberty except in the following cases and in accordance with a procedure prescribed by law:

    a) The lawful detention of a person after conviction by a competent court

    b) The lawful arrest or detention of a person for non-compliance with the lawful order of a court or in order to secure the fulfillment of any obligation prescribed by law

    c) The lawful arrest or detention of a person effected for the purpose of bringing him before the competent legal authority on reasonable suspicion of having committed an offence or when it is reasonably considered necessary to prevent his committing an offence or fleeing after having done so

    d) The detention of a minor by lawful order for the purpose of educational supervision or his lawful detention for the purpose of bringing him before the competent legal authority

    e) The lawful detention of persons for the prevention of the spreading of infectious diseases, of persons of unsound mind, alcoholics or drug addicts or vagrants

    f) The lawful arrest or detention of a person to prevent his effecting an unauthorised entry into the country or of a person against whom action is being taken with a view to deportation or extradition

2. Everyone who is arrested shall be informed promptly, in a language which he understands, of the reason for his arrest and of any charge against him.

3. Everyone arrested or detained in accordance with the provisions of paragraph 1(c) of this Article shall be brought promptly before a judge or other officer authorised by law to exercise judicial power and shall be entitled to trial within a reasonable time or to release pending trial. Release may be conditioned by guarantees to appear for trial.

4. Everyone who is deprived of his liberty by arrest or detention shall be entitled to take proceedings by which the lawfulness of his detention shall be decided speedily by a court and his release ordered if the detention is not lawful.

5. Everyone who has been the victim of arrest or detention in contravention of the provisions of this Article shall have an enforceable right to compensation.

SECTION B - THE LAW OF OBLIGATIONS

FORMATION OF CONTRACT

Get through intro

We frequently enter into contracts in our daily life. Even ordinary transactions such as buying a newspaper or purchasing goods for a certain price from a shop are examples of contracts.

A contract is simply an **exchange of commodities / services between two parties for a price**. Individual owners of commodities meet at a common place, known as a market, and freely enter into negotiations to decide the terms on which they are willing to exchange those commodities.

The **law of contract** is based on an idealised model of how the market operates and has been formulated to **facilitate the smooth functioning of the market**.

This Study Guide deals with the study and analysis of the nature of a contract, when a simple agreement becomes a contract, which contract is a void contract and which is a valid one, the meaning of offer and acceptance etc.

You need to devote considerable time to the study of this topic as you will always have a question on this topic in your examination. In your professional life, knowledge of the law of contracts will always be useful as **contracts are the basis of all commercial transactions.**

LEARNING OUTCOMES

a) Analyse the nature of a simple contract
b) Explain the meaning of offer and distinguish it from invitations to treat
c) Explain the meaning and consequence of acceptance
d) Explain the need for consideration
e) Analyse the doctrine of privity
f) Distinguish the presumptions relating to intention to create legal relations

Introduction

> ## Case Study
>
> On March 4, Hardy, a football player, signed a contract with a football club, 'the Wessex Wanderers'.
>
> A clause stating, "This agreement shall become valid and binding upon each party only when and if it shall be approved by the League Commissioner" was included in the contract.
>
> In late March, Hardy told the Wessex Wanderers that he could not play for them because he had joined another football club, 'Wessex United'.
>
> The commissioner approved the contract on April 14.
>
> Wanderers then sued Hardy for breach of contract.

As students of a professional course you would want to know the meaning of a proper contract system. Was there ever a contract between Hardy and the Wessex Wanderers?

This Study Guide which deals with formation of contract will give you your answers.

1. Analyse the nature of a simple contract

[Learning outcome a]

We need to know the following terms in order to understand the meaning of a contract.

Void: Not valid legally. It is something which has no legal force.

Example
A contract to kill a person is a void contract, as killing is not allowed legally.

Voidable: Something which can be legally rescinded i.e. set aside at the option of the innocent party

Example
A contract entered into by a minor is voidable by the minor. Within a reasonable time after attaining majority, he can claim that he was a minor when he entered into the contract. Hence, he was not competent to foresee that the contract was not beneficial for him. After becoming a major, he may cancel the contract or affirm it.

Ultra vires: Beyond the legal capacity of a person, company or other legal entity.

Example
Under traditional ultra vires doctrine, a corporation that has as its purpose the manufacturing of shoes cannot, under its charter, manufacture motorcycles.

Void ab initio: Invalid, at the very beginning.

Example
In many jurisdictions where a person signs a contract under duress, that contract is void ab initio. Duress means force, threat, coercion or compulsion.

An offer: When one person expresses his willingness to do or to abstain from doing something, to another person, with a view to obtaining the assent of that other person, he is said to be making an offer.

Example

Merry needs to rent a shop. Cherry, her friend, has a shop which is vacant. Merry offers to rent Cherry's shop for £10,000 per year. In this case, In this case, Merry has made Cherry an offer. Merry is the 'offeror' and Cherry is the 'offeree'.

Acceptance: When the person to whom the offer is made agrees to it, it is said that the offer is accepted.

Example

In the above example, if Cherry agrees to give her shop on rent to Merry, the offer is accepted.

Consideration: Consideration is required for a contract to be enforceable. Consideration is something that is done or promised in return for a contractual promise.

Example

In a contract between Amy and Bob for the sale of Amy's car to Bob, Bob's payment of the price of the car (or promise to do so) is the consideration for the contract.

Agreement: When an offer made by the offeror is accepted by the offeree, it becomes an agreement.

Example

Merry promises to pay Cherry an annual rent of £10,000 and Cherry promises to give the keys to the office to Merry. This is an agreement. The availability of the shop is consideration for Merry and £10,000 is consideration for Cherry.

It is important to note that, although, all contracts are agreements, **not all agreements are contracts.** This is because **all agreements are not legally enforceable.**

> **Tips**
>
> **Contract = Enforceable agreement + Consideration**

> **Tips**
>
> **Agreement = Offer + Acceptance**

1.1 Meaning of contract

1. A contract consists of an actionable promise or promises

2. Every such promise involves two parties, a promisor and a promisee

3. It involves a common intention of acceptance

4. There must be a consideration as to the act (i.e. agreeing to) or forbearance promised (i.e not doing something)

Example

Ajay and Ben enter into an agreement. Ajay promises Ben to sell his house for £15,000 and Ben accepts to purchase it for the said amount.

This is a contract between Ajay and Ben where Ajay is the offeror and Ben is the offeree.
The promise to pay £15,000 is the consideration by Ben.
The promise to sell the house is the consideration by Ajay.

Definition

The simplest possible description of a contract is **"an agreement enforceable by law for a consideration"**

Tips

Contract = Agreement + Enforceability + Consideration

Tips

Consideration is the element that makes the agreement a contract

1.2 Legal requirements for the creation of a contract (Essentials of a valid contract)

There are **three essential elements,** which would be examined by a court as the evidence of any contract. These are:

1. Agreement made by offer and acceptance

2. Intention to create legal relations

3. Consideration

Diagram 1: Essentials of a valid contract

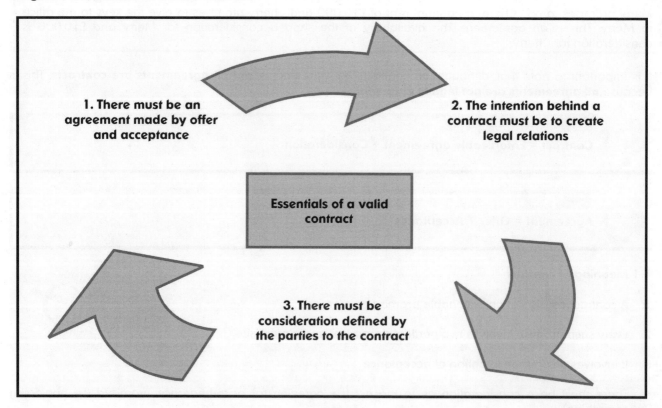

1. The agreement must have an offer and an acceptance: a contract is a **bilateral agreement** between two or more parties. Every contract has to go through the **stages** of:

a) an **offer being made**
b) **negotiations** among the parties which lead to a settlement
c) **acceptance** of the offer **for a consideration**

Therefore the presence of an offer and its acceptance are of utmost importance for any contract to take place.

> **Example**
>
> Lee and Chee enter into an agreement. Lee promises Chee to sell his house for £15,000 and Chee accepts to purchase it for that amount. Lee is said to be the offeror and Chee the acceptor. An offer becomes a promise when it is accepted.

2. The intention behind a contract must be to create legal relations: A contract, which is governed by the law of contract, must be made with a view to creating legal relations.

> **Example**
>
> David is leaving on a business trip. He promises his daughter that he will bring her back a camera. This cannot be considered a contract as he does not intend to bind himself legally.
>
> However, if David while leaving the office makes a written agreement with James that he will bring goods according to his description for a given price then this can be considered a contract. This is because both mutually intend to bind themselves legally.

Case Study
Intension to create legal relation is essential to create a contract

Balfour v Balfour (1919)

In this case the defendant, who was working in Ceylon, went on holiday to England with his wife. At the end of the holiday, his wife fell ill and was advised to remain in England for medical treatment. Before returning to Ceylon, the husband promised to pay £30 a month to his wife for her maintenance. Initially, he sent the amount regularly. However, he stopped paying as certain differences between them led to their separation. By the time of the separation, the allowance had fallen into arrears, so the wife brought an action to recover the arrears.

Court's decision: Her action was dismissed. It was held there was no indication that the arrangement was intended to be a contract.

While rejecting her claim, Lord Atkins observed: "there are agreements between parties which do result in contracts within the meaning of that term in our law. The ordinary example is where two parties agree to take a walk together, or where there is an offer and acceptance of hospitality. However, they are not a contract because the parties did not intend that they shall be attended by legal consequences."

3. There must be consideration defined by the parties to contract: consideration is necessary for the formation of every simple contract. **Consideration is the incentive, price or motive that causes a party to enter into an agreement or contract.**

It is something of value that is given in exchange for receiving something from another person.

An informal promise without consideration is not actionable in law even though the promisor may have acted upon it to his detriment.

> **Example**
>
> John wanted to go for an important meeting. David promised John to drive him to the station at the right time. However David failed to keep his promise, as a result of which John missed the train and ultimately missed the meeting.
> In this situation, John cannot take any action against David for the loss of potential benefits from the meeting as the promise made by David was an informal promise without consideration.

Tips

It is important to understand that every contract is a bilateral agreement (i.e. an agreement between two or more parties) and hence all the parties to the contract must have some agreed consideration.

Example

Alden enters into a contract with Bayol whereby he agrees to pay £500 to Bayol if Bayol's horse wins the race. Bayol's horse wins the race and he claims £500 from Alden.

Bayol is not entitled to get £500 from Alden because there is no consideration from his side. The contract contains no condition because of which Bayol will have to pay Alden some consideration.

Hence this is not a valid contract.

Besides the three essential conditions explained earlier, there are **some additional elements** which decide the validity of a contract. These are:
a) Capacity to contract
b) Legality of object.
c) Certainty of terms of contract

a) Capacity to contract: One of the essential requirements of a **valid contract** is that the parties must be competent to contract. Capacity refers to a person's ability to enter into a contract. In general, all adults of sound mind have full capacity to contract. However the capacity of certain individuals is limited. Normally, the following persons are considered to be incompetent to contract:

i.   Minor
ii.   Incorporated body: If the contract is against the clauses of or outside the scope of its Memorandum of association.
iii. Mental incapacity and intoxication
iv.   Disqualification by law
v.   Free consent

i. Minor: A minor is a person below the age of 18 years. Their contractual capacity is restricted by the law to prevent them from entering into disadvantageous agreements. However, not all contracts entered into by a minor are void.

Agreements entered into by minors may be classified within three possible categories:

➢ Valid contracts
➢ Voidable contracts
➢ Void contracts

Definition

Valid contracts: a valid contract is one which has all the essential elements of contract i.e. agreement, intention to create legal relations and consideration, and which is legally enforceable.

There are again two types of valid contracts which can be enforced against a minor:

✓ Contracts for necessaries

✓ Beneficial contracts of service

Contracts for necessaries: When a contract is relating to a payment for a supply of necessaries to a minor, then such a contract is binding on the minor.

Necessaries refer to things that are necessary to maintain a minor. However, whether any particular goods supplied are necessary or not will depend upon the facts and circumstances of each case.

As pointed out by **Cheshire and Fifoot,** the word necessaries is not confined to articles necessary for the support of life, but include articles and services fit to maintain the particular person in the station of life in which he moves.

Therefore, there is no definition of the term necessaries. Generally it means **goods and services which are most essential for the survival** of human life. It includes:

➢ food
➢ clothing
➢ shelter
➢ education

➢ medical and legal aid etc.

It also varies from person to person subject to his social status and family background. What is a luxury to one person may be a necessary to another.

Example

A car is a luxury for a poor boy whereas it may be a necessary for a prince who hails from a royal family.

The **necessaries must be things which the minor actually needs**. It is not enough that they be of a kind which a person of his condition may reasonably want for ordinary use. Items, which are generally necessaries, will prove to be **unnecessary if** the minor is **already supplied with items of that kind.** Whether the other party knows this fact or not will be held immaterial.

Case Study — Contract for necessities is binding on a minor

Nash v Inamn (1908)

In this case, a tailor supplied an undergraduate minor with some clothing. The minor was studying at Cambridge University. The clothing consisted of 11 fancy waistcoats at the price of two guineas each. It was proved that the Cambridge undergraduate already had a sufficient supply of clothing for his position in life.

Court's decision: It was held by the Appellate Court that the tailor was not entitled to be reimbursed for the supply of clothing as he failed to prove that the clothing was suitable to the minor's actual requirements at the time of sale and delivery.

The crux of the case is that, although the clothes were suitable according to the minor's station in life, they were not **necessary**, as he already had sufficient clothing.

This shows that the supply of more than adequate clothing can be considered **not** to be supply of necessaries.

Beneficial contracts of service: a minor is bound by a contract of apprenticeship or employment, as long as it is, **on the whole, for his / her benefit.**

Case Study — Minor is bound only by benefecial Contracts of service

Doyle v White City Stadium (1935)

Doyle, a minor, was granted a professional boxer's licence, which was treated as a contract of apprenticeship. The licence provided that he would be bound by the rules of the Boxing Board of control. According to one of the rules, the Board had the power to retain any prize money if he was ever disqualified in a fight. Doyle claimed that the licence was void, as it was not for his benefit.

Courts decision: It was held that, in spite of the penal clause, the licence, taken as whole, was beneficial to him. Hence the conditions of the licence were held enforceable.

Definition

Voidable contracts: Voidable contracts are those contracts which may be avoided, that is, set aside, **by one of the parties.** If, however, no steps are taken to avoid the contract, then the contract is considered to be a valid contract.

There are some contracts which may bind the minor. They remain valid until cancelled by the minor.

These contracts are binding on the minor, unless they are expressly disclaimed by the minor during the period of minority or within a reasonable time after attaining the age of majority.

Example

Fancy, a minor and a very famous child artist enters into a contract with a film producer to do a lead role in his film immediately after she becomes a major. However, this contract is voidable at the option of Fancy on becoming a major.

If she does not expressly disclaim fulfilling the contract within a reasonable time after attaining majority, then the contract will be binding on her.

Definition

Void contracts: A void contract is one which is not legally enforceable and the parties thereto are not legally obligated to each other.

Generally, contracts are void because the subject matter is not legal or one of the contracting parties does not have the competency to contract.

The following contracts entered into by a minor are always void:

✓ Contracts entered into by a minor for repayment of money lent or to be lent.

Example

John had lent Ted £10,000. Ted's minor son, Jimmy, entered into a contract with John for repayment of the loan his father had taken.

This is a void contract.

✓ Contracts for goods supplied or to be supplied (other than necessaries)

Example

Lilly, a minor, enters into a contract with Peter to buy his car.
This is a void contract.

Case Study — Contracts with minor are void

Mercantile Union Guarantee Corp v Ball (1937)

A minor was engaged in the haulage business. He had entered into a hire purchase contract which was related to the business.

Courts decision: It was decided by the court that a minor was not liable for the hire purchase entered into by him with regards to the haulage business. Contracts with minor for goods supplied are void.

✓ Contracts for release of rights in property.

Example

Jack, a minor, enters into a contract with his Uncle John whereby Jack agrees to release his right to their ancestral property.
This is a void contract.

Diagram 2: Minor

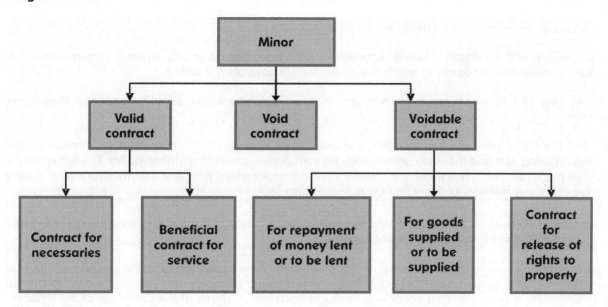

ii.   Incorporated body: Every incorporated body is a legal body created by the law. It can contract only through its agents such as a board of directors or chief officers in accordance with its internal   management.

A company cannot make any contract, which is **inconsistent with the objective set out in the Memorandum of Association.** If the company enters into such a contract, it is ultra vires i.e. beyond its powers and therefore void at common law but under S35 Companies Act 1985 (as amended by the Companies Act 1989) a third party acting in good faith will be able to enforce the transaction against the company.

iii.   Mental incapacity and intoxication: A contract entered into by a person who is of unsound mind or under the influence of drugs, or drunk is prima facie valid. Such contract can be held void if the person in contract proves:

➤   That at the time their mind was so affected that they were incapable of understanding the nature of their actions

➤   That the other party either knew or ought to have known of their disability. In any case, however, the person claiming such incapacity must pay a reasonable price for the goods supplied to them

---

Tips

Prima facie: a Latin term meaning "on the face of it." It is a fact which, unless disproved, is presumed to be true. In day-to-day speech, the term prima facie is used to describe the apparent nature of something at first glance.

Test Yourself 1

Sunny went to a bar. There he met Bobby, who was a painter. Sunny made an offer to Bobby that he paint his farm house for £500. Bobby accepted the offer. Sunny gave him the address of the farm house, the keys and £100 as an advance.

The next day Bobby went to Sunny's farm house and painted the farm house. However Sunny refused to pay the balance amount. He claimed that he was under the influence of alcohol and hence was unable to make a rational decision. In your opinion, is the contract valid?

---

iv.   Disqualifications by law: A person may also be disqualified from entering into a contract by any law to which he is a subject.

Example

A contract entered into with an alien enemy will be void.

An alien is a person who resides in a foreign country. An alien becomes an enemy when the country of which he is a citizen is at war with a country of which the other party to contract is a citizen.

Hence, at the time of a war between these two countries, an agreement with an alien enemy is illegal and therefore void.

In Potts v Bell (1918), it was held that all rights and obligations arising out of a contract with an alien enemy are suspended during war and that the contract may be void on the grounds of public policy. This is because it may promote the economic interests of the enemy state (i.e make money for the enemy country) or it may prejudice the economic interests of the state at war with enemy state.

---

v. Free consent: Two or more persons are said to consent when they agree upon the same thing in the same sense. A consent is said to be free when it is **not caused** by:

a) **Duress (Coercion):** This means committing, or threatening to commit any act against a person's will. Duress is some element of force, either physical or economic, which is used to override one party's freedom to choose whether to enter into a particular contract or not. Such contracts are voidable at the insistence of the innocent party.

In order to benefit from the doctrine of duress, claimants must prove two points:

➤ That the pressure, which has resulted in an absence of choice on their part, was brought on them against their will.

➤ That the pressure was of a nature considered to be illegal by the court.

Example

Armstrong threatened to kill Barton if he did not sign a contract. The contract was set aside due to duress to Barton.

---

b) **Undue influence:** A contract is said to be influenced by 'undue influence' when all the essential elements of undue influence are satisfied i.e.:

➤ The relationship between the parties is such that one of the parties is in a **position to dominate the will of the other**

➤ He **uses that influence to obtain an unfair advantage** over the other and

➤ Unfair **advantage is in fact obtained.**

Example

Alan advances some money to his son Bobby because he has financial problems in his business. When Bobby's financial problems end, Alan obtains a contract from Bobby for a greater amount than the sum due in respect of the advance.

The facts of the case needs to be compared with the essential elements of undue influence that:

1. The relationship between the parties is that of father and son. The father is in a position to dominate the will of his son.

2. The father uses his influence to obtain a greater amount than the sum which is due.

3. Unfair advantage, in fact has been obtained as there is already a contract between Alan and Bobby.

As all the essential elements of undue influence are satisfied, therefore this is a case of undue influence.

Test yourself 2

Brown approaches a bank for a loan at a time when banks generally are not giving loans. The bank declines to make the loan except at an unusually high rate of interest. Brown accepts the loan on these terms.
Do you consider this to be a case of undue influence?

Misrepresentation is not covered in syllabus.

SYNOPSIS

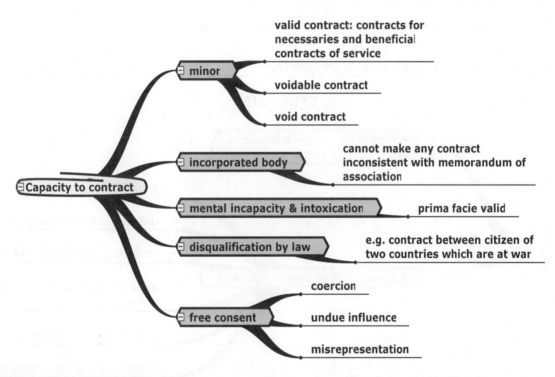

b) Legality of object: The legality of object is yet another essential element of a valid contract. A contract that breaks the law is illegal. The courts have recognised that any contract that tends to prejudice any social or economic interest of the country must be forbidden.

However, contracts that would be contrary to public policy depend on the facts and circumstances of the case under consideration.

Some examples of illegal contracts are:

i.   Contracts prohibited by statute.

Example

A contract to employ a child in a factory. Child labour is illegal and therefore this contract is illegal.

ii.   Contracts to defraud the Inland Revenue.

Example

A contract showing a sale price which is less than the actual price and accepting the difference in cash without disclosing it to the Inland Revenue.

iii. Contracts involving commission of crime.

> **Example**
>
> A contract to kill a person

iv. Contracts against the interest of the UK or friendly states.

> **Example**
>
> A contract to sell weapons to an enemy state

v. Contracts leading to corruption in public life.

> **Example**
>
> An amount paid to secure a high-profile job in government

vi. Contracts which interfere with the court of justice.

> **Example**
>
> A promise to indemnify a person who will do an illegal act

SYNOPSIS

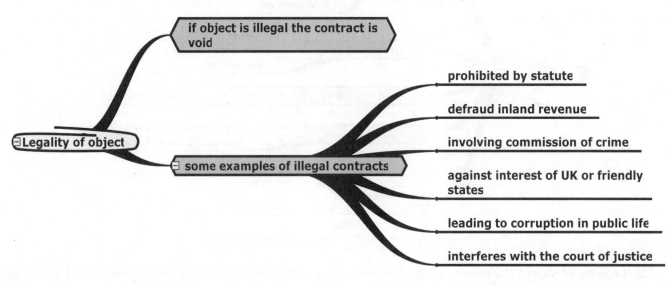

- if object is illegal the contract is void
- **Legality of object**
- **some examples of illegal contracts**
  - prohibited by statute
  - defraud inland revenue
  - involving commission of crime
  - against interest of UK or friendly states
  - leading to corruption in public life
  - interferes with the court of justice

c) Certainty of terms of contract: The contract terms should not be vague. They must be certain and definite. The intentions of the parties to contract must be clearly indicated by the terms of contract.

> **Example**
>
> Annie makes an offer to Bob to supply her with 100 metres of cloth. Here, the terms of offer are not clear since the type of cloth, colour, and price is not mentioned.
>
> Hence this is not a contract.

Case Study
The contract is not enforceable if the terms are vague and uncertain.

Taylor v Portington (1885)

The claimant in this case, promised to take the defendant's house on lease for a period of three years provided, "it is thoroughly repaired and the drawing rooms are decorated according to the latest style.

Courts decision: It was held that the contract is not enforceable, since the terms were vague and uncertain.

Diagram 3: Additional essentials of a valid contract

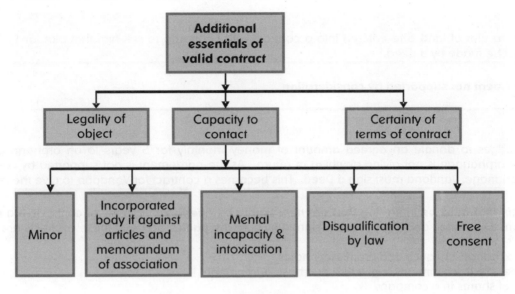

SYNOPSIS

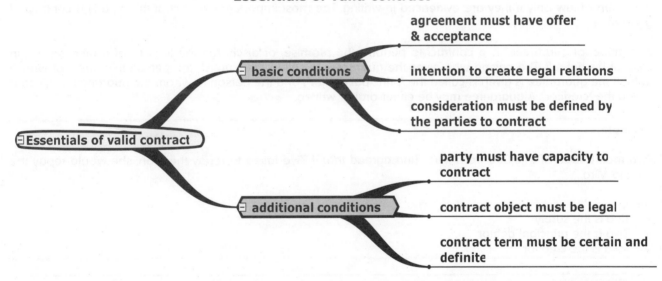

1.3 Form of contract – written or oral or inferred from the conduct of parties: As a general rule, a contract may be made in any form. There is no requirement that a contract has to be in writing. They can be created by **word of mouth or by an action**, as well **as in writing**.

However, the following types of contracts must be in writing

1. Contracts that must be made by a deed: A deed is a legal instrument used to grant a right. A contract by deed must be in writing. The deed must be signed by parties to the deed.

The contracts that must be in the form of a deed are:

a) **Leases of property** for a period of more than 3 years.

Example

Jennifer entered into a contract with Maria to lease her flat to Maria for 10 years. As the lease period is more than 3 years, the contract must be made by a deed.

---

b) Conveyance or **transfer of land**

Example

Marion owns a plot of land. She entered into a contract with Leonardo to sell him that plot for £25,000. This contract must be made by a deed.

---

c) An **agreement not supported by consideration**

Example

Vandana pledges to donate an agreed amount of money monthly for 5 years to an orphanage near her house. The orphanage is not giving anything in return. As the agreement is not supported by consideration from the orphanage, Vandana must sign a Deed. This becomes a contract for Vandana to give the money.

---

2. Contracts that must be in writing (but not necessarily by deed): Some types of contracts are required to be in the form of a written document, usually signed by both the parties. Some of these contracts are:

a) Bills of exchange, cheques and promissory notes.
b) Consumer credit instruments, e.g. a hire purchase agreement
c) Transfer of shares in a company
d) Sale or disposition of interest in land

3. Contracts that must be evidenced in writing: Certain contracts even though made orally, are enforceable in a court of law only if they are evidenced in writing. The most important contract of this type is a contract of guarantee.

A "contract of guarantee" is a contract to perform the promise, or discharge the liability, of a third person in case of his default. The person who gives the guarantee is called the "surety", the person in respect of whose default the guarantee is given is called the "principal debtor", and the person to whom the guarantee is given is called the "creditor". A guarantee may be either oral or written.

Example

Ziya took a loan of £10,000 from Mira. Tina agreed that if Ziya failed to repay the loan, she would repay the loan to Mira.

Here,
➢ Tina is the surety
➢ Ziya is the principal debtor
➢ Mira is the creditor

Test Yourself 3

Is an agreement for service with relatives or friends legally enforceable?

Test Yourself 4

David, a man enfeebled by disease and age, is induced by Baul's influence over him as his medical attendant, to agree to pay Baul an unreasonable sum for his professional services. Is the contract affected by undue influence?

Test Yourself 5

Andrew threatened to have Brian killed if he did not buy Alan's shares in a company of which Brian was the managing director. Is the contract to buy shares by Brian valid?

Test Yourself 6

Fenny promises to pay Campbell £5,000 if he murders her husband. Is the contract valid?

Test yourself 7

Which of the following relationships do not raise the presumption of undue influence?
a) Doctor and Patient
b) Trustee and Beneficiary
c) Landlord and Tenant
d) None of the above

SYNOPSIS

- **Form of contract**
  - oral contract
  - written contract

- **Some contracts must be in writing**
  - **deed**
    - leases
    - transfer of land
    - not supported by consideration
    - must be in writing
  - **in writing**
    - bills of exchange, cheques, promissory notes
    - consumer credit instruments
    - transfer shares in company
  - **evidenced in writing**
    - contract of guarantee

2. Explain the meaning of offer and distinguish it from invitations to treat
[Learning outcome b]

2.1 What is an offer?

Definition

An offer is a definite promise to be bound by particular terms and it must be capable of acceptance.

When one person signifies to another his willingness to do or to abstain from doing anything, with a view to obtain the assent of the other person to such act or abstinence, he is said to make a offer.

The person who makes the offer is the offeror and the person to whom the offer is made is the offeree.

The offer sets out the terms upon which the offeror is willing to enter into contractual relations with the offeree.

2.2   Elements of offer: The following are important elements of an offer:

1. There shall be at least two persons: the offeror and the offeree, who are competent to contract.

2. One person (the offeror) expresses his willingness to another (the offeree) to do, or abstain from doing something.

3. The offeror has the intention of getting the consent of the offeree to do such an act or abstain.

2.3 The offer can be made to whom?
The offer may be made to:

1. One person
2. A class of persons
3. The world at large

An offer need not always be made to a certain person (an ascertained person), but it is necessary that someone should accept it.

Example

If a person offers a reward to anyone who finds his lost diamond ring, the finder can successfully claim the reward.

Where an offer is made to the world at large, acceptance of the offer and performance by the party replying to it will be sufficient to make it an enforceable contract.

Very important case in the law of contract!!

Case Study   Acceptance of the offer

Carlill v Carbolic Smoke Ball Co (1893)

The defendants were proprietors and vendors of 'Carbolic Smoke Ball Co'.
They advertised a reward of £100 to any person who contracted influenza after using the Smoke Ball for a certain period, according to the printed directions. In order to show their sincerity, they also deposited £1,000 in a bank. The claimant used the Smoke Ball according to the printed directions yet she contracted influenza. She brought an action to claim the reward.

Arguments by the defendant company
1. The offer was so vague that it could not form the basis of a contract, as no time limit was specified in the offer.
2. There was no contract between the parties because a notification of acceptance had not been communicated to the company by the offeree.
3. Cannot contract with the whole world
4. Mrs Carlll had not provided any consideration for their promise
5. The advertisement did not constitute an offer but was simply sales talk.
6. There was no intention to create legal relations

Courts decision

The Court disagreed with the company's arguments, and awarded the claimant damages. It was pointed out by the court that:

1. In advertisement cases, an offer may be made to the world at large but it becomes a promise only when it is accepted by an ascertained person

2. The company must protect the user during the period of use- the offer was not vague.

2.4 Who can accept the offer?

1. Only the person or one of the persons **to whom the offer is made** can accept the offer.

2. Only a person who has knowledge of an offer can accept the same.

Example

Rocky loses his wallet and he offers a reward for it without advertising the fact that there would be a reward for it. Jacky finds the wallet and does not know about the reward offered by Rocky. He therefore cannot claim the reward.

SYNOPSIS

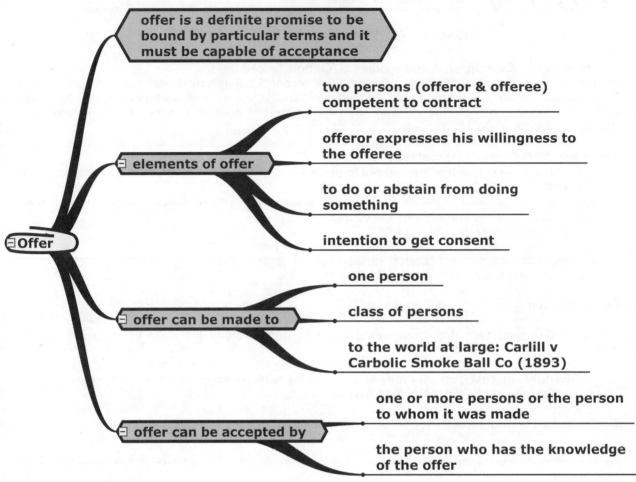

offer is a definite promise to be bound by particular terms and it must be capable of acceptance

Offer

elements of offer
- two persons (offeror & offeree) competent to contract
- offeror expresses his willingness to the offeree
- to do or abstain from doing something
- intention to get consent

offer can be made to
- one person
- class of persons
- to the world at large: Carlill v Carbolic Smoke Ball Co (1893)

offer can be accepted by
- one or more persons or the person to whom it was made
- the person who has the knowledge of the offer

2.5   Essentials of a valid offer

A valid offer must fulfil the following two conditions:

1. **An offer cannot be vague:** offers with uncertain meaning are void.

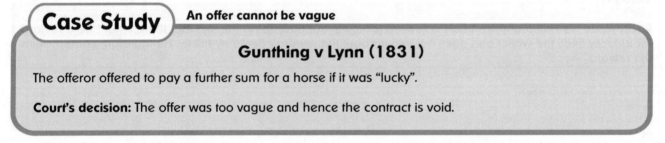

Case Study   An offer cannot be vague

Gunthing v Lynn (1831)

The offeror offered to pay a further sum for a horse if it was "lucky".

Court's decision: The offer was too vague and hence the contract is void.

2. **An offer must be distinguished from supply of information, statement of intention and an invitation to treat.**

a) Supply of information

Information may be necessary for the parties who are negotiating the terms of a contract before a definite offer is made. However, the mere supply of information cannot be a valid offer.

Case Study
Mere supply of information is not an offer.

Harvey v Facey (1893)

The claimant offered to purchase a plot of land, Bumper Hall Pen, belonging to the defendant. He telegraphed the defendant: 'Will you sell us the land known as Bumper Hall Pen? Telegraph lowest cost price".

The defendant sent the reply through the telegraph quoting, 'lowest price for Bumper Hall Pen £900'.

The claimant was ready to purchase the land at the quoted price. He telegraphed, "We agree to buy Bumper Hall Pen for £900".

But the defendant refused to sell the land for £900. On the denial of the defendant to sell the land, the claimant brought this suit.

Court's decision: It was held that no contract was made. The **defendant had not made an offer** by stating the lowest price of the land known as Bumper Hall Pen. He had **merely supplied information**. In other words, no offer had been made by the defendant and no acceptance of the offer was made by the claimant.

b) Statement of intention
A statement showing a present intention, which can be altered in the future as one wishes, is not an offer. Such a statement cannot be the basis of a contract, even though the party to whom it was made acts on it.

Case Study
Statement of intension is not an offer

Harris v Nickerson (1873)

The auctioneer had advertised that an auction sale would be held on a particular day. The claimant saw the advertisement and reached the place of the auction on the specified day. However, due to the auctioneer's illness the proposed sale was postponed.

Court's decision: It was held that the **auctioneer** was **not liable for damages.** An advertisement that an auction would be held at a particular time and place is not an offer to hold an auction. Any person who on the faith of the advertisement had incurred expenses to attend the proposed sale has no right of action if it is cancelled. This advertisement was a **statement of intention**.

c) Invitation to treat
This is an invitation to others to make offers. An offer comes into existence only when a person shows his readiness and willingness to enter into a contract. Where a person invites others to make an offer to him, the invitation made by him is not an offer, but only "an invitation to treat".

The purpose of making an invitation to treat is to receive the offer.

Example

A menu of a restaurant showing the various food items available at that restaurant and their prices. When the restaurant owner gives you the menu card, he is inviting an offer from you.

The contract of the owner of the restaurant serving food and you paying money does not exist.

It is only when you order something from the menu card and the restaurant owner agrees to serve you that the contract begins.

The person extending the invitation is not bound by the offers made to him. If you order some food item which is not on the menu, the hotel owner will reject your offer.

An invitation to treat is different from an offer primarily on the grounds that it is not made with the intention that it become binding as soon as the addressee communicates his assent to its terms. The contract comes into existence only when the offer made by others is accepted by the person who had made the "invitation to treat".

Some of the common situations involving an invitation to treat are:

i.   An advertisement in the newspaper inviting applications for jobs is generally not deemed to be an offer.

     However, a situation where an advertisement specifies the performance of a task or terms that are clear and leave no room for negotiation are exceptions to this. The **Carlill v Carbolic Smoke Ball Co case** shown earlier is a good example of this exception.

ii. Goods exhibited with a price-label in a display case.

> **Case Study**   Goods exibited with a price label are merely an invitation to treat.
>
> ### Fisher v Bell (1961)
>
> In this case, a shopkeeper was prosecuted for offering offensive weapons for sale, by having flick-knives on display in his window.
>
> **Court's decision**: It was held that the shopkeeper was not guilty as the display in the shop window was not an offer for sale but only an invitation to treat.
>
> Unless somebody offers the shopkeeper to purchase those weapons, and he accepts to sell them, he cannot be held guilty.

iii. Circulation of catalogue or price list by a seller

iv. A personal quotation of the price of goods

v.   Prospectus of a company inviting public to subscribe to their shares and debentures

vi. Auction sale

vii. Invitation for tenders is not an offer. A tender which is received in response to such an invitation is an offer.

> **Case Study**   Auction is invitation to treat and not an offer itself.
>
> ### Harris v Nickerson
>
> An auctioneer made an advertisement in the newspaper that an auction of office furniture would be held on a particular day. The claimant came from a distant place to buy the furniture, but the auction was cancelled.
>
> **Court's decision**: It was held by the court that the advertisement of the auction **was only an "invitation to treat" and not an offer itself.**
>
> Since there was no offer, there could not be any acceptance. Hence there was no contract between the auctioneer and the claimant.

Case Study — Goods displayed in shops are invitations to the customer to offer to buy.

Pharmaceuticals Society of Great Britain v Boots Cash Chemicals Ltd (1953)

In this case, the defendant was charged with breaking the law, which stated that certain drugs could only be sold under the supervision of a qualified pharmacist. They had placed the drugs in an open display in their self service store, although a qualified person was stationed at the cash desk.

It was claimed by the claimant that once the customer picked up an article and put it into the basket (supplied by the shopkeeper for the purpose), the contract of sale was complete: the shopkeeper could not then refuse to sell it.

Court's decision: The defendant was found not guilty. It was held that the mere fact that a customer picks up a bottle of medicine from the shelves does not amount to an acceptance of an offer to sell. It is an offer by the customer to buy, and there is no sale confirmed until the buyer's offer to buy is accepted by the acceptance of the price.

SYNOPSIS

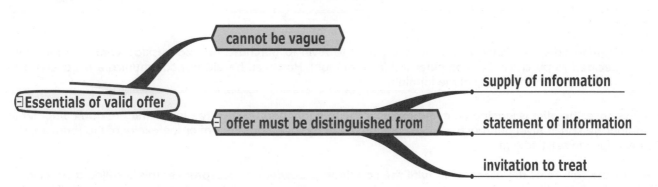

Diagram 4: Essentials of valid offer

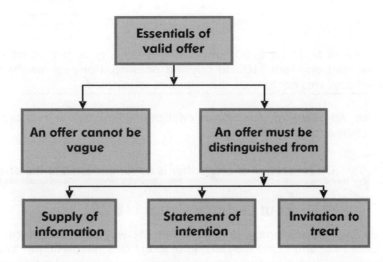

Test yourself 8

Distinguish between an "offer" and an "invitation to treat".

2.6 How can an offer be terminated?

Termination means putting an end to an offer. An offer can be terminated in any one of the following ways:

1. **By rejection of offer:** Expressed rejection of an offer terminates the offer. A **counter-offer** also terminates the original offer.

Case Study
A counter-offers teminates the origianl offer

Hyde v Wrench (1840)

Wrench offered to sell his farm for £1,000. Hyde offered £950, which Wrench rejected. Hyde then informed Wrench that he accepted the original offer of £1,000. But Wrench refused to sell the farm to Hyde.

Court's decision: It was held that there was no contract.

Hyde's **counter-offer** had terminated the original offer and therefore the original offer was no longer open for acceptance. Hyde was now making an altogether new offer to buy Wrench's land for £1,000, and it was for Wrench to decide whether to accept the offer or reject it.

The offeror and offeree have replaced each other.

2. **By lapse of time:** An offer is terminated by the lapse of time prescribed in the offer for its acceptance. If no time for acceptance is mentioned in the offer, then the offer is terminated by the lapse of reasonable time.

Example

Daisy purchased a new laptop. She made an offer to Alvin to purchase her old desktop computer for £250. Alvin decided to purchase the computer within a fortnight. However, he did not communicate his decision to Daisy during or after the expiry of the fortnight.

In this case, the offer is terminated at the expiry of the fortnight and Daisy is free to sell the desktop computer to another person. If Alvin approaches her to purchase the desktop computer after the expiry of the fortnight, she may refuse to sell it to him.

3. **By the failure of the acceptor to fulfil the condition precedent to acceptance:** This is called a conditional offer. Where an offer is subject to any condition for its acceptance, then the offer terminates on non-fulfilment of the condition.

Example

Jaya offers to sell a painting to Maya for £100, provided that Maya gives her an advance of £20 within two days. Maya came on the third day with £100 to buy the painting. However, as the condition of giving an advance of £20 within two days was not fulfilled, the offer was terminated.

4. **By revocation of offer:** An offeror may revoke an offer at any time before its acceptance. Once revoked, it is no longer open to the offeree to accept the offer.

Case Study
On revocation of offer, offer is no longer open to the offeree.

Rout Ledge v Grant (1828)

Grant offered to buy Rout ledge's house and gave him six weeks to accept the offer. However, he withdrew the offer before the end of the 6 weeks. Rout ledge claimed that Grant was bound to buy his house.

Court's decision: It was held that Grant was entitled to withdraw the offer at anytime before the acceptance. As the offer was already withdrawn, Rout ledge could no longer create a contract by accepting the offer.

Important points to note

i. Revocation is not effective until it is actually received by the offeree.

Case Study

Revocation of offer has no effect until it is communicated to the person to whom the offer has been mode.

Byrne v Van Tinehoven (1880)

In this case, on October 1, an offer to sell was mailed by the offeror.

It was received by the offeree on October 11. The offeree accepted the offer by sending a telegram on October 11. On October 15, the offeree again mailed a letter to the offeror to confirm the acceptance.

However, on October 8, a letter was sent by the offeror revoking the offer. On October 20, the offeror received the letter of acceptance sent by the offeree.

Court's decision: It was held that the **revocation was inoperative**.

The court said that "an offer can be withdrawn before it is accepted and it is immaterial whether the offer is expressed to be open for acceptance for a given time or not."

However, withdrawal of offer has no effect until it is communicated to the person to whom the offer has been sent. An uncommunicated revocation is no revocation at all under the law.

Case Study

Implied revocation of offer

Dickinson v Doodds (1876)

Once a person is informed that the item that was offered to him was sold to another person, there is an implied communication of the revocation of the offer and it is too late for acceptance (full case below)

ii. Communication of revocation may be made through a reliable third party.

Example

Charley offered to sell his car to Eddy. However the next day, he sold the car to another person. Charley informed Eddy's wife, that the offer to Eddy is now revoked as he had already sold the car to somebody else. In this case, the revocation is effective as the communication of revocation of the said offer was made through a reliable third party.

Case Study

Communication of revocation of offer may be made by a reliable third party.

Dickinson v Doodds (1876)

Dodds offered to sell a property to Dickinson. He also told Dickinson that the offer would be left open until Friday. On Thursday, Dodds informed Dickson through a person who was acting as an intermediary that he intended to sell the property to someone else. Dickson still attempted to accept the offer on Friday. But the property was already sold before Friday.

Courts decision: It was held that the sale of the property amounted to revocation. The revocation communicated by a reliable third party amounts to effective communication of revocation.

5. By death of one of the parties

a) In the case of personal contract, where the offeree dies, the offer automatically ends.

Example

Rani, a finance consultant offers to handle Mani's financial matters from the month of April. However Rani dies in March. The offer to Mani automatically ends.

b) In the case of non personal contracts e.g. sale of a vehicle, the contract can be enforced by a representative of the deceased.

Example

John offered to buy flowers from Kim's farm in the month of March for £5,000. Kim accepted the offer. However John died in February and his son Jacky took over the charge of his business. In this case, Jacky can enforce the contract against Kim. Kim will have to supply the flowers to Jacky.

SYNOPSIS

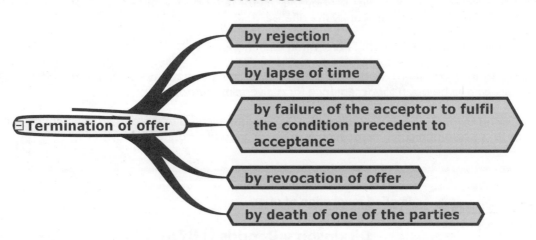

Diagram 5: Termination of an offer

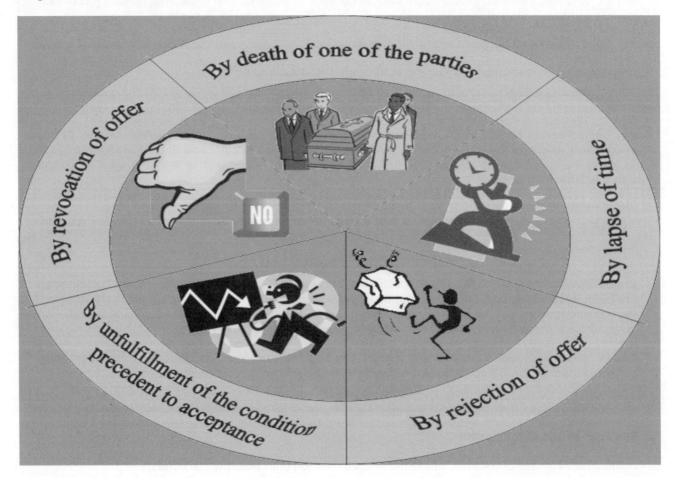

Test yourself 9

Which of the following offers constitute a valid offer?

a) An auctioneer displays a T.V. set before a gathering in an auction sale.
b) John advertises in a newspaper that he would pay £500 to anyone, who finds and returns his lost briefcase containing valuables.
c) Ron who is in possession of three cars purchased in different years says 'I will sell you a car'
d) A clothing store owner announces that prices of formal shirts are reduced by 60%
e) Julie communicates to Lilly that she will sell her car for £4000.

Test Yourself 10

Explain the rules relating to revocation of an offer in relation to the law of contract.

3. Explain the meaning and consequence of an acceptance

[Learning outcome c]

3.1 What is an acceptance?

Definition

"When a person to whom an offer is made signifies his assent to the same, the offer is said to be accepted. Acceptance of an offer is a necessary and vital ingredient towards the creation of a contract".

After an offer has been made, the next important step for the formation of a contract is acceptance. An offer creates no legal rights or duties unless it has been accepted. **Acceptance converts an offer into a contract.**

3.2 Conditions for valid acceptance

For an acceptance to be binding, it must fulfil the following conditions:

1. **Acceptance must be communicated:** Even if the offeree has made up his mind to accept the offer, the agreement is not yet complete. There must be an external expression of assent. The acceptance of an offer must be communicated to the offeror. The communication of acceptance should be clear and unambiguous.

2. **Mode of communication:** Acceptance can be communicated in any of the following three ways:

    a) Acceptance by express words
    b) Acceptance by action
    c) Acceptance inferred from conduct

Case Study — Mode of communication

Felthouse v Bindley (1862)

The claimant wrote a letter to his nephew offering to buy his nephew's horse for £30.15s. He also wrote in his letter, "If I hear no more about him I shall consider the horse to be mine at £30.15s." The nephew did not reply to this letter. However, he told the defendant, an auctioneer, not to sell the horse. **Hence, he intended to reserve the horse for his uncle.** But the auctioneer sold the horse to someone else. The claimant thereupon sued the defendant, the auctioneer.

Court's decision: Dismissing the action, the court held that since the nephew **did not communicate his acceptance**, no contract took place between the claimant and his nephew. Hence, he had no right to make a complaint regarding the sale.

The court also held that the communication of acceptance must be made to the offerer himself or to his agent. Here the communication of acceptance was made to the auctioneer who was a stranger to the claimant.

3. **The offeror cannot impose upon the offeree an obligation to refuse: In Felthouse v Bindley** discussed above, it was also held that the offerer cannot impose upon the offeree the obligation of refusal. The uncle wrote to his nephew, "If I hear no more about him I shall consider the horse to be mine at £30.15s." In this case, **mere silence from the nephew would not constitute acceptance.**

4. **Communication of acceptance must be by a person who has authority to accept:** A communication of acceptance to be valid must be made either by the offeree himself or by his authorised agent. A communication of acceptance by any other person will not be valid.

Case Study — Communication of acceptance must be by a person who has authority to accept

Powell v Lee (1908)

The board of managers of a school passed a resolution selecting the claimant (a candidate) for the post of headmastership but the decision about his selection was not communicated to him. One of the managers, in his individual capacity, informed him about the resolution. Subsequently, the board of managers rescinded their decision and so the claimant was not appointed as the headmaster. The claimant, thereupon, brought an action for breach of contract.

Court's decision: The court held that no contract was concluded because for a communication of acceptance to be valid it must be made by the offeree himself or his authorised agent.

A communication of acceptance from an unauthorised person is not valid.

There are, however, **exceptions to the general rule that acceptance must be communicated.** Communication of acceptance is not required in the following cases:

a) Communication may be waived by the offerer: Since the notification of the communication is for the benefit of the offerer, he may waive it if he deems it fit.

In Carlill v Carbolic Smoke Ball Co, the facts of which were discussed earlier, the court observed that it was sufficient for the claimant to act on the offer without notifying her acceptance of it. The contract was a unilateral contract, where the offer takes the form of a promise to pay money in return for an act.

Case Study

Acceptance through postal services complete when letter of acceptance is posted by the offeree

Adams v Lindsell (1818)

The defendants made an offer to sell wool to the claimant in a letter dated September 2, 1817. This letter arrived on September 5, 1817. The claimant posted his letter of acceptance on the same day, i.e. on the 5th September 1817. The defendants received the letter on September, 9, 1817. But the defendants had already sold the wool to some other party after waiting until 8th September 1817. An action was brought against them by the claimant for the breach of contract.

Court's decision: The court held the defendants liable to pay.
The court observed: "....If the defendants were not bound by their offer when accepted by the claimant until the answer was received, then the claimant ought not to be bound until after they had received the notification that the defendants had received the answer and assented to it. And, so there will be no end to this".
It was therefore decided that the contract was made when the acceptance was posted, regardless of the fact that the letter of acceptance was lost or not received.

b) Where acceptance is through postal services: The general rule is that acceptance is complete as soon as the letter is posted, provided post is a reasonable method of communication. An acceptance by post is a well-established exception to the general rule that acceptance must be communicated.

SYNOPSIS

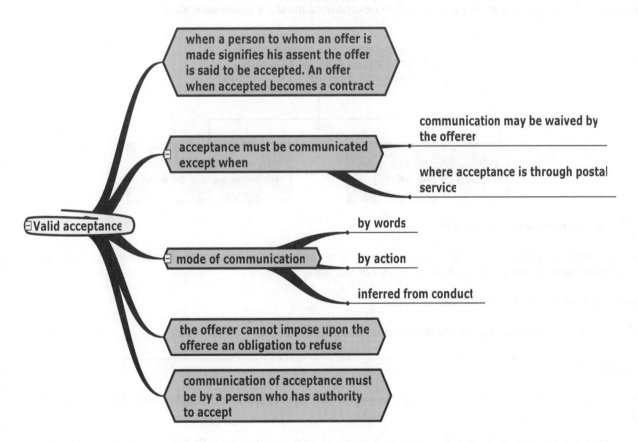

Diagram 6: Conditions for valid acceptance

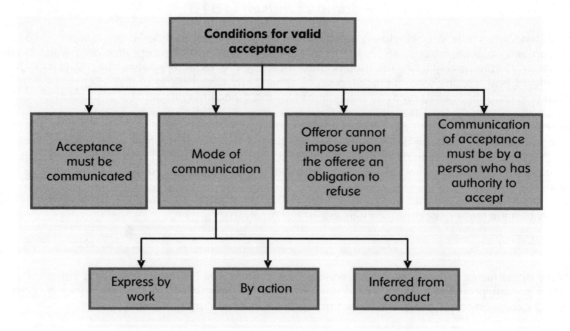

Diagram 7: Exceptions to general rule that acceptance must be communicated

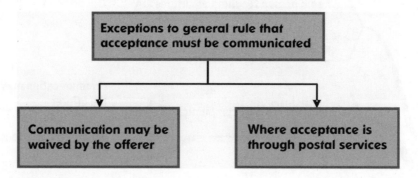

3.3. Some other important points

1. **Conditional contracts:** A conditional contract is a contract to do or not to do something, if any stipulated condition stated in the contract, does or does not happen.

Important elements of conditional contract

a) A valid contract that is currently being contemplated is a conditional contract.

Example

A buyer places a condition that the car (he wishes to buy) must pass a mechanical check before he will purchase it.

Therefore the passing of the mechanical check is the condition without which this contract cannot take place. If the car fails to pass the mechanical check the buyer can choose to cancel the contract. Any deposit that has been paid will have to be refunded.

---

b) Such a contract becomes due for performance either on

i.   The occurrence of a future event or

> **Example**
>
> Roger offers to sell his sports car to Bali if Bali wins a car race. Here, the performance by Roger (selling his car) will become due when Bali wins the car race.

ii.   The non-occurrence of a future event.

Examples of conditional contracts

➤ **Contract of insurance:** The insurer is liable to pay the damages to the insured only when the insured suffers damages to the insured property. The causing of damages is the condition attached for the payment of sum assured by the insured.

➤ **Contract of life insurance:** The sum assured under a life insurance contract is payable to the nominee of the insured only on the death of the person insured. The death of the person insured is the condition stipulated for the payment of the sum insured.

2.   **Collateral contracts:** A collateral contract is a contract which requires some other contract for its fulfilment. A collateral contract may be between one of the parties and a third party.

> **Example**
>
> There are two separate contracts: one between A and B and the other between A and C. The terms of both the contracts require some action between B and C and hence there may be a contract between B and C.

The case study given below will help you to understand this.

Case Study — **Collateral contracts**

Shanklin Pier Ltd v Detel Products Ltd (1951)

In this case, the defendant gave assurances to the claimant that their paints would be satisfactory and durable for repainting the claimant's pier. The pier company, relying upon representations made by the defendant, the paint manufacturer, specified a particular type of paint for the redecoration and protection of their pier. The redecoration work was carried out by a painting contractor who purchased paint from Detel Products. When the product later proved to be defective and failed, the contractor pointed out that the particular type of paint was specified by the pier company itself and he only complied with the pier company's specification.

The defendant (Detel Products Ltd) argued that they had not supplied paint to the claimants (Shanklin Pier Ltd) under a purchase agreement. As there was no contract with Shanklin Pier, they could not therefore recover damages.

Court's decision: However, the court decided that collateral to the redecoration contract, there was an implied agreement between the claimant and the defendant. Owing to this implied agreement, the choice of the defendant's product was made in response to their (false) representations as to its suitability.

Shanklin Pier Ltd therefore recovered damages for breach of this collateral undertaking on the part of the paint supplier.

3.   **Unilateral contract:** A contract where one party promises a reward or action in return for some desired action on the part of the second party is called a unilateral contract. In this case the offeror cannot revoke the contract once the offeree has started executing the action. Errington v Errington (1952)

Example

In Carlill v Carbolic Smoke Ball Co (1893), the company promised to pay £100 to anyone who caught influenza after using their product. There was no force to buy the product. However, once any person bought it and started using it the company was bound by its promise.

Test Yourself 11

Explain the following terms:
(a) A unilateral contract
(b) The rules relating to acceptance of an offer

SYNOPSIS

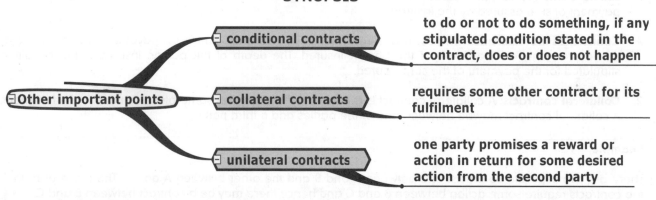

Other important points
- conditional contracts — to do or not to do something, if any stipulated condition stated in the contract, does or does not happen
- collateral contracts — requires some other contract for its fulfilment
- unilateral contracts — one party promises a reward or action in return for some desired action from the second party

---

4. Explain the need for consideration

[Learning outcome d]

4.1 What is consideration?

Another essential element of a contract is the consideration. Consideration, in simple terms is a reasonable equivalent or other valuable benefit passed on by the contractor to the contractee. We will discuss the need for consideration, the adequacy and sufficiency of consideration in this section.

1. Need for consideration

Consideration is necessary for the formation of every contract. An agreement can take the form of a contract only when it is made by the free consent of parties competent to contract, for a lawful consideration and with a lawful object. Therefore consideration is one of the essential ingredients of a contract.

Example

Alan promises to give Baron £100. Baron has to give nothing in return. As there is no consideration, this is a gratuitous promise and not legally enforceable.

---

2. Meaning of consideration

Definition

The term 'consideration' has been defined as:

"A valuable consideration in the eye of law may consist either in some right, interest, profit, or benefit accruing, to one party, or some forbearance and detriment, loss or responsibility given, suffered or undertaken by the other".

From Currie v Misa (1875)

"An act or forbearance of one party, or the promise thereof, is the price for which the promise of the other is bought, and the promise thus given for value is enforceable".

From Dunlop v Selfridge (1915)

Consideration simply, is the price paid for the promise. **Consideration need not be in the form of money only**. It can be in any form such as rights, interest, profits or benefits. Some of the examples of consideration are:

a) The giving of employment
b) Permitting goods to remain in the promisor's possession.
c) The assignment of contract
d) The guarantee of an overdraft

Consideration may also be forbearance, detriment, loss or responsibility suffered, or undertaken by the promisee.

3. **Types of consideration**

Diagram 8: Types of consideration

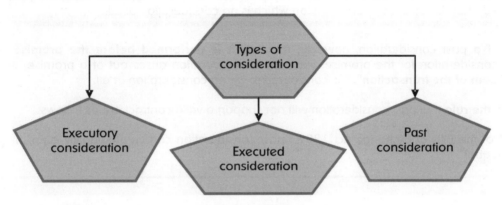

Consideration can be divided into the following three categories:

a) **Executory consideration**: This is a **promise** to perform an action in return **of a promise**, at some future time.

Example

➢ Omar promises to do some work in return for a promise of payment.

➢ Shopkeeper's promise to supply the goods and customer's promise to accept the goods and pay.

In the above examples, neither party has yet done any act but each party has given a promise in order to obtain the promise of the other person. It would be a breach of contract if either party withdrew from his / her promise without the consent of the other.

b) **Executed consideration**: This is an **act in return for a promise.** The promise only becomes enforceable when the offeree has actually performed the required act.

Example

➢ Richard loses his wallet and offers Bogdan a reward if he finds and returns the lost wallet. It is only when Bogdan finds the wallet and duly returns it to Richard that the reward becomes enforceable and the consideration becomes valid.

➢ **In Carlill v Carbolic Smoke Ball Co's case,** Mrs. Carlill's act of using the smoke ball for the prescribed period in response to the company's promise of reward **was therefore executed consideration**.

---

c) **Past consideration:** Such consideration, actually, is **not regarded as a valid consideration**. Usually, consideration is provided either at the time of the creation of a contract or at a later date.

Case Study

Past consideration is no consideration at all.

Re McArdle (1951)

In this case, according to the will of the father a certain number of children were entitled to a house after the death of their mother. In the mother's lifetime one of the children and his wife lived in the house with the mother. The wife made some improvements in the house during this period. All the children subsequently undertook in writing to pay a sum of £488 to the said wife in consideration of her carrying out the improvements. But at the mother's death they refused to pay her any thing.

Court's decision: It was held that the said promise was without consideration for the obvious reason that improvements to the house had been completed before the document containing the promise were signed. Thus, it was a past consideration which is no consideration at all.

In the case of a past consideration, however, the **action is performed before the promise**. So it cannot become the consideration for the promise. Since past consideration arises out of a promise **"subsequent to and independent of the transaction"**, it is considered to be no consideration at all.

Exceptions to the rule that past consideration will not support a valid contract are as follows:

i. Under s.27 of the Bills of Exchange Act 1882, "past consideration can create liability on a bill of exchange (such as cheque)".

> **Example**
>
> Robert mows Mike's lawn and a week later Mike gives Robert a cheque for £10. Robert's work is valid consideration in exchange for the cheque.

ii. Under s.29 of the Limitation Act 1980, "a time barred debt becomes enforceable again if it is acknowledged in writing".

iii. Where the claimant performed the action at the request of the defendant and payment was expected, then any subsequent promise to pay will be enforceable. An illustrative case on this point is:

Case Study

Past consideration .

Lampleigh v Braithwaite (1615)

In this case, the defendant had killed a man and had asked the claimant to obtain royal pardon for him. The claimant did so at his own expense. The defendant then promised to pay him £100. He failed to pay and was sued.

Courts decision: It was held that there was an implied promise to pay and the subsequent promise merely fixed the amount. Hence the consideration (to obtain royal pardon) was valid.

SYNOPSIS

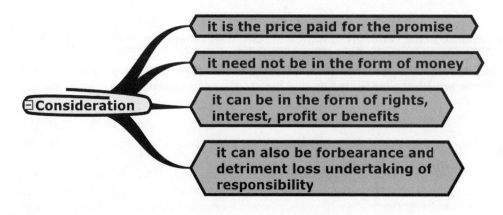

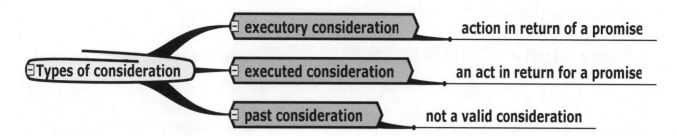

4. Rules relating to consideration

Along with the past consideration rule, some other rules that govern the legal definition and operation of consideration are:

1. **An act, abstinence or promise to be a good consideration, must be something more than what the promissor is already bound to do:** to do something which a person is already bound to do, is not a good consideration. A person may be bound to something in the following two ways:

a) **By law**

For example, performance of a legal duty is no consideration for a promise.

> ### Case Study — Act, abstinence or promise to be a good consideration, by law
>
> #### Collins v Godfroy (1831)
>
> In this case, the claimant had been summonsed to give evidence on behalf of the defendant in a case. He argued that the defendant had promised to pay him six guineas for appearing before the court.
>
> **Courts decision:** There was no consideration for this promise as appearing before the court to give evidence is the duty imposed by statute.

However, when a person has done something more than what he was bound to do by law, then that would be a good consideration.

> ### Case Study — If an act is performed over and above that required by law or public duty, that act is sufficient consideration for a promise.
>
> #### Glassbroke Brothers Ltd v Glamorgan County Council (1925)
>
> In this case, due to a strike in the colliery, a colliery manager requested police protection for his colliery. Rejecting the view of the police that a mobile force was enough, the manager agreed to pay for a special guard at the mine. Later, he refused to pay arguing that the police were already bound to protect the life and property of persons and had done no more than perform their public duty of maintaining order.
>
> **Courts decision:** The court pointed out that the police were bound to protect the life and property of the public. However, if any person wanted any special kind of protection (which was usually not provided for by the police) then the person concerned must pay for it.

b) **By contract**

A person may also be already bound to do something under a pre-existing contract. This pre-existing contract may be:

i. With the third party or

ii. With the promisor himself.

i. **Pre-existing contract with the third party**

If Julie promises Millie a reward if Millie performs her existing contract with Lilly, then Julie is entitled to some right for which she was previously not entitled and Millie is under a new obligation. **Here the question arises of whether a promise for the performance of an existing duty constitutes a good contract?**

The case study given below is a good example to understand this concept.

Case Study — Pre-existing contract with the third party

Shadwell v Shadwell (1860)

In this case, the claimant had promised to marry a girl. The claimant's uncle (the defendant), in consideration of his intended marriage with the said girl, promised, in a letter, to pay him (the claimant) £150 yearly during his (i.e. the uncle's) life or until the claimant's income as a practising lawyer increased to 600 guineas. The claimant married the girl. His annual income never increased to 600 guineas. The annuity fell into arrears as the uncle died. The claimant filed a suit to enforce the said promise.

Courts decision: It was held that entering into the marriage was **sufficient consideration** for the uncle's promise, even though the claimant was already contractually bound to his fiancée. The uncle received benefit from the marriage taking place (in his capacity as a close relative), and the nephew was therefore entitled to the arrears of the promised annuity.

ii. **Pre-existing contract with the promisor himself**

A promise to do a particular thing which the promisee is already bound to do under a pre-existing contract with the promisor will not constitute a good consideration.

Example

In **Pinnel's case (1602),** it was held that if a debtor pays a smaller sum in satisfaction of a large sum, it will not be regarded as a good discharge of the debt because the debtor was already bound to pay the whole amount. The payment of a lower debt for a larger sum is not a good discharge of debt; it is against ethical commercial practices. Hence it is considered a part payment, not a full payment.

2. **Consideration must be sufficient but need not be adequate:** the court will **not inquire into the 'inadequacy of consideration'**. This means:

i. They will not seek to measure the comparative value between the defendant's promise and of the act or promise given by the claimant in exchange for it

ii. They will not denounce the agreement merely because it seems to be unfair

It is presumed that each party is capable of serving his / her own interests. The courts will not seek to weigh the comparative value of the promises or acts exchanged.

The court will not intervene and require equality in the value exchanged as long as the agreement has been freely entered into.

Case Study — Consideration need not be adequate.

Thomas v Thomas (1842)

In this case, by his will, the claimant's husband expressed his wish that his widow should be allowed to use his house during her lifetime. The executors of the husband's will promised to let his widow live in his house, in return for rent of £1 per year. However, they later said that their promise to let her occupy the house was not supported by consideration.

Courts decision: It was decided that £1 was **sufficient consideration to validate the contract,** although it did not represent an adequate rent in economic terms.

3. **Sufficiency of consideration:** Consideration is sufficient if it has some identifiable value. The law only requires an element of bargain, not necessarily that it should be a good bargain.

> **Example**
>
> In **Chappell & Co v Nestle Co (1959)** Nestle offered a record to customers who sent a certain number of chocolate bar wrappers. It was held that a used chocolate wrapper was consideration sufficient to form a contract, although it had no economic value whatsoever to Nestle and was in fact thrown away after it was returned to them.

4. **Performance must be possible:** A binding valid contract cannot be framed if the consideration is the promise to perform an act that is clearly impossible.

Promise to perform an impossible act cannot form the basis of a binding contractual agreement.

> **Example**
>
> ➢ Aurelia agrees to pay Benedict £1,000 if Benedict will marry Aurelia's daughter Claudia. Claudia was dead at the time of the agreement. The agreement is void.
>
> ➢ Ahmed agrees to pay Burquah £1,000 if two straight lines enclose a space. The agreement is void.
>
> ➢ Harry promises to bring a dead body back to life for £100,000. This is impossible hence void

5. **Promissory Estoppel:** The doctrine of promissory estoppel prevents one party from withdrawing a promise made to the second party **if the latter has relied on that promise and acted upon it.**

In law, a promise made without consideration is generally not enforceable. It is known as a bare or gratuitous promise.

> **Example**
>
> If a car salesman promises not to sell a car until the weekend, but does so, the promise cannot be enforced against him. But should the car salesman accept even one penny in consideration for the promise, the promise will be binding and enforceable in court.

Case Study Promissory Estoppel

Central London Property Trust Ltd v High Trees House Ltd (1947)

In this case, the claimants leased a block of flats to the defendants in 1937 at an annual rent of £2,500. However, the defendants were unable to find enough tenants during WWII. Therefore they agreed to accept a reduction in rent to £1,250.

There was no consideration for this promise to accept a lower rent.

At the end of the war the flats were again fully let. The claimants wanted to return to the terms of the original agreement. They claimed the full rent (£2,500) for the future period. They also wanted to recover the rent lost during the war time period when they received only half rent.

Courts decision: It was held that the claimants were entitled to the full rent from the end of the war. However, they were stopped from claiming the rent lost during the wartime period

Estoppel is an exception to this rule.

Estoppel is "a shield not a sword" – it cannot be used as the basis of an action on its own. It can be used in defence by a party sued and cannot be used as a cause of action. It also does not extinguish rights.

> **Example**
>
> In **Combe v Combe,** the court refused to allow using estoppel as a "sword" by an ex-wife to extract funds from the destitute husband.

If a payment is made early then there is consideration for the promise and it is binding. Estoppel can be raised if a party agrees to accept a smaller amount and then changes his mind.

Test yourself 12

Which of the following is false?

a) Consideration must be real
b) Consideration must have some identifiable value
c) Consideration can be inadequate
d) A promise to do something which one is already bound to do by law, will be treated as good consideration

Diagram 9: Rules relating to consideration

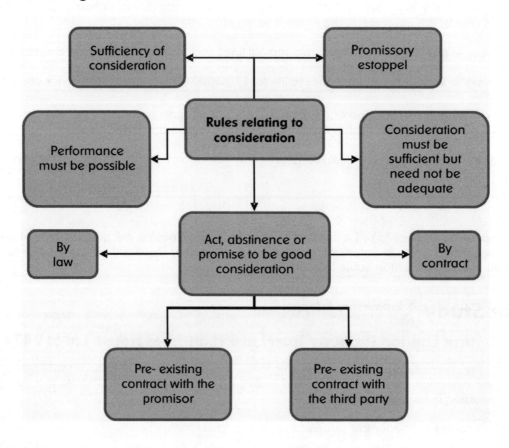

Test Yourself 13

Define consideration.

Test Yourself 14

Explain and distinguish between the following terms:
i. Executory consideration
ii. Executed consideration
iii. Past consideration

Test Yourself 15

Alan offered to pay Tom a sum of £50 if Tom dry-cleaned Alan's suit. Alan subsequently lost his baggage, including his suit, at the hotel. Alan then offered a reward of £100 to Greg to find the suit. Greg found the suit and returned it to Alan who later gave it to Tom to dry-clean. Tom dry-cleaned the suit and handed it back to Alan.

State with explanation which of the above considerations is executory consideration and which is executed consideration.

SYNOPSIS

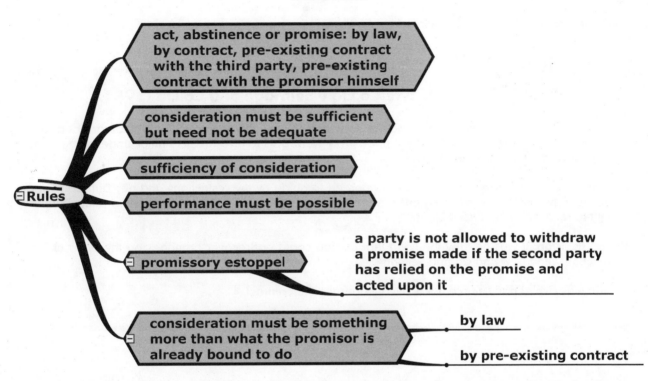

5. Analyse the doctrine of Privity

[Learning outcome e]

The general rule is that, parties to a contract alone can sue and be sued on the contract. Any person other than the parties to contract is a "stranger to the contract". A contract neither confers any rights nor imposes any duties / obligations on such a person.

The principle of privity states that a **person with whom a contract is made is only able to enforce it because he had given the consideration to the promisor. A third party has no right of action except in certain exceptional instances.**

Example

Yen Yen promises to pay Chang £1,000 if Chang gives his car to Lee. In this case, Lee cannot enforce Chang's promise, because he has not provided the consideration for the promise.

Lee is a stranger to the contract between Yen Yen and Chang.

> ### Case Study — Privity of contract
>
> ### Tweeddle v Atkinson (1861)
>
> In this case, on the occasion of marriage of A (claimant) and B, their respective fathers entered into a contract to pay money to A. When one of the parents died without having made the payment, A (claimant) tried to enforce a contract against his estate.
>
> **Courts decision:** It was held by the court that a stranger to the consideration cannot take advantage of a contract although made for his benefit. It was held that A (claimant) could not enforce the contract, as he personally provided no consideration for the promise.

Another important case study on privity of contract:

> ### Case Study — Privity of contract
>
> ### Dunlop Pneumatic Tyre Co Ltd v Selfridge and Co Ltd (1951)
>
> In this case, Dunlop sold tyres to a distributor: Dew and Co. Dunlop instructed the distributor not to sell the tyres and the tubes below the listed price. They were also told to take a similar undertaking from anyone to whom they supplied the tyres.
>
> Dew and Co sold the tyres to Selfridge, who agreed to abide by the restrictions and pay Dunlop £5 for each tyre they sold below the listed price. When Selfridge sold tyres below Dunlop's listed price, Dunlop sought to recover the promised £5 per tyre.
>
> **Courts decision:** It was held by the court that Dunlop could not recover damages on the basis of the contract between Dew and Co and Selfridge.
>
> Dunlop was a third party hence not entitled to enforce the contract.

SYNOPSIS

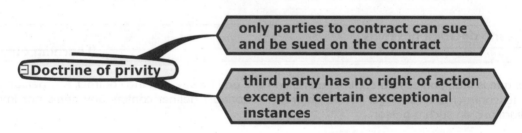

Doctrine of privity
- only parties to contract can sue and be sued on the contract
- third party has no right of action except in certain exceptional instances

5.1 Exceptions to the rule of privity of contract

1. **Common law exceptions**

There are exceptions to the general rule that a third party cannot enforce a contract. These exceptions allow the rights to the third parties to enforce the contract. These are:

a) **Beneficiary sues in some other capacity:** Although a beneficiary cannot sue in his personal capacity because he was not a party to the contract, he can sue in some other capacity e.g. as an executor of a deceased person.

Case Study

Exceptions to the rule of privity of contract

Beswick b Beswick (1966)

In this case, a nephew bought his uncle's coal business. One of the terms was that the nephew would pay support to the uncle's wife upon the uncle's death. When the uncle died, the nephew stopped paying the widow. The widow sued.

Courts decision: The widow was able to sue, not personally, but as an executor of the uncle's estate and on his behalf (the uncle, of course, having been a party to the contract). "Where a contract is made with A for the benefit of B, A can sue on the contract for the benefit of B and recover all that B could have recovered if the contract had been made with B himself."

b) **Collateral Contracts:** This is a contract between the third party and one of the contracting parties. This has been explained at section 3.3 (b) above.

c) **Beneficiary under the trust:** There are usually three parties to the trust.

   i.   **Author of the trust:** The person creating the trust is the author of the trust.

   ii. **Beneficiary of the trust**: The person for whose benefit the trust is created is the beneficiary.

   iii. **Trustee:** The person who is entrusted with the trust property and to execute the trust is called the trustee.

The beneficiary is not a party to the agreement creating a trust. However, he is the person for whose benefit the trust is created. Therefore, the beneficiary of a trust may sue the trustee to carry out the contract.

Example

Jackson formed a trust of his property for the benefits of his daughter Angelina. He appointed Thomas as the trustee of the trust.

Peter, the manager of the trust, misappropriated some of the property of the trust. Thomas refused to file a suit against the manager for misappropriation of trust property.

Here,
Jackson is the author of the trust.
Angelina is the beneficiary.
Thomas is the trustee.

The trust agreement was created between Jackson and Thomas. However, Angelina is the beneficiary of the trust. If Thomas refuses to sue, she can sue the manager for misappropriation of trust property.

---

d) **Contract entered into through agent:** The principal can enforce the contracts entered into by his agent provided the agent has acted in the name of the principal and within the scope of the principal's authority.

Example

Vivian appointed John as her agent. John entered into a contract with Toby to sell goods from Vivian's factory for £50,000. Toby paid an advance of £30,000.

Meanwhile, Vivian terminated her agency with John. Toby refused to pay the balance amount.

Here, Vivian (the principal) can enforce the contracts against Toby entered into by her agent (John).

---

e) **The assignment of rights:** Assignment is a process by which the rights of one person are transferred to another person. The person **assigning the rights is called the assignor** and the person **to whom the rights are assigned** is called the **assignee.**

After assignment, the assignee is entitled to exercise all the rights which could have been exercised by the assignor previously, even though the assignee was not a party to the contract as originally made.

Example

Ram and Vijay were partners. Vijay assigned his partnership rights to his brother Ajay. Ram uses the partnership's money for his personal use. Here, **Ajay is entitled to recover** the partnership money **from Ram.**

Although, Ajay was not a party to the partnership agreement, Vijay has assigned him Vijay's rights in partnership. Therefore, **Ajay (the assignee)** is entitled to exercise all the rights which could have been exercised by the assignor (Vijay) previously.

2. **Statutory exception**

In some cases the doctrine of privity is justified by statute.

Example

In relation to car insurance a third party can claim directly against the insurers of the party against whom they have a claim in respect of damages.

The provisions of the Contracts (Rights of third parties) Act 1999 set out various **circumstances in which a third party can enforce the terms** of a contract:

i.   For the enforcement of a third party right, the contract in question must confer such right on them or it must have been made for their benefit.

ii. The contract must specify the identity of the third party either by name or by a specific description or as a member of particular class of persons.

iii. It is not necessary that the third person must be in existence, when the contract was made. Therefore it is possible to make the contracts for the benefit of unborn children.

The act also provides that where the third party has rights by virtue of this Act, unless the original contract contains an express term to that effect, the original parties to the contract cannot in any way rescind or vary the terms without the consent of third party.

Diagram 10: Doctrine of privity

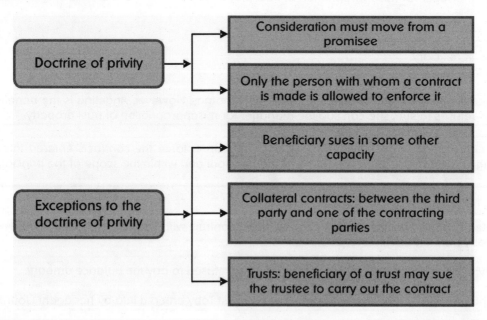

Test Yourself 16

Explain the principle of doctrine of privity and state the exceptions to this rule.

SYNOPSIS

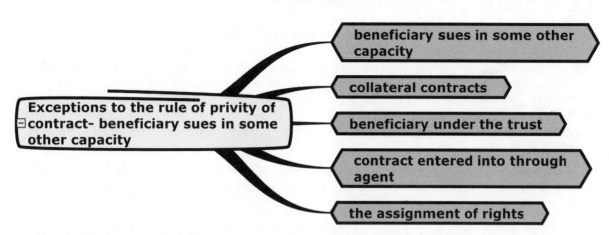

6. **Distinguish the presumptions relating to intention to create legal relations**

[Learning outcome f]

6.1 In ordinary **commercial contracts**, there is a strong presumption that the parties to the contract have an intention to enter into a legally binding relationship. However, this presumption is rebuttable if:

1. Legal binding is expressly disclaimed in the contract or
2. The circumstances indicate that there is no intention to be bound legally by the contract.

Case Study Presumtion relating to intension to create leagal relations

Rose and Frank Co v Crompton Brothers (1923)

In this case, the defendant (a British company) agreed to make the claimant (an American company) its sole vendor in America. The agreement included a clause stating that the document was not a formal one and was not subject to legal jurisdiction in either country.

Subsequently, when the defendant terminated the agreement after notice, the claimant brought an action for damages for the breach of contract and for delivery of goods.

Courts decision: It was held that the documents were not legally binding and consequently the breach of its terms did not give rise to any cause for action.

The court, however, held that where the orders had already been placed, there was a binding contract and the claimant would be entitled to the delivery of goods. The claim for damages for breach of agreement failed, but the claim for damages for non-delivery of goods ordered was upheld.

6.2 In domestic and family arrangements there is a presumption that there is no intention to create legal relations. **(Balfour v Balfour (1919))**

However, the intention not to create legal relations in such relationships is only a presumption. It may be rebutted by the actual facts and circumstances of a particular case.

Case Study

Presumtion relating to intension to create leagal relations

Merritt v Merritt (1970)

In this case, the husband left the matrimonial home, which was jointly owned by the husband and the wife. The husband met the wife after that and promised to pay her £40 per month, from which she undertook to pay the outstanding mortgage on their house. The wife made the husband sign a note stating these terms and an undertaking to transfer the house into her name when the mortgage had been paid off. The wife paid off the mortgage but the husband refused to transfer the house in her name.

Courts decision: It was held that an agreement was enforceable because the circumstances of the case clearly indicate that the parties had an intention to enter into a legally binding contract.

SYNOPSIS

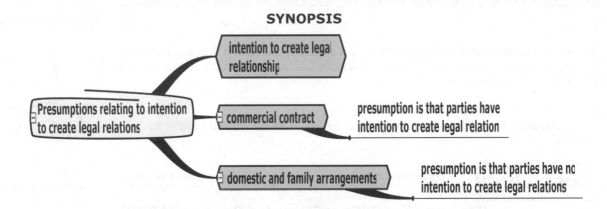

Test yourself 17

Distinguish the presumptions relating to intention to create legal relations.

Answers to Test Yourself

Answer 1

The contract, prima facie, appears to be a valid contract. However, the contract can be held void if Sunny proves that:

1. At the time of making the contract, his mind was so affected that he was incapable of understanding the nature of his actions.

2. The other party i.e. Bobby either knew or ought to have known of his disability.

In any case, however, Sunny must pay a reasonable price for the work done by Bobby.

Answer 2

Perhaps not, because this is a transaction in the ordinary course of business, because:

1. The relationship between Brown and the banker is not of such a nature that the banker can dominate the will of Brown.

2. The banker has not used any influence.

3. Signing loan documents on agreed terms is a usual business practice.

Answer 3

This depends on whether the two parties in question had the intention to enter into a legal relationship when they made their promises. If the promises were made casually on a social occasion, the law would presume that the parties had no such intention. If this presumption can be rebutted and the intention to enter into a legal relationship can be proved, then the agreement would be legally enforceable.

Answer 4

Yes, as the relationship between the attendant and patient is such that the patient may be affected by undue influence. This is because a patient is physically and psychologically dependent on his attendant to look after him and finds himself handicapped without him. He fears that if the amount demanded by him is not paid, the attendant may not work for him or will become less concerned.

Answer 5

This is not valid as the agreement was vitiated under duress.

Answer 6

No, because the object of the contract is unlawful. Hence this contract is illegal.

Answer 7

Correct answer is (c). A contract is said to be induced by undue influence where the relations subsisting between the parties are such that one of the parties is in a position to dominate the will of the other. The relationship of landlord and tenant does not raise the presumption of undue influence.

Answer 8

Basis of distinction	Offer	Invitation to treat
Meaning	It signifies the intention or willingness of a person to enter into a contract	Where a person invites others to make an offer to him, such invitation is not an offer but only an "invitation to treat"
Purpose	An offer is made to obtain acceptance of another person	An invitation to treat is made to obtain an offer from another person.
Legal effect	An offer, if accepted by the other person, results in a "contract"	An invitation to treat if accepted by the other person, results in an "offer"
Status	It is a proposal prior to acceptance	It precedes an offer

Answer 9

The valid offer is the offer in option (e) as there is an offeror (Julie) and an offeree (Lilly). Julie is offering the car as consideration and Lilly will pay £4,000 as consideration. Hence the elements of an offer are complete.

Options (a), (b), (c) and (d) are examples of invitation to offer, as they have not been made to ascertained people and most of the options are vague.

Answer 10

Revocation: Revocation refers to the cancellation of an offer and occurs when the offeror withdraws the offer. The rules relating to revocation are as follows:

i.   An offer may be revoked at any time before acceptance. However, once revocation has occurred, it is no longer open to the offeree to accept the original offer.

ii. Revocation is not effective until it is actually received by the offeree. This means that the offeror must make sure that the offeree is made aware of the withdrawal of the offer, otherwise it might still be open for the offeree to accept the offer.

iii. Communication of revocation may be made through a reliable third party. Where the offeree finds out about the withdrawal of the offer from a reliable third party, the revocation is effective and the offeree can no longer seek to accept the original offer.

Answer 11

a) A contract where one party promises a reward or action in return for some desired action on the part of the second party is called a unilateral contract. In the case of such contracts, the offeree cannot revoke the contract once he has started executing the action.

For e.g., **in Errington v Errington (1952)** a father promised his son and daughter in law that he would give the ownership of the house to them if they paid off the outstanding mortgage. After the father's death, his widow sought to revoke the promise. It was held by the court that the promise cannot be withdrawn as the payments were made regularly.

b) **Acceptance:** Acceptance is necessary for the formation of a contract. Once the offeree has accepted the terms offered, a contract comes into effect and both the parties to the contract are bound by the contract. Thereafter the offeror cannot withdraw his offer, nor can the offeree withdraw his acceptance.

Rules relating to acceptance:

i. Acceptance must correspond with the terms of the offer. Therefore, the offeree must not seek to introduce new contractual terms into their acceptance.

ii. A counter-offer does not constitute acceptance (Hyde v Wrench). Also, a conditional acceptance cannot create a contract relationship.

iii. Acceptance may be in the form of express words, either oral or written or may be implied from conduct.

iv. Generally, acceptance must be communicated to the offeror. Consequently, silence cannot amount to acceptance.

Where acceptance is communicated through the postal service then it is complete as soon as the letter, properly addressed and stamped, is posted. The contract is concluded even it the letter subsequently fails to reach the offeror.

However the postal rule will only apply where it is in the contemplation of the parties that the post will be used as the means of acceptance.

If the parties have negotiated either, face to face, in a shop, for example or over the telephone, then it might not be reasonable for the offeree to use the post as a means of communicating their acceptance and they would not gain the benefit of the postal rule.

Answer 12

(d) is false whilst the others are all true.

Answer 13

Consideration is one of the basic elements for the formation of the contract. Without consideration an agreement cannot be enforced and be a binding contract.

The term 'consideration' has been defined as:

"A valuable consideration in the eyes of law may consist either some right, interest, profit, or benefit accruing, to one party, or some forbearance and detriment, loss or responsibility given, suffered or undertaken by the other". **From Currie v Misa (1875)**

"An act or forbearance of one party, or the promise thereof, is the price for which the promise of the other is bought, and the promise thus given for value is enforceable". **From Dunlop v Selfridge (1915).**

Answer 14

Consideration can be divided into the following categories:

i.   **Executory consideration:** it is the promise to perform an action at some future time. One party to a contractual agreement may pay money to another on the understanding that the latter will perform some act for them in the future.

ii. **Executed Consideration:** this is an **act in return for a promise.** The promise only becomes enforceable when the offeree has actually performed the required act.

iii. **Past Consideration:** normally consideration is provided either at the time of the creation of a contract or at a later date. In the case of past consideration, however the action done is performed before the promise. Such prior action is not deemed sufficient to support the later promise.

In **Re McArdle (1951)**, according to the will of the father a certain number of children were entitled to a house after the death of their mother. In the mother's lifetime one of the children and his wife lived in the house with the mother. The daughter-in-law made some improvements in the house during this period. All the children subsequently undertook in writing to pay a sum of £488 to the said wife in consideration of her carrying out the improvements. But at the mother's death they refused to pay her any thing.

It was held that the said promise was without consideration for the obvious reason that improvements to the house had been completed before the document containing the promise was signed. Therefore, it was a past consideration which is no consideration at all.

Answer 15

1.   Executory consideration is the promise to perform an action at some future time. One party to a contractual agreement may pay money to another on the understanding that the latter will perform some act for them in the future.

     In the given case, consideration of £50 by Alan to Tom is executory consideration as it is payable when Tom dry-cleans Alan's suit and returns it to Alan.

2.   Executed Consideration is an **act in return for a promise.** The promise only becomes enforceable when the offeree has actually performed the required act.

     In the given case, the consideration of £100 promised by Alan to Greg is the executed consideration. Because it is payable only when Greg finds Alan's suit and duly returns it to Alan.

Answer 16

According to this principle, consideration must move from a promisee. A person with whom a contract is made is only able to enforce it as consideration must have been given by him to the promisor. A third party has no right of action except in certain exceptional instances.

Exceptions to the rule of privity of contract:

There are exceptions to the general rule, allowing the rights to third parties and some impositions of obligations. These are:

a)   **Beneficiary sues in some other capacity**
     Although, a beneficiary cannot sue in his personal capacity because he was not a party to contract, he can sue in some other capacity e.g. an executor of a deceased person.

b)   **Collateral Contracts**
     Between the third party and one of the contracting parties

c)   **Trusts**
     The beneficiary of a trust may sue the trustee to carry out the contract.

d)   **Statute**
     In some cases the doctrine of privity is justified by statute. For e.g., in relation to car insurance, a third party can claim directly against the insurers of the party against who they have a claim in respect of damages.

Answer 17

In ordinary **commercial contracts**, there is a strong presumption that parties to contract **have intention to enter into a legally binding relationship**.

However, this presumption is rebuttable if

a) Binding by legal relations is expressly disclaimed in the contract or

b) The circumstances indicate that there is no intention to be bound legally by the contract.

In **domestic and family arrangements** there is a presumption that there is no intention to create legal relations

However, this presumption may be rebutted by the actual facts and circumstances of a particular case.

Quick Quiz

1.   State true or false

a) All contracts are agreements but all agreements are not contracts.

b) Every contract must be in writing.

c) Acceptance may also be communicated by an unauthorised person

d) Acceptance must be communicated in writing only.

e) Contract without consideration is not enforceable.

2.   Choose the correct option

i. Communication of acceptance made by post is complete as against the offeror when the letter of acceptance
a) Reaches the offeror
b) Is posted to him
c) Is in transit
d) Is signed by the offeree

ii. Under which of the following instances, does the offer automatically lapse?
a) If it is revoked by the offeror at any time before its acceptance
b) If the offeror or offeree dies
c) Upon failure to fulfill a condition precedent to acceptance
d) All of the above

iii. Rani accepts Sunny's invitation to dinner by phone. This is not a contract because
a) Acceptance is given orally
b) There is no intention to create legal relations
c) There is no consensus between the two parties
d) None of the above

iv. Alan took up the responsibility of providing education to Jessica who is a minor. Which of the following is true?
a) The contract is void
b) Alan can rescind the contract
c) Jessica is liable to reimburse Alan out of her property
d) Jessica is not liable to reimburse Alan and can claim exemption as she is minor

Answers to Quick Quiz

1.
a) **True,** because all agreements are not legally enforceable.

b) **False,** a contract can be written or oral or inferred from conduct of parties.

c) **False,** acceptance must be communicated by acceptor or his authorised agent or by a reliable third party.

d) **False,** as acceptance can be in either of three ways:
   i. Acceptance by express words
   ii. Acceptance by action
   iii.Acceptance inferred from conduct

e) **True.**

2.
a. Correct answer is (b)

b. Correct answer is (d)

c. Correct answer is (b)

d. Correct answer is (c). A minor's estate is liable to a person who supplies necessaries (both goods and services) to a minor. The provision of education falls under the category of necessary services.

Self Examination Questions

Question 1

An invitation to treat is not an offer: explain.

Question 2

All illegal agreements are void but all void agreements are not illegal: explain.

Question 3

Define consent. When can consent be said to be free consent?

Question 4

Alvin agrees to sell his car to Charley for £1,500. Is the contract valid?

Question 5

Distinguish between an agreement and a contract.

Question 6

Merry deals with antique sculptures. One morning, John approached Merry to sell her an antique piece in his possession for £20,000. Merry was willing to pay £12,000 only. John replied that he would sell it for £15,000. Merry then said that she needed some time to buy it for that price. John agreed not to sell the piece to any other person until Merry phoned him back in five days time with her final decision.

After sometime, John phoned Merry but as she was out he placed a message with her assistant that he was not willing to sell her the antique piece.

On the same evening, Merry met Lilly at a party and while talking to her Merry came to know that Lilly was looking for the same antique that John wanted to sell and she was willing to pay even £30,000 for that antique.

The next day, Merry called John to tell him that she was ready to buy the antique piece for £12,000. However, John informed her that he had already sold it to Sunny for £22,000.

Analyse the situation in relation to the provisions of law of contract.

Question 7

Ronny, a retail trader, displayed goods in his shop with prices marked on them. Kelly a consumer asked to sell the goods at the prices mentioned on the goods. Ronny refused to sell the goods at that price by saying the prices had increased. Kelly demanded that Ronny sold the goods for the displayed prices; otherwise she would sue Ronny for breach of contract.

Which of the following statement(s) is / are correct?

a) Kelly can sue Ronny for breach of contract
b) Display of prices on goods amounts to a valid offer
c) Display of prices on goods amounts to an invitation to make an offer
d) Refusal to sell the goods at the prices mentioned on them will amount to breach of contract.

Answers to Self Examination Questions

Answer 1

An invitation to treat is merely an **invitation** to others **to make offers**. It is **not an offer**.

An offer is made when one party proposes to another that it should **buy a particular item** on particular terms, including:

i. the precise nature of the item,
ii. the price to be paid,
iii. the mode of delivery
iv. the date of payment etc.

An offer must not be confused with an invitation to treat. An invitation to treat is intimation by one party to another that:

i. It may be willing to do business in relation to a particular article on particular terms and
ii. The other party, **if interested** should **make the first party an offer in relation thereto.**

Hence, an invitation to treat if accepted by the other party does not form a contract.

Examples of common situations involving invitations to treat are:

The display of goods in a shop window: the classic case in this area is Fisher v Bell (1961), in which a shopkeeper was prosecuted for offering offensive weapons for sale, by having flick-knives on display in his window. It was held that the shopkeeper was not guilty as the **display in the shop window was not an offer for sale but only an invitation to treat.**

The display of goods on the shelf of a self-service shop: in Pharmaceutical Society of Great Britain v Boots Cash Chemists (1953), it was held that the display of goods on the shelf was only an invitation to treat and that in law, the customer offered to buy the goods at the cash desk.

Answer 2

An agreement may become void due to various reasons, such as:

i. Object is not lawful
ii. Contract terms are vague
iii. No consideration is provided by the parties
iv. Consent to contract was caused by duress, undue influence or misrepresentation.

Void agreements are not necessarily illegal, for e.g., the agreements, the terms of which are uncertain, are void but not illegal.

A void agreement does not involve any punishment. It also does not invalidate the collateral transactions and the law may enforce them. An illegal agreement not only vitiates the primary transaction but also any collateral transactions.

Illegal agreements are **void abinitio** (i.e. void from the beginning) but, at times, valid contracts may subsequently become void for certain reasons.

Answer 3

Free consent is one of the essentials of valid contract. Two or more persons are said to consent when they agree upon the same thing in the same sense.

Consent is said to be free when it is not caused by:

i.   Duress
ii. Undue influence
iii. Fraud
iv. Misrepresentation

Answer 4

Yes, because all the elements for valid contract are present.

i.   The contract is made because of the offer by Alvin and acceptance by Charley
ii. The object (the ownership of car) is lawful
iii. Charley's promise to pay £1,500 is the consideration for Alvin's promise to sell the car and Alvin's promise to sell the car is the consideration for Charley's promise to pay £1,500.

Answer 5

Basis of distinction	Agreement	Contract
Meaning	Offer when accepted becomes an agreement	An agreement enforceable by law is a contract
One in another	All agreements are not contracts	All contracts are agreement
Enforceability	An agreement may or may not be enforceable by law	All contracts can be enforced by law

Answer 6

The areas cover in this case study are offer, counter-offer, revocation of offer, communication of revocation of offer by a reliable third party, etc.

Offer and counter-offer

John offered Merry to sell a piece of antique for £20,000. Merry made a counter-offer to buy the antique for £12,000. This counter-offer by Merry resulted in termination of the original offer. Then John again offered to sell the piece for £15,000. This counter-offer by John resulted in rejection of Merry's offer of £12,000.

In **Hyde v Wrench (1840) case,** Wrench offered a price of £1,000 to sell his farm. Hyde offered £950, which Wrench rejected. Hyde then informed Wrench that he accepted the original offer of £1,000. But Wrench refused to sell the farm to Hyde. It was held that there was no contract. Hyde's **counter-offer** had terminated the original offer and therefore the original offer was no longer open for acceptance. Hyde was now making an altogether new offer to buy Wrench's land for £1,000, and it was for Wrench to decide whether to accept the offer or reject it. The offeror and offeree has replaced each other.

Revocation of offer and communication of revocation of offer by a reliable third party

An offeror may revoke an offer at any time before its acceptance. Once revoked, it is no longer open to the offeree to accept the offer. John phoned Merry to inform her about the revocation of his offer to her. However as she was out, he informed the same to her assistant.

In **Dickinson v Dodds (1876),** it was held that communication of revocation of offer may be made by a reliable **third party.**

The facts of this case are as follows:

Dodds offered to sell a property to Dickinson. He also told Dickinson that the offer would be left open until Friday. On Thursday, Dodds informed Dickson through a person who was acting as an intermediary that he intends to sell the property to someone else. Dickson still attempted to accept the offer on Friday. But the property was already sold before Friday.

It was held that the sale of the property amounted to revocation. The revocation communicated by the reliable third party amounts to effective communication of revocation.

In our case, it can be concluded that John has revoked his offer to Merry before she accepted it. This was successfully communicated to her through her assistant. Hence there was no contract between John and Merry for sale of antique. Merry, therefore, cannot force John to sell her the antique.

Answer 7

A contract basically evolves from an offer by one party and acceptance of the same by the other party. The offer needs to be clear, definite and complete. An offer should be differentiated from an invitation to make an offer. For example, a catalogue with prices indicated on it is not an offer to sell; it is an invitation to make an offer. A person interested in buying the product specified in the catalogue may make an offer to buy and it is left to the discretion of the seller to either accept or reject the same.

Kelly cannot insist that Ronny sells the goods for the prices mentioned on them. Ronny has not made an offer. He has only made an invitation to make an offer.

Therefore option (c) is a true statement

SECTION B - THE LAW OF OBLIGATIONS

CONTENT OF CONTRACTS

Individual owners of commodities meet at a common place, known as a market, and freely enter into negotiations to **decide conditions** on which they are willing to exchange those commodities.

Some of the **conditions are statements** of such **major importance** that the parties would not have entered into the contract without it. These statements will become the **terms of the contract**.

However, some of these statements are **mere representations** which mean that they are **statements made to induce** another person to enter into a contract.

This Study Guide discusses the difference between a representation and a term of contract and also explains the different types of terms of contract like warranties, exclusion clauses etc.

As terms of contract form the essence of any contract understanding this Study Guide will be beneficial to you in the examination as well as in your professional life.

LEARNING OUTCOMES

a) Distinguish terms from mere representations
b) Define the various contractual terms
c) Explain the effect of exclusion clauses and evaluate their control

Introduction

Mark wanted to participate in a car race. He gave an advertisement in a local newspaper that he wanted to buy a sports car and any person interested may contact him. Alex approaches Mark and tells him that he wants to sell his sports car as he is moving to another country. While describing the features of the car, Alex makes a statement that the car gives good average mileage, it is insured, the speed of the car runs is 80km/hour, and Mark will definitely win the race if he uses that car. Mark purchases the car. In the purchase agreement, the average per litre of petrol, the insurance, speed etc were covered. However, Mark lost the car race.

Mark demanded refund of his money as the car proved useless for winning the car race. Alex refuses to refund the money as according to him, the car worked fine and the specifications given by him were proved true and Mark lost the race because of his inability to drive fast.

From the above example, it is clear that the seller made a number of representations for selling the car from which some statements like insurance and average per litre of fuel were the terms of contract i.e. without which Mark would not have entered into the contract. However, it is not right to say that Mark purchased the car only because Alex told him that he will definitely win the race if he uses that car.

Mark can not rescind the contract on the ground that he lost the race even when it was assured by the seller of the car that he will win.

1. Distinguish terms from mere representations

[Learning outcome a]

During negotiations and before the final contract, many features may be discussed. Some of these **features** may have **induced the other party**, to enter into the contract. However, such features are **mere representations**. They may **not form a part of the contract**.

Parties to the contract will normally be bound by any promise that they have made in the contract.

Therefore, it is very important to decide **which promise to include** in the contract.

It is essential to **determine** whether the **features** discussed are terms of contract **terms or mere representations**.

> **Definition**
>
> **Representation:** A representation is a pre-contractual statement of fact made to induce another person to enter into a contract. Although, such statements **induce the other party to enter into a contract,** the person who makes the statement **does not guarantee its compliance or validity**. If the statement proves to be incorrect, it cannot be enforced as it is not a term of the contract. It may prove to be a misrepresentation for which other remedies are available.

Example

A salesman came to Mary to sell a shampoo. He told her that a very famous actress also uses the same shampoo. This statement made by a salesman regarding the product that the may constitute misrepresentation.

> **Definition**
>
> **Term:** Where the statement is of such **major importance** that the promisee would not have entered into the agreement without it will be construed as a term. The **validity and compliance of such statement is guaranteed** by the person who made the statement. A term is a part of contract.

Example

Alan has entered into a contract to buy Jenny's car. He has made it clear to Jenny that he wants to buy her car because the model is very old and hence rare. The model of the car is a term of this contract. Alan would not have agreed to buy the car if it is a model of a later period.

The difference between a representation and a term is important because if a statement which was:

➢ A 'term' of contract proves to be **untrue**, the party who has been misled can claim for the **breach of contract**.
➢ A 'mere representation' of contract proves to be **untrue**, the party misled can claim for the **misrepresentation**

Tips

Remedies for misrepresentation are different than for breach.

The four tests for distinguishing a contractual term from a mere representation are:

Diagram 1: Four tests of distinguishing a contractual term from a mere representation

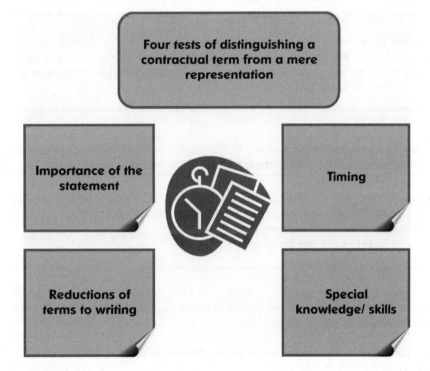

1. **Importance of the statement:** If a statement is so important that the promisor would not have entered into the agreement without it then it will be construed as a term.

Case Study | Importance of the statement

Bannerman V White (1861)

In this case, the defendant wanted to buy hops for brewing purposes and told the claimant that the hops should not be treated with sulphur. He also told the claimant that he would not have even entered into negotiations if the hops had been treated with sulphur. **The claimant replied explicitly that no sulphur had been used.** However, the defendant discovered later that the hops had been treated with sulphur; he refused to pay for the hops.

Court's decision: It was held that the claimant's statement about the sulphur was a fundamental term of the contract. The defendant would not have entered into the contract without that statement. Since it was incorrect, the defendant was entitled to cancel the contract.

2. **Timing:** The court will consider the lapse of time between the making of the statement and the conclusion of the contract. If the **interval is short** the statement is more likely to be a **term.**

Case Study — Lapse of time

Roultedge V Mckay (1954)

In this case, the defendant, while discussing the possible sale of his motorcycle to the claimant on 23 October said that the motorcycle was a model of 1942. On 30 October, a written contract for the sale of bike was made which did not refer to the year of the model. The bike was actually a model of 1930.

Court's decision: The buyer's claim for damages failed because it was held that the statement about the date was a pre-contractual representation.

In the above case, if buyer had claimed that he want to buy the motorcycle only if it is a model of 1942 then it would have became a term of the contract. In that case, the buyer's claim for damages could have succeeded.

3. **Reductions of terms to writing:** The court will consider whether the statement discussed during the negotiations was not included in writing in the formal contract drawn up later. If the written contract does not incorporate the statement, this would suggest that the parties did not intend the statement to become a contractual term.

Example

In **Routledge v McKay (1954)** discussed above, if the statement that the motorcycle to be purchased is a model of 1942 is incorporated in the contract then it is a term not a mere representation.

4. **Special knowledge / skills:** If the maker of the statement had some special knowledge or was in a better position than the other party to verify the accuracy of the statement, then:
➢ The statements made **by them** will be **terms but**
➢ The statements made **to them** will **not be terms.**

Example

In **Oscar Chess Ltd v. Williams (1957),** a person selling a car to a second-hand car dealer stated that it was a 1948 Morris, when in fact it was a car made in1939.

It was held that the **statement did not become a term.** The main reason for this decision was that the seller had no special knowledge as to the age of the car, while the buyers were car dealers, and so in at least as good a position as the seller to know whether the statement was true.

Case Study — Special knowledge / skills

Dick Bentley Productions Ltd v Harold Smith (Motors) Ltd (1965)

In this case, Harold sold Dick a car saying that it had run only 20,000 miles since it had major repairs done. Harold bought the car. It turns out that the car had done much more then 20,000 since the last major repair.

Court's decision: It was held that the **defendant's statement was a 'term'** to the contract and the claimants were entitled for damages. The main reason for this decision was that the car dealer (the defendant) was clearly in a better position than the buyer (the claimant) to know whether the representation was true.

Test Yourself 1

Explain term and representation.

Test Yourself 2

State the tests to distinguish contractual term from mere representation?

Test Yourself 3

Determine whether the following statements are terms of contract or mere representations.

a) Daffy met Desmond, to purchase his nursery garden, meanwhile Daffy met Mathew in a party who offered her a proposal to buy his mobile ice cream parlour which fascinated her more and she decided to buy the mobile ice cream parlour. After a couple of months, Daffy bought Desmond's nursery garden and found that the position of the garden was not very sound.

b) Joey instructs his secretary to purchase some paintings made in the year 1852 which are very rare. The secretary selects some paintings and shows them to Joey. However, Joey finds out that those paintings were not made in 1852.

c) Melvin has a small café. He tells his supplier to provide him with a table cloth which would be made of such material so that it doesn't get wet, nor holds stains and is not even affected by very hot dishes on it. The supplier assures him of such a material.

d) Lolla wanted some cosmetics made by a famous beautician Monica and which would last longer with the same effects. The supplier assures her that the cosmetics are from Monica's beauty parlour and has the desired effects.

SYNOPSIS

Distinguish terms from representation

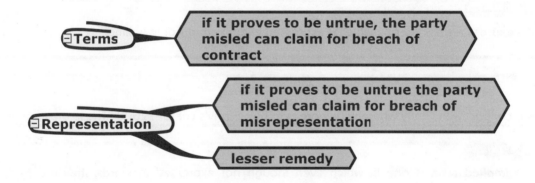

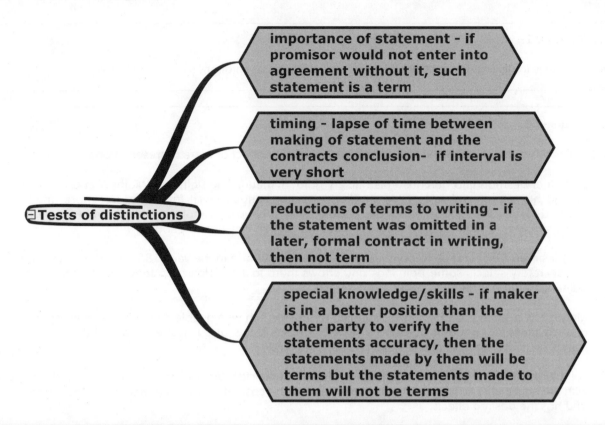

importance of statement - if promisor would not enter into agreement without it, such statement is a term

timing - lapse of time between making of statement and the contracts conclusion- if interval is very short

reductions of terms to writing - if the statement was omitted in a later, formal contract in writing, then not term

Tests of distinctions

special knowledge/skills - if maker is in a better position than the other party to verify the statements accuracy, then the statements made by them will be terms but the statements made to them will not be terms

2. Define the various contractual terms

[Learning outcome b]

2.1. Expressed terms and implied terms

Definition

An **express term** is the one which is expressed either verbally or in writing.

Example

John **signs** a contract with Ginny whereby he agrees to buy Ginny's car for £2000. These are express terms.

Definition

An **implied term** is one in which even though not expressed in words, they are part of the contract due to implication.

Example

In the case of **Smith v Wilson,** the tenant of a farm was given notice to leave the farm. Since he had already sown seeds in the farm before he was asked to leave, he asked for compensation.

The court said that he was **entitled to compensation** for the seeds he had sown.

This was because, **although** there was **no such term in the agreement** between landlord and tenant, paying such compensation was the **established custom in that locality**.

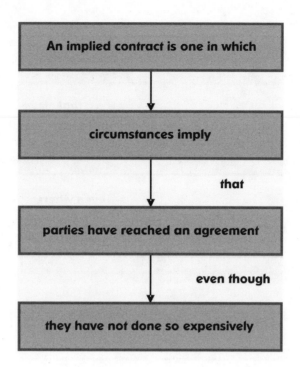

An implied contract is one in which

↓

circumstances imply

that

↓

parties have reached an agreement

even though

↓

they have not done so expensively

1. A term implied in fact

Example

By going to a doctor for a physical check-up, a patient agrees that he will pay a fair price for the service. If he refuses to pay after being examined, he has breached an implied term (implied in fact).

---

2. A term implied in law: Terms may be implied in a contract because of one of the following three sources:

a) **Custom:** A term which can be shown to be the **certain and general custom** of a **particular industry,** is **implied to be in the contract** even where it is **not actually specified** in the contract **by the parties.**

Case Study

Hutton V Warren (1836)

The tenant of a farm was asked to leave and given six month's notice. In accordance with the custom followed in that area, his landlord stated that he should continue to cultivate the land during the notice period. Referring to the same custom, the tenant argued that he was entitled to a fair allowance for the seeds sown and work carried out on the land.

Court's decision: It was held that customary usage permitted a farm tenant, on quitting his tenancy, to claim an allowance for seed and labour.

Tips

Custom cannot override the express terms of an agreement

Example

In the above case, it was expressly agreed while making the contract between the landlord and the tenant that no allowance for seed and labour can be claimed by the tenant at the time of quitting his tenancy.

In that case, even though customary usage permits allowance for seed and labour on quitting tenancy, such an allowance will not be allowed to the tenant, as it is expressly denied by the agreement.

---

b) **Statute**

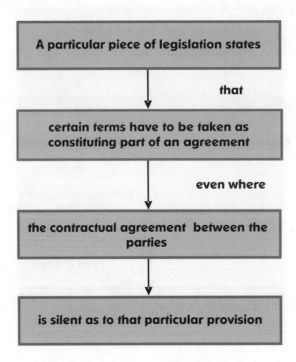

It is a means for the courts to remedy situations in which one party would be unjustly enriched wherein he or she is compensated by the other when it is not required to do so.

Some of the examples of terms implied by statute are as follows:

a) Sale of Goods Act 1979 contains implied terms about quality or fitness of the goods sold. Section14 subsection (2) of this Act provides that where the seller sells goods in the course of a business, there is an implied term that the goods supplied under the contract are of satisfactory quality.

b) Some statues include implied terms which apply unless stated otherwise in the contract.
The Table A model relating to the articles of association is an example of an implied term in company law. Unless specifically excluded, the provisions of Table A apply, even if the actual articles make no reference to the provision.

c) Some implied terms are very inflexible and cannot be removed.
Under the Supply of Goods and Services Act 1982, for e.g., contracts for service (other than simple employment, and some other specific types of contract) include an implied term that the service will be carried out within a reasonable time, with reasonable care and skill, and for a reasonable price. Similarly, sale of goods contracts include implied terms relating to the description, quality and fitness for the purpose which **cannot be removed** even with the consent of the parties to the contract.

---

c) **The courts:** It is assumed that parties to a contract should (in general) be free to deal with each other on the terms they themselves fix. It is generally presumed they know what they are doing. Where practicable, the law should help the parties to make the contract actually 'work'.

So, in general, where parties to a contract have made a contract which is sufficiently clear (whether by express agreement – or omission), the courts will not interfere. Where on the other hand it is necessary to imply a particular term into a contract in order to give it 'business efficacy' (or in other words, the contract won't work without it), then the Courts will imply such a term.

(Source: www.egos.co.uk/Freelanc/freela22.htm)

Example

Within the context of the **employer / employee relationship,** the courts have used this principle to imply terms that the employee will carry out his work with reasonable skill and care, and will indemnify the employer against any loss caused by his negligence.

In a Landlord / Tenant relationship, the courts have used this principle to imply a term requiring a landlord to maintain the common parts of a block of flats.

Case Study · Terms implied by court

Wilson v Best Travel (1993)

Wilson booked a holiday in Greece with Best Travel. He fell through a glass door in the hotel and was injured and claimed that (a) there was an implied term that the hotel would be reasonably safe, or (b) there was a breach of a duty to provide services with care and skill under Sec.13 of the Supply of Goods and Services Act 1982.

Court's decision: The court said that the defendants would not have agreed to such a term, as the defendants had no control over the hotel. The hotels were inspected and as they met Greek standards the defendants had acted with care and skill. Therefore the claimant's claim failed.

Case Study · Terms implied by court

Liverpool City Council v Irwin (1976)

The condition of a council tower block deteriorated; there were defects in the stairs and lifts. The claimant (Irwins) alleged a breach on the part of the council of its implied contract for their quiet enjoyment of the property.

Court's decision: The House of Lords held that it was an implied term of a lease of a flat in a Council block that the landlord should take reasonable care to keep the common parts of the block in a reasonable state of repair.

Test Yourself 4

Determine whether the following terms are expressed terms or implied terms:

a) A contract for the sale of washing machines is made. The date of the delivery is to be decided afterwards. The date of delivery was communicated by a letter send by post by the purchaser.

b) Jack buys a second hand bike from a private seller, but at the time of purchasing the bike he forgets to ask whether the seller is the real owner of the bike or not.

c) A real estate agency lets the house on the tenth floor of the building. No reference is made to the fact that there are no windows to the house.

d) A tour company keeps the rights to change the place of the tour and date of the customer's destination.

2.2. Conditions and warranties

Definition

Condition: Condition is a **stipulation essential to the main purpose of the contract. Condition is a fundamental term** of the agreement and is something which goes to the root of the contract.

The **breach of a condition** to contract gives the right to the innocent party to **terminate the contract.**

Example

Jolly has a retail shop dealing with appliances. Jenny, a customer asks for a clothes washer that can handle 15 pounds of laundry at a time.

Thus, suitability of the model to handle 15-pound loads is a condition. If the washer can handle maximum 10-pound load at a time, then the condition of fitness for 15-pound loads is breached. Therefore, Jenny has the right to terminate the contract.

Definition

Warranty: Warranty is **stipulated collateral to the main purpose of the contract.**

Warranty is a subsidiary obligation. It is comparatively a minor term. If a warranty is broken, the innocent party may claim the damages but does not have the right to terminate the agreement.

Example

Jolly has a retail shop dealing with appliances. Jenny, a customer asks for a durable and good quality clothes washer. Jolly recommended a model and Jenny purchased it. However, within two months, the cloths washer started making noise.

Thus, good quality was the warranty given by Jolly and as the warranty is broken Jenny may claim **damages.**

1. **Distinction between condition and warranties:** Whether a stipulation in a contract is a condition or a warranty **depends on the construction of the contract**. A term may be a condition even though it is called a warranty in the contract.

Whether a term is a condition or a warranty depends on a number of factors such as:

a) **Decided by statute**: Sometimes, whether a term is a condition or a warranty is made clear by the statute.

Example

Sale of Goods Act 1979 implies a condition into every contract for the sale of goods that seller has the right to sell.

b) **Declared by the parties:** The parties to the contract may expressly declare that a particular term in the contract is a condition, the breach of which may result in termination of contract.

Example

When a hotel is booked in order to organise a business event, the term that the hotel should be made available on the date of the event is a condition in the contract.

c) **Decided on the basis of facts of the case**: Whether a particular term is a condition of the contract or a warranty will be decided by the courts on the basis of existing circumstances.

Case Study   **Breach of condition**

Poussard v. Spiers & Pound (1876)

In this case the claimant had entered into a contract with the defendants to sing in an opera that they were producing. As she fell ill, she was unable to sing on the first few nights. When she recovered, the defendants refused her services as they had hired a replacement for the entire run of the opera.

Court's decision: It was held that her failure to appear on the opening night had been a **breach of a condition**, and the defendants were at liberty to treat the contract as discharged.

Case Study — Breach of warranty

Bettini v. Gye (1876)

In this case, the claimant had entered into a contract with the defendants to complete a number of engagements. He had also agreed to be in London for rehearsals six days before his opening performance. As he fell ill, he arrived only three days before the opening night, and the defendants refused his services.

Court's decision: It was held that failure to appear for rehearsals was only a **breach of warranty**. The defendants were entitled to damages, but could not treat the contract as discharged

2. **Conditions and warranties can be either expressed or implied.**
   Express conditions and warranties are those which, are expressly provided in the contract. Implied conditions and warranties are those which are implied by laws or customs.

> **Example**
>
> In the case of a contract of sale, there is an implied condition on the part of the seller, that he has a right to sell the goods.

3. **Condition implied by custom or trade usage:** An implied warranty or condition as to quality or fitness for a particular purpose may be decided by the usage of trade.

   In certain sale contracts, the purpose for which the goods are purchased may be implied from the conduct of the parties or from the nature or description of the goods. In such cases, the parties enter into the contract with reference to those known usages.

> **Example**
>
> If a person buys a medicine the purpose for which it is purchased is implied from the thing itself, the buyer need not disclose the purpose to the seller.

Diagram 2: Conditions and warranties

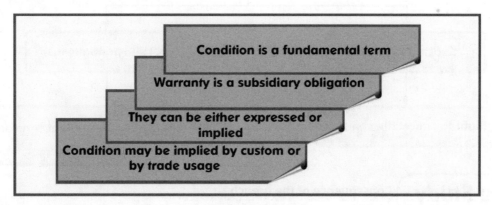

- Condition is a fundamental term
- Warranty is a subsidiary obligation
- They can be either expressed or implied
- Condition may be implied by custom or by trade usage

4. **Innominate terms:** In this case, whether the term breached is a condition or a warranty depends on the consequence of the breach.

If the breach **deprives** the innocent party of '**substantially the whole benefit of the contract**', then the **right to repudiate will be permitted**, even if the term might otherwise appear to be a mere warranty.

If, however, the innocent party **does not lose** 'substantially the whole benefit of the contract', then they will **not be permitted to repudiate** but must settle for damages, even if the term might otherwise appear to be a condition.

Hong Kong Fir Shipping Co Ltd v Kawasaki Kisen Kaisha Ltd (1962) was the first case to consider an innominate term.

Case Study

Hong Kong Fir Shipping Co Ltd v Kawasaki Kisen Kaisha Ltd (1962)

Kawasaki entered into a contract with Hong Kong Fir to charter a vessel for a period of 24 months. A provision in the contract guaranteed that the vessel was "fitted in every way for ordinary cargo service" and that the owners would "maintain her in a thoroughly efficient state ... during service". Not long after the voyage began, it was discovered that the vessel was in poor condition and in need of many repairs.

At first, the vessel was delayed for repairs for five weeks mid-voyage. However, more damage was discovered and so further repairs requiring 15 weeks to complete, were required before the vessel was seaworthy.

Once the vessel had been made seaworthy, Kawasaki was still free to use it for a period of 17 months. However, they repudiated the contract. They claimed that they were entitled to do so as the term regarding seaworthiness was a condition of the contract and had been breached. Hong Kong Fir brought an action for wrongful repudiation.

Court's decision: The Court of Appeal held that the term regarding the seaworthiness of the vessel was neither a warranty nor condition, but an innominate term. Therefore, in deciding whether the defendants could terminate the contract, the consequences of the breach needed to be examined to see if the innocent party had been deprived of substantially the whole benefit he should have received under the contract.

In this case, this was not true. Kawasaki was not deprived of "substantially the whole benefit" as most of the rental period remained available to use the vessel.

The defendants were held entitled only to monetary compensation in the form of damages (but not to repudiate the contract).

Diagram 3: Effects of innominate terms

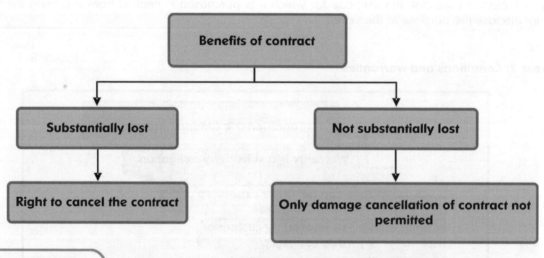

Case Study   Consequence of the breach

Cehave v. Bremer (The Hansa Nord) (1976)

In this case, there was a contract for the sale of a cargo of citrus pulp pellets, to be used in making cattle food. One of the terms of the contract was that they were to be delivered in good condition.

On delivery, the buyers rejected the cargo as it was not in good condition. They claimed back the money that they had paid to the sellers. The sellers refused to repay the money.

Evidence showed that the pellets had remained useable in cattle food. Subsequently, when the cargo was sold off, the same buyers obtained the pellets and used them for making cattle food.

Court's decision: It was held that the buyers had not been free to reject the cargo, **but could claim damages.** The goods cannot have been so bad if they were actually used for their intended purpose.

The parol evidence rule

Any evidence not included in written contract documents is parol evidence. Parol evidence may include information about what was said during contract proposals, negotiations or conversations.

Under the parol evidence rule, **a written contract's terms cannot be altered or explained by parol evidence**.

When parties enter into an agreement, all terms of the agreement are included in the contract. **Therefore, parol evidence does not constitute a part of a contract.** As a result, parol evidence cannot be admitted to explain the meaning of any contract terms.

Simply stated, the **final agreement made by the parties supersedes any terms discussed in earlier negotiations**

A written contract strengthens the presumption that the written document is complete and final.

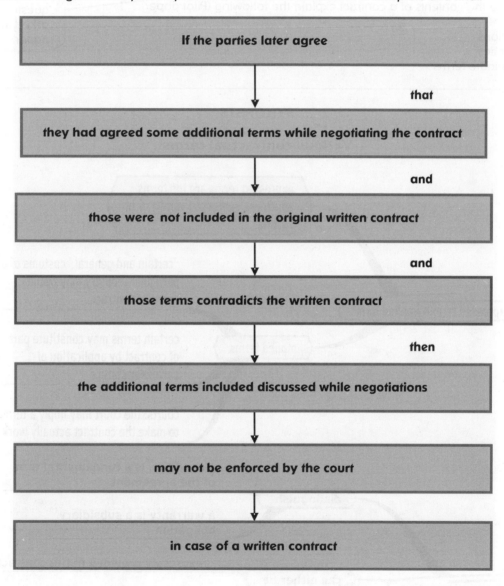

There are some exceptions to the parol evidence rule. Evidence of the following is admissible:

a) Oral evidence can be admitted to show a custom or trade usage that is part of the contract.

b) Oral evidence is admissible to clarify any unclear language used in the written contract.

c) Oral evidence is admissible to show that the written document represents only part of the agreement.

d) Oral evidence is admissible to show that due to a mistake of the parties, their agreement has been recorded incorrectly.

e) Oral evidence may be given to show that the written agreement between the parties was entered into subject to a verbal condition that has not been fulfilled.

f) Oral evidence may be given to show that the written contract is not binding because there is evidence of fraud or duress.

g) Oral evidence can be given to show that a subsequent oral agreement rescinded the original written agreement.

h) Oral evidence can be given to show that there is a collateral contract in existence.

Test Yourself 5

In relation to the contents of a contract explain the following (Pilot paper)
a) Terms
b) Conditions
c) Warranties
d) In nominate terms

Such straight forward questions are often asked in the question paper.

SYNOPSIS

Various contractual terms

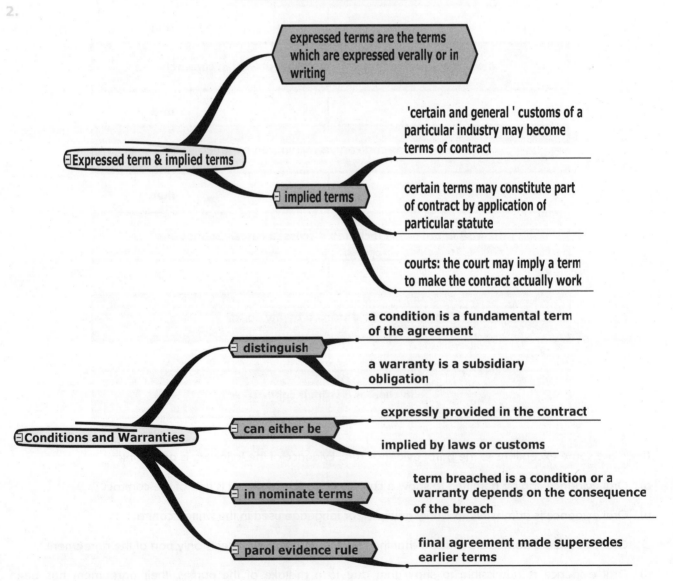

expressed terms are the terms which are expressed verally or in writing

Expressed term & implied terms

implied terms

'certain and general ' customs of a particular industry may become terms of contract

certain terms may constitute part of contract by application of particular statute

courts: the court may imply a term to make the contract actually work

Conditions and Warranties

distinguish

a condition is a fundamental term of the agreement

a warranty is a subsidiary obligation

can either be

expressly provided in the contract

implied by laws or customs

in nominate terms

term breached is a condition or a warranty depends on the consequence of the breach

parol evidence rule

final agreement made supersedes earlier terms

3. Explain the effect of exclusion clauses and evaluate their control

[Learning outcome c]

An exclusion clause is a clause inserted in a contract which aims to exclude or limit the party's liability for breach of contract or negligence.

Exclusion clauses generally fall into one of the following categories:

1. **True exclusion clause:** This clause recognises a potential breach of the contract, and then excuses the liability for the breach. Alternatively, the clause is constructed in such a way that it only includes reasonable care to perform duties on one of the parties.

Example

For many products, the manufacturer inserts an exclusion clause which states that no replacement will be granted for any breakage or damages due to improper handling of the product. The product will be replaced only for any manufacturing defects.

---

2. **Limitation clause:** This clause places a limit on the amount that can be claimed for a breach of contract, regardless of the actual loss.

Example

Alan and Beth enter into a contract according to which Beth was to supply Alan with a painting at a fixed price and in a good condition within one week from the signing of the contract. The contract also states that in the event Beth does not keep her part of contract then Beth will be liable to pay Alan £500 as breach of contract. Due to this term, the liability of Beth for breach of contract is limited to £500.

---

3. **Time limitation:** This clause states that an action for a claim must start within a certain period of time or the cause of action becomes extinguished.

Example

When a bank send monthly statements to its customers, many banks include a term that any discrepancies in it should be reported by the customer within a week of the receipt of statement. If no communication is received with the stipulated time, the statement will be taken as final.

Traditionally, the courts have sought to limit the operation of exclusion clauses. The law seems to explicitly recognise the greater possibility of exploitation of the consumer by businesses.

The consumers are protected from the harsher effects of the exclusion clauses by stating that for an exclusion clause to be effective, it must be:

a) Properly incorporated into the contract
b) Strictly interpreted

Its validity will then be tested under:

➤ the Unfair Contract Terms Act 1977 and
➤ the Unfair Terms in Consumer Contracts Regulations 1999

a) **Incorporation of exclusion clauses:**
   The courts have traditionally held that exclusion clauses only operate if they are actually part of the contract. There are three methods of incorporation:

Case Study — Incorporation by signature

L'Estrange v Graucob (1934)

In this case, the claimant bought a cigarette machine for her cafe from the defendant and signed a sales agreement (which was in very small print) without reading it. The agreement provided that "any express or implied condition, statement or warranty ... is hereby excluded". The machine failed to work properly. In an action for breach of warranty the defendants were held to be protected by the clause.

Court's decision: Scrutton LJ said "When a document containing contractual terms is signed, then, in the absence of fraud, or, I will add, misrepresentation, the party signing it is bound, and it is wholly immaterial whether he has read the document or not".

i. **Incorporation by signature:** If the claimant signs a document which has a contractual effect and contains an exclusion clause, it will automatically form part of the contract, and he will bound by its terms. This is regardless whether he has not **read the document or not or whether he has understood it or not**.

However, even a signed document can be rendered wholly or partly ineffective if the other party has made a misrepresentation as to its effect.

Case Study — Incorporation by signature

Curtis v Chemical Cleaning Co (1951)

In this case, the claimant took a wedding dress to be cleaned by the defendants. She was asked to sign a piece of paper headed 'Receipt' When Curtis enquired why, the company's employee said it was to disclaim liability for damage done to 'beads and sequins' on the dress. The receipt in fact contained a clause excluding liability "for any damage howsoever arising". When the dress was returned it was badly stained. Curtis sued the cleaning co.

Court's decision: It was held that the cleaners could not escape liability for damage to the material of the dress by relying on the exemption clause because Curtis's signature was obtained by misleading her.

Curtis's signature was induced by a misrepresentation. Therefore, it cuts down the protection of the exclusion clause.

ii. **Incorporation by notice:** The general rule is that an exclusion clause will said to be incorporated into the contract if the person relying on it has taken reasonable steps to draw other parties' attention to this incorporation.

➤ The notice must be given **at or before the time of concluding** the contract
➤ The **terms** must be **contained in a document** which was intended to have contractual effect and
➤ Reasonable steps must be taken to bring the terms to **the attention of the other party.**

Example

The notice excluding the liability for inconvenience suffered by the heart patients in the Giant Wheel ride displayed at the entrance.

 Tips

An exclusion clause cannot be introduced into a contract after it has been made.

Case Study   **Incorporation by notice**

Olley v Marlborough Court (1949)

In this case, the claimant stayed at the defendants' hotel for a week. On the back of her bedroom door, a notice stated that "the proprietors will not hold themselves responsible for articles lost or stolen unless handed to the managers for safe custody." A stranger managed to enter her room and stole her mink coat.

The claimant sued the hotel for the loss of her coat. The Hotel argued that the notice disclaiming liability for theft protected them against the suit.

Court's decision: The Court of Appeal held that the notice was not incorporated in the contract between the claimant and the hotel owners. As the contract was made in the hall of the hotel, before the claimant reached her bedroom and therefore had an opportunity to see the notice, the disclaimer was not part of the contract. The hotel could therefore not rely on the disclaimer.

However it is difficult to determine exactly at what point of time the contract was entered into. This is needed to decide whether the terms of the contract were included before or after the contract was made.

Case Study   **Incorporation by notice**

Thornton v Shoe Lane Parking (1971)

In this case, Thornton parked his car in a commercial car park. He was given a ticket by an automatic machine, which stated that it was issued subject to conditions displayed inside the car park. The car park displayed a sign in small print to the effect that cars were parked at the owner's risk.

Thornton (the claimant) was injured partly due to the defendant's negligence and sued for damages.

Court's decision: Lord Denning said that the liability exemption condition did not apply because the contract was concluded when the claimant put his money into the machine. It was held that the customer is bound by those terms which are brought to his notice before entering into a contract, but not otherwise. He is not bound by the terms printed on the ticket if they differ from the notice, because the ticket came too late (the claimant having already paid). The contract has already been made.

So the terms disclaiming liability for personal injury were held unreasonable.

iii. **Incorporation by previous course of dealings**: Terms (including exclusion clauses) may be incorporated into a contract if the course of dealings between the parties were "**regular and consistent**". The interpretation of this usually depends on the facts.

However, the courts have indicated that the equality of bargaining power between the parties may be taken into account. If the parties are of equal bargaining power then one previous dealing may be sufficient to incorporate the exclusion clause, as in British Crane Hire v Ipswic Plant, whereas if the parties are not of equal bargaining power, three or four previous dealings over a period of five years may not be sufficient, as in Hollier v Rambler Motors

Relevant case studies regarding this point are:

Case Study

Incorporation by previous course of dealings

Spurling v Bradshaw (1956)

The defendant delivered eight barrels of orange juice to the claimants' warehouse, for storage. The defendant received a document from the claimant a few days later, which acknowledged receipt of the barrels. The document contained a clause "exempting the warehousemen from liability for loss or damage because of negligence, wrongful act or default" caused by themselves, their employees or agents".

When the barrels were collected from the warehouse, some contained dirty water and others were empty. The defendant refused to pay the storage charges and the warehousemen sued the defendant.

Court's decision: It was held that, as a result of regular transactions between the parties over several years in which documents similar to the one received by the defendant had been issued, the clause had been included in the contract. Therefore, although the defendant did not receive the document containing the exclusion clause until after the conclusion of the contract, he was now bound by the terms contained in it.

Case Study

McCutcheon v MacBrayne (1964)

McCutcheon asked his brother-in-law, McSporron, to send his car to Islay on MacBrayne's ferry. Exclusion clauses were contained in 27 paragraphs of small print inside and outside of a ferry booking office and in a 'risk note' which passengers sometimes signed.

The ferry sank. McCutcheon claimed for damages. McBrayne argued that its conditions of business were displayed at the port, and were printed on its receipts.

Court's decision: The exclusion clauses were held not to be incorporated. The receipts issued were not contractual documents.

MacBrayne argued that it had done business with McSporron before, and he ought to have known of the terms. However, the court ruled that these dealings, although regular, were not of a sufficiently consistent nature to claim incorporation by prior business.

(Source:www.kevinboone.com/lawglos SpurlingLtdVBradshaw1956.html)

Case Study

Hollier v Rambler Motors (1972)

Over a five-year period, the claimant, Hollier, had used the defendant's garage three or four times. On some occasions he had signed a contract, which excluded the defendant from the liability for damages by fire. On the occasion in question, Hollier had not signed a contract. A fire broke out which badly damaged his car, so he sued for damages.

Court's decision: It was held that three or four dealings over five years did not amount to a course of dealings. Consequently the defendants were liable to pay damages.

Diagram 4: Exclusion clause

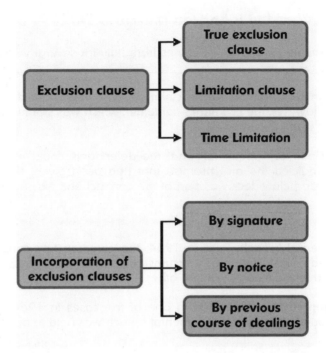

b) **Interpretation of exclusion clause:**

Once, it is established that an exclusion clause is incorporated, the whole contract will be construed (i.e. interpreted) to see whether the clause covers the breach that has occurred.

> **Tips**
>
> **The basic approach is that liability can only be excluded by clear words.**

The main rules of construction are as follows:

i. **Contra proferentem rule:** It means that an **ambiguity** will be construed in **favour of the party disadvantaged by the clause.** If there is any ambiguity or uncertainty as to the meaning of the exclusion clause, the court will construe it contra proferentem, i.e. against the party who inserted it in the contract.

Case Study — Contra proferentem rule

Baldry v Marshall (1925)

In this case, the defendants were motor car dealers. The claimant asked them to supply a car that would be suitable for touring purposes. The defendants suggested a car, which the claimants bought. A clause excluding the defendant's liability for any "guarantee or warranty, statutory or otherwise" was included in the written contract. The claimant discovered that the car was not suitable for touring. So he rejected it and filed a suit against the car dealer to recover the price he had paid.

Court's decision: The Court of Appeal held that the requirement that the car be suitable for touring was a condition. The exclusion clause inserted in the contract did not exclude the liability for breach of a condition and therefore the claimant was not bound by it. **Hence, the defendants were held liable to pay damages.**

ii. **The main purpose rule:** Under this rule, a court can strike out an exemption clause which is inconsistent with the main purpose of the contract.

Case Study — The main propuse rule

Evans Ltd v Andrea Merzario Ltd (1976)

In this case, the claimants had imported machines from Italy for several years. The defendants were their forwarding agents.

The defendants gave an oral promise to the claimants that their machines would continue to be stored below the deck. However, the claimant's container, which was stored on the deck, slid, fell into the sea and was lost.

Court's decision: The Court of Appeal held that the defendants could not rely on an exemption clause because it contradicted the oral promise that had been given. The oral promise that the machines would be stored below-deck was part of the contract and was held to override the written exclusion clause.

iii. **The doctrine of fundamental breach:** Prior to 1964, the common law considered that a fundamental breach could not be excluded or restricted in any circumstances. This was because it would amount to giving something with one hand and taking it away with the other.

However, the rule of law approach was rejected in one of the cases in 1964. Thereafter, the question of whether a clause could exclude liability for a fundamental breach was held to be a question of construction of the clause.

Case Study — The doctrine of fundamental breach

Photo Productions v Securicor Transport (1980)

In this case, Securicor Transport agreed to provide a night patrol service to Photo Production's factory to protect them from theft, fire etc. An employee of Securicor Transport, who was on duty, lit a fire to keep himself warm. This led to a fire which burnt down the factory.

Securicor Transport's standard form of contract had a condition which stated that:" the company will not be liable for injurious acts or defaults of the employees, unless it could have been foreseen and avoided by due diligence of the employer, nor for loss by burglary, theft or fire or any other cause, except so far as it is attributable to the negligence or the company's employees acting within the course of their employment."

Further provisions limited the liability of the Company to the stated amounts. Photo Production claimed damages of £648,000 for breach of contract and / or negligence.

Court's decision: The court observed that it was not disputed that the employee acted in breach of their contract with Securicor Transport. As it rendered further performance of the contract impossible, it is not unnatural to say that it was a "fundamental breach". However, the exclusion clause in this particular case was wide enough to the cover the events that took place. Therefore, Photo Production's action failed.

(Source: netk.net.au/ContractLaw/ContractCasesP.asp)

Diagram 5: Exclusion clause / exemption clause

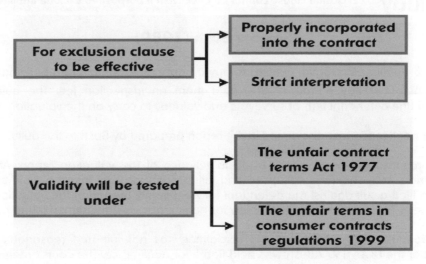

The Unfair Contract Terms Act (UCTA) 1977 and its effect on exclusion clauses

The basic purpose of UCTA 1977 is to restrict the extent to which liability in a contract can be excluded for breach of contract and negligence. However the main area of concern is the principle of 'freedom of contract', which says that adults of full capacity who make contracts with each other should be expected to abide by them, including those terms that are unwelcome.

So when the Unfair Contract Terms Act 1977 was drafted, it tried **to balance freedom of contract against the need to prevent injustice.**

THE SCOPE OF UCTA 1977
The Act does **not** apply to:

➢   insurance contracts
➢   the sale of interest in land
➢   contracts relating to companies formation or dissolution.
➢   the sale of shares

Most of the provisions of the Act apply only to what is termed "business liability" i.e. liability arising from things done by a person in the course of a business or from the occupation of business premises.

In principle, a private person may restrict liability as much as they wish.

For controlling the exclusion clauses, two techniques are used:

a)   Some types of clauses are void, whereas
b)   Others are subject to a test of reasonableness.

a)   **Void clauses**

i.   A trader **cannot** by the use of an exclusion clause in the contract **exclude his liability** for death or personal injury **resulting from negligence**

Case Study

Exclusion clause cannot be effective if it purpose to exclude liability for negligence

Smith v Bush (1989)

In this case, the claimant Mrs. Smith wanted to buy a house. She applied to a building society for a mortgage to help her buy a house. She paid them an inspection fee. The building society instructed Bush (the defendant firm of surveyors and valuers) to carry on the valuation of the house.

The liability for negligence was disclaimed in the report prepared by Bush to the building society.

Mrs. Smith purchased the house for £18000 in reliance of the valuation report. After eighteen months, the bricks from chimneys collapsed and fell through the roof into the main bedroom and loft. Mrs. Smith filed a suit against the defendant for negligently preparing the valuation report and claimed damages. Bush argued that the liability for negligence was disclaimed in the report.

Court's decision: The judge held that the disclaimer was not fair and reasonable and hence ineffective under the UCTA 1977.Bush was held liable for negligence. The court ordered him to pay damages.

ii. If a trader is selling or hiring goods to a consumer he cannot use a contractual term or condition to restrict or exclude his legal obligations:
  ➢ To provide goods as described in the contract and
  ➢ To provide the goods of satisfactory quality.

Example

If a customer has ordered a pineapple cake of 2 pounds with a chocolate icing. The baker cannot exclude to provide chocolate icing by putting in a clause that no icing will be provided if the person doing icing job is on leave. He has to provide goods as described.

---

b) **Clauses subject to reasonableness.**

i. An exclusion clause can be used in a contract to restrict the liability for other loss or damage resulting from negligence, so long as the clause satisfies the test of reasonableness.

ii. If a trader hires or sells goods to a person who is not a consumer, he can insert a clause excluding his liability to provide goods which meet the description and are of acceptable quality, only if the clause satisfies the test of reasonableness.

iii. A trader can stipulate a clause in a contract requiring a consumer to compensate him for any loss that he may incur through breach of contract or negligence, only if the clause satisfies the test of reasonableness.

iv. When a trader provides a service to a consumer, he can only restrict or exclude his liability for breach of contract or unsatisfactory service if he can prove that the clause satisfies the test of reasonableness.

v. When a trader provides a service for any person (who may or may not be a consumer) on his own written terms of business, a written term can be used to exclude or restrict his liability for breach of contract or allow himself to provide an unsatisfactory service only if he can show that the term satisfies the test for reasonableness.

Summary of the effect of UCTA on exclusion of liability Comparative

Source of liability	Definition of liability (where relevant)	Effect on consumer	Effect on non-consumer
Negligence leading to death or injury		void s.2(1) UCTA	void s.2(1) UCTA
Negligence leading to loss or damage		acceptable if reasonable s.2(1) UCTA	acceptable if reasonable s.2(1) UCTA
Sale of goods with defective title	s.12 Sale of Goods Act 1979	void (UCTA s.6(1))	void (UCTA s.6(1))
Sale of goods that do match their description	s.13 Sale of Goods Act 1979	void (UCTA s.6(2)a)	acceptable if reasonable (UCTA s.6(3))
Sale of goods that do match their sample	s.15 Sale of Goods Act 1979	void (UCTA s.6(2)a)	acceptable if reasonable (UCTA s.6(3))
Sale of goods that are of unsatisfactory quality	s.14 Sale of Goods Act 1979	void (UCTA s.6(2)a)	acceptable if reasonable (UCTA s.6(3))
Any other passage of goods where the goods are of unsatisfactory quality or do not match their sample or description		void (UCTA s.7(2))	acceptable if reasonable (UCTA s.7(2))
Breach of standard-form contract		acceptable if reasonable (UCTA s.3)	not affected
Misrepresentation	s.3 Misrepresentation Act 1967	acceptable if reasonable (UCTA s.8(1))	acceptable if reasonable (UCTA

(Source: www.kevinboone.com/ucta.html)

Test Yourself 6

State the main rules of construction in interpretation of exclusion clause

Test Yourself 7

What are the two techniques used to control exclusion clause under the scope of UCTA 1977.

SYNOPSIS

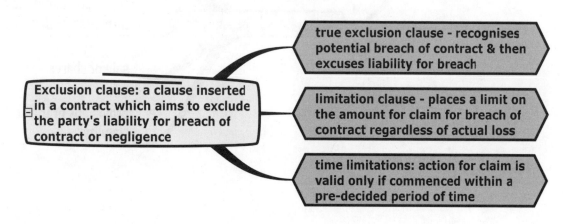

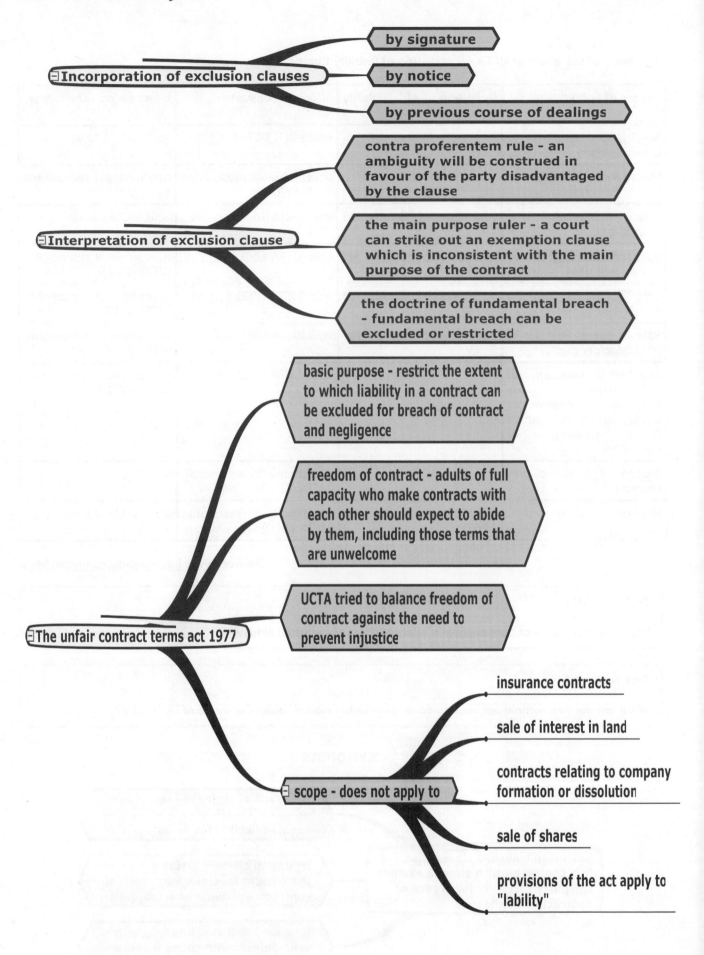

Incorporation of exclusion clauses
- by signature
- by notice
- by previous course of dealings

Interpretation of exclusion clause
- contra proferentem rule - an ambiguity will be construed in favour of the party disadvantaged by the clause
- the main purpose ruler - a court can strike out an exemption clause which is inconsistent with the main purpose of the contract
- the doctrine of fundamental breach - fundamental breach can be excluded or restricted

The unfair contract terms act 1977
- basic purpose - restrict the extent to which liability in a contract can be excluded for breach of contract and negligence
- freedom of contract - adults of full capacity who make contracts with each other should expect to abide by them, including those terms that are unwelcome
- UCTA tried to balance freedom of contract against the need to prevent injustice
- scope - does not apply to
  - insurance contracts
  - sale of interest in land
  - contracts relating to company formation or dissolution
  - sale of shares
  - provisions of the act apply to "lability"

Answers to Test Yourself

Answer 1

Representation: A representation is a **pre-contractual** statement of fact made to induce another person to enter into a contract. Such statements, although, induce the other party to enter into a contract, the maker of the statement does not guarantee its truth. If the statement proves to be incorrect, it cannot be enforced, as it is not a term of the contract, but it may prove to be a misrepresentation, whereupon other remedies are available.

Term: Where the statement is of such major importance that the promise would not have entered into the agreement without it, it will be construed as a term. A term is similar to a representation, but the truth of the statement is guaranteed by the person who made the statement.

Answer 2

There are four tests for distinguishing a contractual term from a mere representation. These are:

i.   **Importance of the statement:** Where the statement is of such a major importance that the promisor would not have entered into the agreement without it, it will be construed as a term.

ii. **Timing:** The court will consider the lapse of time between the making of the statement and the contract's conclusion if the interval is short the statement is more likely to be a term.

iii. **Reductions of terms to writing:** The court will consider whether the statement was omitted in a later formal contract in writing. If the written contract does not incorporate the statement, this would suggest that the parties did not intend the statement to be a contractual term.

iv. **Special knowledge / skills:** If the maker of the statement had specialist knowledge or was in a better position than the other party to verify the statement's accuracy, then the **statements made <u>by</u> <u>them</u> will be terms but the statements made to them will not be terms.**

Answer 3

a) Mere representation. This is because Desmond only informally provided the information about his garden to Dafty with intention to induce her to buy the garden.

b) Term. This is because a painting made in the year 1852 is the basic requirement of the contract. The contract would not have been entered into if it was known earlier that is was not made in 1852.

c) Term. This is because the specific requirements about the quality of the table cloth were given which is the condition of the contract.

d) Mere representation. This is because the statement by supplier is only to induce Monica to buy the cosmetics.

Answer 4

a) Expressed term as the terms about delivery of washing machine are expressly stated in the letter.
b) Implied Term: As per the provisions of the Sale of Goods Act, 1979 it is an implied ownership in all the contracts where one person sells goods to another.
c) Implied Term because a house is implied to be fit for dwelling purposes.
d) Express Term as it is expressly made clear by the tour company.

Answer 5

a) **Terms:** Contractual terms are a part of the contract. The parties to a contract have to perform whatever they have agreed to perform or not to perform in a contract. If their action is in contravention to the contract then they have said to have breached the contract. This breach can have a remedy, however that will depend on the nature of the breach. There can be cases like where some statements do not form a part of the contract but one of the parties must have entered into the contract due to its inducement. Thus these statements which are made before the contract and on that basis a contract takes place are called pre-contractual representation. Therefore a contract contains expressed terms and implied terms.

b) **Conditions:** It is the base of any contract. When a condition is breached then the party at loss can either terminate the contract or refuse to perform their part of the contract, or can sue for the damages or losses incurred by them. Condition is essential for the main purpose of the contract, the breach of which gives a right to treat the contract as repudiated. Condition is a fundamental term of the agreement and is something which goes to the root of the contract.

c) **Warranties:** Warranty is collateral to the main purpose of the contract, the breach of which gives rise to a claim for damages but not a right to reject the goods and treat the contract as repudiated. Warranty is a subsidiary obligation. It is comparatively a minor term. If a warranty is broken, the innocent party may claim the damages but does not give the right to terminate the agreement.

d) **Innominate terms:** These are the terms, in case of which whether the term breached is a condition or a warranty, depends on the consequence of the breach. If the breach deprives the innocent party of 'substantially the whole benefit of the contract', then the right to repudiate will be permitted, even if the term might otherwise appear to be a mere warranty. If, however, the innocent party does not lose 'substantially the whole benefit of the contract', then they will not be permitted to repudiate but must settle for damages, even if the term might otherwise appear to be a condition.

Answer 6

When an exclusion clause is incorporated, the whole contract is construed (i.e. interpreted) to see whether the clause covers the breach taken place. The basic approach is that liability can only be excluded by clear words. The main rules of construction are as follows:

a) **Contra proferentem rule:** It means that an ambiguity will be construed in favour of the party disadvantaged by the clause. If there is any ambiguity or uncertainty as to the meaning of exclusion clause the court will construe it contra proferentem, i.e. against the party who inserted it in the contract.

b) **The main purpose rule:** Under this rule, a court can strike out an exemption clause which is inconsistent with or repugnant to the main purpose of the contract.

c) **The doctrine of fundamental breach:** Prior to 1964, the common law considered that a fundamental breach could not be excluded or restricted in any circumstances as this would amount to giving with one hand and taking with the other. This became elevated to a rule of law.

Answer 7

For controlling the exclusion clauses, two techniques are used:
a) Void clauses
b) Clauses subject to a test of reasonableness

a) **Void clauses**

i. An exclusion clause cannot be used in the contract just to exclude one's liability for death or personal injury resulting from negligence.

ii. A contractual term or condition to restrict or exclude one's legal obligations cannot be included just to provide goods which are as described and of satisfactory quality.

b) **Clauses subject to reasonableness.**

i. An exclusion clause can be used in the contract which restricts the liability for loss or damage resulting from negligence provided it satisfies the test of reasonableness.

ii. A clause can be used in the contract only when one requires a consumer to indemnify him against any loss he may incur through negligence or breach of contract.

iii. An exclusion clause can be used by a trader who is selling or hiring goods to a person who is not a consumer to restrict his legal liability to provide goods which are as described and of satisfactory quality provided that it satisfies the test of reasonableness.

iv. When services are being provided than one can restrict or exclude his liability for breach of contract or allow himself to provide an inadequate service if he can show that the term or condition satisfies the test of reasonableness.

When one undertakes to provide a service on his own written terms of business then he can only use those written terms to exclude or restrict his liability for breach of contract or allow himself to provide an inadequate service if he can show that the term in question satisfies the test or reasonableness.

Quick Quiz

True or False

1. If a statement which was a 'term' of contract proves to be untrue, the party misled can claim for the breach of contract.

2. If the written contract does not incorporate the statement, this would suggest that the parties did not intend the statement to be a contractual term.

3. A contract may be deemed to incorporate a term which can be shown to be the 'certain and general' custom of a particular industry.

4. Implied conditions and warranties are those which, are expressly provided in the contract.

5. An exclusion clause is a term inserted in a contract which aims to exclude or limit on party's liability for breach of contract or negligence.

6. Terms implied by custom can not be overridden.

Answers to Quick Quiz

1. True. If a term proves to be untrue the misled party is entitled to breach the contract.
2. True.
3. True. Such terms are implied by customs.
4. False. Implied conditions are not expressly provided in the contract.
5. True. Exclusion contract prima facie excludes the liability.
6. False. Expressed terms can override the implied terms.

Self Examination Questions

Question 1

Why doesn't the Unfair Contract Terms Act 1977 prohibit all exclusion clauses?

Question 2

Explain express terms of contract.

Question 3

Explain what an exclusion clause / exemption clause is.

Question 4

State the methods of incorporation of exclusion clauses.

Question 5

Tom contracts with Flowers Inc to provide Tom with a dozen Red Roses on the 12 February. 20X1. Flowers Inc provides the Roses to Tom on the stipulated day but they were Yellow Roses. Tom does not accept the Roses. Explain what is Tom's right?

Question 6

James is developing a subdivision near Houston. On February 14, 2005, he entered into a written contract to sell a lot in the subdivision to Pearl as for £50,000. During negotiations, Leon assured Paola that the property was zoned outside of the 50-year flood plain. The written contract made no mention of this. When, after signing the contract and paying James for the lot, Pearl applied for a building permit, she was notified that the lot was within the 50-year flood plain (meaning both that it was substantially more prone to flooding and that it would be much more expensive to insure the house that Paola intended to build on the lot).

If Pearl sued James for breach of contract, would evidence of James's oral representation be admissible at trial, notwithstanding the parol evidence rule?

(Source: www.lexisnexis.com/lawschool/study/qanda/contracts.asp)

Answers to Self Examination Questions

Answer 1

The basic premise of the law of contract is that of freedom of contract, with both parties being free to negotiate whatever terms they want. However, the law now recognises that freedom of contract is unrealistic for some people when there is inequality of bargaining power. The law has intervened to protect vulnerable people in a variety of ways, one being the restriction of exclusion clauses in a consumer contract which enable a person in breach to avoid liability.

However, where the parties are of equal bargaining power the courts will not generally interfere with the concept of freedom of contract and will permit exclusion clauses in contracts between commercial people.

Answer 2

Express terms are statements actually made by one of the parties with the intention that they become part of the contract and thus binding and enforceable through court action if necessary. It is this intention that distinguishes the contractual term from the mere representation, which, although it may induce the contractual agreement, does not become a term of the contract. Failure to comply with the former gives rise to an action for breach of contract, whilst failure to comply with the latter only gives rise to an action for misrepresentation. Such express statements may be made by word of mouth or in writing as long as they are sufficiently clear for them to be enforceable.

Answer 3

An exclusion clause is a term inserted in a contract which aims to exclude or limit   on party's liability for breach of contract or negligence.
Exclusion clauses generally fall into one of these categories:

a) **True exclusion clause**: The clause recognises a potential breach of the contract, and then excuses the liability for the breach. Alternatively, the clause is constructed in such a way that it only includes reasonable care to perform duties on one of the parties.

b) **Limitation clause**: The clause places a limit on the amount that can be claimed   for a breach of contract, regardless of the actual loss.

c) **Time limitation:** The clause states that an action for a claim must be   commenced within a certain period of time or the cause of action becomes extinguished.
   Traditionally, the courts have sought to limit the operation of exclusion clauses. The law seems to explicitly recognize the greater possibility of exploitation of the consumer by businesses. The consumers are protected from harsher effects of exclusion clauses by putting that for an exclusion clause to be effective, it must be:
   ➢ Properly incorporated into the contract,
   ➢ Strict interpretation

Answer 4

Incorporation of exclusion clauses:

The courts have traditionally held that exclusion clauses only operate if they are actually part of the contract. There seems to be three methods of incorporation:

i.   **Incorporation by signature:** If the document is signed by the claimant which has contractual effect containing an exclusion clause, it will automatically form part of the contract, and the terms are then binding on him even though he has not read the document and regardless of whether he understands it or not.

ii. **Incorporation by notice:** An exclusion clause should be incorporated into the contract if the party relying on it takes reasonable steps to draw it to the other parties' attention.

iii. **Incorporation by previous course of dealings:** Terms (including exclusion clauses) may be incorporated into a contract if course of dealings between the parties were **"regular and consistent"**. What this means usually depends on the facts, however, the courts have indicated that equality of bargaining power between the parties may be taken into account.

Answer 5

Tom can sue for breach of contract due to the fact that Flowers Inc agreed to supply him with Red Roses not Yellow Roses and hence it is breach of condition.

Answer 6

Yes. Even if the trial court finds the contract to be unambiguous and fully integrated as a matter of law, there are numerous parol evidence rule exceptions that might permit the admission of James's oral assurance to Pearl that the property was zoned outside of the 50-year flood plain.

First, if both James and Pearl were mistaken when they entered into the contract as to the flood-plain zoning of the property, and that zoning materially affected the value of the transaction to one or both parties, parol evidence may be admissible to establish a **mutual mistake** that would allow either party to avoid the contract.

Second, if James should have known that the property was within the 50-year flood plain, or did not know one way or the other whether the property was outside the 50-year flood plain, parol evidence may be admissible to establish a **material misrepresentation** that would allow Pearl to avoid the contract.

Third, if James knew that, in fact, the property was inside the 50-year flood plain, parol evidence may be admissible to establish **fraudulent inducement**.

Fourth, if Pearl would never have purchased the property if she had known it was zoned within the 50-year flood plain, but did so believing that she was receiving a property that was not flood-prone in exchange for her promise to pay James, parol evidence may be admissible to establish **lack or failure of consideration**.

And, fifth, if Pearl's agreement to purchase the property was conditioned on it's not being situated within the 50-year flood plain, parol evidence may be admissible to establish the existence of an **unsatisfied condition precedent**.

BREACH OF CONTRACT AND REMEDIES

Get through intro

A **contract** is an **exchange** of commodities / services **between two parties** for a price.

Whenever two or more parties are involved in any transaction, **the possibility of disputes can never be eliminated.** The law of contract contains **provisions which govern the settlement of disputes** (if any) between the parties to a contract.

The parties to a contract are not relieved of their obligations until the contract has been discharged in the manner which has been agreed. **The failure to discharge a contract in a desired way results in breach of contract.**

This Study Guide takes you through the meaning of a breach of contract, the consequences of a breach of contract and the remedies for a breach of contract.

The knowledge of the remedies available in the case of a breach of a contract is essential for the successful discharge of a contract and will help you in your professional life. It will also help you to solve the question in the examination with confidence.

LEARNING OUTCOMES

a) Explain the meaning and effect of breach of contract
b) Explain the rules relating to the award of damages
c) Analyse the equitable remedies for breach of contract

Introduction

Vir enters into a contract with Zara to sell his motor car for £3,000. Zara accepts to purchase the motor car.

This is a contract between Vir and Zara and both the parties have contractual obligations. Vir has an obligation to deliver his car to Zara for £3,000 and Zara has an obligation to purchase the motor car by paying a price of £3,000.

If either of the parties, i.e. Vir or Zara fails to perform the contractual obligation, this amounts to breach of contract.

1. Explain the meaning and effect of breach of contract
[Learning outcome a]

The parties to the contract are freed from their contractual obligations only when the contract is discharged completely and the terms and conditions are fulfilled. A contract is discharged when the rights and liabilities created by the contract come to an end.

Meaning

> **Definition**
>
> Discharge of contract means termination of contractual relations between the parties to a contract.

A contract may be discharged in any of the following ways.

Diagram 1: A contract is discharged in the following ways

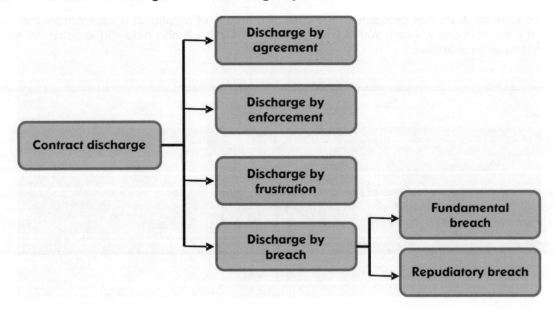

1. Discharge by agreement

When both parties agree to terminate the contract, this is called a discharge of contract by agreement. Some contracts provide for discharge by agreement, for example, by expressly stating that the contract can be discharged by notice.

Example

Jack owned a lorry which he hired out to Ted. Ted agreed to pay a monthly rent of £100 for the use of the lorry. The arrangement continued for five months after which the vehicle started giving trouble. Ted wanted Jack to repair the lorry. However, Jack didn't want to spend any money on repairing the lorry. Hence they mutually agreed to terminate the contract.

---

2. Discharge by frustration

When a contract is terminated because it became impossible or illegal to perform the contract, this is called a discharge of contract by frustration.

> **Example**
>
> Mack entered into a contract with Jack, according to which Jack was to paint Mack's office for a sum of £1,500 within eight days' time. However, the next day, the building where the office was situated was seized by the police, acting under a court's order. As a result, Jack could not perform the contract and the contract was discharged by frustration.

3. Discharge by performance

The most common way to discharge a contractual obligation is through performance of the contract by the parties to it. As a general rule, discharge requires complete and exact performance of the obligation in the contract.

> **Example**
>
> In contracts for the sale of goods, **s13 Sale of Goods Act 1979** imposes the condition that the goods delivered must correspond to the description given in the contract. This requirement of s13 is illustrated in **Re Moore and Landauer (1921)** which is explained below.

Case Study

Discharge of contract requires complete and exact performance of the obligation in the contract

The cases below illustrate this point:

1. **Cutter v Powell (1795)**
   In this case, a sailor's wages were due to be paid after **the end of a voyage.** He died a few days before reaching the port and his wages were claimed by his widow.

   Court's decision: It was held that the sailor **had not fulfilled** his contractual obligation. As a result, his wages could not be collected by his widow.

2. **Re Moore and Landauer (1921)**
   In this case, the parties made an agreement for the sale of 3,000 tins of canned fruit packed in cases of 30 tins. When the cases of tins were delivered, although the total number of tins was 3,000, many cases contained not 30 but 24 tins. The market value was not affected.

   Court's decision: It was held that, under s13 of the Sale of Goods Act, the buyer could reject the consignment as the goods did not match their description.

However, in these cases, the defendants appear to have benefited in the following ways:

➢ They did not have to pay anything (given no consideration).
➢ They obtained a part of the consideration that the claimant had promised to deliver.

Hence, certain exceptions to the general rule regarding complete performance have been developed. These exceptions which secure the interest of both the parties are:

a) **Divisible contracts**

Contracts can be divided into two categories: entire and divisible. In an entire contract, the contractual liability of one party does not begin until the other party has completed its performance of the contract. In a divisible contract, part performance of one party will lead to a partial liability for the other party.

> **Case Study**   Divisible contracts
>
> **1) Taylor v Laird (1856)**
>
> In this case, the claimant had agreed to captain a ship up the River Niger at a rate of £50 per month but quit before finishing the job. He claimed his pay for the months he had worked.
>
> **Court's decision:** It was held that, under the contract, the performance and corresponding payments were divisible by the number of months. The claimant was therefore entitled to £50 for each complete month of service.
>
> **2) Bolton v Mahadeva (1972)**
>
> In this case, a contract had been made that the claimant would install central heating in the defendant's house for a one-off payment of £560. After the central heating had been installed, the defendant found that it was faulty and refused to pay. The judge found that the system provided varying levels of heat to different rooms and also gave off unpleasant fumes. The cost of rectifying these defects was £174.
>
> **Court's decision:** The Court of Appeal held that the claimant had not carried out any substantial performance and was therefore not entitled to receive any payment. However, an agreement to supply a bathroom suite was found to be separate from the overall agreement and therefore the payment for this service could be recovered.

b) **Acceptance of partial performance**

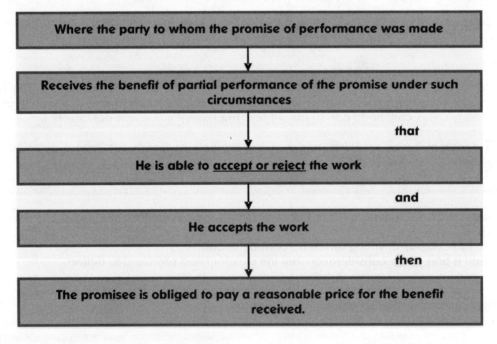

It is very important here that mere performance by the promisor is not enough; it must be open to the promisee to accept or reject the benefits of the contract.

Example

Alisha orders 20 tins of a soft drink from John. John only has 16 tins in stock. So he delivers 16 tins to Alisha. In this case, Alisha has the right either to accept the 16 tins or to reject them. If she accepts the 16 tins, then she **has to pay the price of 16** tins.

She **cannot claim** that she is not liable to pay anything since she had ordered 20 tins and John had delivered only 16 tins.

c) Completion of performance prevented by the other party

Where a party to an entire contract is prevented by the promisee from performing all his obligations, then he can recover a reasonable price for what he has done on a quantum meruit basis (See 2.3 (2) (e) below)

Tips

Quantum meruit: The expression quantum meruit means "the amount one deserves" or "what the job is worth". In most instances, it denotes a claim for a reasonable sum.

Case Study — Performance prevented by the other party

Planche v Colburn (1831)
In this case, the claimant had agreed to write a book on 'Costume and Ancient Armour' for the defendant's library series. He was to receive £100 on completion of the book. After he had done the necessary research but before the book had been written, the publishers abandoned the series. The claimant claimed remuneration on a quantum meruit.

Court's decision: The court held that the contract had been discharged by the defendants' breach. Therefore, the claimant could obtain 50 guineas as **reasonable remuneration on a quantum meruit.**

d) Substantial performance

When the essential element of an agreement is performed completely but some minor part or fault needs to be corrected, the party who performed the act can claim the contract price. When making the payment, the other party can deduct some amount for the work which remains to be done.

Case Study — Substantial performance of contract by the party gives that party the right to recover the corresponding contractual price.

1. Hoenig v Isaacs (1952)
In this case, the claimant was employed by the defendant to decorate and furnish his flat for the total price of £750. However, the furniture had some faults which would cost £56 to be rectified. The defendant argued that the claimant was only entitled to reasonable remuneration as the work did not meet the expected standards.

Court's decision: It was held that, as the claimant had substantially completed the contract, he was entitled to the total price of contract (£750) minus the amount to rectify the defects (£56) (i.e. £750 -£56 = £694)

2. Dakin v Lee (1916)

In this case the defendants were contracted to build a house. However, the completed house did not meet all the specifications, for e.g., certain rolled steel had the wrong joining and the concrete was not four feet deep.

Court's decision: The Court of Appeal held that the builders were entitled to receive the contract price reduced by an appropriate amount regarding the defective items.

e) Time of performance

Under common law, time is given prime importance. When a contract condition relating to the **time** of performance is **'of the essence'** of a contract, a party's failure to meet that condition gives the other party the right to terminate the contract.

Section 41 Law of Property Act 1925 provides that **if time** is **not of the essence**, a **right to damages accrues but not a right to terminate** the contract.

Time is **not regarded** as being of the **essence, except** in three circumstances:

i. The contract expressly states that time is of essence.

Example

Stephen enters into a contract with Eve to make catering arrangements for her birthday party. The contract clearly states that the contract has to be performed on 23 August (her birthday) otherwise it will be treated as terminated.

Here, time of performance is of the essence as it is expressly stated in the contract.

---

ii. Time was made of the essence by a notice (during the currency of the contract) to perform the contract within a reasonable time.

Example

On 1 July, Steve entered into a contract with Kate to decorate the interior of her house. It was agreed that Steve would complete his work before the month of October. However, on 1st August, Kate informed Steve by **sending a letter** that she wanted the work to be completed before 25th October. She clearly stated in the letter that if the work was not completed before 25th October, she would treat the contract as terminated.

Here, the time of performance was not of the essence originally. However, it was made of the essence later on when Kate sent the notice to Steve.

---

iii. Where, from the nature of the surrounding circumstances or from the subject matter of the contract, it is clear that time is of the essence.

Example

Peter enters into a contract with Alan to buy flowers from Alan's farm for £2,500.

Here, flowers are perishable goods. If Peter fails to take the delivery of flowers within a reasonable time, the flowers will perish. Hence, (even though it is not clearly stated), from the subject matter of the contract it is clear that time is of the essence of performance of the contract.

Test Yourself 1

Isha enters into a contract with Nisha to design Nisha's wedding dress. Nisha's wedding date is 15 July. Is time of the essence in performance of this contract?

SYNOPSIS

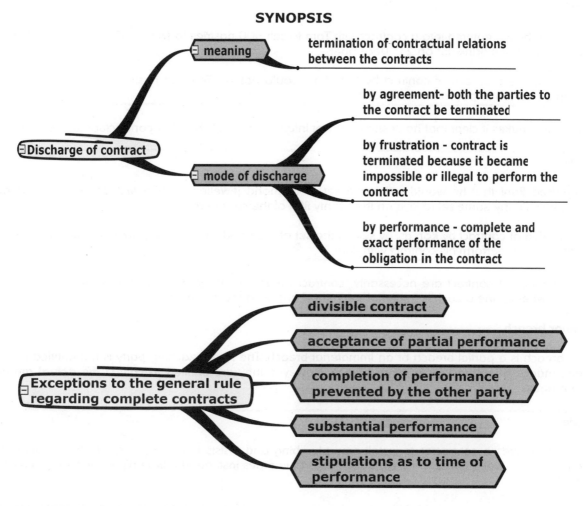

1.1 Meaning and effects of breach of contract

Meaning

Breach, in simple terms, means breaking or violating a law, right, or duty, either by commission or omission.

> **Definition**
>
> **Breach of contract** is an **unjustified failure** to fulfil the duties under the contractual terms when the performance is due.

A contract can be breached in the following ways:

1.   One party does not perform as he or she had promised.

Example

Jaya promised Maya that she would handle all the financial accounts of Maya's boutique for a monthly payment of £200. At the end of the month, Maya refuses to pay.

This is breach of contract because Maya did not perform as she had promised.

---

2.   One party does something that makes it impossible for the other party to perform his / her duties under the contract.

Example

Sam, who is a baker, entered into a contract with Tom to sell 500 pastries to Tom on Christmas day. However, Tom declared himself bankrupt on 21st December.

In this case, this is a breach of contract by Tom. Sam could not sell Tom the pastries as Tom was bankrupt and not in a position to pay for the pastries.

3. One party makes it clear that he or she does not intend to perform his / her contractual duties.

Example

Ron promised Rani that he would sell her a set of diamond jewellery on the first day of the next month. However, he sold the same set to Riya on the twenty fifth of the current month.

This is a breach of contract by Ron as, by selling the set of diamond jewellery to Riya, Ron made it clear that he does not intend to perform his contract with Rani.

Not all breaches of contract are necessarily "contract killers" which would end up in a lawsuit. Much would depend on whether the breach is "material" or "minor" and who the parties are.

a) **Minor breach**

A minor breach is a partial breach or an immaterial breach. The non-breaching party is not entitled to compel the performance of contract for a minor breach. However, they are entitled **to collect the actual amount of their damages.**

Example

A homeowner hires a contractor to install new plumbing and insists that the pipes, which will ultimately be sealed behind the walls, are red. The contractor uses blue pipes instead. The blue pipes function just as well as the red pipes.

Although the contractor breached the literal terms of the contract, the homeowner cannot compel the contractor to take out the blue pipes and fit the red pipes.

However, he can recover the amount of his damages. Since no damages were inflicted, the homeowner receives nothing.

If the breach is minor, the non-breaching party has the option to:

➤ ignore or excuse the defect and continue as if nothing occurred
➤ point out the problem to the breaching party and give him an opportunity to rectify it
➤ refuse to pay anything more until it is rectified, or
➤ correct the work himself and deduct the cost from any payment due to the breaching party

b) **Material breach**

A material breach is any failure to perform that **permits the other party to the contract to either compel performance, or collect damages because of the breach.**

Example

Consider that, in the above example, the contractor was instructed to use copper pipes. Instead he used iron pipes which do not last as long as copper pipes.

The homeowner can recover the cost of correcting the breach i.e. taking out the iron pipes and replacing them with copper pipes.

Diagram 2: Breach of contract

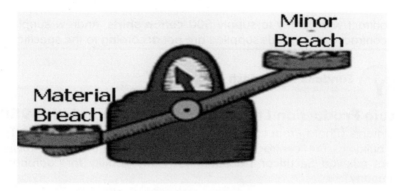

Test Yourself 2

Fill in the table with appropriate marks (✔ or x)

	Minor breach	Material breach
Collect damages		
Compel performance		

SYNOPSIS

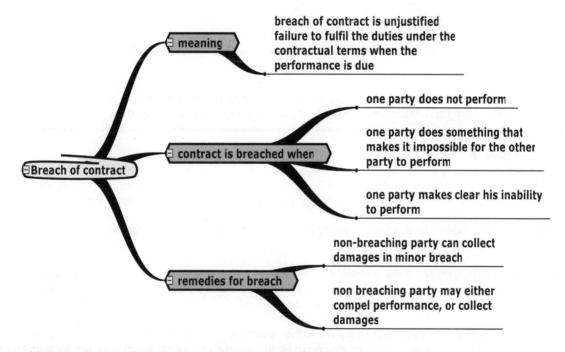

1. 2 Breach giving the aggrieved party right to terminate the contract

Breach of contract places an obligation on the defaulting party to pay damages to the innocent party. The primary obligation to perform according to the terms of contract remains in force.

However, in the following types of breach, the aggrieved party has a **right to terminate the contract altogether.**

1. Fundamental breach

A fundamental breach is a breach so fundamental that:
➤ it permits the aggrieved party to terminate performance of the contract and

➤ to sue the defaulting party for damages.

Example

Andrew enters into a contract with Jimmy to supply 500 **cotton shirts**. Andrew supplied 500 **skirts.** This is a fundamental breach of contract as the goods supplied are not according to the specification.

Case Study — Fundamental breach

Photo Production Ltd v Securicor Transport Ltd (1980)

In this case, the claimants (Photo Production Ltd) hired the defendants (Securicor Transport) to guard Photo Production's building. The contract between Securicor and Photo Productions contained an exclusion clause that relieved Securicor Transport from any liability for "damages caused by any employee of the company."

One of the security guards of Securicor Transport, while patrolling Photo Production's building, intentionally started a fire that destroyed the whole building.

The issue was whether Securicor could rely on the exclusion clause to escape liability for their employee's conduct.

Photo Productions argued that the exclusion clause could not apply. They claimed that Securicor Transport had entirely failed to perform their contract. Therefore, the doctrine of fundamental breach is applicable whereby the whole agreement is invalid.

Court's decision: It was held that the exclusion clause precluded all liability even when harm was caused intentionally.

Hence, Photo Production's claim for fundamental breach was rejected.

Tips

In the above case, if the exclusion clause had not been inserted in the contract, then the claimant's claim for fundamental breach of contract might have succeeded.

2. Repudiatory breach

To repudiate means to reject or to disclaim. Where a party to a contract, either by words or by conduct, indicates that he does not intend to honour his contractual liability, this is a repudiatory breach of contract.

The repudiatory breach does not automatically discharge the contract but gives the aggrieved party the choice of:

➢ **either to affirm the contract:** If the innocent party opts to affirm the contract, then he may continue with his preparation for performance and recover the agreed price for his services. Any claim for damages will be assessed on the basis of what the claimant has actually lost.

➢ **or to treat the contract as repudiated by the other party:** In this case, the breach not only gives rise to a cause for action for **damages** but also **discharges** the aggrieved party **from** any **performance** still due from him.

Case Study — Repudiatory breach

White & Carter v McGregor (1961)

McGregor contracted with the claimant to have advertisements placed on litter bins which were supplied to local councils. He then wrote to cancel the contract but the claimants elected to advertise as agreed. They produced and displayed the adverts as required under the contract and then claimed the payment.

Court's decision: It was held that the **claimants were not obliged to accept** the defendant's **repudiation**. Repudiation does not, of itself, bring the contract to an end. It **gives the innocent party** the **choice to affirm or reject** the contract. The claimants were held entitled to recover the agreed price for their services.

3. Anticipatory breach

Anticipatory breach arises when one of the parties to a contract repudiates the contract **before the time of performance**. There is a clear indication that the party will not perform when performance is due, or a situation in which future non-performance is foreseeable.

Example

Lara, a singer, enters into a contract with John, the manager of the theatre, to sing at his theatre on the Christmas Eve. The contract was entered into on 1 November. John agrees to pay her £5,000 for the performance. However, on 15 November, John enters into a similar contract with a celebrity singer.

The invitation cards and advertisement boards of the event do not mention of Lara's name. Moreover, John does not even call Lara for rehearsals for the event.

John's conduct indicates that he does not intend to honour his contract with Lara. This is a repudiatory breach of contract.

The repudiation by the party to perform the contract may be either expressed or implied.

Expressed anticipatory breach occurs when the party who breaches the contract **declares expressly** that they will not perform the act **(Hochster v De La Tour (1853))**.

Implied anticipatory breach occurs when a party carries out some act which makes the performance impossible **(Omnium Enterprises v Sutherland (1919))**.

An anticipatory breach gives the non-breaching party the option to treat the breach as immediate, and, if repudiatory, to terminate the contract and sue for damages (without waiting for the breach to actually take place).

Case Study Anticipatory Breach

Hochster v De La Tour (1853)

In this case, the claimant was engaged by the defendant to enter into his services as a courier and accompany him on a tour. The claimant was to begin service on 1 June. On 11 May he was informed by the defendant that his services were no longer required. The claimant brought an action on 22 May i.e. even before the scheduled time of performance had arrived.

The defendant claimed that any action against him can be taken only after 1st June.

Court's decision: It was held that the claimant was entitled to bring the action even before the time of performance.

Diagram 3: Types of breach in which aggrieved party has right to terminate the contract.

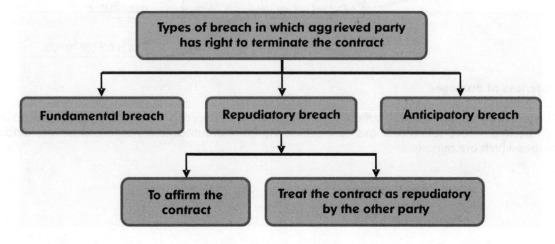

Test Yourself 3

Explain the term anticipatory breach of contract.

SYNOPSIS

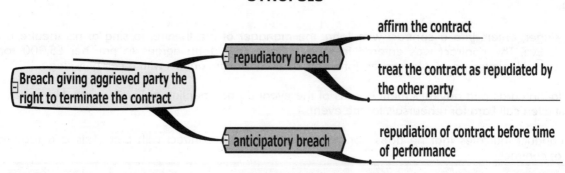

2. Explain the rules relating to the award of damages

[Learning outcome b]

2.1 Damages

Damages are intended to compensate the innocent party for the loss that he has suffered as a result of the breach of contract. In order to get compensation for the breach of contract the injured party must establish that:

> actual loss has been caused by the breach;
> the type of loss is recognised as giving an entitlement to compensation;
> the loss is not too remote; and
> the quantification of damages to the required level of proof.

A breach of contract can be established even if there is no actual loss. In that case there will only be an entitlement to nominal damages.

SYNOPSIS

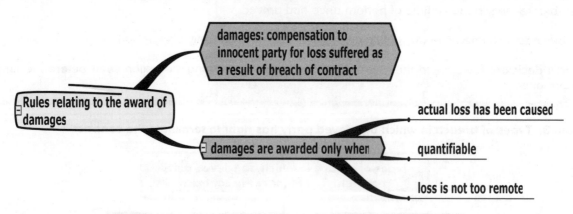

2.2 Remoteness of damages

Even if it is proved that the claimant suffered loss because of the breach of contract, he cannot claim all the loss which he might have suffered. In this connection, the general principle is not to compel the defendant to pay damages which are remote.

Case Study — Remoteness of damages

Hadley v Baxendale (1854)

In this case, **Hadley's** (the claimant) mill stopped due to breakage of the crankshaft, a vital part of the mill. The claimant, therefore, wanted to send the shaft to a certain maker in Greenwich. The shaft was to be used as the model for a new shaft to be manufactured by the maker in Greenwich.

The claimant delivered the shaft to **Baxendale** (a carrier) for delivery to the makers in Greenwich. Baxendale was told that the article to be carried by them was the broken shaft of a mill and that the claimants were the millers of that mill. Delivery of the shaft to the manufacturers at Greenwich was delayed due to some negligence on the part of Baxendale (the defendant).

The claimant, therefore, did not receive the shaft for several days and consequently the mill could not start in time. This resulted in loss of profits to the claimant (which they would have earned, had they received the shaft in time).

The defendant resisted the claim on the ground that the damages were too remote.

Court's decision: It was held that the claimant was entitled to recover **only the general damages** from the breach of contract.

The court reasoned that Baxendale had no way of knowing that the claimant would lose profits if the shipment of the shaft was delayed. This information wasn't communicated directly to them. The loss of profits was not discussed by both the parties when they made the contract. Although the fact that the mill was closed was communicated, it wasn't made completely clear to the defendants that the mill was closed because of the broken shaft and couldn't re-open again until it was fixed.

Summary: Indirect or consequential damages are only recoverable if:

➤ the damages were reasonably foreseeable by both parties at the time of the contract; and
➤ the damages were a "natural" consequence of the breach.

This legal concept is still alive today – 150 years later. If the claimant had made it clear that the mill's operation was dependent upon getting the new crank shaft, they would have been able to receive damages.

Tips
The defendant is liable only if he knows of the special circumstances from which the abnormal consequence of breach could arise.

This famous case **Hadley v Baxendale (1854)** created a new rule. The court found that an aggrieved buyer of services will be unable to recover consequential losses resulting from breach **unless the losses are:**

1. a "natural" consequence of the breach; or

2. the buyer brings the circumstances which would generate the losses expressly to the seller's attention.

Tips
A claimant can claim for losses only when the circumstances which would generate the losses are within defendant's knowledge

Case Study

Damages could be recovered in regard to the normal profits, because loss was the normal consequence of the breach of the contract

Victoria Laundry (Windsor) Ltd v Newman Industries Ltd (1949)

In this case, the claimants were launderers and dyers and wanted to expand their business. With this aim in mind, they entered into a contract with the defendants for purchase of a new boiler. The defendants agreed to deliver the boiler on June 5 but actually delivered the boiler in November. Consequently, the claimants brought action for loss of profit which they would have earned had the boiler been delivered on June 5.

Court's decision: The court **upheld the claim of the claimant** for, in his view, the defendants knew at the time of the contract that the claimants were launderers and dyers and needed the boiler for immediate use in their business.

Case Study

Remoteness of damages

Ha Parsons (Livestock) v Uttley Ingham (1978)

This case involved the purchase of a bulk food storage hopper from Uttley Ingham the manufacturer. The hopper was delivered and set up. However, by mistake, the ventilator hatch was left shut. The pig food which was stored inside became mouldy. As the pigs were given this food, they fell sick and some of them died.

It was suggested that this type of illness was not well known, and that the pigs were particularly susceptible to this disease. A large number of the pigs died, causing considerable financial loss.

Court's decision: Some degree of illness of the pigs was to be expected as natural consequences. As illness was to be expected, **death from illness was not too remote**. Hence the **defendants' claim failed**.

If the loss caused is not too remote, the defendant may be liable for serious consequences.

Test Yourself 4

Explain in brief the test of remoteness of damages as set out in Hadley v Baxendale (1854).

SYNOPSIS

Remoteness of damages — losses can be claimed if
- losses are natural consequences of breach
- defendant was aware of the circumstances from which the abnormal consequence of breach could arise

2.3 Measures for damages

The principle for measuring damages is that the party injured by the breach should receive **compensation** which is, as far as possible the **equivalent of the benefits** he would have **received** had the **contract** been **performed.** It is essential to establish a connection between the breach and the damages sought.
The injured party may **recover the profits or benefits** which it would have obtained by performance if it can establish them with reasonable certainty.

Generally, there are two main methods of calculating damages:

Diagram 4: Measures of damages

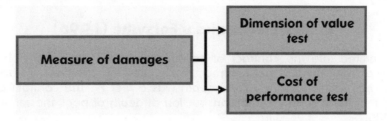

1. Diminution of value test

The **damages** are decided on the basis of **the difference between** what was **contracted for** and what was **received.** Legislation makes it the prima facie rule in contracts of sale of goods.

> **Tips**
>
> **Prima facie:** This is a Latin term meaning 'on the face of it'. It is a fact which, unless disproved, is presumed to be true. In day-to-day speech, the term prima facie is used to describe the apparent nature of something at first glance.

According to this test, where there is an available market for the goods in question,

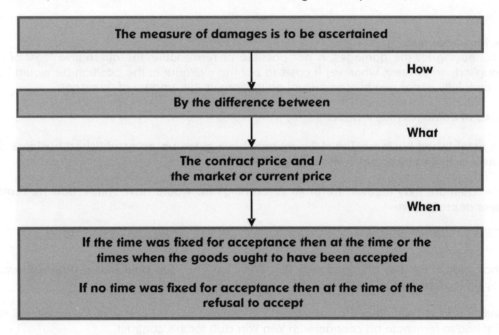

The diminution of value method is applied as a prima facie rule in sale of goods cases because the claimant is required to mitigate his or her damages.

Example

Ronaldo entered into a contract with John to sell apples for £1,000 on July 1. The apples were delivered on July 4. This forced John to buy apples from another source on July 1. The cost of these apples was £1,300.

So, the damages to be awarded are £300 (i.e. the difference between the contract price and the market price on the date of sale, according to the contract.)

---

2. Cost of cure test: The alternative rule of damages requires the defendant to pay the cost of putting things right after defective performance. Here the claimant does not have to accept the difference in value caused by the defective workmanship but can claim the cost of the work necessary to carry out the contract in accordance with its specifications.

However, in Ruxley Electronics v Forsythe (1996), it was held that the cost of cure may not always be appropriate and that it is necessary to consider whether the cost of cure is disproportionate to the benefit obtained.

Case Study

Ruxley Electronics v Forsythe (1996)

The parties have entered into the contract of construction of a swimming pool and surrounding building. At the time of fixing the terms of contract, they agreed that the pool will be 7feet 6" deep but after construction it was found that the actual depth was 6 feet 7". The contract price was £70,000. When it was found that there is an error in construction of depth of pool, the reconstruction cost was calculated at £20,000.

The issue was decided by the trial judge stating that the damages to be paid for breach of contract was to be calculated as the difference between the value of pool actually provided and the value of the pool contracted for. When this difference was calculated, it was coming to 'nil' and so as a loss of enjoying facility, the court awarded Forsythe £2,500.

The defendants appealed in higher court and so the Court of Appeal then awarded the full cost of reconstruction.

This verdict was not final, there was further appeal and so the House of Lords considered that in determining damages of construction contracts, there were two possibilities.
(a) The difference in value, or,
(b) The costs of reinstatement.

3. Cost of performance test:

If mitigation, i.e. paying for the damages, is not possible or reasonable, the alternative "cost of performance test" can be applied. In this test, whatever it costs to put the claimant in the position he would have been in, had the defendant fully performed his contractual obligations, is the amount of damages.

Other measures of damages may include:

a) **Giving up established business**: The claimant may have **given up an established business** or profession **to enter into new activities** by contract with the defendant.

On breach, the claimant may recover the profit or earnings he would have made **had he remained in his former business** or profession.

Example

Jim is a football player. He was engaged with Win Win club. The club paid him a monthly remuneration of £2,100 for playing football for their club.

Jim entered into a contract with Roger for coaching. The contract was for one year for an overall remuneration of £30,000. Jim had to terminate his contract with Win Win club for this contract.

Jim left the football club and started training Roger. However, after two months of training, Roger lost his interest in football and hence terminated the contract with Jim.

In this case, the damages calculated according to the cost of performance test will be Jim's salary from Win Win club at the rate of £2,100 per month, which he had lost.

---

b) **Future profits from existing business**: The success of the business usually depends upon a variety of circumstances, and the outcome is therefore too uncertain to provide a tangible basis for calculation of future profits. However, in some businesses, past experience provides a reasonably certain basis for the calculation of the claimant's probable loss as a result of the breach.

c) **Claimant's expenditures**: If, because of uncertainty, difficulty of proof or another reason, the claimant is unable to establish a claim for lost profits then damages have to be awarded on the basis of expenses.

This is calculated as total of:

➢ the amount of the claimant's expenses; and
➢ the costs and expenses incurred in reliance on a contract.

> **Example**
>
> Jimmy entered into a contract with John to design accounting software for John's business. Relying on this contract, Jimmy purchased a laptop to perform the software designing work.
>
> John breached the contract.
>
> Here, the cost of laptop can be recovered as damages as Jimmy had purchased the laptop in reliance on the contract with John.

4. Cost of Cure

i. Quantum meruit

In some situations, a claim may be made on a quantum meruit basis. The expression quantum meruit means the amount he deserves" or "what the job is worth" and in most instances denotes a claim for a reasonable sum.

Tips
The phrase "quantum meruit" means 'as much as is earned' i.e. in proportion to the extent of work.

A claim on quantum meruit **does not usually arise** if there is an **existing contract** between the parties to pay an **agreed sum**.

Quantum meruit **can be used** in situations where:

a) No contract exists; or
b) A contract exists but for some reason is unenforceable.

But there may be a quantum meruit claim where there is:

i.   An **expressed agreement** to pay a **reasonable** sum i.e. a specific amount was not decided by the contract.

ii. **No price is fixed**. If the contractor does the work under a contract (expressed or implied), and no price is fixed by the contract, he is entitled to be paid a reasonable sum for his labour and the materials supplied.

iii. **Work outside the scope of contract:** Where there is a contract for specified work but the contractor does work outside the contract at the employer's request then the contractor is entitled to be paid a reasonable sum for the work done outside the contract on the basis of an implied contract.

To recover damages under the doctrine of quantum meruit, the claimant must prove the following four basic elements:

➢   that valuable **services were rendered**
➢   that the services were rendered **to the defendant**
➢   that the services were **accepted, used, and enjoyed by the defendant** and
➢   that the defendant was aware that the **claimant**, in performing the services, **expected to be paid** by the defendant

Diagram 5: Cost of performance test

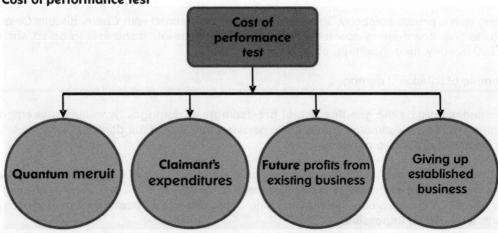

Test Yourself 5

Donald agrees to buy 100 dozen of apples from Ricky's farm for £5,000. However, he suddenly refuses to buy the apples. In the meantime, the market value of the 100 dozen apples has been reduced to £3,500. Donald claims against Ricky for damages. What amount of damages is likely to be awarded?

SYNOPSIS

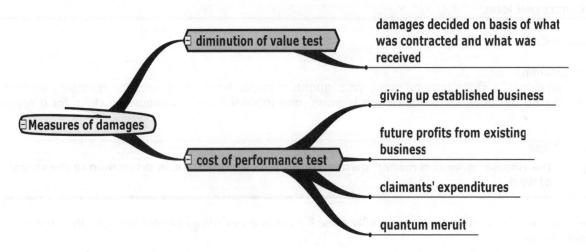

Measures of damages

diminution of value test — damages decided on basis of what was contracted and what was received

cost of performance test
- giving up established business
- future profits from existing business
- claimants' expenditures
- quantum meruit

2.4 Liquidated damages and penalty clauses

Liquidated damages

Meaning

Definition

When the parties to a contract agree to the payment of a certain sum as a fixed and agreed upon compensation for not doing certain things specifically mentioned in the agreement, the sum is called liquidated damages.

Tips

Liquidated damages are fixed in **anticipation of the breach.**

The parties may specify a certain sum as compensation at the time of formation of a contract. This specified compensation is liquidated damages. The purpose of specifying the amount of compensation in advance is to avoid uncertainty and expenses of proving damages in court.

These clauses are referred to as liquidated damages clauses due to the fact that a court is **not required to quantify the losses** sustained by a party.

Example

Mary is working with a private company. She has entered into a contract with Cherry Biscuits Co according to which she has to give one month's notice if she wants to leave her job. If she fails to do so, she has to pay damages of £50 per day, for a maximum of 30 days.

This is an example of liquidated damages.

Liquidated damages must be the **genuine actual pre-estimate** of damages by mutual agreement among the parties to contract. If the pre-estimated sum is **not a genuine** estimate of the damages which are likely to result as a result of breach, the sum is a **penalty.**

The court will acknowledge the liquidated damages only when they **show a genuine pre-estimate figure of damages** and the **intention of the party is not to charge a penalty** to the other party in breach. The **genuine pre-estimate** of breach is acceptable because making a **precise pre-estimation** of damages in the event of breach of contract is **almost impossible.**

Case Study

Dunlop Pneumatic Tyre Co Ltd v Selfridge and Co Ltd (1915)

In this case, the claimants, who were manufacturers of motor tyres, covers and tubes, sold some tyres to Dew and Co under an agreement. The agreement provided that Dew and Co would not sell or offer any Dunlop motor tyres, covers, tubes etc. below the claimant's list price. Dew and Co was not allowed to give a discount to any customer, including a cash discount. It was also decided that, if this condition to contract was breached, then an amount of £5 would be payable as damages for every tyre, cover and tube sold or offered by Dew and Co.

Dew and Co, in turn, sold certain tyres to the defendant and obtained a similar contract regarding:
➤ the maintenance of list price; and
➤ promise to pay the sum of £5 for each tyre sold or offered below the list price.

The defendants sold tyres below the list price and were sued by the claimants for the breach of contract.

Court's decision: It was held that the damages agreed in the contract were liquidated damages and the claimant could recover the damages from the defendant.

Even though the parties may use the word 'penalty' or 'liquidated damages' in respect of a clause, the court must verify that the payment stipulated is indeed a penalty or liquidated damages

If the provisions are considered to be a penalty by the court, it will set aside the so-called liquidated damages and will award damages in the normal way, that is, **unliquidated damages.**

Case Study

Duffen v FRA Bo SpA. (1998)

In this case, the agreement stated that, on the dismissal of the agent, £100,000 would be paid to him as liquidated damages. The agreement specifically stated that a reasonable pre-estimate of the damages which the agent would suffer on termination of agreement was £100,000.

Court's decision: It was held that the so-called liquidated damages were, in fact, a penalty clause and hence could not be enforced. The court concluded that, although the wording of the agreement was influential, the more important fact was that the amount of damages did not alter in proportion to the time remaining to be served in the agreement. The court only allowed normal damages to the agent.

The question of whether a sum stipulated in the contract is a penalty or liquidated damages is a question of construction. It has to be decided upon the terms and inherent circumstances of each particular contract. This is judged at the time of making the contract, not at the time of the breach.

In **deciding whether a liquidated damages clause is a penalty or not**, the court will take into consideration:

a) whether the contract refers to the clause as a liquidated damages clause or a penalty;

b) where the estimate of loss is imprecise, whether the sum is a genuine pre-estimate of the losses that would be sustained or whether it is disproportionate to the actual losses sustained. (A stipulated sum is not disproportionate simply because it is notably greater than the actual losses sustained.)

c) whether the sum stipulated is an excessive amount in comparison with the greatest loss that could conceivably be proved to have followed from the breach.

Test Yourself 6

Adam bought a new bungalow. He hired Moses to buy and install a barbecue stand in his garden. Adam specified that the stand should be 25 metres long, 10 metres wide and 5 metres high. He wanted a special exhaust system to be fitted to clear the smoke immediately. This work was due to be completed by April. Adam meanwhile entered into another contract with Joshua to plant the lawn of his garden, starting on the 1st of May.

Moses finished his work on 29 April and handed it over to Adam. On testing the barbecue stand, Adam discovered that its height was only 3 metres and the exhaust system fitted did not clear the smoke immediately as specified in the contract. In the process, he suffered a severe asthma attack, which made him bedridden for a week and resulted in his losing a very valuable contract. However, Moses did not know that Adam was asthmatic.

Meanwhile Joshua called up Adam and expressed his inability to perform the second contract as he had other engagements. Adam could find only one other person who charged him £500 more than what Joshua had agreed upon for doing the same work.

Required:

i. Can Adam ask Moses to reconstruct the barbeque as specified and, if not, what is the alternative remedy available to him? Can he claim compensation for the loss he suffered due to the exhaust system fitted by Moses, which did not meet the given specifications?

ii. Can he ask Joshua to plant the lawn of his garden and, if not, what alternative remedy is available to him?

---

3. Analyse the equitable remedies for breach of contract

[Learning outcome c]

3.1 Meaning

Remedies are of two types: legal and equitable. An example of a legal remedy is monetary damages. An example of an equitable remedy is an injunction.

A single wrong may give rise to a right to several different remedies.

Example

A breach of contract might entitle the injured party to an amount of money sufficient to compensate for the breach (compensatory damages) or an order from the court commanding the breaching party to perform its contractual obligations (specific performance).

In today's legal system, the distinctions between law and equity have been largely abolished and the court will usually have the power to grant both legal and equitable relief.

3.2 Why equitable remedies?
Sometimes the remedy of damages will be an inadequate compensation to the victim of a breach of contract.

Example

The claimant may have contracted to purchase a particular plot of land from the defendant for which compensation cannot provide a satisfactory equivalent in the event of the defendant's breach. The reason might be that the particular plot had a beautiful landscape ideal for a resort, which was the dream project of the claimant.

Therefore, a number of remedies have been developed which are discretionary in nature. They ensure that a claimant is not unjustly treated by being compensated to the extent of damages only.

3.3 Types of equitable remedies: Equitable remedies mainly include:

1. Specific performance
2. Injunctions
3. Rescission

1. Specific performance

Specific performance of a contract is a remedy that seeks to award performance specifically as agreed. The party who has been harmed by a breached contract may not be interested in monetary damages, but would prefer to have the contract fulfilled. Specific performance seeks to ensure the benefit of the contract by compelling the breaching party to do what it had agreed to do.

a) **Generally, this remedy for breach of contract is available as a substitute for monetary damages when the remedy of monetary damages is inadequate or impracticable.**

The right to claim monetary damages is, of course, generally available for a breach of contract. However, sometimes the right to claim monetary damages will not adequately compensate the non-breaching party to the agreement.

Example

Annia runs a boutique in Paris. Julia places an order for a wedding dress worth £200. When the dress was ready it looked so beautiful that Annia decided to exhibit it in a fashion exhibition. She refused to sell the dress to Julia.

Here, Julia may be able to bring a lawsuit to force Annia to sell the dress to her at the agreed price.

---

b) **Specific performance is not available for a breach of every type of contract.** Some relevant points are:

i. The **existing agreement** must be valid.

Example

If the contract is for sale of packets of tobacco to school students, it violates a public policy consideration. Therefore, the court will not order that the contract be enforced.

---

ii. If monetary damages are an adequate remedy, then the powers of the court will not be exercised to order specific performance, but rather the court may order monetary damages.

Example

George entered into a contract with Peter to sell his shares of stock. However, George refuses to sell his shares.

Here, if the shares of stock are readily available on the market, the court will not order specific performance of a contract for their sale. It will only allow monetary damages for breach of contract.

However, if shares of stock cannot be readily obtained on the market, specific performance of a contract for their sale is allowable.

---

iii. If a party seeks specific performance, the main question to decide is whether monetary damages are an adequate remedy. The party seeking specific performance must show that there are some special circumstances or unique factor regarding this particular contract that:

➢ make **specific performance appropriate**; and

➢ make **monetary damages inadequate.**

Example

Contracts relating to real estate may generally be specifically performed because each plot of real estate is unique. As a result, subject to certain exceptions, one can sue to compel a party to a real estate agreement to do as they have contracted to do.

---

iv. Specific performance of contracts will **never be ordered in the case of employment or other contracts involving performance of personal services.** This is because these contracts require performance over a period of time and the court cannot ensure that the defendant will comply fully with the order. In short, the court cannot supervise the enforcement.

Case Study

Ryan v Mutual Tontine Westminster Chambers Association (1893)

The landlords of a flat appointed a porter. His jobs included constantly attending to services such as cleaning common passages and stairs and delivering letters. However, the porter used to spend much of his time working as a chef at a nearby club. In his absence, his duties were performed by other people or by the cleaner. So the claimant filed a case for enforcement of the contractual undertaking.

The issue was whether the claimants could compel the porter to provide these services?

Court's decision: It was decided that there would not be an order for specific performance from the court available to compel the porter to provide these services. However, the remedy in the form of damages was awarded.

v. In order to receive full and equitable relief it is also possible to receive **other forms of relief, in addition to specific performance** of the contract.

Example

The non-breaching party may be entitled to **monetary damages** for the time period between the breach of the agreement and the court's order for specific performance.

In a real estate matter, the court might also order cancellation of other transactions entered into with knowledge of the contract to be specifically performed, in order to grant a clear title to the property.

Tips

A minor will generally not be awarded specific performance of contract.

2. Injunctions

a)   In simple terms, injunctions are court orders which prevent a party from carrying out a certain act. An injunction is an equitable measure which directs a party not to break its contract.

Example

An injunction might be obtained to prevent a copyright infringer from reprinting copyrighted materials.

b)   Unlike specific performance, an injunction has the effect of enforcing a contract of personal services.

Case Study

An injunction may be made to enforce a contract of personal service

Warner Bros Pictures Inc v Nelson (1937)

In this case, the defendant, an actress, Bette Davis, had entered into a contract according to which she agreed to work for a year for the claimants (a British film producer). The contract terms stipulated that she would work exclusively for the claimant for the period of one year and would not engage in any other occupation without the consent of the claimants.

During the year when she had agreed to work only for the claimants, she came to England to work for someone else.

Hence the claimant applied for an injunction to prevent her from working for someone else.

Court's decision: The court granted the order of injunction to the claimants. In doing so, it rejected Davis's argument that granting the injunction would force her either to work for the claimant or not to work at all which was equivalent to abandoning her livelihood.

c) Injunction can only be granted to enforce negative clauses within the agreement and cannot be used to enforce positive obligations.

Case Study — An injunction is limited to enforcing negative contract terms.

1. Metropolitan Electric Supply Co v Ginder (1901)

In this case, the defendant contracted to take all the electricity required by him, from the claimants. On the defendant's attempt to obtain electricity from other suppliers, the claimants sued him for injunction.

Court's decision: It was held that the terms of contract to take electricity only from one supplier implied a negative restriction. Hence an injunction was granted to the claimants.

2. Whitwood Chemical Co v Hardman (1891)

In this case, Hardman, the defendant had entered into a contract to give his entire time to the claimants, his employers. However, he occasionally worked for others. The claimants applied for an injunction to prevent him from working for anyone else.

Court's decision: No injunction was granted. The defendant had said what he would do, not what he would not do. Therefore, there was no negative promise to enforce.

Mareva Injunctions

This is the name of a type of injunction, which comes from the case of **Mareva Compania Naviera SA v International Bulkcarries SA (1975).**

This is a special form of injunction which stops a party from disposing its assets or removing them from the jurisdiction (out of the country).

A Mareva Injunction will be granted only if the claimant can show that:
➤ The assets of the defendant are within the jurisdiction
➤ There is a real risk that the defendant will remove the assets from the jurisdiction and that any order the claimant might obtain for damages will remain unsatisfied.

Example

There may be a fear that money in a bank account will be withdrawn and dissipated, or that an expensive car which had been purchased as asset will easily be concealed and disposed of for cash.

In such cases, the defendant may be awarded an injunction. The injunction will restrict the defendant from removing it's assets from the jurisdiction/ disposing its assets.

3. Rescission

a) To rescind the contract means to cancel or to reject the contract. When a contract is rescinded, the parties to the contract are returned to their pre-contract conditions.

b) An equitable right to rescind a contract is applicable in certain circumstances only, such as where the contract is voidable.

c) The right to rescind a contract must be exercised within a reasonable time.

d) The contract can be rescinded only when all the parties to the contract are in a position to return to the pre-contract conditions.

Example

Tina was living in the outskirts of the city. She wanted a place in the centre of the city.

Alan entered into a contract with Tina to let out his flat to her for a monthly rent of £175. Tina paid him a deposit of £800.

Before Tina could move into the flat, Alan informed her that he had decided to cancel the contract as he needs the flat for his own use. He also refunded the deposit paid by Tina.

Here, on the rescission of the contract, the parties to the contract reverted back to their pre-contract conditions.

Whereas, if Tina had already terminated her contract with her previous landlord, she would have had no place to live. In that case, she would not be in a position to return to the pre-contract conditions. Therefore, the contract could not be rescinded. If Alan refused to let out his flat, this would be a breach of contract.

Diagram 6: Types of equitable remedies

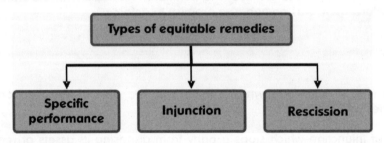

Limitations of action for breach

According to the provisions of the Limitation Act 1980, any action with reference to a contract can be taken within the requisite period only.

Any action on a contract is "barred" if not brought with the stipulated time prescribed by the Act.

This time period is **six years for a simple contract** and **twelve years for contracts by deed** from the date of breach of contract, subject to the following conditions.:

1. The period of six years or twelve years is normally **reduced to three years** if the **claim** includes **damages from personal injuries or death**.

2. The Act also provides that the **three-year period** can be **extended** by the court **if the injury does not become apparent within the period**.

The following are the situations where the six-year / twelve-year period begins later than the date of breach of contract.

1. **Minor:** If the claimant is a minor or there is any contractual disability associated with him such as his being a person of unsound mind or insane at the point of breach of contract, then this period will begin only after he becomes a major or his disability ceases.

2. **Fraud:** If there is any fraud or mistake by the defendant with regard to the right of action, then this six-year period will only begin when the fraud or mistake is discovered by the claimant.

3. The **period of six years** can be extended when information relevant to the claim is deliberately concealed after the six-year period has already begun.

Test Yourself 7

Why is it necessary to have equitable remedies to a breach of contract other than damages?

SYNOPSIS

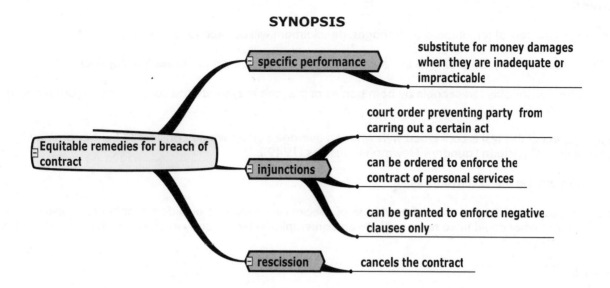

Equitable remedies for breach of contract

specific performance — substitute for money damages when they are inadequate or impracticable

injunctions
- court order preventing party from carring out a certain act
- can be ordered to enforce the contract of personal services
- can be granted to enforce negative clauses only

rescission — cancels the contract

Answers to Test Yourself

Answer 1

Yes, in the given situation, time is of the essence in performance of the contract.

Here, it is **not expressly stated** in the contract that the dress has to be delivered before 15 July (the wedding date). However, it is obvious that a wedding dress has to be delivered before the wedding date. If it is delivered late it is of no use.

Hence, from the subject matter of the contract it is clear that time is of the essence in this contract.

Answer 2

	Minor breach	Material breach
Collect damages	✔	✔
Compel performance	X	✔

Answer 3

Breach of contract, in simple terms, means breaking or violating a law, right, or duty, either by commission or omission. Breach of contract is an unjustified failure to fulfil the duties under the contract terms when the performance is due.

Anticipatory breach is the outcome of the repudiation of the contract by one of the parties to the contract **before the due date of performance.** It is clear that the party will not perform when performance is due, or a situation exists in which it can be implied that performance is not foreseeable. An anticipatory breach gives the non-breaching party the option to treat such a breach as immediate, and, if repudiatory, to terminate the contract and sue for damages (without waiting for the breach to actually take place).

For e.g., Dr. Mark is appointed as a dentist in City Hospital, on an annual remuneration of £75000, on 1 January 20X5. Under the terms of appointment, his appointment is for a minimum period of two years and either party can terminate the contract by giving 3 months' notice. Failure by either party to give the required notice would require that party to pay £5,000 in compensation.

On 31 December 20X5, Dr Mark gave notice to City Hospital that he would join another hospital from 15 January 20X6.

In this case it is clear that Dr. Mark does not intend to work for the notice period of three months. Hence City Hospital can retain £5,000 as compensation from his monthly remuneration.

Answer 4

According to the test of remoteness of damages, the claimant will be able to recover losses only if:

1. They arise naturally, according to the ordinary course of things, from the breach of contract itself; and

2. They are reasonably foreseeable by both parties at the time they made the contract, as a probable result of the breach.

The first aspect of this test is concerned with what an average person would consider to be the "ordinary course of things" (Victoria Laundry v Newman Industries (1949)).

This will depend on the circumstances.

The second aspect of the test covers knowledge of special circumstances outside the ordinary course of things. The question is what could have reasonably been contemplated by the party in breach with knowledge of the special circumstances.

Answer 5

According to the **diminution of value test**, the damages are to be ascertained by the difference between:

a) the contract price; and
b) the market or current price

Therefore, likely damages = (£5,000 - £3,500) = £1,500

Answer 6

In the above case, there is a breach of contract between Adam and Moses – the first is that the height of the barbeque stand did not meet the specifications mentioned by Adam and, secondly, the exhaust system did not function as he expected. There is an anticipatory breach of contract in the case of contract between Adam and Joshua.

i   Remedies for breach of contract:

The party who breaks the contract is liable to provide monetary compensation to the other party to the extent of the damages or loss suffered due to the breach of the contract.

Remoteness of damage

Even if it is proved that the claimant suffered loss because of the breach of contract, he cannot claim all the loss which he might have suffered. In this connection, the general principle is not to compel the defendant to pay damages which are remote.

There is a very famous case, Hadley v Baxendale (1854), in this area. A new rule was created in this case: The court found that an aggrieved buyer of services will be unable to recover consequential losses resulting from breach unless the losses are:

1. a "natural" consequence of breach; or
2. the buyer brings the circumstances which would generate the losses expressly to the seller's attention.

A claimant can claim for losses only when the circumstances which would generate the losses were within the defendant's knowledge.

ii Measures for damages

The basic object of damages is compensation. In the law of contracts, the theory is that the party injured by the breach should receive as closely as possible the equivalent of the benefits of the performance. It is essential to establish a causal connection between the breach and the damages sought.
The injured party may recover for the profits or benefits which it would have obtained by performance if it can establish them with reasonable certainty.
Therefore, on this background, we can apply the statements of law to the problem of Adam as follows:

i. A specific performance order will only be granted by the Court where the common law remedy of damages is inadequate. Also the enforcement of contract will not be granted in case of contracts of employment or personal services. Hence, in the given case, Adams cannot force Moses to carry out the remedial action to rectify the height of the barbeque; he can only claim the damages. The extent of the value of the difference in the heights specified and constructed would be granted.

ii. Moses will be liable for the breach of contract for not fitting the exhaust system as specified by Adam, However, he will not be liable for the damages occurred as a consequence of the breach of the contract as he was unaware of Adam's illness.

iii. Joshua had expressly shown his inability to perform the contract resulting in anticipatory breach. Now it is Adam's decision whether to accept the repudiation or take action against him at the time of performance. Adam cannot force Joshua to work for him but he can claim damages to the extent of the extra rate he will have to bear due to the breach of contract.

Answer 7

The victim of a breach of contract may find that the **remedy of damages compensated is inadequate.** For example, a claimant bought a plot of land on which he wanted to construct the house of his dreams, and employed constructor for this job. However, the defendant breached the contract and did not complete even fifty percent of the work the claimant expected. Here, the claimant will not be satisfied with the compensation he gets from the defendant for the breach of contract.

Therefore, other equitable remedies have been developed, discretionary in nature, which are designed to ensure that a claimant is not unjustly treated by his being confined to the common law for remedy of damages.

Quick Quiz

1. Match the pairs

A	B
1. Rescission	a. Can be granted to enforce negative clauses within the agreement but cannot be granted to enforce positive obligations
2. Injunction	b. Seeks to order the benefit of the contract by compelling the breaching party to do that which it agreed to do.
3. Specific performance	c. The parties to contract are returned to their pre-contract conditions.

2. True or False

a. The parties to the contract are freed from their contractual obligations only when the contract is discharged.

b. A claimant can claim for losses only when the circumstances which would generate the losses are within the defendant's knowledge.

c. A court can always enforce a contract of employment or personal services.

d. In diminution of value test, the damages are decided on the basis of the difference between what was contracted for and what was received.

e. Unlike specific performance, an injunction has the effect of enforcing a contract of personal services.

3. Answer in one line

a) What is meant by performance of a contract?

b) On 1 April 20X5, Annie entered into a contract with Jimmy to sell her house to him for £100,000, on 10 August 20X5. However, on 2 July 20X5, Jimmy expressed his intention to repudiate the contract as he did not have enough money to purchase the house. Identify the type of breach of contract.

Answers to Quick Quiz

1. 1- (c), 2- (a), 3 (b)

2. True: a, b, d, e
   False: c

3. a) When both the parties have performed their legal obligations arising out of the contract, the contract is said to be discharged by performance.
   b) This is an anticipatory breach of contract because one party to the contract expressed his inability to perform the contract, before the due date of its performance.

Self Examination Questions

Question 1

Explain in relation to remedies for breach of contract:
a. Liquidated damages
b. The duty to mitigate losses

Question 2

State and explain the remedies available for breach of contract (**this is a very important question as it is repeatedly asked the exam**).

Question 3

State and explain the types of equitable remedies for a breach of contract.

Question 4

Mr. Alan enters into a contract with MGM garment showroom to supply 500 shirts at £100 each on or before 31 December 20X5. However, on 10 November 20X5, Alan informs the MGM garment showroom that he is not willing to supply the goods as the price of each shirt has gone up to £200. Examine the rights of MGM garment showroom in this regard.

Question 5

Lily, a film actress, agreed to work exclusively for a period of two years, for a film production company. However, during the two-year period, she entered into a contract to work for another film company. Discuss the rights of the aggrieved film production company under the provisions of the Contract Act.

Answers to Self Examination Questions

Answer 1

a) Liquidated damages

In many cases, the parties to the contract provide for possible breach in advance by stating the amount of damages that will be recovered or paid if there is a breach of contract. The **provisions made for such damages are called liquidated damages.** The provisions should be made by estimating the loss which would arise as a consequence of the breach of contract. The court will not acknowledge the provision if it is intended as a penalty on the other party for the breach and will instead grant only damages.

For example, Bob was appointed as a chef in Todd's restaurant. According to the terms of contract, Bob has to give two month's notice if he wants to leave the job. On his failure to give such notice, damages at the rate of £100 per day, for a maximum of 60 days, will be recovered from him.

In this case, the predetermined damages of £100 per day (maximum 60 x £100 = £6,000) are the liquidated damages.

In Dunlop Pneumatic Tyre Co Ltd v Selfridge and Co Ltd (1915), the claimants, who were manufacturers of motor tyres, covers and tubes, sold some tyres to Dew and Co under an agreement. The agreement provided that Dew and Co would not sell or offer any Dunlop motor tyres, covers, tubes etc. below the claimant's price list and not offer any customer a cash discount, or any other discount, on these products.. It was also decided that if the condition to contract was breached then the amount of £5 would be payable as damages for every tyre, cover and tube sold or offered by Dew and Co.

Dew and Co, in turn, sold certain tyres to the defendants and obtained a similar contract regarding the maintenance of the price list and a promise to pay the sum of £5 for each tyre sold or offered below the list price. The defendants sold tyres below the list price, were sued by the claimants for the breach of contract.

It was held that the damages agreed were liquidated damages and the claimant could recover the damages from the defendant.

b)   The duty to mitigate losses
The duty to mitigate losses is the duty placed on the aggrieved party to reduce his loss to a minimum.
For example, Alex approached Bindu to buy goods from her and Bindu agreed. However, Bindu failed to supply the goods to Alex. In this case it is the duty of Alex to buy the goods from a seller at the lowest possible price. The same principle also applies to the seller; he has to sell the goods at a reasonable price and not at an exaggerated price by taking undue advantage of Alex's situation.

Answer 2

1. A contract can be breached in the following ways:

a.   One party does not perform as he or she had promised
b.   One party does something that makes it impossible for the other party to perform the duties under the contract
c.   One party makes it clear that he or she does not intend to perform the contract duties

A breach of contract can be rectified by offering remedies. The remedies for damages can be classified under the following headings:
i.   Damages
ii.   Remoteness of damages
iii.   Measures of damages
iv.   Alternative remedies to damages

i   Damages
Damages are intended to compensate the innocent party for the loss that he has suffered as a result of the breach of contract.
In order to establish an entitlement to substantial damages for breach of contract the injured party must establish that:

➢ actual loss has been caused by the breach;
➢ the type of loss is recognised as giving an entitlement to compensation;
➢ the loss is not too remote; and
➢ These damages can be quantified with the required level of proof.
A breach of contract can be established even if there is no actual loss. In that case, there will only be an entitlement to nominal damages.

ii   Remoteness of damages
Even if it is proved that the claimant suffered loss because of the breach of contract, he cannot claim all the loss which he **might have suffered.** In this connection, the general principle is not to compel the defendant to pay damages which are remote.

There is a very famous case, Hadley v Baxendale (1854), in this area. A new rule was created in this case: The court found that an aggrieved buyer of services will be unable to recover consequential losses resulting from breach **unless the losses are:**

➢ a "natural" consequence of breach; or
➢ the buyer brings the circumstances which would generate the losses expressly to the seller's attention.

A claimant can claim for losses only when the circumstances which would generate the losses are within the **defendant's knowledge.**

iii Measures for damages

The principle of awarding damages is that the party injured by breach should receive as closely as possible the equivalent of the benefits of performance.

It is essential to establish a causal connection between the breach and the damages sought.

The injured party may recover the profits or benefits which he would have obtained by performance if he can establish them with reasonable certainty.

Generally, there are **two main methods** of calculating damages:

a) Diminution of value test: The damages are decided on the basis of difference between what was contracted for and what was received
Provincial legislation makes it the prima facie rule in sale of goods contracts. Where there is an available market for the goods in question, the measure of damages is to be ascertained, in the absence of evidence to the contrary, by the difference between the contract price and the market or current price at the time or times when the goods ought to have been accepted, or if no time was fixed for acceptance, then at the time of the refusal to accept. The diminution of value method is applied as a prima facie rule in the sale of goods cases because the claimant is required to mitigate his or her damages.

b) Cost of performance test:
If mitigation is not possible or reasonable, the alternative cost of performance test can be applied. In this test, whatever it costs to put the claimant in the position he would have been in, had the defendant fully performed his contractual obligations, is the amount of damages.

Measures of damages may include:

➢ Giving up established business.
➢ Future profits from existing business.
➢ Claimant's expenditures.
➢ Mental or physical suffering.
➢ **Quantum meruit**- In some situations, a claim may be made on a quantum meruit basis. The expression quantum meruit means "the amount he deserves" or "what the job is worth" and in most instances denotes a claim for a reasonable sum.

A claim on a quantum meruit does not usually arise if there is an existing contract between the parties to pay an agreed sum. However, there may be a quantum meruit claim where:

➢ there is an express agreement to pay a reasonable sum.
➢ the contractor does work under a contract expressed or implied, and no price is fixed by the contract
➢ there is a contract for specified work but the contractor does work outside the contract at the employer's request

iv) Alternative Remedies
Remedies are of two types: legal and equitable. An example of a legal remedy is monetary damages. An example of an equitable remedy is an injunction. The court of general jurisdiction will usually have the power to grant both legal and equitable relief. Sometimes the remedy of damages will be inadequate compensation to the victim of a breach of contract.

A number of remedies have been developed, discretionary in nature, which are designed towards ensuring that a claimant is not unjustly treated by his being confined to the common law for remedy of damages.

Equitable remedies mainly include:
a. Specific performance
b. Injunctions
c. Rescission

a) Specific performance
Specific performance of a contract is a remedy that seeks to award performance specifically as agreed. The party who has been harmed by a breached contract may not be interested in money damages, but would prefer to have the contract fulfilled. Specific performance seeks to order the benefit of the contract by compelling the breaching party to do that which it agreed to do.

b) Injunctions

Injunctions are court orders which prevent a party from carrying out a particular act. This is an equitable measure which directs a person not to break their contract. Unlike specific performance, an injunction has the effect of enforcing a contract of personal services.

c) Rescission

To rescind the contract means to cancel or to reject the contract. When a contract is rescinded, the parties to the contract are returned to their pre-contract conditions. An equitable right to rescind a contract is applicable in certain circumstances only, such as where contract is voidable. The right to rescind a contract must be exercised within a reasonable time. Contract can be rescinded only when all the parties to contract are in a position to return to the pre-contract conditions.

Answer 3

The types of equitable remedies are:
a) Specific performance
b) Injunctions
c) Rescission

a) Specific performance

Specific performance of a contract is a remedy that seeks to award performance specifically as agreed. The party who has been harmed by a breached contract may not be interested in money damages, but would prefer to have the contract fulfilled. Specific performance seeks to order the benefit of the contract by compelling the breaching party to do that which it agreed to do.

i.   Generally, this remedy for breach of contract is available as a substitute for money damages when the remedy of money damages is inadequate or impracticable. The right to collect money damages is, of course, generally available for a breach of contract. However, sometimes the right to collect money damages will not adequately compensate the non-breaching party to the agreement.

ii.   Specific performance is not available for a breach of every type of contract. Some relevant points are:

First, there must be a valid, existing agreement.

Furthermore, if some of the essential terms of the agreement were left open for the parties' future determination or agreement, the contract is not sufficiently certain or complete to permit specific performances.

If monetary damages are an adequate remedy, then the powers of the court will not be exercised to order specific performance, but rather the court may order money damages.

If a party seeks specific performance, the traditional area of dispute is whether monetary damages are an adequate remedy. As a result, the party seeking specific performance must show that there are some special circumstances or unique factor regarding this particular contract that makes specific performance appropriate, and that makes monetary damages inadequate. For example, Annia runs a boutique in Paris. Julia placed an order for a wedding dress to be delivered to her two days before her wedding. However, Annia could not deliver the dress before the wedding date and instead delivered it two days after the wedding. Here, even if Annia did not charge any price for the dress, the monetary damages in this form could not compensate the loss which Julia suffered due to breach of contract by Annia.

As a general rule, monetary damages are available to provide a remedy for a breach of a contract for the sale of a personal property. However, if the item of property has a peculiar, unique or sentimental value, specific performance may then be available.

Specific contracts will **never be ordered in the case of employment or other contracts involving personal services** because this would require performance over a period of time and the court cannot ensure whether the defendant has complied with the order. In **Ryan v Mutual Tontine Westminster Chambers Association (1893),** the landlords of the flat appointed a porter. His job involved constantly attending to services such as cleaning common passages and stairs and delivering letters. However the porter used to spend much of his time working as a chef at a nearby club. In his absence, his duties were performed by the other people or by the cleaner. So the claimant claimed for specific performance.

It was decided that even if there was a breach of the contract by the landlords, there would not be an order for specific performance from the court. However, remedy in the form of damages was awarded.

It is also possible to receive other forms of remedy in addition to specific performance of the contract in order to receive full and equitable relief,

b) Injunctions

Injunctions are court orders which prevent a party from carrying out a certain act. An injunction is an equitable measure which directs a person not to break their contract. For example, an injunction might be obtained to prevent a copyright infringer from reprinting copyrighted materials.

Unlike specific performance, an injunction has the effect of enforcing a contract of personal services. In **Warner Bros Pictures Inc v Nelson (1937)**, the defendant, the actress, Bette Davis, had entered into a contract whereby she agreed to work for a year for the claimants (a British film producer). The contract terms stipulated that she would work exclusively for the claimant for the period of one year and would not engage in any other occupation without the consent of the claimants. During the year when she had agreed to work only for the claimants, she came to England to work for someone else. Hence the claimant applied for an injunction to prevent her from working for someone else.

The court granted the injunction. In doing so, it rejected Davis's argument that granting the injunction would force her either to work for the claimant or not to work at all, which was equivalent to abandoning her livelihood.

An injunction can only be granted to enforce negative clauses within the agreement and cannot be used to enforce positive obligations.

In **Metropolitan Electric Supply Co v Ginder (1901)**, the defendant contracted to take all the electricity required by him, from the claimants. On the defendant's attempt to obtain electricity from other suppliers, the claimants sued him for an injunction.

It was held that the terms of contract to take electricity only from one supplier implied a negative restriction. Hence an injunction was granted to the claimants.

c) Rescission

To rescind a contract means to cancel or to reject the contract. When a contract is rescinded, the parties to the contract are returned to their pre-contract conditions.

An equitable right to rescind a contract is applicable in certain circumstances only, such as where contract is voidable. The right to rescind a contract must be exercised within a reasonable time.

Contract can be rescinded only when all the parties to contract are in a position to return to the pre-contract conditions.

Answer 4

Where the party refuses to perform a contract before the performance of contract is due, this is called an anticipatory breach. The effect of anticipatory breach is that the aggrieved party may exercise any of the following two options:

➢ **either to affirm the contract:** He may continue with his preparation for performance and recover the agreed price for his services.

➢ **or to treat the contract as repudiated by the other party:** This gives rise to a cause of action for damages and also discharges the aggrieved party from any performance still be due from him.

For e.g., Mr. Alan has communicated to MGM garment showroom his non-willingness to perform the promise to supply 500 shirts, resulting in an anticipatory breach. Mr. Alan cannot claim that, due to an increase in the price of shirts to £200 each, it is impossible to fulfil the contract, because an increase in price results in commercial impossibility only, and it is not impossible or unlawful to perform the contract.

The right of action depends upon the course of action MGM garment showroom chooses on receipt of intimation of anticipatory breach from Mr. Alan.

1. If the company **decides to wait until the due date of contract i.e. 31 December 20X5**, and Alan fails to supply the shirts on or before that date, the company shall be entitled to recover the damages equal to the difference between the price of the shirts on 31 December 2005 and the contract price i.e. £150.

2. If the company decides **to treat the contract as repudiated by the other party**, it shall be entitled to recover damages equal to the difference between prices on 10 November 20X5 i.e. £200 and contract price i.e. £150.

Answer 5

Non-performance of terms and conditions of contract amounts to breach of contract. In the given case, Lily has violated the terms and conditions of her contract with the film production company since she has entered into a contract to work with another film producer.

The film production company can claim the following remedies:

1. The company can rescind the contract

2. The company can recover back any advance paid to Lily

3. The company can claim damages for loss caused due to breach by Lily.

4. The company can also apply to court to obtain an injunction order from the court restraining Miss Lily from committing the breach of contract and continue to work with the company. In **Warner Bros Pictures Inc v Nelson (1937)**, the defendant, the actress Bette Davis, had entered a contract whereby she had agreed to work for a year for the claimants (a British film producer). The contract terms stipulated that she would work exclusively for the claimant for the period of one year and would not engage in any other occupation without the consent of the claimants. During this year, she came to England to work for someone else. Hence the claimant applied for an injunction to prevent her from working for someone else.

The court granted the injunction. In doing so, it rejected Davis's argument that granting the injunction would force her either to work for the claimant or not to work at all which was equivalent to abandoning her livelihood.

THE LAW OF TORTS

Get through intro

The word tort simply means **"wrong."** A tort occurs when someone **deliberately or carelessly** causes harm or loss to another person or their property. There are many situations where people are harmed by someone else's action, but no crime has taken place. For e.g., violation of a duty not to injure the reputation of other person results in tort of defamation, violation of a duty not to interfere with the possession of land by another person results in tort of trespass to land.

The purpose of the law of torts is not to punish offenders but to provide damages to victims as compensation for their losses. For e.g. monetary settlements are used to restore, as far as possible, the lives of accident victims to their condition before the accident.

From road accidents to noisy neighbours, from mishaps causing injury at work to dogs biting the postman, the tort world covers pretty much the full range of human experience. The Law of Torts is a dynamic subject which deals with a vast range of human experience. While studying the subject, students will gain an insight not only into an essential branch of the law but also into how the law affects the majority of social and economic activities. This is not a dry or abstract subject but rather one which vitally influences everyday life in the domestic as well as business spheres. Accordingly, there is a lively interaction between legal principles and social and economic policy. Hence, study of the law of torts is important and interesting.

As this has been added recently, it is likely that there will be questions on this topic in the exam paper.

LEARNING OUTCOMES

a) Explain the meaning of tort
b) Identify examples of torts including 'passing off' and negligence
c) Explain the duty of care and its breach
d) Explain the meaning of causality and remoteness of damage
e) Discuss defences to actions in negligence

Introduction

> ### Case Study
>
> Negligence is a tort for which existence of duty of care is a pre-requisite of liability
>
> ### Donoghue v Stevenson (1932)
>
> On the evening of Sunday 26 August 1928, May McAlister was in the Wellmeadow Café in Paisley with a friend. They were approached by the café owner, Francis Minghella. May's friend ordered and paid for a ginger beer. The owner brought the order and poured part of a bottle of ginger beer into a tumbler containing ice cream. May consumed part of the bottle of ginger beer – as part of an ice-cream float. May drank some of the contents and her friend lifted the bottle to pour the remainder of the ginger beer into the tumbler. On doing so, it was claimed that the remains of a snail in a state of decomposition plopped out of the bottle into the tumbler. May later complained of stomach pain, and her doctor diagnosed her as having gastroenteritis. She also claimed to have suffered emotional distress as a result of the incident.
>
> She sued the manufacturer of the ginger beer – David Stevenson.
>
> The House of Lords held that there could be a remedy in tort. A manufacturer had a duty of care in negligence to the ultimate consumer of his products. **Lord Atkin stated that "you must take reasonable care to avoid acts or omissions which you can reasonably foresee would be likely to injure your neighbour".** However, the case was ultimately settled out of court, and the facts were never established in a court of law.
>
> The importance of the case lies in the legal principle which it established. The House of Lords expressed the opinion that the manufacturer owes a duty of care to those whom he intends to consume his products. Therefore, the House of Lords answered the question "Who in law is my neighbour?" and their decision shaped legal thinking throughout the common-law world. It has given rise to modern principles of product liability and it remains an important part of the law of "tort" (called "delict" in Scotland) which deals with civil wrongs.

This Study Guide discusses various torts.

1. Explain the meaning of tort

[Learning outcome a]

In a person's day-to-day relations, he must be careful that his behaviour does not cause injury to other people or their property. **Tort law sets standards for behaviour and provides remedies if these standards are not met. It imposes on each member of society the duty to take reasonable care to avoid causing harm to others**. It provides legal recourse to those who suffer harm as a result of the breach of this duty. A person who has suffered such harm may have the right to obtain compensation for the injury in a civil action.

The word 'tort' is derived from a Latin term 'tortum' which means 'to twist'. It includes conduct which is not straight or lawful but is twisted or unlawful. **It is equivalent to the English term 'wrong'. This branch of law consists of various 'torts' or wrongful acts whereby the wrongdoer violates some legal right vested in another person.** The law imposes a duty to respect the legal rights vested in members of the society and the person who breaches these rights is said to have committed a wrongful act.

> **Example**
>
> Bob digs a ditch on a public road. Jack, a passer-by, falls into the ditch and gets injured. Bob is liable to compensate Jack under the law of torts.

As a 'crime' is a wrongful act, which results from the breach of duty recognised by criminal law, a 'breach of contract' is the non-performance or default of a duty voluntarily undertaken by a party to a contract. Similarly, **'tort' is a breach of duty recognised under the law of torts and is part of the civil law.**

Tort is a private or civil wrong or injury for which a court of law may provide a remedy through a lawsuit for damages in the form of compensation. When a person violates his / her duty to others created under general (or statutory) law, a tort has been committed.

> **Example**
>
> A person's actions may cause injury to others through negligence, committing of a nuisance, or damaging another's reputation by libel or slander.

Tort is an area of law concerned with injuries to people or property that come about due to a breach of duty imposed by the law rather than by some contractual arrangement between people. **Individual torts include trespass, defamation, nuisance, negligence and passing-off.**

1. Trespass

Trespass means interruption or interference with the possession of the land. Violation of a duty not to interfere with the possession of land by another person results in the tort of trespass.

> **Example**
>
> Jack is the owner of land of one hectare. Ted has interfered with the possession of the land for six months. So this is a case of trespass.

2. Defamation

Defamation is making a statement which harms the status of the claimant. Violation of a duty to not injure the reputation of someone else results in the tort of defamation.

> **Example**
>
> Without giving any specific reasons, the Association of Doctors has removed the right of a doctor to practise medicine. This act by the Association of Doctors may lead to defamation.

3. Nuisance

Nuisance involves unreasonable interference with or disrupts the use and enjoyment of another person's property.

> **Example**
>
> Ginny's neighbour often burns garbage. The smell and smoke drift over to her property making it very unpleasant for her to sit outside.

4. Negligence

Negligence means failure to act reasonably. Business activities that involve negligence, such as not caring for a customer or selling defective goods, involve a tort.

> **Example**
>
> A railway passenger, who got injured due to the negligence of the driver, has a right to sue the railway company.

5. Passing-off

Where an individual or company claims to produce goods or offer services as somebody else or with the express permission of somebody else in such a manner that deceives the consumer into believing that they are purchasing the goods or services of that individual or company that they trust and recognise, this is a tort of passing off.

> **Example**
>
> A small shoe-maker may represent that he or she made goods which were in fact made by the branded show company to pass off his own business as a branch of that company.

The nature of a tort can be understood by distinguishing:
➢ Tort and crime
➢ Tort and breach of contract

Distinction between tort and crime

A tort and a crime are not the same thing. The basic difference between the two is as follows:

a) Torts are private wrongs whereas crimes are public wrongs. The former are the violation of private or civil rights belonging to an individual whereas the latter are breach and violation of public rights and duties which affects the whole community.

However, there are various wrongs which find their place both under criminal law and the law of torts.

Example

When someone deliberately injures another person in the case of assault and battery, criminal charges may be laid against that person. The injured person may also seek monetary compensation in a private civil action under the law of torts. The intent of the criminal action is to punish the wrongdoer while the intent of the civil action is to compensate the injured person.

---

b) Another difference between the two is that, since tort is considered to be a private wrong, the injured person himself has to file a suit as a claimant. The injured party may, at any time, agree to a compromise with the defendant and withdraw the suit filed by him.

In the case of crime, on the other hand, even though the immediate victim is an individual, the criminal wrong is considered to be a public wrong, i.e. a wrong against the public at large. The criminal proceedings against the wrongdoers are, therefore, not brought by the injured person but by the State.

c) While some torts are also crimes punishable with imprisonment, the primary aim of tort law is to provide relief for the damages incurred and deter others from committing the same harms. The injured person may sue for an injunction to prevent the continuation of the tortuous conduct or for monetary damages.
In the case of crime, the wrongdoer is punished.

> **Tips**
>
> A tort is a concept of civil law: a **wrong against an individual**; whereas a crime is a concept of criminal law: a **wrong against "society"**.

Distinction between tort and breach of contract

a) A breach of contract results from the breach of a duty undertaken by the parties themselves. The violation of the agreement, which is made by the parties with their free consent, is known as a breach of contract. A tort, on the other hand, results from the breach of such duties which are not undertaken by the parties themselves but which are imposed by law.

Example

A person has a duty not to defame anyone or to commit nuisance not because he has voluntarily undertaken any of these duties but because the law imposes such duties on him.

---

b) In a contract, the duty is based on the privity of contract and each party owes a duty only to the other contracting party.

Example

If Jimmy and Johnny make a contract, Jimmy's duty is towards Johnny and Johnny's duty is towards Jimmy. Jimmy and Johnny do not owe any duty in respect of this contract to any person other than each other.

> **Tips**
>
> A stranger to a contract cannot sue for breach of contract.

On the other hand, the duties imposed by the law of torts are not towards any specific individual or individuals but towards the world at large. However, even in a tort, only the person who suffers damages by the breach of the duty will be able to sue.

c) Damages are the main remedy both in an action for the breach of contract as well as in an action for tort. However, in a breach of contract the damages may be 'liquidated' whereas in an action for tort, they are **always 'unliquidated'**.

Tips

Damages are liquidated when a sum payable by way of damages is predetermined. When the amount of damages payable is not fixed and the court is at liberty to award such an amount as it thinks just, the damages are known as 'unliquidated' damages.

Test Yourself 1

Is tort a crime?

Essentials of a tort

The four elements which must be present in a tort lawsuit are:

a) **The existence of a legal duty owed by a person to others**: The existence of a legal duty towards the other person is an essential element of a tort. If the legal duty is not present, the tort cannot be claimed.

Example

If somebody fails to help a starving man or save a drowning child, it is only a moral wrong and therefore, no liability can arise for that unless it can be proved that there was a legal duty to help the starving man or save the drowning child.

b) **The breach of the duty by one person**: The person who legally owed a duty to the other person must have breached his duty. Unless there has been a violation of a legal right, there can be no action under the law of torts.

Example

Every person is under a duty not to cause any inconvenience to another person. If the person breaches his duty and commits an act which causes inconvenience to another person then there is a liability for tort.

c) **The breach of the duty being the "proximate cause" of damage suffered by a person**: When a person claims damages in tort, it is to be proved that the other person's breach of duty under the law of torts is the cause of the damage. The harm would not have occurred without the defendant's actions.

d) **Damage actually incurred by a person**: The claimant must have suffered actual damage (medical costs, lost wages, pain and suffering, etc.).

The law of tort **deals with situations in which people suffer harm or injury to themselves or their property because of the actions or negligence of another person.**

A tort is a civil law matter where only the interests of the particular individual are involved. The main purpose of tort law is for the wrongdoer to compensate (pay back) the person who has suffered a loss or injury, not to punish the person who is responsible. Much of the process of tort law involves determining who is at fault and the extent of the damage. The wrongdoer must compensate the injured person. This usually means paying a sum of money.

Tips

The purpose of tort law is to decide if the person sued is at fault, determine the extent of the injury and provide a remedy such as ordering the wrongdoer to pay monetary compensation to the injured person.

Diagram 1: Essentials of tort

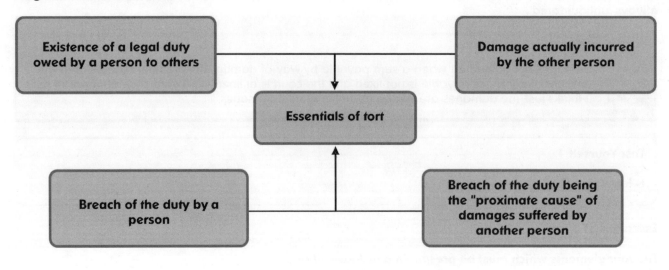

SYNOPSIS

Categories of tort

Torts fall into three general categories:

a) **Intentional torts** are those wrongs which the defendant knew or should have known would occur through their actions or inactions.

Example
Intentionally hitting a person or assaulting a person.

b) **Negligent torts** occur when the defendant's actions were unreasonably unsafe due to negligence.

Example
Causing an accident by failing to obey traffic rules.

Case Study — Negligent tort

Paris v Stepney Borough Council (1951)

The claimant in this case was blind in one eye and the defendant was aware of this fact. There was some risk of eye injury where the claimant was working. However, this risk was not enough for the claimant to ask the employer to provide goggles to all the other workers with two good eyes. A chip of metal got into the claimant's healthy eye resulting in injury.

Court's decision: It was held that it was the employer's duty to provide goggles to all employees. The employers did not provide goggles and they were therefore negligent in performing their duties. There was a risk of eye damage for all the workers but, for the claimant, the injury to his healthy eye led him to total blindness.

c) **Strict liability torts:** Strict liability torts do not depend on the degree of carefulness by the defendant, but are established when a particular action causes damage. In order to collect damages an injured party is required to prove only that he or she was harmed in a specified way, even if the person found strictly liable was not at fault or negligent.

Example

A manufacturer of goods is liable for making and selling defective products. If any consumer suffers any injury because he used those goods, the manufacturer is responsible for damage suffered by the consumer. The injured claimant has to prove that the product caused harm but does not have to prove exactly how the manufacturer was careless.

Case Study — Strict liability

Rylands v Fletcher (1968)

In this case, Rylands employed independent contractors to construct a mill on his land. During the excavation of the construction site, the contractors discovered some disused mine shafts. They failed to investigate where the shafts led, and admitted negligence on this front. The shafts led to Fletcher's land and water from the mill's reservoir, without negligence, flooded into the shafts and into Fletcher's land. Fletcher sued Rylands.

The court had to decide whether inherently dangerous activities could be subject to the doctrine of strict liability. Fletcher argued that Rylands should be liable for the damages caused by the storage of water on his land, an inherently dangerous activity. In other words, Fletcher argued that a strict doctrine of negligence should be applied. Rylands, on the other hand, argued that the flooding was a straightforward accident for which he could not be held responsible.

Court's decision: The court found in favour of Fletcher and ordered Rylands to pay for all the property damage to the mine. The court agreed that Rylands, as owner of the reservoir, was responsible for all damage caused by it, explaining that anyone who keeps "anything likely to do mischief" on his land, must take responsibility for any damage which is "a natural consequence of its escape". According to the court, the only case in which the defendant would be exempt from liability would be it the damage was caused by force majeure or an Act of God.

Rylands appealed to the House of Lords. The Lords gave the same verdict, except that the liability was restricted to there being a non-natural use of the land (i.e. the water in Ryland's reservoir had collected there as a result of man's intervention and not as a result of a natural process).

Note: The case is called Rylands v Fletcher even though the claimant was Fletcher. This is because Rylands appealed against the verdict at the House of Lords (a higher court) and so the original case name was reversed.

For the application of the **Rylands v Fletcher** rule, there must be:

i.   some dangerous thing bought or collected by a person on his land.
ii. escape of the thing collected.
iii. non-natural use of land.

i.   **Dangerous thing:** The thing collected should be capable of causing damage if it escapes. The rule has been applied to water, gas, electricity, poisonous trees, sewages, explosives, noxious fumes and rusty wire.

ii. **Escape:** If the damage is caused within the premises where the defendant had collected the thing, the liability under the rule does not arise. (Read v Lyons and Co Ltd).

iii. **Non-natural use of land:** Collection of water in such a big quantity in Rylands v Fletcher was held to be a non-natural use of land. Keeping water for domestic purposes is a natural use. Fire in a house in a grate is an ordinary, natural, proper, everyday use of the fireplace in the room and if this fire spreads to the adjoining premises, the liability under the rule cannot arise.

Exceptions to the Rylands v Fletcher rule

➢ **Claimant's own default:** The damage caused by the escape due to the claimant's own default was considered to be a good defence in Rylands v Fletcher itself.

➢ **Act of God:** If the escape was unforeseen and because of forces outside human control and the damage due to the escape could not have been avoided by taking reasonable care, the "Act of God" plea can be put forward. For e.g., if the embankments of ornamental lakes give way due to extraordinary rainfall, the owners of these lakes would not be liable under the rule. (Nichols v Marshland).

➢ **Consent of the claimant:** If the claimant had consented to the accumulation of the dangerous thing on the defendant's land, the liability under the rule does not arise. Such consent is implied where the source of danger is for the common benefit of both the claimant and the defendant.

➢ **Act of third party:** If the harm had been caused due to the act of a stranger, who is neither the defendant's servant nor agent and the defendant has no control over him, the defendant will not be liable under the rule.

➢ **Statutory Authority:** An act done under the authority of a statute is also a defence when an action under the rule in Rylands v Fletcher is brought.

Test Yourself 2

How is tort different from breach of contract?

Diagram 2: Categories of torts

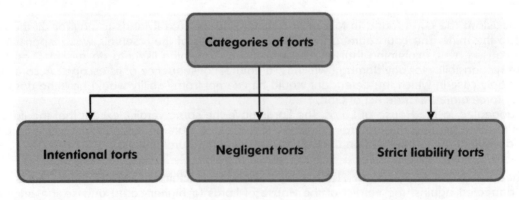

SYNOPSIS

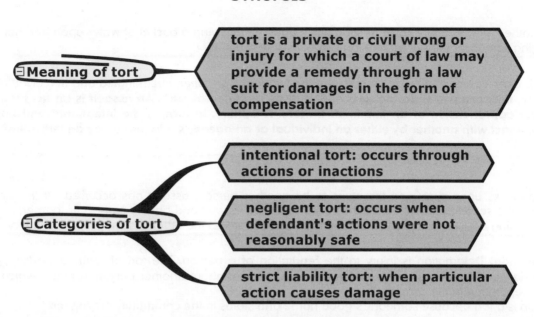

---

2. Identify examples of torts including 'passing off' and negligence
[Learning outcome b]

The law of torts covers different types of torts, each of which comes with a distinct set of procedures and remedies.

Some torts recognised under common law are:

1. Assault & battery
2. Defamation
3. Nuisance
4. Negligence
5. Passing off

1. **Assault & battery**

Assault: Assault refers to an **overt attempt to physically injure a person or create a feeling of fear and apprehension of injury.** No actual physical contact need take place for an assault to occur.

An assault involves:

a) An **intentional,** unlawful threat or "offer" to cause bodily injury to another by force
b) Under circumstances which create in the other person a well-founded fear of imminent danger
c) Where there exists the apparent present ability to carry out the act if not prevented

Note that an assault can be completed even if there is no actual contact with the claimant, and even if the defendant had no actual ability to carry out the apparent threat.

Example

A defendant who points a realistic toy gun at the claimant may be liable for assault, even though the defendant was fifty feet away from the plaintiff and had no actual ability to inflict harm from that distance.

Battery: Battery, on the other hand, is an intentional tort that results from physical contact. In general, two different types of contact may constitute a battery:

a) The first type of contact includes any type of physical harm including a cut, scrape, bruise, burn or fracture, no matter how slight. Physical pain, without any scar or physical "reminder" can also constitute a battery.

b) The second type of contact includes any type of connection or impact which does not result in physical harm, but which is done without consent.

> **Example**
>
> Poking another with an angry finger spitting upon another, throwing a bucket of water upon another, or kissing and hugging someone without permission can constitute a battery.

A battery is often confused with an assault, and the two terms are often intermingled and perceived as one tort. **In actuality, they are two separate torts** and must be regarded as such. **An assault is an act that creates a reasonable apprehension of an imminent battery. A battery, in turn, is the intentional and unpermitted physical contact with another by either an individual or an agency set in motion by an individual.**

> **Example**
>
> If a person picks up a chair and threatens to hit another person, assault has occurred. If the person then actually hits the second person, battery has occurred. Both assault and battery can occur if a person threatens another, causing apprehension and fear, and then actually strikes the other, resulting in actual injury.

2. **Defamation:** Defamation is injury to the reputation of a person. The tort of defamation happens when someone deliberately or negligently makes a false statement about another person in public which lowers or injures his reputation in the community.
Defamation is a tort because someone's good name and status in the community are injured.

There are **two types of defamation:**
a) **Libel** is a representation made in some permanent form e.g. printed, written, filmed or recorded statements

> **Example**
>
> A newspaper prints a false statement about a candidate involved in a local elections that he has not paid his taxes.

Factors for libellous statement:
➢ It must be false
➢ It must hurt the other person
➢ It must be intentional
➢ It must be communicated to other people

b) **Slander** is a representation of a defamatory statement in a temporary form e.g. spoken in words or conveyed by gestures.

> **Example**
>
> If someone calls you a liar in public or accuses you of committing a crime, then you may sue that person for slander. The statement, however, must be false.

The distinction between libel and slander is important for two reasons:
i. Under criminal law, only libel has been recognised as an offence. Slander is no offence.
ii. Under the law of torts, slander is actionable only on proof of special damage. Libel is always actionable without the proof of any damage.

> **Example**
>
> Bill told John that Jimmy is a cheat, and, as a result, John refused to do business with Jimmy. If Jimmy wants compensation from Bill, he has to prove that he lost business with John because of what Bill said.
>
> Bill would have to compensate Jimmy for the loss of John's business, but not for the general damage to his reputation.

However, in the following four cases, a slander lawsuit may succeed without the claimant proving financial loss. Even though there's no permanent record of the slander, the law will presume damages, as if there were libel, if someone:
➢ accuses claimant of a **crime**
➢ accuses the claimant of having a **contagious disease**
➢ makes **negative remarks** about the claimant in his trade or business such as that he is incompetent, dishonest or unfit for the profession

Tips	**Mnemonic: RCC**
	R- Remark (negative) C- Crime C- Contagious disease

3. **Nuisance:** The tort of nuisance happens when someone unreasonably interferes with or disrupts the use and enjoyment of other person's property.

The nuisance must, however, be serious or continuing. The minor problems that often occur between neighbours are usually not nuisances for which legal remedies are provided.

The common remedies for nuisance are monetary compensation and / or a court order to stop the nuisance from happening again (injunction).

Case Study — Nuisance

Davey v Harrow Corporation (1958)

The claimant's land had been penetrated by the roots of trees which were growing on the adjoining corporation property, owned by the defendant. The claimant's house was badly damaged by these roots.

Court's decision: The claimant won the case. Lord Goddard stated that if damage is caused by the encroachment of a tree, regardless of which part of the tree causes the damage and whether it is self-sown or deliberately planted, an action for nuisance will lie.

4. **Negligence:** In the law of torts, negligence may be defined as the failure to act reasonably, i.e. as a reasonable man would act. The law of negligence requires that every person acts reasonably towards other people and their property.

Example

The law of negligence requires that a homeowner takes reasonable care to make sure that persons visiting her or his home are not injured. If a visitor slips on icy steps and is injured, the homeowner may be liable for negligence. Although the visitor may have suffered a tort, the homeowner has not committed an offence. If a court finds the homeowner negligent, then he or she may be ordered to compensate the injured visitor.

The elements of tort of negligence

➤ **Duty:** A person owes a duty of care to another when a reasonable person would foresee that the other will be exposed to the risk of injury if the particular acts or omissions are continued.

Example

The driver of a vehicle owes a duty to anyone within the area of risk when moving, i.e. other road users, pedestrians, and the owners of adjacent land and buildings, to drive carefully.

Similarly, manufacturers are responsible for adequately warning consumers of any dangers in the use of their products. Failure to do so will usually make the manufacturer liable to those injured as a result.

➤ **Breach of duty:** Breach of duty means non-observance of a duty which is required in a particular situation. Once it is established that the defendant owed a duty to the claimant, the second question is whether the duty was breached. The test is both subjective and objective. If the defendant actually realised that the claimant was being put at risk, taking the decision to continue that exposure to the risk of injury breaches the duty. If the defendant did not actually foresee that the claimant might be put at risk, but a reasonable person in the same situation would have foreseen the possibility that another might be injured, there will be a breach.

Case Study

Haley v London Electricity Board

In this case, the claimant, a blind man, was walking carefully with a stick along a pavement in a London suburb, on his way to work. The servants of the defendants, London Electricity Board, dug a trench there in pursuance to statutory powers and in its front they put a long-handled hammer. The head of the hammer was resting across the pavement while the handle was on a raising two feet above the ground. The claimant tripped over the obstacle, fell into the trench and was injured. In an action for damages against the Electricity Board, it was found that there were 285 blind persons registered in that area. The hammer gave adequate warning of trench to persons with a normal sight, but it was insufficient for blind persons.

Court's decision: The House of Lords held that since the city pavement was not a place where a blind man could not be expected, not providing sufficient protection for him was negligence for which the defendants were held liable.

> **Causation:** For the defendant to be held liable, it must be shown that the particular acts or omissions were the cause of the loss or damage sustained. For this purpose, a distinction is made **between loss and damage which is "proximate", and loss or damage which is "remote".**

Study the following example to understand the concept.

While driving, John collides with a second vehicle. Unknown to John, this second vehicle is carrying explosives to be used for rock blasting in a local mine. There is an explosion in the street. Other road users and pedestrians are directly injured, adjacent properties are damaged, and people in the immediate vicinity are injured by flying glass and falling debris. Around the corner, a pedestrian, Bob, is so shocked by the sound of the explosion that he drops his laptop computer which is irreparably damaged. Half a mile away, the wife of the man who supervises the blasting at the local mine hears the explosion, looks at her watch, and faints when she realises that the explosion is half-an-hour too early. She suffers a miscarriage. Later, police officers and ambulance crews attending the street scene are traumatised by the carnage. The general rule is that a claim will only succeed for reasonably foreseeable loss or damage. This limits claims to those reasonably foreseeable at the time of the breach and for loss or damage of the same kind as that actually suffered. All those on the street at the time of the explosion (or their surviving relatives) will be able to claim. However, although the wife of the mine employee would not have been injured "but for" the explosion, she is a remote claimant because she is physically far removed from the area of risk. If the injury to her had been foreseeable, the defendant must take the claimant as found which would include her pregnancy. The police and ambulance crews may be removed from the area of risk in terms of time, but it is always foreseeable that such officers will attend the scene of a serious accident, and their psychological injuries may be considered foreseeable depending on the relevant rules in each jurisdiction. Once it is established that the breach was not too remote a cause of some injury, the precise nature and extent of the actual damage need not be foreseeable.

Hence, the fact that a pedestrian around the corner might suffer economic loss outside the area of physical risk, might not have been foreseen by the defendant. However, this is not necessarily a defence because it is foreseeable that such people may suffer shock when hearing the sound of an accident (which may involve loss of earnings or other financial losses), and the consequence of dropping things carried is not too remote in those circumstances. For these purposes, it does not matter what the claimant actually foresaw. The test is purely objective.

> **Damage:** The claimant must have suffered loss or damage flowing naturally from the breach of the duty of care if damages are to be awarded. This may be physical (e.g. personal injury), economic (e.g. pure financial loss), or both (e.g. financial loss of earnings consequent on a personal injury), or reputation (e.g. in a defamation case).

Example

John's car came from behind and hit George's bike, damaging the bike. Here, it is clear that, John owed a duty under the law of torts that he should not cause any injury to any other person through his driving. He breached his duty by hitting George's bike. The damage caused was due only to the accident i.e. the cause of damage is proximate and not remote. Actual damage was caused. Hence, this is a case of negligence on behalf of John.

3. Passing off

Passing off is a tort that seeks to protect victims where an individual or company claims to produce goods or offer services as somebody else or with the express permission of somebody else in such a manner that deceives the consumer into believing that they are purchasing the goods or services of that individual or company that they trust and recognise.

Passing off is concerned with the protection of the goodwill earned by a business and / or product and / or service. It often occurs when a party uses another's trademarks, brand names or other features without permission, in order to mislead consumers. They are therefore "passing off" or misrepresenting their products as those of another party.

Example

This is more easily explained by way of an **example.**

A consumer is searching the Internet for original **'Softgame'** figures, produced in the early 1970's, for purchase. The consumer does not know who the licensed company was that produced these figures, but nonetheless searches for those figures lawfully endorsed by George Lucas.

The consumer discovers a website that claims to be a seller of **'Softgame'** figures. In fact, these figures are not **'Softgame'** but are imitations of the officially licensed producer of **'Softgame'** goods and therefore the company is misrepresenting to the consumer that the goods are something which they are not (i.e. genuine). The motive of the company in misrepresent its goods in this way is to take advantage of the official company's (i.e. **'Softgame's')** reputation and sell their goods in place of the authentic merchandise that the consumer wants and expects.

This has the following effects:

➢ The consumer is deceived into purchasing goods that he does not want,
➢ The officially licensed company is deprived of revenue which they may have reasonably expected to secure,
➢ The officially licensed company's reputation may be damaged if the bootlegged version is defective or of poor quality.

The 'pirate company' has unlawfully received payment for their goods which otherwise would not have been purchased but for their misrepresentation.

Passing off is a tort, a legal wrong. If one company establishes an identity which attracts people to its products, another company should not, by dressing up its own products to cause confusion, trade on the first company's reputation. It must not pass off its goods or services as those of another.

The principle aim of bringing an action in passing off is to prevent one person benefiting from the goodwill inherent in the business, product or service of another.
The claimant has to give evidence that shows:

➢ **The goodwill exists**
The claimant has to show that he had required a reputation or goodwill connected with the goods or services he supplied in the mind of the buyers and such goods or services were known to the buyers by some distinctive feature.

➢ **Misrepresentation by the defendant**
The claimant has to show that the defendant had, whether or not intentionally, made misrepresentations to the public leading them to believe that the defendants' goods or services were that of the claimants, and

➢ **That misrepresentation damages the goodwill**
The claimant has to show that he had suffered or was likely to suffer damage because of the erroneous belief engendered by the defendant's misrepresentation.

Diagram 3: Types of tort

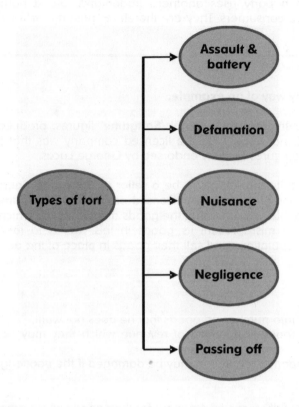

Test Yourself 3

What is the difference between assault and battery?

SYNOPSIS

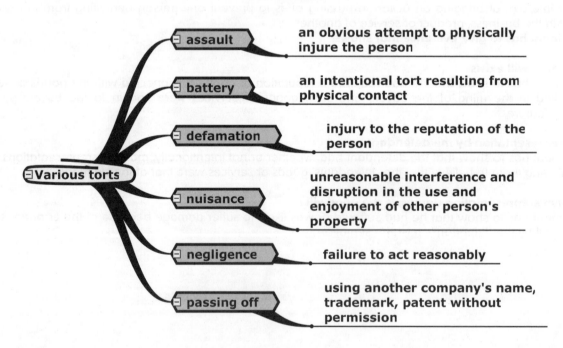

3. Explain the duty of care and its breach

[Learning outcome c]

What is duty of care?

Duty of care is **the obligation to exercise a level of care towards an individual, as is reasonable in all the circumstances, to avoid injury to that individual or his property**. Duty of care is based upon the relationship of the parties, the negligent act or omission and the reasonable foreseeability of loss to that individual. A negligent act is an unintentional but careless act which results in loss. **Only a negligent act will be regarded as having breached a duty of care.**

Example

In Booker v Wenborn (1962), the defendant boarded a train which had just started moving but kept the door of the carriage open. The door opened outside and created a danger to those standing on the platform. The claimant, a porter, who was standing on the edge of the platform was hit by the door and injured. It was held that the defendant was liable because a person boarding a moving train owed a duty of care to a person standing near it on the platform.

Breach of a duty of care

Once it has been shown that a duty of care exists it is then necessary to show that it has been 'breached'.

The duty would have been breached if the **defendant failed to take reasonable care as judged against the conduct of a reasonable person in that person's position.**

The general **rules for establishing a breach of a duty of care** are:

1. The act or omission **was negligent.**
2. The act or omission was **voluntary.**
3. The act or omission must have as its **foreseeable and natural consequence harm to another individual.**

Example

If a specialist doctor does not attend to a patient admitted in the emergency ward of a hospital, this is a breach of a duty of care.

Assessing the breach involves the use of the "reasonable man test" in which the court assesses if a duty of care is owed by one individual to another, whether the harm was reasonably foreseeable under the circumstances of the case in question and the actual harm which occurred.

Remedies for a breach of a duty of care

Remedies for anyone who has suffered loss in the commission of a tort are either a **claim for damages or an action to stop their wrongful conduct by seeking an interdict in the civil courts in Scotland or an injunction in the courts of England, Wales and Northern Ireland.**

Not all harm will result in payment of damages or interdict / injunction. Certain losses can be regarded by the courts as too remote to give rise to a claim. **Generally, damages will only become payable if the harm suffered was a direct result of the wrongful conduct.**

Sometimes there doesn't even have to be physical harm to the person or property as the courts now recognise a pure economic loss in certain restricted circumstances where the individual's only loss is financial and there is no associated harm to the individual's person or property. This is particularly relevant to negligent misstatements in references, although it must be noted that the law has traditionally held the economic interests of an individual to be less worthy of protection than either his physical or property interests.

Test Yourself 4

Discuss the concept of duty of care

(pilot paper)

SYNOPSIS

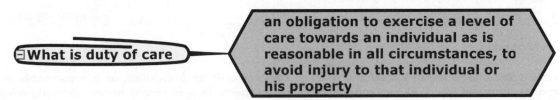

What is duty of care — an obligation to exercise a level of care towards an individual as is reasonable in all circumstances, to avoid injury to that individual or his property

4. Explain the meaning of causality and remoteness of damage

[Learning outcome d]

What is remoteness?

After the commission of a tort, the question of the defendant's liability arises.

Tips

Causality here is the principle that everything that happens must have a cause.

Example

A cyclist negligently hits a pedestrian who was carrying a bomb in his pocket. The pedestrian and four other persons on the road die and twenty other persons are severely injured due to the explosion. A building nearby is set on fire due to the same explosion and some women and children therein are severely injured. The question is can the cyclist be liable for all these consequences?

He is liable only for those consequences which are not too remote from his conduct. No defendant can be made liable infinitely for all the consequences which follow his wrongful act. On practical grounds, a line must be drawn somewhere and certain kinds or types of losses, although a direct result of the defendant's conduct may remain uncompensated.

As Lord Wright has said: "The Law cannot take account of everything that follows a wrongful act, it regards some subsequent matters as outside the scope of its selection, because it was infinite for the law to judge the causes of causes, or consequences of consequences. In the varied web of affairs, the law must abstract some consequences as relevant, not perhaps on ground of pure logic but simply for practical reasons."

Remote and proximate damage

How and where does such a line need to be drawn? To answer this question it has to be decided whether the damage is too remote a consequence of the wrongful act or not. **If it is too remote, the defendant is not liable**. If, on the other hand, the act and the consequences are so connected that they are **not too remote but are proximate, the defendant will be liable for the consequences**. It is not necessary that the immediate consequences of an event are proximate and any further consequences are too remote. The following case study is a good example to understand this concept.

Case Study

The claimant's carelessness need not be a cause of damage but it is essential to show that it contributed to the damage suffered.

Scott v Shepherd

In this case, the defendant threw a lighted firecracker into a crowd, it fell upon a person, say Matt. Matt in order to prevent injury to himself, threw it further and it fell upon John. John, in turn, did the same thing and it then fell on the claimant, as a result of which the claimant lost one of his eyes.

Court's decision: The defendant was held liable to the claimant. His act was the proximate cause of the damage even though his act was furthest from the damage in so far as the acts of Matt and John had occurred in between.

Case Study

Haynes v Harwood

In this case, the defendant's servant negligently left a horse van unattended in a crowded street. When a child threw stones at the horses, the horses ran away and a policeman was injured in an attempt to stop them from injuring a woman and some children who were on the road.

One of the defences pleaded consequences, i.e. the mischief of the child was the proximate cause and the negligence of the defendant's servants was the remote cause.

Court's decision: It was held that the defendant was liable even though the horses had bolted when a child threw stones at them, **because such a mischief on the part of children was anticipated.** "It is not true to say that where the claimant has suffered damage occasioned by a combination of the wrongful act of a defendant and some further conscious act by an intervening person, that of itself prevents the court from coming to a conclusion in the plaintiff's favour if the accident was the natural and probable consequences of the wrongful act."

Case Study

It has to be shown that the defendant's wrongful act was the real cause of the damage.

Haynes v Harwood

In this case, due to the negligence of the defendant, the claimant, a married woman, suffered an injury that resulted in her severe disfigurement. Sometime afterwards, she was separated from her husband. She wanted to claim damages for this separation.

Court's decision: It was found that the real cause of the desertion of the claimant was not her disfigurement but the estranged relations between the claimant and her husband, which existed even before the accident. Therefore, the defendant was held not liable on that ground.

There may be various causes for damage to the plaintiff. In order that the action against the defendant succeeds, it has to be shown that the defendant's wrongful act was the real cause of the damage.
There are two main tests to determine whether the damage is remote or not:

1. The test of reasonable foresight
According to this test, if the consequences of a wrongful act could have been foreseen by a reasonable man, they are not too remote. If, on the other hand, a reasonable man would not have foreseen the consequences, they are too remote. **According to this test, if a person commits a wrong, he will be liable only for those consequences which he could foresee, whatever could not have been foreseen is too remote a consequence of his wrongful act.**

Case Study

The defendant is not liable for all the direct losses; the kind of harm sustained must be reasonably foreseeable.

Hughes v Lord Advocate (1963)

Employees of the post office negligently left an open manhole unattended in the street. It was covered by a canvas tent and surrounded by paraffin warning lamps. Two boys, out of curiosity, entered the tent and the claimant; an eight year old boy, took one of the lamps in with him. The lamp was knocked over inside the hole and caused a violent explosion in which the claimant suffered severe burns.

Court's decision: The defendants were held liable. Even though, in the circumstances, the explosion was unforeseeable, the kind of damage which occurred, i.e. the burns, was foreseeable.

2. The test of directness
The test of reasonable foresight was rejected and the test of directness was considered to be more appropriate by the Court of Appeal **in Re Polemis and Furness, Withy & Co Ltd. According to the test of directness, a person is liable for all the direct consequences of his wrongful act, whether he could have foreseen them or not, because consequences which directly follow a wrongful act are not too remote.**

Case Study — Consequences directly following a wrongful act are not too remote.

Re Polemis and Furness, Withy and Co Ltd (1921)

In this case, the defendants chartered a ship and the cargo included some tins of benzene and / or petrol. Due to leakage of the tins, some of their contents collected in the hold of the ship. Owing to the negligence of the defendant's servants a plank fell into the hold, a spark was caused and consequently the ship was totally destroyed by fire.

Court's decision: The owners of the ship were entitled to recover nearly £200,000 as the loss was a direct consequence of the wrongful act of the defendants although the destruction of the ship by fire could not have been reasonably foreseen by them.

The only question which has to be answered in such a case is whether or not the defendant's act is wrongful, i.e. could he have foreseen some damage? If the answer to this question is in the affirmative i.e. he could have foreseen damage to the claimant, then he is liable not merely for those consequences which he could have foreseen but for all the direct consequences of his wrongful act.

Case Study

Smith v London & South Western Railway Company

The first authority for the view advocating the directness test is the case of **Smith v London & South Western Railway Company,** where it was observed : "Where there is no direct evidence of negligence, the question what a reasonable man might foresee is of importance in considering the question whether there is evidence for the jury of negligence or not....but when it has been once determined that there is evidence of negligence, the person guilty of it is equally liable for its consequences, whether he could have foreseen them or not. What the defendant might reasonably anticipate is only material with reference to the question, whether the defendants were negligent or not, and cannot alter their liability if they were guilty of negligence."

In **Smith v London & South Western Railway Co,** the railway company was held negligent in allowing a heap of trimmings of hedges and grass near a railway line during dry weather. A spark from the railway engine set fire to the material. Due to high wind, the fire was carried to the plaintiff's cottage which was burnt down. The defendants were held liable even though they could not have foreseen the damage to the cottage.

The test of directness as laid down in Re Polemis has been considered to be incorrect and the same was rejected by the Judicial Committee of the Privy Council in 1961 in Overseas Tankship Ltd v Morts Dock and Engg. Co Ltd (Wagon Mound Case) in an appeal from New South Wales and it was held that the test of reasonable foresight was a better test.

Case Study — Test of reasonable foresight was held to be the better test.

Overseas Tankship Ltd v Morts Dock and Engg. Co Ltd. (Wagon Mound Case) (1961)

In this case, the Wagon Mound, an oil-burning vessel, was chartered by the defendants' overseas tankship Ltd and was taking fuel oil at Sydney port. The claimants' (Morts Dock and Engg. Co,) owned a wharf 600 ft away where welding on another ship was taking place. Due to the negligence of the defendant's servants, a large quantity of oil was spilt into the water. The oil spread into the water under the claimants' wharf. After about 60 hours, molten metal from the wharf fell on the floating cotton waste which had also collected there and, as a result, the oil on the surface of the water also caught fire. This fire caused great damage to the wharf and the equipment on the wharf. In an action by Morts Dock for damages for negligence it was found as a fact that the defendants did not know and could not reasonably have been expected to know that the oil was capable of catching fire when spread on water

Court's decision: The Privy Council held that the defendants were not liable in negligence for the damage which they could not foresee even though the damage was the direct result of their negligence.

Although the Wagon Mound, being the decision of the Privy Council, is not itself applicable in England and has only a persuasive value, the same decision appears to have been considered good law by the House of Lords in Hughes v Lord Advocate (1963). The Court of Appeal in Doughty v Turner Manufacturing Co Ltd (1964) has expressly stated that it is the Wagon Mound and not the Re Polemis which is the governing authority.

Case Study   Wagon Mound followed in subsequent cases

Hughes v Lord Advocate (1963)

In this case, the post office employees opened a manhole for the purpose of maintaining underground telephone equipment. The manhole was covered with a tent. One evening, it was left surrounded by paraffin lamps but otherwise unguarded. A child of eight years entered the tent and started playing with one of the lamps. The lamp fell into the manhole and caused a violent explosion. As a result, the boy fell and suffered severe burns. It was foreseeable that a child could get burnt by tampering with the lamp, but the explosion could not be foreseen.

Court's decision: The House of Lords held that since the kind of damage was foreseeable although the extent was not, the defendants were liable. Lord Reld said: "The appellant's injuries were mainly caused by burns and it cannot be said that injuries from burns were unforeseeable. As a warning to traffic, the workmen had set lighted red lamps round the tent which covered the manhole, and if boys did enter the dark tent, it was very likely that they would take one of these lamps with them. If the lamp fell and broke, it was not at all unlikely that the boy would be burnt and the burns might well be serious. No doubt, it was not to be expected that the injuries would be as serious as these which the claimant in fact sustained. But the defendant is liable, although the damage may be a good deal greater in extent than was foreseeable."

The test of reasonable foresight as stated in the Wagon Mound case was also applied in Doughty v Turner Manufacturing Co Ltd.

Case Study   Wagon Mound followed in subsequent cases

Doughty v Turner Manufacturing Co Ltd (1964)

The claimant was employed by the defendants. Some other workmen of the defendants let an asbestos cement cover slip into a cauldron of hot molten liquid. This resulted in an explosion and the liquid thereby erupted, causing injuries to the claimant, who was standing nearby. The cover had been purchased from reputed manufacturers and nobody could foresee that any serious consequences would follow by the cover falling into the cauldron.

Court's decision: It was held that the damage resulting from the explosion could not reasonably have been foreseen, and therefore the defendants were not liable.

Test Yourself 5

Explain the test of reasonable foresight and the test of directness in relation to the remoteness of damages.

SYNOPSIS

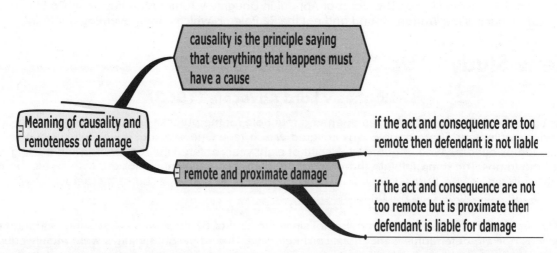

---

5. Discuss defences to actions in negligence

[Learning outcome e]

Notwithstanding that the claimant can prove elements of Duty of care, Breach of duty, Causation, Damage and Remoteness above, the defendant may have a complete or partial defence to the tort. Where the defence is complete, the claimant will be denied any remedy - i.e. damages by the court. Where the defence is partial, the claimant's award of damages will be reduced to the extent of the partial defence.

Complete defence

A common complete defence is where the defendant proves that the claimant consented either expressly or by implication to the risk of damage.

Example

If a regular spectator at an ice hockey match is injured when a player strikes the puck in the ordinary course of play, causing it to fly out of the rink and hit him or her, this is a foreseeable event and regular spectators are assumed to accept that risk of injury when buying a ticket.

Another defence is where defendants can show that by a notice, sign or otherwise, they have validly excluded liability for the damage the claimant is seeking a remedy for.

Example

On most educational books, the authors give the disclaimer that, although they have taken all reasonable efforts to make the book error-free, they do not guarantee the validity of the text. They will not be liable for any losses suffered by any person believing the information given in the book.

Partial defence

A common partial defence is **contributory negligence**. This is where the defendant proves that the claimant acted negligently and that this negligence contributed to the damage the claimant suffered from the defendant's negligent act. In other words, when the claimant, by his own want of care, contributed to the damage caused by the negligence of the defendant, he is considered to be guilty of contributory negligence.

Example

A simple example is where Bob's negligent driving caused Peter damage, but Peter's negligent failure to wear a seatbelt at the time was also a partial cause of the damage. In other words, had Peter worn a seatbelt, his injuries would not have been as severe as they in fact were.

Case Study — Contributory negligence

Owens v Brimmell (1977)

In this case, the claimant and the defendant went on a pub-crawl together and each consumed about eight or nine pints of beer. On the journey home the defendant negligently drove into a lamp post.

Court's decision: Even though the claimant himself was too drunk to know how drunk the driver was, he knew the driver to be drunk. The claimant was held contributorily negligent in getting into the car with the driver whom he knew to be drunk.

Where contributory negligence is proved, the court will reduce the claimant's damages by the extent to which the claimant's negligence contributed to his loss.

Diagram 4: Defences to actions in negligence

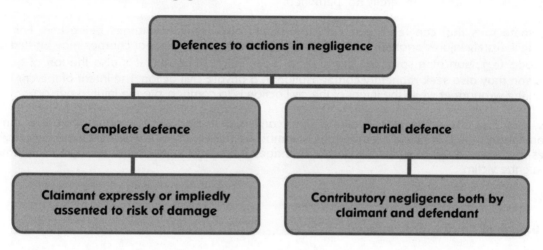

Test Yourself 6

Explain the defences to actions in negligence and state their classification.

SYNOPSIS

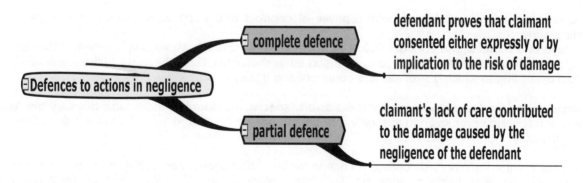

Answers to Test Yourself

Answer 1

A tort and a crime are not the same thing. The difference between a crime and a tort is that a tort allows a person, usually the victim ('claimant'), to obtain a remedy that serves their own purposes (for e.g., the payment of damages if they have been injured in a car accident, or obtaining an injunction to stop a person interfering with their business). Criminal actions on the other hand are pursued not to obtain remedies to assist a person (although often criminal courts do have the power to grant such remedies), but to punish a person for their actions. This punishment may be in the form of a monetary fine or imprisonment.

Since a tort is considered to be a private wrong, the injured person himself has to file a suit as a claimant. At any stage, the injured party may agree to a compromise with the defendant and withdraw the suit filed by him. In the case of a crime, on the other hand, even though the immediate victim is an individual, the criminal wrong is considered to be a public wrong, i.e. a wrong against the public at large. The criminal proceedings against the wrongdoers are, therefore, not brought by the injured person but by the State. Moreover, a settlement in criminal cases is generally not permitted.

However, some torts that can lead to a civil action may also result in charges being laid. For e.g. when someone deliberately injures another person as in the case of assault, criminal charges may be laid under the Criminal Code. (e.g., punching someone in the nose is the crime of assault, it is also the tort of battery). The injured person may also seek monetary compensation in a private civil action. The intent of the criminal action is to punish the wrongdoer while the intent of the civil action is to compensate the injured person.

Generally, torts that are also crimes involve a significantly worse kind of misconduct than torts that are not crimes. Tort liability results in monetary damages that must be paid in order to compensate the victim. Torts that are crimes also carry a risk of a special kind of damages intended to punish the wrongdoer and not just to compensate the victim.

Answer 2

Tort and breach of contract distinguished

a) A breach of contract results from the breach of a duty undertaken by the parties themselves. The agreement, the violation of which is known as a breach of contract is made by the parties with their free consent. For e.g., John undertakes to supply Ron a music system and then fails to perform the obligation. This is a breach of contract as John has voluntarily undertaken the obligation.

A tort, on the other hand, results from the breach of such duties which are not undertaken by the parties themselves but which are imposed by the law. For e.g., every person has a duty not to commit a nuisance not because he has voluntarily undertaken this duty but because the law imposes this duty on every person.

b) In a contract, the duty is based on the privity of contract and each party owes a duty only to other contracting party.
For e.g., Jaya and Maya sign a contract. Jaya's duty owes a duty towards Maya only. Similarly, Maya does not owe any duty in respect of this contract to any person other than Jaya. This is because of the principal of privity of contract according to which a stranger to a contract cannot sue.

Duties imposed by the law of torts are not towards any specific individual or individuals but they are towards the world at large. However, even in tort, only that person will be entitled to sue who suffers damages by the breach of the duty.

c) Damages are the main remedy both in an action for breach of contract as well as in an action for tort. In a breach of contract, the damages may be 'liquidated' whereas in an action for tort, they are always 'unliquidated'.

Damages are liquidated when the sum payable by way of damages is predetermined, for e.g., by the clause in the contract. When the amount payable is not a predetermined sum of money but the court is at liberty to awards the sum at its discretion, the damages are known as 'unliquidated'.

There may be certain cases when the same fact results in a breach of contract as well as a tort. For e.g., if due to the negligence of the driver, a railway passenger is injured, the railway authorities are liable for the breach of contract of safe carriage, there is also a tort of negligence which results in damages to the passenger.

In such cases, both suits (for tort and breach of contract) can be filed parallel to each other

Answer 3

The terms assault and battery are often used interchangeably. An **assault can be defined as the threat of the use of unlawful force to inflict bodily injury on another.**

The threat, which must be believed to be imminent, must cause reasonable apprehension in the claimant. Therefore, where the defendant has been threatened by some use of force, but the apprehensive reaction of the claimant is not reasonable, an assault has not occurred. The focus, for the purpose of determining whether a particular act is an assault, must be on the reasonableness of the claimant's reaction. For e.g., if the defendant points an unloaded gun at the claimant and says "I am going to shoot you," an assault will likely have occurred, as long as the claimant was unaware that the gun was, in fact, not loaded.

In order to have a valid assault claim, the claimant must be able to show that the defendant threatened to use unlawful force to exact bodily harm which was imminent and which the defendant was actually capable of carrying out, which created a reasonable reaction of apprehension in the claimant.

In comparison to assault, **a battery is the intentional and unpermitted contact with another.** For e.g., a defendant who spits on a claimant, even though there is little chance that the spitting will cause any injury other than to the claimant's dignity, has committed a battery.

Battery, for practical purposes, is the end-product of an assault. Battery does not actually require a physical injury, although it may in many cases. For e.g., battery may also occur when the defendant jabs a finger in the air at the claimant or where the defendant grabs onto the claimant's coat.

Battery need not result in actual injury, but only needs to be an unlawful and unpermitted contact with another, or with the property of another. In addition, it is not necessary for the contact to be with an object in the possession of the claimant or the claimant's body. An unpermitted contact with property of the claimant, located within the claimant's proximity, may also constitute battery.

Answer 4

In the law of torts, a duty of care is a legal obligation imposed on an individual requiring that they exercise a reasonable standard of care while performing any acts that could foreseeable harm others. For an action in negligence, there must be an identified duty of care in law.

Duty of care may be considered a formalisation of the implicit responsibilities held by an individual towards another individual within society. Duty of care is based upon the relationship of the parties, the negligent act or omission and the reasonable foreseeability of loss to that individual. A negligent act is an unintentional but careless act which results in loss.

For e.g., **in Booker v Wenborn (1962),** the defendant boarded a train which had just started moving but kept the door of the carriage open. The door opened outside and created a danger to those standing on the platform. The claimant, a porter, who was standing on the edge of the platform was hit by the door and injured. It was held that the defendant was liable because a person boarding a moving train owed a duty of care to a person standing near it on the platform.

Answer 5

Remoteness of damage

The consequences of a wrongful act may be endless. No defendant can be made liable indefinitely for all the consequences which follow his wrongful act. He is liable for all those circumstances only which are not too remote from his act.
There are two main tests to determine whether the damage is remote or not. They are the test of reasonable foresight and the test of directness.

i. Test of reasonable foresight

According to the test of reasonable foresight, if the consequences of the wrongful act can be foreseen by a reasonable man, they are not too remote. If, however, the consequences could not be foreseen by a reasonable man, they are considered to be remote. According to the opinion of Pollock C.B. in Rigby v Hewitt (1850) and Greenland v Chaplin (1850), the liability of the defendant is only for those consequences which could have been reasonable foreseen.

ii. Test of directness

The test of reasonable foresight was rejected and the test of directness was considered to be more appropriate by the Court of Appeal in Re Polemis and Furness, Withy and Co Ltd (1921). According to the test of directness, a person is liable for all the consequences which directly follow his wrongful act whether he could have foreseen them or not because the consequences which directly follow a wrongful act are considered to be not too remote. Therefore, when a railway company negligently allowed a hay stack to remain by the side of a railway line and the hay stack caught fire by a spark from an engine and the fire was carried by high wind to a nearby cottage, the railway company was held liable for the destruction of the cottage as that was considered to be the direct consequences of the defendant's negligence (Smith v London and South Western Rly Co (1870).

In Re Polemis and Furness, Withy and Co Ltd (1921), the defendants chartered a ship and the cargo included some tins of benzene and / or petrol. Due to leakage, some of the contents of the tins collected in the hold of the ship. Owing to the negligence of the defendant's servants a plank fell into the hold, a spark was caused and consequently the ship was totally destroyed by fire. The owners of the ship were entitled to recover nearly £200,000 as the loss was a direct consequence of the wrongful act of the defendants although the consequences could not have been reasonably foreseen by them.

The test of directness as laid down in Re Polemis has been considered to be incorrect and the same was rejected by the Judicial Committee of the Privy Council in 1961 in Overseas Tankship Ltd v Morts Dock and Engg. Co Ltd (Wagon Mound Case) in an appeal from New South Wales and it was held that the test of reasonable foresight was the better test.

In that case a large quantity of fuel oil was discharged from the defendant's ship into Sydney Harbour owing to their carelessness. The oil spread into the water under the claimants' wharf at 600 ft away where welding on another ship was being carried out. After about 60 hours, molten metal from the wharf fell on the floating cotton waste which had also collected there and, as a result, the oil on the surface of the water also caught fire. This fire caused great damage to the wharf and the equipment on the wharf. In an action by Morts Dock for damages for negligence it was found as a fact that the defendants did not know and could not reasonably have been expected to know that the oil was capable of catching fire when spread on water. The Privy Council, therefore, held that the defendants were not liable in negligence for the damage which they could not foresee even though the damage was the direct result of their negligence

Answer 6

In the law of torts, a defendant may have complete or partial defence to tort. A claimant will not be awarded damages by the court or any other remedies if the defence is a complete defence. **Complete defence** means the claimant on his own either expressly or by implication assented to the risk of damage i.e. he himself contributed to the risk of damage.

If there is partial defence a claimant will be awarded damages by the court which will be reduced to the extent to which the claimant's negligence contributed to his loss. **Partial defence** is the contributory negligence which means both the claimant as well as the defendant has acted in a wrongful way. In these circumstances, the defendant will prove that the claimant acted negligently and thereby contributed to the damages which he suffered from the defendant's negligent act. The claimant is considered to be guilty of contributory negligence.

Quick Quiz

State true or false
a) A tort is a crime.
b) Assault and battery are the same tort.
c) Defamation is injury to the reputation of a person.
d) The claimant must have suffered loss or damage as a natural consequence of the breach of the duty of care if damages are to be awarded for tort.

Answers to Quick Quiz

a) False: A tort is a civil wrong. The difference between a crime and a tort is that a tort allows a person, usually the victim ('claimant'), to obtain a remedy that serves their own purposes (for e.g., the payment of damages to a person injured in a car accident, or a person obtaining an injunction to stop someone else from interfering with their business). Criminal actions on the other hand are pursued not to obtain remedies to assist a person (although often criminal courts do have the power to grant such remedies), but to punish a person for their actions

b) **False:** They are two separate torts. An assault is an act that creates a reasonable apprehension of an imminent battery. A battery, on the other hand, is the intentional and unpermitted physical contact with another by either an individual or an agency set in motion by an individual.

c) **True**

d) **True**

Self Examination Question

Question 1

Explain what tort is and what the different categories of tort are?

Answer to Self Examination Question

Answer 1

A 'tort' is a breach of duty recognised under the law of torts. With the help of the law of torts, a person who has suffered from harm may have the right to obtain compensation for the injury in a civil action.

The following are the different categories of tort:
a)   Intentional tort
b)   Negligent tort
c)   Strict liability tort

a)   **Intentional tort:** This is a tort which arises from the actions or inactions of the defendant and which the defendant could reasonably have foreseen as the outcome of his actions / inactions.

b)   **Negligent tort:** Due to the negligence on the defendant's behalf, an unsafe situation arose.

c)   **Strict liability tort:** Strict liability torts do not depend on the degree of carefulness by the defendant, but are established when a particular action causes damage.

PROFESSIONAL NEGLIGENCE

Get through intro

Mark is a businessman. He has appointed James, a professional accountant, to take care of all his financial affairs and to comply with the legal requirements. However, James failed to register Mark's business for VAT, even though this is mandatory as Mark's turnover has exceeded the limit set out by the tax department. Because of this, Mark has to pay heavy penalties. Therefore, James has behaved negligently as he was under a duty to comply with all the legal requirements of his client's business.

Every person who enters into a learned profession undertakes to carry out that profession with reasonable care and skill. A member of the accounting profession is expected to possess the required skill and competence to carry out their work. The degree of reliance on their work is very high. Either absence of the requisite skill or failure to exercise reasonable skill can give rise to an action for damages for professional negligence.

A professional is expected to exercise a reasonable degree of skill and care in his / her work. Where a professional fails to do so and the client suffers a loss as a result, then the client may well be entitled to claim for that loss.

This Study Guide examines professional negligence and the consequences of the same.

LEARNING OUTCOMES

a) Explain and analyse the duty of care of accountants and auditors

Introduction

A point, on which there was a doubt 15 years ago, was whether the statutory auditor of a company had a duty of care to the public at large or even the potential investors in a company.

Case Study

Caparo Industries Plc v Dickman (1990)

The Court of Appeal held that there was **no relationship** between an auditor and a potential investor sufficiently proximate to give rise to a duty of care under common law. However, there was such a relationship with individual shareholders that an individual shareholder, who suffered loss by acting in reliance on negligently prepared accounts whether by selling or retaining or purchasing shares, was entitled to recover compensation in tort.

The auditors filed an appeal to the House of Lords while Caparo Industries Plc filed a cross appeal with reference to their claim that the auditor owed them a duty of care as potential investors. The House of Lords unanimously allowed the appeal and dismissed the cross appeal.

The three criteria which had to be met for there to be a duty of care identified by Lord Bridge of Harwich in Caparo Industries Plc v Dickman (1990) are:

1. There has to be reasonable foreseeability of damage.

2. A relationship between the party owing the duty and the party to whom it was owed should be of sufficient proximity.

3. The imposition of a duty of care has to be just and reasonable in all circumstances.

---

1. Explain and analyse the duty of care of accountants and auditors

[Learning outcome a]

Case Study Duty of care

Stephenson Blake v Streets Heaver (1992)

Stephenson Blake, a family firm whose managers had little familiarity with computers, was looking to upgrade its accounting systems. An IT consultancy, Streets Heaver, made assumptions about Stephenson Blake's business, which turned out to be wrong and the resulting system turned out to be unfit for purpose, even though it met the requirements set out in the original specification.

Streets Heaver argued that Stephenson Blake should have anticipated the problems, or, if it didn't understand them, should have queried them before the contract was signed. It argued that Stephenson Blake, and not them, had responsibility for getting the system into working order.

Court's decision: The judge, however, disagreed. He felt that Streets Heaver was an **expert in the field, and had a duty to "think ahead" and "think for" its client.**

As with other professions, auditors and accountants **owe a duty of care to their clients.** This duty arises from the law of negligence, contract, fiduciaries, or, in the case of auditors of corporate clients, from business corporations' legislation. However, auditors and accountants have **often also been held liable to third parties** who have relied on their professional advice to a client.

The duty of care has been defined as doing the things that a prudent man would do in the circumstances and refraining from those things he would not do. In the case of an auditor engaged to audit a company's accounts, this presumably means that the audit will be conducted in accordance with the accepted accounting standards and standards of audit practice.

> **Example**
>
> ISA 620 Using the work of an expert requires that the an auditor is entitled to rely on the work performed by others, provided he exercises adequate skill and care and is not aware of any reason to believe that he should not have so relied.
>
> Hence, when an auditor plans to use an expert's work, he should satisfy himself as to the expert's skill and competence by considering the expert's professional qualifications, licence or membership in an appropriate body and his experience and reputation in the field. If he fails to do so, he has not exercised adequate care.

When a professional accountant offers his services to the public, he presents himself to the public as an accountant qualified to undertake such assignments. Therefore, when he is appointed to carry out certain professional assignments, it is presumed that he shall carry out the work with the care and diligence expected of a member of profession.

> **Example**
>
> While evaluating the inventory, an accountant is expected to physically verify the inventory. If he certifies the inventory without verifying it, he has not performed his work with reasonable care.

The financial statements on which the auditor reports are designed to serve the needs of a variety of users who have direct economic interest in the concerned business enterprises such as the owners, creditors, suppliers, potential investors, bankers, management, taxation authorities, employees and customers. There are also others who have indirect interest such as financial analysts and advisers, stock exchanges, lawyers, regulatory bodies, financial press, trade associations and labour unions. When auditors or accountants provide an opinion on a client company's financial statements, they usually expect that the client will share the opinion with others who may rely on it.

However, all these parties are not in privity with the auditors. So should they be allowed to recover the losses they incurred as a result of the auditors breach of duty of care, from the auditors? If yes then the accountants (and auditors in particular) could **face liability in any amount to a virtually unlimited number of third parties.**

The courts generally considered this to be an **extreme and undesirable result.** To hold the negligent accountant / auditor liable "in an indefinite amount for an indefinite period to indefinite parties" will be stretching the limits too far.

And so, over the past few decades, the law has evolved to limit the scope of the duty of care owed by auditors for financial statements. **The liability for professional negligence may arise if the following three elements are present:**

➢ **Existence of duty** or responsibility owed by one party to another to perform some act with a certain degree of care and competence.

➢ Occurrence of **breach of such duty**

➢ **Loss being suffered** by the party to whom the duty was owed as a result of negligence.

Definition

> Definition
>
> **The professional negligence,** in relation to accountants and auditors, would constitute **failure to perform duties according to "accepted professional standards" resulting in some loss or damage to a party to whom the duty is owed.**

To who is the duty owed?

While studying the Law of contract, we have discussed the doctrine of privity of contract whereby only parties to a contract can enforce the rights under the contract. Any person other than the parties to the contract is a "stranger to the contract". A contract neither confers any rights nor imposes any duties / obligations on such person, apart from when the Contract (Rights of Third Parties) Act 1999 applies

> **Example**
>
> In **Winberbottom v Wright (1842), it was held that an injured passenger, who was not a party to a contract to maintain a stage coach, could not sue on the contract.** The learned judge observed that "there is no privity of contract between these parties and if the claimant can sue, every passenger, or even any person passing along the road who was injured by the upsetting of the coach, might bring a similar action ." Therefore the liability was limited to the parties to whom the duty actually is owed.

Accountant's duty of care: This can be summarised as follows:

1. An accountant must possess the skills that an ordinarily prudent accountant would have and exercise the degree of care that an ordinarily prudent accountant would exercise.

2. By his contract with his client, an auditor owes a duty to perform the audit, report or investigation for which he was engaged exercising reasonable care.

3. The duty of care would require that:

a) The audit is properly pre-planned given the inherent risks of the client company.
b) The audit is carried out by qualified personnel who in turn are supervised by experienced audit leaders.
c) The audit is reviewed by an audit partner.
d) Any anomalous situations should be the subject of further investigation to eliminate the possibility of mistake or fraud. It is now well-established that the audit team may not blindly rely on statements made by management.

4. The skill and care of an ordinarily prudent accountant are reflected in the:

a) Generally Accepted Accounting Principles ("GAAP") promulgated by the Financial Accounting Standards Board (FASB).

b) Generally Accepted Auditing Standards ("GAAS"), promulgated by the American Institute of Certified Public Accountants (AICPA).

5. An accountant conforming to GAAP or GAAS, and acting in good faith, will normally not be held liable for incorrect judgments or for relying on incorrect information.

6. On the other hand, a violation of GAAP or GAAS will be prima facie evidence of the accountant's negligence, subject to the accountant clearly qualifying his / her opinion or disclaiming liability for particular errors.

Duty of care to third parties

Now the question arises of whether the auditors owe the duty of care to lenders and other creditors. The question of accountant's liability to third parties directly came up for consideration in the case of Candler v Crane Christmas & Co.

Case Study
Accountant's duty of care to third party

Candler v Crane Christmas & Co

In this case, a firm of accountants had been engaged by a company to prepare the company's accounts. The accountants knew that the statements would be shown to third parties. Relying on the statements of account reported upon by the accountants, the claimant had invested money in the company and it was lost. The statements in question had been prepared negligently but there was no fraud.

Court's decision: Cohen and Asquith L J (Denning, LJ. Dissenting), held that a false statement made **carelessly, as contrasted with one fraudulently** made by one person to another, although acted on by that other to his detriment was not actionable in the absence of any contractual or fiduciary relationship between the parties.

Lord Denning, however, dissented, and said:

".............................. The Accountant, who certifies the accounts of his client is always called upon to express his personal **opinion whether the accounts exhibit a true and correct "view of his client's affairs; and he is required to do this not so much for the satisfaction of his own client but more for the guidance of shareholders, investors, revenue authorities, and others who may have to rely on the accounts in serious matters of business.** If we should decide this case in favour of the Accountants there will be no reason why Accountants should ever verify the word of the man in a one man company, because there will be no one to complain about it. The one man who gives them wrong information will not complain if they do not verify it. He wanted their backing for misleading information he gives them and he can only get it if they accept his word without verification. It is just what he wants so as to gain his own ends. And the persons who are misled cannot complain because the accountants owe no duty to them. If such be the law, I think it is to be regretted, for it means that the accountant's certificate which should be a safeguard becomes a share for those who rely on it. I do not myself think it is the law. **In my opinion Accountants owe a duty of care only to their own clients; but also to those who they know will rely on their accounts in the transactions for which these accounts are prepared."**

After these two different opinions in **Candler v Crane Christmas & Co,** in Hedley Byrne & Co Ltd (1963), the subject of liability to third parties for negligence of a professional person was comprehensively studied and proved to be the turning point of the entire issue. **In this case, the House of Lords unanimously overruled the majority decision in Candler v Crane Christmas & Co and upheld Lord Denning's dissenting opinion in that case.**

The auditors are usually not found liable to creditors of whom they were not aware at the time of the audit. However, there have been many cases where the courts held auditors liable to their clients' creditors (often a client's bank) **where the auditors knew that that creditor might rely on the audited financial statements**. The test to decide arises whether the auditors owe the duty of care to lenders and other creditors is whether **a creditor known to the auditor can also show that the financial statements were prepared for the purpose for which the creditor relied on them.** In the case of a routine annual audit, this will ordinarily not be possible.

In unusual cases, an auditor's actions can create a duty of care to a third party who could not meet this test at the time of the audit.

Example

The auditor met with a client's prospective investor and confirmed that the financial statements which were prepared for the company some time earlier were accurate. In such a case, the direct relationship formed with the investor at the meeting created a duty of care.

Conclusion on accountant's liability to third parties

➢ An accountant only owes a duty of care to those persons for whose primary benefit the accountant's statements were intended, namely:
✓ Persons in privity with the accountant
✓ Third parties whose relationship with the accountant was "so close as to approach that of privity".

➢ Accountants are also liable to third parties
✓ For whose benefit and guidance the accountant intends to supply the information or knows that the recipient intends to supply it

✓ Whom the accountant intends the information to influence or whom the accountant knows that the recipient intends the information to influence

Case Study — Damages awarded for negligent misstatement

Cann v Wilson (1888)

In this case, the defendants, who were the valuers of the property, over-valued a certain property. At that time, they knew that the property was being valued for the purpose of a mortgage. On the basis of the valuation, the claimant granted a loan to the owner of the property. When the owner of the property defaulted in repayment, the claimant found that the true value of the property was not sufficient to satisfy the mortgage debt. He wanted to satisfy the loss from the defendants.

Court's decision: The defendants were held liable because in these circumstances, they owed a duty towards the claimant to use reasonable care in the presentation of the document.

Confidentiality and privilege

An accountant's working papers

The notes, calculations, memoranda, copies and other papers that make up the accountant's work product remain the property of the accountant, subject to the following provisos:

➢ The client has the right to have access to those working papers which relate to the client
➢ The accountant must obtain the client's permission before transferring the working papers to another accountant or otherwise making them available for review by someone other than the client.

Accountant - Client privilege

Communications between an accountant and his client are confidential and treated as privileged. They may not be disclosed without the client's permission.

Conclusions

1. An auditor's duty of care to third parties is only triggered when the auditor intends that its statement will be relied upon by an identifiable person for a particular purpose regarding a specified transaction.

2. Similarly, the auditor can only be held liable for losses flowing from the inaccuracy of their audit statement, not all losses suffered by a claimant.

Test Yourself 1

Tony made an investment in the shares of a company on the basis of an auditor's report about the financial soundness of the company and lost on his investment. Tony sued the auditor of the company for making a false report. Tony claimed that auditors could easily have anticipated that someone (including existing shareholders) might rely on their client's audited financial statements in making an investment in the client and could be harmed if the statements were wrong. In your opinion, does the auditor owe any duty of care to Tony?

SYNOPSIS

⊟ Professional negligence — failure to perform duties according to 'accepted professional standards' which results in loss to party to whom duty is owed

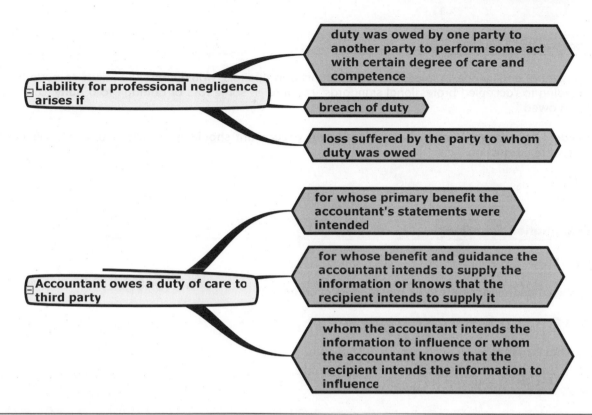

Answer to Test Yourself

Answer 1

The situation is to be dealt with in the light of the following two questions as:
> Who is owed a duty of care?
> What use is made of an auditor's or accountant's opinion?

With respect to the **"who?" question,** it is an established fact that the auditors did not owe a duty to anyone and everyone who might be harmed by reliance on a negligent misstatement in the financial statements. An auditor will only owe a duty of care to someone who the professional actually knows might rely on the advice given.

Tony fell into this category.

Dealing with the **second question, "for what use?"** the established rule is that an auditor will only be liable to someone who used the advice for the specific purpose or transaction for which the advice was given.

In the case of an audit opinion, ordinarily, the purpose is to assist shareholders in overseeing the management and affairs of the company, not to assist in making personal investment decisions. **Therefore, the auditors cannot be held liable to shareholders for their individual investment losses.** Auditors can be liable to their clients' shareholders if the shareholders as a group suffer a loss because inaccurate financial statements prevented them from holding the management of the company to account for some problem.

On the basis of the above discussions, it can be concluded that the auditor is not liable for action for breach of duty of care to Tony.

Quick Quiz

1. Define professional negligence.

2. State true or false:

a) Communication between accountant and client is treated as privileged.

b) The auditor can only be held liable for losses flowing from the inaccuracy of their audit statement, not all losses suffered by a claimant.

Answers to Quick Quiz

1. Professional negligence, in relation to accountants and auditors, would constitute failure to perform duties according to "accepted professional standards" resulting in some loss or damage to a party to whom the duty is owed.

2. a) **True:** This communication is confidential. An accountant should not disclose anything without their client's permission.

   b) **True.**

Self Examination Questions

Question 1

What is the criterion that needs to be met for duty of care?

Question 2

Explain what is meant by an accountant's duty of care.

Answers to Self Examination Questions

Answer 1

The following is the criterion to be met for the duty of care:

1. The damages have to be reasonably foreseeable.
2. A sufficient proximity should exist between the party owing the duty and the party to whom it was owed.
3. In all circumstances, imposition of the duty of care should be **just** and **reasonable.**

Answer 2

Accountant's duty of care

1. An accountant must possess the skills that an ordinarily prudent accountant would have and exercise the degree of care that an ordinarily prudent accountant would exercise.

2. By his contract with his client, an auditor owes a duty to perform the audit, report or investigation for which he was engaged exercising reasonable care.

3. The duty of care would require that:

   a) The audit be properly pre-planned given the inherent risks of the client company
   b) The audit is carried out by qualified personnel who in turn are supervised by experienced audit leaders.
   c) The audit be reviewed by an audit partner
   d) Any anomalous situations are the subject of further investigation to eliminate the possibility of mistake or fraud. It is now well-established that the audit team may not blindly rely on statements made by management.

4. The skill and care of an ordinarily prudent accountant are reflected in the:

   a) Generally Accepted Accounting Principles ("GAAP") promulgated by the Financial Accounting Standards Board (FASB).
   b) Generally Accepted Auditing Standards ("GAAS"), promulgated by the American Institute of Certified Public Accountants (AICPA).

5. An accountant conforming to GAAP or GAAS, and acting in good faith, will normally not be held liable for incorrect judgments or for relying on incorrect information.

6. On the other hand, a violation of GAAP or GAAS will be prima facie evidence of the accountant's negligence, subject to the accountant clearly qualifying his / her opinion or disclaiming liability for particular errors.

SECTION C - EMPLOYMENT LAW

CONTRACT OF EMPLOYMENT

Get through intro

The contract of employment governs and regulates the relationship between the employer and the employee.

People who work for another person / company / firm and get a salary from them are employees. People who have their own business are self-employed.

This Study Guide deals with the test to differentiate between employees and the self-employed and the nature of the contract of employment.

The contract of employment deals with, and is important for, people employed in any profession or trade and is very common in a working person's life.

You need to study this Study Guide carefully as it is important from an examination point of view as well as in your professional life.

LEARNING OUTCOMES

a) Distinguish between employees and the self-employed
b) Explain the nature of the contract of employment and give examples of the main duties placed on the parties to such a contract

Introduction

As soon as you take up a job, you should ask for a contract of employment which sets out the relationship between you and your employer. The contract should be based on issues and tasks you feel should be legally binding between you and your employer, and can both agree upon. A contract gives both you and your employer certain rights and obligations. The most common example is that you have a right to be paid for the work you do. Your employer has a right to give reasonable instructions to you regarding your work. These rights and obligations are called contractual terms.

It is always best to draw up a contract of employment rather than to do this verbally; as this will prevent any disputes arising from what was said or not said when the employment was taken on. Also, written contracts should be worded clearly to avoid ambiguity or misinterpretation. The document should be signed and dated by both parties.

1. Distinguish between employees and self-employed

[Learning outcome a]

Who is an 'employer': An employer is any person or organisation for whom an individual performs or has performed any service, of whatever nature, as an employee. The term "employer" includes not only individuals and organisations in a trade or business, but organisations such as religious and charitable organisations, educational institutions, clubs, social organisations, and societies.

Who is an 'employee': An employee generally includes any individual who performs services if the relationship between the individual and the person for whom the services are performed is the legal relationship of employer and employee.

> **Definition**
>
> Employee means an individual who has entered into or works under a contract of employment:
> s.230 ERA.

Employment contract: An employment contract is an agreement stating the terms and conditions of employment, which are agreed by both the employer and employee. In principle, a contract is created as soon as the person agrees to work for the employer provided the conditions of employment (pay, hours, etc.) have been duly outlined.

Usually it is very clear whether a particular person is employed or self-employed. However, sometimes there are borderline cases. For example, in the case of an employee with a number of part-time jobs, it is difficult to decide whether he is employed or self-employed.

The difference between being an employee or self-employed will affect that person's employment rights.

Directions have evolved from court cases over the years as to whether an individual is an employee or self-employed. That direction has often been grouped in the form of several "tests". These tests are explained below.

1. Control test

In an employer / employee relationship, the employer has the right to control the employee's manner of doing his / her work. The employer determines what is to be done and how it is to be done.
In the case of a self-employed individual, the work to be done is controlled but not the manner of doing it. This means the employer determines what is to be done but not how it is to be done.

A person, who is working under a contract of service, is an employee and a person who is working under a contract for services is self-employed.

The control test was applied in cases concerning the assignment of employees by their employer to a temporary employer. Is the temporary employer or the original employer liable for the tortuous acts of the employees? The control test was used to determine which of the two potential employers would be vicariously liable for the torts of employees.

Case Study — Control test

Walker v Crystal Palace Football Club (1910)

Crystal Palace Football Club had employed Walker as a professional footballer. There was a dispute among the parties in deciding whether his contract with the football club was a contract of service or a contract for services.

Court's decision: It was decided by the court that he was employed under a contract **of** service (or employment). The decision was based on the fact that he was under the control of the club in the form of training, discipline and method of play.

Case Study — Control test

Mersey Docks and Harbour v Coggins & Griffith (Liverpool) Ltd (1947) AC 1

In this case, a firm of stevedores hired a crane from the Harbour Board. Along with the crane, the driver of the crane was also provided by the Harbour Board. The wages of the driver, however, were paid by the stevedores. An employee of the stevedores was injured through the negligence of the crane driver. The issue for consideration for the court was whether the Harbour Board or the stevedores were vicariously liable, as employers, for the crane driver's negligence.

Court's decision: The House of Lords emphasised that the issue would depend on the facts of the case. It was held that the Harbour Board retained responsibility for the crane driver's negligence. This decision was based on the fact that, although the driver was under the temporary directions of stevedores for the relevant operation, they had no power to direct how the crane driver should control the crane. The ultimate control over the method of performing the work had not been transferred by the Harbour Board to the stevedores.

The control test by itself is often found to be too inflexible. Hence it is always combined with other criteria which include:

➢ The ownership of facilities and tools

Example
Does the individual supply his / her own facilities and tools?

➢ The chance of profit and risk of loss

Example
Does the individual earn a fixed amount and incur few costs or does the individual incur various costs without certain knowledge of recovery and profit?

2. Integration test

The integration test examines the role of the individual in the organisation. If the work done is an integral part of the organisation's business, the individual is an employee.

If the work done can be only accessory to the business and can be severed from the organisation this may be an indication that the individual is self-employed.

Case Study — Intergration test

Whittaker v minister of Pensions and Nationals Insurance (1967)

Whittaker was a trapeze artist in the circus. She was required to do general tasks in the functioning of the circus which indicates that she was an employee rather than self-employed.

Court's decision: As she was an employee of the circus, she could claim compensation for injuries sustained during the period of her employment.

Case Study — Intergration test

Cassidy v Minister of Health (1951)

Cassidy was a doctor in a hospital. The question which arose was whether he was an employee of the hospital or an independent contractor.

Court's decision: Although Cassidy was not controlled by the hospital for his method of working, he was considered an employee because he was part of the institution of the hospital.

The integration test has the advantage of seeming a fairly straightforward one, although it proved to be of limited use since, in asking if a person is an integral part of the organisation, it was unclear precisely what constituted "integration" into an "organisation".

3. Economic reality / multiple test

Rather than relying on one single factor, this test uses a more general assessment of the circumstances. No single factor would be conclusive, all factors are considered and weighed to decide whether someone is an employee. The economic reality test examines the opportunity for profit (or loss) and investment in facilities. The absence of chance of profit and risk of loss may indicate an employee relationship.

Alternatively, the potential that unforeseen expenses or hours of work will have to be absorbed in a fixed-price contract may indicate self-employed status.

Case Study — Multiple test

Ready Mixed Concrete v ministry of pensions (1968)

Ready Mixed Concrete made a contract with a lorry driver. He had his own lorry which he drove on company business. He followed the instructions stated by the company and he had to wear the company's uniform. He purchased his own lorry on a hire purchase basis and it was painted in the colours of the company. If the driver fell ill, he could have the substitute driver. The driver received money on the basis of the mileage and the quantity of the goods he delivered. The expenses for repairs and maintenance were borne by the driver himself. He had to pay for his own national insurance and income tax. It was the case that the Minister of Pensions claimed that the lorry driver was an employee of Ready Mixed Concrete and it was hence required that the company had to make the employer's insurance contributions.

Court's decision: It was held that even if there was some control over the lorry driver by the company, the other aspects were not consistent with there being a contract of service. The important thing was that he owned his own lorry and he was functioning at his own financial risk up to some extent. So it was decided that he was an independent contractor.

The various elements which decide whether a person is employed or self-employed are:

a) **Control:** The degree of direction or control a contractor has over a worker is an important factor to consider. The greater the degree of control by the contractor, the more likely it is that the worker is an **employee**. It is important to establish who has control over
  ➤ What work is done
  ➤ When it is done
  ➤ How it is done

An employee is always controlled by the employer. He has to obey the instructions given by his employer such as what work is to be done, how to do it, when to do it, where to do it.

Self-employed people are not subject to someone else's control. They take their own decisions regarding their work.

b) **Financial risk involved:** The greater the degree of **financial risks** for the worker, the more likely it is that he or she will be **self-employed.** The basis of payment and the surrounding financial circumstances of the arrangement will therefore be important.

Example

If you pay a worker for all hours of attendance at an hourly rate, he or she faces little, if any, financial risk, and is, therefore, more likely to be an **employee**.

On the other hand, a worker may be contracted to carry out a defined task or activity at a fixed price. If the completion of this task is vulnerable to delay, for example because of bad weather or it proves more difficult than anticipated, it is more likely that the worker will be regarded as **self-employed.**

c) **Equipment:** If a worker supplies any **expensive / heavy equipment** which is necessary to do the work, this suggests **self-employment.**

On the other hand, if a worker is engaged to operate equipment or plant that has been hired by the employer from another source, it is much more likely that the worker will be regarded as an **employee.**

This factor will be very important in the case of drivers / operators of heavy plant, such as JCBs, lorries, heavy equipment, demolition plant, etc.

d) **Assistance:** Employees are required to do their work themselves. Self-employed people usually delegate their work to staff or to subcontractors and only supervise them.

e) **Work correction:** Mistakes made by employees during their work are usually corrected by the employees themselves during the working hours. They therefore get paid for the original work as well as for making corrections. If the work performed by a self-employed person is unsatisfactory, the client will expect him to make the corrections and not be paid for the time taken. In fact, the self-employed person may have to pay a penalty for delay of work due to rectification of the mistakes.

f) **Holidays: An employee gets holiday pay and sick pay from his company. The company pays a self-employed person only for the days when he works and not for holidays.**

g) **Number of persons contracted with:** Usually, employees work for a single employer. Self-employed people normally have number of companies that they work for.

Example

The simplest way to understand contracts of employment is to take an example from the trades. The terms self-employed and an employee differ in a very simple way. The conceptual difference is easily understood by taking the example of hiring a plumber.

1. If you call a plumbing company you are hiring the company and not the individual plumber. So you may get several different qualified plumbers, even if you have an ongoing contract.

2. It is up to the plumbing company to provide you with the right plumber for specific jobs. If your project moves from one stage to another then the company will assign the right qualified person for that job. It is not up to the customer to understand or demand different expertise for different project phases.

3. Plumbers are not your employees, so they decide when their day begins and ends.

4. Customers have to specify what problems need fixing. You cannot tell a plumber to work 9 to 5 and just do some plumbing.

5. Customers do not have control over a plumber's holiday entitlement. Deciding on entitlement for 2 weeks holiday is up to the plumbing company.

---

6. Plumbers will invoice customers for specific projects jobs: "Replaced dishwasher pipe and pumped out toilet".

7. Customers don't fill out plumbers time sheets and receive all invoices on the plumbing companies' letter head.

8. Customers don't supervise plumbers. The plumber will listen to the customers needs, but as he is the profession he may not take the customers direction.

9. The plumber has all his own tools and equipment as he has invested in his own company.

10. All financial risks are borne by the plumber (i.e. capital costs and rent). This goes beyond his customers' solvency.

Tips **How do you remember these seven elements?**

Make some meaningful word by using the first letter of each of them.
For example, using the first letters of each of above are C, R, E, A, W, H, N then we can **remember Ho!! NEW CAR?** Where:

H - Holidays
N - Number of persons connected with
E – Equipment
W - Work correction
C - Control
A - Assistance
R - Risk involved (financial risk involved)

Diagram 1: Difference between employee and self-employed

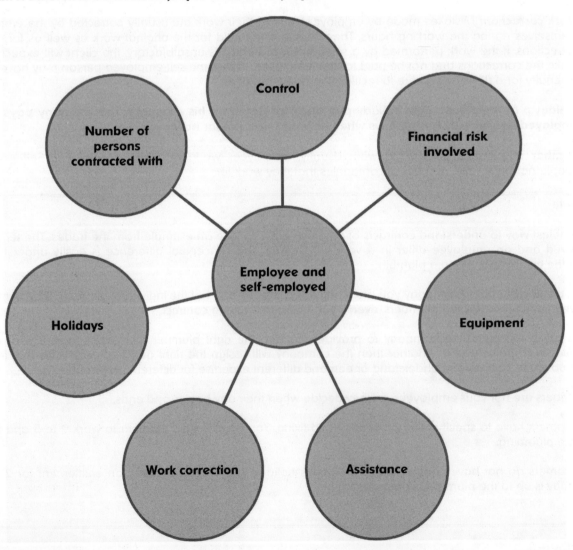

Test Yourself 1

What are the elements that are used to decide whether an engagement of a person to a job is in the capacity of employee or self-employed?

SYNOPSIS

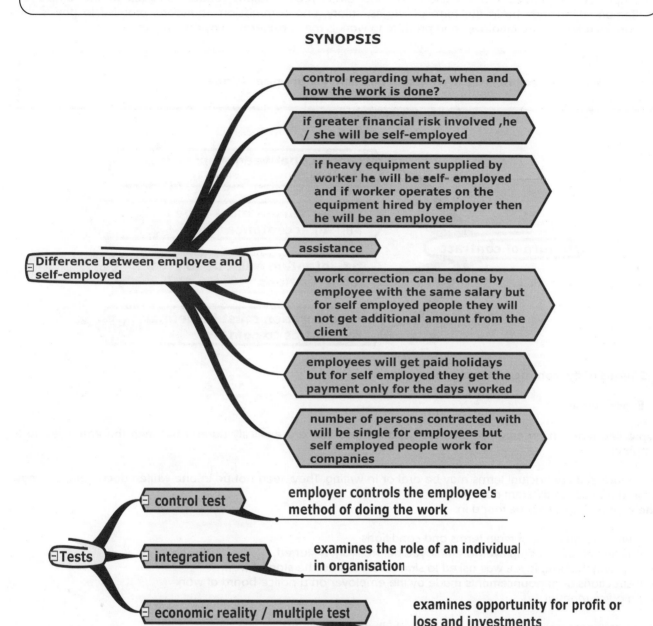

control regarding what, when and how the work is done?

if greater financial risk involved ,he / she will be self-employed

if heavy equipment supplied by worker he will be self- employed and if worker operates on the equipment hired by employer then he will be an employee

assistance

work correction can be done by employee with the same salary but for self employed people they will not get additional amount from the client

employees will get paid holidays but for self employed they get the payment only for the days worked

number of persons contracted with will be single for employees but self employed people work for companies

Difference between employee and self-employed

Tests

control test — employer controls the employee's method of doing the work

integration test — examines the role of an individual in organisation

economic reality / multiple test — examines opportunity for profit or loss and investments

---

2. Explain the nature of the contract of employment and give examples of the main duties placed on the parties to such a contract

[Learning outcome b]

2.1. Nature of the contract of employment

There are two parties in the contract of employment: the employee and employer. An employer normally gives an offer to an employee and employee accepts that offer on terms as mutually agreed.

A contract of employment is a contract of service hence the basic rules of contract also apply to the employment contract. There are **three essential elements**, which would be examined as the evidence of any contract. These are:

1. **The agreement must have an offer and an acceptance:** The employer offers the employee the opportunity to work for the employer and the employee agrees to work for him.

2. **The intention behind a contract must be to create legal relations:** An employment contract is formulated with the objective of creating a legally-binding relationship between the employer and employee.

3. **There must be consideration defined by the parties to contract:** An employer agrees to provide the employee an agreed remuneration and the employee in return renders services to the employer. Remuneration may be in the form of wages, salary, and commission. Therefore, promise to pay is the consideration by the employer and promise to work is the consideration by the employee.

> **Tips**
>
> **An employee promises to work and an employer promises to pay.**

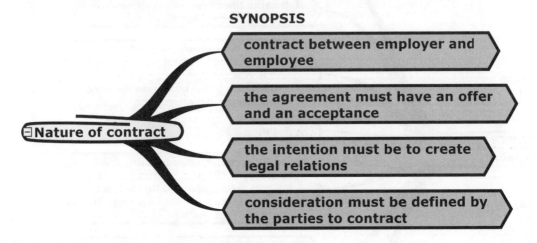

SYNOPSIS

Nature of contract

- contract between employer and employee
- the agreement must have an offer and an acceptance
- the intention must be to create legal relations
- consideration must be defined by the parties to contract

2.2 Terms of the contract of employment

1. Expressed terms

Expressed terms in an employment contract are those that are explicitly agreed between the employee and employer.

The expressed contractual terms may be oral or in writing. They need not be in one written document, but may be in a number of different documents.
The express terms may be found in:

➢ A written statement of main terms and conditions
➢ Any letters sent by employer to employee before work is started
➢ Anything that employee was asked to sign when or since he started work
➢ Instructions or announcements made by the employer on a notice board at work
➢ An office manual

There are some points which are usually made in writing such as:

a) The names of employer and employee.

Example

Between: LUXURY LIMITED (the' Employer')
15 Town Road – Leeds

And: MIKE TURNER (the 'Employee')
12 Small Town Road - Birmingham

---

b) Date of the employment

Example

Employment Start Date: 26 November 20X5

---

c) Pay-scale and intervals
d) Working hours

e) Holidays
f) Pension schemes
g) Notice period in case of termination on either side.
h) Name of the post which is offered to the employee.

Example

The Employee's job title is: Production Controller
The Employee's main task is to assist the Production Manager in maintaining a consistent flow of production.

---

i) Place of the work
j) Sometimes details of disciplinary procedures and grievance procedures are also mentioned
k) Other general clauses that are agreed

2. Implied terms

Implied terms in an employment contract are those which are not specifically agreed between the employer and employee.

Some example of implied terms

a) **General terms** which are implied in most contracts of employment

i. The employee and employer have a duty of trust to each other.

Example

If the employee gives his employer's industrial secrets to a competitor, he has broken an implied contractual term of trust.

---

ii. The employer and employee have a duty of care towards each other and other employees.

Example

The employer should provide a safe working environment for the employee and the employee should use machinery safely.

---

iii. The employee has a duty to obey any reasonable instructions given by the employer. There is no legal definition of reasonable, but it would not be reasonable to demand an employee to do something unlawful.

Example

A lorry driver should not be told to drive an uninsured or untaxed vehicle.

---

b) **Terms implied by custom and practice**: When dealing with a particular employment problem, there may be no express contractual term covering the matter. In such a case, it is helpful to look at what has happened to other employees in the workplace.

Example

Holiday on Christmas.

SAMPLE EMPLOYMENT AGREEMENT

This employment contract is executed and entered into by and between:

A. Employer:

_____

Address:

_____

P.O. Box No. : _____ Tel. No.:_____

B. Employee: _____

Civil Status: _____Passport No.: _____
Date & Place of Issue: _____
Address:

_____

For good consideration, the Company employs the Employee on the following terms and conditions.

1. **Term of Employment:** subject to the provisions for termination set forth below this agreement will begin on _____, 20___, unless sooner terminated.

2. **Salary:** the Company shall pay Employee a salary of £_____ per year, for the services of the Employee, payable at regular payroll periods.

3. **Duties and Position:** the Company hires the Employee in the capacity of _____. The Employee's duties may be reasonably modified at the Company's discretion from time to time.

4. **Employee to Devote Full Time to Company:** the Employee will devote full time, attention, and energy to the business of the Company, and, during this employment, will not engage in any other business activity, regardless of whether such activity is pursued for profit, gain, or other pecuniary advantage. Employee is not prohibited from making personal investments in any other businesses provided those investments do not require active involvement in the operation of said companies.

5. **Confidentiality of Proprietary Information:** the Employee agrees, during or after the term of this employment, not to reveal confidential information, or trade secrets to any person, firm, corporation, or entity. Should Employee reveal or threaten to reveal this information, the Company shall be entitled to an injunction restraining the Employee from disclosing same, or from rendering any services to any entity to whom said information has been or is threatened to be disclosed, the right to secure an injunction is not exclusive, and the Company may pursue any other remedies it has against the Employee for a breach or threatened breach of this condition, including the recovery of damages from the Employee.

6. **Reimbursement of Expenses:** the Employee may incur reasonable expenses for furthering the Company's business, including expenses for entertainment, travel, and similar items. The Company shall reimburse Employee for all business expenses after the Employee presents an itemized account of expenditures, pursuant to Company policy.

7. **Vacation:** the Employee shall be entitled to a yearly vacation of ____ weeks at full pay.

8. **Termination of Agreement:** without cause, the Company may terminate this agreement at any time upon ___ days' written notice to the Employee. If the Company requests, the Employee will continue to perform his / her duties and may be paid his / her regular salary up to the date of termination. In addition, the Company will pay the Employee on the date of the termination a severance allowance of £_____ less taxes required to be withheld.

9. **Death Benefit:** should Employee die during the term of employment, the Company shall pay to Employee's estate any compensation due through the end of the month in which death occurred.

10. **Restriction on Post Employment Compensation:** for a period of _____ (___) years after the end of employment, the Employee shall not control, consult to or be employed by any business similar to that conducted by the company, either by soliciting any of its accounts or by operating within Employer's general trading area.

11. **Grievance and Disciplinary Procedures**: The Company's Grievance and Disciplinary procedures can be viewed electronically on the Company's systems and are also available from the Administration Office. It is the Company's policy to deal fairly with disciplinary issues and grievances, which arise, in accordance with these

procedures. If an employee have a grievance relating to his employment or wish to appeal against disciplinary action or decisions, he/she should, in the first instance, notify his/her line manager in writing making it clear that he/she is raising it formally. If the grievance is against his/her line manager personally, he/she should notify his/her grievance or appeal in writing to a member of the Executive Committee.

12. Oral modifications not binding: this instrument is the entire agreement of the Company and the Employee. Oral changes have no effect. It may be altered only by a written agreement signed by the party against whom enforcement of any waiver, change, modification, extension, or discharge is sought.

Signed this____ day of _____ 20___._____   _____

13. Company

Employee

Witness

_____   _____
(Witness no. 1)   (Witness no. 2)

Tips

Note for students: This is only a sample employment agreement to give an idea of how an employment contract would be drafted. The clauses and terms of the said employment agreement can be duly modified by the parties to the contract according to their requirements.

SYNOPSIS

expressed terms

Terms of contract of employment

implied terms

general terms

terms implied by custom and practice

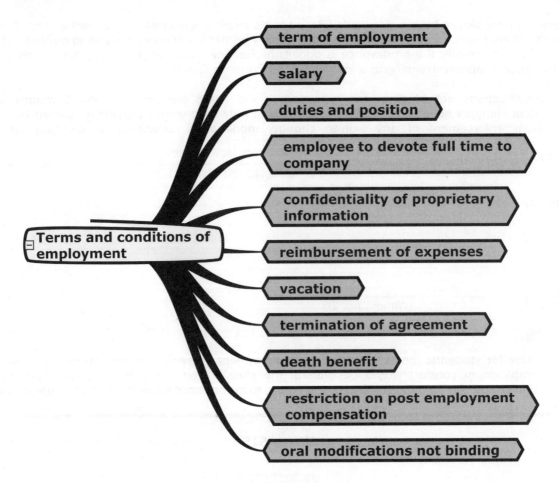

2.3 Employment Act 2002

Some provisions of the Act are given below

1. Flexible working policy: From 6 April 2003 the provisions of the Employment Act of 2002 allowed the parents of children under the age of six, or of disabled children under the age of eighteen, the **right to request** that their employer gives consideration to requests for flexible working options. The only service provision being that the employee has six months' continuous service.

2. Paternity rights: The Act provides for two weeks' paternity leave following the birth of a child as paternity leave. This right is (despite its name) available to both men and women so long as the individual is to be 'parenting' the child and is the 'partner' of the child's mother.

An employee can take statutory paternity leave if he:

➤ Is an employee, with a contract of employment
➤ Is the biological father of the child, or is the mother's husband or partner (including a mother's partner in a same-sex relationship) and
➤ Has been continuously employed for at least 26 weeks by the 14th week before the expected week of childbirth.
➤ Will be fully involved in the child's upbringing.

During the paternity leave, an employee will be paid Statutory Paternity Pay which is lower of:
1. £100 per week

2. 90% of the employee's average weekly earnings.

3. Maternity leave: An employee is entitled to maternity leave as long as she advises her employer of her pregnancy no later than the end of the 15th week before the expected week of childbirth. This has increased from 18 weeks to 26 weeks. Employees with 26 weeks' continuous employment are entitled to Additional Maternity Leave of a further 26 weeks (unpaid). Statutory Maternity Pay is £102.80 per week (increasing to £106 in April 2005). An employee can receive 90% of her average weekly earnings for the first six weeks and from then on will receive Statutory Maternity Pay (SMP).

SYNOPSIS

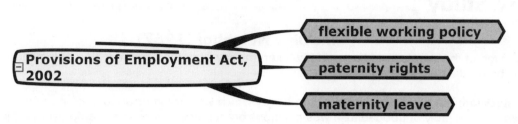

2.4 Main duties on the parties to employment contract

1. Duties of employee

An important duty of an employee is to give his best service in the faithful manner. The following are the main duties of an employee:

a) **An employee should show reasonable competence in his work:** An employee must exercise reasonable care and skill in the performance of her / his work. If the employee is negligent he / she may be liable to indemnify the employer (or contribute) for losses sustained by the employer·

This duty only applies to work for which the employee has been hired to do and which he / she has claimed he / she is competent to do.

> **Example**
>
> An electrician who breaks valuable artwork which he was told to move, is not liable because he only warrants being a skilful and competent electrician and not a furniture mover.

b) **An employee should obey the reasonable and lawful instructions given by his employer:** An employee has a duty to obey lawful and reasonable orders relating to the performance of duties relative to the scope of employment.

Wilful failure to obey such commands can render an employee liable to summary dismissal. However, this depends on the nature of the order / command and the degree of refusal

Case Study

Pepper v Webb (1968)

An employer had given an instruction to a gardener, i.e. an employee, to plant some plants. But the gardener had declined to obey the instruction.

Court's decision: It was held that the gardener had breached the duty of obedience. It was also clear that he was rude. So he was qualified for the summary dismissal.

c) **Duty to take reasonable care of their own safety:** It shall be the duty of every employee while at work to take reasonable care for his own safety, health and welfare and that of any other person who may be affected by his acts or omissions while at work.

d) **Duty to provide honest services / act in good faith:** This duty covers a broad scope and depends on the facts. Some of the most common are as follows:

➢ An employee must not use her / his position to derive secret profits / benefits.
➢ An employee must account to employer for all money and property received in the course of employment.
➢ An employee must not solicit the employer's customers while she / he is employed (e.g. with a view to setting up a business in competition).
➢ An employee must not abuse trade secrets of an employer (e.g. engaging in work in spare time for a commercial rival).
➢ An employee has a duty to make available to the employer inventions made in the course of employment. This is so even if the employee has not been particularly employed for the purpose of the invention.

Case Study

Sinclair v Neighbor (1967)

An employee of the shopkeeper had secretly taken money from the cash machine of the shop. The very next day he repaid the money.

Court's decision: The employee had acted in a way which was not in good faith of the employer. So he had breached the duty of good faith. It was a serious breach of contract so the employer was justified in summarily dismissing that employee.

An employee would normally be required to disclose information relevant to the employer's business (such as the dishonesty of fellow employees) to the employer. This is so especially if the employee is in a management / supervisory role

Case Study

Hivac Ltd v Park Royal Scientific Instruments Ltd (1946)

In a company manufacturing sophisticated components for hearing aids, there were two employees who did the same job for a rival company at the weekends.

Court's decision: An injunction was granted on the grounds that there was potential for leakage of secret information.

e) **Duty to render personal service:** Whatever work is assigned to an employee has to be completed by him only. He cannot delegate the work to other employees without the permission of the employer.

f) **Duty to comply with statutory obligations:** An employee must comply with all relevant legislation, particularly in the area of occupational, health and safety and depending upon their role and responsibility must be able to act with authority to prevent hazards or risks from occurring in circumstances where harm or injury is likely.

SYNOPSIS

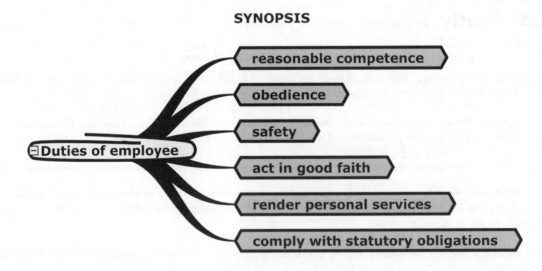

- reasonable competence
- obedience
- safety
- Duties of employee
- act in good faith
- render personal services
- comply with statutory obligations

2. Duties of employer

An employer and employee should have **confidence and mutual trust** between them. The following are the duties that an employer has to perform:

a) **Duty to pay remuneration to the employees:** This is an implied duty as it has to be fulfilled even if there is no express provision regarding pay in the employment contract. This duty generally exists even if there is no work to be done, especially in relation to fixed term contracts.

b) **Duty to indemnify the employee for the expenses and losses incurred during the course of employment:** The employer must indemnify the employee for expenses legitimately incurred by the employee in carrying out the work instructed.

c) **Competent employees:** It is the duty of an employer to hire competent employees, who possess the appropriate skill and qualifications required for the job.

d) **Duty to take care of the employees' health and safety at work:** This duty is both a tort (e.g. negligence in failing to provide a safe system of work) and an implied term in a contract of employment.

It is closely linked with other statutory duties contained in worker's compensation and occupational health and safety legislation.

Case Study

Latimer v AEC Ltd (1953)

Due to a flood, there was huge damage to the factory of AEC Ltd. Because of the water, the floor of the factory became very slippery. The employers carefully strew sawdust over the factory floor to prevent the employees slipping on the floor before it could be properly cleared. A small patch of the floor was not covered by the sawdust. Latimer slipped on that piece of floor and was injured.

Court's decision: It was held that the employers did their duty to provide a safe working environment. So the employers were not liable to Latimer for his injuries.

e) **Duty to provide work to the employee:** There is generally no duty to provide work (if pay is still continuing), but this is dependent on the type of employment contract:

Case Study

Devonald v Rosser and Sons (1906)

Rosser and Sons employed Devonald. But they found that they could not carry on the business with the profit. So they gave Devonald, a pieceworker, one month's notice. However, the factory was closed down immediately. So the damages lost during this period were claimed by Devonald. He also claimed that it was implied that he would be provided with the work during the period of notice.

Court's decision: It was decided that it was reasonably implicit in the contract that the employer would find work up to the expiration of the notice period. If the employee wants to work in order to maintain particular skills, then to refuse this would be a breach of this duty.

Case Study

Collier v Sunday Referee Publishing Co Ltd (1940)

Sunday Referee Publishing Co had employed Collier as a sub-editor of their newspaper. The company sold the newspaper but still continued to pay Collier although he wasn't given any work. Collier claimed that it was his employer's duty to provide him with work.

Court's decision: It was held that the employer had breached the duty of providing work as Collier had been appointed to perform a particular job.

Types of contract

i.   **Casual contracts:** Due to nature of casual relationship, there is no duty to provide work.

ii. **Contracts where pay is linked to performance** (e.g. piece work, bonus, time-rate contracts): Since the employee's pay is dependent on his / her productivity, the employer generally will be obliged to provide sufficient work to enable the employee to earn a reasonable living.

iii. **Contracts where an employee needs to acquire skills** (e.g. apprenticeship or training contracts) or maintain skills (e.g. surgeons): the employer generally will be obliged to provide a reasonable level of work.

iv. **Contracts involving the enhancement of reputation:** Such as where public notoriety and reputation are essential for career potential (e.g. professional actor, professional sportsperson).

SYNOPSIS

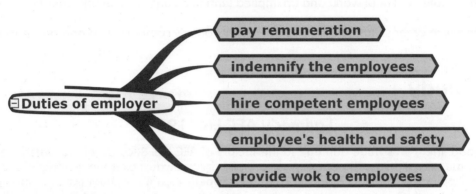

3. **Statutory duties of employer**

The following are the statutory duties of an employer:
a) Pay
b) Time off Work
c) Maternity Rights and the 'Work-Life Balance'
d) Health and Safety
e) Working Time

a) Pay: There are two main Acts that deal with pay: the Equal Pay Act 1970 and the National Minimum Wages Act 1998.

i. Equal Pay Act 1970: According to the provisions of this Act, payments should be at least favourable to the opposite sex. Rules regarding sick pay, holiday pay and working hours are applicable to all full-time and part-time work.

Case Study   Equal pay for work of equal value

Hayward v Cammell Lairds Shipbuilders (1986)

In this case, a canteen cook employed on a shipyard demanded equal pay with painters, joiners and thermal insulation engineers employed in the same shipyard. She claimed that her work was of equal value.

Court's decision: The House of Lords upheld the claim. It was held that the claimant was employed on work of equal value.

ii. National Minimum Wages Act 1998: An employee is entitled to receive at least the national minimum wages, which are increased annually.

b) Time off work: Almost all employees have a statutory right to take paid time off work for the following:

➢ To carry out duties as a trade union official
➢ To carry out duties as a trade union health and safety representative
➢ To look for work if faced with redundancy

c) Maternity rights: A woman who is pregnant has rights to time off work, maternity leave, additional maternity leave, the right to return to work after maternity leave and so on.

d) Parental leave: An employee, who had been continuously in employment for one year, is entitled to a parental leave to care for that child. The period of leave allowed is 13 weeks for each child born or adopted after 15 December 1999. This leave is unpaid leave.

e) **Work-life balance:** Almost every employee is entitled

➢ to take paternity leave,
➢ to take adoption leave
➢ to ask for flexible working hours to care for a child

f) **Health and safety:** It is the duty of the employer to provide health and safety measures to his employees such as safe handling of articles, maintenance of work place etc.

g) **Working time:** Working time should not be beyond the time stated in the employment contract.

Test Yourself 2

Explain the duties of an employee according to the contract of employment.

Test Yourself 3

Tina is employed by Edom Ltd, a big manufacturing company, as an assistant to the Finance Officer. Jack, who is a dry fruit shop owner, offers to pay her £50 per month if she agrees to do the accounting for his business at weekends. If this offer is accepted by Tina, will she be liable for breaching her contract of employment with Edom Ltd?

SYNOPSIS

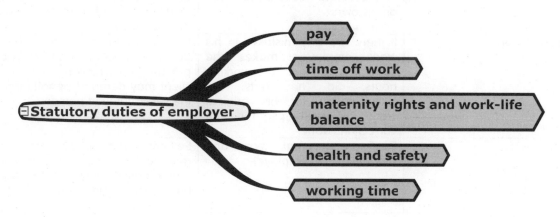

Answers to Test Yourself

Answer 1

Basis of Distinction	Employee	Self-employed
Control	Employee is always controlled by the employer. He has to obey the instructions given by their employer such as which work is to be done, how to do it, when to do it, where to do it.	Self-employed people are not subject to anyone else's control. They take their own decisions regarding their.
Financial risk involved	Employee does not have his own capital in the business, so there is no financial risk for an employee. Evan if, there is any loss in the organisation, employee gets his remuneration	Financial risk involved is more in the case of self-employed person as he has invested his capital in the business. There may be profit or loss in the business that affects him directly.
Equipments	Equipment necessary to carry out the work is provided to an employee by his employer.	Self-employed person has to use his own equipment.
Assistance	Assistance is not there for employee, he has to do his work on his own.	Generally, a self-employed person allocates or delegates his work to his staff and supervises the work.
Work correction	If there are any mistakes in his work, employee makes the correction during his working hours. So he gets the remuneration for his original work as well as for the corrections done.	For self-employed person, if there are any mistakes, client will not pay for the corrections done and client may demand penalty from the self-employed person.
Holidays	Employee gets paid leave and sick leave from employer.	Self-employed person does not get paid leaves; he gets his remuneration only for the days he works and not for the holidays.
Number of persons contracted with	Normally, employees work for a single employer or a company or a firm.	Self-employed people generally have more than one company with which they are dealing.
Taxation	Tax deductions from the employee's income are made by the employer from his salary under PAYE (Schedule E) under income tax.	Self-employed are taxed under schedule D under income tax.
Employment protection	An employee is protected under the contract of service i.e. minimum period of notice.	There is no employment protection for self-employed person as, if company is wound up, it is self-employed person himself who will do this.
Wrongful act	Employer is generally liable for wrongful act of employee done in the duration of employment.	Liability of person hiring contractor is limited.
Bankruptcy	In case of bankruptcy, employee has preference in the payment of outstanding dues.	As there is liquidation of the company there is no question of clearance of the outstanding dues in case of self-employed person.

Answer 2

There are two parties in the contract of employment: an employer and employee. The following are the duties of an employee under the Contract of Employment:

a) **Reasonable care and competence:** In the performance of the employee, he should show reasonable care and competence. If the employee has not performed his duties very well then he will be liable for the loss suffered by an employer.

b) **Obedience of the lawful instructions given by an employer:** An employee has to obey all the lawful instructions given by the employer. If he wilfully has not obeyed the instructions given by the employer, then he will be liable for summary dismissal.

c) **To take reasonable care of their own safety:** An employee is responsible for taking care of his own safety, health and welfare.

d) **To act in good faith:** It is the main duty of the employee to act in good faith and to be honest. He should not make secret profit out of the company's funds. He should not share the trade secrets of the employer.

e) **Rendering of personal services:** It is the duty of the employee to render personal services. He should perform all the duties on his own. He should not delegate the duties to other people.

f) **To comply with the statutory obligations:** An employee has to comply with all the statutory obligations such as occupation, health and safety.

Answer 3

An employee owes a duty of honesty and confidentiality towards the employer. It is an implied duty of an employee not to cause any harm to the employer's business. Hence, if the employee's working for another business would harm the employer's business, then the employee must not work for such other business.
In the case of Hivac v Park Royal Scientific Instruments (1946), the skilled employees of the claimant had worked for the competitor firm in their spare time. It was held by the court that the employees were in breach of the duty even if they did not disclose any confidential information.

However, in the case of Nova Plastics v Frosatt, an employee was held not liable for breach of his duty of honesty even if he worked with the competitor because he had no potential to harm his employer.

In the above case, Jack is not a competitor of Edom Ltd as the two companies run entirely distinct businesses. Therefore, Tina has very little potential to harm her employer Edom Ltd as she is not working with the company's competitor and the work she is doing for Jack is not similar to that she is doing for the company. So it is unlikely that Edom Ltd will get an injunction to stop her from doing extra work in her spare time.

Self Examination Questions

Question 1

What are the statutory duties of the Employer?

Question 2

Matt has been employed as a personal trainer by Solo Health Club Ltd for three years. He receives wages with tax deductions at source on a PAYE (Pay As You Earn) basis.

According to the instructions of the company, he is required to become self-employed in order to reduce the cost. The company has asked Matt to sign a new contract. Matt will continue to receive his previous payment from the company. He will do the same work he has always done and his working hours will also be the same. The company insists that Matt cannot work independently on his own account.
Advise Matt on:

a) The importance of the distinction between contracts of service and contracts for services.
b) The procedure of the court when deciding whether someone is self-employed or is an employee.
c) Whether Matt will be an employee or self-employed.

(December 2003).

Question 3

What should be included in an employment contract?

Answers to Self Examination Questions

Answer 1

a) Pay

There are two main Acts that deals with pay: the Equal Pay Act 1970 and the National Minimum Wages Act 1998.

i. **Equal Pay Act 1970**: According to the provisions of this Act, payments should be at least favourable to the opposite sex. Rules regarding the sick pay, holiday pay, working hours are applicable to all full-time and part-time work. In **Hayward v Cammell Laird Shipbuilders (1986)**, a canteen cook employed on a shipyard demanded equal pay with painters, joiners and thermal insulation engineers employed in the same shipyard. She claimed that her work was of equal value.
The House of Lords upheld the claim. It was held that the claimant was employed on work of equal value. Hayward's application was the first successful claim for equal pay for work of equal value.

ii. **National Minimum Wages Act 1998:** An employee is entitled to receive at least the national minimum wage, which is increased annually.

b) Time off work

Almost all employees have a statutory right to take paid time off work for the following:

➢ To carry out duties as a trade union official
➢ To carry out duties as a trade union health and safety representative
➢ To look for work if faced with redundancy

c) Maternity rights

A woman who is pregnant has the rights to time off work, maternity leave, additional maternity leave, the right to return to work after maternity leave and so on.

d) Health and safety

It is the duty of the employer to provide health and safety measures to his employees such as safe handling of articles, maintenance of work place etc.

e) Working time: Working time should not be beyond the stated time in the employment contract.

Answer 2

a) When a person is working under the contract of service, then he is an employee and a person who is working under the contract for services is self-employed. For the protection of employees there are various laws but self-employed people do not have any protection.

b) With the help of the following tests it will be easier to decide whether someone is self-employed or is an employee.

Control test: Control is an effective tool in deciding whether a person is self-employed or an employee. An employee is always under the control of the employer. He has to obey the instructions given by the employer, while a self-employed person is not controlled by anyone.

In Walker v Crystal Palace Football Club (1910), the Football Club had employed Walker as a professional footballer. There was a dispute among the parties in deciding whether his contract with the football club was a contract of service or a contract for services.

It was decided by the court that he was employed under a contract **of** service (or employment). The decision was based on the fact that he was under the control of the club in the form of training, discipline and method of play.

Integration test: This test scrutinises the jobs performed by the individual in the organisation. If the jobs performed are primary and essential component of the organisation, the individual is treated as an employee of the organisation.

In Whittaker v Minister of Pensions and National Insurance (1967), Whittaker was a trapeze artist in the circus. She was required to do general tasks in the functioning of the circus which indicates that she was an employee rather than self-employed.

It was held that she was an employee of the circus. Hence, she can claim compensation for injuries sustained during the period of her employment.

Multiple test: This test scrutinises the opportunity for profit or loss and investment facilities. If unforeseen expenses or hours of work have to be absorbed in a fixed-price contract, it is likely that the individual is self-employed.

In Ready Mixed Concrete v Ministry of Pensions 1968, Ready Mixed Concrete had made a contract with a lorry driver. He had his own lorry which he drove on company business. He followed the instructions stated by the company and he had to wear the company's uniform. He purchased his own lorry on a hire purchase basis and it was painted in the colours of the company. If the driver fell ill, he could have the substitute driver. The driver received money on the basis of the mileage and the quantity of the goods he delivered. The expenses for repairs and maintenance were borne by the driver himself. He had to pay for his own national insurance and income tax. The Minister of Pensions claimed that the lorry driver was an employee of Ready Mixed Concrete and it was hence required that the company had to make the employer's insurance contributions.

It was held that even if there was some control over the lorry driver by the company, the other aspects were not consistent with there being a contract of service. The important thing was that he owned his own lorry and he was functioning at his own financial risk to some extent. So it was decided that he was an independent contractor.

c) It is more likely that Matt will be treated as an employee if the principles of the control test are applied. The manner in which he pays tax might indicate that he is self-employed. But the most important fact is that Solo Health Club Ltd controls Matt. Matt has to work for Solo Health Club Ltd and cannot work independently on his own account. So he is an employee.

Answer 3

The employment contract should contain details of the following:

a) Names of both the employer and employee
b) Starting date of the employee
c) Job title and description
d) Address of the workplace(s)
e) Details of pay – hourly rate / salary and when it is paid (weekly / monthly)
f) Hours worked each week
g) Holiday entitlement
h) Sickness entitlement
i) Details of any pension schemes
j) If the employee is to work overseas – the period that they will work overseas and the currency in which remuneration will be paid for this period
k) Grievance arrangements
l) Termination of contract notice
m) Redundancy
n) Disciplinary procedures
o) Signatures of both the employer and employee

DISMISSAL AND REDUNDANCY

Get through intro

An employer can dismiss an employee whenever he wants to. It does not matter whether he has a good reason or not under common law. However he has to abide by the employees signed contract and give full notice. The employee can do nothing, even if his contract has been breached, if the employer follows these measures.

The law has now moved on from the above position and incorporates "fairness" into employment contracts.

The employer must be able to show that he has been consistent and has not dismissed the employee for doing something that he would normally let other employees do.

An employee may be able to claim unfair dismissal against the employer provided he can prove that he was treated unfairly and unjustly by the employer.

Understanding this Study Guide will help you to better understand the rights of employees.

LEARNING OUTCOMES

a) Distinguish between wrongful and unfair dismissal including constructive dismissal
b) Explain what is meant by redundancy
c) Discuss the remedies available to those who have been subject to unfair dismissal or redundancy

Introduction

Employees and employers may at some stage in their careers need information on unfair or wrongful dismissal as a job is no longer for life.

Not following the terms of a contract to the letter, can lead an employer to face wrongful dismissal cases. Even if someone is dismissed for a good reason, if the employer doesn't follow the terms of the contract, it can still be classed as unfair. This has wide ranging implications for employers, as it means they may be unable to enforce restrictive covenants and other contractual terms in their contracts.

An unfair dismissal result occurs when a fair reason (redundancy etc) and fair procedure are not followed.

An employee can raise a grievance, and if this grievance is not satisfied then they can resign and claim constructive dismissal if their employer has fundamentally breached their contract.

1. Distinguish between wrongful and unfair dismissal including constructive dismissal
[Learning outcome a]

What is dismissal?

Dismissal is when an employer, with or without notice, ends the employment of an employee. It can also happen when a fixed-term contract isn't renewed or when an employer forces someone to retire. Dismissal can be done verbally or in writing.

Wrongful dismissal

This is where an employer **breaches the contract duly explicit by him in dismissing the employee**, normally by dismissing the employee without notice or without following a procedure required in the contract. A person who has been wrongfully dismissed has to show that:
1. The employer terminated the contract without notice or with inadequate notice
2. The employer was not justified in doing so.

Example

Anthony was working with Cool Company. According to the contract of employment, the employment was only for one year at the end of which either a new contract would be signed or the employment would be terminated. If the employment were terminated by the employer then the employee would be given compensation equal to two months' salary. Anthony's employment was terminated after the end of the year and the employer refused to pay the agreed compensation. As a result Anthony suffered loss of earnings. This is a case of wrongful dismissal.

Where an employee has, for example, a three month notice clause in his contract and the employer dismisses the employee with immediate effect, then prima facie the employee is entitled to make a claim for wrongful dismissal for damages which will reflect the three month notice that he should have received. The employee will also be entitled to other contractual benefits, such as accrued holiday pay.

Unfair dismissal

A dismissal is unfair when it is 'harsh, unreasonable or unjust'. An unfair dismissal happens when an employee is dismissed from the job and the employer **doesn't have a valid reason for dismissing him / her or if an employer has not used proper or fair procedure to dismiss the employee.**

Example

Pixy was an employee of Audrey Company. She was the personal assistant of the Managing Director. She arrived at the office half an hour late on the day of the company's annual general meeting due to personal reasons. In this case, her employer could have given her a warning but instead he dismissed Pixy from her employment. This is a case of unfair dismissal.

To establish unfair dismissal, following steps are followed:

1. Was the employee qualified to bring a claim for unfair dismissal? The employee must prove that he or she is qualified.

2. If so, was the employee dismissed? The employee must prove that he or she has been dismissed.

3. If so, what was the reason for the dismissal? The reasons are:
    ➤ Capability
    ➤ Conduct
    ➤ Redundancy,
    ➤ Breach of statue, and
    ➤ Some other substantial reason.
    The employers must prove that they held one of these five reasons.

4. If the employers prove one of the so-called potentially fair reasons, was the dismissal reasonable? If they do not, the dismissal was unfair, and the tribunal goes immediately to stage 5.

5. Which remedy is the tribunal to award? The tribunal must look at the remedies in the order: reinstatement, re-engagement and compensation.

Case Study   Unfair dismissal

Ransome v The Harley Medical Group, (2001)

In this case, the claimant was a secretary and worked on a part-time basis following maternity leave, leaving at 5.30 pm. The defendants reorganised and needed her to stay to 6.00 pm to answer the phone and meet patients. The claimant could get childcare help on Tuesdays and Wednesdays but could not arrange for her child to be picked up from nursery by 6.00 pm on Mondays. The defendants suggested that she gave up working on Monday afternoon altogether but this was not acceptable to her. She was dismissed with notice.

Court's decision: It was held that the defendants had not shown a real need for her to be there until 6.00 pm and dismissed her without prior warning that her job was at risk, so her dismissal was unfair

---

It is also important to note that it is **not only dismissal for an unfair reason,** which gives an employee the right to claim unfair dismissal. **The conduct and manner in which an employer dismisses an employee is of paramount importance.** This is because a dismissal can and will amount to an unfair dismissal in the eyes of a tribunal if the manner in which the dismissal was handled is unfair.

Example

If an employee is not consulted and / or given a fair chance to improve / rectify the wrong the dismissal may be found to be unfair.

It is important to note that there are situations in which an employer is entitled to summarily dismiss, i.e. dismiss an employee without any notice. This would be in cases where the employee is guilty of gross misconduct such as stealing or selling confidential company information. In these situations, the employer can simply "fire" an employee without any notice.

On what grounds can an employee claim unfair dismissal?

Certain reasons for dismissal are automatically unfair. It is automatically unfair to dismiss an employee, or select for redundancy, if the reason or main reason is for:

1. Dismissal for trade union reasons: This applies where an employee has been dismissed for actual, or proposed, membership of a trade union, or is dismissed for taking part in trade union activities. It applies equally where an individual has refused to join a trade union. Dismissal of individuals involved in a strike, lock out, or other industrial action is not unfair as long as all of those engaged in the action are dismissed. The employer cannot select which individuals to dismiss from the general body of strikers.

2. Dismissal on grounds of pregnancy or childbirth: s.99 ERA 1996 provides that dismissal is automatically unfair where the principal reason for the dismissal is related to the employee's pregnancy or other reasons connected to her pregnancy; or following her maternity leave period, for childbirth or any reason connected with childbirth.

3. **Dismissal in relation to health and safety issues:** s.100 ERA 1996 provides that employees have a right not to be dismissed for carrying out any health and safety related activities for which they have been appointed by their employer; or for bringing to the employer's attention any reasonable concern related to health and safety matters. Nor can they be dismissed for leaving their place of work in the face of a reasonably held belief that they faced serious danger.

4. **Dismissal for making a protected disclosure:** This is covered by s.103 (A) ERA and protects 'whistle blowing' employees who have reported their employer for engaging in certain reprehensible activity. Such protected activity is set out in s.43 ERA and covers criminal activity, breach of legal obligations, breach of health and safety provisions, and activity damaging to the environment.

5. **Dismissal for asserting a statutory right:** s.104 ERA provides that a dismissal is automatically unfair where the principal reason for it is victimisation of the employee for having taken action against the employer to enforce their statutory rights. Rights under the Working Time Regulations 1998 and the National Minimum Wage Act 1998 are specifically covered in s.101 (A) and 104 (A) ERA.

Potentially fair reasons for dismissal

A **dismissal** is 'potentially fair' if it's because of:

➢ **Employee conduct:** This includes quite an extensive range of circumstances including theft, fighting, bad time-keeping, taking drugs or being drunk at work, abusive behaviour, and accessing the internet for personal use.

➢ **Capability or qualification:** Dismissal of an employee who is incapable of performing their job either through ill health or incompetence is potentially fair. As is the dismissal if it transpires that the employee does not have the necessary qualifications for the job.

➢ **Redundancy:** Dismissal on the grounds of redundancy is potentially fair, provided the employer follows a fair procedure for selection.

Case Study

Clarke v Eley Ltd (1982)

In this case the Eley Ltd was making a large round of redundancies. They implemented a practice to make part time staff redundant first, then a "last in first out" practice to full time workers. In total 26 full time women , 20 full time men and all 60 women part time workers where made redundant. If the company had applied the "last in first out" rule to the entire workforce, then the claimants (Ms Clarke and Ms Powell) would not have been made redundant.

Court's decision: The EL found that the "part timers first" practice imposed a requirement or condition that was to the detriment of the two women and ultimately wrong. A judgement of indirect discrimination was found.

If an employee is made redundant for a reason related to her request to work flexibly or where she is working flexibly, it will be indirect discrimination unless justified.

Case Study

Martin v Westhill Insurance Services Ltd (2002)

Mrs Martin was dismissed from Westhill Insurance as she asked for her hours to be reduced.

Court's decision: The tribunal found that this dismissal was unfair. This is not an adequate reason for dismissal. The defendants took no steps to discover if the claimants' hours could be covered by other employees, either for the hour reductions or for her dismissal. The tribunal found that no reasonable employer would dismiss someone, even if for another reason, without looking into the matter further.

➢ A **legal reason** that prevents an employee from doing his job (for example, losing your driving licence if you're a delivery driver)

➢ **Another substantial reason** almost any other reason one can think of - from not getting on with your colleagues, through "sound business reasons", to refusal to reorganise along with others.

If the employee is dismissed while taking part in any industrial action that's unofficial or unlawful, he may lose the right to claim **unfair dismissal.**

Constructive dismissal: Constructive dismissal occurs when an employer commits a repudiatory or serious breach of an express or implied term of the contract of employment. If due to the employer's action, there is a fundamental breach of contract i.e. breach of mutual trust and confidence between employer and employee, then the employee can resign and claim constructive dismissal. The employee must prove that he has left due to the breach of contract terms by the employer.

Example

Alan has been working with a company for the last three years. His employment contract contains a provision that his place of work will never be changed. However, his boss unreasonably changes the location of Alan's work to a location far away from his residence due to which it is not possible for him to work in the company. He resigns from the job. His resignation is due to his boss's breach of contract terms. There is a fundamental breach of contract between employer and employee; hence the employee can claim Constructive Dismissal.

Case Study

Bushnell v Yellow Pages Sales Ltd (2000)

The employment tribunal held that the claimant had been constructively dismissed as changing the claimant's place of work was a fundamental breach of contract. Although the reason for dismissal was a reorganisation, which affected many people, the employer was allowed to make this change. However, no consideration was given to the claimant's personal circumstances or contract. This made it an unfair dismissal.

Case Study

Animashaun v First Media Ltd (2001)

The claimant in this case worked nights. Her husband babysat their child whilst she worked. The claimant had no written contract, but her employment was based on an offer which allowed her hours of work to be changed at the management's discretion. There was no condition that stated her hours of work could be reduced. The claimant was offered daytime hours and her hours where reduced. She could not accept this due to childcare.

Court's decision: The employment tribunal discovered in her employment offer an implied term that any changes would be discussed, negotiated and agreed on. It was found that there was a breach of the claimant's contract as her time and hours of work had been changed without negotiation or agreement. The claim for constructive dismissal was upheld.

It is an employee's responsibility to prove that he has been constructively dismissed. He must show that:

➢ There was conduct by the employer that entitled him to leave and this entitled him to terminate the contract of employment without notice.

Example

Maria is the Assistant Manager of Tasty Ltd. They manufacture biscuits and other sweets and chocolates. She has worked in this role for 10 years. The New Managing Director Don does not like Maria and thinks she is too friendly with the staff. He tells Maria that she is not up to the job and he demotes her without any disciplinary process. He has not sacked her but the demotion would amount to a fundamental breach of contract entitling Maria to resign and claim constructive dismissal.

➢ There must be both an unambiguous repudiation of the contract by the employer and an unambiguous acceptance by the employee of the repudiation.

Diagram 1: Types of dismissal

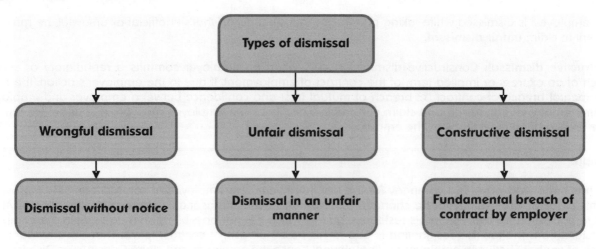

The following are the points of distinction between wrongful and unfair dismissal including constructive dismissal:

Basis of distinction	Wrongful dismissal	Unfair dismissal
Meaning	Dismissal without notice.	If an employer has dismissed an employee in an unfair manner then the dismissed person can claim for unfair dismissal.
Justifications of dismissal	Wilful disobedience, misconduct, dishonesty, incompetence, negligence, immorality, drunkenness.	Capability or qualification, conduct of employee, redundancy, legal prohibition, other reasons.

Test Yourself 1

State the reasons for justifications of unfair dismissal?

SYNOPSIS

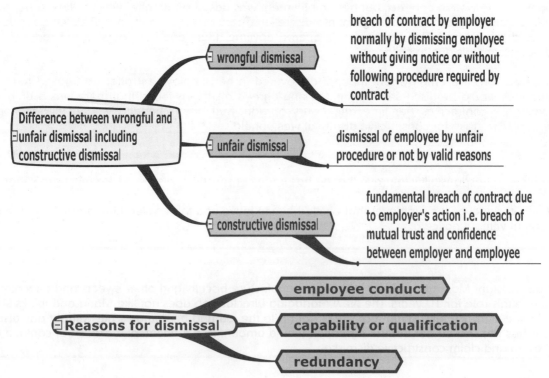

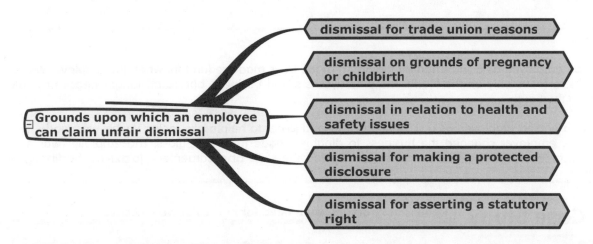

dismissal for trade union reasons

dismissal on grounds of pregnancy or childbirth

Grounds upon which an employee can claim unfair dismissal

dismissal in relation to health and safety issues

dismissal for making a protected disclosure

dismissal for asserting a statutory right

2. Explain what is meant by redundancy

[Learning outcome b]

On occasions, an employer is forced to make a job position redundant. Sometimes a number of positions, or even a department or site team have to be made redundant.

Redundancy is simply dismissal from employment because the job or the worker has been deemed no longer necessary.

Definition
According to Employment Rights Act 1996, an employee is said to be made redundant if the only or main reason for his dismissal is:

1. the fact that the employer has ceased, or intends to cease:
 ➤ to carry on the business for the **purposes** of which the employee was employed by him,
 ➤ to carry on that business in the **place** where the employee was so employed; or

2. the fact that the requirements of that business for employees to carry out work of a particular kind, or for employees to carry out work of a particular kind in the place where he was so employed, has ceased or diminished or are expected to cease or diminished.

Three basic situations are covered in the definition:

➤   Where the employer ceases to run the business in the place where the employee was employed
➤   Where the employer ceases to run the business on a temporary or permanent basis
➤   Where the employer no longer needs as many employees to do a specific type of work (whether in general or in the place where the employee was employed), or no longer requires any employees at all.

In order to claim a redundancy payment from the employer the employee must have been **"dismissed"**.

Once it is established that the employee has been dismissed, s. 163(2) raises a presumption that the dismissal is by reason of redundancy, which means that the burden is on the employer to disprove it.

Another important element to claim redundancy relates to length of service. In order to qualify for redundancy payments an employee must have been continuously employed by the same employer, or associated company for a period of two years.

A dismissal is treated as caused by redundancy if the only or the main reason for dismissal is that:

1. The need for the worker has diminished or ceased: a redundancy situation may arise where a business continues to operate but there is no longer a need for the skills for which the employee was taken on (s. 139 (1) (b))

Example

A person employed as a salesman for the South of the UK is made redundant when the employer changes the business to focus only on the North. The employer is still in business, but he no longer needs any sales staff based in the South.

For e.g., a person employed as a skilled carpenter and joiner to help make racing yachts was made redundant when the employer changed the business to dinghies made from fibre-glass. The employer was still in the business of boat building, but he no longer needed the skills of a carpenter / joiner as the fibre-glass was moulded.

Case Study | Redundancy occurs when need for particular work ceases

European Chefs v Currell

When the demand for éclairs and meringues decreased and that for continental pastries increased, the cook who specialised in making éclairs and meringues was dismissed and a new cook who specialised in making continental pastries was appointed.

Court's decision: It was held that the dismissal of the cook was caused due to redundancy as the need for the particular work he was contracted to do had ceased.

2. New systems in the workplace

Redundancy may also arise if an employer reorganises the business to improve its efficiency, so that fewer people are needed to do the same amount of work. The introduction of the new system or technology will not automatically mean that the employee is redundant. He will be redundant only if the new system is the direct cause of his work no longer needing to be done.

Example

In the business of manufacturing spare parts for cars; the new technology is introduced into the factory. Due to this, there is a reduction in the number of persons required to perform a particular job. This results in redundancy.

3. The job no longer exists because other workers are doing the work the redundant employee carried out

This covers a situation where the tasks the employee was doing still need to be done, but have been handed over to other people to do.

Example

In a furniture-making business called Woods Ltd, Jack performed the job of wood-cutting and Matt performed the job of welding the furniture. But Matt has started doing the job performed by Jack along with his original job of welding.

4. The workplace has closed, or is closing down

The most common example of a situation in which someone's work is no longer needed is where the business or part of the business has closed down or is closing down.

Example

Rosy has been working with Sun Inc for more than five years. But the employer has decided to close down the business due to some unavoidable circumstances. So it is obvious that Rosy is going to lose her job.

5. The business moves

If the place where the employee works, or the whole business moves, and the employee cannot continue to work in the new location, a redundancy will arise.

Example

Rob was working with Steel Ltd. His employer changed the location of the business. Rob was unable to move to the new place of work. This resulted in redundancy as the employer ceased to carry on the business at the place where Rob was working.

However, if the employer offers the employee a similar job at the new location, which involves the employee in no added inconvenience, then the employee cannot claim redundancy (Managers (Holborn) Ltd v Horn (1977)

6. The business is transferred to another employer

If made redundant because of a transfer of employer's business to another employer then this may be unfair dismissal.

Example

Peter has been working with Spades Ltd for five years, under a work bond of eight years. However, the employer has passed the business to another employer in the same field. As the new employer does not need more staff, he refuses to employ Peter.

Offer of fresh suitable employment

This section deals with cases where an employee who is about to be made redundant is offered another job by his employer.

An employee who is about to be made redundant and who is offered a "suitable alternative employment" by his original employer, or an associated employer, will lose his redundancy payment if he accepts the job, or if he unreasonably refuses the offer (s.141)

What is an offer of "suitable alternative employment"?

An offer of "suitable alternative employment" is one which:
➢   Is made by the original employer or an associated employer
➢   Is made before the employee is made redundant
➢   Begins as soon as the employee is made redundant or within four weeks of his redundancy
➢   Is either on the same terms and conditions as his previous job or on other suitable terms.

It is an objective question whether an offer is "suitable". But, whether it was reasonable for the employee to refuse depends on his personal situation.

What is the effect of an offer of suitable alternative employment?

If the employee is offered a new job on terms which are different from his old job, he has a four-week trial period. If he accepts the new job, and completes the trial period, his employment continues as if he was never redundant. Consequently, he will lose his redundancy payment and the right to claim for unfair dismissal. If the employee refuses to take the job unreasonably, he will also lose his redundancy payment and, probably, any claim for unfair dismissal. However if the refusal is reasonable then he may be entitled to redundancy payment and may have an unfair dismissal claim.

If the employee is made redundant and the employer cannot offer him a suitable alternative job, the employee is entitled to the following provided he has worked for the employer **for at least two years:**

a)   Adequate notice
b)   A statutory lump-sum redundancy payment
c)   Reasonable time off work to look for a new job or to make arrangements for retraining

SYNOPSIS

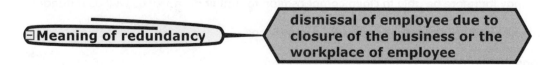

Meaning of redundancy — dismissal of employee due to closure of the business or the workplace of employee

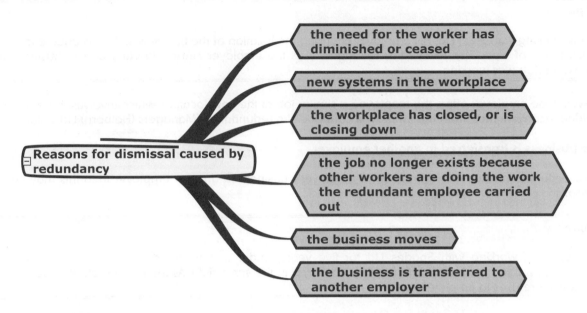

2.1. Redundancy notice

The minimum legal period of notice for redundant employees is dependent on the number of years of service.

➢ If the employee has been **employed for more than a month, but less than two years**, they are entitled to **at least one week's notice.**

➢ If the employee has been **employed for two years, they are entitled to at least two weeks' notice.**

➢ If an employee has been employed **for more than two years, but less than twelve years**, they are entitled to **at least one week's notice for every year of continuous service.**

Example
If the redundant employee has been employed for 8 years then he is entitled to 8 weeks' notice.

➢ If an employee has been employed **for twelve years or more**, they are entitled to **at least twelve weeks' notice.**

If 20 or more employees are made redundant at one time then the notice period is as follows:

20 - 99 employees	at least 30 days
100 or more employees	at least 90 days

SYNOPSIS

2.2. Redundancy pay

The employer must use a procedure which is fair, objective and non-discriminatory, using objective criteria. Unfair selection for redundancy is a type of unfair dismissal. Someone who has been unfairly selected for redundancy may therefore be able to claim compensation for unfair dismissal as well as redundancy pay.

The amount of a statutory redundancy payment depends on:

➢ How long the employee has worked for the employer
➢ Employee's age
➢ Employee's weekly pay

> **Example**
>
> Rob was working with Steel Ltd. His employer changed the location of the business. Rob was unable to move to the new place of work. This resulted in redundancy as the employer ceased to carry on the business at the place where Rob was working.

However, if the employer offers the employee a similar job at the new location, which involves the employee in no added inconvenience, then the employee cannot claim redundancy (Managers (Holborn) Ltd v Horn (1977)

6. The business is transferred to another employer

If made redundant because of a transfer of employer's business to another employer then this may be unfair dismissal.

> **Example**
>
> Peter has been working with Spades Ltd for five years, under a work bond of eight years. However, the employer has passed the business to another employer in the same field. As the new employer does not need more staff, he refuses to employ Peter.

Offer of fresh suitable employment

This section deals with cases where an employee who is about to be made redundant is offered another job by his employer.

An employee who is about to be made redundant and who is offered a "suitable alternative employment" by his original employer, or an associated employer, will lose his redundancy payment if he accepts the job, or if he unreasonably refuses the offer (s.141)

What is an offer of "suitable alternative employment"?

An offer of "suitable alternative employment" is one which:
➢ Is made by the original employer or an associated employer
➢ Is made before the employee is made redundant
➢ Begins as soon as the employee is made redundant or within four weeks of his redundancy
➢ Is either on the same terms and conditions as his previous job or on other suitable terms.

It is an objective question whether an offer is "suitable". But, whether it was reasonable for the employee to refuse depends on his personal situation.

What is the effect of an offer of suitable alternative employment?

If the employee is offered a new job on terms which are different from his old job, he has a four-week trial period. If he accepts the new job, and completes the trial period, his employment continues as if he was never redundant. Consequently, he will lose his redundancy payment and the right to claim for unfair dismissal. If the employee refuses to take the job unreasonably, he will also lose his redundancy payment and, probably, any claim for unfair dismissal. However if the refusal is reasonable then he may be entitled to redundancy payment and may have an unfair dismissal claim.

If the employee is made redundant and the employer cannot offer him a suitable alternative job, the employee is entitled to the following provided he has worked for the employer **for at least two years:**

a) Adequate notice
b) A statutory lump-sum redundancy payment
c) Reasonable time off work to look for a new job or to make arrangements for retraining

SYNOPSIS

Meaning of redundancy — dismissal of employee due to closure of the business or the workplace of employee

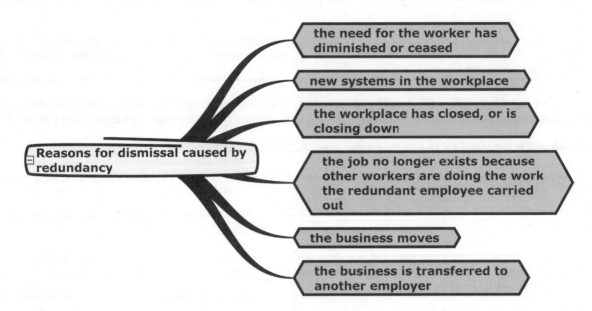

2.1. Redundancy notice

The minimum legal period of notice for redundant employees is dependent on the number of years of service.

➤ If the employee has been **employed for more than a month, but less than two years**, they are entitled to **at least one week's notice.**

➤ If the employee has been **employed for two years, they are entitled to at least two weeks' notice.**

➤ If an employee has been employed **for more than two years, but less than twelve years**, they are entitled to **at least one week's notice for every year of continuous service.**

Example

If the redundant employee has been employed for 8 years then he is entitled to 8 weeks' notice.

➤ If an employee has been employed **for twelve years or more**, they are entitled to **at least twelve weeks' notice.**

If 20 or more employees are made redundant at one time then the notice period is as follows:

20 - 99 employees	at least 30 days
100 or more employees	at least 90 days

SYNOPSIS

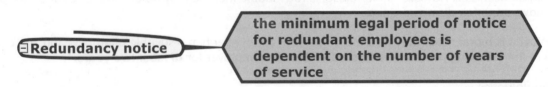

2.2. Redundancy pay

The employer must use a procedure which is fair, objective and non-discriminatory, using objective criteria. Unfair selection for redundancy is a type of unfair dismissal. Someone who has been unfairly selected for redundancy may therefore be able to claim compensation for unfair dismissal as well as redundancy pay.

The amount of a statutory redundancy payment depends on:

➤ How long the employee has worked for the employer
➤ Employee's age
➤ Employee's weekly pay

The employee will be paid for redundancy as follows:

➢ Half a week's pay for each complete year of continuous service below the age of 21
➢ A full week's pay for each complete year of continuous service between the ages of 22 and 40, and
➢ A week and a half's pay for each complete year of continuous service above the age of 41

The period of employment is restricted to a maximum of 20 years.

The payment is restricted to, either the amount owed, or the limit of £290 per week, whichever is lower.

Test Yourself 2

Peter is made redundant at the age of 43, having worked for the employer company for 14 years. His pay at this time is £300 a week. Calculate redundancy pay.

> **Tips**
> **Redundancy pay is the amount which is paid at the time of dismissal with reference to age, length of service, final remuneration.**

Redundancy pay cannot be given to an employee in the following circumstances:

1. If an employee does not fit in the statutory definition of 'employee'
2. If an employee resigns voluntarily
3. Normal retirement age is passed
4. Misconduct of an employee
5. If the employer gives the employee an offer of alternative or fresh employment but the employee clearly refuses to accept that offer
6. Time limit for making the claim for redundancy pay is exceeded, i.e. period of *six* **months** beginning on the date on which notice of a fixed term expired and if notice was not given then the date on which termination took place.

SYNOPSIS

Redundancy pay — amount paid at time of dismissal with reference to age, length of service and final remuneration

2.3. Time off for job hunting

An employee, who has been continuously employed for two years by the date his notice expires, will be allowed a reasonable amount of time off during his notice period to:
➢ Look for another job
➢ Arrange training

Whatever the amount of time off the employee takes, the employer only has to pay him **up to two fifths of a week's pay for it.**

Example

If an employee works 5 days a week and take 4 days off in total during the whole notice period, his employer only has to pay him for the first 2 days.

Test Yourself 3

State the reasons where the dismissal is treated as caused by redundancy.

3. Discuss the remedies available to those who have been subject to unfair dismissal or redundancy

[Learning outcome c]

If there has been an unfair dismissal, an employee must make a claim to the **employment tribunal within three months** of the date of effective termination.

On the unfair dismissal or redundancy claim being proved, the tribunal can order the following remedies:

1. Reinstatement: Getting the job back with no loss of money or security

> **Definition**
>
> Reinstatement is returning to the same job without any break of continuity.
>
> s.114

It means going back to work as if there had been no break and removes totally the effects of dismissal.

2. Re-engagement: Getting another job with the same employer with or without loss of money or security

> **Definition**
>
> Re-engagement means that the employee is given new employment with the employer (or his successor or associate) on terms specified in the order.

In this case, the employment tribunal must first consider reinstatement and then re-engagement taking into account the wishes of the complainant, if it is practicable for the employer to comply with such an order and so on.

3. Compensation: If reinstatement or re-engagement is not ordered by the tribunal then the tribunal may award compensation.

Compensation has three levels:

a) Basic Award

The basic award, which was introduced to compensate employees for the loss of job security following dismissal, is very similar to a redundancy payment, and is calculated according to a strict mathematical formula based upon age, length of service and average gross weekly pay to arrive at a figure. **The average weekly pay figure is limited to a maximum of £290 per week and the maximum number of years that will be considered is 20 years.**

The basic award is calculated in detail as follows:

i.   Years of service below 22 years of age, the weekly pay is multiplied by 0.5
ii. Years of service between 22 and 41, the weekly pay is multiplied by 1
iii. Years of service from 41 onwards, the weekly pay is multiplied by 1.5

Hence, the absolute maximum that could be awarded for the basic award is 20 years at £290 x 1.5 = £8,700.

The basic award is not payable to employees aged 65 or over. From 64 to 65 the award is reduced 1/12th for every month up to 65 when it becomes nil.

The tribunal will reduce the Basic Award in the following circumstances:

➢ If the employee refuses an offer to be reinstated and it is unreasonable to refuse the offer
➢ If an employee is in some manner responsible for his own dismissal
➢ Any misconduct by the employee before they were dismissed, even if it is not linked with the actual dismissal
➢ Redundancy payments already paid to the employee where the dismissal was due to redundancy

b) Compensatory award

The idea of the compensatory award is to compensate the employee for the financial loss suffered as a result of being dismissed including expenses and loss of benefits. **The tribunal will award what it considers to be 'just and equitable'** in all of the circumstances given the losses sustained as a consequence of the dismissal. The award is subject to an overall ceiling which is revised every February. **For dismissals in the year beginning the 1 February 20X6, the maximum award is £58,400.** It is calculated on a net basis and is payable even if the claimant has reached or passed 65 so long as they are below the employer's normal retirement age.

c) Additional or special award

Where a tribunal orders reinstatement or re-engagement and the employer fails to comply, the tribunal will make an additional award unless the employer is able to prove that it was impractical to comply. Where the tribunal finds that it was unreasonable for the employer not to comply, then it **can award 26-52 weeks' pay on top of the basic and compensatory awards.**

Diagram 2: Remedies available for unfair dismissal

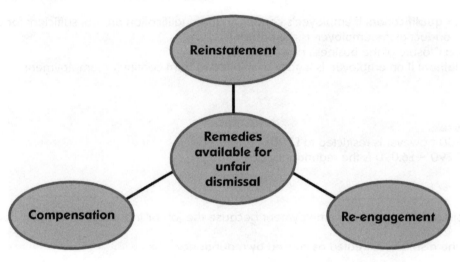

Test Yourself 4

Explain the compensation remedy available for unfair dismissal.

SYNOPSIS

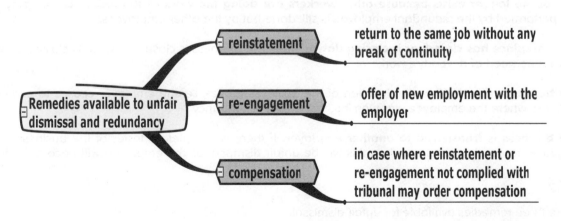

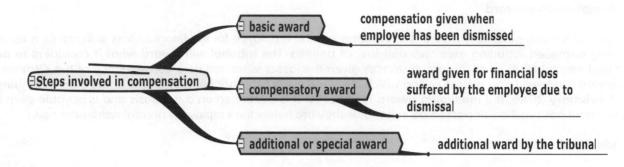

basic award — compensation given when employee has been dismissed

Steps involved in compensation

compensatory award — award given for financial loss suffered by the employee due to dismissal

additional or special award — additional ward by the tribunal

Answers to Test Yourself

Answer 1

There are different reasons for the justification of dismissal such as:

1. **Capability or qualification**: If employee's capability and qualification are not sufficient for employment.
2. **Conduct**: If conduct of the employee is not proper.
3. **Redundancy**: Closure of the business or workplace.
4. **Legal prohibition**: If an employee is legally prohibited to from continuing employment.

Answer 2

(14 x1.5) = 21 weeks
Weekly pay is £300 however is restricted to £290
Therefore, 21 x £290 = £6,090 is the redundancy pay.

Answer 3

Redundancy is simply dismissal from employment because the job or the worker has been deemed no longer necessary.
Reasons where the dismissal is treated as caused by redundancy:

1. **The need for the worker has diminished or ceased:** It might be the case that the business will continue to operate but no longer requires the skills of the worker.

2. **New systems in the workplace:** There is an installation of a new system which reduces the burden of the work so that the same amount of work can be done by fewer people. This will only be redundancy if the new system means that the work of some employees is no longer needed by the organisation.

3. **The job no longer exists because other workers are doing the work of the redundant employee:** The job performed by the redundant employee is still done but by the other employees.

4. **The workplace has closed, or is closing down:** When the business is closed down or is closing down then there is no need of anybody's work.

5. **The business moves:** When the location of the business moves, i.e. the employer ceases to carry on the business where the employee was working, then this is redundancy.

6. **The business is transferred to another employer**: If there is complete transfer of the business from the employer to another employer then this will be unfair dismissal as the employee will become redundant.

Answer 4

There are three remedies available for unfair dismissal:
1. Reinstatement
2. Re-engagement
3. Compensation

Compensation: Compensation can be ordered by the tribunal in a case where reinstatement or re-engagement is ordered by the tribunal.
Compensation has levels:

© GTG   Dismissal And Redundancy: C2.13

b) Compensatory award

The idea of the compensatory award is to compensate the employee for the financial loss suffered as a result of being dismissed including expenses and loss of benefits. **The tribunal will award what it considers to be 'just and equitable'** in all of the circumstances given the losses sustained as a consequence of the dismissal. The award is subject to an overall ceiling which is revised every February. **For dismissals in the year beginning the 1 February 20X6, the maximum award is £58,400.** It is calculated on a net basis and is payable even if the claimant has reached or passed 65 so long as they are below the employer's normal retirement age.

c) Additional or special award

Where a tribunal orders reinstatement or re-engagement and the employer fails to comply, the tribunal will make an additional award unless the employer is able to prove that it was impractical to comply. Where the tribunal finds that it was unreasonable for the employer not to comply, then it **can award 26-52 weeks' pay on top of the basic and compensatory awards.**

Diagram 2: Remedies available for unfair dismissal

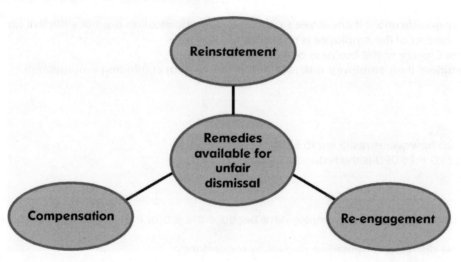

Test Yourself 4

Explain the compensation remedy available for unfair dismissal.

SYNOPSIS

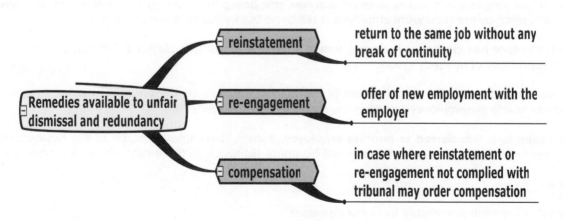

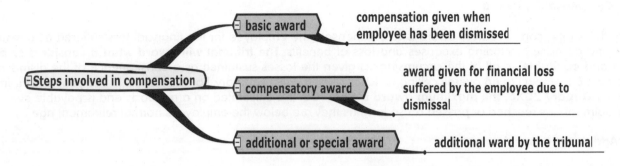

Answers to Test Yourself

Answer 1

There are different reasons for the justification of dismissal such as:

1. **Capability or qualification**: If employee's capability and qualification are not sufficient for employment.
2. **Conduct**: If conduct of the employee is not proper.
3. **Redundancy**: Closure of the business or workplace.
4. **Legal prohibition**: If an employee is legally prohibited to from continuing employment.

Answer 2

(14 x1.5) = 21 weeks
Weekly pay is £300 however is restricted to £290
Therefore, 21 x £290 = £6,090 is the redundancy pay.

Answer 3

Redundancy is simply dismissal from employment because the job or the worker has been deemed no longer necessary.
Reasons where the dismissal is treated as caused by redundancy:

1. **The need for the worker has diminished or ceased:** It might be the case that the business will continue to operate but no longer requires the skills of the worker.

2. **New systems in the workplace:** There is an installation of a new system which reduces the burden of the work so that the same amount of work can be done by fewer people. This will only be redundancy if the new system means that the work of some employees is no longer needed by the organisation.

3. **The job no longer exists because other workers are doing the work of the redundant employee:** The job performed by the redundant employee is still done but by the other employees.

4. **The workplace has closed, or is closing down:** When the business is closed down or is closing down then there is no need of anybody's work.

5. **The business moves:** When the location of the business moves, i.e. the employer ceases to carry on the business where the employee was working, then this is redundancy.

6. **The business is transferred to another employer:** If there is complete transfer of the business from the employer to another employer then this will be unfair dismissal as the employee will become redundant.

Answer 4

There are three remedies available for unfair dismissal:
1. Reinstatement
2. Re-engagement
3. Compensation

Compensation: Compensation can be ordered by the tribunal in a case where reinstatement or re-engagement is ordered by the tribunal.
Compensation has levels:

a) **Basic award:** This is the award given to the employee for the job lost by him / her. It is similar to the redundancy payment which is calculated on the basis of age, length of service and average gross weekly pay to arrive at a figure. There are some circumstances where the tribunal will not give compensation e.g. where the employee has refused an offer of re-instatement or, to some extent, an employee is responsible for his own dismissal etc.

b) **Compensatory award:** This is the award given for the financial loss incurred by an employee because of his dismissal. The tribunal will award what it considers to be 'just and equitable'. The basis of calculation is net.

c) **Additional or special award:** When there is failure by an employer to re-engage an employee, then the additional award will be ordered by the tribunal unless the employer has stated that it is impracticable to perform.

Quick Quiz

1. State true or false.

a) A 'harsh, unreasonable or unjust' dismissal is wrongful dismissal.

b) Constructive dismissal occurs when an employer commits a repudiatory or serious breach of an express or implied term of the contract of employment.

2. Answer in one sentence.

a) What is redundancy?

b) What is re-engagement?

Answers to Quick Quiz

1. True or False

a) **False**, it is unfair dismissal.
b) **True.**

2. Answer in one sentence.

a) Redundancy is simply dismissal from employment because the job or the worker has been deemed no longer necessary.

b) Re-engagement means that the employee is given new employment with the employer on the terms specified in the order.

Self Examination Questions

Question 1

What is meant by 'constructive dismissal'?

Question 2

Zeta College Ltd provides private tuition. The college is administered by Ted. He also handles the personal matters of the employees of the college.

Due to some problem, there is a reduction in the number of clients of the college. So the management has decided to reduce the number of employees by 8. In total, 40 employees are working in the college in different departments. Matt, Rose and Nicole are amongst the 40 professors working in the college. All of them have been working for Zeta College for the last four years. Matt has been a part of the staff trade union for two years and he has had many arguments with Ted regarding the rights of the professors, Rose has taken maternity leave twice in the four years. There was some problem regarding the health and safety matters of the college. Nicole reported this problem to the authorities and the college had to pay a large fine for violation of safety and health matters. The management decides that Matt, Rose and Nicole are amongst the 8 employees to be selected for dismissal. All 8 members believe that this is because of the Ted's personal argument with them.

Now, from the above information, advise Matt, Rose, Nicole and the other five members of staff to be dismissed, what action they can take against their employer.

Answers to Self Examination Questions

Answer 1

If an employee has been treated extremely badly by his employer, he has the right, under s.95(1) (c) of the Employment Rights Act 1996, to resign from employment and claim compensation on the grounds of constructive dismissal. For example, if a male employer regularly makes unwanted advances towards a female employee, she is entitled to resign and claim constructive dismissal. A famous case in this area is Western Excavating v Sharp (1978).

In Western Excavating v Sharp (1978), Western Excavating employed Sharp for twenty months. Under the terms of his contract, if he worked overtime he was allowed to take compensatory time off. In February 1976, he asked for three hours off to play a team card game but his request was denied as there was a lot of work. Sharp ignored the refusal and played the card game. The next morning he was dismissed for failing to carry out a reasonable order.

CA Lord Denning, in his definition of fundamental breach, stated that if an employer breaches or indicates that he no longer wishes to be bound by one of the integral terms of the contract of employment, the employee may consider himself as discharged from further performance. Otherwise, the contract may be terminated on the basis of the employer's behaviour. **Sharp was held to have been constructively dismissed.**

Answer 2

This is a case of both redundancy and unfair dismissal.

Redundancy is breach of a contract by an employer due to the closure of the business or closure of workplace of an employee.

With regard to the person's age, length of continuous service, weekly rate pay subject to statutory maxima, redundancy payment can be claimed by the employee.

Unfair dismissal is the dismissal of the employee by unfair procedure. The conduct and the behaviour of the employer are very important in deciding whether the case is one of unfair dismissal.

A dismissal can be automatically unfair in the following circumstances:

1. Dismissal for trade union reasons
2. Dismissal on grounds of pregnancy or childbirth
3. Dismissal in relation to health and safety
4. Dismissal for making a protected disclosure
5. Dismissal for asserting a statutory right

So, from the above, it can be concluded that Matt, Rose, Nicole have been dismissed in an unfair manner. The remedies for unfair dismissal are therefore applicable here. In this case, reinstatement or re-engagement is not possible but they can be awarded compensation. The other five members who have been dismissed can claim unfair dismissal and additional compensation which may depend upon whether it was fair of the college to select them. If the procedure of selecting the other five members was fair, then they would be entitled to redundancy payments because they have not been dismissed in an unfair manner.

a) **Basic award:** This is the award given to the employee for the job lost by him / her. It is similar to the redundancy payment which is calculated on the basis of age, length of service and average gross weekly pay to arrive at a figure. There are some circumstances where the tribunal will not give compensation e.g. where the employee has refused an offer of re-instatement or, to some extent, an employee is responsible for his own dismissal etc.

b) **Compensatory award:** This is the award given for the financial loss incurred by an employee because of his dismissal. The tribunal will award what it considers to be 'just and equitable'. The basis of calculation is net.

c) **Additional or special award:** When there is failure by an employer to re-engage an employee, then the additional award will be ordered by the tribunal unless the employer has stated that it is impracticable to perform.

Quick Quiz

1. **State true or false.**

a) A 'harsh, unreasonable or unjust' dismissal is wrongful dismissal.

b) Constructive dismissal occurs when an employer commits a repudiatory or serious breach of an express or implied term of the contract of employment.

2. **Answer in one sentence.**

a) What is redundancy?

b) What is re-engagement?

Answers to Quick Quiz

1. True or False

a) **False**, it is unfair dismissal.
b) **True.**

2. Answer in one sentence.

a) Redundancy is simply dismissal from employment because the job or the worker has been deemed no longer necessary.

b) Re-engagement means that the employee is given new employment with the employer on the terms specified in the order.

Self Examination Questions

Question 1

What is meant by 'constructive dismissal'?

Question 2

Zeta College Ltd provides private tuition. The college is administered by Ted. He also handles the personal matters of the employees of the college.

Due to some problem, there is a reduction in the number of clients of the college. So the management has decided to reduce the number of employees by 8. In total, 40 employees are working in the college in different departments. Matt, Rose and Nicole are amongst the 40 professors working in the college. All of them have been working for Zeta College for the last four years. Matt has been a part of the staff trade union for two years and he has had many arguments with Ted regarding the rights of the professors, Rose has taken maternity leave twice in the four years. There was some problem regarding the health and safety matters of the college. Nicole reported this problem to the authorities and the college had to pay a large fine for violation of safety and health matters. The management decides that Matt, Rose and Nicole are amongst the 8 employees to be selected for dismissal. All 8 members believe that this is because of the Ted's personal argument with them.

Now, from the above information, advise Matt, Rose, Nicole and the other five members of staff to be dismissed, what action they can take against their employer.

Answers to Self Examination Questions

Answer 1

If an employee has been treated extremely badly by his employer, he has the right, under s.95(1) (c) of the Employment Rights Act 1996, to resign from employment and claim compensation on the grounds of constructive dismissal. For example, if a male employer regularly makes unwanted advances towards a female employee, she is entitled to resign and claim constructive dismissal. A famous case in this area is Western Excavating v Sharp (1978).

In Western Excavating v Sharp (1978), Western Excavating employed Sharp for twenty months. Under the terms of his contract, if he worked overtime he was allowed to take compensatory time off. In February 1976, he asked for three hours off to play a team card game but his request was denied as there was a lot of work. Sharp ignored the refusal and played the card game. The next morning he was dismissed for failing to carry out a reasonable order.

CA Lord Denning, in his definition of fundamental breach, stated that if an employer breaches or indicates that he no longer wishes to be bound by one of the integral terms of the contract of employment, the employee may consider himself as discharged from further performance. Otherwise, the contract may be terminated on the basis of the employer's behaviour. **Sharp was held to have been constructively dismissed.**

Answer 2

This is a case of both redundancy and unfair dismissal.

Redundancy is breach of a contract by an employer due to the closure of the business or closure of workplace of an employee.

With regard to the person's age, length of continuous service, weekly rate pay subject to statutory maxima, redundancy payment can be claimed by the employee.

Unfair dismissal is the dismissal of the employee by unfair procedure. The conduct and the behaviour of the employer are very important in deciding whether the case is one of unfair dismissal.

A dismissal can be automatically unfair in the following circumstances:

1. Dismissal for trade union reasons
2. Dismissal on grounds of pregnancy or childbirth
3. Dismissal in relation to health and safety
4. Dismissal for making a protected disclosure
5. Dismissal for asserting a statutory right

So, from the above, it can be concluded that Matt, Rose, Nicole have been dismissed in an unfair manner. The remedies for unfair dismissal are therefore applicable here. In this case, reinstatement or re-engagement is not possible but they can be awarded compensation. The other five members who have been dismissed can claim unfair dismissal and additional compensation which may depend upon whether it was fair of the college to select them. If the procedure of selecting the other five members was fair, then they would be entitled to redundancy payments because they have not been dismissed in an unfair manner.

SECTION D - THE FORMATION AND CONSTITUTION OF BUSINESS ORGANISATIONS

AGENCY LAW

One of the most common legal relationships in business is agency. With the growth of industry, the intervention of a third party in the process of marketing, selling and licensing a company's products is a common feature. The channel of distribution involves distributors, retailers, company and independent sales representatives. The contractual arrangement between these various entities is critical.

The agreement between the parties must be very clear, detailed and unambiguous. This Study Guide deals with an agency relationship, how an agency relationship is created, and the legal authority an agency has under the provisions of law.

Agents play an important role in society and so a sound knowledge of this topic will be needed in your professional life.

The questions on this topic are frequently asked in the examination. You need to devote considerable time to studying and understanding this topic.

LEARNING OUTCOMES

a) Define the role of the agent and give examples of such relationships paying particular regard to partners and company directors
b) Explain how the agency relationship is established
c) Define the authority of the agent
d) Explain the potential liability of both principal and agent

Introduction

The increasing number of commercial transactions reflects an increasing need for the rights and liabilities of principal and agent. In the case of large business entities, it is not possible for one person to travel everywhere to negotiate all the transactions necessary to maintain or expand the business. In the case of corporations, these problems are aggravated because it is a fictitious legal person and it can only act through human agents. Hence, agents are appointed by entities to act on their behalf for trading their goods or services. Under the contract the principal is held liable for the agent's acts. If the agent has done what he or she was instructed to do by the principal, the result is held to be the same as if the principal had done it directly.

Third parties approached by a person who identifies himself as an agent another person or entity trust that the agent has the authority to represent the person or entity. In the busy commercial world, it would not be cost-effective to check whether everyone who is represented as having the authority to act for another actually has that authority. Deals are done at face value in the majority of routine situations. If it should later appear that the alleged agent was acting without the consent of the principal, the principal will usually be held liable. Any other decision would be unduly disruptive to the usual flow of trade. This commercial necessity has led to the creation of a body of law that applies in any situation, commercial or otherwise, where one person is seen to be acting for another.

1. Define the role of the agent and give examples of such relationships paying particular regard to partners and company directors

[Learning outcome a]

What is 'Agency?'

As a general rule, one person cannot, by contract with another, confer any rights that impose liabilities upon a third party. However, one person may employ another person for the purpose of bringing him into a legal relationship with a third party. Employment for this purpose is called "Agency".

> **Definition**
> An agent is a person employed to do any act for another or to represent another in dealing with a third person, the person for whom such act is done, or who is so represented, is called the principal.

Therefore, in effect, an agent is the connecting link between the principal and the third person - a sort of conduit pipe or an intermediary. This intermediary has the power to create a legal relationship between the principal and the third party. He has the competency to make the principal responsible to the third party.

It is very important to understand here that the contract entered into is between the principal and the third party, the agent has no personal rights or liabilities in relation to the contract and cannot be bound by the contract.

1.1 Essential elements of agency: The following are the essential elements that constitute agency.

1. **Principal must be competent to contract**

As an agent is acting on behalf of the principal, it is essential that the principal has the full contractual capacity because, ultimately, the party to contract is the principal and not the agent.

Example

A minor is not competent to appoint an agent because a minor does not have full contractual capacity.

2. **Any person may become an agent**

As the agent is not actually entering into a contractual relationship with a third person, there is no requirement that the agent have contractual capacity. In other words, full contractual capacity is not necessary to enable a person to represent another as an agent.

Example

Even a minor can act as an agent. However, even though a minor may become an agent, since he is incompetent to contract, he will not be responsible to his principal.

No consideration is necessary for the creation of an agency: No consideration is necessary to create an agency. (This is yet another exception to the general rule that an agreement without consideration is void.) Normally, however, commission is paid for an agent's services.

Diagram 1: Essential elements of an agency

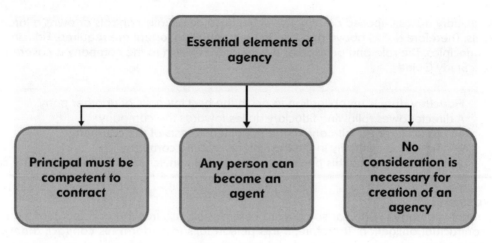

1.2. Different kinds of agents

Various examples of agency relationships can be encountered in day-to-day life.

> **Example**
>
> As their name suggests, estate agents and travel agents are expressly appointed to facilitate particular transactions. In certain circumstances, employees may act as agent of their employers.

Broadly, there are two types of agents:

1. **General agents:** They act generally for the principal in relation to some particular area of business.

> **Example**
>
> Partners of a firm or directors of a company are authorised to carry out all acts which relate to the firm or the company.

2. **Special agents:** They have the authority to carry out only certain specific acts or transactions.

> **Example**
>
> An auctioneer is appointed to carry out a particular auction.

Some forms of agency are listed below:

a) **Partners**
This is the most important example of agency. Partners are agents to each other. If any contract is signed by one partner in the firm's name, it is binding on all the partners of the firm. The firm as a whole is liable for each partner's actions. Partnership will be discussed in further detail in Section D Study Guide 2.

> **Example**
>
> Annie, Benny, Conny are partners of Grasim pharmaceuticals. Benny enters into a contract with Candila medicines for the partnership firm. Therefore this contract is binding on Annie and Conny as Benny has acted as an agent on behalf of the partnership firm.

b) **Directors**
A director is the agent of the company. He executes his duty with other directors as part of a board, or on his own when duties are delegated to him by other directors. In the latter he is the agent of the board. A director needs to know whether he has done the right thing. Referencing the duties of an agent and a managing agent can provide directors with clarity on their conduct.

The duties of a director are:
a) To act in good faith
b) To act with care and skill
c) To act in obedience to lawful instructions
d) Personal performance

A director has fiduciary duties imposed on him. This is because he usually controls or owns a large part of the company's assets. Therefore duties above and beyond a commercial agent are required. Fiduciary duties are based on trust principles. The role and position of a director in relation to the company is covered in greater detail in the next Study Guide.

> **Tips**
>
> **Fiduciary duty** is an obligation to act in the best interests of another party.
> A director owes following fiduciary duties towards the company.
> ➢ To act in good faith and in the genuine interests of the company
> ➢ To use his authority in the best interests of the company
> ➢ To take care that his personal goals do not conflict with the interests of the company.

c) Del credere agents

A del credere agent is an agent who, for some extra commission, assures the principal that the other party will perform their contractual obligation. Therefore, if this person fails to perform his contract, a del credere agent will be responsible to the principal for failure. A del credere agent guarantees that, in the event of the buyer's failure to pay for the goods received, he will make good the loss.

Example

Emma is an agent of Elsa, who enters into a contract on behalf of Elsa with Emily for the sale of mangos at a rate specified by Elsa. However, Elsa's experience with Emily is that she delays the payment and also gives less payment than was agreed. Therefore Emma assures Elsa that, if Elsa is ready to pay her higher commission, she will take the responsibility that Emily pays the entire amount on time. In such case, if Emily fails to pay the price in due time, Emma has to bear the loss incurred by Elsa.

---

d) Factor

A factor is an agent who is entrusted with the possession and control of the goods to be sold by him for his principal. He has the possession of the goods, authority to sell them in his own name, and a general discretion as to their sale. He may sell on the usual terms of credit, may receive the price and give a good discharge to the buyer. **His authority** to dispose of the goods **cannot**, even under common law, be restricted as against third parties by instructions privately communicated to him by his principal. This is because he has the authority to carry out any transactions which are within the normal course of his business.

Example

Robert has been appointed as a factor by Basil to sell the apples from Basil's orchards. The apples are plucked, packed and delivered to Robert's place of business. As the apples are of good quality, Basil expects a good margin of profit for the sale. However, due to riots, the markets are not open for the next four or five days. Robert checks the condition of the apples to see if they can be preserved for four or five days, and finds that they are already very ripe and should be sold as soon as possible so he forms a deal with Cathy who agrees to buy the apples at a price lower than the market price. Basil is disappointed to receive a profit which is below his expectations. However, he cannot recover his loss from Robert as Robert has the authority to dispose of the apples in any manner which is within the normal course of business. As apples are perishable, they had to be disposed of as soon as possible.

---

e) Brokers

A broker is an agent who is employed by a principal to enter into contracts for sale or purchase on behalf of the principal. He is not given possession of the property. A broker can neither enter into a contract in his own name nor can he receive payment. He cannot even cancel a contract which he has entered into on behalf of his principal.

Therefore a broker is an agent primarily employed to negotiate a contract between two parties in which he is a broker for sale, he has no possession of goods to be sold, and he does not have the authority which a factor enjoys, nor does he have the authority to sue in his own name by virtue of contracts made by him.

Example

Hugh is Sue's broker, who buys or sells shares on behalf of Sue. Sue wants to sell some of her shares, as the market conditions are suitable. She instructs Hugh to get the best price for her shares. Hugh enters into a contract with Lou for the sale of the shares and negotiates the sale price with him. He communicates this sale price to Sue. Sue then shows her approval and she arranges a meeting with Lou where the sale takes place. In this meeting, possession of the shares is passed from Sue to Lou and the sales price is also received directly by Sue.

---

f) Auctioneer

An auctioneer is an agent who sells property goods at a public auction. He is primarily an agent for the seller, but upon the property being sold / knocked down he also becomes the agent of the buyer. He has the authority to sell, but not to give warranties as to the property sold, unless expressly authorised by the seller.

Example

Honey has become bankrupt and has to pay off her debts so needs to sell her house. She is not able to do this herself so she appoints Boney as her agent to sell her property at a public auction. Boney sells the property on behalf of Honey.

---

g) Estate agents

An estate agent is an intermediary who is entrusted with the job of finding a buyer for the principal's property. Estate agents are governed by Estate Agents Act 1979.

Example

Sam and Jenny run a business in partnership. They decided to start a division. As their office place was too small for the new division, they decided to move the business to a new, more spacious place. As both Sam and Jenny were busy in their business, they appointed Ted to find a suitable place for their business. They agreed to pay him a commission for his duties. Here, Ted is an estate agent.

---

h) Commercial agents

A commercial agent is a self-employed intermediary who has continuing authority in relation to the **sale or purchase of goods**. Continuing authority means that one-off sale transactions, such as an auction, are not included. An individual or a company can act as a commercial agent.

Example

Raj is a trader of IC components. He buys these components from a fixed number of suppliers and provides them to his list of clients regularly.

Diagram 2: Kinds of agents

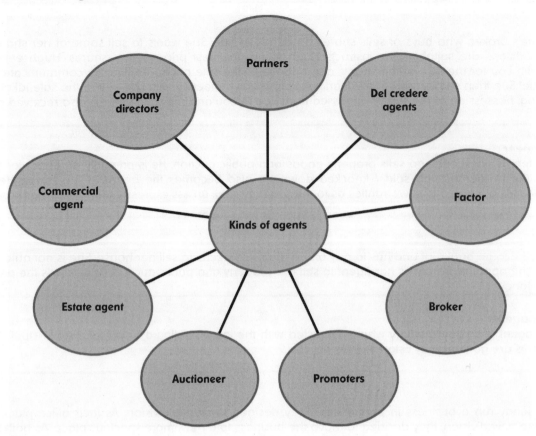

Test Yourself 1

Name the essential elements of agency.

Test Yourself 2

What are the different kinds of agency?

SYNOPSIS

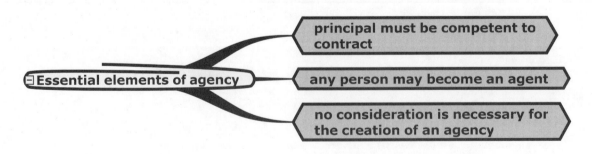

Essential elements of agency
- principal must be competent to contract
- any person may become an agent
- no consideration is necessary for the creation of an agency

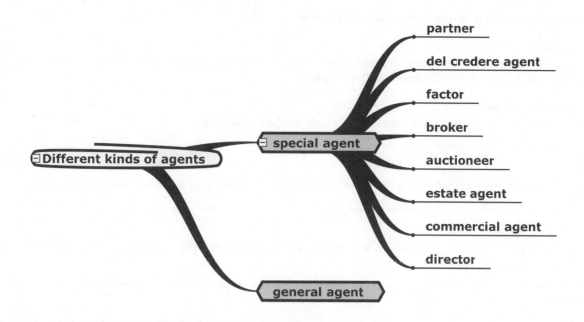

2. Explain how the agency relationship is established

[Learning outcome b]

The agency relationship is created by mutual consent, although the consent need not be expressly stated.

Case Study

Principal-agent relationship cannot be created without mutual consent.

White v Lucas (1887)

A firm of estate agents claimed to act on behalf of the owner of a particular property, although that person had denied them permission to act on his behalf. When the owner sold the property to a third party, introduced by the estate agents, they claimed their commission.

Court's decision: It was held that the estate agents were not entitled for commission because the property owner had not agreed to their acting as his agent.

Diagram 3: Creation of agency

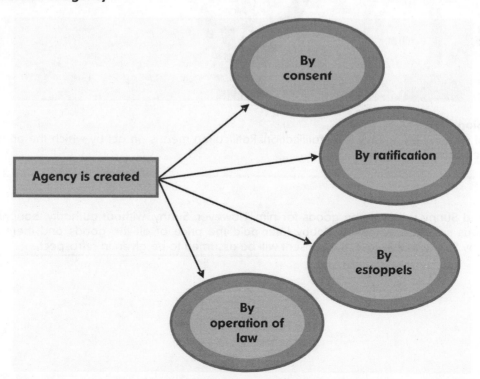

Agency may be created in any of the following ways:

1. By consent

The most common way an agency is created is when a principal gives actual authority to contract to his agent. The authority of an agent may be expressed or implied.

a) Expressed authority

An authority is said to be expressed when it is verbally spoken or written.

Example

An agency may be created when a principal gives power of attorney to a person who will then become the agent.

---

b) Implied authority

An authority is said to be implied when it is to be inferred from the circumstances of the case or by their relationship with each other.

Example

Employer and employee, company and company director are implied agency relationship. Although an express agreement is not created, a director, by his position, has the implied authority to act on behalf of his company.

Diagram 4: Implied and expressed authority

2. By ratification

Another way of creating an agency is by ratification. Ratification means an act by which the principal confirms the unauthorised acts of the agents.

Example

Bobby appointed Sunny to buy some goods for him. However, Sunny, without authority, bought other goods along with goods specified by Bobby. Bobby later paid the price of all the goods and thereby ratified the contract made by Sunny. In this case, the consent will be assumed to be given in retrospect.

Where the principal elects to ratify the contract, it gives retrospective validity to the action of the self-styled agent.

It may, however, be noted that for a ratification to be valid, it must satisfy certain conditions:

a) The agent must have acted on behalf of the principal

The first essential condition for ratification is that the agent must admit that he or she was acting as an agent for the principal. It is not always necessary for the agent to disclose the name of the principal but the principal must be identifiable. If the agent acts in his own name and does not disclose the name of the principal then the principal cannot later ratify his act.

Case Study An undisclosed principal cannot ratify a contract

Keighly, Masted & Co v Durant (1901)

In this case, the claimant authorised a corn merchant to buy wheat at a certain price jointly for himself as well as the claimants. The corn merchant acted in excess of his authority by purchasing the wheat at a higher price and did so in his own name. Subsequently, the claimants ratified his transaction. They, however, refused to take delivery of the wheat.

Court's decision: The claimants were held not liable to take delivery of the wheat. The so-called ratification was invalid and therefore ineffective because, while purchasing the wheat, the corn merchant did not profess to be acting on behalf of another.

---

b) The principal must be in existence at the time of agent's act

The obvious reason for this rule is that the ratification relates to the time when the contract was originally made by the agent on behalf of the principal.

Case Study The principal must have been in existence at the time of agent's act

Kelner v Baxter (1866)

In this case, the claimants entered into a contract as promoters of an unincorporated company. After the formation of the company was complete, the company ratified the contract. Subsequently the company went into liquidation. When the defendants were sued for breach of contract, they took the defence that since the company had ratified the contract, they were not liable for the breach of contract.

Court's decision: The court rejected the contention of the defendants by stating that, the ratification can only be by a person ascertained at the time of the act carried out by an agent.

---

c) The principal must have the legal capacity to contract

In order to be able to ratify a contract, a principal must be competent to contract both at the time the act was carried out and at the time of the purported ratification.

d) The contracts must be valid and legal: Ratification can be made only for lawful acts.

Case Study Legal capacity of the principal

Boston Deep Sea Fishing and Ice Co Ltd v Farnham (1957)

The claimant, a company of trawler owners, took control of a French trawler lying in an English port when France fell to the German army. The French company claimed to ratify their acts.

Court's decision: Since the French Company was an alien enemy under common law at the time that the acts were carried out, it could not have carried out the acts itself. Therefore, it did not have the legal capacity to contract and hence could not ratify the contract.

> **Example**
>
> Acts causing injury to third person cannot be ratified.

e) The principal must adopt the whole of the contract

Principals are not at liberty to pick and choose some parts of the contracts for ratification, they must accept all its terms. The contract should be ratified in its entirety.

> **Example**
>
> Bee appoints Lee as an agent to buy him a certain plot of land and lease it, Afterwards, he gives some authority to Lee and, at the same time, he puts in a clause to restrict Lee's authority as the clause stipulates that Lee may accept payments only in cheque and not in cash. Bee finds that, due to this clause, Lee's flexibility of operations is hampered, resulting in a delay for Bee. Bee therefore considers altering the clause. In this case, Bee will have to ratify the whole contract and not just that part of it.

f) Ratification must be within a reasonable time

What is a reasonable time depends on the facts and circumstances of each particular case. However, where the third party with whom the agent contracted becomes aware that the agent has acted without authority, a time limit can be set, within which the principal must indicate their adoption / ratification of the contracts for it to be effective.

Diagram 5: Conditions to make ratification valid

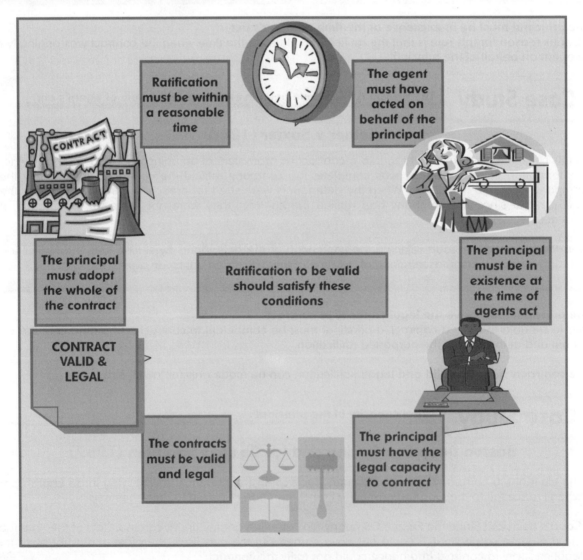

3. By estoppel

The **principal** may, by words or conduct, **create an inference** that an authority has been conferred upon an agent even if, in fact, no authority was given. In this case, if the agent contracts within the limits of his apparent authority, although without actual authority, the principal will be bound to the third party by his agent's act.

The doctrine of apparent authority is really an application of the principle of estoppel. **Estoppel means that a person is not permitted to resist an inference which a reasonable man would draw from his words or conducts.**

However, there are certain important points:

a) An agent himself cannot, by his representation, create an agency by estoppel. It must be made either **by principal** or by his authority.
b) The **third party must rely on the representation** of the agent that he has the authority to act as an agent.
c) It must not be in the knowledge of the third party that the agent has, in fact, no authority.

Example

Francis, a dealer in food items, directed his brother James not to give any guarantee of the freshness of packed food items while selling them. Despite this, James gave a guarantee to Annette that the juices he sold to her were fresh and that he would replace the entire carton if the juices were sour. The entire carton of the juice boxes had turned sour. Annette asked for the replacement.

Here, Francis is liable to replace the goods. His brother had the authority to sell the goods. On the basis of this, he also had ostensible authority to give the guarantee on the basis of which Annette purchased the juices. Francis could escape the liability only if Annette knew that Francis had instructed his brother not to give any guarantee. In the above case, Annette had no knowledge of Francis' instruction to James. Therefore, Annette was not bound by the instructions which Francis gave privately to his brother.

Case Study

To rely on agency by estoppel, the principal must have made a representation as to the authority of the agent.

Freeman & Lockyer v Buckhurst Park Properties Ltd. (1964)

In this case, the property company had four directors on its Board of Directors. One of the directors, without being appointed as managing director, acted as managing director and asked the claimants, who were architects, to perform some work for the company. The other directors, however, were aware of this activity. The company afterwards disowned any liability for the work and resisted the claim of payment contending that the person was not authorised to act on behalf of company.

Court's decision: It was held that the company was liable to pay, as the board which had the actual authority to bind the company had presented the individual director as having the necessary authority to enter such contracts. It was, therefore, a case of agency by estoppel.

---

d) **Agency by operation of law**

The most common instance in which agency arises by operation of law is the case of agency by necessity. According to Halsbury, "Agency of necessity arises whenever a duty is imposed upon a person to act on behalf of another apart from the contract, and in circumstances of emergency, in order to prevent irreversible injury. It may also arise where a person carries out the legal or moral duties of another in the absence of default of that other, or acts in his interest to preserve his property from destruction".

For agency of necessity to arise, some conditions have to be satisfied:

i. **There has to be a genuine emergency**

A person may become an agent by necessity because of a certain emergency. It is necessary to prove that the course adopted was the only practical one under the circumstances.

Case Study

In order for agency by necessity to arise, there needs to be a genuine emergency. Great Northern

Railway Co v Swaffield (1874)

In this case, the railway company transported the defendant's horse and when no one arrived to collect it at its destination, it was placed in a livery stable. However the defendant denied paying the cost of stabling incurred by the company.

Court's decision: It was held that, the company was entitled to recover the cost of stabling, as necessity had forced them to act as they had done as the defendant's agent.

ii. There must be no practical way of contacting the principal to obtain further instructions
The circumstances have to be such that the person acting as the agent by necessity did not have enough time or opportunity to communicate with the principal.

Case Study

In order for agency by necessity to arise, the agent must have no practical way of contacting the principal to obtain further instructions.

Springer v Great Western Railway Co (1921)

In this case, a consignment of tomatoes arrived at port after a delayed journey due to storms. A railway strike would have caused further delay in getting the tomatoes to their destination, so the railway company decided to sell the tomatoes locally.

Court's decision: It was held that the railway company was not an agent of necessity as it could have contacted the principal to seek his further instructions. The railway company was held responsible to the claimant for the difference between the price achieved and market price of tomatoes in London.

iii. The person seeking to establish the agency by necessity must have acted in good faith
This means that he must act in the interests of the principal rather than in his own interests.

Case Study

The agent must have acted bona fide in the interests of the principal.

Sachs v Miklos (1948)

The claimant stored his furniture in a room of the defendant, free of charge. After a lapse of about three years the defendant wanted to use this room because his premises had been damaged due to bombing. He made efforts to communicate with the claimant for this purpose, but could not find his whereabouts. Consequently, he sold the furniture in an auction.

Court's decision: It was held that there was no agency by necessity since no emergency had arisen and the defendant sold the furniture for his own convenience.

Diagram 6: Agency by operation of law

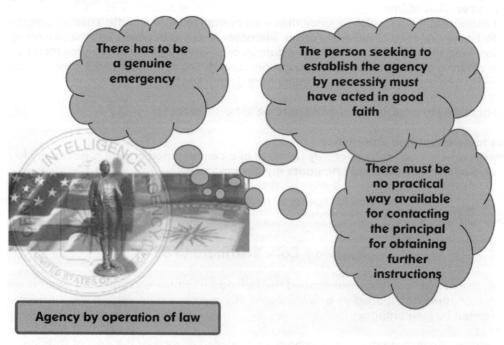

There has to be a genuine emergency

The person seeking to establish the agency by necessity must have acted in good faith

There must be no practical way available for contacting the principal for obtaining further instructions

Agency by operation of law

Test Yourself 3

Explain how an agency relationship can be established in the following ways:
➢ By agreement
➢ By ratification
➢ By estoppel
➢ By necessity

(December 2003)

SYNOPSIS

How the agency relationship is established

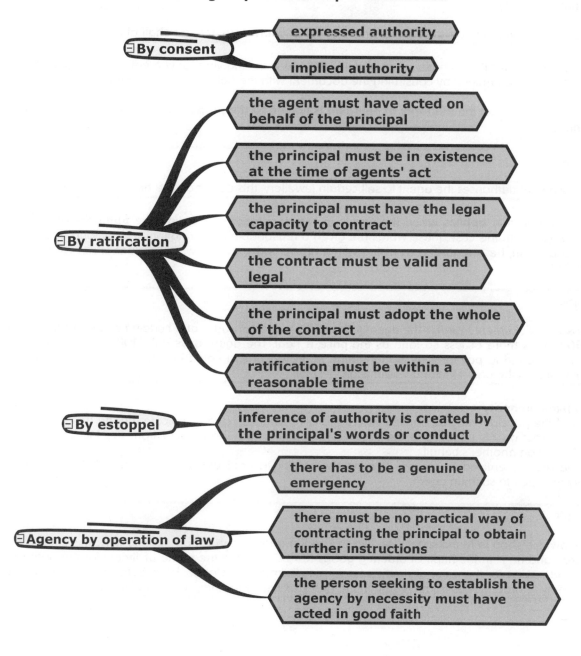

By consent
- expressed authority
- implied authority

By ratification
- the agent must have acted on behalf of the principal
- the principal must be in existence at the time of agents' act
- the principal must have the legal capacity to contract
- the contract must be valid and legal
- the principal must adopt the whole of the contract
- ratification must be within a reasonable time

By estoppel
- inference of authority is created by the principal's words or conduct

Agency by operation of law
- there has to be a genuine emergency
- there must be no practical way of contracting the principal to obtain further instructions
- the person seeking to establish the agency by necessity must have acted in good faith

3. Define the authority of the agent

In order to bind a principal into a contract with a third party, the agent must have the necessary authority. There are two types of authority:

1. Actual authority
2. Apparent authority

1. **Actual authority** : This is again of two types:
a) **Expressed authority:** Expressed authority is conferred by the contract of agency and is usually in writing.

Example

As a regular feature of trade, an agent is given power of attorney to act on behalf of the principal.

Generally, whenever the authority of an agent is defined in writing via a document duly executed, the scope of that authority is determined by construing the document with the help of two simple rules:

i. The first rule is that the **authority of an agent is limited to the purpose for which it has been given** by the principal.

Example

If the document authorises the agent to sell certain jewellery, this does not give him the authority to pledge it.

---

ii. The second rule **applies when the words in the document concerning the authority of the agent are ambiguous.** In this case, these words are given a reasonable interpretation and, as long as the agent acts in good faith, he is regarded as acting within his authority, even if what he does is not what the principal intended.

Example

Suppose the document instructs the agent to buy 500 tonnes of sugar at a certain price and adds that he may buy 50 tonnes more or less so long as the price is right. The agent buys only 400 tonnes at that price. The principal is bound to pay for it as the language in the document could be reasonably interpreted to provide that authority to the agent [Ireland v Livingston (1872)].

---

b) **Implied authority**
Assent of the principal may be implied where the circumstances clearly indicate that he has given authority to another to act on his behalf and the assent of the agent may be implied from the fact that he has acted intentionally on another's behalf.
Third parties are entitled to assume that agents holding a particular position have all the powers that are usually provided to such an agent.

Example

Jimmy owns a shop in Manchester. He lives in London and visits the shop occasionally. This shop is managed by Baron and he is in the habit of ordering goods from George in the name of Jimmy for the purposes of the shop, and paying for them out of Jimmy's funds with Jimmy's knowledge. Here, Baron has an implied authority from Jimmy to order goods from George in the name of Jimmy for the purposes of the shop.

Case Study
Creation of agency by way of implied authority

Watteau v Fenwick (1893)

Fred owned a hotel. He sold it to the defendants, who then hired him as the hotel manager. Fred continued to hold the licence for the hotel, which was placed over the door. The claimants in the case supplied cigars to Fred on credit. The claimants believed Fred was the hotel owner. They didn't know that the defendants (the actual owners), whom they had never heard of, had forbidden Fred to buy cigars on credit. The claimants learnt of this and sued for the outstanding amount.

Court's decision: The court declared that a manager of such an establishment had authority to purchase cigars. If limitations where imposed on this authority, then these limitations needed to be communicated to third parties to make the limitations effective.

2. Apparent authority

This arises when the principal's words or conduct reasonably cause the third parties to believe that the agent has been authorised to act on his behalf. It is an aspect of agency by estoppel considered in this Study Guide in 2.C above. It can arise in the following two ways:

a) Where a principal, from his conduct, suggests to third parties that a particular person is his agent: In such a case, the principal is bound by the acts of the agent. This also applies where the principal knows that the agent claims to be his / her agent and does not correct that impression.

Example

Ira wanted to buy a wooden cupboard. So she entered a furniture store. The owner of the store, who was sitting on the cash counter, welcomed Ira and told her that an attendant would attend to her. A man in a suit introduced himself to Ira and asked if he could help her. On informing him what she wanted, the man showed Ira a piece of furniture. Ira told the man that she liked the furniture and wanted to purchase it, she handed the man a cheque and was told that the furniture would be delivered to her in about a month. After waiting over a month for the furniture to be delivered to her, Ira contacted the furniture store. She learned, to her surprise, that there was no record of her transaction and that there was no man known to have worked there who helped her out.

In this case, the store owner from his conduct suggested to Ira that the person who took the cheque was his agent. Hence he is bound by the act of the so-called agent.

---

b) Here a principal has previously represented to a third party that an agent has the authority to act on their behalf.

Example

If a father regularly pays the debts incurred by his daughter at a local shop, then he may be denied the right to prove that she was not acting on his behalf if he should on some subsequent occasion refuse to pay. He has led the supplier to believe, reasonably, that she is acting on his behalf. Hence he will be liable to pay the debts incurred by his daughter, unless he has informed the shop owner that he will not pay any debts incurred by his daughter anymore.

Diagram 7: Types of authority

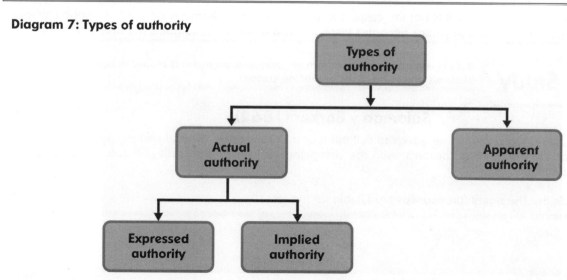

Test Yourself 4

Give an example for each of the following:
a) Apparent authority
b) Expressed authority
c) Implied authority

SYNOPSIS

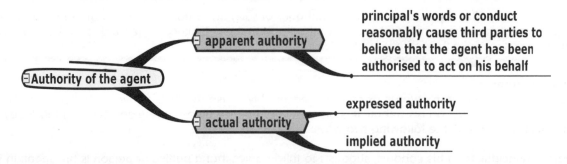

apparent authority — principal's words or conduct reasonably cause third parties to believe that the agent has been authorised to act on his behalf

Authority of the agent

actual authority — expressed authority / implied authority

4. Explain the potential liability of both principal and agent
[Learning outcome d]

The principal is usually liable to third parties for contracts formed by agents within his authority. However, the agent owes some duties towards the principal and enjoys certain rights. This Study Guide deals with the rights and duties of an agent and an agent's relationships with third parties.

4.1 Rights and duties of an agent

The rights and duties of the principal and agent depend upon the terms of the contract which they enter into. Besides these terms, the mere establishment of the relationship between principal and agent gives rise to certain rights and duties.

1. The following are the duties of an agent

a) Duty to perform the business according to the direction of the principal
The agent is bound by contractual obligation to carry out the agreed business in accordance with the principal's instructions in so far as these are lawful and reasonable. Even if he believes that non-compliance with the principal's instructions will be in the principal's best interest, he should not disobey the instructions. However, any agent may refuse to perform an illegal act. If there are no instructions from the principal, an agent is bound to conduct the business according to the custom which prevails in carrying out business of the same kind and in the same place where the agent conducts the business. If the agent does not conduct the business according to the directions of the principal or in the absence of such directions, according to the prevalent custom, he will be liable for any loss sustained.

Example

James is a broker. In his business, it is not the custom to sell the goods of Anthony on credit to Bobby, whose credit is very high. Bobby, before payment, becomes insolvent. **James must make good the loss to Anthony.**

Case Study

If there are no instructions from the principal, an agent is bound to conduct the business according to the prevailing custom.

Soloman v Barker (1862)

A broker was entrusted with some goods to sell them at a proper price. Without making an estimate of the value of the goods in accordance with the prevailing custom of that trade, he sold them at an inadequate price.

Court's decision: The agent (broker) was held liable for the loss.

Case Study   The agent is bound to perform what he has contracted to perform.

Turpin v Bilton (1843)

An insurance agent contracted to arrange for insurance for the principal's ship. He failed to arrange the insurance and ship was lost at the sea.

Court's decision: The agent was held liable to compensate the principal.

b) Duty to apply reasonable skill and care

Whether the relationship is contractual or gratuitous, an agent is bound to act with reasonable care and skill. The agent must perform his duties with a normal degree of diligence. If the agency is gratuitous, he is expected only to employ as much skill as he would to conduct his own affairs. A somewhat higher standard is required of him if the agency is for reward.

Example

Peter, an insurance broker employed by Lee to arrange insurance on a ship, doesn't notice that the usual clauses are inserted in the policy. The ship was later lost at sea. In consequences of the omission of the clauses nothing can be recovered from the insurance company. As Peter failed to exercise due care, he is bound to compensate Lee for the loss.

In **Keppel v Wheeler (1927),** the defendant estate agents were held liable for failing to secure the maximum price for a property.

c) Duty to perform personally

An agent owes a duty to perform the task himself. It is the duty of the agent not to delegate his functions to a sub-agent. An agent cannot, except with the express or implied authorisation by the principal, delegate the work. The principal will not be bound by the act or contract of the sub-agent whose appointment is not sanctioned by the principal. However, where it is usual to appoint sub-agent by the ordinary custom of trade, a sub-agent may be employed.

On the other hand, where an agent, having the authority for his principal expressly or by implication, names another person to act for the principal in the business of agency, such a person will not be deemed to be a sub-agent. He will, in fact, be deemed to be an agent of the principal for that part of the business of agency that is entrusted to him.

Example

Alan directs John, his solicitor, to sell his estate by auction, and to employ an auctioneer for the purpose. John names Bob, an auctioneer, to conduct the sale. Here, Bob is not a sub-agent, but is Alan's agent for the conduct of the sale of estate by auction.

d) Duty to render accounts

An agent who enters into any transaction on behalf of his principal is under an implied duty to render proper accounts to the principal. The agent is required to account for all monetary considerations and other property received on behalf of his principal and should ensure that his personal property / money is kept separately from that of the principal.

e) Duty to avoid conflict of interests

It is the duty of the agent to ensure that his personal interests does not conflict with the interests of his principal. If there is any possibility of a conflict of interest, the agent must disclose this possibility to the principal. Upon full disclosure by the agent, it is for the principal to decide whether or not to allow a particular transaction. If an agent deals on his own account in the business of the agency, without first obtaining the consent of his principal and acquainting him with all material circumstances which have come to his knowledge on the subject, the principal may repudiate the transaction. If it later comes to the notice of the principal that any fact was dishonestly concealed from him by the agent, the principal may repudiate the transaction

Example

Where an agent is employed to sell some goods, he cannot himself purchase the goods unless full disclosure is made to the principal and the transaction is allowed by the principal.

Case Study

Agent must not allow his personal interest and his duty to conflict with each other.

De Bushe v Alt. (1984)

In this case, a ship was consigned by the claimant to a company in China for sale, fixing a minimum price of £90,000 payable in cash. The company, with the consent of the claimant, employed the defendant (an agent in Japan) to sell the ship. The defendant made efforts to sell the ship but failed. The defendant thereupon, purchased the ship himself and paid £90,000 for it. After some time, the defendant resold the ship for £160,000. When this fact came to the knowledge of the principal, he brought an action to recover the profits gained by the defendant.

Court's decision: It was held that the defendant was bound to account for the profits gained by him for resale of the ship. The court observed that it was wrong on the part of agent to buy the property himself, which he received from his principal for sale, he can do so only by disclosing the fact to the principal. If he does not disclose this fact to principal, the principal is entitled to avoid the transaction and may also recover any profit which the agent makes from such a transaction.

Case Study

Agent must avoid conflict of interest

McPherson v Watt (1877)

In this case, a solicitor was engaged to sell a property. He nominated his brother to purchase the property.

Court's decision: It was held that the sale could be set aside as the solicitor had allowed a conflict of interest to arise. The fact that a fair price was offered for the property, was immaterial.

f) Duty not to make secret profits

It is also the duty of the agent that he should not make a secret profit or gain from the agency. An agent is bound to disclose and account for all the profits he makes out of the agency.

Case Study

Agent can not make any secret profit.

Happisley v Knee Brothers (1905)

In this case, the defendants, the auctioneers, were engaged by the claimants for the sale of a certain property. The claimant agreed to pay them a certain commission and certain other expenses. While charging the full amount from the claimant, they did not deduct the discount received from printers and advertisers.

Court's decision: It was held that the defendants were bound to disclose to the claimant the discounts received by them.

Example

Cathy directs Annie, her agent, to buy a sports car from Kevin. Annie, through discussion with Kevin, finalises a price of £2,000. To purchase the car, Annie must take only £2,000 from Cathy and give this amount to Kevin. She should not take £2,500 from Cathy and give only £2,000 to Kevin, keeping £500 for herself.

If an agent accepts from the other party any commission or reward as an inducement to make the contract with him, this is considered to be a bribe and the contract is fraudulent.

Case Study
Agent can not make any secret profit

Boston Deep Sea Fishing & Ice Co Ltd v Ansell (1957)

Ansell was the managing director of Boston Deep Sea Fishing & Ice Co Ltd. Some goods were to be purchased on behalf of the company. Ansell accepted commission from a supplier to order goods from that supplier. On discovering this fact, the company removed him from the directorship.

Court's decision: An agent is in a fiduciary relationship with the principal. Ansell was held to be liable for breach of fiduciary duty. The company could recover the commission paid to him.

Where it is found that an agent has taken a bribe, the following civil remedies are available to the principal:

> To repudiate the contract with the third party
> To dismiss the agent without notice
> To refuse to pay any money owed to the agent or to recover such money already paid.
> To claim the amount of bribe from the agent
> To sue both the agent and the third party who paid the bribe, to recover damages for any loss.
> To seek prosecution of the agent under the Prevention of Corruption Act 1916.

Example

Keppel wanted to buy a flat to live in. He appointed Dennett as his agent to buy a residential flat for him. Dennett knew that Sunny wanted to sell his residential flat urgently as he was moving to another city for employment. He contacted Sunny and told him that he could arrange to sell Sunny's flat to Keppel if Sunny agreed to pay him £2,000. Sunny, as he wanted to sell the flat urgently, agreed to this and paid Dennett £2,000. Afterwards, Dennett arranged for the purchase of Sunny's flat by Keppel for £30,000.

Here Keppel can:
> repudiate the contract with Sunny to purchase the flat
> dismiss Dennett without notice
> refuse to pay any balance of agency commission payable to Dennett
> recover the commission paid to Dennett for undertaking this transaction of buying a flat for him
> claim £2,000, the amount of the bribe from Dennett
> seek prosecution of the agent under the Prevention of Corruption Act 1916

Diagram 8: Duties of an agent

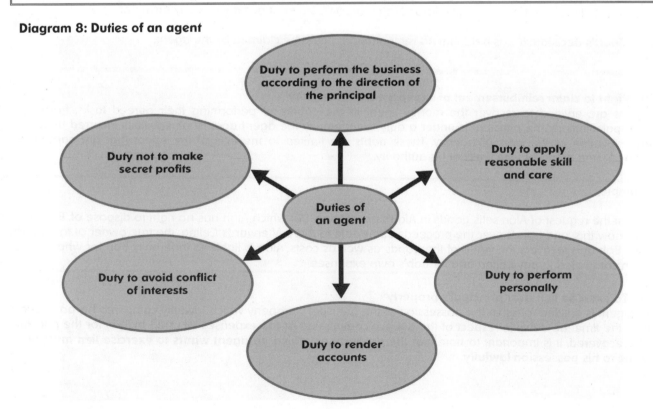

SYNOPSIS

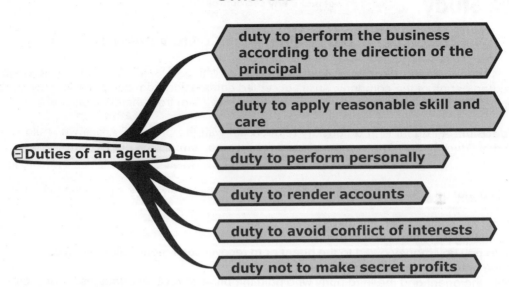

Duties of an agent
- duty to perform the business according to the direction of the principal
- duty to apply reasonable skill and care
- duty to perform personally
- duty to render accounts
- duty to avoid conflict of interests
- duty not to make secret profits

2. **The following are the rights of an agent:**

a) **Right to receive remuneration**

It is the right of an agent to receive, from his principal, the agreed remuneration. If remuneration was not agreed, he will be entitled to receive reasonable remuneration with regard to the nature of the work performed by him.

It may however be noted that the agent is entitled to receive his remuneration only after he has carried out his duties. Also, where the remuneration is payable in accordance with an expressed contract, no implied term can be added to or vary the terms of the expressed contract.

Case Study | Remuneration

Re Richmond Gate Property Co Ltd (1965)

In this case, the terms of agreement stated that the remuneration of the agent would be determined by the directors of the company. Actually, the directors had not decided on any payment.

Court's decision: It was held that no remuneration could be claimed by the agent.

b) **Right to claim reimbursement of expenses and indemnity**

Agents are entitled to recover the money spent in the course of performing their agreed tasks, from their principal. Similarly the principal is under a duty to indemnify the agent against all liabilities incurred by him in the execution of the work of agency. These rights are limited to the acts of the agent that are carried out properly and are within the limits of his authority.

Example

Bob at the request of Alan sells goods in Alan's possession, but which Alan has no right to dispose of. Bob does not know this, and hands over the proceeds of the sale to Alan. Afterwards Celina, the true owner of the goods, sues Bob and recovers the value of the goods as well as costs. Alan is liable to indemnify Bob for what he has been compelled to pay Celina and for Bob's own expenses.

c) **To exercise lien over principal's property**

An agent is entitled to retain the possession of the principal's property which lawfully came into his possession, until the time the debts in respect of the agency commission or the expenses incurred by him for the principal are recovered. It is important to note that **the property on which an agent wants to exercise lien must have come to his possession lawfully.**

> **Example**
>
> An agent has been appointed to purchase a piece of land on behalf of the principal. The agency commission agreed is £5,000. The agent purchases the land and gets it duly transferred in the principal's name. The principal pays the cost of land to the seller but does not pay the agent's commission. In this case, the agent can exercise lien on the property papers in his possession from the seller. However, he cannot forcefully take in his possession the car of the principal and exercise lien on it.

SYNOPSIS

- Rights of an agent
  - right to receive remuneration
  - right to claim reimbursement of expenses and indemnity
  - right to exercise lien over principal's property

3. The relationship between the agent and third parties

Once the agent creates a contract between the principal and a third party, prima facie he has no further responsibility. The contract entered into is between the principal and the third party and the agent has no personal rights or liabilities in relation to the contract.

This is generally applicable where the principal's existence is disclosed i.e. although the actual identity of the principal need not be mentioned, where the agent indicates that he is acting as an agent. Exceptionally, in the case of a disclosed relationship, an agent may be held personally liable as a party to contract where:

a) The agent has expressly accepted liability with the principal in order to encourage the third party to enter the contract.

b) The agent has signed the contractual agreement in his own name without clearly expressing that he is merely acting as a principal's representative.

> **Example**
>
> Where an agent signs a deed without having a power of attorney in his favour, he will be personally liable for it.

c) The agent acts for a nonexistent or fictitious principal, the other party is entitled to take action against the self-styled agent.

Where the principal is undisclosed, and also the agent fails to disclose the fact that he is acting for a principal to the third party, then the following consequences arise:

➤ The third party can enforce a contract against the agent. (Refer also to the rules governing the rights and liabilities between the undisclosed principal and the third party stated above).

➤ An undisclosed principal cannot ratify any contract made outside of the agent's actual authority.

  i.   Disclosed principal
  ii. Partially disclosed principal
  iii. Undisclosed **principals**

i   Disclosed Principal

When a person dealing with an agent knows that the agent is acting for a principal and knows of the principal's identity, then the principal is a disclosed principal. The contract made by the agent of a disclosed principal is between the principal and the third party. The agent neither has any liability under the contract nor has any right to enforce the contract. However, in some cases, agent may hold liable for the contract. Some of these cases are as follows:

➤ If, while signing any contractual document, the agent fails to indicate that he does so in a representative character on behalf of the principal.

Example

A company director, to avoid any personal liability, should sign "for and on behalf of ABC Ltd".

Where an agent signs a bill of exchange without sufficiently indicating that he or she is merely acting as the agent of the named principal, he or she will become personally liable.

➢ Where by custom of trade, the agent is liable.

Example

Advertising agents are liable to the media for contracts made on behalf of their clients.

➢ Where the principal is fictitious or non-existent, the agent himself is liable as the principal to the third party.

➢ Where the agent showed his intention to undertake personal liability.

Example

An agent signs a written contract in his own name i.e. without mentioning that he is acting on behalf of the principal.

ii   Partially disclosed principal

When a person dealing with an agent knows of the agency but does not know the name or identity of the principal, the relationship is a partially disclosed principal. If, at the time of the transaction, the other party has notice that the agent is or may be acting for a principal but does not have notice of the principal's identity, the principal is a partially disclosed principal.

Where a principal is a partially disclosed principal, then:

➢ Both the agent and the principal are considered parties to the contract, and both the partially disclosed principal and the agent have separate liability to, and may be sued by, a third party without joining of the other.

➢ Moreover, an agent of a partially disclosed principal is not relieved from liability by the fact that the third party obtains a judgement against the principal, where that judgement remains unsatisfied.

Example

Alan sold goods to Bob on behalf of a partially disclosed principal, John. However, all these goods were damaged. Bob sued John and recovered half the amount of the price paid, as compensation. However, Bob felt that his loss was more than what he recovered. Hence, he is entitled to sue Alan for the loss.

iii   Undisclosed principals

When a person dealing with an agent does not know the agent is acting for a principal, the principal is undisclosed. In other words, if, at the time of a transaction conducted by an agent, the other party has no notice that the agent is acting for a principal, the principal is an undisclosed principal. An undisclosed principal cannot ratify any contract made outside of the agent's actual authority

Undisclosed principal and agent

The rights and duties between the principal and the agent in an undisclosed principal situation are basically the same as in a disclosed principal situation. These mainly include:

➢ Rights and duties contained in the agency agreement or implied in the custom of the trade of the agent, to be supplemented by common law rules etc.

➢ The agent is to be treated as a trustee for the undisclosed principal of any goods or payments received or any benefit that he derives from the contract with the third party.

➢ He is liable to account to the principal for these goods, payments or benefits, as in the case of a disclosed principal.

Example

If an agent received additional commission from the party to whom he sold some goods on behalf of an undisclosed principal, then it is the agent's duty to account to the undisclosed principal for the commission.

Undisclosed principal and third party: Before the undisclosed principal may enforce any right or be liable for any obligation under a contract apparently made between the agent and the third party, two conditions have to be met:

➢ The agent must have actual authority, whether expressed or implied, to enter into the contract in question with the third party, and

➢ The agent, on entering into the contract with the third party, must have intended to act on behalf of the undisclosed principal, but not for his own benefit.

The rules governing the rights and liabilities between the undisclosed principal and the third party are as follows:

➢ An undisclosed principal **can sue and be sued** by the third party under the contract.

➢ An undisclosed principal **remains liable to a third party** for the price of goods sold or services provided under a contract between the agent and the third party. The undisclosed principal's liability will not be discharged even if he has made the payment to the agent with an instruction that the agent passes this amount to the third party, and the agent fails to pay the third party.

➢ If the third party is to take action for recovery of any amount payable to him under the contract, the third party must elect to sue either the undisclosed principal, if and when his identity is discovered, or the agent, within a reasonable time of discovering the fact. The third party cannot sue both the principal and the agent.

➢ The third party who commences **legal proceedings** against either agent or principal **may withdraw** them **before judgement is given and sue the other**.

➢ Once the third party obtains a judgement on breach of contract, he cannot sue the other even if the judgement is unsatisfactory.

Example

Alex enters into a contract with Glen to sell sports goods and afterwards discovers that Glen was acting as an agent for Peter. Who is liable to Alex for the price of goods sold? What are the rights of Alex against Glen and Peter?

Here,

➢ If Alex wants to take legal action for recovery of the price of goods he sold, he has to elect whether he wants to take action against Peter or against Glen. He cannot sue both of them.

➢ If Alex commences legal proceedings against Glen but then decides that action should be taken against Peter, he can withdraw the suit against Glen and commence the proceedings against Peter. However, this has to be done before judgement is given for the suit against Glen.

➢ If Alex files a suit against Peter and obtains judgement on it, he cannot, after that file a suit against Glen for the same matter.

SYNOPSIS

- The relationship between the agent and third parties
  - disclosed principal
  - partially disclosed principal
  - undisclosed principal
    - undisclosed principal and agent
    - undisclosed principal and third party

4. Termination of agency

a) Termination by act of parties

i. By revocation
An agency is terminated by the principal by revocation of the agent's authority. Revocation may be expressed or implied by the conduct of the principal or the agent respectively.

> **Example**
>
> Ajay empowered Bonny to let out his house. Afterwards, Ajay lets the house himself. This is an implied revocation of Bonny's authority.

ii. By lapse of time
If the agency is created for a stipulated time then, on the expiry of that time, the agency will come to an end.

> **Example**
>
> Matthew appointed a share broker to sell and purchase securities for him, for one year. At the end of the year, the agency will terminate automatically. If Matthew wants the share broker to continue working for him, he has to renew the agency contract.

iii. By performance
An agency comes to an end when the business of the agency is completed by due performance.

> **Example**
>
> Nancy appointed an agent to sell her house. The agent sold the house to Lily. The property papers were transferred in Lily's name and the price was paid by Lily to Nancy. As the business of the agency has been completed, the agency relationship comes to an end.

iv. Irrevocable agreements
In some cases, it is not possible to revoke an agency agreement. Where the agency is coupled with an interest it cannot be terminated unless the interest is also realised.

> **Example**
>
> Axe owes Rose a certain amount and cannot repay it. He makes Rose the agent for selling his estate and whatever amount is realised will be adjusted against the debt. Here, Axe cannot terminate the agency until the debt is repaid.

b) Termination by operation of law

i. By frustration
Like any other contract, the contract of agency is also subject to discharge by frustration. When a contract is terminated because it became impossible or illegal to perform the contract, this is called discharge of contract by frustration. In other words, where no impossibility existed at the time of formation of contract but subsequently it becomes impossible to fulfil the contract, then the contract is said to have been discharged by frustration.

> **Example**
>
> John appointed Toby as his solicitor. However, Toby was later found guilty in a case of misconduct according to the Law Society regulations. Hence, he was prohibited from acting as a solicitor for a period of five years. It therefore became illegal for Toby to continue working as a solicitor. Here, the contract of agency is discharged by frustration.

ii. By death or insanity of the principal or the agent
An agency comes to an end on the death or insanity of either the principal or agent.

iii. By bankruptcy of principal or agent
An agency comes to an end on the bankruptcy of either the principal or agent.

SYNOPSIS

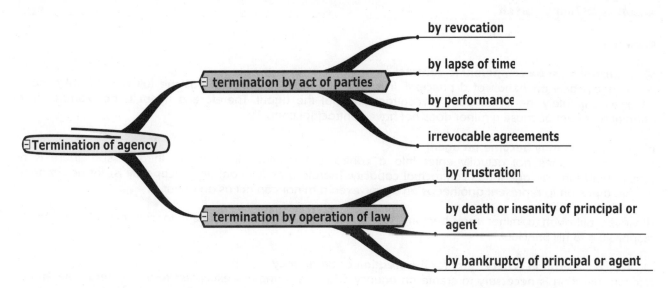

Diagram 9: Termination of agency

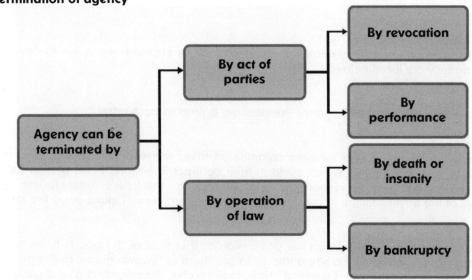

Test Yourself 5

Chan was appointed as an agent by Chris Tucker for the purpose of procuring him a house in Edinburgh. Chan bought a cottage for £20,000 in the name of Ms. Jane. He then purchased the house from Ms. Jane at a price of £24,000. He then sold this house to Mr. Tucker for £26,000. Later on, Mr. Tucker became aware of Chan's trickery and tried to recover the excess amount paid to Chan. Is he entitled to recover the excess amount paid to Chan? If yes, how much and why?

Answers to Test Yourself

Answer 1

a) Principal must be competent to contract

As an agent acts on behalf of a principal, it is essential that the principal has the full contractual capacity because, ultimately, he is the party to contract and not the agent. Therefore a minor is not competent to appoint an agent because a minor does not have contractual capacity.

b) Any person may become an agent

As the agent does not actually enter into a contractual relationship with the third person, there is no requirement that the agent has contractual capacity. Therefore as full contractual capacity is not necessary to enable a person to represent another as an agent, even a minor can act as an agent.

However, although a minor may become an agent, since he is incompetent to contract, he will not be responsible to his principal.

c) No consideration is necessary for the creation of an agency

No consideration is necessary to create an agency. (This is yet another exception to the general rule that an agreement without consideration is void). Normally, however, commission is paid to agents for their services.

Answer 2

There are various examples of agency relationships which may be encountered in day-to-day life.
Some forms of agency are listed below:

i. Partners

This is the most important example of agency. Partners are agents to each other.

ii. Del credere agents

A del credere agent is an agent who, for extra commission, takes the responsibility that the person with whom he contracts on behalf of the principal will perform their contract. Therefore, if this person fails to perform his contract, a del credere agent will be responsible to the principal for this failure. A del credere agent guarantees that, in the event of the buyer's failure to pay for the goods received, he will make good the loss.

iii. Factor

A factor is an agent who is entrusted with the possession and control of the goods to be sold by him for his principal. He has possession of the goods, authority to sell them in his own name, and a general discretion as to their sale. He may sell on the usual terms of credit, may receive the price and give a good discharge to the buyer. **His authority** to dispose of the goods **cannot**, even under common law, **be restricted** as against third parties by instructions privately communicated to him by his principal, because he has authority to carry out any transactions which are within the normal course of his business.

iv. Brokers

A broker is an agent who is employed by the principal to enter into contracts for sale or purchase on behalf of his principal. He is not given possession of the property. A broker can neither enter into contract in his own name nor can he receive payment. He cannot also cancel a contract which he has entered into on behalf of his principal.

Therefore a broker is an agent primarily employed to negotiate a contract between two parties. Where he is a broker for sale, he has no possession of the goods to be sold, and he does not have the authority which a factor enjoys. Nor has he the authority to sue in his own name on contracts made by him.

v. Auctioneer

An auctioneer is an agent to sell a property at a public auction. He is primarily an agent for the seller, but upon the property being sold / knocked down he becomes also the agent of the buyer. He has the authority to sell, but not to give warranties as to the property sold, unless expressly authorised by the seller.

vi. Estate agents

An estate agent is an intermediary who is entrusted with the job of finding a buyer for the principal's property. Estate agents are governed by Estate Agents Act 1979.

vii. Commercial agents

A commercial agent is a self-employed intermediary who has continuing authority in relation to the **sale or purchase of goods.** Continuing authority means that one-off sale transactions, such as an auction, are not included.

Answer 3

a) By agreement
The principal appoints an agent to perform a particular duty or to get it done from a third party. Such an appointment brings about a legal relationship between the principal and the agent. There are no legal requirements for appointing an agent, but in case the principal wants him to execute some duties where he will require some authority to execute those duties, the principal has to give this authority to him in writing e.g. power of attorney.

b) By ratification
An agency can be created by ratification. Ratification means an act by which the principal confirms the unauthorised acts of the agent. Where the principal elects to ratify the contract, this gives retrospective validity to the action of the self-styled agent.

It may, however, be noted that a ratification to be valid must satisfy certain conditions:

i. The agent must have acted on behalf of the principal
The first essential condition for ratification is that the agent must disclose that he or she was acting as an agent for the principal. If he does not want to disclose the identity of the principal, the principal must be a real person and identifiable. However, the principal cannot ratify if the agent acts in his own name and does not disclose the name of the principal.

ii. The principal must be in existence at the time of agent's act
This is very important because if the original contract between the principal and the agent does not exist then there cannot be any valid contracts based on it.

iii. The principal must have the legal capacity to contract
In order to be able to ratify a contract, a principal must be competent to contract both at the time the act was carried out and at the time of the purported ratification to make the contract.

iv. The contracts must be valid and legal
Ratification can be made only of lawful acts.

v. The principal must adopt the whole of the contract
Principals are not at liberty to pick and choose some parts of contracts for ratification, they must accept all of a contract's terms.

vi. Ratification must be within a reasonable time
What is reasonable time depends on the facts and circumstances of each particular case.

c) By estoppel
The principal may, by words or conduct, create an inference that an authority has been conferred upon an agent even though no authority has, in fact, been given. In such cases, if the agent's contract is within the limits of his apparent authority, although without actual authority, the principal will be bound to third parties by his agent's act.

The doctrine of apparent authority is really an application of the principle of estoppel. Estoppel means that a person is not permitted to resist an inference which a reasonable man would draw from his words or conducts.

However, there are certain important points as given below:

i. An agent himself cannot, by his representation, create an agency by estoppel. It must be made either by principal or by his authority.

ii. The third party must rely on the representation of the agent that he has the authority to act as an agent.

iii. It must not be in the knowledge of the third party that the agent has, in fact, no authority.

d) By necessity
The most common instance in which agency arises by operation of law is the case of agency of necessity. According to Halsbury, "Agency of necessity arises whenever a duty is imposed upon a person to act on behalf of another apart from contract, and in circumstances of emergency, in order to prevent irreversible injury. It may also arise where a person carries out the legal or moral duties of another in the absence of default of that other, or acts in his interest to preserve his property from destruction".

For agency of necessity to arise, some conditions have to be satisfied:

i.   **There has to be a genuine emergency:** A person may become an agent of necessity because of an emergency.
ii. **There must be no practical way of contacting the principal to obtain further instructions:** The circumstances have to be such that the person acting as an agent of necessity does not have enough time or opportunity to communicate with the principal.
iii. **The person seeking to establish the agency by necessity must have acted in good faith:** This means that he must act in the interest of the principal rather than in his own interest.

Answer 4

a) Apparent authority

Where a person represents a person or firm to third parties as having the authority to act as his agent without actually appointing the person / firm as his agent. In this case, the principal is bound for the actions of the agent. The person who has been given the apparent authority also does not take any effort to correct the impression to the third party about his status.

For e.g., Rex and James are partners in their business and Rex wants to sell his car which he mentions while having lunch with his business associates along with James. He also tells them that any information and action in this regard in his absence can be given to James. Rex left for New York in the coming week and James sold his car to the business associate with its accessories such as the car air conditioner and tape recorder. Rex did not want to part with these accessories but he cannot claim them back as he is responsible for James' action.

Where it has already been intimated by the principal to the third party that he has given the authority to his agent carry out the necessary transaction on his behalf, here the principal will be liable for the actions of the agent even if he has changed the agent or revised his duties unless he informs the third party of the changed structure.

For e.g., Holmes is a resort owner and Xando is his manager, who has been working with him for ten years, looking after the day-to-day administration, purchases, sales etc. Mr. Holmes has full faith in Xando, but due to Xando's ill health, he has to appoint a manager to handle purchases and sales, leaving Xando to look after administration. A supplier, Mr. Ken, who knows only Mr. Xando, supplies goods as he used to supply before and the new manager refuses to accept them as they are not up to the desired standard. Mr. Ken approaches Mr. Xando who receives the goods. The new manager does not approve the payment of the goods, so Mr. Ken takes up the matter with Mr. Holmes, who has to make the payment as Mr. Ken was not informed of the new arrangement. Mr. Holmes is therefore responsible for the behaviour of Xando and has to release Mr. Ken's payment.

b) Expressed authority

This is a type of actual authority which is bestowed by the principal upon the agent. The principal instructs the agent about his duties and what kind of performance is expected and for that what authority is required to accomplish the task is given to him.

For e.g., if the principal wants to sell his house and appoints an agent to sell it, he has to give the agent the authority to hold the keys of the house, to enter the house in his absence and to allow visitors or clients into the house. He also has to give the agent the authority to represent him before the lawyer to get the sale deed done and the duties & taxes paid. All the authority needed to sell the house is given to the agent but authority to represent the principal for his trade or business or sale of any other article is not given to him.

c) Implied authority

This is also a type of actual authority and increases the scope of expressed authority. Here, the third parties, if not informed about the authorities held by an agent by the principal, can assume that the agent must possess all the authorities that an agent in that position has.

For e.g. Jimmy owns a shop in Manchester, living himself in London, and visiting the shop occasionally. This shop is managed by Baron and he is in the habit of ordering goods from George in the name of Jimmy for the purposes of the shop, and paying for them out of Jimmy's funds with Jimmy's knowledge. Here, Baron has an implied authority from Jimmy to order goods from George in the name of Jimmy for the purposes of the shop.

In the case of **Watteau v Fenwick (1893)**, a hotel was taken over by new owners and most of the staff was absorbed in the new venture. The manager also was absorbed in the normal course of taking over. The new owners expressly gave him instructions to buy some consumable goods which also included cigarettes. According to the instructions of his new employer, the manager bought the goods from a third party. The payments for these goods were not made and so the third party sued the owners for payment as they were the manager's principal. The court held that the cigarettes were purchased in the normal authority given to the manager in his normal course of work. If the owners deny giving any such authority to their manager, then the onus of informing the third party about the limited authority given to the manager is on the owners.

Answer 5

Duties of an agent

a) Duty to perform the business according to the direction of the principal
The agent is bound by contractual obligation to carry out the agreed business in accordance with the principal's instructions in so far as these are lawful and reasonable. Even if he believes that non-compliance with the principal's instructions will be in principal's best interests, he should not disobey the instructions. However, any agent may refuse to perform an illegal act.

b) Duty to apply reasonable skill and care
Whether the relationship is contractual or gratuitous, an agent is bound to act with reasonable care and skill. The agent must use ordinary diligence in the discharge of his duties. If the agency is gratuitous, he is expected only to employ as much skill as he would in the conduct of his own affairs. A somewhat higher standard is required of him if the agency is for reward.

c)   Duty to perform personally
An agent owes a duty to perform the task himself. It is the duty of the agent not to delegate his functions to a sub-agent. An agent cannot, except with expressed or implied authorisation from the principal, delegate the work. The principal will not be bound by the act or contract of the sub-agent whose appointment is not sanctioned by the principal.

However, where it is usual to appoint a sub-agent by the ordinary custom of trade, a sub-agent may be employed.

d) Duty to render accounts
An agent who enters into any transaction on behalf of his principal is under an implied duty to render proper accounts to the principal. The agent is required to account for all money and other property received on behalf of his principal.

e) Duty to avoid conflict of interests
It is the duty of the agent to ensure that his personal interests do not come into conflict with those of his principal.

f)   Duty not to make secret profits
It is also the duty of the agent that he should not make secret profits or gains from agency. An agent is bound to disclose and account for all the profits he makes out of the agency.

If he accepts from the third party any commission or reward as an inducement to make the contract with him, this is considered to be a bribe and the contract is fraudulent. Where it is found that an agent has taken a bribe, the following civil remedies are available to the principal:
➢   To repudiate the contract with the third party
➢   To dismiss the agent without notice
➢   To refuse to pay any money owed to the agent or to recover such money already paid.
➢   To claim the amount of bribe from agent
➢   To sue both, the agent and the third party who paid the bribe, to recover damages for any loss.
➢   To seek prosecution of the agent under the Prevention of Corruption Act 1916.

Tucker had engaged Chan to be his agent and purchase a house for him. However, Chan purchased the house in Jane's name on behalf of Jane and then purchased it himself on behalf of Tucker, thereby enhancing the cost of the house and making a personal profit of £4,000. This act was not disclosed to Tucker.

Non-disclosure of profit of £4,000 made by Chan amounts to a breach of duty of Chan as an agent. Tucker is entitled to claim the secret profit of £4,000 made by Chan.

Quick Quiz

State whether the given statements are correct.

1. A minor cannot be appointed as an agent as he is not competent to contract.

2. A minor can appoint an agent.

3. No consideration is necessary for the creation of an agency.

4. An agency comes to an end on the death or insanity of either the principal or agent.

Answers to Quick Quiz

1 **Incorrect.** A minor can be appointed as an agent. However, he is not personally liable for any of his acts. The principal will be liable to the third parties for the acts of the minor agent.

2 **Incorrect.** A contract entered into by an agent, is ultimately between the principal and the third party. A minor is incompetent to contract. Hence he cannot be the principal and cannot therefore appoint an agent.

3 **Correct**, although normally commission is paid to an agent.

4 **Correct.**

Self Examination Questions

Question 1

When is an agent held to be personally liable for the contracts entered into by him while representing his principal?

Question 2

State the various situations where it is held that the agency is terminated.

Question 3

Explain the term undisclosed principal. What are the rights of the third party when the principal is undisclosed.

Question 4

John owned 5 acres of land. The land was in a remote area. John was not able to visit the place often. John came to know that people from a nearby locality had started using his land. John then decided to sell the land. He directed Mack to sell his estate. When Mack visited the estate, in order to look it over before selling it, he came to know about a mine on the estate which was unknown to John.

After coming back, Mack informed John that he wished to buy the estate for himself, but concealed from John the existence of the mine.

John sold the land to Mack and later came to know about the mine. He also discovered that Mack knew of the mine at the time he bought the estate.

What remedies are available to John against Mack?

Answers to Self Examination Questions

Answer 1

The agent does not act for himself but on the behalf of his principal. All the dealings or transactions with third parties are for the principal. Therefore the principal is responsible for and can be held liable for the contracts entered by the principal's agents.
However, there are certain exceptions to this rule, for e.g.:

i.   Where the principal's name is not disclosed by the agent, the third party sues the agent in the case of breach of contract.

ii. When it is mentioned in the contract that, for certain actions or deeds, the agent himself will be personally liable.

iii. A person acts as an apparent agent for his own personal benefit.

iv. Where the agent represents a non-existent principal and acts on behalf of him.

v.   Where the agent uses authority which is not given by the principal to him.

vi. When a person pretends to act as an agent of a principal, and the principal does not own up his actions.

vii. When an agent receives or pays money by mistake on behalf of the principal or attempts a fraud.

viii. When an agent breaches his authority.

ix. When an agent signs a negotiable instrument without disclosing his status.

Answer 2

The agency can be terminated in either of the ways given below:

a) Termination by the Parties

i.   By mutual agreement:
The parties can agree to end the relationship on terms mutually agreed upon. If the agency was formed for a particular purpose, it will automatically come to an end after the purpose is achieved or if the agency was engaged only for a definite time period, after the expiry of the period or due date the agency comes to an end.

ii. By the action of one of the parties
Either of the parties can terminate the agency by giving a notice of termination to the other. However, where the principal receives a notice from his agent for termination of agency when the task has not been fully completed and the principal may incur heavy losses due to the termination, then he can take action for damages.

iii. Irrevocable agreements
Where the agency is coupled with an interest it cannot be terminated unless the interest is also realised.

For e.g., Axe owes Lily a certain amount and cannot repay it. He makes Lily the agent for selling his particular estate and whatever amount is realised is to be adjusted against the debt. Here, Axe cannot terminate the agency until the debt is repaid.

b) Termination by operation of law

i.   By death of principal or agent
An agency relationship is created between a principal and an agent, so therefore the death of either of them brings an end to the agency.

ii. By insanity of either party
As stated above, the insanity of either of the parties brings the agency to an end.

iii. By frustration
Like any other contract, the contract of agency is also subject to discharge by frustration. When a contract is terminated because it became impossible or illegal to perform the contract, this is called discharge of contract by frustration. In other words, where no impossibility existed at the time of formation of contract but subsequently it becomes impossible to fulfil the contract, then the contract is said to be discharged by frustration.

For e.g. John appointed Toby as his solicitor. However, Toby was later found guilty of misconduct according to the Bar council regulations. Hence, he was prohibited from acting as a solicitor for a period of five years. It is therefore illegal for Toby to continue working as a solicitor. Here, the contract of agency is discharged by frustration.

iv. **By bankruptcy of principal or agent**
An agency comes to an end on the bankruptcy of the principal. However the bankruptcy of an agent will only result in the termination of the agency when it renders him unfit to act as an agent.

Answer 3

When a person deals with an agent and does not know that the agent is acting on behalf of a principal, in this situation it is said that the principal is undisclosed. In other words, if, at the time of a transaction conducted by an agent, the other party has no notice that the agent is acting for a principal, the principal is an undisclosed principal.

Undisclosed principal and third party
Before the undisclosed principal may enforce any right or be liable for any obligation under a contract apparently made between the agent and the third party, two conditions have to be met:

i.   The agent must have actual authority, whether expressed or implied, to enter into the contract in question with the third party, and

ii. The agent on entering into the contract with the third party must have intended to act on behalf of the undisclosed principal, but not for his own benefit.

The rules governing the rights and liabilities between the undisclosed principal and the third party are as follows:

1. The third party can sue an undisclosed principal under the contract.

2. The third party can hold an undisclosed principal liable for the price of goods sold or services provided under a contract between the agent and the third party. The undisclosed principal's liability will not be discharged even if he has made payment to the agent with an instruction that the agent passes this amount to the third party, if the agent fails to pay the third party.

3. If the third party has to take action for recovery of any amount payable to him under the contract, the third party must sue either the undisclosed principal, if his identity is discovered, or the agent, within a reasonable time of discovering the fact. The third party cannot sue both principal and agent at the same time.

4. The third party who commences legal proceedings against either the agent or the principal may withdraw them before judgement is given and sue the other.

5. Once the third party obtains a judgement on breach of contract, he cannot sue the other even if the judgement is unsatisfactory.

6. The third party can enforce the contract on the agent and the agent, in turn, can enforce the contract on the third party. In either of the cases, the principal can enter the picture to defend or to enforce the action for his behalf.

7. Where the third party has a special reason to contract with the agent as in irrevocable contracts, the principal cannot intervene. The third party has the right to set off debts against the agent.

Answer 4

It is the duty of the agent to ensure that his personal interests do not come into conflict with those of his principal. If there is any possibility of a conflict of interest, the agent must disclose this possibility to the principal. Upon full disclosure by the agent, it is for the principal to decide whether or not to allow the particular transaction. If an agent deals on his own account in the business of the agency, without first obtaining the consent of his principal and acquainting him with all material circumstances which have come to his knowledge on the subject, the principal may repudiate the transaction. If it is later comes to notice of the principal that any fact was dishonestly concealed from him by the agent, the principal may repudiate the transaction. Also, an agent should not make secret profits or gains from agency. An agent is bound to disclose and account for all the profits he makes out of the agency. If he accepts from the other party any commission or reward as an inducement to make the contract with them, this is considered to be a bribe and the contract is fraudulent.

In the given case, therefore, John can repudiate (reject) the sale.

SECTION D - THE FORMATION AND CONSTITUTION OF BUSINESS ORGANISATIONS

PARTNERSHIPS

Get through intro

This Study Guide deals with various provisions governing partnership relationships. In simple terms a partnership is the relationship between persons who have agreed to share the profits and losses of a business run by all or any one of them acting for and on behalf of them all.

IS349-017 www.imagesource.com

Whenever two or more persons come together to carry out any task, there is always the advantage of sharing and multiplying resources. However, there may also be differences of opinions.

The study of the provisions of partnership law helps you to understand what the advantages of entering into partnership are, as well as what problems may arise and how they can be resolved.

Questions from this topic are regularly asked in your examination. Hence you should devote considerable time to studying this Study Guide.

LEARNING OUTCOMES

a) Demonstrate a knowledge of the legislation governing the partnership, both unlimited and limited
b) Discuss how partnerships are established
c) Explain the authority of partners in relation to partnership activity
d) Analyse the liability of various partners for partnership debts
e) Explain the way in which partnerships can be brought to an end

Introduction

A partnership is the most basic form of collaborative business. Like a sole proprietorship, it has the advantage of simplicity. A partnership is defined as the relationship between persons who have agreed to share the profits and losses of a business run by all or any one of them acting for and on behalf of them all .The governing law is principally the Partnership Act 1890.

However, this traditional model is not equipped to meet the multi-competency, multi-disciplinary and multi-location requirements of today's global and domestic clients. The main shortcoming of a general partnership is the lack of limited liability for the partners. Due to the legal stipulation of unlimited liability among partners, partnerships are mostly restricted to family members and persons who know each other thoroughly. Hence a new form of partnership was introduced known as the limited liability partnership (LLP).

LLP is a form of partnership which has the characteristics of a company. LLP limits the liability in the case of a business failure or professional negligence litigation against the partner responsible. A limited liability partnership is a form of organisation which shields a partner's assets from limitless liabilities that may accrue from the omissions and commissions of other partners. This Study Guide covers the study of both these models of partnership.

1. Demonstrate a knowledge of the legislation governing the partnership, both unlimited and limited

[Learning outcome a]

Definition of 'partnership'

> **Definition**
>
> Section 1 of the Partnership Act (PA) 1890 defines partnership as "the relation which subsists between persons carrying on a business in common with a view of profit".

Definition of 'firm'

> **Definition**
>
> Persons who have entered into partnership with one another are collectively called a 'firm'.

Definition of 'partner'

> **Definition**
>
> Persons who have entered into partnership with one another are individually called 'partners'.

A partnership relationship is divided into three main types:

1.1. Standard partnership (governed by Partnership Act 1890)
1.2. Limited partnership (governed by Limited Partnership Act 1907)
1.3. Limited liability partnership (governed by the Limited Liability Partnership Act 2000)

1.1. Standard partnership: A standard partnership is a contractual association of two or more persons or entities to operate a common enterprise and to share in the management and profits and losses of the stipulated business. A standard partnership can be formed by either an agreement or by the conduct of the parties, express or implied. Written articles are not necessary to create a standard partnership, although they are advisable as a method of defining the rights and obligations that the partners intend to assume. As with a sole proprietorship, the advantages of a general partnership are the flexibility and simplicity of formation and operation.

> **Example**
>
> Jack and Jill buy 100 bales of cotton, which they agree to sell jointly. They agreed to share the profits and losses from the activity equally and jointly form a firm called cotton organisation. Jack and Jill are therefore partners of the firm cotton organisation.

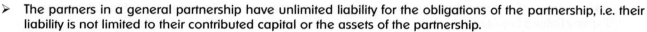

Liability of partners in a standard partnership

➢ The partners in a general partnership have unlimited liability for the obligations of the partnership, i.e. their liability is not limited to their contributed capital or the assets of the partnership.
➢ Every partner is an agent of the general partnership and can act on behalf of the business and bind the other partners.
➢ Each partner is jointly and severally liable for the debts and obligations of the business, including those arising from the wrongful actions of another partner.
➢ The liability in a standard partnership extends to the personal assets and benefits of the partners to the partnership.

1.2. Limited partnership: A limited partnership is a partnership formed by two or more persons / entities, one or more of whom are general partners and one or more of whom are limited partners. This form is unavailable if no one is willing to assume the risks of a general partner. The primary purpose of the limited partnership is to enable one or more persons to invest in a partnership without incurring the unlimited liability of a general partner. A limited partnership is more or less similar to a standard partnership except that the liability of one or more partners (but not of all partners) for a partnership debt is limited to their capital contribution in the partnership. The partnership must be registered with the Companies' Registry.

Example

Om, Jay and Jagdish entered into a partnership. All the partners contributed a capital of £20,000 and all are equal partners. However, the agreement provided that Jagdish's liability towards the partnership debts will be limited to the capital contributed by him i.e. £20,000. This is a limited partnership as the liability of one partner for a partnership debt is limited to his capital contribution to the partnership. Two of the partners have an unlimited liability.

Liability of partners in a limited partnership

➢ In a limited partnership, the liability of limited partners for the obligations of the partnership is limited to their investment.
➢ General partners, however, still have unlimited personal liability.
➢ The limited liability partner is not usually permitted to participate in the management of the business enterprise and cannot usually bind the partnership in any transaction. If he does so, he becomes liable as a general partner for all debts and liabilities incurred during the period of his participation.
➢ The firm is not affected in its working by a limited partner's death, bankruptcy or insanity.
➢ The limited partner can transfer his shares with the consent of the general partners.
➢ The limited partner cannot dissolve the partnership by notice.
➢ The general partners may introduce a new partner without consulting the limited partner. In the event of dissolution, the affairs of the firm are wound up by the general partners.

1.3. Limited liability partnership: The limited liability partnership ("LLP") is a form of partnership that differs from standard partnership and limited partnership in that all partners have a limited liability. Although the formalities in organising an LLP are sometimes more extensive than those for organising a limited partnership or standard partnership, the LLP has become a popular business structure, particularly for professional firms.

The essence of a limited liability partnership for practical purposes is as a vehicle to contain a partnership of any size where partners may be at risk from the careless or accidental negligence of a colleague.

Example

Partners in international accountancy firms would be protected from personal liability if a claim was successfully pursued by a major client.

Partners in a construction business would be protected if a new building collapsed, causing high level claims against them.

Liability of partners in a limited liability partnership

➤ Unlike partners of a general partnership or the general partner of a limited partnership, all partners of an LLP enjoy limited liability.

➤ Typically, the partners remain liable for contractual debts, but their liability with respect to the tort debts of the business is limited. Contractual debts refer to liability arising out of contract whereas tort debt is a liability due to negligence. Partners of a LLP enjoy limited risk arising from the careless or accidental negligence of a colleague.

➤ All partners may participate in the control of the business and still maintain their limited liability, unlike the limited partners of a limited partnership.

Regardless of which type, all partnerships are considered to be an aggregate of their partners, rather than a separate entity. Unlike corporations, in which stock can be freely traded (assuming a willing buyer), a partner involved in the management of a partnership can only transfer his interest with the consent of the other partners. If the mutual consent to form a partnership breaks down, the partnership breaks down as well.

Tips

The liability of a partner in a limited liability partnership is limited to the extent of their capital contribution.

Diagram 1: Types of partnerships

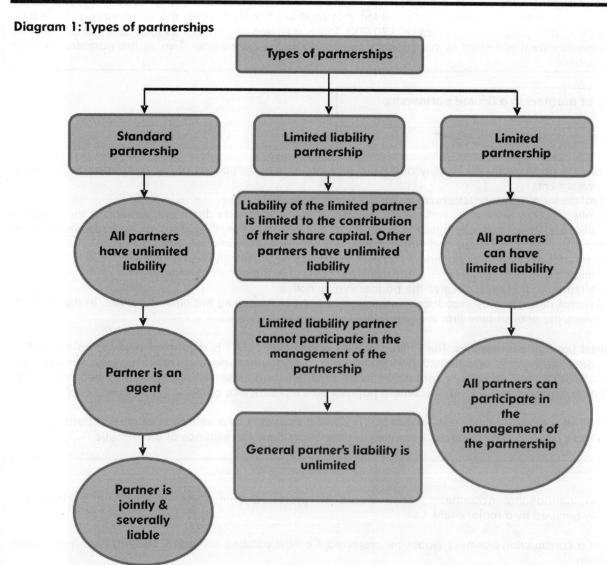

SYNOPSIS

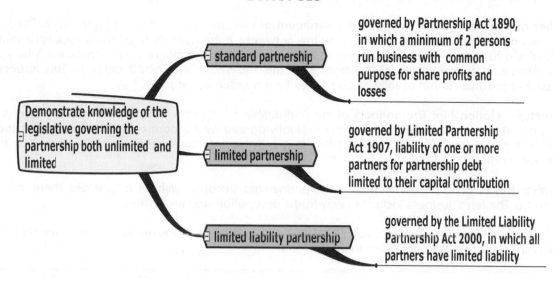

standard partnership — governed by Partnership Act 1890, in which a minimum of 2 persons run business with common purpose for share profits and losses

Demonstrate knowledge of the legislative governing the partnership both unlimited and limited

limited partnership — governed by Limited Partnership Act 1907, liability of one or more partners for partnership debt limited to their capital contribution

limited liability partnership — governed by the Limited Liability Partnership Act 2000, in which all partners have limited liability

---

Test Yourself 1

Explain the liability of the members of partnerships formed under the following Acts:
a) Partnership Act 1890
b) Limited Partnership Act 1907
c) Limited Liability Partnership Act 2000

(December 2003)

For easy understanding, this Study Guide is divided into two sections. The first section deals with a standard partnership and the other section deals with limited liability partnership.

Standard Partnership

In general terms, a partnership is where a business is formed and run by a number of joint owners i.e. partners. These partners:

➢ share the responsibility of running the business
➢ agree on any decisions made and actions taken
➢ share profits and losses as agreed
➢ share any liabilities that are accumulated regardless of which partner was originally responsible for generating the debt

After sole-traders, a partnership is the second most popular type of business and is more commonly associated with professional services such as accountants, solicitors and doctors.

It is also common in partnerships for each partner to specialise in a specific area of the business.

Example

In an accountancy service, one partner may specialise in book-keeping, another partner may specialise in financial advice and taxation, and so on...

Definition of partnership

Definition

Section 1 of the Partnership Act (PA) 1890 defines a partnership as "the relation which subsists between persons carrying on a business in common with a view of profit".

In relation to this definition, there are some important points that need to be noted, as under:

a) **Number of members:** There have to be a **minimum of two** members to form a partnership. The standard **maximum** number of members permitted by law is **twenty**. If the number of partners exceeds twenty, they are expected to form a registered company. However, some professional partnerships, such as solicitors, accountants and surveyors etc. are exempt from this maximum limit of 20 partners. This is because a professional practice cannot usually be carried on by a registered company.

b) **Contractual relationship:** The partners of the partnership are contractually bound with the firm and with each other. The terms of the partnership are mutually agreed by the partners and hence, unless the terms conflict with the express provisions of PA 1890, they may be enforced by the law in the same way as other contractual terms.

c) **Business:** This is an essential element of a partnership because without a business there can be no partnership. The term business includes every trade, occupation and profession.

➢ A business requires the existence of some activity. If two or more persons are merely the joint owners of the property then this fact does not make them partners.

Example

Mary and Matt are the joint owners of a flat given on rent. They share the amount of rent equally. Mary and Matt are not partners in this case because they do not carry out any joint activity.

Case Study

Merely receiving a share in profits without jointly carrying out an activity is not sufficient to form partnership

Britton v Commissioner of Customs & Excise (1986)

In this case, a wife received a share of the profit of her husband's business. It was claimed that she had become partner of the firm as she received a share in the partnership's profit.

Court's decision: It was held that the wife was not a partner in the business as the wife receiving the husband's share of the profit was purely a domestic arrangement.

➢ It is not necessary that the business should be permanent and long-lasting. A single commercial transaction may constitute a business.

Example

If two solicitors, who are not partners, are appointed jointly to plead a case and they agree to divide the profits, they become partners in respect of that particular case.

---

d) **Profit sharing:** The business must be carried on with a view to profit. Charitable or mutual benefit schemes are not considered to be partnerships.

Diagram 2: Partnerships

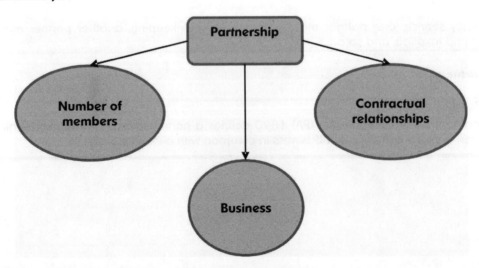

Advantages of a partnership

➤ The workload can be shared between partners
➤ Each partner may specialise in their own area of the business
➤ More finance can be raised than, say, sole-traders, due to more owners investing in the business
➤ Due to the business being generally larger than a sole-trader, it has a better chance at generating other sources of finance e.g. bank loans, etc.
➤ There are no legal formalities to complete prior to starting the business
➤ Partners can cover each other during times of absence, e.g. holidays or illness

SYNOPSIS

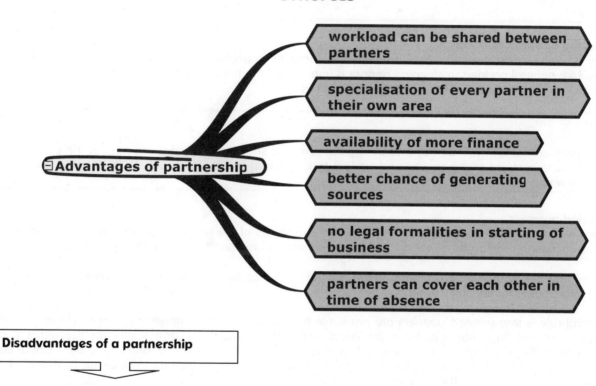

Disadvantages of a partnership

➤ Profits are shared between partners
➤ Decisions may take time to be reached due to disagreements between partners
➤ Partners are equally responsible for liability even to the extent of their personal wealth in Standard Partnership Act (stated by The Partnership Act, 1890)
➤ Any action or decision based on the business is legally binding on all partners

SYNOPSIS

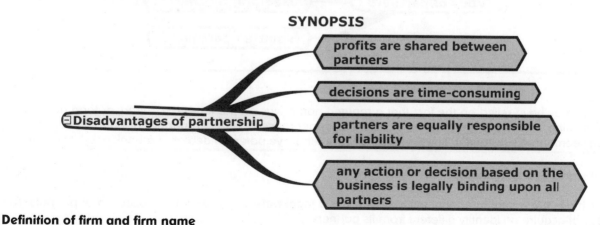

Definition of firm and firm name

Definition

Persons who have entered into partnership with one another are collectively called a firm, and the name under which their business is run is called the firm-name.

Types of partners: There are two main types of partners:

a) **General partners**

General partners **invest** in the business, **take part in running** it and **share in its profits**. Each general partner is **fully liable for any debts** that the **partnership** may have. This means that they could lose more than their initial investment in the business if it gets into difficulty, and that their personal assets could be at risk. Every partnership must have at least one general partner.

Example

Adams, Barker, and Connell form a general partnership with ownership interest of 40%, 30%, and 30%, respectively. They will share all the income, losses, or capital gains of the partnership business in the proportion of 40:30:30 respectively. They trust one another and know that any one of them can bind them all to a transaction.

---

b) **Sleeping or dormant partners**

Sleeping partners invest money in the business and share in its profits, but do not take part in running the business. Like general partners, a sleeping partner is liable to all the third parties for the partnership's debts. It is immaterial that his identity is not known to the third parties.

Example

Mike is a partner in a firm with James and Danny. He takes no share in the active business of the partnership, but is entitled to a share of the profits, and subject to a share in losses. Here, Mike is a sleeping partner or dormant partner.

---

c) **Salaried partners**

A **partner** who has no right to participate in the profits and losses of the partnership and who is paid salary by the firm is a salaried partner He, generally, has no voting rights in relation to the partnership.

Any act carried out by the salaried partner in the normal course of business is binding on all the partners and they are jointly liable for the firm's debts.

The general rule is that salaried partners are not liable for the debts of the partnership, since they are merely employees and not 'true' partners. However, a salaried partner would become liable for the debts if he presented himself as a partner to a creditor, or knowingly allowed others to do so, and where the creditor can show that he relied on the representation that the salaried partner was a partner in deciding to make credit available to the firm (section 14(1) Partnership Act 1890).

SYNOPSIS

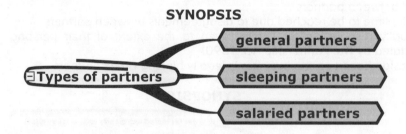

Example

The creditor may have relied on the fact that a reputed name was on the firm's letterhead, or loan application form, in deciding whether to grant the firm credit. The appearance of an extra partner or partners can make a small firm seem more substantial, and therefore a more attractive potential debtor to a bank or other creditor.

The legal status of a partnership

A partnership is not a separate legal entity i.e. it is not a legal person; it is merely a collection of partners. The firm does not acquire an identity different from its partners.

However, according to the provisions of Section 4 of the Partnership Act 1890, the business can be carried out under the firm's name. Therefore, if the partnership is the claimant or defendant in legal proceedings, it sues or is sued in the name of the firm.

Also the procedural Rules of the Supreme Court, Order 81, as stated in the Civil Procedure Rules 1998, provides that legal action may be taken by and against the partners in the firm's name. Any awards against the partnership may be executed against any of the individual partners.

Illegal partnership

If a partnership is formed to carry out an illegal purpose then it is an illegal partnership.

Example

John and Matt formed a partnership to carry out the business activity of smuggling weapons and selling them. This is an illegal partnership as the purpose is illegal.

If a partnership carries out a legal purpose in an illegal manner it is an illegal partnership.

Example

John and Matt formed a partnership to carry out the business of selling weapons with the proper license and approvals. However, they sold weapons to minors who are not licensed to use these weapons. As the business is carried out in an illegal manner, this is an illegal partnership.

In such situations, no rights attached to the partnership are allowed to the so-called partners by the court. However, the innocent third parties, who were not aware of the illegality, can recover any damages suffered by them from the persons involved in the illegal partnership.

Example

Jack and Ted formed a partnership to run a construction business. Some customers booked flats in one of their schemes and paid an advance on booking of £50,000 each. However, these flats were constructed on land which was not registered in the name of the partnership. The lawful owner of the land took objection and hence the ownership of the flats could not be transferred to the customers However, the customers were not aware of the fact that the partnership was illegal as the partners forcefully took possession of the land from the landlord. Therefore, these customers can recover any damages suffered by them.

According to the provisions of section 716 of the Companies Act 1985, partnerships which consist of more than 20 persons are generally not considered to be lawful. However, certain professional partnerships, such as solicitors, accountants and surveyors etc. are exempt from this maximum limit.

Test Yourself 2

Ian and Steve have formed a partnership in order to run a restaurant. It is stated in the partnership agreement that all the necessary utensils and equipment required for the business will be provided by Rob. It is also stated in the agreement that, if any partner needs to incur any liability of more than £5,000, he should first consult with the other partner. Even though all the initial capital of the firm has been contributed by Ian, he does not actively participate in the business and also does not visit the place of the business very often. Steve works full-time for the firm and receives a salary.

Steve has ordered utensils worth £8,000 from Ted. Advise Ian what he should do in this situation.

SYNOPSIS

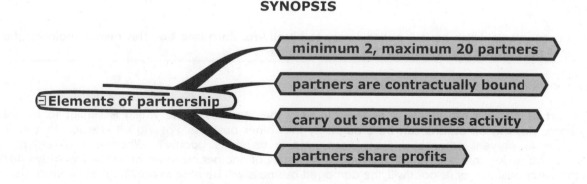

2. Discuss how partnerships are established

[Learning outcome b]

Important points to remember with regard to the formation of a partnership:

➢ The formation of a partnership requires a voluntary "association" of persons who "co-own" the business and intend to conduct the business for profit.

➢ Persons can form a partnership by written or oral agreement, and the partnership agreement often governs the partners' relations to each other and to the partnership firm.

➢ The partnership comes into existence from the date of agreement and not from the date on which the firm starts trading.

➢ The term person generally includes individuals, corporations, and other partnerships and business associations. Accordingly, some partnerships may contain individuals as well as large corporations. Family members may also form and operate a partnership.

➢ Certain conduct of persons may lead to the creation of an implied partnership. Generally, if a person receives a portion of the profits from a business enterprise, the receipt of the profits is evidence of a partnership.

Example

Two brothers living together inherited a property on the death of their father. They sold the property for £15,000 and invested the amount in a new business. There was no formal agreement but it appears that they intended to share profits. Hence the relationship between the two brothers in the new business is that of a partnership.

➢ If, however, a person receives a share of profits as repayment of a debt, wages, rent, or an annuity, such transactions are considered "protected relationships" and do not lead to a legal inference that a partnership exists.

Example

Alex and Bahaman started a business in partnership. Alex's father contributed £5,000 towards their business. It was decided that, every year, the firm would give £500 to Alex's father. In this case, Alex's father is not a partner even though he has invested funds in the partnership. The nature of receipts received by Alex's father is of annuity hence he is not a partner of the firm.

Tips

The term **annuity** refers to any fixed payments over a specified period of time.

The firm's name

A partnership is merely a group of individual partners. However, according to the provisions of Section 4 of the Partnership Act 1890, the business can be carried out under the firm's name. Therefore if the partnership is the claimant or defendant in legal proceedings, it sues or is sued in the name of the firm.

A partnership may use any name of its choice. Partnerships cannot use the word 'Limited' or its abbreviation 'Ltd' in its name although they may, and frequently do, uses the name 'Company' or its abbreviation 'Co'.

Example

A firm of accountants which have 5 partners may call itself **'Ira, Zara and Co'**. This merely indicates that the names of all the partners are not included in the firm's name.

However, there are **two restrictions** as follows:

a) **The tort of passing off:** Where a partnership uses the business name which is similar to an existing business, passing off actions can be brought by that other business. Passing off is a tort that entitles a business to prevent other businesses from unfairly using its goodwill. When a business misleads prospective buyers into believing that its goods are those of another business, and thereby causes damage to the other business or its goodwill, the damaged business will be able to prevent that conduct. The court may grant an injunction stopping the partnership from using the name.

Example

Rosy runs a boutique selling ready-made clothes called "Make over". She represents that her shop is actually a branch of a branded ready-made clothes company also called "Make over". However, her business is actually not in any way related to this company. Here, she is trying to use the goodwill of the company to promote her own business.

Here, the company may prevent her from running her business in the name "Make over" by applying to the court for an injunction.

Case Study The court may grant injuction stopping the partnership from using the name

Croft v Day (1843)

In this case, two people called "Day" and "Martin" set up a business making boot polish, with the intention of taking business from a well-known boot polish manufacturer called Day and Martin.

Court's decision: The court granted an injunction to the manufacturer to prevent the new partnership from trading under the name "Day and Martin".

b) **The Business Names Act 1985**: The provisions are explained below:

➢ The Business Names Act 1985 requires that, where a partnership is trading under names other than those of its partners, the partnership has to display the names of individual partners and an address at which documents can be served.

➢ This information must be displayed both at business premises and on business stationery. It must also be supplied in writing at the request of any person with whom the firm is doing business.

➢ For firms with more than 20 partners, the individual names need not be listed on each document, but a list must be available at the firm's principal place of business.

➢ According to provisions of this Act, in order to use certain words in the name, the approval of the Secretary of State is required. Some examples of these words are Royal, Prince, Queen, International etc.

➢ Criminal sanctions are imposed for failure to comply with the provisions of BNA, 1985.

Test Yourself 3

Does a firm have to publish any details of the partnership?

SYNOPSIS

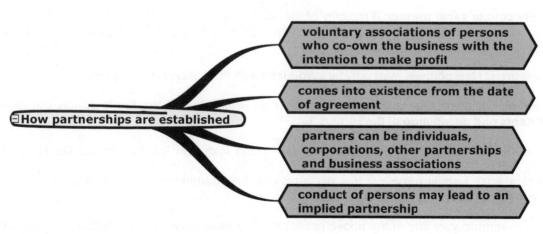

3. Explain the authority of partners in relation to partnership activity
[Learning outcome c]

Subject to any agreement expressed or implied between the partners, the interests of partners in the partnership property and their rights in relation to the partnership must be determined by the provisions of the Partnership Act 1980:

1. **Profit sharing:** All the partners are entitled to a share in the capital and profits of the business, according to the agreed terms. They must also contribute towards the losses, whether of capital or otherwise, sustained by the firm. In the absence of a contrary agreement, the profits and losses are shared equally.

Example

If there are two partners in the business and they earn a profit of £20,000, they may share the profits equally i.e., £10,000 each or in any other agreed proportion, say one fourth and three fourths i.e. £5,000 and £15,000

If the partners decide to share profits in a certain proportion; then losses are also to be shared in the same proportion.

2. **Indemnity:** The firm must indemnify every partner in respect of payments made and personal liabilities incurred by him or her:
   - in the ordinary and proper conduct of the business of the firm, or
   - for anything done out of necessity to preserve the business or property of the firm

3. **Interest on capital:** A partner making, for the purpose of the partnership, any actual payment or advance beyond the amount of capital that he or she has agreed to subscribe is entitled to interest at a fair rate (usually 5%) from the date of the payment or advance.

4. **Active part in management:** Every partner may take part in the management of the partnership business; however, as discussed above, sleeping partners invest money in the business and share in its profits, but do not take part in running the business.

5. **Change in business:** Any difference arising due to ordinary matters connected with the partnership business may be decided by a majority of the partners, but no change may be made in the nature of the partnership business without the consent of all existing partners.

6. **Access to records and books of accounts:** The partnership books are to be kept at the place of business of the partnership, or the principal place, if there is more than one, and every partner may, when he or she thinks fit, have access to and inspect and copy any of them.

7. **Majority cannot expel partner:** A majority of the partners cannot expel any partner unless a power to do so has been conferred by express agreement between the partners and the power is exercised in good faith.

8. **New partners:** New partners must only be introduced with the consent of all existing partners.

9. **Dissolution:** On dissolution, any partner can insist on **realisation of the firm's assets, payments of the firm's debts and distribution of the surplus.**

10. **Good faith:** The partnership relationship is one of good faith and The Partnership Act 1890 specifically requires that-
    - **Disclosure:** Each partner must give true accounts and full information to the other partners or their legal representatives (s 28).

If the partners want to vary any of the above provisions they must draw up their own partnership agreement specifying what the rights, duties and liabilities of the partners are. Although the Partnership Act 1890 provides a default code it is advisable for the partners to draft their own partnership agreement.

Case Study | The Duty of partners to disclose

Law v Law (1905)

One of the partners of a partnership firm offers to sell his share in the partnership to another partner of the firm. The other partner accepted his offer. However, the first partner later came to know that the purchasing partner had not disclosed to him certain partnership assets. He took action against the purchasing partner to have the contract set aside.

Court's decision: It was held that the purchasing partner had breached the duty of disclosure therefore the agreement could be set aside.

> **Account:** A partner must account for any profit he makes from using the firm's name, connection etc (s 29).

Case Study | The Duty of partners to account

Bentley v Craven (1853)

Craven and Bentley ran a sugar refinery business in partnership. Craven purchased the sugar on his own account and sold it with a profit to the partnership. He did not disclose his interest in the transaction to the other partner.

Court's decision: It was held that Craven was in breach of s 29 and partnership was entitled to recover the profits earned by Craven in the transaction.

> **Not to compete:** A partner must account for any profit made in a competing business where the competing business is carried on without the consent of the partners (s 30).

Case Study | The duty of partners not to compete

Glassington v Thwaites (1823)

A partnership firm was engaged in the production of a morning newspaper. One of the partners was engaged in the production of an evening newspaper.

Court's decision: The partner was held to account for the profit he earned from the publishing of the evening paper.

Diagram 3: Authority of partners in relation to partnership activity

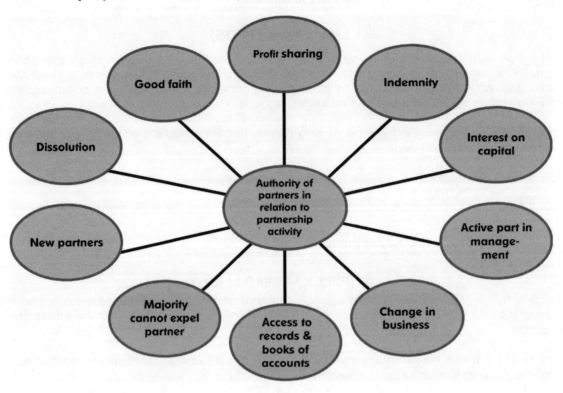

Test Yourself 4

In 1995, Frank, Greg, Hank and Ivan formed an engineering partnership. Last year, Frank sold his share in the partnership to the other members. Frank has now found out that, prior to the sale, the others had entered into a very valuable contract without informing him. The future profits from that contract should have ensured that the value of his share in the partnership was considerably more than the price he actually received.
Furthermore, last year, Greg bought some land and later sold it to the partnership without revealing that he was the true owner of the land. He made a personal profit of £50,000 on the deal.
It has now emerged that Hank is running a business in direct competition to the partnership.

Required:

Analyse the above situation from the point of view of the duties owed between partners and advise the various parties as to any legal action that they may take or that might be taken against them.

(June 2003)

SYNOPSIS

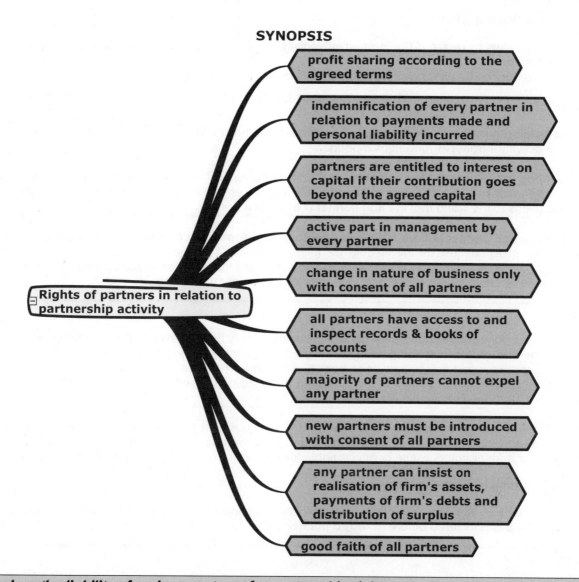

Rights of partners in relation to partnership activity

- profit sharing according to the agreed terms
- indemnification of every partner in relation to payments made and personal liability incurred
- partners are entitled to interest on capital if their contribution goes beyond the agreed capital
- active part in management by every partner
- change in nature of business only with consent of all partners
- all partners have access to and inspect records & books of accounts
- majority of partners cannot expel any partner
- new partners must be introduced with consent of all partners
- any partner can insist on realisation of firm's assets, payments of firm's debts and distribution of surplus
- good faith of all partners

4. Analyse the liability of various partners for partnership debts

[Learning outcome d]

Joint and several liabilities (s9)
A partner in a firm is jointly liable with the other partners for all debts and obligations of the firm incurred while he or she is a partner.

Example

Ron and Todd are the partners of a partnership firm running a garage. A car belonging to a customer, which had been brought to the garage for wheel alignment, was damaged badly due a short circuit at the garage. So both Ron and Todd will be jointly liable for the damages to be paid to the customer.

After a partner's death, his or her estate is also severally liable in the course of administration for those debts and obligations, so far as they remain unsatisfied, but subject to the prior payment of his or her separate debts.

Liability for wrongs (s10)
Where, by any wrongful act or omission of any partner acting in the ordinary course of the business of the firm, or with the authority of his co-partners, loss or injury is caused to any person not being a partner in the firm, or any penalty is incurred, all the partners of the firm are jointly and severally liable to the same extent as the partner so acting or omitting to act.

Liability for holding out (s14)

➢ Holding out refers to where a non-partner advertises himself or alternatively is advertised to the world as being a partner.
This holding out can be either expressed and / or implied.

Example

Expressed holding out: This would occur where a non-partner has his name on the company letterhead or if a non-partner actively introduces himself as a partner.

Implied holding out: Where the firm permits a non-partner to 'sign off' on company accounts or documents or where a non-partner has an office next to the partner's or even enjoys the perks of the true partners; these are implicit indications to the world that the non-partner is actually a partner.

In this case, the **non-partner will be held to be liable as a partner**. The **true partners will also be liable** for the non-partner's actions just as they would be for the actions of a true partner. This is provided that the relevant third-party was reasonably unaware of the non-partner's true position in the business and the conduct on the non-partner could be described as in the ordinary course of the business.

Example

George, a retired partner, although no longer a partner in the firm, holds himself out as still being a partner. He also allows the firm to continue using old stationery which bears his name as a partner. George's repeated appearances could suggest that he has gone back to work and, if he were to continue to involve himself in the business of the firm to such an extent that third parties believed he had not really retired at all, he could incur liability under s 14 of the Partnership Act 1890.

➢ Note that where, after a partner's death, the partnership business is continued in the old firm-name, the continued use of that name, or of the deceased partner's name as part thereof shall not, of itself, make his executors or administrators estate or effects liable for any partnership debts contracted **after his death**.

Liability of incoming and retiring partner (s17)

a) A new partner admitted to an existing firm is liable for debts incurred only after he becomes a partner. He is not liable for debts incurred before he was a partner unless he agrees to become liable.

Example

Mark and Sam formed a partnership firm to run a business activity. Rob joined them four months after the formation of the partnership. As a result, Rob will only be liable for the debts incurred after his joining. He is not liable for debts incurred before he was a partner unless he agrees to become liable.

➢ The **partner who retires** is still **liable for any outstanding debts incurred while he was a partner, unless the creditors have agreed to release him** from liability. He is also liable for debts of the firm incurred after his retirement if the creditor knew him to be the partner and was not given notice of his retirement.

Case Study

Tower Cabinet v Ingram (1949)

Cabinet and Ingram formed a business which was called 'Merry's'. The partnership dissolved, however, Cabinet continued to run the business alone, under the same name, even after the dissolution of the partnership. After one year, the claimant received an order from Merry's to supply goods. This was the first order to the claimant from Merry's. The order was on the old letterhead, i.e. Merry's, including the name of Ingram as well as Cabinet. Cabinet used the old letterhead without obtaining permission from Ingram. The claimant supplied the goods according to the order but Cabinet did not pay for the goods. So the claimant went to court and got the judgement against Merry's. He then sought to enforce this judgement against Ingram.

Court's decision: It was held that Ingram was not liable. The judgement was based on the fact that:
1) As it was the first transaction of the claimant with Merry's, the claimant was not aware that Ingram was a member of the partnership and so Ingram was not under the obligation to give notice of his retirement to the claimant.
2) Ingram had not knowingly allowed Cabinet to hold him as a partner under s14 of the Partnership Act 1890.

Partnership property (s20)

A partnership property is owned collectively by all the partners. A personal property of any one of the partners, even though used by the partnership firm, remains the personal property of that partner.

> **Tips**
>
> Property belonging to an individual partner does not become the firm's property simply by being used for the purpose of the partnership.

According to section 20 of the Partnership Act 1890, all property originally brought into the partnership stock or subsequently acquired, by purchase or otherwise, on account of the partnership is partnership property.

Whether a particular property belongs to the partnership or not depends upon the circumstances of the case.

Case Study   Partnership property

Miles v Clarke (1953)

Clarke ran a photography business as a sole trader. He then decided to run the business in partnership with Miles. According to the agreement of the partnership, it was decided that profit would be divided equally among the partners. After the partnership was dissolved, there was a dispute among the partners regarding the ownership of the assets used by the partnership.

Court's decision: The court decided that only consumable stock in trade could be considered partnership property. The ownership of the lease of the business premises and other plant and equipment remained the personal property of the partner, Clarke, who had introduced them into the business.

Distinguishing between partnership property and personal property is essential for the following reasons:

i   **Partnership property must be used exclusively for partnership purposes:** The partners should not use the partnership property for their personal use or personal profit. If this is done by the partners they would be liable to account to the partnership for any profit made.

ii **Any increase in the value of partnership property belongs to the partnership:** If there is any increase in the value of the partnership property then such increased value will be divided between the partners.

iii **Any increase in the value of personal property belongs to the person who owns it:** If there is any increase in the value of the personal property, the increase will belong to the person who owns the property. Other partners cannot share this amount.

iv **On the dissolution of the firm, partnership property is used to pay debts before personal property:** As provided by s 39, when the partnership firm is dissolved the partnership property is used to pay debts before personal property.

Test Yourself 5

In 2003 Hal, Ina and Jo formed a partnership to engage in property development. Hal introduced £50,000 into the partnership and Ina and Jo each put £250,000 into the business. The partnership agreement expressly stated that the partnership business was to be limited exclusively to the purchase, development and sale of property in London.

Hal was the real expert in improving houses but, as he had no prospect of raising any more money it was agreed between the partners that, although they would share profits equally, his maximum contribution and liability for any partnership debts would be fixed at his original input of £50,000.

In January 2004, Ina withdrew £25,000 from the partnership's bank, drawn on its overdraft facility. She told the bank that the money was to finance work on partnership property but in fact she used the money to pay for an extension to her own house. In March, Jo entered into a £250,000 contract on behalf of the partnership to buy a derelict house in Scotland. She thought they could make a large profit on it but the others refused to have anything to do with the purchase. In the event, the Scottish property proved so dilapidated that it could not be restored, resulting in a consequential loss of £100,000. By May, the partners realised that their business had proved disastrous and that it had realisable assets of only £200,000 and debits of £400,000.

Required:

Analyse the scenario from the perspective of partnership law, advising the parties as to their various rights and liabilities.

(June 2005)

SYNOPSIS

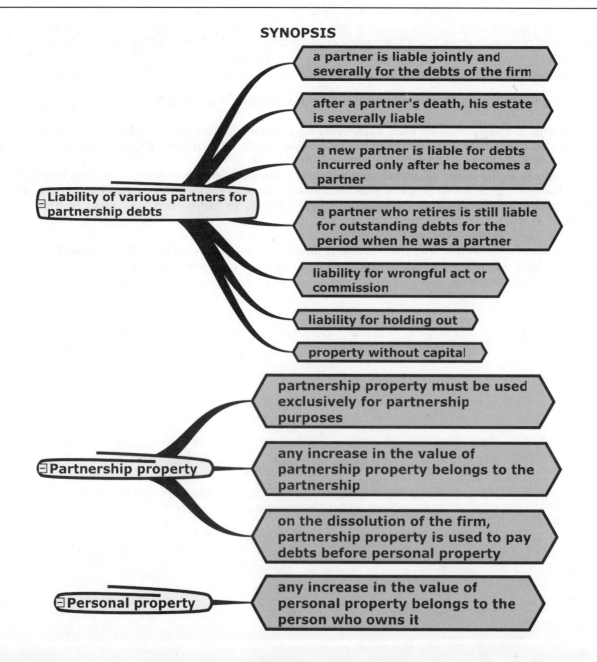

5. Explain the way in which partnerships can be brought to an end

1. **Dissolution by expiration or notice**

   Subject to any agreement between the partners a partnership is dissolved:

   a) If entered into for a fixed term, by the expiration of that term.

   b) If entered into for a single venture or undertaking, by the termination / completion of that venture or undertaking.

   c) If entered into for an undefined time, by any partner giving notice to the other or others of his intention to dissolve the partnership. In this case, the partnership is dissolved as from the date mentioned in the notice as the date of dissolution, or, if no date is mentioned, from the date of the communication of the notice.

2. **Dissolution by bankruptcy, death or charge**

   a) Subject to agreement between the partners, a partnership can be dissolved by the partners, by the death or bankruptcy of any partner. However, the partnership can continue as before by giving the share to the representative of the deceased partner.

   b) If a partner suffers his share in the partnership to be charged under the Act for his separate debts, his partners may dissolve the partnership.

3. **Dissolution by illegality of partnership**

   A partnership will be dissolved if an event occurs that makes it unlawful for the business of the firm to be carried out or for the members of the firm to continue the partnership.

Case Study

Hudgell, Yeates and Co v Watson (1978)

For practising solicitors it is necessary to have a certificate of practice. One of the three partners failed to renew his practice certificate. He was therefore not legally entitled to act as a solicitor.

Court's decision: It was held that due to the non-renewal of the practice certificate, the partnership had been brought to an end. However, a new partnership could be started by the other two partners of the old partnership.

4. **Dissolution by the court**

   On application by a partner, the court **may** pass a decree of dissolution of the partnership in any of the following cases:

   a) When a partner, other than the partner suing, becomes permanently incapable of performing his part of the partnership contract.

Example

In a partnership, one of the partners is an old woman who is not able to perform her duties because of her age. On this basis the partnership would be dissolved by the court.

   b) When a partner, other than the partner suing, has been found guilty of conduct that will, in the opinion of the court, prejudicially affect the operation of the business.

Example

Rashnae and Rosel were the partners of a solicitors' firm. Rosel was found guilty of bribing a government officer. As this verdict could damage the integrity and morality of the firm, the court can order the dissolution of the firm on this ground.

   c) When a partner, other than the partner suing, wilfully or persistently commits a breach of the partnership agreement, or otherwise conducts himself in matters relating to the partnership business in a way that makes it impractical for the other partner or partners to run the business in partnership with him.

Example

Ted and Lan ran business in partnership. They had the firm's bank account with a bank and the bank required the signatures of both the partners before honouring any cheque. As a result of a minor dispute with Lan, Ted refused to sign the cheque. So it became impractical for Lan to continue running the business.

d) When the business of the partnership on at a loss.

Example

John and Jack form a partnership to run a restaurant and to earn profit. However, after a few months of operation, their business suffers a loss. So, instead of running the partnership at a loss, John and Jack can avoid losses by bringing the business of the partnership to an end.

---

e) In the event, circumstances have arisen which, in the opinion of the court, renders it **just and equitable** that the partnership be dissolved.

Example

There were 19 members in a partnership firm which carried out the business of selling electronic products. Two other members joined and hence the total number of members became 21. However, the standard **maximum** number of members permitted by law is **twenty.** Hence these are just and equitable grounds to demand dissolution of the firm.

Diagram 4: Dissolution of partnership

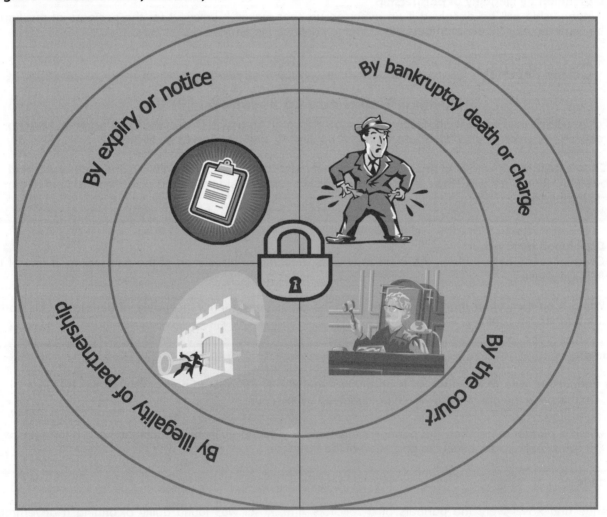

Test Yourself 6

Detail the grounds upon which a partnership can be terminated.

(December 2002)

SYNOPSIS

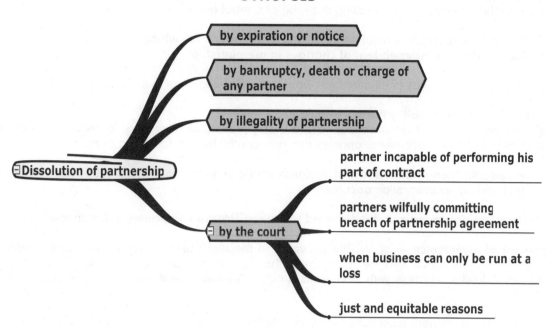

by expiration or notice

by bankruptcy, death or charge of any partner

by illegality of partnership

Dissolution of partnership

by the court

partner incapable of performing his part of contract

partners wilfully committing breach of partnership agreement

when business can only be run at a loss

just and equitable reasons

Limited liability partnership

An LLP is an alternative corporate business vehicle (introduced 6 April 2001) that gives the benefits of limited liability but allows its members the flexibility of organising their internal structure as a traditional partnership.

> **Definition**
>
> A limited liability partnership (LLP) is a form of business entity formed under the 2000 Act, which has a separate legal personality from its partners and where the liability of the partners is limited.

Important points for consideration:

➢ The LLP will be a **separate legal entity** and while the **LLP itself will be liable to the full extent of its assets, the liability of the members will be limited.**

➢ The **LLP is a body corporate.** That means it has a legal personality separate from that of its members. Like a limited company, a LLP can do all the things an individual or company can do. It can make contracts, sue or be sued, hold property or become insolvent.

➢ Under certain circumstances, however, claims for economic loss can be made against individual members who have been negligent. Any such claim would be a civil action outside the contract as the party would have contracted with the LLP.

➢ By and large, partnership law does not apply to an LLP, but the arrangements between the partners may closely follow a traditional partnership agreement.

➢ Despite the similarity with a limited company, **the partners in a LLP are not employees** of the partnership, whereas the directors of a limited company are employees of the company.

➢ **The LLP would typically select a "Designated Member" or members** (who have a similar responsibility to a directors / secretary of a limited company). He would be responsible for maintaining communications with Companies House, preparing accounts and acting for the LLP if, for some reason, it is dissolved.

➢ **Any new or existing firm of two or more persons will be able to incorporate as an LLP** in England, Scotland or Wales. There is no maximum limit on membership.

➢ **It is not possible to convert a company into an LLP or vice versa.**

➢ LLP's are **not available to charities**; there must be a view to profit.

➢ LLP can hold property in its own right.

➢ LLP's are similar to companies in the respect that they will be required to provide financial information equivalent to that of companies, including the filing of annual accounts.

➢ The LLP itself will be a separate legal entity owned by the members which means that the LLP will be **able to continue in existence independent of changes in membership.**

➢ The rights and responsibilities of all members would usually be laid out in a 'Deed of Partnership'.

1. Formation of a Limited Liability Partnership (LLP) :

In order to form an LLP, the subscriber to the incorporation document or a solicitor engaged in the formation of the LLP must submit the appropriate form containing the following details:

a) At least two people **"carrying on a lawful business with a view to profit"** must **subscribe their names** to a document called an "incorporation document".

b) The incorporation document must be delivered to the **registrar of companies** at Companies House.

c) **A statement of compliance** must also be delivered to the registrar (wherein the members undertake that there has been compliance with the requirement that at least two persons, associated for the purpose of carrying on a lawful business with a view to profit, have subscribed their names to the incorporation document).

d) The incorporation document must include this information:
   ➢ the **name** of the LLP, which must end with the words "Limited liability partnership" or the abbreviation LLP.
   ➢ whether the **registered office** is to be situated in England and Wales, (in Wales or in Scotland, the address of the registered office).
   ➢ the **name and address of the persons** who are to be members on incorporation.
   ➢ specification of those persons who are to be designated members or statement that every person who from time to time is a member of the limited liability partnership is a designated member.

e) There is also a **registration fee of £95.**

f) On registration, the registrar will issue a certificate of incorporation.

2. Designated members

A designated member has the same rights and duties towards the LLP as any other member. These rights and duties are governed by the Limited Liability Partnership Agreement and general law. However, the law on LLP's places extra responsibility on designated members. In particular, they are responsible for:

➢ the appointment of an auditor.
➢ signing the accounts on behalf of the members.
➢ delivering the accounts to the registrar.
➢ notifying the registrar of any membership changes or change in the registered office address or name of the LLP.
➢ preparing, signing and delivering to the registrar the annual statement of return
➢ acting on behalf of the LLP if it is wound up or dissolved.

Designated members are also accountable in law if they fail to carry out these responsibilities.

3. Members as agents

Every member of a limited liability partnership is the agent of the limited liability partnership.
However, a limited liability partnership is not bound by any act carried out by a member in dealing with a third party if:
➢ the member in fact has no authority to act for the LLP, and the third party knows that he has no authority.
➢ the person has ceased to be a member of a limited liability partnership.

4. Dissolution of LLP

An LLP is a separate legal entity which is distinct from its members. Hence it continues in existence even upon the death, insolvency or resignation of members. An LLP must therefore be wound up by application of winding up provisions, similar to company winding up provisions.

5. Ceasing to be a member of LLP

The membership of the member of LLP ceases on the following circumstances:

a) **Death:** On the death of a member of the LLP.

b) **Dissolution (if the member is a corporation):** If the company or the corporation is a member of the LLP, then, on the dissolution of the company, membership of the LLP ceases.

c) **On gaining the agreement of the other members:** On obtaining the mutual consent of other members of the LLP.

d) **After giving of reasonable notice:** If it is provided in the agreement that a member can withdraw his membership by giving reasonable notice, then his membership of the LLP is brought to an end after such notice.

6. Difference between partnership and LLP

Points of differences	Partnership (E&W) (other than a limited partnership)	LLP
Status	Not a separate legal entity	Separate legal entity
Registration & public records	Registration **not required**	Incorporation **requires registration** at Companies House
	Accounts **not open** to public inspection	Accounts etc. open to public inspection
	No corresponding requirement	Registrar must be **notified** of membership changes
Governing law & constitution	**Partnership law and the Partnership Act 1890** applies	**LLPA, 2000 applies.**
Partnership agreement	**No obligation** to enter formal arrangements between members – there are default provisions in the Partnership Act which will apply, in the absence of agreement to that effect.	**No obligation** to enter formal arrangements between members – there are default provisions in the LLP Act which will apply, in the absence of agreement to that effect.
	Interest of a member **will not generally pass** to another, and e.g. death, bankruptcy will generally operate so as to dissolve the partnership	If the interest in the LLP of a member **passes to another** (e.g. death, bankruptcy), the other **may not interfere** with the management but will be entitled to receive whatever would otherwise have been due to the member
	No corresponding requirement	At least 2 members must be **'designated members'** and notified to Companies House as such; and they thereby have additional responsibilities for *inter alia* administrative and filing duties
Liability to third parties	Liability of partners for partnership debts is **not limited**	Liability of partners for partnership debts **limited**
	Liability of partners for wrongful acts done in ordinary course of the partnership business or with the authority of the partners is **not limited**	Liability of partners for wrongful acts done in ordinary course of the partnership business or with the authority of the partners is **limited**
	Provisions of Partnership Act apply to partnerships	Many provisions of company and insolvency law apply to LLPs with appropriate modifications, generally to protect those dealing with LLPs
	A partnership is not an independent legal entity in its own right; a contract with a partnership is a contract with all its members.	An LLP is an independent legal entity in its own right; a contract with an LLP is therefore not a contract with any of its members.

7. Similarity between partnership and LLP

Points of similarity	Partnership (E&W) (other than a limited partnership)	LLP
No. of members	Requires **at least 2** partners	Requires **at least 2** people to incorporate a LLP
Agreement	A person may become a member **by agreement** with existing members – and may leave by death, dissolution, or by agreement (or by giving reasonable notice, in the absence of agreement to the contrary)	A person may become a member **by agreement** with existing members – and may leave by death, dissolution, or by agreement (or by giving reasonable notice, in the absence of agreement to the contrary)
Power to bind	Each member has **power to bind** the partnership, unless the person with whom he is dealing knows he does not have that power	Each member has **power to bind** the LLP unless the person with whom he is dealing knows he does not have that power
Powers of departed members	Departed members also have **power to bind** the partnership, to his acts unless the person with whom he is dealing knows he has departed, or the departure has been formally notified. A wrongful act of a member towards a third party in the course of the partnership business or with its authority makes the partnership also liable.	Departed members also have **power to bind** the LLP unless the person with whom he is dealing knows he has departed, or the departure has been formally registered. A wrongful act of a member towards a third party in the course of the LLP's business or with its authority makes the LLP also liable.

Test Yourself 7

Hal, Irma and Jon have decided that they have sufficient complementary skills and sufficient capital to conduct a business together. They all want to be involved in the day-to-day business activity and they want to limit control of the business strictly to themselves. They also wish to place a limit on the amount of capital they can lose. The have been told that there are several different ways in which their business could be organised, but they are currently undecided as to which they should choose.

Required:

(a) Explain the various legal forms under which their business could be conducted and consider the advantages and disadvantages of each of these possibilities.
(b) Advise Hal, Irma and Jon as to which of the forms considered best suits their intentions.

(December 2004)

SYNOPSIS

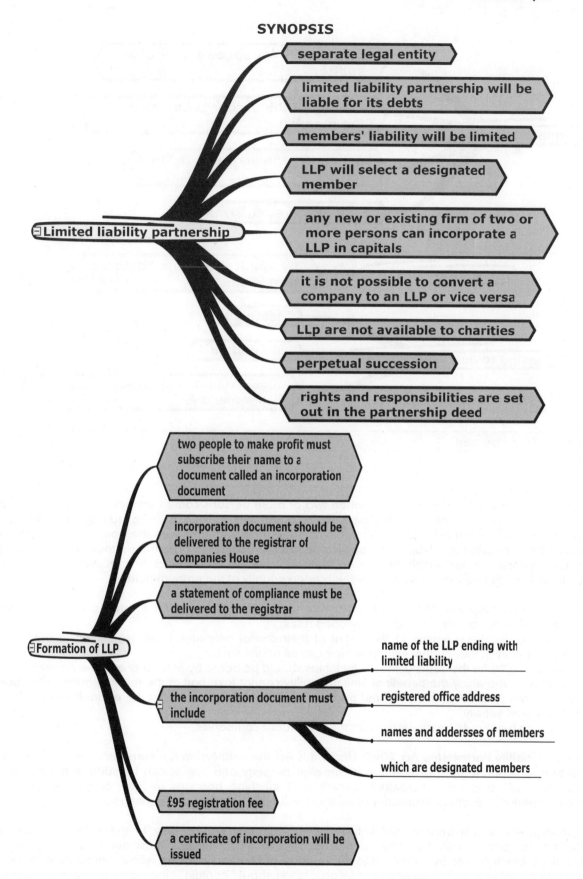

Limited liability partnership
- separate legal entity
- limited liability partnership will be liable for its debts
- members' liability will be limited
- LLP will select a designated member
- any new or existing firm of two or more persons can incorporate a LLP in capitals
- it is not possible to convert a company to an LLP or vice versa
- LLp are not available to charities
- perpetual succession
- rights and responsibilities are set out in the partnership deed

Formation of LLP
- two people to make profit must subscribe their name to a document called an incorporation document
- incorporation document should be delivered to the registrar of companies House
- a statement of compliance must be delivered to the registrar
- the incorporation document must include
  - name of the LLP ending with limited liability
  - registered office address
  - names and addersses of members
  - which are designated members
- £95 registration fee
- a certificate of incorporation will be issued

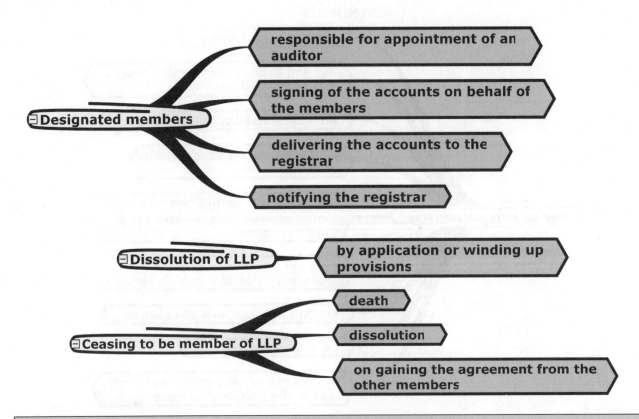

Designated members
- responsible for appointment of an auditor
- signing of the accounts on behalf of the members
- delivering the accounts to the registrar
- notifying the registrar

Dissolution of LLP
- by application or winding up provisions

Ceasing to be member of LLP
- death
- dissolution
- on gaining the agreement from the other members

Answers to Test Yourself

Answer 1

a) **Partnership Act 1890:** This states that when two or more persons come together for the common motive of running a business and making profits, this is called a partnership. There is unlimited liability on the partners. They are jointly and severally liable for the debts of the partnership firm, even their personal property will be considered while clearing the debt. This is applicable to both active and dormant partners. The third party can take action against the partnership firm or an individual partner. If damages are recovered from only one partner, then the other partners have to bear the burden equally of the amount paid.

b) **Limited Partnership Act 1907:** This states that the partnerships can be formed under limited liability, however they have to comply the below-mentioned rules:
➢ The partners' liability is limited to the extent of their capital only and it will not extend to their personal property. However, they cannot withdraw their capital at any time.
➢ Unlimited liability for the debts of the partnerships should be borne by at least one of the partners.
➢ The partners who enjoy the benefit of limited liability cannot take part in the management of the business and not even contract on behalf of the partnership. If this is overruled then the partners will not have the right to limited liability.
➢ This partnership should be registered with the registrar of companies.

c) **Limited Liability Partnership Act 2000:** Under this Act, the partnership is a corporation which has a distinct legal existence separate from its partners. It can own property and sue or can be sued in the name of the corporation. It will also enjoy perpetual succession if anything happens to the partners i.e. additions or departure of partners, death or insolvency of partners, will have no effect on its continuation.

Every partner will benefit from limited liability i.e. their liability will be only to the extent of their capital contribution. To form a limited liability partnership, two or more persons must apply for the certificate of incorporation, which should be submitted to the registrar of companies along with a statement of compliance prepared by an advocate. The document of incorporation should contain – the name of the entity, address of its registered office, the names and addresses of the potential partners or members of the entity and the names and addresses of at least two partners who will be carrying out the full administrative duties. If the names of such designated partners are not submitted then all the partners are assumed to be designated partners.

Answer 2

According to the Partnership Act 1890, a partnership is a contractual relationship between two or more partners to carry out some business activity in order to earn a profit. In a partnership, each partner is liable for the debt of the firm.

In the above case, Ian is the dormant / sleeping partner in the firm. A sleeping partner is a person who invests in the firm and share in the profits / losses of the firm but does not take active part in the operations of the business. Like general partners, a sleeping partner is liable to all the third parties for the partnership's debts.
A salaried partner is one who does not have the right to share in the profits and losses of the firm. He is paid salary by the firm and normally he does not have the voting rights with regard to partnership.
In the above situation, Steve is a salaried partner. Any act which is carried out by him within the normal course of the business is binding upon all the partners and all the partners are jointly liable for the debts of the company.
At the time when Steve makes the contract with Ted regarding the purchase of utensils worth £8,000, he is acting outside the powers granted to him by the partnership agreement (as the partnership agreement specifically requires that the utensils should be purchased only from Rob). Therefore Steve is breaching the partnership agreement by making the contract with Ted. So it is possible for Ian to sue Steve for the breach of the partnership agreement and recover the damages for any losses incurred by him.

As the partnership agreement is not published, it is obvious that Ted could not be aware that Steve has overstepped his powers. Hence the contract for sale of utensils to the firm is a valid contract and is binding upon both the parties. Both partners are liable to Ted for the sales price.

Answer 3

The Business Names Act 1985 requires all businesses trading under names other than those of their owners to display their owners' names and an address at which documents can be served.

Therefore, a partnership trading under names other than those of its partners has to display the names of individual partners and an address at which documents can be served.

This information must be displayed both at business premises and on business stationery. It must also be supplied in writing at the request of any person with whom the firm is doing business.

Where the partnership consists of more than 20 persons certain exceptions apply to the business stationery requirements. In this case, the individual names need not to be listed on each document, but a list must be available at the firm's principal place of business.

Answer 4

Two or more people come together to run a business with an aim to make profits, they have to follow the terms of the partnership which is agreed in the agreement of partnership. These terms are fixed and agreed upon by the partners themselves. If something is not covered then it is decided on the basis of the common law existing on partnerships. Each partner acts as an agent, principal and equity for the partnership firm.

a) **Duty to disclose:** The partners should give full and true information of all the factors which affects the accounts of the partnership firm or its partners.
b) **Duty to account:** The partners should give an account of all the benefits made by the partner from the partnership firm, without obtaining consent for e.g. the goodwill of the partnership firm, its business connections.
c) **Duty to not to compete:** The partner should not compete with the partnership business without obtain the prior consent of the other partners. If he does not obtain any consent beforehand then he has to account for the profits made in his personal business. Full disclosure of the partner's activities is necessary.

In this above case, it is evident that the partners have not complied with their duties of disclosure and have not imparted full information to the partnership firm. Frank will therefore renegotiate the sale of his partnership to obtain a better selling price as there has been a breach of duty by one of the partners.
Greg too, had not disclosed his interest in the property of the partnership. Therefore he has to account for the profit earned by him from the transaction i.e. £50,000.
Hank will be held liable for the profits he has made by entering into competition with the partnership firm. If, in the partnership deed, it is specifically mentioned that any partner engaged in business that competes with partnership business should be expelled, then Hank will be expelled and the partnership will be reconstituted without him.

Answer 5

In partnerships the partner's liability is unlimited. If the partnership is registered under the Limited Liability Partnership Act (LLP) then only the partner's liability is limited to the extent of his capital contribution. However, to obtain this facility the partners have to maintain certain rules. They are:
1. The partnership should be registered with the registrar of companies.
2. The partners cannot withdraw their capital contribution at any given point of time.
3. At least one of the partners should have unlimited liability to bear the debts of the partnership if any.
4. The partners who enjoy the benefit of limited liability should not take part in the management of the partnership in its daily routine matter.

If any of the above is overruled then the partners do not get the benefit of limited liability. Therefore, in the above case Hal cannot benefit from limited liability as the partnership has not taken appropriate procedures for its commencement of business. Furthermore, Hal had taken active participation in the management of the business of the partnership. If the partnership had been registered under the LLPA 2000, the partners would have continued to enjoy the benefit of unlimited liability in spite of taking active participation in the day-to-day business of the entity. However, in this case Hal is liable for the debts of the partnership and will have to bear the debts beyond his capital contribution i.e. £50,000. He can recover the excess amount over his contribution from the other two partners if they are in a position to pay this amount, according to the terms of the partnership deed which they have entered.

On the other hand, Ina has also misrepresented herself to obtain a loan from the bank for an unauthorised purpose. However, when the bank claims back the loan amount, the partnership cannot repudiate the claim and hence will have to settle the third party and then recover the amount from Ina and can even close down the partnership as she had breached her duty as a partner.

Jo's activity was limited to London and not beyond that area, but she purchased a house in Scotland, therefore the partnership will be held liable and hence Jo will be further liable to the other two partners for the loss incurred in the transaction.

The partnership therefore has a debt of £200,000 and, as it is not in a position to settle the debts fully, its partners will be held liable for the uncleared amount.
Ina is liable to the other two partners for £25,000 and Jo is liable for £100,000 due to their breaches towards their duty. After recovering these amounts from them, there is still a deficiency of £75,000. This £75,000 will have to be borne by all three partners in the proportion of their share capital or according to the partnership agreement. So, if Hal has to pay more than £50,000, then he can sue the other two partners to recover the excess amount paid by him.

Answer 6

There can be several reasons for partnerships closing down. The grounds on which a partnership can be dissolved according to the Partnership Agreement 1890 are:

a) **Dissolution by expiration or notice:** According to the agreement between the partners, a partnership can be dissolved. If the partnership is entered into for a fixed period of time, then after the expiry of this period, the partnership is dissolved. Similarly, it is formed to undertake a specific venture or goal then, after the venture or goal has been achieved, the partnership is dissolved. If one of the partners does not want to continue then he can give notice to the others for dissolution of the partnership and the partnership may be dissolved from the date mentioned in the notice or, if not mentioned, the date of communication of the notice.

b) **Dissolution by bankruptcy, death or charge:** According to the agreement between the partners, every partnership is dissolved if any of the partners dies or becomes bankrupt of insolvent. If any partner had to pay the partnership property in his share for settling his personal debt then the other partners can opt to dissolve the partnership.

c) **Dissolution by illegality of partnership**: A partnership is automatically dissolved if it gets involved in unlawful dealings for the business of the firm. In **Hudgell, Yeates and Co v Watson (1978),** one of the three partners failed to renew his practice certificate. For practising solicitors it is necessary to have a certificate of practice. So he was not legally entitled to act as a solicitor.

It was held that due to the non-renewal of the practice certificate, the partnership had been brought to an end. However, the new partnership may be carried on with the other two partners of the old partnership.

d) **Dissolution by the court:** On application by a partner, the court **may** order dissolution of the partnership in any of the following cases:

i   When a partner, other than the partner suing, becomes permanently incapable of performing his part of the partnership contract.

ii   When a partner, other than the partner suing, has been found guilty of fraud or breach of duty or conduct which, in the opinion of the court, is calculated to prejudicially affect the operation of the business.

iii Where the business can only be run at a loss.

iv   Where it is just and equitable to do so.

Answer 7

a) The various business forms are as follows:

1. **Standard partnership:** A standard partnership is a contractual association of two or more persons or entities to operate a common enterprise and to share in the management and profits and losses of the business. A standard partnership can be formed by either agreement or conduct of the parties, expressed or implied. Written articles are not necessary to create a standard partnership. The partners have unlimited liability for the obligations of the partnership. Every partner is an agent of the partnership and can act on behalf of the business and bind the other partners. Each partner is jointly and severally liable for the debts and obligations of the business, including those arising out of the wrongful actions of another partner.

2. **Limited partnership:** A limited partnership is a partnership formed by two or more persons, one or more of whom are general partners and one or more of whom are limited partners. This form is unavailable if no one is willing to assume the risks of a general partner. The primary purpose of the limited partnership is to enable one or more persons to invest in a partnership without incurring the unlimited liability of a general partner. A limited partnership is more or less similar to a standard partnership except that the liability of one or more partners (but not of all partners) for a partnership debt is limited to their capital contribution in the partnership. The partnership must be registered with the Companies' Registry.

3. **The limited liability partnership & the private company:** The LLPA 2000 has provided a new form of business entity. Although it is a partnership it is formed to be a corporation which has a distinct legal existence separate form its members or partners. It enjoys all the advantages of a company registered under the company's legislation.

➢ Unlike partners of a general partnership or the general partner of a limited partnership, all partners of an LLP enjoy limited liability.

➢ Typically, the partners retain liability for contract debts, but their liability with respect to the tort debts of the business is limited.

➢ All partners may participate in the control of the business and still maintain their limited liability, unlike the limited partners of a limited partnership.

Regardless of type, all partnerships are considered to be an aggregate of their partners, rather than a separate entity. Unlike corporations, in which stock can be freely traded (assuming a willing buyer), a partner involved in the management of the partnership can only transfer his interest with the consent of the other partners. If the mutual consent to form a partnership breaks down, the partnership breaks down as well.

b) Hal, Irma and Jon have to choose between a limited liability partnership and a private limited company as both options allow participation of day-to-day management with limited liability to the partners.

Quick Quiz

Correct or incorrect?

1. A partnership may be formed with two partnership firms as partners.

2. A bankrupt person can become a partner in the partnership firm..

3. A new partner can be introduced in partnership by the decision of majority of partners.

4. If a non-partner holds himself out as a partner, he will be liable for the debts of partnership.

Answers to Quick Quiz

1. **Incorrect.** A partnership is a relationship between persons. The term 'person' does not include a firm. Since firms do not have a separate legal entity of their own, two partnership firms cannot enter into a partnership.

2. **Incorrect.** A person, upon being declared bankrupt, cannot become a partner. Also, when a partner of an existing firm is declared bankrupt, he ceases to be a partner.

3. **Incorrect.** Under the Partnership Act 1890 a new partner can be introduced only with the **consent of all the existing partners.** (but the provisions of the Partnership Agreement specify otherwise)

4. **Correct.**

Self Examination Questions

Question 1

Sharing of profits is not conclusive evidence of the creation of a partnership: Explain.

Question 2

Tom, Dick and Harry are partners in a courier company, which operates from Tom's residence. The capital contributions of each of them were £15,000, £12,000 & £9,000 respectively. A rent of £150 was agreed to be paid to Tom for the use of his residence. The profits and losses were to be shared in proportion to their capital contribution.

The courier company was doing well, so it was necessary to appoint more staff and bring in furniture. Dick bought the furniture from his own expenses which cost £650 and showed it as a loan to the company, which he will recover from its profits.

However, that year the courier company had huge competitors and could not make the profits they had estimated. As a result, they decided to close down the courier company.

The assets of the partnership amounted to £12,000 and loans went up to £1,550, unpaid rent was £450. The value of Tom's residence was £50,000.

Required:

i   Can the property of Tom be used to clear the debts of the courier company?
ii State how the dissolution of the courier company should be conducted regarding the distribution of its assets and liabilities.

Question 3

Ascertain the form of the following partnerships:

i   NOMY Company is a partnership formed by the partners Jack, Matt and Rob. NOMY is registered with the Companies' Registry. The business of the firm is buying and selling electronic goods. All the partners have decided to smuggle these electronics goods. The liability of Jack for a partnership debt is limited to his capital contribution in the partnership.

ii Soothing and Cooling is a partnership formed by the partners Rosy, Ted and Greg for the same purpose i.e. buying and selling electronic goods. They decided to share the profits arising from the business equally. Among these three partners, Ted is the sleeping partner. He does not take an active part in running the partnership. He also does not visit the place of the business very often.

iii Machine Electronics is a partnership formed by John, Bob and Carol. The business of the firm is buying and selling electronic goods. All the partners i.e. John, Bob and Carol have a limited liability. If Bob is carelessly or accidentally negligent in performing his duties, the other partners John and Carol may be at risk.

Answers to Self Examination Questions

Answer 1

Sharing of profits or gross returns arising from property by persons holding a joint or common interest in that property does not of itself make these persons partners. The sharing of profits is not, prima facie, evidence of partnership.

The true test in determining whether a partnership exists or not is to see whether the relationship of principal and agent exists between the parties. There must be mutual **agency relationship between the partners** (Cox v Hickman). It implies that every partner is the agent of all others and all others are his agents as far as the business of the firm is concerned. Every partner is bound by the acts of others and all others are bound by his acts (Section 18).

Answer 2

i   The assets of the partnership or property can be owned by the partnership or by its partners. According to Section 20 of the Partnership Act 1890, partnership property is the property brought into the inventory or bought for the trading purpose of the entity. Section 21 states that any property bought by the firm's finances is the firm's property. It is very important to separate the personal property of the partners from the property of the partnership firm at the time of dissolution of the firm. The property owned by the partnership should be used for the purpose of the business of the partnership firm only. Even if the value of the property appreciates over time it will remain the property of the partnership firm alone. Similarly, the appreciation in the value of the personal property of any of the partners will remain his personal property. At the time of dissolution, the partnership's property is first used to clear the debts before the personal property. While treating the claims of the creditors both the properties are treated separately although the partner's liability is unlimited. However, here the personal creditor of the partner will have no share or claim in the partnership's property. The amounts owed to creditors total £1,550, the loan from is Dick £650 and the unpaid rent is £450, both of these can be cleared by disposing the partnership firms' assets worth £12,000. The excess of £9,350 can be distributed in the proportion of the capital of the partners. Tom's residence will not be taken as all the debts are cleared by the partnership's property alone.

ii   When the partnership is closed the assets of the partnership are disposed and the amount realised is distributed in the following ways:

➢   First the debts of the creditors are cleared.
➢   Second the outstanding payments of partners which are payable by the partnership are paid off in excess of their capital contribution.
➢   Thirdly the capital contribution of the partners.
➢   Fourthly, if anything still remains then it is divided among the partners in the same proportion of sharing their profits.

However, if the opposite situation exists where the partnership's funds are insufficient to pay off the creditors, then the shortfall has to be brought in from the previous profits or from the partners' capital contributions in the proportion of their profit sharing ratio.

Here the business premises are Tom's residence. They are therefore the property of Tom and their value cannot be included in the value of the partnership's property to settle the creditor's debts.

The partnership's assets should be sold to pay off the creditors. The assets are worth £12,000 and the debts of the third parties amount to £1,550, unpaid rent £450 and loan from Dick £650. Here the value of asset is sufficient to clear all the debts, so Tom and Dick will also be paid their debt in full. The amount remaining is to be distributed among the partners in the ratio of their profit sharing against their capital contribution. Therefore Tom, Dick and Harry do not get the full amount they had invested of £15,000, £12,000 & £9,000 respectively; instead they receive £3,896, £3,117 & £2,337. Therefore, Tom Dick and Harry suffer a loss of £11,104, £8,883 & £6,663 respectively.

Answer 3

i NOMY, is a partnership which is registered with the Companies' Registry. It is a **limited partnership** as the liability of Jack, for partnership debt is limited to his capital contribution to the partnership. The primary purpose of the limited partnership is to enable one or more persons to invest in a partnership without incurring the unlimited liability of a general partner. The business is buying and selling electronic goods, but it is carried out for the purpose of smuggling these goods. Hence the object is illegal; therefore it is an **illegal partnership.**

ii The partnership of Soothing and Cooling is a **standard partnership** as the liability of none of the partners is limited. All three partners share the profits equally. Ted is the dormant partner as he does take an active part in the operation of the business and also he visits the place of the business very rarely. Nevertheless, shares in the profit of the business.

The partners in a general partnership have unlimited liability for the obligations of the partnership, i.e. their liability is not limited to their contributed capital or the assets of the partnership. Every partner is personally and severally liable for all the debts and liability extends to the personal assets and benefits of the partners to the partnership.

iii The partnership of Machine Electronics is a partnership which is registered under the **Limited Liability Partnership Act, 2000**. The liability of all the partners is limited in this form of partnership.

D 3

SECTION D - THE FORMATION AND CONSTITUTION OF BUSINESS ORGANISATIONS

CORPORATIONS AND LEGAL PERSONALITY

Get through intro

This Study Guide deals with the **different choices available when deciding** which type of business organisation is the most appropriate form in which to **conduct business.** The **structure one chooses** for conducting business should **fit like a pair of comfortable shoes.** Just as **ill fitting shoes pinch the wearer, a poor choice** of business structure can prove **detrimental in the long run.**

'Ownership and legal form,' refer to the way a **business is organised, managed and it determines its rights and obligations under law.**

However, **ownership** primarily represents **percentage holdings** in a particular business while the legal form determines the control of the business.

This Study Guide will help students understand factors such as **type and size of business, taxation, and finance requirements and the establishment** costs. All these factors need to be considered, whilst making the right choice about business structure.

LEARNING OUTCOMES

a) Distinguish between sole traders, partnership and companies
b) Explain the meaning and effect of limited liability
c) Analyse different types of companies, especially private and public companies
d) Illustrate the effect of separate personality
e) Recognise instances where separate personality will be ignored

Introduction

The previous Study Guide examined that the liability of partners in a limited liability partnership is limited in the same way as the members of a limited company. Then what is the difference between a LLP and a limited liability company (LLC)?

The main difference is that whereas Limited Companies are required to abide by the terms and conditions set out in their Memorandum & Articles, a Limited Liability Partnership has a much more flexible structure.

An LLP is not required to hold formal board meetings or annual general meetings or pass resolutions, note, under s.288 (5) CA 2006 a private company is not required to hold an AGM

A Limited Liability Partnership is treated as a partnership for the purpose of taxation.

This brings up the question of why businesses want an LLP over an LLC. The answer is simple. The professional regulatory body may prohibit forming an LLC, but not an LLP. In a case like this, the LLP at least gives a business contract liability protection.

1. Distinguish between sole traders, partnerships and companies
[Learning outcome a]

In the UK, enterprises or organisations can be described as being either within the public or private sector. The public sector comprises central and local government and public corporations. The private sector comprises three basic types of ownership or legal forms: sole proprietorships (or sole traders), partnerships and companies.

The simplest way of doing business is as a sole trader with or without employees. If the business is owned by more than one person, the owners may choose to form a partnership firm. An alternative to either is to trade through a limited company.

The three main distinct business structures are discussed in more detail below:
1. Sole trader.
2. Partnership (sometimes called a firm).
3. Limited company – either a private company or a Plc (Public Limited Company)

Corporations are founded in a number of ways:

a) **By royal charter:** This is issued by the Crown and is used mostly for non- commercial bodies.

Example

The BBC, the Bank of England, and the older universities

---

b) **By statute:** This is similar to the royal charter, but is issued by the government instead.

Example

Local government authorities and new universities.

---

c) **By registration:** This is the most common method, used to form companies incorporated under the Companies Act, 2006. Companies must register with the registrar of companies, and are issued with a certificate of incorporation.

Comparative analysis of sole trader, partnership firm and company is as follows:

	Sole trader	Partnership firm	Company
No. of members	**Only one person** can start a business	**Minimum two** partners and **maximum twenty** partners. (except LLP)	The **Private Co** can have only **one** member The **public Co** can have **one** member. There are **no maximum** limit on number of members.
Formation procedure	Starting business is relatively easy.	Although an agreement is not compulsory, Partnerships always formulate agreement and registered with the Registrar.	To register (incorporate) a company under the Companies Act, one needs to: ➤ contact the Registrar of Companies ➤ fulfil the formalities. ➤ pay for the legal registration process.
Liability	Liability of a sole trader is unlimited i.e. even his personal property is liable to be attached for paying business debts	Liability of partners is usually unlimited (Except the limited liability partnership)	Liability of shareholders is limited to the extent of capital contributed by them. Personal assets can not be attached in any event.
Separate entity	The identity of sole trader is not separate from his business.	A partnership is a relationship between two or more persons but it is not a separate legal entity'	A company exists as a formal and legal entity in its own right. It is separate from its shareholders.
Succession	No perpetual succession. Business comes to an end on death of the proprietor or the closure of business by the proprietor.	No perpetual succession. Business comes to an end on death or retirement or resignation or dismissal of the partner unless specifically provided for in the partnership deed.	Perpetual succession. Company continues to exist even on the death or resignation of all the shareholders. The company comes to an end only by winding up / or dissolution.
Sharing of profits	Sole trader is entitled to all the profits.	The profit is shared among the partners in agreed profit sharing ratio.	Entire profit belongs to company. Some profit is distributed to shareholders in the form of dividends.
NIC contributions	National Insurance is low.	Partners are taxed individually on their share in profits of the partnership. Hence, National Insurance is low.	National Insurance payments are higher.
Funds generation	Limited options for raising funds.	Able to raise money by introducing new partners.	It is easier to raise large sums of money or to sell a part of the business to generate funds.
Ownership of assets	All assets of the business are owned by proprietor.	All assets of business are owned jointly by the partners or as mutually agreed.	All assets of the business are owned by company.
Audit / Accounting	A proprietor can keep simple un-audited accounts	Partnership accounts are relatively less complicated than company accounts	Annual accounts are generally more complicated and are required to be delivered to the registrar.
Withdrawal of capital	Withdrawal of capital is very easy.	Relatively straightforward for a partner to withdraw his capital.	Rules regarding repayment of subscribed capital are strict.
Owner's interest	Transferable at the option of the owner.	Partners cannot assign their interest in the firm without express consent of all the partners.	Shares in the company are freely transferable in a manner relating to the regular procedure.

Test Yourself 1

Give one advantage of each of the following forms of organisations over the other forms:

a) Sole trader
b) Partnership Firm
c) Company

Test Yourself 2

Choose the correct option:
Four out of six members of a public company die. Such a company:

a) Becomes a private company
b) Becomes a defunct company
c) Continue to exist with the two members.
d) Is automatically dissolves

Diagram 1: Number of persons / members in different business structures

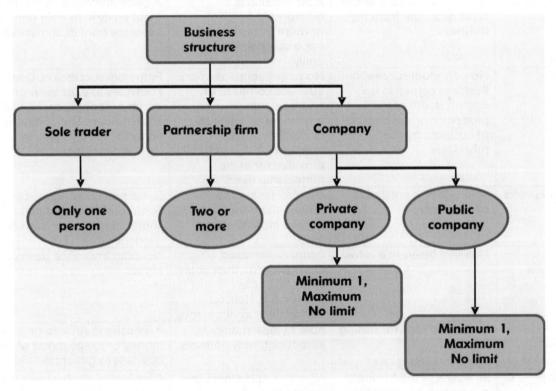

SYNOPSIS
Difference between sole trader, partnership and company

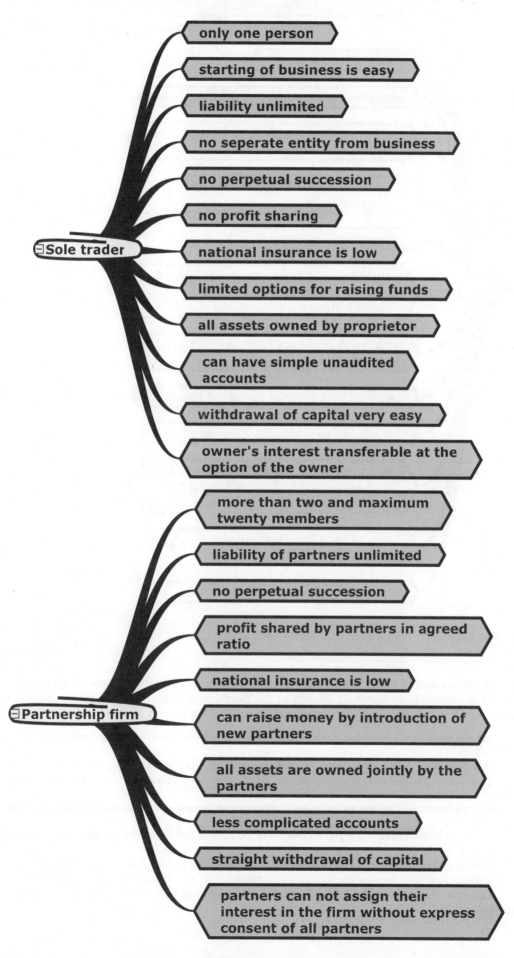

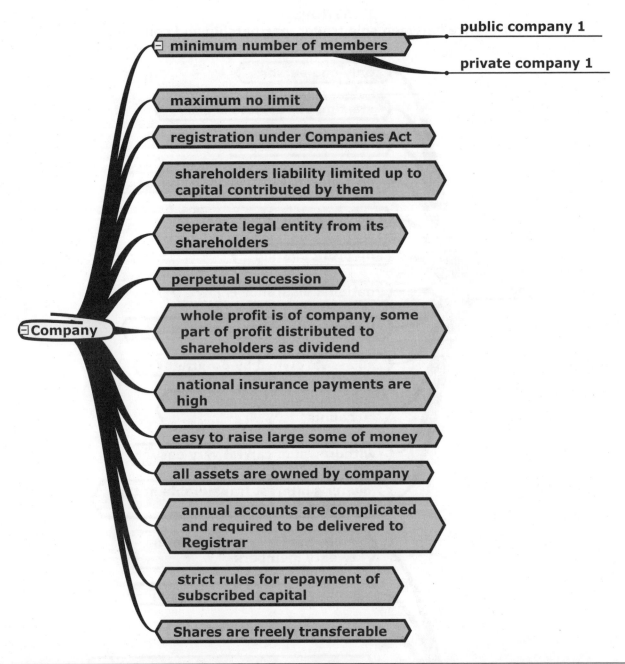

public company 1

private company 1

minimum number of members

maximum no limit

registration under Companies Act

shareholders liability limited up to capital contributed by them

seperate legal entity from its shareholders

perpetual succession

Company

whole profit is of company, some part of profit distributed to shareholders as dividend

national insurance payments are high

easy to raise large some of money

all assets are owned by company

annual accounts are complicated and required to be delivered to Registrar

strict rules for repayment of subscribed capital

Shares are freely transferable

2. Explain the meaning and effect of limited liability

[Learning outcome b]

What owners of Private and of Public companies have in common is that the liability of the owners for debts of their companies is limited. Their liability is limited to the paid-up value of the shares they own. In other words, their liability is limited to the amount they had agreed to pay for the shares when they purchased them.

Definition

Limited liability is a shelter given to certain types of enterprises. It suggests that the liability of shareholders for debts of a corporation or limited company is limited to the nominal value of their shares.

In other words, their personal assets are not at risk if the company becomes insolvent and is liquidated.

When companies become insolvent and cease to trade, they are liable without limit for all its debts. But the shareholder's liability is strictly limited by law to the amount he / she agreed to pay for the shares when he / she bought them. The owner is protected by law; his / her personal possessions cannot be used to repay the company's debts.

Example

If the nominal value of the share in a company is £10 and a member has already paid £7 per share then he can be called upon to pay not more than £3 per share during the lifetime of company. This is because his total liability by contributing to company's share is £10 out of which he has already paid £7. Hence the balance of £3 only can be his maximum liability for the company's debts.

Tips

It is the member, not the company, whose liability for the company's debts may be limited.

So there is a greater risk for those dealing with companies if the companies become insolvent. In the company form of organisation, the owners risk to the greater extent is transferred to suppliers (creditors), customers and employees.

Example

Jacuzzi Ltd's share capital is £20,000 contributed by its two members equally. The company entered in a big deal and unfortunately incurred heavy losses of £30,000 and hence liquidated. In this case, the members cannot be asked to bring in more funds to pay off the company's debts, because they have already paid their share of capital to the company and their liability is limited to that extent only. Hence the loss of £10,000 is to be borne by the creditors, customers or employees of the company and they cannot recover the amount from the shareholders.

Hence such enterprises generally have to indicate to those who have dealings with them:
➢   that the enterprises' owners have passed some of the risk to suppliers and customers,
➢   that those dealing with the enterprise may not be repaid if it ceases to trade.

In the UK, for e.g., the law requires the company's name to include specified words, or their specified abbreviations, which in effect state the type of company and that suppliers and customers may lose their money if they have dealings with this company. A private company's name has to end with the word 'Limited' or the abbreviation 'Ltd': s. 59 CA 2006. A public company's name has to end with the words public limited company or plc'. : s. 58 CA 2006

Note that even though a shareholder's liability is limited in its capacity as a shareholder, the shareholder may still be directly liable for his own acts.

Example

If the president (who happens to be a shareholder) of a small corporation negligently hits someone while on company business, the president (as well as the company) is still liable for his own negligence; however, the other shareholders are not liable for the president's negligence, unlike a general partnership where all partners are liable for each other's negligence.

Test Yourself 3

What does limited liability mean in relation to the company?

SYNOPSIS

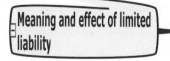

| Meaning and effect of limited liability | liability of shareholders limited to the nominal value of shares | members liability is limited to debts but not of the company |

3. Analyse different types of companies, especially private and public companies
[Learning outcome c]

Diagram 2: Types of companies

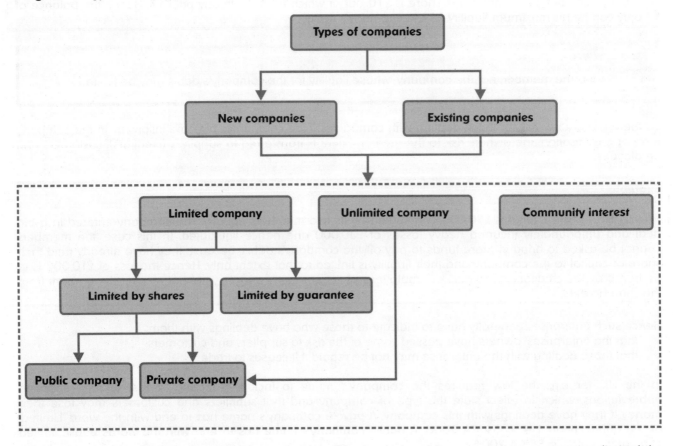

There will be a limited and unlimited companies, Private and public companies, companies limited by guarantee and community interest companies. The companies formed under the Companies Act 2006 will be known as New Company and companies formed prior to Companies Act 2006 as existing companies but the provisions will apply to both the new and existing companies.

New companies will generally have unlimited capacity, its objects are unrestricted unless articles specifically restricts the objects.

1. Unlimited company: Every member of an unlimited company is, in the event of its winding up, jointly and severally liable for all the obligations of the company and is therefore in this respect is in the same position as a partner in a partnership.

Only a private company can have liability of its members to be unlimited. A public limited company can not register as an unlimited company.

An unlimited company would usually only be appropriate if the company will merely be used to hold land or other investments and will not trade. It may be a useful vehicle where incorporation is necessary or desirable and one or more of the following applies:

➢ The company will operate in a field where limited liability is disapproved. For example, as a service company for a professional firm i.e. in circumstances where limited liability is not vital but perpetual succession is important.

➢ The risk of insolvency is minimal.

➢ It is thought that a reduction in the company's share capital may become desirable (in this regard an unlimited company may reduce its capital at will, provided the articles of association permit it, without requiring the sanction of the court).

Important privileges enjoyed by an unlimited company are:

➢ It has separate legal entity and perpetual succession.

➢ It is not required to deliver copies of its annual accounts and reports to the Registrar of Companies(provided it meets certain conditions directed at ensuring that it is not a subsidiary or parent of an undertaking which is limited - section 254 of the Companies Act 1985.)

➢ It can buy back its shares from its members without many formalities.

➢ An unlimited company may or may not have a share capital. If a company has no share capital, a member may resign or terminate his membership only if the Memorandum or Articles so provide, and only in the circumstances and in accordance with the conditions set out therein.

2. Limited company

a) A company limited by guarantee: A company limited by guarantee has members, rather than shareholders, whose liability is limited by an amount guaranteed by each member, which becomes due in the event of the company being wound up. The memorandum includes a non-profit distribution clause and these companies are usually formed by professional, trade or research associations. After incorporation the company can be registered with the charity commission.

In this type of company, the liability of the member is limited to such amount as he may undertake to contribute to the assets of the company, in the event of its being wound up. Members can not be called upon to contribute beyond that stipulated amount.

Example

A company is formed with the following objectives:

a) To promote the awareness and appreciation of classical and associated music from around the world.
b) To provide entertainment and recreation for residents and visitors, during the time of the festival.

10 members from various fields gathered and registered a company with the 'charity commission' under the name "Find the Peace Ltd" and agreed to pay £10,000 each in the event of winding up of the company.

This is a company limited by guarantee.

---

b) A company limited by shares: In this type of company, the liability of the shareholder is limited to the extent of unpaid amount of the shares.

The majority of companies are those limited by shares. Members or shareholders hold one or more shares issued to them by the company in return for payment. A shareholder's liability to the company's creditors is normally limited to the amount of the shares that have been issued to them and which they have not been fully paid for.

A company limited by shares can be incorporated either as a Public company or a Private company.

Example

Sindi and Vandy were two fashion designers. They decided to form a company with each contributing a capital of £25,000. The business of the company was to design clothes according to the traditions and trends of various countries. The Memorandum of the company prohibits the company from accepting public deposits and inviting the general public to subscribe to its share capital.

This is a private company.

---

i Public company

> **Definition**
>
> The Companies Act 2006 defines a public company as a company Limited by shares or by guarantee. Its certificate of incorporation must state that it is public company: s.4(2) CA 2006

A public limited company is a company which is registered and complies with the following:

The certificate of incorporation must state that it is a public company: s.4 (2) CA 2006
> ➤ The name **must end** with the words 'Public Limited Company' or 'PLC' or their Welsh equivalents, 'ccc', for a Welsh company (s 33).

> ➤ The memorandum **must** be in the form specified in Table F of the Tables of Companies Regulations 1985 or as near to that form as circumstances permit. This is wrong, the memorandum has a much more restricted position under the CA 2006

> ➤ The liability of members of the public limited company is limited.
> New companies will no longer be required to specify their authorised share capital, a mere statement of capital will be sufficient. For existing companies it will be continue to be a requirement.

> ➤ It must have an (**authorised share capital**) of at least £50,000(s.763 CA 2006). The amount of share capital stated in the memorandum of association is the company's 'authorised' capital. There is no maximum to any company's authorised share capital

> ➤ It must have **an (issued share capital)** of at least £50,000.
> Issued capital is the value of the shares issued to shareholders. A company need not issue all its capital at once, but a public limited company must have at least £50,000 of allotted share capital   i.e. before it can start business, it must have allotted shares to the value of at least £50,000. (s 117)

> ➤ The capital must be paid up to the extent of 25% (s 101).

Example

The issued capital is £50,000; £12,500 must be paid up.

It is important to note that each allotted share must be paid up to at least 25% of its nominal value together with the whole of any premium.

Example

If a share with a nominal value of £1 is sold for £6, then it is said to have a premium of £5. This premium must be paid to the company, together with a minimum of 25% of the nominal value of each share. That is £0.25p plus £5, making a total payment of £5.25 per share.

> ➤ A newly formed Plc **must not** begin business or exercise any borrowing powers until it has a certificate issued under section 756 CA 2006confirming that the company has issued a share capital of at least the statutory minimum (currently £50,000).

A company can get this certificate from Companies House by completing Form 117. **Once issued, the certificate is proof that the company is entitled to do business including monetary transactions.**

Advantages of a public limited company

> ➤ A Plc has access to capital markets and can offer its shares for sale to the public through a recognised stock exchange.
> ➤ It can also issue advertisements offering any of its securities for sale to the public.

ii. Private company

S. 4 CA 2006 states that a private company is any company that is not a public company. The words 'limited' or 'Ltd' in the name denotes a private company.
The liability of members of a private company may be limited by shares or by guarantee or it may be unlimited.

Private companies have certain **advantages over public companies as:**

➢ A private company may commence business immediately upon the issuing of certificate of incorporation by the Registrar of companies.

A public company on the other hand needs to obtain a certificate of commencement of business from the Registrar of Companies under s.756 CA 2006

➢ There is a minimum amount of £50,000 for a public company;

No minimum amount is required for a private company.

➢ A private company is limited by shares or by a guarantee (but not an unlimited one) and needs only one member. The sole member may be the same person as the sole director.

Whereas, if a public company (or an unlimited company) carries on business for more than 6 months with less than two members, a member during this period may be held personally liable for company's debts – s.118 CA 2006

➢ The provisions relating to the retirement of directors on reaching the age of 70 do not apply to a private company (unless the company is the subsidiary of a public company) – s.163 CA 2006

➢ The statutory restrictions which apply to a company making a loan,, to its directors apply less rigorously to a private company (unless it is the subsidiary of a public company); - s.198 CA 2006

➢ A private company   need not to hold annual general meetings –s.288(5) CA 2006

➢ Private companies may purchase their own shares out of the capital and can also provide financial assistance for the purchase of their own shares.

➢ Public companies are strictly forbidden from doing so.

➢ Private companies have to keep its accounting records for three years whereas a public company has to keep its accounting records for six years.

➢ A private company can, by way of a resolution, dispense with the provision relating to appointment of auditors annually, giving account before annual general meeting (AGM). It need not hold an AGM unless they expressly resolve to have them, instead decisions can be made by written resolution.

➢ A public company, however, has to comply with all the above requirements.

➢ In a private company, a resolution can be passed by way of circulation. It means that whatever might be done by way of a resolution of a general meeting or a meeting of a class of members may instead be achieved by a resolution in writing, signed by all members of company, without actually convening any general meeting.

➢ This facility is not available to public company.

➢ Private companies will no longer have to have a company secretary

➢ On the other hand, a private company has certain disadvantages as compared to a public company. These include:

➢ A private company is **prohibited from making an offer to the public** (whether for cash or otherwise) of shares or debentures of the company and also may not allot or agree to allot shares or debentures of the company with a view of them being offered for sale to the public – s.755 CA 2006

➢ A private company's **shares or debentures cannot be listed or dealt with at the Stock Exchange**

Test Yourself 4

What is the meaning of the term "Company"?

Test Yourself 5

What are the different types of company?

SYNOPSIS

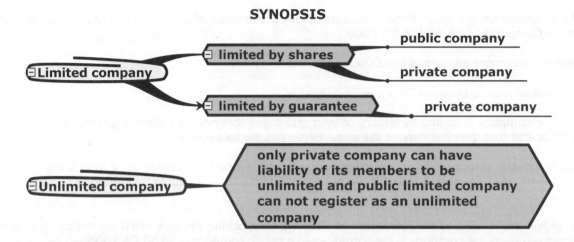

4. Illustrate the effect of separate personality

[Learning outcome d]

On incorporation, a company becomes a separate legal entity distinct from its members. The company is different and distinct from its members in law. It has its own name and its own seal, its assets and liabilities are separate and distinct from those of its members. It is capable of owning property, incurring debt, and borrowing money, having a bank account, employing people, entering into contracts and suing and being sued separately.

In Salomon v Salomon Co Ltd (1987) the House of Lords laid down that a company is a person distinct and separate from its members.

Case Study — A Company is a person distinct and separate from its members

Salomon v Salomon Co Ltd (1897)

In this case, Salomon incorporated a company named "Salomon & Co Ltd" with seven subscribers consisting of himself, his wife, four sons and one daughter. This company took over the personal business assets of Salomon for £38,782 and in turn, Salomon took 20,000 shares of £1 each, debentures worth £10,000 of the company with a charge on company's assets and the balance in cash. His wife, daughter and four sons took up a one £1 share each. Subsequently, the company went into liquidation due to a general trade depression. The unsecured creditors contended that Salomon could not be treated as a secured creditor of the company, in respect of the debentures held by him, as he was the managing director of the one-man company, which was not different from Salomon and company was a sham and fraud.

Court's decision: The claim of the unsecured creditors was rejected. It was held by Lord MacNaghten that the Company is at law a different person altogether from the subscribers to the memorandum, and though it may be that after incorporation the business is precisely the same as it was before and the same person are managers, and the same hands receive the profits, the company in law is not the agent of the subscribers. The **company has its own existence** and as a result, a shareholder cannot be held liable for the acts of the company even though he holds virtually the entire share capital.

4.1 The effects of separate personality

1. **Perpetual succession**: Perpetual succession is the continuation of a company's existence despite the death of any owner or member, or any transfer of stock. The company does not die or cease to exist unless it is specifically wound up or the purpose for which it was formed has been completed. Membership of a company may keep on changing from time to time but that does not affect the life of the company. Death or insolvency of member does not affect the existence of the company.

   Perpetual succession is one of the legal distinctions between a business and a company. A company has perpetual succession meaning that a change in the membership does not affect the existence of the company. The other forms of business such as sole trading or partnership do not enjoy perpetual succession.

Example

In the case of a partnership a change in the membership affects the existence of partnership.

Tom and Harry were the two partners of a partnership firm. Tom decided to move to India and resigned from the partnership. Hence, the partnership will dissolve. A Partnership cannot continue when the partners separate themselves from the firm.

---

2. **Separate property**: A company is a distinct legal entity. The company's property is its own. A member cannot claim to be owner of the company's property during the existence of the company.

3. **Common seal**: A company is an artificial person and does not have a physical presence. Therefore, it acts through its Board of Directors for carrying out its activities and entering into various agreements. Such contracts may be under the seal of the company. The common seal is the official signature of the company.
   Most companies have a company seal that they use on important documents like conveyances, mortgages and share certificates. **However, since 1989, a company seal is not mandatory.**

4. **Transferability of shares**: Shares in a company are freely transferable. When a member transfers his shares to another person, the transferee steps into the shoes of the transferor and acquires all the rights of the transferor in respect of those shares.

5. **Contractual capacity**: A company can enter into any contract in its own name and it is liable on any such contract. The extent of company's liability, as opposed to members' liability, is unlimited. A company can sue or be sued in its own name as distinct from its members.

6. **Separation of ownership from management**: A company is administered and managed by its managerial personnel i.e. the Board of Directors. The shareholders are simply the holders of the shares in the company and need not be necessarily be the managers of the company.

Test Yourself 6

Zigzag Ltd and Tin Tang Ltd are the two companies engaged in the business of manufacturing electronics goods? Can Zigzag Ltd become a member of Tin Tang Ltd?

Diagram 3: Effects of a separate personality

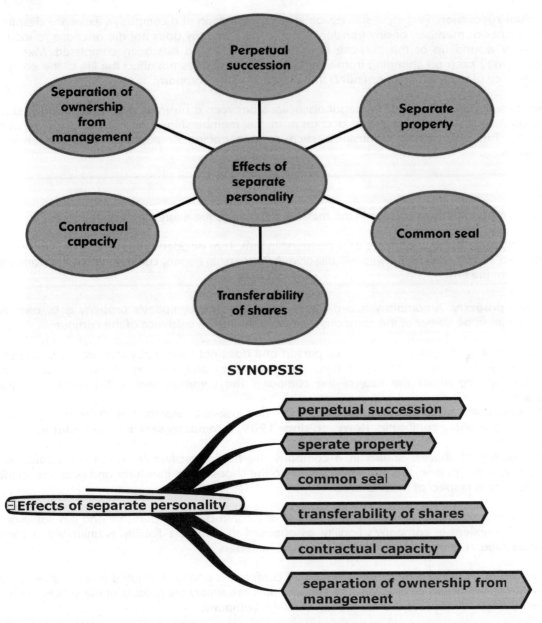

SYNOPSIS

5. Recognise instances where separate personality will be ignored

[Learning outcome e]

A company limited by shares, once registered, is regarded as a legal person, separate and distinct from the directors and shareholders who manage and own the company respectively (**Salomon v Salomon & Co Ltd (1897)**).

The basic principle established in Salomon in relation to single companies was extended to groups of companies by a comparatively recent decision of the Court of Appeal in **Adams V Cape Industries PLC (1990)**.

Case Study

Adams V Cape Industries Plc (1990)

This is a complicated case. Cape is an English registered company, which was involved in mining asbestos in South Africa. Cape has become the subject of a class action law suit in the USA. On jurisdictional grounds, Cape attempted to avoid fighting the case. The claimants managed to get a judgement in the US courts against the English company. However as Cape no longer had assets in the US, the claimants attempted to bring the judgement against the main company in the English courts.

Court's decision: The court declared that the use of Cape Industries' corporate group structure had been to ensure that a particular group's legal liability would fall on that particular group, and not on the entire company based in England. The judge's decision was "Whether or not this is desirable, the right to use a corporate structure in this manner is inherent in our corporate law. ... In our judgement Cape was in law entitled to organise the group's affairs in that manner ..."

The Court of Appeal held the judges decision on the principle of the law. It stated that under the principles of the law it could not life the corporate veil. The court rejected the fact that a separate personality could be ignored. A group of companies are entitled to operate as a single economic entity.

What is meant by lifting of the corporate veil?

This means looking behind the company as a legal person, i.e. disregarding the corporate entity and paying regard to the realities behind the legal facade. Where the courts ignore the company and concern themselves directly with the members or managers, the corporate veil is said to have been lifted.

Only in appropriate circumstances as discussed below are the courts willing to lift the corporate veil.

In general, the Courts will not allow the corporate form to be used:

➢ for the purposes of fraud or dishonestly for the express purpose of depriving a claimant of the ability to exercise his lawful rights.
➢ as a mere façade to conceal the true facts or,
➢ where it is established that there has been dishonesty or abuse of the corporate form.
➢ Sole Corporate directors are now not allowed and all companies are required to have at least one actual person as director.

The various **situations where the separate personality will be ignored** are discussed in more detail below:

1. Fraud: These occur where individuals have used the separate legal entity to do something they are personally and legally forbidden from doing.

The courts are prepared to ignore the separate personality and pierce the corporate veil when the court feels that fraud is or could be perpetrated behind the veil of incorporation.

Case Study   Separate personality of a company ignored in a case of fraud.

Gilford motor company Ltd v Horne

As an ex-employee of the Gifford Motor Company, Mr Horne was contractually prevented from soliciting the companies' customers. To get around this and to be able to solicit Gifford Motor Companies' customers, Mr Horne incorporated a limited company in his wife's name. Gifford Motor Company brought legal action against him.

Court's decision: A court injunction prevented Mr Horne from soliciting customers from Gifford Motor Company. The court ruled "the company was formed as a device, in order to mask the effective carrying on of the business of Mr. Horne". Mr Horne was purposefully perpetrating fraud by incorporating the new company. The new company was regarded a cloak to hide this fraud and was in affect a sham. The corporate veil was lifted and Mr Horne's' own company was made subject to the injunction as the judge ruled that the limited company and Mr Horne where the same entity.

1. Group enterprises

Sometimes in the case of group of enterprises, the Solomon principal may not be adhered to and the court may lift the veil in order to look at the economic realities of the group itself.

> **Tips**
>
> **Salomon principal:** A company is a person distinct and separate from its members.

Case Study Subsidiary companies may be treated as a part of the same economic entity or group.

DHN Food Distributors Ltd v London Borough of Tower Hamlets (1976)

A subsidiary company of DHN owned land. London Borough of Tower Hamlets issued a compulsory purchase order on that land. DHN claimed compensation for the land owned by its subsidiary.

Court's decision: The courts held that DHN was able to claim compensation because it and its subsidiary was a single economic unit. It has been said that the courts may disregard the view / judgement in Solomon's case whenever it is just and equitable to do so.

In **Stocznia Gdanska SA v Latvian Shipping Co (2002),** a parent company was held liable for indirectly inducing the breach of a contract between its subsidiary and a third party using unlawful means through failure to comply with an agreement to fund the subsidiary's purchase of goods.

In many respects a group of companies are treated together for the purpose of accounts, balance sheet, and income statement.
Whether the court will pierce the corporate veil depends on the facts of the case. The nature of shareholding and control would be indicators as to whether the court would pierce the corporate veil.

2. Agency

This applies where the companies form other companies as their subsidiaries to act as their agents. In certain cases the courts have found that holding companies were in fact carrying on business through the agency of its subsidiary company. Where the activities of the subsidiary company are so closely controlled and directed by the parent company the latter can be regarded as merely an agent, conducting the parent companies business.

Case Study When the courts recognise an agency relationship, the separate personality of a company is ignored

Smith Stone and Knight Ltd v Birmingham Corporation (1939)

Smith Stone and Knight owned land and a subsidiary company. The subsidiary company operated its business on the land. Birmingham Corporation decided to purchase the land and issued a compulsory purchase order. The order stated that any company who owned the land would receive payment for it. They would also compensate the owner of the land for and business they where running on the land. Birmingham Corporation claimed they owed no compensation to the subsidiary as they didn't own the land.

Court's decision: The court held that the subsidiary company was an agent of Smith Stone and Knight and therefore Birmingham Corporation had to pay them compensation.

Example

To get tax advantages and protect itself from LSE listing rules, an English registered company set up a foreign subsidiary. This subsidiary company issued bonds to banks which where guaranteed by the holding company.

In this case, the company has acted as a nominee or as an agent either for another party or for its main shareholder. In these kinds of case a court would ignore the law on separate personality and base its decisions accordingly.

A sham or something like a sham should not be suggested on the grounds that a subsidiary company only has a small paid up capital and a board of directors which is made up of directors and senior executives from its holding company.

In cases where the agency agreement holds good and the parties concerned have expressly agreed to such a agreement then the corporate veil shall be lifted and the principal shall be liable for the a acts of the agent.

3. Trust

The courts may pierce the corporate veil to look at the characteristics of the shareholders. In the case of **Abbey and Planning** the court lifted the corporate veil. In this case a school was run like a company but the shares were held by trustees on educational charitable trusts. They pierced the veil in order to look into the terms.

4. Tort

Usually the English courts have not lifted the veil on the ground of tort. This is a phenomenon not witnessed in most common law jurisdictions apart from Canada.

5. Enemy character

In times of war the court is prepared to lift the corporate veil.

Case Study

Daimler Co Ltd v Continental Tyre and Rubber Co (1916)

An English company, (**Continental Tyre and Rubber Co**) was formed for selling in England the tyres produced by a German company in Germany. The bulk of the English company's shares were held by the German company. All the shareholders of the company, except one, and all the directors were German nationals residing in Germany. The English Company filed a suit during the World War I to recover a trade debt. Daimler argued that they should not pay the debt to German individuals to prevent money going towards Germany's war effort.

Court's decision: The court held that **Continental Tyre** was German although it is incorporated as English Co.

---

6. Tax

At times tax legislations warrant the lifting of the corporate veil. The courts are prepared to disregard the separate legal personality of companies in case of tax evasions or liberal schemes of tax avoidance without any necessary legislative authority.

Example

Directors of a company can be held personally liable in certain circumstances if it can be established that there has been "fraudulent trading" and / or "wrongful trading" under Sections 213 and / or 214, Insolvency Act 1986;

---

7. Statutory support of lifting the veil

The Companies Act 2006 includes a number of exceptions to the general rule imposed by Salomon v Salomon & Co Ltd.

➢ If the number of members of public company is below two, i.e. there is a single member (who is aware that he is the only member) for more than six months, he is personally liable for any debts incurred during that period.

➢ However, he is liable for the debts incurred after the expiry of the period of 6 months only.

➢ Groups of companies must produce accounts acknowledging their internal relationship, and the profits and losses of different subsidiaries can be offset for taxation purposes.

➢ Employees of a company can be liable for the company's actions in the following circumstances:

a) A public company must have incorporation / trading certificate (s.756 CA 2006). If it operates without one, a director may be personally liable for any debts incurred.

b) A company cheque must bear the name of a company exactly, otherwise the director who signs are liable if the cheque is not cleared. This applies even if the omission is due to a printing error.

> **Example**
>
> A Director of Michael Jackson Ltd was held personally liable for a cheque he signed bearing the company name M Jackson Ltd.

c) If a company is wound up, its director may not carry out similar business with a similar name for five years. Double glazing companies are a good example of this; before this legislation, Directors would pay themselves high bonuses and run a company into the ground, then they would buy the assets of the insolvent company cheaply and set up a virtually identical company with a similar name to transfer the goodwill.

d) Under the Company Directors Disqualification Act 1986, a person who is disqualified from being a director can be personally liable if they act as a director during their disqualification period.

e) If directors know a company is close to insolvency but continue trading, they may be personally liable.

> **Example**
>
> Courts Furniture Ltd recently continued taking orders and deposits despite the directors knowing the business was close to closing.

8. **Where the director is found liable for the fraud in their personal capacity:** Courts have treated the conduct or characteristics of its directors, managers or shareholders as attributable to the company itself.

> **Example**
>
> A public limited company newly incorporated must not "do business or exercise any borrowing power" until it has obtained from the registrar of companies a certificate that has complied with the provisions of the act relating to the raising of the prescribed share capital.
>
> If the company enters into any transaction contrary to this provision, the company and its officers in default, are liable to pay fines. If the company fails to comply with its obligations in that connection within 21 days of being called upon to do so, the directors of the company are jointly and severally liable to indemnify the third parties in respect of any loss or damage suffered by reason of the company's failure.

> **Test yourself 7**
>
> The number of members of a public limited company falls below 2 on 1 April 20X2. The company continues to carry on its business with the reduced number till 11 November 20X2. During the intervening period between 1 April 20X2 to 1 August 20X2, the company contracts a debt of £10,000. The company incurred no other liability till 11 November 20X2 other than this debt of £10,000. Will the continuing member be severally liable for the whole debt?

SYNOPSIS

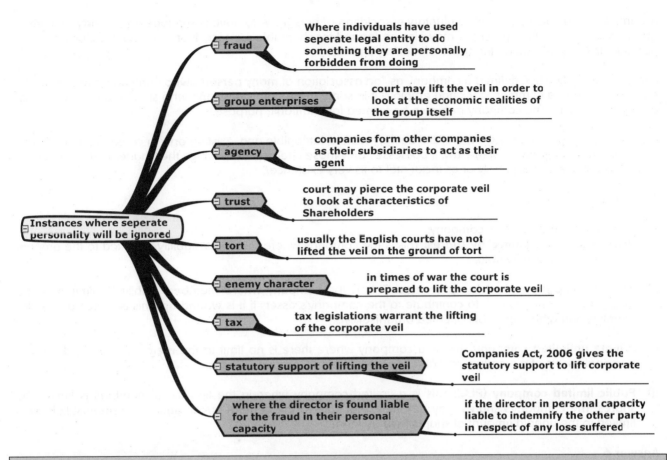

fraud	Where individuals have used seperate legal entity to do something they are personally forbidden from doing
group enterprises	court may lift the veil in order to look at the economic realities of the group itself
agency	companies form other companies as their subsidiaries to act as their agent
trust	court may pierce the corporate veil to look at characteristics of Shareholders
tort	usually the English courts have not lifted the veil on the ground of tort
enemy character	in times of war the court is prepared to lift the corporate veil
tax	tax legislations warrant the lifting of the corporate veil
statutory support of lifting the veil	Companies Act, 2006 gives the statutory support to lift corporate veil
where the director is found liable for the fraud in their personal capacity	if the director in personal capacity liable to indemnify the other party in respect of any loss suffered

Instances where seperate personality will be ignored

Answers to Test Yourself

Answer 1

a) **Sole trader:** A Sole Trader can withdraw his capital easily and in case of Partnership Firm also a partner can withdraw his capital in a simple way. But it is not the case of Company. There are strict rules regarding repayment of subscribed capital.

b) **Partnership:** Resources and efforts can be combined like a company yet partners are taxed like individuals on their share of income.

c) **Company:** Liability of members of the company for company's debts is limited to the extent of capital contributed by them. Also company has perpetual succession which means members may come and go the company will exist unless it is wound up.

Answer 2

The correct option is C. A company has perpetual succession and continues to exist unless it is wound up.

Answer 3

When it is said that a particular company is a Limited Liability company it means that the liability of the shareholder in the event of the winding up of the company, is limited to the extent of nominal value of the shares owned by them. A member's personal property can not be attached to pay off the company's debts.

For e.g., If Kelly buys stock in a corporation for £10,000; she cannot lose more than that amount.

It is important to note that only member's liability is limited not the company's liability. A company is a legal entity distinct and separate from its members.

As per the law certain words should be specified in the name of the company like name of the private company should end with the word 'Limited' or 'Ltd' and public companies name should end with 'Company' or 'Co'. Even if the Shareholders liability is limited, he may be directly liable for its own acts.

Answer 4

A Company" may be defined as a voluntary association of persons who have come together to carry on some business and sharing the profits, or may also be formed for charitable purpose. Not all companies, unlike partnerships, are formed for the urose of making a profit.

Lord Justice Lindley has defined a company as "an association of many persons, who contribute money or, money's worth to a common stock and employs it in some trade or business and who share the profit and loss, arising there from. "The company may also be formed for charitable purpose.

A company is also defined as "an artificial being, invisible, intangible and, existing only in contemplation of the law. Being a mere creation of the law, it possesses only those characteristics which the Charter of its creation confers upon it, either expressly or as incidental to its very existence."

Answer 5

There are mainly four types of company:
a) **Private company limited by shares:** This is the company where members' liability is limited to the amount unpaid on shares they hold.

b) **Private company limited by guarantee:** This is the company where members' liability is limited to the amount they have agreed to contribute to the company's assets if it is wound up. This is more suitable for charities and other non profit oriented organisations.

c) **Private unlimited company:** This is a company where there is no limit to the members' liability. Even the personal assets of a member are liable for repayment of company's debts.

d) **Public limited company (PLC):** This is a limited company wherein the liability of members is limited by shares. The company's shares may be offered for sale to the general public and the members' liability is limited to the unpaid amount of shares held by them.

Answer 6

A company is a legal person in the eyes of law. It has all the powers that of a human. A company can enter into any contract in its own name and it is liable on any such contract. Hence, it can buy shares of any other company and can exercise all the rights of a member.

Answer 7

No, because, the member is so liable for the debts incurred after the expiry of the period of 6 months only. In this case, the debts are incurred before the expiry of 6 months since the number of members reduced below 2. In other words, members can be held personally liable for any debts incurred after 1 September 20X2.

Quick Quiz

1. State whether the following statements are true or false

a) If the members composing the company die or disassociate themselves, the company becomes extinct.

b) For company's debts, creditors can sue the members of the company.

c) The assets of company are owned by the shareholders of the company.

d) A private company is prohibited from making an offer to the public.

2. **Choose the correct option.**
i. The liability of members in a company limited by shares
a) is limited to the called-up value on share
b) is limited to the guarantee given by members
c) is nil, if the shares are fully paid up.
d) Is unlimited

ii. Since a company is regarded as an entity separate from its members,
a) Then assets and liabilities of the company are also the assets and liabilities of the members
b) The shareholders can enter into contracts with the company
c) The shareholders are the agents of the company
d) The members of the company can be sued for the debts of the company.

iii. If a company uses the words 'Plc' at the end of its name, it must have a minimum authorised share capital of:
a) £500,000
b) £25,000
c) £5,000
d) £50,000

Answers to Quick Quiz

1. a) **False**, a company is a separate entity distinct from its member and it has perpetual succession.
   b) **False**, company is a separate legal person competent to contract in its own name.
   c) **False**, company is a separate legal person and hence it can own property in its own name.
   d) **True**

2. a). The correct option is (c)
   b). The correct option is (b)
   c). The correct option is (d)

Self Examination Questions

Question 1

What are the restrictions on Plc?

Question 2

When can a Plc start business?

Question 3

State any five points of difference between a public company and a private company.

Question 4

The Board of directors of a private company, N, by resolution dated September 21, 1972, decided to sell certain immovable property of the company for £5,000. The purchasers were the wives of two of the directors, who were brothers. The wives did not have their own source of income. The purchasers paid £7,000 to one of the directors i.e. husband of the first purchaser, and the sale deed was executed by the company on 20 March, 20X5.

Soon after that company went into liquidation, one of the creditors of company filed a suit objecting to the transaction of sale of property and to their rights in title and interest over the suit property.

Reading the facts of the case, is that the transaction of sale between the appellants and the company a sham and bogus and was it entered into to avoid the vesting of the suit property in the name of the creditors? Students should give reasons for their conclusions.

Answers to Self Examination Questions

Answer 1

There are two main restrictions on Plc:

a) A Plc normally has only seven months after the end of its accounting reference period to deliver its accounts to the Registrar.

b) A Plc cannot take advantage of many of the provisions and exceptions applying to private companies under the Act, such as audit exemptions for small private companies.

Answer 2

A newly formed Plc must not begin business or exercise any borrowing powers until it has a certificate issued under s 4 CA 2006.confirming that the company has an issued share capital of at least the statutory minimum (currently it is £50,000).

Answer 3

	Private company	Public company
Minimum amount of capital	No minimum amount prescribed.	Minimum amount of £50,000
Public offer	Prohibited from offering its shares and debentures to public.	Can issue its shares and debentures to public.
Commencement of business	Can commence business on incorporation.	After incorporation, before starting business, has to obtain a certificate from the registrar.
Name	The name includes the words 'limited' or 'Ltd'	The name must end with the words 'public limited company' or 'Plc'
Listing of shares	Shares or debentures cannot be listed or dealt with at The Stock Exchange	Shares and debentures can be listed or dealt with at The Stock Exchange

Answer 4

A transaction of sale of its immovable property by a company in favour of the wives of the directors is alleged to be sham and collusive. In this case it would be justified to pierce the veil of incorporation to ascertain the true nature of the transaction. Also to discover who were the real parties to the sale and whether it was genuine and bona fide or whether it was between the husbands and the wives acting from behind the facade of the separate entity of the company.

The facts under consideration for holding that the transaction was sham are:

a) The resolution appears to be an ante-dated document

b) Though the resolution mentioned the sale consideration as £5,000, there was no explanation as to why it was enhanced to £7,000;

c) The purchasers did not exercise their rights as purchasers over the suit property till the date of the suit;

d) The transaction of sale was between the husbands and the wives and they had no independent source of their income, which fact could not be ignored altogether as irrelevant.

COMPANY FORMATIONS

Get through intro

This Study Guide takes students through the **basic concepts regarding company formation procedures.**

The Company's Act 2006 herein2006 herein after called as Company's Act has established a **strict procedure,** which a company has to comply with, before it can commence its legal operations.

The **procedural aspects and formalities** to be **fulfilled by a company for incorporation** are explained in this Study Guide. Understanding these concepts is very important for the examination as questions on this topic generally find their way into the examination paper.

Important concepts like the **role and fiduciary duties of promoters** and important documents such as **the Memorandum of Association and Articles of Association of the company** are dealt with in this Study Guide. A thorough understanding of these concepts is required in order for accountants to effectively perform their roles.

LEARNING OUTCOMES

a) Explain the role and duties of company promoters
b) Describe the procedure for registering companies, both public and private
c) Describe the statutory books, records and returns that companies must keep or make
d) Describe the contents of Model articles of association
e) Analyse the effect of a company's constitutional documents
f) Explain how articles of association can be changed

Introduction

Michael, a resident of the UK, has been employed in Superb Ltd since 1990. He now wants to start his own business, trading in electronic goods. However, he doesn't have sufficient funds to start a business. He is also not aware of which type of organisation it would be most appropriate for him to start.

He thinks that forming a sole trading business is the best option available to him. Is he correct?

No, this is not the best option as he doesn't have sufficient funds to run the business efficiently.

On the other hand, if Michael chooses to form a company, it would be easier for him to raise money to invest in the business. Forming a company also carries with it various other advantages, such as the company having a separate legal personality from its shareholders, the limited liability of shareholders and the absence of a limit on the maximum number of members. As a result, it is more appropriate for Michael to form a company, rather than a sole trading business or partnership. If Michael decides to form a company, he will have to comply with all the legal requirements, including the terms of the Companies Act 2006

In this Study Guide, the advantages of forming a company over other types of organisation and the procedure of company formation are examined.

1. Explain the role and duties of company promoters

[Learning outcome a]

1.1 Promoter

It is an individual or group of individuals, commonly known as promoters, who conceive a project and incorporate a company to implement the project. It is they who invest their money, time and expertise. Their stakes both in terms of value of money and time is high and no one other than the promoters would be more concerned with the successes of the company. Therefore, the active role played by promoters in the affairs of a company cannot be ignored.

The promoter is the person or persons who conceive the idea of forming the company with reference to the given object and then to get it going. They do the necessary preliminary work vital to the formation of a company.

> **Definition**
>
> In Phosphate Sewage Co v Hart mount, a promoter was defined as "a **person who as principal, procures or aids in procuring the incorporation of a company**".

Promoter is a person who originates the idea of the formation of the company and makes the efforts to form actually form it.

Whether a person is a promoter of a company or not depends upon the role performed by him in the formation of the company. Basically, promoters are the persons who set in motion the machinery by which the Companies Act enables them to create a registered company. But if a person is employed merely in a technical or professional capacity, he will not be a promoter. For example, a solicitor appointed for preparing the Articles of Association of a proposed company. He will not be a promoter because he is working for a limited purpose under supervision and under the directions of the promoters.

But if any such person acts beyond the scope of his professional duty and helps in any way in the formation of a company, he becomes the promoter.

Example

Annie is a professional accountant hired by Johnny and James, who were forming a company. The business to be undertaken by the proposed company was to design clothes. Annie had a keen interest and an extensive know-how of that field. So she started taking interest and initiative in meeting various designers, making catalogue of designs, and promoting the brand name.. Acknowledging her capability of promoting the business, to keep her interest alive, they decided to give her an incentive by allotting her 10% of shares in the company after its formation.

It is clear from the above stated case that Annie even though initially appointed as an Accountant for the proposed company, becomes the promoter of the same company.

1. Who can be a promoter?

No specific qualifications are laid down for being a promoter. Any person whether an individual or a body corporate or any association or group of person can be a promoter.

2. Functions of promoters

The promoters of a company take every effort to bring a company into existence and they are undertaking almost all the functions necessary to form a company. Some of these functions are outlined below:

➢ Generating the idea of starting a business and forming a company.
➢ Conducting a feasibility study to determine whether the proposed business is profitable.
➢ Deciding the name of company, and place of registered office.
➢ Settling the details of the Articles of Association.
➢ The nomination of directors, bankers, solicitors, secretary and other key officials of company.
➢ Filing the required documents with registrar.
➢ Arranging for issue of a prospectus, where public issue is necessary.
➢ Safe custody of important documents such as certificate of incorporation and certificate of commencement of business.

3. Fiduciary duty of promoters

The fiduciary duty is a **legal relationship** between two or more parties. A fiduciary is expected to be extremely loyal to the person to whom they owe the duty (the "principal"): they must not put their personal interests before the duty, and must not profit from their position as a fiduciary, unless the principal consents. A promoter stands in a fiduciary relation to the company which he promotes. Fiduciary duty, in a general sense, is the obligation someone has to act wisely on behalf of another, or to act solely in the best interest of another. This includes acting honestly and in good faith and exercising reasonable care and skill while performing tasks on behalf of the business.

Example

A company promoter may receive £10,000 from an investor in a company and instead of banking the money into the company bank account and using it for company purposes, he uses it for his own purposes. Here, he is not acting in the interest of the company. He is breaching his fiduciary duties towards the company.

The fiduciary position of a promoter is:
➢ Promoters have the general duty to **apply reasonable skill and care** in their functions.
➢ The promoter should **not make any secret profit**, either directly or indirectly or through a nominee etc., at the expense of the company which is being promoted, unless the company after full disclosure of the facts consents.
➢ The promoter must **account for any benefits obtained** through acting as a promoter. The disclosure may be made either:
    i. to an independent Board (i.e. Board which is not influenced by the promoters),
    ii. or to the prospective shareholder by means of prospectus
➢ The promoter must not allow his **own interest to conflict with those of the company.**

Example

Where the promoter purchases some property for the company, he cannot rightfully sell that property to the company at a price higher than he got for it. If he does so, the company may, on discovering it, rescind the contract or compel the promoter to surrender the profit.

➢ A promoter should keep proper records of all transactions undertaken by him in relation to the incorporation of company and must account for all monies.

4. Remedy for breach of fiduciary duty

When the fiduciary duties are violated, it is known as breach of fiduciary duties. Some common remedies can be
➢ If any profit is found made by the promoter, which are not disclosed by him, the company may compel him to account for and surrender such profit.
➢ If any wrongful contracts are made by promoter, the company may rescind the contract and recover its money.
➢ A promoter may also be sued for damages for breach of his fiduciary duties.

1.2 Pre-Incorporation contracts

Promoters who are entering into business ventures and who are in the process of incorporating a company, often enter into contracts, called pre-incorporation contracts.

> **Definition**
>
> A pre-incorporation contract is a contract purported to be made by a company or its agent at a time before the company has received its certificate of incorporation.

Those contracts are intended for the benefit of the company to be incorporated but the company to be incorporated cannot enter into a contract because it does not become a legal entity until the certificate of incorporation is issued.

Even after it is incorporated it cannot "ratify" or "adopt" a contract apparently made on its behalf because the promoters are unable to act for a principal which does not exist.

However promoters are often keen to take advantage of a business opportunity while their attorneys are incorporating companies on their behalf. They may for example wish to buy or sell, a business, equipment, a restaurant or do a deal which must be finalise immediately.

The remedy to this is "novation". Novation means the substitution of a new contract for an old one; or the substitution of one party in a contract with another party. **A company may enter into a new contract** on similar terms **after it has been incorporated.** However, there has to be sufficient evidence that the company has made a new contract. Mere recognition of the pre-incorporation contract by performing it or accepting benefits under it is not the same as making a new contract.

The following points need to kept in mind
1. A corporation cannot ratify a contract that a promoter purported to enter into on behalf of the corporation before the corporation came into existence.
2. A promoter can be liable on a pre-incorporation contract but only if it can be said that it was intended in the circumstances that the promoter be a party to the contract.

> ## Case Study A corporation cannot ratify a contract
>
> ### Kelner v Baxter (1866)
>
> In this case, the defendant accepted the terms of an agreement on behalf of a corporation not yet in existence. Both parties were aware that the proposed corporation was not yet in existence. The claimant fulfilled his obligations under the agreement. The corporation was created and sought to adopt the agreement. The corporation then became insolvent before fulfilling its obligations to the claimant. The claimant then sued the defendant in breach.
>
> **Court's decision:** It was held that if the promoter purports to contract on behalf of an unformed company, he will be personally liable provided he is a party to the contract, even though it is expressed that he was contracting only as an agent.

> **Test Yourself 1**
>
> What are pre-incorporation contracts? Are such contracts binding on the company even after its incorporation?

> **Test Yourself 2**
>
> "A company cannot ratify a pre-incorporation contract" comment.

SYNOPSIS

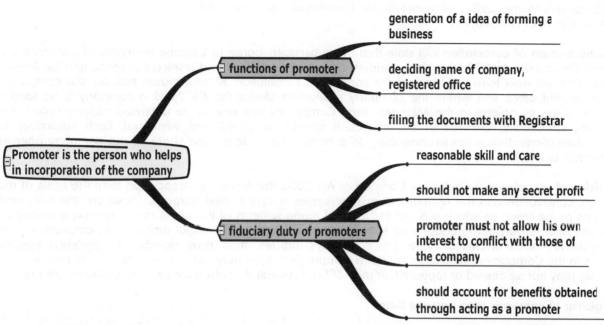

functions of promoter
- generation of a idea of forming a business
- deciding name of company, registered office
- filing the documents with Registrar

Promoter is the person who helps in incorporation of the company

fiduciary duty of promoters
- reasonable skill and care
- should not make any secret profit
- promoter must not allow his own interest to conflict with those of the company
- should account for benefits obtained through acting as a promoter

---

2. Describe the procedure for registering companies, both public and private

[Learning outcome b]

Usually, a company is incorporated by its registration under Companies Act 2006. The following are the steps to be undertaken for incorporation of a company:

1. Deciding the name:

This is governed by Part 6 CA 2006, which is designed to prevent third parties dealing with the company from being misled.. The CA 2006 includes new sections, ss 70-40, which provide for the appointment of company name adjudicators in cases where there is a dispute over registering a company name.
Part 5 CA 2006 introduces significant changes to provisions on a company's name

Most names are acceptable to the Companies House when forming a limited company, but there are a few exceptions. These exceptions are

a) S54 CA 2006 provides that the approval of the Secretary of State is needed if a name gives the impression that the company is connected with Her Majesty's Government
b) Proposed name must be different from that of a company already incorporated.: s.69-74 CA 2006
c) Certain words like "Group" or "International" must be substantiated by providing evidence of other related companies or companies operating in at least two different countries.
d) Names containing words likely to cause offence are not allowed, s.53 CA 2006
e) sensitive words require the approval of the Secretary of State p s.55(1) CA 2006
f) S57(1) CA 2006 provides that the Secretary of State may make provision by regulations as to the letters or other characters, signs or symbols and punctuation that may be used.

2. Documents to be submitted

The following must be submitted to register a new UK Company:

a) S9(1) CA 2006 states that the Memorandum of Association must be delivered to the Registrar together with the following details:

➢ Company's proposed name
➢ Whether the company's registered office is to be situated in England and Wales, in Scotland or in Northern Ireland.
➢ Whether the liability of the members is to be limited by shares or by guarantee
➢ Whether the company is to be a public or a private company
➢ Whether the company is to have a share capital
➢ A statement of the company's proposed officers
➢ A statement of the company's intended address

> A copy of the proposed Articles of Association (to the extent that the company does not intend to use the model articles under s20 CA 2006
> Company's Memorandum of Association in a new-look 'short form' style
> A statement of compliance.

The Memorandum of association will state that the subscribers agree to become members of the company. Under the Companies Act 2006 the Memorandum now serves a limited and restricted purpose and the Articles of Association will now form the basis of the company's constitution. Memorandum sets out the company's name, registered office and where the company is situated. Under the CA 2006 a company is no longer required to state its objects in the Memorandum. Companies will now have unlimited objects, unless the objects are specifically restricted in the Articles. It should be dated and witnessed. Each subscriber to Memorandum of association has to undertake to subscribe for at least one share of the company after its incorporation. (s.1 (1)).

The Articles of association – Under the Companies Act 2006 the Articles of Association form the basis of the company's constitution and the Memorandum now serves a very limited purpose. These are the rules and regulations or the bye-laws which sets out the internal managements of the company. A company limited by shares may alternatively opt to endorse its Memorandum as 'registered without articles of association'. In that case, the default model articles become the company's articles. It is now possible to entrench specific provisions in the Company's constitution so that a company's articles may not provide that specific provisions in the articles may not be altered or repealed, or may only be repealed or altered if certain conditions are me.

3. **Registrar of company then ensures that:**

a) All the requirements of Companies Act 2006 have been complied with.
b) The name of the company is lawful.
c) In the case of public company, its share capital is not less than the authorised minimum (Which is at least £50,000).
d) The Memorandum and Articles of Association do not contravene the provisions of Companies Act.

4. **Issue of certificate of incorporation**

Once the registrar is satisfied that all the requirements are complied with, he will issue a certificate of incorporation. Such a certificate is conclusive evidence that
a) All requirements of the Companies Act in respect of registration and of matters precedent and incidental thereto have been complied with.
b) The company has been properly incorporated.
c) It places the existence of company as a legal person beyond doubt.

Specimen copy of a certificate of Incorporation

CERTIFICATE OF INCORPORATION OF A PRIVATE LIMITED COMPANY

Company Number 104210

I hereby certify that EDINBURGH TECHNOLOGY TRANSFER CENTRE LIMITED is this day incorporated under the Companies Act 2006 as a Private company and that the Company is limited

Signed at Edinburgh
9 NOVEMBER 2007

Registrar of Companies

C 13 Od8925729 6M 8/87 R.P. (53791)

5. Further requirement for a public company

A private company can start its business and exercise its borrowing powers as soon as the certificate of incorporation is issued. A public company, however, cannot start a business or borrow money until it has obtained an additional certificate called Certificate of Commencement of business from the registrar under s.756 of Companies Act 2006.

a) To obtain the certificate under s.756 CA 2006 i.e. certificate of business commencement, a public company has to   make an application. and comply with the provisions of s763 CA 2006

b) This application is to be signed by director or the secretary.

c) A statutory declaration to be made by the person signing the application to the effect that:

  i   The nominal value of the allotted share capital is not less than £50,000
  ii The paid up capital is not less that 25% of the nominal value of allotted capital (amount of premium, if any, not to be included in paid up capital for this purpose)
  iii The amount, or estimated amount, of the preliminary expenses of the company and the persons by whom any of those expenses have been paid or are payable; and
  iv Any amount or benefit paid or given or intended to be paid or given to any promoter of the company, and the consideration for the payment or benefit.

Consequences if public company starts business before obtaining business commencement certificate under s.756 CA 2006.

➤ If a public company does any business or borrows before obtaining a certificate of commencement of business, the transaction is valid as a company is a legally existing company. Hence the other party dealing with the company is protected.

➤ However, the company and any officer in default are punishable with a fine not exceeding £500.

➤ The other party may call on the directors to obtain a certificate of business commencement under s.756.

➤ On failure to do so within 21 days, directors of the company shall be jointly and severally liable to indemnify the other party to the transaction in respect of any loss or damage suffered by him by reason of the failure of the company to comply with those obligations (s.756 CA 2006).

➤ If a public company fails to obtain s.756 certificate within a period of one year after incorporation, a petition may be presented for its compulsory winding up. (s.122(1) (b) Insolvency Act 1986.

Diagram 1: Procedure for registering the companies

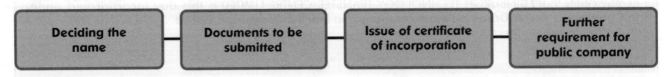

| Deciding the name | Documents to be submitted | Issue of certificate of incorporation | Further requirement for public company |

Test Yourself 3

What are the steps involved in the process of registering the company?

Test Yourself 4

A public limited company duly incorporated under Companies Act , purchases goods worth £1,200 on credit from Mr. David. Two days after the transaction, David came to know that the company was not holding a certificate under s.756 and hence not entitled to carry on business. Is the transaction between the company and Mr. David valid? What are the alternatives available to David to recover his amount?

SYNOPSIS

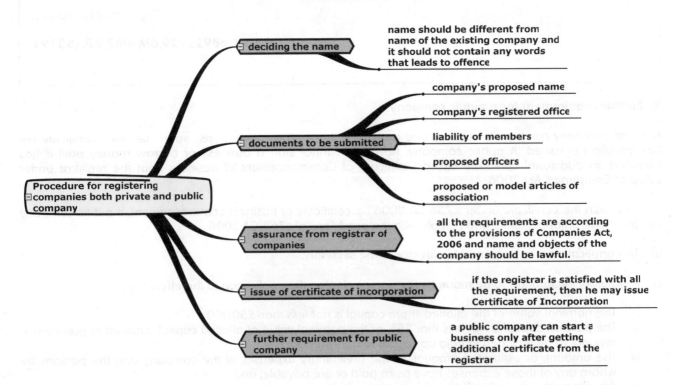

3. Describe the statutory books, records and returns that companies must keep or make
[Learning outcome c]

3.1 Statutory books

Every incorporated company maintains certain books and registers for the purpose of record as well as to secure efficiency in operation. Some of these books have to be maintained compulsorily by all companies under the provisions of Companies Act . These are known as statutory books. To facilitate the easy inspection by people who are entitled to have access to these books the company must keep them either at registered office or other specified place. Companies Act 2006 enable a Company to use electronic storage or paper for its records provided there can be paper printouts of electronic records.

The Companies Act requires every English, Scottish or Welsh registered company, to have available at its registered office various records which contain information relating to the company **including**
- A register of members (s 113(1) CA 2006.
- A register of directors and secretaries along with their service address (s 162 CA 2006)
- A register of directors' interests .(s.808 CA 2006)
- A register of charges (s.860 CA 2006).
- Minutes of proceedings of any general meeting of the company (s.383).
- Minutes of directors and managers meetings (s248 CA 2006)).
- A register of written resolution (s.288-289 CA 2006)).
- A register of members holding substantial interest (i.e. 3% or more of the nominal value of any class of shares) in company.

1. Register of members

Under s 113(1) CA 2006, every company must keep a register of members. It contains:

a) Name and address of every member.

b) in case the company has a share capital, the register shall contain particulars regarding:
   i. The number of shares held by each member. If the shares have distinguishing numbers, the member's shares must be identified in the register by those numbers.
   ii. Where there is more than one class of shares for e.g. ordinary shares or preference shares, then the member's shares in the register must be distinguished by their class.

c) The date on which a person was admitted as a member and the date on which she / he ceased to be a member.

Place of keeping register of members

- At the registered office.
- At another office of the company in England and Wales, provided such office is notified to registrar.
- At the office of professional registrar in England and Wales, provided such office is notified to registrar.

2. Register of directors and secretaries (s.162 CA 2006)

This register must contain following details of the directors and secretaries:
a) Present and former forenames and surnames.
b) Service address.
c) Date of birth.
d) Nationality.
e) Business occupation.
f) Particulars of other directorship, if any, held in last 5 years.

The register must

- Contain **particulars of all directors** including shadow directors (to be studied later).
- **Open to inspection** by any member free of charge and by non-member for a fee.

Tips

Shadow director: Person not appointed as director of the company but according to whose instructions, the Board of Directors of the Company is accustomed to act.

3. Register of directors' interests (s.808 CA 2006)

This register is maintained to
a) Record each director's interest in shares and debentures.
b) The director's interest includes interests of a director's spouse and minor children.
c) The director must notify the interest within five days of his becoming aware of it.
d) The company must then amend the register within three days.
e) The register is to be kept either at the registered office or where the register of members is kept.

4. Register of charges (s.860 CA 2006)

A **charge** is a security created in favour of a creditor at the time of accepting a loan for the payment of a debt by the company. Charges can be either fixed or floating. All the charges are required to be registered with the Companies Registrar within 21 days of their creation (CA s.395 and s.396).

The company must maintain a register of charges which must contain
a) Details of charges affecting the company property or undertaking.
b) Brief description of property charged.
c) The amount of the charge.
d) The name of the person in whose favour the charge is created.

The register must

➢ Be kept at registered office.
➢ Be **open to inspection** by any member and creditors free of charge and by non-member for a fee.

Test Yourself 5

What are the registers that a company is statutorily required to maintain under the provisions of Companies Act 2006?

3.2 Accounting records

S.386 of Company's Act 2006 requires companies to keep at their registered office (or at any other place as the directors see fit) accounting records which should be sufficient to show and explain the company's transactions.
➢ To ensure that the income statement and balance sheet of company complies with statutory requirements.
➢ To disclose with reasonable accuracy, the financial position of company.

These records contain

➢ Entries from day to day of all sums of moneys received and spent by the company and the matter in respect of which the receipts and expenditure takes place.
➢ A record of companies' assets and liabilities.
➢ Statements relating to holding of stock.
➢ Records of stock-taking.
➢ Statements of all goods sold and purchased in sufficient detail to enable identification of the goods and the buyers and sellers.

Other important points

➢ These records must be kept for a **minimum period of three years by a private company** and a **minimum of six years by a public company**.
➢ Failure to keep such accounting records will result in a criminal offence, unless the company officers can show that they acted honestly, and that the default was excusable in the circumstances.
➢ The accounting records must be **open to inspection by the company's officers** at all times. The term officers in this context include the directors, secretary and managers.
➢ The **members of the company do not have a statutory right to inspect** the accounting records but under the Model Article, they may gain such right by ordinary resolution or through authorization by a director.

3.3 Annual returns

➢ An annual return is a snapshot of general information about a company's directors and secretary, registered office address, shareholders and share capital.

➢ If the annual return is filed late, or not at all filed, the company and its director(s) and secretary can be prosecuted.

➢ Every company must deliver an annual return to Companies House.

➢ a company's director(s) and secretary are responsible for ensuring that the annual return
   i.   Is delivered to Companies House within 28 days after the anniversary of incorporation or the anniversary of the date of the last annual return; and
   ii.   Gives a true picture of the management structure and capital (if applicable) of the company at the date on which return is made.

➢ The return must be signed by a director or a secretary and accompanied by a fee of £15.

Tips

Remember: Not delivering the company's annual return within 28 days of their preparation is a **criminal offence**, for which company secretaries and directors may be prosecuted.

➢ An annual return must contain the following information:

   i.   The name of the company.
   ii.   Its registered number.
   iii.   The type of company it is, for example, private or public.
   iv.   The registered office address of the company.
   v.   The address where certain company registers is kept if not at the registered office.
   vi.   The principal business activities of the company.
   vii.   The name and address of the company secretary.
   viii.   The name, address, date of birth, nationality and business occupation of all the company's directors. No longer have to give residential addresses but can provide a service address, in order to protect their privacy
   ix.   The date to which the annual return is made-up (the made-up date).

     And if the company has share capital, the annual return must also contain:

   x.   The nominal value of total issued share capital;
   xi.   The names and addresses of shareholders and the number and type of shares they hold or transfer from other shareholders.

Test Yourself 6

When must the annual return be delivered to Companies House?

Test Yourself 7

Every company is required to maintain, at its registered office, proper books of account. What is meant by 'proper' books of accounts?

SYNOPSIS
Statutory books, records, returns that companies must keep or make

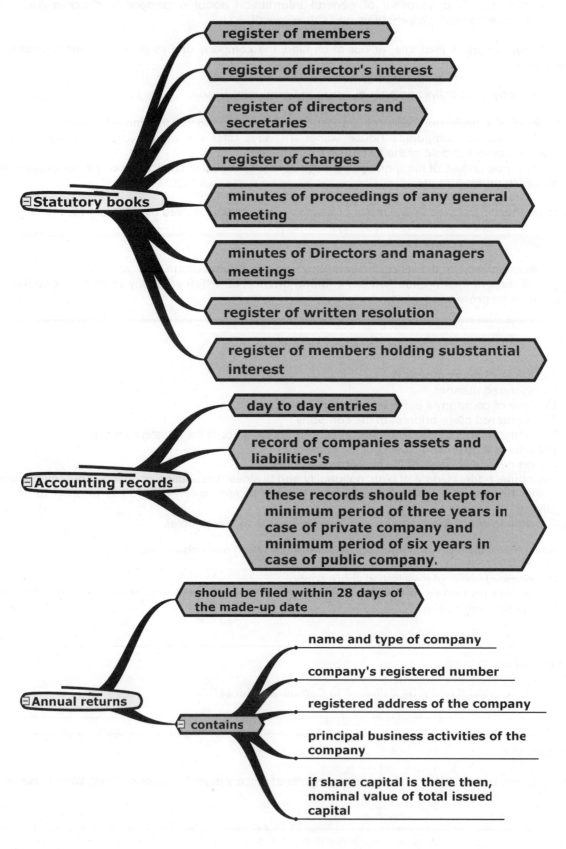

4. Describe the contents of Model articles of association

The Articles sets out the rules and regulations for the running of the company's internal affairs and form the company's constitution. It is the most important document to be filed with the registrar at the time of incorporation of the company. A company's Articles of Association are its internal rulebook. They typically deal with such matters as decision-making by the company's directors and members and the rights of its members to receive dividends on their shares.

Definition

The true nature of Articles can be understood by the observation of Lord Cairns in Ashbury Railway Carriage and Iron Co v Riche- "The Articles proceed to define the duties, the rights and the powers of the governing body as between themselves and the company at a large, and the mode and form in which the business of the company is to be carried on, and the mode and form in which changes in the internal regulations of the company may, from time to time, be made".

Important points to consider

➤ The articles are the dominant document, with the Memorandum having little significance under CA 2006

➤ The Articles can not override the Companies Act.

➤ The Companies Act may permit companies to do something if their articles also authorize them to do so.

Example

According to Act, a company may reduce its capital if its articles give power to do so. Hence, where company want to reduce its capital but its articles do not contain this clause then the company has to first alter its articles to include the necessary power.

Contents of Articles

Articles usually contain the following matters:
a) The exclusion, whole or in part, of Model Article.
b) Appointment of managing personnel such as directors, secretary, their remuneration, qualifications, powers etc.
c) Proceedings of Board meetings.
d) Appointment and remuneration of auditors.
e) Rights of different classes of shares.
f) Issue of shares.
g) Transfer of shares.
h) Alteration of capital structure.
i) Accounts and audit.
j) Dividends and reserves.
k) Conduct of general meeting.
l) Borrowings powers.

Articles must

➤ Be printed.
➤ Be divided into paragraphs numbered consecutively.

B be signed by each subscriber of the memorandum in the presence of at least one witness.

Where the articles are delivered to the registrar in legible form and are authenticated by each subscriber to the memorandum in such manner as is directed by the registrar, then the formalities regarding signature in the presence of at least one witness and attestation of the signature are not required to be fulfilled.

Model articles

While the articles are always subject to rules of general company law, companies are given considerable freedom to make their own rules in their articles. Alternatively, a company may adopt the whole of Model Article as its articles or any part of it.

What is Model Article?

Model Article is a specimen set of articles for a company limited by shares. It is used as the basis for most companies' articles. The current version of Model Article is to be found in s20 CA 2006.

A company limited by shares which has adopted the whole of Model Article without modification does not need to deliver a copy for registration. However, company must attach a letter to the application for incorporation stating that.

"Companies Act 2006, sec. 18 provides that the terms of Model Article apply to every company except insofar as they are not excluded, and it is possible to register a company without articles in which case the company has all of Model Article as its articles".

> **Test Yourself 8**
>
> What are the Articles of Association and state their contents.

SYNOPSIS

Contents of model articles of association

- appointment of directors, secretary
- appointment and remuneration of directors
- issue of shares
- transfer of shares
- accounts and audit
- dividends and reserves

5. Analyse the effect of a company's constitutional documents

[Learning outcome e]

The Articles constitutes a statutory contract between the company and its members

The effect of articles:

1. The position is now governed by s 33(1) CA 206 which replaces s14(1) CA 1985. Its effect is that the provisions of a company's constitution constitute a special kind of contract, whose terms bind the company and its members from time to time. Unlike s14 CA 1985, s33 CA 2006 refers to the company's constitution rather than its memorandum and articles.

Case Study   The articles are enforceable by the company against the shareholders

Hickman v Kent or Romney Marsh Sheep Breeders Association (1920)

The Company's Articles provide that any dispute between the company and its members were to be referred to arbitration. A member, however, instead of referring the dispute to arbitrator, brought court proceedings against the company.

Court's decision: The Company was held entitled to insist the member to comply with articles which provided that disputes between the company and member should be referred to the arbitrator. The company could enforce the arbitration clause against the member. The proceedings were stayed.

2. The company is contractually bound to each member to abide by the terms of document.

Case Study — The articles are enforceable by the shareholders against the company

Pender v Lushington (1877)

The Company's Articles provided that every member will have one vote per hundred shares subject to a maximum of hundred votes. One of the shareholders holding more than one thousand votes transferred the surplus shares to a nominee and directed him how to vote. The chairman refused to accept the nominee's vote.

Court's decision: The member was held entitled to enforce his constitutional right to vote at a company meeting.

3. Members are bound to each other.

Case Study — The articles constitute a contract between the members.

Rayfield v Hands (1960)

In this case, the articles of the company provided that where shareholders wished to transfer their shares, they should inform the directors of the company who were obliged to take the shares equally between them at fair value. The directors refused to purchase the claimant's shares.

Court's decision: The court held that the directors were bound as members by the articles and therefore had to comply with the procedure set out there.

It is however important to note that memorandum and articles creates a contractual relationship in respect of membership rights only. The non-members or members acting in other capacity cannot enforce the provisions of these documents.

Case Study — Rights under the constitutional documents can be enforced only by members

Eley v Posotive Government Life Assurance (1876)

The articles provided that Aley should be the solicitor for the life of the company and would not be removed from office except for misconduct. He was also a member of the company. Eley worked as solicitor to the company for some years but he was removed from service without any charge of misconduct. He sued the company for damages for breach of contract.

Court's decision: It was held that he had no cause of action. The articles only constitute a contract between the company and its members, and although Aley was a member of the company, he was not suing in that capacity but in a different capacity as the company's solicitor

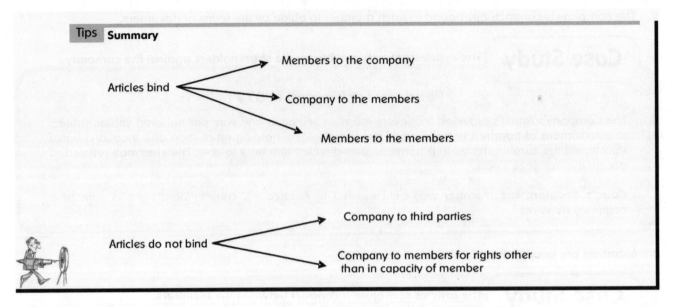

SYNOPSIS

| Effect of company's constitutional documents | company is contractually bound to each member and members are bound to each other. |

6. Explain how articles of association can be changed

[Learning outcome f]

A company has wide powers to alter its Articles to suit its requirements from time to time. A company can alter its Articles by passing a special resolution s.21(1 CA 2006). But care must be taken to ensure that the alteration must not conflict with provisions of Companies Act 2006.

Important points to remember

1. The power to alter Articles is a **statutory power** and, therefore, no company can deprive itself of this power either by a provision in the Articles or by a contract with a third party. (Walker v London Tramways Co).

2. Section 22(1) CA 2006 states that a company's articles may provide that specified provisions of the articles may not be altered.

3. An article can not be made unalterable by providing that a larger majority of votes shall be required on a special resolution to make an alteration. (Malleson v National Insurance & Guarantee Corporation 1894)

4. A clause in the Articles that no alteration shall be made without the consent of a particular person is ineffective.(Bushel v. Faith)

A special resolution by circulation is also sufficient to alter the Articles i.e. if all the members of the company agree to an alteration of Articles, the resolution can be held passed if they all sign the resolution when circulated to them without actually holding a general meeting.

Once an alteration is duly made, it shall be valid as if originally contained in Articles. The altered Articles shall be binding on the members in the same way as original articles and such altered articles may again be altered by special resolution

Restrictions on alteration of articles

The Articles may be altered by passing a special resolution. However, an alteration of Articles shall be subject to the following restriction:

a) An alteration can not be inconsistent with companies Act i.e.
➢   Any rights given to members by the Act cannot be taken away by alteration of Articles.

Example

Tasty Ltd altered its Articles to empower the company to make discrimination of rights between the various classes of members. However, such discrimination of rights is against the Act. Hence, no alteration can be made to the Articles of the company for this purpose.

➢   Any restriction imposed on the company can not be removed by alteration of Articles.

Example

Alteration can not be made to Articles to empower a company to adopt any pre-incorporation contract entered in by the promoters.

---

b) An alteration must not be unlawful or against the public policy.
c) An alteration must not compel the members to assume additional liability by subscribing for additional shares without the consent of the shareholder (s.16).
d) An alteration must be bona fide and in the interest of the company as a whole.

Case Study   An alteration must be bona fide and in the interest of the company as a whole.

Brown v British Abrasive Wheel (1920)

The company's articles were altered to enable the majority to purchase the shares of the minority at a fair value. The intention behind such a clause was to purchase the shares of some minority members who were refusing to bring in more capital into the company. They objected to the alteration.

Court's decision: The alteration was held ineffective. It was considered that the alteration was not bona fide as it would benefit the majority shareholders rather than the company as a whole.

SYNOPSIS

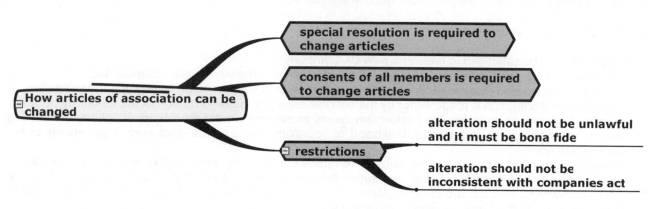

special resolution is required to change articles

consents of all members is required to change articles

How articles of association can be changed

restrictions

alteration should not be unlawful and it must be bona fide

alteration should not be inconsistent with companies act

Answers to Test Yourself

Answer 1

Pre-incorporation contracts are the contracts made by promoters, with parties to acquire some property on right for and on behalf of a company that is yet to be formed.

Where the promoters of a company have, before its incorporation, entered into contracts for the purposes of the company and such contracts are **warranted by terms of incorporation,** the contract may be specifically enforced by or against the company, if the company has accepted the contract and communicated such acceptance to the other party to the contract.

The contract should be for the purposes of company operations. The other party can also enforce the contract if the company has adopted it after incorporation and the contract is within the terms of incorporation.

Answer 2

It is correct to say that a company cannot ratify pre-incorporation contracts after its incorporation. This is because only a principal who is in existence at the time of contract is competent to ratify such contract. However, a company is not in existence until it is legally incorporated under the Company's Act. Since the company not in existence at the time of making the contract, the ratification is not possible. In **Kelner v Baxter,** it was held that a company could not ratify a pre-incorporation contract. The position remains unchanged even if the company has received some benefits under the contract.

Therefore the only remedy open for the company is to enter into a fresh contract after being incorporated a similar / same terms and conditions and carry out the contract made by its promoters.

Answer 3

According to the provisions of the Companies Act, the following steps are involved in the process of registering the company:

1. Deciding the name

Most names are acceptable to Companies House when forming a limited company,   but there are a few exceptions. These exceptions are:
➢ Proposed name must be different from that of a company already incorporated.
➢ Certain words like "Group" or "International" must be substantiated by providing evidence of other related companies or companies operating in at least two different countries.
➢ Names containing words likely to cause offence are not allowed.

2. Documents to be submitted

The following must be submitted to register a new UK Company.
➢ summary of a company's first directors, secretary, other officers, registered office address, etc
➢ A statutory declaration that the information filed as part of, or in support of, an incorporation application is correct. Such declaration is made either by the solicitor engaged in the formation of the company or by the proposed director or secretary. The declaration allows prosecution under the Perjury Act of anyone making false statements and so reduces the likelihood of applicants avoiding the disclosure requirements of the Companies Act.
➢ Memorandum of Association setting out the company's name, registered office, where the company is situated. It is to be signed by at least two subscribers or one in case of single member private company, dated and witnessed. Each subscriber to Memorandum of association has to undertake to subscribe for at least one share of the company after its incorporation.
➢ Articles of Association containing the rules and regulations or the bye-laws which sets out the internal managements of the company. A company limited by shares may alternatively adopt, the statutory Model Articles.
➢ A registration Fee

3. Registrar of company then ensures that:

a) All the requirements of Companies Act have been complied with.
b) The name of the company is lawful.
c) In the case of public company, its share capital is not less than the authorised minimum. (which is at least £50,000)
d) The memorandum and articles of association do not contravene the provisions of Companies Act.

4. Issue of certificate of incorporation

Once the registrar is satisfied that all the requirements are complied with, he will issue a certificate of incorporation. Such a certificate is conclusive evidence that all requirements of the companies Act in respect of registration and of matters precedent and incidental thereto have been complied with.

5. Further requirement for public company

A private company can start a business as soon as getting the certificate of incorporation; but public company can start a business only after getting the additional certificate for commencement of business.

Answer 4

If a public company does any business or borrows before obtaining a certificate of commencement of business, the transaction is valid as a company is a legally existing company. Hence the other party dealing with the company is protected. However, the company and any officer in default are punishable with a fine not exceeding £500. Thus the transaction between the company and David is a valid transaction and therefore binding upon the company.

If a public company does any business or borrows before obtaining a certificate of commencement of business, the other party may call on the directors to obtain a certificate of business commencement under s 756. On failure to do so within 21 days, directors of the company shall be jointly and severally liable to indemnify the other party to the transaction in respect of any loss or damage suffered by him by reason of the failure of the company to comply with those obligations. Therefore, David can call on the directors of the company to obtain a certificate of business commencement under s 756. If they fail to do so, David is entitled to be indemnified by the directors for losses he had suffered.

Answer 5

Following are the registers that a company is statutorily required to maintain under the provisions of Companies Act,.
➢ Register of members containing names and addresses of all the members.
➢ Register of directors and secretaries containing names and forenames of all directors, secretaries, nationality, address, date of birth and so on.
➢ Register of directors' interests containing each director's interest in shares and debentures.
➢ Register of charges containing details of charges, property charged, amount of charge, name and person who is responsible for charge.

Answer 6

The annual return must be delivered to Companies House within 28 days of return date. Return date for this purpose is
➢ the anniversary of incorporation or
➢ the anniversary of the date of the last annual return

Answer 7

Proper books of account must fulfil the following
➢ they must exhibit and explain the transactions and financial position of the business of the company, including books, containing sufficiently detailed entries of daily cash receipts and payments.
➢ where the business of the company is involved with dealings in goods, statements of the annual stock takings (except in the case of goods sold by way of ordinary retail trade) of all goods, sold and purchased and the buyers and sellers, thereof, should be shown in sufficient detail to enable these goods and these buyers and sellers to be identified.
➢ they must include the cost accounting records and stock records, apart from normal books of account.
➢ the records should, inter alia, contain prescribed particulars of elements of cost, viz., - material, labour, overheads, etc.

Similarly, the proper maintenance of stock records is also a necessity, as, in the absence of proper stock records, the truth and fairness of the annual statement of account cannot be properly understood.

Answer 8

The Articles sets out the rules and regulations for the running of the company's internal affairs. The articles now form the basis of the company's constitution and the memorandum is of little significance under CA 2006. Articles are the most important document to be filed with the registrar at the time of incorporation of the company. A company's Articles of Association are its internal rulebook. They typically deal with such matters as decision-making by the company's directors and members and the rights of its members to receive dividends on their shares.

The true nature of Articles can be understood by the observation of Lord Cairns in Ashbury Railway Carriage and Iron Co v Riche. "The Articles proceed to define the duties, the rights and the powers of the governing body as between themselves and the company at a large, and the mode and form in which the business of the company is to be carried on, and the mode and form in which changes in the internal regulations of the company may, from time to time, be made".

Articles must be printed, be divided into paragraphs numbered consecutively and be signed by each subscriber of the memorandum in the presence of at least one witness who must attest the signature.

It is important to note that Articles of Association can not override the Companies Act. The companies Act may permit companies to do something if their articles also authorize them to do so. For example, a company may reduce its capital if its Articles give power to do so. Hence, where company want to reduce its capital but its Articles do not contain this clause then the company has to first alter its Articles to include the necessary power.

A company may adopt the whole of Model Article as its articles or any part of it.

Contents of Articles

Articles usually contain the following:
➢ The exclusion, whole or in part, of Model Article.
➢ appointment of managing personnel such as directors, secretary, their remuneration, qualifications, powers etc
➢ Proceedings of Board meetings.
➢ Appointment and remuneration of auditors.
➢ Rights of different classes of shares.
➢ Issue of shares.
➢ Transfer of shares.
➢ Alteration of capital structure.
➢ Accounts and audit.
➢ Dividends and reserves.
➢ Conduct of general meeting.
➢ Borrowings powers.

Where the articles are delivered to the registrar in legible form and are authenticated by each subscriber to the memorandum in such manner as is directed by the registrar, the requirements in subsection (3) (c) do not apply. It means the formalities regarding signature in the presence of at least one witness and attestation of the signature are not required to be fulfilled.

Model Article whilst the articles are always subject to rules of general company law, companies are given considerable freedom to make their own rules in their articles.

Quick Quiz

1. **State true or false**
   a) Even a registered company may act as a promoter.
   b) A company can ratify a pre-incorporation contract entered into by its promoters, after its incorporation.
   c) The certificate of incorporation, once issued, is conclusive evidence that the company has been duly registered.
   d) Not filing an annual return with stipulated time is a criminal offence for which company secretaries and directors may be prosecuted.

2. Choose the correct alternative.

   a) The Articles of Association of Tick Tock Ltd contained a clause which stated that Anil would be the company's solicitor for 20 years and shall not be removed except on the grounds of misconduct. After 2 years, Anil was removed by the company as solicitor on the grounds other than on misconduct. Which of the following statement(s) is/are correct?
   i. The removal of Anil is not valid.
   ii. The removal of Anil is valid.

iii.The Articles cannot create contract between company and outsiders.
iv.The Articles cannot create contract between its members and the company.
v. both (ii) and (iii)

b) The Articles of Growth Well Ltd empowers the company to create lien on partly paid share only. Jimmy, holder of fully paid shares of the company, owed money to the company. Growth Well Ltd altered the Articles so as to give it a lien on fully paid-up shares also. Which of the following statement(s) is/are correct?
i. The alteration of the Articles is not valid as it amounts to infringement of individual rights.
ii. The alteration of the Articles is not valid as it amounts to oppression against the shareholder
iii.The alteration is ultra vires the company.
iv.The alteration of articles is valid
v. None of above.

3   Define the Certificate of incorporation?

4.   On which documents must the company name be displayed?

Answers to Quick Quiz

1. a) True
    b) False
    c) True
    d) True

2. a)   The correct option is (v)
The Articles do not confer any contractual rights upon outsiders against the company or its members, even though the outsider is mentioned in the articles. An outsider cannot rely on articles of association for his action against the company.

In the given case, Anil cannot sue the company as the Articles of Association will not create any contract between the company and the outsiders.

b)   The correct option is (iv)
The Companies Act provides very wide powers to companies to alter its articles. But the alteration of Articles
➢ Must not be inconsistent with the Companies Act.
➢ Must not sanction anything illegal.
➢ Must be bona fide for the benefit of the company as a whole.

In the given case also, the alteration of articles is made for the benefit of the company and is valid.

3. The certificate of incorporation is the birth certificate of the company. It is a certificate issued by the registrar of companies to the effect that, all legal formalities having been complied with, a company have come into being.

4. The company must state its name, place of registration and the registration number, address of registered office, and if the company is an investment company, the fact that it is such a company, in legible lettering, on the following:
i.   all the company's business letters
ii.   all its notices and other official publications
iii. all bills of exchange, promissory notes, endorsements, cheques and orders for money or goods purporting to be signed by, or on behalf of, the company all its bills of parcels, invoices, receipts and letters of credit
iv. Iv on all its websites

Self Examination Questions

Question 1

Distinguish between the Memorandum and the Articles.

Question 2

State the effect of the provisions of the Articles of Association' upon the contractual relations between different parties upon registration of a company? To what extent are they binding?

Answers to Self Examination Questions

Answer 1

Basis of distinction	Memorandum	Articles
1. Definition	Memorandum means the Memorandum of Association of a company as originally framed or as altered from time to time in pursuance of the companies Act 2006.	'Articles' means the Articles of Association of a company as originally framed or as altered from time to time in pursuance of the companies Act 2006 including, so far as they apply to the company, the regulations contained in Model Articles.
2. Nature of document	Memorandum has a limited purpose under CA 2006	Articles are constitution of Company.
3. Powers v Rules	Memorandum states that the subscribers agree to become member of the company.	Articles contain the rules and regulations for the internal management of the company
4. Hierarchy	In case of any inconsistency, the Articles shall prevail over the Memorandum.	The Articles dominate over the memorandum.
5. Requirements for alteration	Alteration of Memorandum is simple	Alteration of Articles is restricted as compared to alteration of Memorandum.
6. Retrospective amendment	The Memorandum can be amended retrospectively.	The Articles cannot be amended retrospectively.
7. Effect of contravention.	Any act done in contravention of provisions contained in the Memorandum can be enforced against the company, as per the doctrine of indoor management.	Any act done in contravention of object clause of Articles is ultra vires the company and is wholly void, as per the doctrine of ultra vires.
8. Mandatory or not	Every company must have its own Memorandum.	A public company limited by shares may adopt Model Articles, and in such a case it need not have its own Articles.

Answer 2

1. The company is bound to members

a) **A member can enforce his individual rights.** Every member is given some individual rights under the Act and the articles. If a company derives any of its members of such rights, such a member can sue the company for enforcement of such rights.

b) **The company must comply with the articles.** The company is bound to comply with all the terms and conditions contained in the articles.

2. Members are bound in company

When articles are registered, it shall be deemed that they were signed by every member of the company individually and therefore, every member shall be bound to comply with the provisions contained in the articles. Thus, every member is bound to act in accordance with the provisions contained in the articles of the company. In case of non-compliance, the company may sue a member.

Any money that is due to the company from the member under the articles shall be deemed to be a debt due from the member.

For example in **Boreland Trustees V Steel Bros. Co Ltd,** the articles of a company provided that in case of insolvency of any member his shares shall be liable to be sold by the directors of the company at a price to be fixed by the Board. A member became insolvent. His official assignee was held to be bound by the terms contained in the articles.

3. Members are bound inter se (i.e with each other)

Every member is bound to all the other members. However, there is no privity of contract between the members. Therefore, a member may enforce his rights against another member only through the company and not directly. Therefore, defaulting member may be sued by the company at the instance (i.e. application) of any other member.

4. The company is not bound to outsiders

The Articles do not bind a company to the outsiders. Similarly, the outsiders are not bound to the company by the terms contained in the Articles.

In other words, the Articles do not constitute a contract between the company and the outsiders. Therefore, an outsider cannot proceed against the company on the basis of any provision contained in the articles.

Member as an outsider: If a person is an outsider as well as a member, he cannot sue the company for breach of a provision contained in the articles, if his rights in the capacity of a member are not affected.

For e.g. **in Eley V Positive Government Security Life Assurance Co,** Eley was the secretary of a company. The articles of the company provided that Eley shall not be removed from service except in case of proven misconduct. Eley afterwards became a member of the company. After some years, Eley was removed from service, even though there was no misconduct on his part. Eley claimed compensation from the company on the ground of breach of contract as between the company and Eley since Eley was an outsider (even though he was a member, but since his rights as a member were not affected, he was held to be an outsider and not a member).

SECTION E - CAPITAL AND THE FINANCING OF COMPANIES

SHARE CAPITAL

When a company **commences** its business it **requires funds**.

This Study Guide has already discussed, that **a private company is not allowed to raise funds from the general public**. So, the capital required by a private company, is obtained mainly from family members, relatives and friends.

However, **a public company can raise capital by selling its shares to the general public**.

This Study Guide will help students gain **the requisite knowledge** about the **meaning of share capital, various classes of share capital, and the rights of shareholders and the procedures to alter these rights**.

Qualified accountants have the responsibility to guide the company in the formation process, right from the promotion stage. Accountants have to advise clients about **the relative advantages\disadvantages of the various types of shares that can be issued** and guide them in **selecting the most appropriate type of shares to be issued**.

This Study Guide is also important from the examination point of view.

LEARNING OUTCOMES

a) Examine the different meanings of capital
b) Illustrate the difference between various classes of shares
c) Explain the procedure for altering class rights

Introduction

Why should a company issue shares?

The ability to acquire financial resources is, aside from the actual business plan, a precondition for successful business undertaking. Thanks to sufficient capital, a company may successfully implement its goals and react to emerging business opportunities as well as the competitor's activities.

Companies, however, also pay their dues for opportunities brought on by the growing globalisation of business undertakings. The dues are in the form of ever growing demands on survival amongst the competition of multinational entities with strong capital. For medium sized and larger companies, optimisation of their capital expenditures is a necessity. Such optimisation is carried out by a suitable combination of debt financing and financing through shares. The most frequent form of acquiring share capital is an issue of shares.

The advantage of raising money by way of shares is that companies don't have to pay the money back or pay interest to the investors. Instead, shareholders are entitled to a share of the distributed profits of the company, known as dividends.

Selling shares in a company on a stock market can provide:

➢ new finance
➢ an exit for founding investors who want to realise their investment
➢ a mechanism for investors to trade shares
➢ a market valuation for the company
➢ an incentive for staff using shares or share options
➢ the business with an acquisition currency in the form of shares
➢ a way to raise a business' profile

1. Examine the different meanings of capital

[Learning outcome a]

The term capital is used in a variety of meanings.

It means one thing to economists, another to accountants, still another to businessmen and lawyers. In case of companies the term capital is used to mean the funds raised by a company.

Capital raised by a company can be of two types:

a) Share capital (by issue of shares)
b) Loan capital (by issue of debenture)

In this chapter we are going to study the concept of share capital.
In simple words, the amount raised by the **issue of shares** is called the share capital.

1.1 Types of share capital

The share capital of a company can be of the following types:

1. Authorised capital

This is also known as nominal or registered capital. The company Law Review recommended that the requirement for a company to have an authorised share capital should be abolished and so CA 2006 does not require a company to state in its memorandum the amount of its share capital as the capital of the company with which it is to be registered. It was the maximum capital that can be issued by the company during its lifetime.

Some important points to remember:

a) There is no maximum to any company's authorised share capital and no minimum share capital for private limited companies. However, a public limited company must have an authorised share capital of at least £50,000 or the prescribed sterling or euro equivalent (and, if it is trading, issued capital of £50,000).

b) The authorised capital amount must be divided into shares of fixed denomination. For example (authorised capital of £100,000 divided into 10,000 shares of £10 each).

c) There is no requirement that companies issue shares to the full extent of their authorised capital.

2. Issued capital

This is the capital which has actually been issued by the company to the public. A company need not issue all its share capital at once. If company issues only some part of its capital the remaining part is called as "unissued capital".

Example

A company has authorised capital of £10, 00,000 divided into 100,000 shares of £10 each; it may decide to issue 40000 shares of £10 each. In this case the issued share capital shall be £400,000. The balance of £600,000 is the unissued capital of the company.

There are no statutory regulations in relation to private companies **but public companies must have a minimum issued capital of £50,000,** of which, 25% of the nominal value of each share and any premium must be paid up before it can start business or borrow money.

3. Called up capital

This is the **part of the issued capital which has been called up** or demanded by the company. Usually the company does not demand the entire amount due on the share at a time, but calls the amount in two or more instalments. The capital not yet called is the **"uncalled capital"**

Example

A company with an issued capital of £400,000 (40,000 shares @ £10 each), has called £5 per share, then the called up capital of the company is £200,000.

---

4. Paid up capital

Sometimes, some of the shareholders fail to pay the full amount called up by the company. The **portion of called up capital which is actually paid** by the shareholders is called as paid up capital. The capital called up but not yet paid is the "unpaid capital".

Example

A company with issued capital of £400,000 (40,000 shares @ £10 each), has called £5 per share, but received only £180,000 instead of £200,000. In this case, the paid up capital of the company is £180,000.

---

5. Reserve capital

This is the part of uncalled capital of the company which the company by **special resolution** has decided, not to call except in the event of company being wound up. When once the reserve capital has been created, the company can not demand the payment of money on those shares during its life time. Also, this portion of capital cannot be charged or mortgaged as security for any loan raised by company.

Diagram 1: Types of share capital

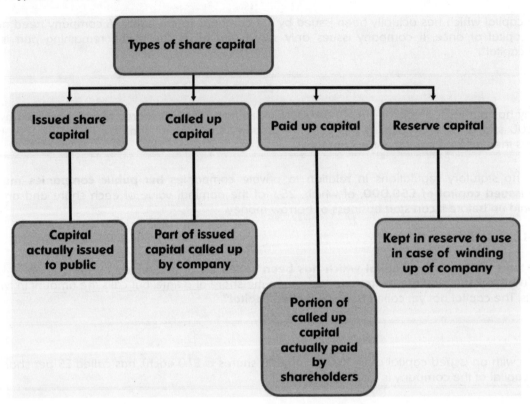

Test Yourself 1

Discuss the various types of share capital.

SYNOPSIS

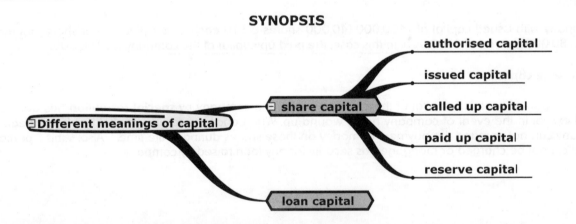

---

2. Illustrate the difference between the various classes of shares

[Learning outcome b]

What is a share?

The capital of a company is divided into a number of indivisible units of a fixed amount. These units are known as shares.

Definition

A share symbolises a shareholders interest in a company. This is measured in monetary terms, firstly for liability and secondly for interest. It also represents a set of mutual covenants which all shareholders enter into.

Shares are the units which represent a participation of an owner in the company. By taking a share in a company a person agrees to invest some of his personal money, or assets, or intellectual rights or property into a company. For this he acquires the right to participate in the profits of the company, in proportion to his share. Also, usually a shareholder receives the right to participate in the decision-making process of the company by applying their voting rights.

2.1. Types of shares

1. Ordinary shares

Also known as **equity shares**, ordinary shares are standard shares with no special rights or restrictions. They have the potential to give the highest financial gains, but have the highest risk. Ordinary shareholders are the last to be paid if the company is wound up.

The features of ordinary shares are:

a) **Voting rights:** These shares contain the controlling powers of the company. The holders of ordinary shares are entitled to exercise their voting rights in the general meeting of company.

b) **No fixed dividend:** The equity shareholders are not entitled to fixed dividends. They are paid dividends only from the profits remaining after dividends has been paid to preference shareholders.

c) **No priority in return of capital:** The equity share capital is repaid only after full payment of liabilities and after the capital has been repaid to preference shareholders.

Advantages of ordinary shares

➢ Since there is no liability for repayments, it is a source of permanent capital.

➢ There is no legal obligation to pay dividends. Therefore, dividend payment can be conveniently skipped till the project starts generating adequate surplus.

➢ Equity capital constitutes the basis for raising debt. In general the larger the equity base, the higher is the ability to raise debt capital.

However since dividends are paid out of post-tax profits, there is no tax shield available to the firm on account of this outflow.

2. Preference shares

These shares typically carry a right that gives the holder preferential treatment. The preference shares have the following features:

a) **Preferential right to dividend**

When annual dividends are distributed to shareholders, the preference shareholders have a preferential right to receive the dividend. However, the dividend to preference shareholders is paid **according to a fixed rate** or **a fixed amount**. Which means that a shareholder would not benefit from an increase in the business' profits?

Tips

Preference shareholders have no entitlement to receive any additional dividend over and above their specified rate.

b) **Preferential right as to repayment of capital**

Where a business is wound up, they are likely to be repaid the par or nominal value of shares **before** repayment of capital of ordinary shareholders.

c) **Cumulative preference shares**

These shares give holders the right that, if a dividend cannot be paid one year, it will be carried forward to successive years. Dividends on cumulative preferred shares must be paid, despite the earning levels of the business.

Example

A company has issued 5% cumulative preference shares. The company can not pay any dividend to the shareholders in one year. Their claim for dividend will be carried forward to next year. In that year the company could not pay any dividend again. Again their claim for the previous year and the current year will be carried forward to the next year. Then in third year if company pays dividends, it will pay a 15% dividend.

Tips

Unless stated otherwise, the right to receive a preference dividend is deemed to be cumulative.

Important points to remember

If a company has arrears of unpaid preference dividends goes into liquidation, the right to receive the arrears of dividend ceases, **unless:**

➢ Before commencement of liquidation, the dividend has **been declared though not paid.**
➢ The **articles provide** that in case of liquidation, the **dividend arrears will be paid in priority to return of capital** to members.

3. Redeemable shares

At the time of issuing these shares, the company enters into an agreement with the purchaser that it will buy the shares back at a future date - this can be at a fixed date or at the choice of the business. A company cannot issue redeemable shares only.

Example

If a company issues 1,000 shares and makes an agreement with the purchaser that the company will buy back that 1,000 Shares at a certain future date then these shares are redeemable shares.

Test Yourself 2

Define the term "shares". What are the different types of shares which a company can issue?

SYNOPSIS
Difference between various classes of shares

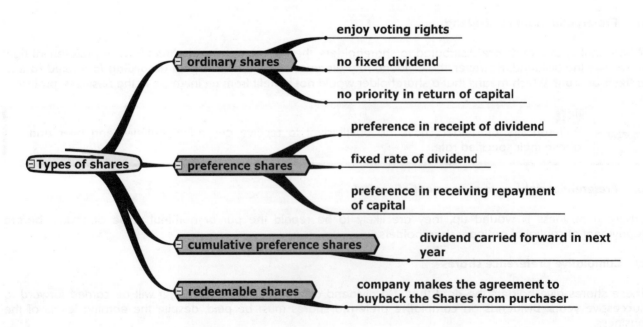

3. Explain the procedure for altering class rights

3.1 What is class right?

Class rights denote the **rights attached to a particular type of share** as authorised by the company's constitutional documents.

A company can issue shares of only one class i.e. all the shares are carrying the same rights or a company can issue shares with different rights. The common examples of types of shares with different rights are preference shares and ordinary shares. The company may attach different rights to different types of shares in relation to:
➢ Dividends.
➢ Repayment of capital.
➢ Voting powers.
➢ The right to appoint directors.
➢ Right to bonus issue.

3.2 Alteration of class rights

This denotes the variation in rights and duties of shareholders of a particular type of shares. A company may alter the rights attached to any class of shares.

3.3 Procedure for alteration of class rights

Altering the rights of a class of share depends on whether the rights originate from the or from elsewhere. Class rights will no longer be contained in the Memorandum. Class rights will be contained in the Articles, terms of issue or shareholder's agreement.

Diagram 2: Procedure for alteration of class rights

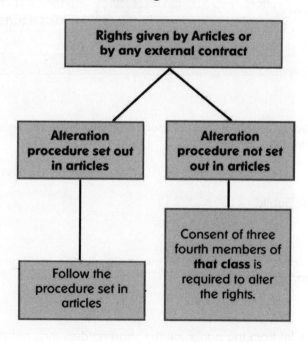

1. When the procedure for alteration of class rights is set out by the Articles of Association, then that procedure is to be followed,

Example

The terms of issue of shareholders' agreement states that preference share holders have voting rights similar to ordinary shares. The Articles contain a detailed procedure for altering the rights of shares. In this case, even if the voting right to preference shares is given the procedure described by the Articles will be followed to alter this right.

2. When the rights attached to shares are granted by the Articles or any external contract, and there is no pre-established procedure, then the alteration requires consent of a 75% majority of nominal value of shares in that class. A sanction of that class of shareholders by an extraordinary resolution passed at a separate general meeting is necessary for such variation.

Example

The Articles of the company provided that the dividend to preference shareholders will be paid within one month of AGM. If this period has to be increased from one month to six months, and if there is no procedure set out in Articles to carry out such alteration then the consent of holders of 75% of preference share capital by an extraordinary resolution will be required.

3.4 Right of dissenting shareholders to prefer an appeal to court:

➤ Dissenting shareholders who hold at least 15% of the issued shares of that class may apply to the court to have the variation cancelled.

➤ They must do this within 21 days after consent was given or a resolution passed to vary the rights.

➤ The company must deliver a copy of the court order to Companies House within 15 days of it being made.

The court can either approve the variation or cancel it as 'unfair'. It can not, however, modify the terms of the variation.

SYNOPSIS

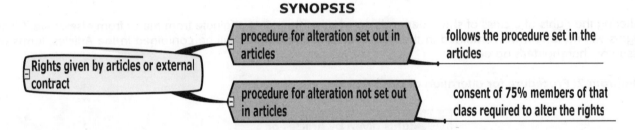

Answers to Test Yourself

Answer 1

Share capital is the capital which is being raised by the company from the issue of shares. There are different types of share capital which are follows:

a) Issued capital

This is the capital which is issued to the public.

c) Called up capital

This is the capital of the company which is actually called by the company. The amount of capital which is not yet called by the company is called uncalled capital.

d) Paid up capital

When the company demands the capital from the public, all the shareholders may not pay the amount which is called by the company. The part of the called up capital which is actually paid by the public is called as the paid up capital.

e) Reserve capital

This is the amount of capital which is kept aside which can not be called upon except in the event of the liquidation of the company.

Answer 2

A share is a unit of capital. A shareholder is the owner of the company. The following are the different types of Shares that can be issued by the company:

a) **Ordinary shares** are also known as equity shares. The holders of these shares do not have a preference to receive a dividend. The rate of dividend is not fixed for the Equity Shareholders. They can get higher rate of dividend but the risk involved is greater. Equity shareholders can vote in the general meeting of the shareholders.

b) **Preference shares** enjoy the preferential right to receive a dividend. The rate of the dividend is fixed which can not be changed even if profits increase. As the name suggests the holders of these shares have preference in the repayment of capital in the winding up of the company.

c) **Cumulative preference shares** are shares which allow non paid dividends to be carried forwarded to successive years.

d) **Redeemable shares** are shares which the company issues with an agreement with the purchaser that the company will buy back these shares at a future date.

Quick Quiz

State true or false

1. The priority to receive a dividend is the right to merely to receive a dividend at the specified rate before a dividend to equity shareholders is declared or paid. It is not a right to compel the company to pay a dividend.

2. The right to receive a preference dividend is deemed to be cumulative unless the contrary is stated.

3. Preference shareholders are entitled to receive additional dividends over and above their specified rate like equity shareholders.

4. Except priority to dividend and repayment of capital, the preference shares have equal rights to ordinary shares in all other respects, unless otherwise stated.

Answers to Quick Quiz

1. **True,** as company can even decide to transfer its profits to reserves instead of paying dividends either to equity shares or preference shares. It was decided in **Bond v Borrow Haematite Steel Co 1902**, that a company can retain its profits to make good the losses suffered on disposal or demolition of current assets or to provide against the diminishing value of non current assets or for any other reason it thinks appropriate. The court would not overrule the director's decision that 'the state of accounts did not admit the payment of dividends'.

2. **True**

3. **False,** preference shareholders have no entitlement to receive any additional dividend over and above their specified rate.

4. **True**

Self Examination Questions

Question 1

Explain the procedure for the alteration of class rights.

Question 2

What are the rights of the minority in relation to alteration of class rights?

Question 3

From the following information, identify whether the holders of the shares are preference shareholders or ordinary shareholders?

a) Jack has subscribed for 200 shares of Epson Ltd at £10 each. In the AGM, the company declared the dividends at 6% in 20X5 and 8% in 20X6. In 20X7, no dividends were declared.

b) John had purchased 500 shares of Epson Ltd at £10 each. Every year he got a dividend of 10% on his capital. In 20X5, the company could not pay the dividend so it was paid in 20X6 along with 20X6 dividends.

c) Bob had purchased 1,000 shares of Epson Ltd at £20 each. It was agreed with the company that 50% of these shares will be purchased back by the company after 5 years of issue of the shares.

Answers to Self Examination Questions

Answer 1

Variation of class rights

➢ When the right is granted by Articles or by a separate contract and the Articles set out the procedure to alter the rights attach to any class of shares, then a company needs to follow that procedure.

➢ When the right is granted by Articles and the Articles do not set out the procedure to alter the rights attach to any class of shares, then the **Consent of three fourth members of that class** is required to alter the rights.

Answer 2

As per s 633 CA 2006 whenever rights of a particular class of shares are altered, a minority of holders of shares of that class may appeal to the court to have the variation cancelled. The objecting minority together must:

➢ Hold not less than 15% of the issued shares of that class of shares.
➢ Not themselves have consented to or voted in favour of the variation.
➢ Apply to the court within 21 days of the consent being given by the class of shares which rights are altered.

The court can either approve the variation or cancel it as 'unfair'. It can not, however, modify the terms of the variation.

Answer 3

a) Jack is an ordinary shareholder as the rate of dividend is not fixed and he receives the dividend only if it is declared by the company.

b) Jack is the holder of cumulative preference shares as he receives the dividend at a fixed rate, and if the dividend is not paid in one year then it is carried forward to the next year.

c) Bob is the holder of redeemable preference shares as there is an agreement with the company that the company will buy back these shares at a future date.

LOAN CAPITAL

Get through intro

This Study Guide deals with the formalities governing a company's borrowing power. It mainly covers debentures, types of debentures, the rights of debenture holders, and the creation and registration of charges over the assets of company,

The key considerations in deciding whether to issue shares or debentures for raising funds mainly include **cost, control and flexibility.**

Loan capital is considered to be a **cost effective option** of raising funds. Usually, cost of debt is lower than the cost of equity because interest payable is a **tax-deductible expense**, while dividends are paid out of after tax profits.

As the shareholders are the owners of the company, with every new issue of shares, control of existing shareholders is diluted. However, debenture holders not being **entitled to exercise any control** over the affairs of the company, the issue of debentures enable the shareholders to retain control of company operations.

Financial flexibility refers to the ability of a company to raise further capital from any source it wishes to tap so as to meet the future financing needs. Therefore to maintain financial flexibility, every company should **maintain certain reserve-borrowing powers to enable it to raise debt capital to meet largely unforeseen circumstances.**

Accountants are expected to guide client companyies as to whether it is beneficial to issue shares or debentures for raising funds, what are the effects, and what are the costs involved in both options . Study of this Study Guide will help students understand the concept of loan capital thoroughly.

Questions from this topic are regularly asked in examinations.

LEARNING OUTCOMES

a) Define companies' borrowing powers
b) Explain the meaning of debenture
c) Distinguish loan capital from share capital
d) Explain the concept of a company charge and distinguish between fixed and floating charges
e) Describe the need and the procedure for registering company charges

Introduction

Raising capital by way of debentures sometimes is more beneficial than raising capital through issuing shares? For e.g., suppose a company's capital requirement is £50,000. It therefore raises the capital by an issue of 5,000 equity shares each having a nominal value of £10. It earns a profit of £5,500 on its investment of £50,000. Thus the return on investment is 11%.

Instead, if the company raises only £25,000 by way of shares and £25,000 by issuing 8% debentures. In that case, the company has to pay interest of £2,000 (£25,000 x 8%) out of its profit of £5,500. Thus the effective return is £3,500. The return of investment in relation to the above example is 14%.

Total funds raised	£50,000	£50,000
Mode of raising capital	by issue of 5,000 shares @£10 each	1) £25,000 by issue of 2,500 shares @£10 each 2) £25,000 by issue of 8% debenture.
Profit earned on total investment of £50000	£5,500	£5,500
Interest expenses	NIL	£2,000 (on £25,000@8%)
Net profit available for shareholders.	£5,500	£3,500
Rate of return of shareholders funds.	5,500/50,000X100=11%	3,500/25,000X100=14%

It is clear from the above example that the company is actually earning at higher rate on the shareholder's investment when funds are raised through debentures.

1. Define companies' borrowing powers

[Learning outcome a]

A company's borrowing power refers to the limit or extent to which a company can raise funds by means of borrowing from sources other than its members which includes; bank loans, public deposits, and issue of debentures.

A company has the power to borrow even if the Articles does not specifically authorise the company to do so. In other words, a company can borrow money even if the power to borrow money is not specifically given in the Articles of the company.

Legal requirements regarding borrowing

1. A public company is required to obtain a trading certificate of commencement of business under section 761 CA 2006 before it borrows any money.

2. The power to borrow money is generally exercised by the directors but the Articles usually provide for certain restrictions on their power to borrow.

Example

Articles of a company may contain a provision that the director's power to borrow shall be limited to £50,000 only.

If the Articles do limit the borrowing powers of the directors and the directors propose to exceed these powers, then any member can apply for an injunction to restrain the director fom doing so, s 40(4)) CA 2006

S40(1) CA 2006 protects a third party dealing with a company in good faith and he does not need to be concerned about whether a company is acting within its jurisdiction

Remedies of the lender in cases where money is borrowed by the directors exceeds their borrowing powers.

➤ Lender will be able to enforce the contract by virtue of s.s39 and 40 CA 2006

Example

Articles of a company state that the director's power to borrow shall be limited to £20,000 only. For borrowing beyond this amount they shall have to seek the prior approval of shareholders in general meeting. In such a case, borrowing beyond £20,000 without the shareholders approval will still be binding under s40.

Test Yourself 1

What is meant by a company's borowing power.

SYNOPSIS

┌Companies borrowing powers ⟩──⟨ **limit on amount of raising of funds through debentures, bank loans**

2. Explain the meaning of debenture

[Learning outcome b]

Definition

It is a document in writing, usually under seal, issued as evidence of a debt or the granting of security for a loan of a fixed sum at a rate of interest (or both). The term is often used in relation to loans secured by charges, including floating charges, over companies' assets.

Palmer describes debentures as "an instrument under seal, evidencing a deed, the essence of it being the admission of indebtedness"

According to Gower, "Debenture is a name applied to certain types of documents evidencing an indebtedness which is normally, but not necessarily, secured by a charge over property.

A debenture is defined in company law as including debenture stock, bonds or other securities of a company whether secured or not

In simple words, a debenture is a written acknowledgement of a debt containing provisions as to payment of interest and terms of repayment of the principal. A debenture is an instrument issued by a company as evidence of a debt or other obligation. It includes debenture stock, bonds and any other securities of a company, whether or not it forms a charge on the assets of the company.

2.1 Debentures may be issued in a variety of ways

1. A single debenture

When the company approaches a bank or other lending institution for a loan or overdraft facility, the bank will want to ensure that they will get their money back. In such cases, a debenture may be issued to a single creditor e.g. to a bank to obtain a secured loan or overdraft facility.

2. Series of debentures

Alternatively, the company may raise the funds by issuing debentures to different lenders of different amounts. Then the sum of all individual loans is made up. Debentures issued in a series with a **pari passu** (at the same rate) clause which entitles them to be discharged rateably **though issued at different times**. Each lender of that particular series is ranked equally in terms of rights and security. New series of debentures cannot rank pari passu with the old series unless the old series allows this.

3. Debenture stock

Debenture stock is a debt carrying interest at a fixed rate. It is similar to debenture but instead of each lender having a separate debenture bond, they get a certificate entitling then to a specified portion of one large loan. Only a public company is entitled to issue debenture stock. An offer document offered to the public to subscribe to a company's debenture stock is considered as a company's prospectus. If the debentures are to be listed on the Stock Exchange, then the required rules must be followed. A company has to maintain a debenture stockholders register.

2.2 Types of debentures

1. On the basis of transferability, debentures are classified into:

a) Bearer debentures

These are unregistered debentures and are payable to the bearer. They are negotiable instruments and are transferable from one person to another by delivery. The name of debentureholder is not specified in the debenture certificate, and so the transfer of debentures from one person to another does not require any registration of transfer.

b) Registered debentures

These are payable to the registered holder whose name appears both on the debentures and in the Register of Debenture Holders maintained by the company. Registered Debentures can be transferred but have to be registered again. Registered Debentures are not negotiable instruments. A registered debenture contains a commitment to pay the principal sum and interest. It also has a description of the charge and a statement that it is issued subject to the conditions endorsed therein.

2. On the basis on convertibility debentures are classified into:

a) Non convertible debentures (NCD)

These instruments retain the debt character and can not be converted in to equity shares.

b) Partly convertible debentures (PCD)

A part of these instruments are converted into equity shares in the future at the notice of the issuer. The issuer decides the ratio for conversion. This is normally decided at the time of subscription.

> **Example**
>
> Tulips Ltd issued 5,000 debentures of £100 each, redeemable after 10 years from the date of issue. It was agreed with the subscribers to the debentures that at the time of redemption, 40% of the debentures will be converted into equity shares of the company and the balance of 60% will be redeemed. The ratio of conversion will be 12 equity shares of £10 for each debenture. Thus, the 5,000 debentures are partly convertible debentures, 40% of which will be converted into equity shares at the time of redemption of debentures. In other words, the debenture holders will be entitled to receive (5,000 x 40% = 2,000 x12 = 24,000 equity shares of Tulips Ltd.

c) Fully convertible debentures (FCD)

These can be fully converted into Equity shares at the issuer's notice .The ratio of conversion is decided by the issuer. Upon conversion the investors enjoy the same status as ordinary shareholders of the company.

> **Example**
>
> Tulips Ltd issued 5,000 debentures of £100 each, convertible into equity shares after 10 years of the date of issue. The ratio of conversion will be 15 equity shares of £10 for every two debenture. Thus, the 5,000 debentures are fully convertible debentures. The debenture holders will be entitled to receive (5,000 x 15/2= 37,500 equity shares of Tulips Ltd.

d) Optionally convertible debentures (OCD)

The investor has the option to either convert these debentures into shares at a price decided by the issuer/agreed upon at the time of issue.

3. On basis of security, debentures are classified into:

a) Secured debentures

These instruments are **secured by a charge on the fixed assets** of the issuer company. So if the issuer fails on payment of the principal or interest amount, his assets can be sold to repay the liability to the investors.

b) Unsecured debentures

These instruments are unsecured in the sense that if the issuer defaults on payment of the interest or principal amount, the debenture holder's stand along with other unsecured creditors of the company. They will be considered to be the unsecured creditors and paid accordingly. In the event of company's liquidation, the unsecured creditors are paid after the debts of secured creditors, liquidation expenses and liquidator's remuneration and the debts of holders of floating charge are paid.

2.3 Features of debentures

➤ Debentures are instruments for raising long-term debt capital.
➤ Debenture holders are creditors of the company.
➤ The obligation of the company towards its debenture holders is similar to that of a borrower who promises to pay interest and capital at specified times.
➤ The interest payment on debentures is a statutory obligation, unlike dividend payments on equity shares.
➤ The interest paid on debentures is a tax-deductible expense.
➤ Debentures have to be compulsorily retired in accordance with the terms of the issue, whereas equity share capital need not be redeemed.
➤ Debenture holders are not entitled to vote.
➤ Debentures are usually secured by a charge on the immovable properties of the company.
➤ The interests of the debenture holders are usually represented by a trustee and this trustee is responsible for ensuring that the borrowing company fulfils the contractual obligations embodied in the contract.

2.4   Debenture trust deed: When the amount borrowed by a company is large, the company commonly executes a trust deed. The object of such a trust deed is:

1. To convey the specific property to the trustees of the deed by way of legal mortgage. This will have appropriate provisions for enabling them, in the event of non-repayment of debt by the company, to enforce security. This will allow the trustees to enter into possession and carry on the business of the company, or to sell it and distribute the proceeds.

2. To organise the debenture-holders and constitute in the trustees of the deed, a body of experienced business men who can watch over the interests of the debenture-holders and take steps for their protection if necessary.

Benefits of appointment of debenture trustees

a) As they are small in numbers (usually four to five) it results in timely decisions. Also it enables the debenture holders to enjoy the benefit of a legal mortgage over the company's land. This would not be possible without trustees as the provisions of Law of Property Act 1925 provides that, legal estate in a land cannot be vested in more than four persons. Hence land, even though a fixed charge is created on it, cannot be vested with all the debenture holders.

b) Generally, professionals are appointed as debenture trustees. Hence it is beneficial for the debenture holders as it facilitates sound decisions and closer watch on the working of the company.

c) The debenture trustees are entrusted with strict duties and onerous responsibilities. This ensures the protection of the interest of the debenture holders.

2.5 The pros and cons of raising funds by way of debentures

Advantages

1. The cost of debt capital represented by debentures is much lower than the cost of preference or equity capital.
2. Debenture financing does not result in dilution of control since debenture holders are not entitled to vote.
3. The call provision found in many debenture issues provides flexibility in changing the capital structure.
4. In a period of rising prices, debenture issue is advantageous. The burden of servicing debentures, which entails a fixed monetary commitment for repayment of interest and principal, decreases in real terms as price level increases.

Disadvantages

1. Debenture interest and capital repayments are obligatory payments. Failure to meet these payments jeopardises the solvency of the company.
2. Various provisions are associated with a debenture issue in order to protect the interest of debenture holders. Some of these provisions are registration of charges, maintaing debenture holders registers, and adherence to the provisions of articles and memorandum. The protective covenants associated with a debenture issue may prove restrictive.

Test Yourself 2

What are debentures? What are the main features of the debenture'?

SYNOPSIS

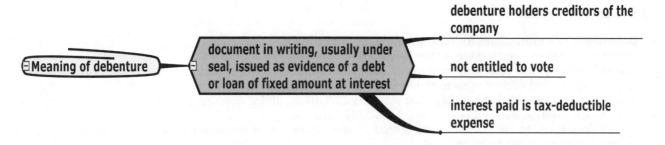

Meaning of debenture	→	document in writing, usually under seal, issued as evidence of a debt or loan of fixed amount at interest	→	debenture holders creditors of the company
			→	not entitled to vote
			→	interest paid is tax-deductible expense

---

3. Distinguish loan capital from share capital

[Learning outcome c]

Loan capital mainly covers debentures. The distinction between shares and debentures is as follows:

Basis of distinction	Shares	Debentures
1. Capital V debt	Amount raised by issue of shares represents the **capital** of the company. For example, if a company issues 10,000 equity shares at £10 each then its capital is £100,000. The company need not to repay this capital to its shareholders during its lifetime. At the time of winding up the company, shareholders are paid if any balance remains after paying all company liabilities.	Amount raised by issue of debentures represents the **indebtedness** of the company. A company has to repay the loan amount as per the agreed terms.
2. Status	The shareholders are the **owners** of the company.	The debenture holders are the **creditors** of the company.
3. Form of return	The return paid to shareholders is termed as **dividend**	The return paid to debenture holders is called as **interest.**
4. Quantum of return	Dividend on shares is an **appropriation of profits**. This means it is not deductible as an expense for calculating company's taxable profit. For e.g., if a company's profit before tax is £50,000 and it pays a dividend of is £10,000. Here, the company have to first pay tax on its profits of £50,000. The dividend of £10,000 is not deductible as an expense for calculating company's taxable profit	Interest on debentures is a **charge on profits**. Hence, it is a deductible expenses for calculating company's taxable profit. For example, if a company's profit before tax is £50,000 and it pays an interst of is £10,000 on debentures. Here, the company's taxable profit is £40,000 and it have to pay tax on its profits of £40,000 only. The interst of £10,000 is deductible as an expense for calculating company's taxable profit.
5. Return v profits	The amount of **dividend varies** with the amount of profit.	The amount payable as **interest is fixed** irrespective of quantum of profits.
6. Voting rights	Shareholders have **voting rights.**	Debenture holders do **not have any voting rights.**
7. Security for payment	**No security is created** in favour of shareholders.	**Generally, security is created** in favour of debentures.
8. Conversion	Shares **cannot be converted into any other security.**	Debentures **may be converted into shares,** if the terms of issue of debentures so provide, i.e. in case of convertible debentures.
9. Discount	Shares may not be issued at discount.	Debentures may be issued at discount.
10. Repayment of Capital	Shareholders are the last people to be paid on winding up.	Debentureholders are paid before Shareholders.

Test Yourself 3

What are the advantages of subscribing to a company's debentures ?

SYNOPSIS
Difference between shares and debentures

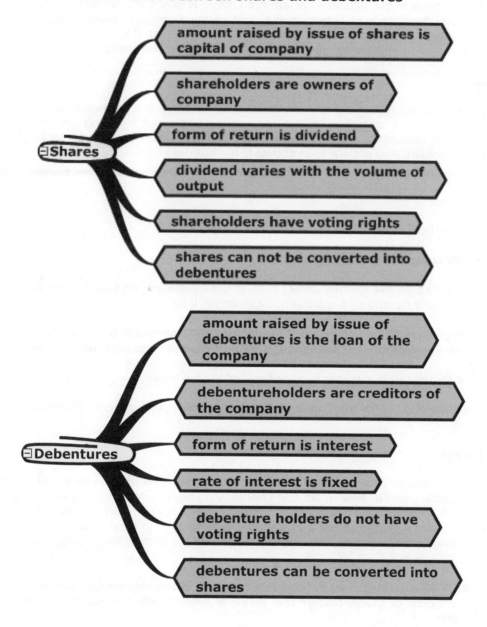

Shares
- amount raised by issue of shares is capital of company
- shareholders are owners of company
- form of return is dividend
- dividend varies with the volume of output
- shareholders have voting rights
- shares can not be converted into debentures

Debentures
- amount raised by issue of debentures is the loan of the company
- debentureholders are creditors of the company
- form of return is interest
- rate of interest is fixed
- debenture holders do not have voting rights
- debentures can be converted into shares

4. Explain the concept of a company charge and distinguish between fixed and floating charges

[Learning outcome d]

A **charge** is a security created in favour of a creditor at the time of accepting a loan for the payment of a debt by the company. It is important to note that creation of charge does not pass 'property' or any right to possession of the property to the person to whom the charge is given. The ownership and possession of the property remains with the company. However, the right of the borrower company to deal in the property charged becomes subject to the rights of the lender. The lender is entitled to recover his money by selling the property charged if the company fails to repay the loan as per the agreed terms.

Definition

A charge is a right given to the creditor/lender to have a designated asset of the debtor appropriated to the discharge of the indebtedness, but not involving any transfer either of possession or ownership. In case of company, the charges over assets are usually granted to the debenture holders who provide loan capital to the business.

4.1 Types of charges

Charges can be either fixed or floating.

1. Fixed or specific charges

A fixed charge is **created on the specific asset** i.e. asset is **determined and defined at the time of creating the charge**. It is generally created on fixed assets, for example, land or plant and machinery or buildings.

Once the fixed charge is created on any asset of the company, the **company is not entitled to:**
➢ Sell or otherwise transfer that asset even though the possession of that asset remains with the company.

➢ To create a subsequent charge (either fixed or floating) having priority over such charge.

In the event of non-payment of the loan amount, the charge holder can dispose off the asset and recover his dues.

2. Floating charges

A floating charge is a **charge that does not affect the assets charged until some event 'crystallises' (fixes) the charge to a certain point in time**. A floating charge is a charge which is not attached to any definite or particular asset. It is a charge on the 'undertaking and the asset of the company' for example, debtors or stock-in-trade. However it is not restricted to current assets only and applies to fixed as well as to current assets. The essence of such charge is that it remains inactive (dormant) until the undertaking charged ceases to be a going concern.

The features of the floating charges as defied in Re Yorkshire Woolcombers Association are:
a) It is a charge on class of assets, present and future. In other words, the floating charge is created on a category of assets.

b) The class is one which, in the ordinary course of business, is changing from time to time.

c) Until the creditors take steps to enforce the charge, the company may continue to deal with the assets charged in an ordinary course of business i.e.

i. The company can sell the entire asset.
ii The company can create the subsequent fixed charge which will have priority over the floating charge already created.

On crystallisation of the floating charge, the right of the company to deal in the assets charged ceases. In other words, once the charge is crystalised

➢ The company cannot sell such an asset
➢ The company cannot create a subsequent charge (whether fixed or floating) having priority over this charge.

> **Example**
>
> Creditors of Chocochips company has a floating charge on its stock and due to a problem, the company ceases to carry on its business. In that case crystallisation of the floating charge occurs. So therafter the company cannot sell the stock and cannot create a subsequent charge on stock (whether fixed or floating) having priority over this charge.

Crystallisation of a floating charge:

Crystallisation **refers to the conversion of a floating charge into a fixed charge**. After crystallisation, the charge becomes subject to all the restrictions applicable to a fixed charge. **Events causing crystallisation** are as follows:

a) The winding up of the company.
b) Where the company ceases to carry on its business.
c) When creditors take steps to enforce their security e.g. by appointment of receiver.
d) If some events, the happening of which would amount to crystallisation as per the terms and conditions of the charge created.

Case Study

The terminology used by the parties is not conclusive evidence to decide whether a charge is a fixed or foating charge

Siebe Gorman And Co Ltd v Barclays Bank Ltd (1979)

The company had a charge created over its book debts. The company was allowed to collect the debts and pay them into a bank account in the companies name with the bank. This account could either be with the lender bank (chargee) or with another bank. They company was not allowed to dispose of the uncollected debts or have unrestricted access to the bank account.

It was argued that this was a floating charge based on two facts:
1. Concept of charges – a charge on a fluctuating asset is always a floating charge. Therefore this has to be a floating charge as the assets are fluctuating.
2. Commercial - Book debts are part of circulating capital and make up a vital source of cash flow. This makes it difficult to subject them to a fixed charge without adversely affecting the business.

Court's decision: Slade J found that it was clear that the company was only allowed to receive payment of the book debts. It could not, sell, discount, assign, factor, charge or deal with them in any other way. The court also decided that after the proper construction of the debenture, the company was not permitted to withdraw money from the bank account without the express permission of the bank, even when the account was in credit. The Judge finally held that the **charge was a fixed charge** over the book debts and their proceeds.

Case Study

The terminology used by the parties is not conclusive evidence to decide whether a charge is a fixed or foating charge

Re Keenan Bros Ltd (1986)

A charge was enacted by the bank on the book debts of the company. The company was prevented from disposing of and from creating any other charges over its book debts without consent from the bank. This was set out in the terms of debenture. The company could collect the book debts, but it had to pay all the proceeds into a special bank account with the bank. The company where not permitted to withdraw money from this bank account unless the bank gave them written consent. Again this was all set out in the debenture deed.

Court's decision: McCarthy J stated that "mere terminology" did not determine the nature of a charge to be floating or fixed. He also declared that we need to look "not to the declared intentions of the parties alone, but to the effect of the instruments whereby they purported to carry out that intention."

The court declared that the charge was a fixed charge as all the proceeds of the book debts where paid into a designated account where withdrawals where prohibited unless written consent was obtained by the bank.

Case Study

R in Right of British Columbia v Federal Business Development Bank (1988)

In this case, the bank had a charge over the company's entire property. It was termed as a fixed and specific mortgage and charge. However, the bank was permitted the company w to use inventory sales to maintain the viability of its enterprise. The bank also permitted the company to sell inventory to pay wages and, necessarily, payroll deduction obligations.

Court's decision; It was held that it was a floating charge and not a fixed charge.

Difference between fixed and floating charge

Basis of distinction	Fixed charge	Floating charge
1. Who can create?	Any person can create a fixed charge on any asset owned by it.	Only an incorporated body (e.g. a company) is authorised to create a floating charge.
2. Identifiable property v property of general description	Is created on some identifiable (i.e. specific) property of the company. In other words, the asset on which the charge is created is definite. For example, a charge on a particular land owned by company.	A floating charge is created on a class of assets, present as well as future. In other words, a floating charge is created on a category of assets. For example, charge on company's inventory.
3. Nature of assets on which charge is created	Fixed charges are generally created on fixed assets, e.g. land and building, plant and machinery etc.	Floating charges are generally created on such assets as are always circulating, i.e., the assets which keep on changing very frequently, i.e., the assets in which the company deals in the ordinary course of business, e.g. inventory and receivables.
4. Power to deal in the asset charged	The company cannot deal in the asset charged in case of a fixed charge. For e.g., if a company has created a fixed charge on its warehouse, it cannot sell that warehouse as there is a fixed charge on it.	The company can deal in the asset charged in the ordinary course of business. For example, if a charge is created on company's inventory, the company can sale or use the goods from inventory. The inventory need not be kept at exact quantity/value as it was at the time of creation of charge.
5. Crystallisation	There is no question of crystallisation in case of a fixed charge.	A floating charge crystallises when the right of the company to deal in the asset charged comes to an end. For example, if the company is ordered to wind up then the floating charge created on its inventory crystalises and then it becomes a fixed charge of creditors on inventory. After that, the company is not entitled to deal in the inventory.

4.2 Priority of charges

1. Fixed charge followed by a floating charge-the fixed charge shall have priority over the floating charge.

> **Case Study**   A fixed charge can be created even after issuing a floating charge
>
> ### Wheatley v Silkstone and Haigh Moor Coal Co (1885)
>
> In this case, it was to be decided whether a fixed charge can be created on an asset which is already subjected to a floating charge.
>
> **Court's decision:** It was decided by the court that the floating charge has been brought out particularly with the objective for facilitating the companies to deal with their assets in the normal routine of their functioning without being subject to any intervention from the party holding the floating charge. As a result, the courts held that a fixed charge can be created even after issuing a floating charge in order to secure later borrowings in the course of the business

It is possible, however, for the debenture creating the original floating charge to include a provision preventing the creation of a later fixed charge taking priority over that floating charge. This provision gives rise to the issue that whether such restriction has any effect on subsequent debenture holders.

> **Example**
>
> Jumbo Ltd had issued 500 debentures in 20X4 with a floating charge on company's current assets. There was a provision agreed by the debenture holders and the company that the company will not be entitled to create a later fixed charge taking priority over this floating charge. In 20X5, the company issued a further 500 debentures. The question is whether the restriction of not creating any subsequent fixed charge will also apply to these debentures issued in 20X5?
>
> The current position is that such a restriction is also applicable for the holder of the subsequent charge **provided they have knowledge of the specific restriction in the original debenture.**

> **Case Study**   A restriction on creation of a later fixed charge is also applicable for the holder of the subsequent charge provided they have knowledge of the specific restriction in the original debenture
>
> ### Wilson v Kelland (1910)
>
> In this case, an issue came up for decision that where the debenture creating the original floating charge included a provision preventing the creation of a later fixed charge taking priority over that floating charge, whether such restriction also applies to the subsequent debenture holders.
>
> **Court's decision:** It was decided that a restriction in a floating charge on the creation of subsequent charges with priority does not bind a subsequent chargee unless the latter had notice of both the charge and the restriction. In other words, such a restriction is also applicable for the holder of the subsequent charge provided they have knowledge of the specific restriction in the original debenture. This is because a registration of charge has been held only to give constructive notice of the existence of a debenture, and not its contents.

2. **Fixed charge followed by another fixed charge**- the fixed charge created first shall have priority over the subsequent fixed charge.

3. **Floating charge followed by fixed charge**- the fixed charge shall have the priority over the floating charge.

4. **Floating charge followed by another floating charge**- the floating charge created first shall have the priority over the subsequent floating charge.

Tips

Summary
1. **Fixed charge followed by a floating charge** - the fixed charge shall have priority over the floating charge.
2. **Fixed charge followed by another fixed charge** - the fixed charge created first shall have priority over the subsequent fixed charge.
3. **Floating charge followed by fixed charge** - the fixed charge shall have the priority over the floating charge.
4. **Floating charge followed by another floating charge** - the floating charge created first shall have the priority over the subsequent floating charge.

Tips

A fixed charge shall always have priority over a floating charge.

Test Yourself 4

State five points of differences between fixed and floating charges.

Diagram 1: Types of company charges

```
                    Types of company charges
                            │
            ┌───────────────┴───────────────┐
            ▼                               ▼
      Fixed charge                    Floating charge
            │                               │
            ▼                               ▼
  Created by any person who       Created only by incorporated
     owns the asset                        body
```

SYNOPSIS

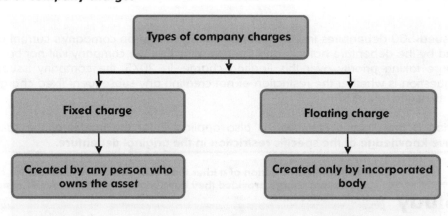

⊟ **Concept of company charge - fixed and floating** — right given to creditor to have particular asset of debtor to discharge of indebtedness but should not involve any transfer either of possession or ownership

⊟ **Fixed charge**
- created on the fixed asset e.g. land and building, plant and machinery
- company can not sell or transfer the charged asset and can not create subsequent charge to have priority over such charge

⊟ **Floating charge**
- does not affect the assets charged until some event crystallises
- charge on class of assets, present or future
- company can sell whole of such assets and also can create subsequent fixed charge which will have priority over floating charge

5. Describe the need and the procedure for registering company charges
[Learning outcome e]

All charges, including both fixed and floating charges, have to be registered with the Companies Registry within 21 days of their creation s 860 CA 2006

5.1 Need for registering company charges
Registration of charges in due time is extremely important because:

➤ Failure to deliver the documents for registration of the charges makes the company and its officers **liable to a fine. (S 860 cA 2006**.

➤ Non-delivery of the documents in the determined time period results in the **charge being void against an administrator, liquidator or any creditor of a company**.

➤ The sum secured by the charge becomes **payable immediately** at the option of the charge holder

5.2 Procedure for registering the charges

1. Which charges needs to be registered?

The following charges generally required to be registered:

➤ A charge to secure any issue of debentures.
➤ A charge on the uncalled share capital of the company.
➤ A charge on land (wherever situated), or any interest in it, exceeding for any rent or other periodical sum arising from land. Technically, land includes property.
➤ A charge on book debts of the company. Book debts are debts that in the ordinary course of a company's business are commonly entered in its books.
➤ A floating charge on the company's undertaking or property.
➤ A charge on calls made but not paid.

> **Tips**
>
> **Memory tip:** If the issue price of the share is payable in instalments, such instalments are called calls.

➤ A charge on a ship or aircraft or any share in a ship.
➤ A charge on goodwill, or on a patent, trademark, registered design, copyright or design right or a license under or in respect of any such right.

2. Registration is to be undertaken by whom?

a) **Company**: It is the duty of the company to register the charges.
b) **Chargee**: If the company does not send the charge for registration, then the chargee (the person to whom property is charged) or some other interested person can register the required documents.

3. Mode of registration

The copies of instrument by which the charge is created should **be sent to the Registrar (s395)**.

4. Time limit for registration of charges

The charges created by a company should be registered with the registrar **within 21 days** of being created. (s 860 cA 2006 0The Court has the power to allow the lateRegistration.

5. Certification of registration

a) The registrar files the particulars of charge date / amount / property / person in the companies charges register which he maintains and notes the date of delivery.

b) The registrar will send the company, the particulars of the charge such as:
➤ The date when the charge was created.
➤ The amount of debt which it secures.
➤ The property to which the charge applies.
➤ The person entitled to it.

c) The registrar also issues a certificate which is conclusive evidence that the charge has been duly registered on the date stated in the certificate. Mistakes in Register are only rectified by the Court Order.

Register of charges. Every company is required to keep a copy of documents creating a charge, and a register of all charges at company's registered office.

6. Effects of non-registrtaation of charges

If the charges are not registered then the charge is void, i.e., ineffective, against any other creditor or the liquidator of the company; but it is still valid against the company. This means that the charge holder loses priority against other creditors.

5.3 Remedies available to debenture holders

1. Remedies available to **unsecured debentureholders**

The unsecured debenture holders rank along with other unsecured creditors of the company. Their relationship with the company is a contractual relationship and hence they are entitled to seek a remedy for breach of contract.

Accordingly following remedies available to the unsecured debentureholders:

a) **To sue the company for debt**: The debenture holders may file a suit against the company for recovery of the debt due to them and may seize the company's property if the judgements for debts are unsatisfied.

b) **Petition for winding up**: The Insolvency Act 1986 empowers the creditor to file a petition to the court for the compulsory winding up of the company, if the company is unable to pay its debts. Therefore, where a company fails to redeem the debentures on maturity, the debenture holders may make a petition to the Court stating that the company is unable to pay its debts, and therefore, it is liable to be wound up.

2. Remedies available to **secured debentureholders**

a) **Power to sell assets:** The debenture holders are entitled to sell the asset and recover their debt provided the debenture is executed as a deed.

b) **Power to take possession of asset:** The fixed charge holders can take the possession of the asset. The floating charge holder can take the possession of the asset charged only if the contract provides so.

c) **Right of foreclosure:** The debenture holders may make an application to the court for foreclosure. 'Foreclosure' means that the right of the company to deal with the security shall come to an end and the secured asset shall vest in the debenture holders.

d) **Appointment of an administrator:** The debenture trustees may appoint an administrator if the debenture trust deed authorises the appointment of such, in case of default by the company. But, if the debenture trust deed does not authorise the trustees to appoint an administrator, the debenture trustees may apply to the court for the appointment of an administrator

N.B. since the passing of the Enterprise Act 2002, it is no longer possible for the holder of a floating charge to appoint an administrative receiver but he can appoint an administrator.

Test Yourself 5

Briefly explain the procedure for registration of charges.

SYNOPSIS

Need and Procedure for Registering Company Charges

need → if charge not registered a fine may be imposed

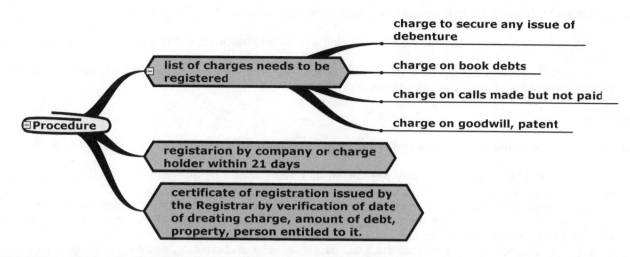

Answers to Test Yourself

Answer 1

A company's borrowing power is the limit or extent to which a company can raise funds by means of borrowing from sources other than by way of issuing shares. These sources include issue of debentures, accepting public deposits, borrowings from banks and financial institutions etc.

A company can borrow money if borrowing is within the powers of Directors and not specifically restricted by its Articles of Association.

Company has an implied power to borrow hence it can borrow money even if the Articles does not specifically auhtorise the company to borrow money.

A public company is required to obtain a trading certificate of commencement of business under section s761 cA 2006 before it borrows any money.

Answer 2

A debenture is an instrument which is issued as evidence of debt which is generally secured by the charge over the property of the company. The features of the debentures are as follows:
➢ Debentures are instruments for raising long-term debt capital.
➢ Debenture holders are creditors of the company.
➢ The obligation of the company towards its debenture holders is similar to that of a borrower who promises to pay interest and capital at specified times.
➢ Interest payment on debenture is a statutory obligation, unlike dividend payments on equity shares.
➢ Interest paid on debentures is a tax-deductible expense.
➢ Debentures have to be compulsorily retired in accordance with the terms of the issue, whereas equity share capital need not be redeemed.
➢ Debenture holders are not entitled to vote.
➢ Debentures are usually secured by a charge on the immovable properties of the company.
➢ The interests of the debenture holders are usually represented by a trustee and this trustee is responsible for ensuring that the borrowing company fulfils the contractual obligations embodied in the contract.

Answer 3

Advantages of the debentures to the debenture holders are as follows:

➢ Debentures are a safe investment as interest is paid on the Debenture at fixed rate irrespective of volume of the Profit.
➢ Debentures represent the indebtedness of the company hence they are repaid by the company as stated in the agreed terms.
➢ Debentures can be convertible debentures which means that they can be converted into shares at an agreed date.
➢ Debentures are paid in preference to shareholders at the time of winding up of company.
➢ Generally, debentures are secured by a charge on company's assets. Hence, even if the company becomes insolvent, the debenture holders can recover their money.

Disadvantages of Debentures to the debenture holders are as follows:

➢ Debenture holders are not entitled to vote. Hence they cannot participate in the management of the company.
➢ The interest on debentures is paid at fixed rate. Hence, the debenture holders are not entitled to additional benefits even if the company is earning huge profits.

Answer 4

The following are the differences between fixed and floating charges:

a) A fixed charge can be created by **any person** on any asset owned by him, whereas floating charges can be created **only by an incorporated body.**
b) A fixed charge is created on the particular property of the company e.g. land and building, plant and machinery. On the other hand, the floating charge is created on the class of the assets, present as well as future e.g. book debts of company.
c) A fixed charge is normally created on the fixed assets i.e. land and building, plant and machinery etc., but a floating charge is created on the assets which are generally in the changing stage e.g. inventory, book debts.
d) In case of the fixed charge a company can not deal in the assets charged but in case of floating charge a company can deal in the assets charged.
e) In case of floating charge, the charge crystallises when a company's right to deal in the assets charged comes to an end. Crystallisation means conversion of floating charge into the fixed charge. This provision is not applicable to fixed charge.

Answer 5

It is normally the company's duty to register the charges. However, if the company does not send the charge for registration, then the chargee (the person to whom property is charged) or some other interested person, can register the required documents. The provisions of s s860of Companies Act 2006 requires that copies of instrument by which the charge is created should **be sent to the Registrar and** the charges created by a company should be registered with the registrar **within 21 days** of being created. However, the Court has the power to allow the late registration. Once the required documents are submitted to the registrar, the **registrar files the particulars of charge** date / amount / property / person in the companies charges register which he maintains and notes the date of delivery.

The registrar will then **send the company the particulars of the charge** such as:

➢ The date when the charge was created.
➢ The amount of debt which it secures.
➢ The property to which the charge applies.
➢ The person entitled to it.

The registrar also **issues a certificate** which is conclusive evidence that the charge has been duly registered on the date stated in the certificate. Any mistakes in the register can only be rectified by a Court Order.

If the **charges are not registered then the charge is,** ineffective, against any other creditor or the liquidator of the company; but it is still valid against the company. This means that the charge holder loses priority against other creditors.

Quick Quiz

State true or false

1. Whenever a company pays dividend to its shareholders, it has also to pay interest to debentures holders.

2. Interest paid on debentures is deducted from pre-tax profits whereas share dividends are not.

3. A public company can borrow funds immediately after its incorporation.

4. The application for registration of charges can be made by the company only.

5. Debenture holders are not entitled to vote.

6. A charge cannot be registered after 21 days.

7. A floating charge is a charge that does not affect the assets charged until some event crystallises the charge, fixing it to a certain point in time.

Answers to Quick Quiz

1. **True**, but it does not mean that a company has to pay interest only when it pays dividend. **Even if the company does not pay dividend, it has to pay interest to the debenture holders.**

2. **True.**

3. **False**, a public company is required to obtain a trading certificate of commencement of business before it borrows any money.

4. **False**, it is the duty of the company to register the charge. But if the company fails to do so, registration of charges may also be affected on application of the chargee or any other person interested in the charge.

5. **True.**

6. **False**, late registration is possible with the Court's permission.

7. **True.**

Self Examination Questions

Question 1

Explain the meaning and effect of fixed charge.

Question 2

Explain the concept of crystallisation of a floating charge. When does crystallisation occurs?

Question 3

Jolly Jelly Ltd issued 1,000 debentures to Afro Bank against a loan £100,000. The company has created a charge on its book debts. The agreement with the debenture holders contains the following terms:

a) It was agreed that the company will not be entitled to dispose off any of the uncollected debts.
b) The company will be free to collect the book debts, the proceeds of which will be deposited into an account in its name with the bank. This account could be with Afro bank or any other bank. After that the company will not be authorised to access that account unless written permission from the bank is obtained.
c) It was agreed that the company will not be entitled to create other charges over them without the consent of the bank.

Required:

Students are required to carefully study the facts given relating to Jolly Jelly Ltd and decide whether the charge created over the book debts of the company are a fixed charge or a floating charge and why?

Answers to Self Examination Questions

Answer 1

Under a fixed charge, a specific asset of the company is made subject to a charge in order to secure a debt. A fixed charge is normally created on assets such as land, building, plant and machinery. Once a charge is created on a particular asset, the company cannot dispose off that asset without the consent of the person holding the fixed charge over that asset. If the company fails to honour its commitments, the charge holder can sell the asset and recover his money.

For example, creditors of Choco company has a fixed charge on its plant and machinery. In this case, the company neither can sell the plant and machinery nor it can create a subsequent charge (whether fixed or floating) having priority over this charge. If the company fails to repay the money of creditors on an agreed date and as per agreed terms, the plant and machinery will be sold and the creditor's debt will be satisfied from the sale proceeds.

Answer 2

Crystallisation refers to conversion of a floating charge into a fixed charge. After crystallisation, the charge becomes subject to all the restrictions applicable to fixed charge i.e. once the charge is crystalise :
➢ The company cannot sell such an asset.
➢ The company cannot create a subsequent charge (whether fixed or floating) having priority over this charge.

Events causing crystallisation are as follows:

➢ The winding up of the company.
➢ Where the company ceases to carry on its business.
➢ When creditors take steps to enforce their security, e.g. by appointment of receiver.
➢ If an event occurs which would amount to crystallisation as per the terms and conditions of the charge created.

Answer 3

A **charge** is a security created in favour of a creditor at the time of accepting a loan for the payment of a debt by the company. Charges can be either fixed or floating A fixed charge is one which is **created on the specific asset** i.e. asset is **ascertained and defined at the time of creating the charge**. It is generally created on the fixed assets, for example, land or plant and machinery or building. A floating charge is a charge which is not attached to any definite or particular asset. It is a charge on the'undertaking and the class of asset' of the company which is changing from time to time, in the ordinary course of business ' for example, debtors or stock-in-trade. This however it is not restricted to current assets only and applies to fixed as well as to current assets. The essence of such charge is that until the creditors take some steps to enforce the charge, the company may continue to deal with the assets charged in an ordinary course of business i.e.:

i. The company can sell the entire asset.
ii. The company can create the subsequent fixed charge which will have priority over floating charge already created.

In the given case, as the charge is on book debts i.e. a fluctuating asset, one may form an opinion that it must be a floating charge.

The same issue was dealt with in **Siebe Gorman and Co Ltd v Barclays Bank Ltd (1979). It was argued that the charge on book debts of the company with the similar provisions as in the above question was a floating charge.** The case argued that this was a floating charge as it was a charge on fluctuating assets because:

1. Concept of charges – a charge on a fluctuating asset is always a floating charge. Therefore this has to be a floating charge as the assets are fluctuating.

2. Commercial - Book debts are part of circulating capital and make up a vital source of cash flow. This makes it difficult to subject them to a fixed charge without adversely affecting the business.

However, the court took a different stand. It was clear from the facts of the case that company was only permitted to receive payment of book debts and could not assign, factor, discount, sell, charge or otherwise deal with them. Slade J found that, on a proper construction of the debenture, the company was not free to draw on its account without the consent of the bank even when the company was in credit. **Accordingly he held that the charge on the uncollected book debts and their proceeds was a fixed charge.**

In Re Keenan Bros Ltd (1986), McCarthy J confirmed that "mere terminology" was not determinative of whether a charge was fixed or floating. One had to look "not to the declared intentions of the parties alone, but to the effect of the instruments whereby they purported to carry out that intention."

In the given case, the company was prevented from disposing of and from creating any other charges over its book debts without consent from the bank. This was set out in the terms of debenture. The company could collect the book debts, but it had to pay all the proceeds into a special bank account with the bank. The company where not permitted to withdraw money from this bank account unless the bank gave them written consent. Again this was all set out in the debenture deed. Hence on the basis of decisions given in **Gorman and Co Ltd v Barclays Bank Ltd (1979) and In Re Keenan Bros Ltd (1986),** the charge is more likely to be a **fixed charge** than to be a floating charge.

SECTION E - CAPITAL AND THE FINANCING OF COMPANIES

CAPITAL MAINTENANCE AND DIVIDEND LAW

Get through intro

Share capital is the share holder's investment in the company. The Companies Act had made specific rules for controlling the capital of the company by specifying what a company can and can not do with its share capital. The ultimate objective is to protect the creditor's interest and at the same time enables the company to give its shareholders the maximum return on their investment. This Study Guide deals with provisions relating to capital maintenance.

This Study Guide also deals with the rules relating to the distribution of dividends. The Companies Act, 2006 provides that dividends can be paid only out of the accumulated profits and not out of the capital. This Study Guide throws light on the various elements of the distribution of profits.

LEARNING OUTCOMES

a) Explain the doctrine of capital maintenance and capital reduction
b) Examine the effect of issuing shares at either a discount, or at a premium
c) Explain the rules governing the distribution of dividends in both private and public companies

Introduction

Can a company buy its own shares to seek capital reduction?

Generally speaking, share capital once introduced by the company cannot be paid back by the company. If a company is allowed to buy back its shares, it would reduce security available to the creditors, thereby increasing the risk of the creditors. This is due to the fact that the stake of the owners will be reduced, which is the very basis on which the creditors lend money to the company. However, the case study given below has changed this whole scenario.

Case Study

Re Hunting Plc (2004)

In this case, the company issued share capital consisting of ordinary shares and convertible preference shares. **Under the company's Articles of Association, the preference shareholders were not entitled to attend or vote at the companies general meetings, unless, among other things, a resolution was proposed at that meeting which modified any of the rights that were attached to preference**   **shares.**

The preference **share certificates stated** that preference shareholders would be entitled to attend and vote at a meeting where a resolution was proposed **"reducing the capital of...or modifying or abrogating any special rights attaching to the preference shares."** Therefore, there was a **conflict between what was stated in the company's Articles, and what was stated on the share certificates.**

The company decided to purchase the preference shares at par value as a way to reduce the company's share capital, which was permitted by section 135 of the UK Companies Act 1985 and the company's Articles. A resolution authorising this was made at a meeting of ordinary shareholders only.

The preference shareholders challenged this resolution on **two grounds**:

1. The share certificates stated that the preference shareholders should be present and vote at meetings concerning a reduction in share capital, and
2. It was unfair that the shares could be purchased at par value, when the shares were trading above par value on the market.

Court's decision:

1. The preference share certificates had misstated the terms of the Articles by incorrectly summarising the voting rights of the preference shareholders. These terms could not override the Articles' restrictions on attendance and voting at meetings.

2. **Reducing the share capital to relieve the company from the cost of maintaining preferred shareholdings is a proper purpose for the reduction,** if doing so is in the best interests of the company. Receiving par value for the shares was all that the preference shareholders were entitled to receive under the company's Articles. The court stated that "the company is not entitled out of feelings of sentiment...to hand over part of its share capital to a class of shareholder which has no entitlement to it under the Articles of Association."

In short, the court held that the company could proceed with the share purchase to reduce its share capital.

1. Explain the doctrine of capital maintenance and capital reduction

[Learning outcome a]

The liability of the shareholders of the company is limited to the extent of the nominal value of shares. Hence, the need to protect the interest of the creditors resulted in the development of the doctrine of capital maintenance. The rules arising from the doctrine of capital maintenance are basically formed to ensure that the capital which is intended to be raised is both received and maintained by the company as a fund within the limits of regular risks of the business for the protection of the company's creditors. This is very important from the creditor's point of view because in a company limited by shares, when a company fails to perform its liabilities, the creditors will not be able to receive any right of recourse other than against the company. The creditors of a limited liability company rely on both i.e. a certain amount of capital already paid and the responsibility of its members for the capital remaining at call. Thus, the doctrine of capital maintenance prevents the direct or indirect way of returning of the capital to the shareholders while permitting a reduction of capital or payment out of capital under strictly restricted situations. The creditors of the company have a right to expect that no part of the capital paid to the company has been subsequently paid out, except in the genuine course of business.

In Trevor v Whitworth (1887), the House of Lords established the principal that a company cannot return any of the capital to the members, unless there is a suitable reduction of capital properly authorised by the courts. It was also held that a company did not have a power to acquire its own shares even though there was an express authorisation to do so in its memorandum.

The capital maintenance rules require that

1. The company achieves the capital which it has intended to raise.

Example

If a company has issued 10,000 £10 shares on which £2 per share is still not called up. The company has intended to raise 10,000 x £10 = £100,000. Hence it has to receive the full amount of £100,000. Till now, the company has received only £10,000 x £8 = £80,000. The company **cannot release its members of their liability to pay £2 per share**.

---

2. The company cannot return capital to the shareholders.

Example

If a company has issued 10,000 £10 shares fully paid-up. It has to maintain this capital. It **can not return** £2 per share to its members as in that case, the company's capital will only be £80,000.

---

3. Once the capital is raised it has to be maintained. To achieve this, the law has provided following limitations:

a) **A company is prohibited from acquiring its own shares (s.658):** In Trevor v Whitworth (1887), it was held that a company did not have power to acquire its own shares even though there was an express authorisation to do so in its memorandum. However there are certain exceptions.

➤ (s.641) Reduction of capital: Section 641 of Company's Act permits reduction of capital provided confirmation from the court has obtained.
➤ (s.685) Redemption of redeemable shares: Where the shares issued to members were redeemable shares, then the company can purchase them back after the expiry of the term fixed.
➤ (s.690) Purchase of own shares: A company can purchase its own shares from its shareholders provided they are cancelled after acquisition.

b) **A company is prohibited from giving any financial assistance for the acquisition of its own shares (s.678):** A company cannot give any direct or indirect assistance (whether by way of loan, guarantee, and surety or otherwise) for purchase of its own shares.

c) **A company is prohibited from paying dividend out of capital (s.s 829 - 853):** The most fundamental condition of payment of dividend is that the dividend must be paid out of profits, and not out of capital. Payment of dividend out of capital amounts to unauthorized reduction of capital.

Capital maintenance

Duty of directors on the serious loss of capital

1. Where the **net assets of a public company are half or less of its called-up share capital,** the directors shall duly **convene an extraordinary general meeting** of the company. This meeting must be convened within **28 days from the earliest day on which that fact is known to a director of the company. The date of meeting** must not later than 56 days from that day. At this meeting, the members have to consider whether any, and if so what, steps should be taken to deal with the situation.

2. If there is a failure to convene an extraordinary general meeting, each of the directors of the company is liable to be fined if:
   a) He knowingly and wilfully authorises or permits the failure, or

   b) After the expiry of the period during which that meeting should have been convened, knowingly and wilfully authorises or permits the failure to continue.

Example

Net assets of Jelly Ltd become less than half of its called up capital on 15 April 20X6. Brown, a director of the company came to know the fact on 1 May 20X6. In this case, the general meeting has to be convened before 29 May and the date of the meeting can not be later than 10 June 20X6 (56 days from 15 April). If the director wilfully and knowingly permits the failure to convene such a meeting, then he is liable to be fined.

Capital reduction

Capital reduction covers two aspects:
a) Reduction of authorised capital.
b) Reduction of issued capital.

1.1 Reasons for reduction of capital

There are a number of reasons why a company may wish to reduce its share capital. The most common one is to eliminate accumulated losses which would otherwise prevent a company from having the distributable profits available to declare a dividend.

Example

GTG is currently a profit-making company but had been hampered by accrued losses on its income statement arising from a previous acquisition of a loss-making company. These losses had prevented it from declaring a dividend to its shareholders when in reality it is in relatively strong financial and trading position since the acquisition.

Other reasons for a reduction may include:

➤ Returning surplus capital to shareholders where such capital is surplus to the company's requirements for the foreseeable future.

Example

Ambry Company has 10,000 equity shares of £10 each fully paid up. The company finds that available funds are in excess of the needs of the company. The company may return back a portion of paid up share capital, say £4 on every share. The share capital of the company will then consist of 10,000 equity shares of £6 fully paid up.

➤ Where shares have been issued partly paid up and a company decides that it no longer has any use for the unpaid fraction of those shares, it can release the shareholders from their liability of paying the balance due on those shares by extinguishing the unpaid capital.

Example

Sweet Jelly Ltd issued 100,000 shares at £10 each, £8 paid up on each share. If there is no requirement of funds for the company as company is doing well the company may decide to release the shareholders from paying £2 on each share. In that case the share capital of the company will be 100,000 shares at £8 each.

> Creating a distributable reserve for purposes other than declaring a dividend, for example if a company wishes to buy back its own shares from shareholders which can only be done out of distributable profits; and,

> Simplifying a company's share structure by cancelling and extinguishing any deferred shares to which little or no rights are attached.

Tips

Deferred shares are the shares which are generally issued to company founders and on which dividends can not be paid until dividends have been distributed to all other classes of shareholders.

Example

BMC Ltd has issued 100 £25 shares at £5 each as deferred shares to its 5 promoters. The dividends on these shares was payable only after 10 years of the company's incorporation and too a maximum 3% rate. Thus, the company may decide to purchase back these shares from the promoters and cancel them.

1.2 Methods of capital reduction

Reduction of authorised capital: A limited company is permitted to cancel its unissued shares without any restriction. Thus a company can reduce its authorised capital by cancelling its unissued shares. This will not alter the financial position of the company in any way.

Reduction of issued capital: A company can reduce its issued capital **in any of the following ways:**

1. By extinguishing / reducing the liability on partly paid shares

A company can reduce its issued share capital either by reducing or totally waiving the shareholder's liability on partly paid up shares.

Example

A company has issued 10,000 equity shares of a nominal value of £10 each. On all these shares, £6 per share have been called up and paid. The company may resolve to reduce the nominal value of its shares to £6 each. When such reduction becomes effective, the members will not be required to pay the balance liability of £4 per share. This is called as an extinguishment of liability on partly paid up shares.

However, if the company decides to reduce the value of share to £7 each then the members will not required paying £3 per share because the value of each share shall stand reduced to £7. This is called reducing the liability on partly paid up shares.

2. By cancelling lost paid up share capital

The company can reduce its capital by cancelling any paid-up share capital which is lost i.e. which is not represented by the available assets. This way of reduction of capital enables the company to bring a reality to the position shown on the balance sheet. Also a company can continue to make payments without making good any past losses.

Example

A company has issued 10,000 equity shares of a nominal value of £10 each. The company has accumulated losses of £60,000. The company can write off whole accumulated losses of £60,000 against capital. If the liability is extinguished, the share capital of company shall henceforth consist of 10,000 equity shares of £4 each fully paid up. If the liability is not fully extinguished, the share capital of the company shall consist of 10,000 equity shares of £10 each, £4 paid up. Alternatively the company may also write off only part total losses say £40,000.

3. By paying off part of the paid up share capital

Another way of reducing capital is the company can pay back a portion of capital already paid on the shares.

> **Example**
>
> The company may reduce the value of its fully paid share from £10 to £7 and repay £3 per share to the shareholders.

1.3 Procedure of capital reduction

The procedure is laid down by s 641 CA 2006 and a company must follow the procedure:

1. **Power in the articles of the company:** A **specific provision in the articles** is required for reducing the share capital of the company. If this power is not in the articles, then the company needs to alter its articles to this effect by passing a special resolution.

2. **Special resolution:** A company **has to pass a special resolution** setting out the terms of reducing the share capital.

3. **Obtaining confirmation from court (s.641):** Confirmation from court is required, in the case of a public company before effecting the reduction of capital.

4. A private company limited by shares may reduce its capital without applying to the court for confirmation but it must pass a declaration of solvency, s 642.

5. **Protection of creditors:** Prior to exercising its jurisdiction, the court will want to be satisfied that the interest of creditors is safeguarded at the time of the application. When the court receives an application for reduction of capital, it follows the following procedure:

   a) If the reduction is by way of extinguishment / reducing the liability or paying off part of paid up share capital, then the court **must** generally require that the creditors shall be invited by advertisement to state their objections (if any) to the reduction.

   Where the company requests the court to dispense with advertising for creditors' objections then the court may require the company to:

   ➢ Pay off all creditors before application is made to the court or,

   ➢ Produce to the court a guarantee that its existing debts will be paid in full.

   b) If the reduction is by cancelling lost paid up share capital, the court **may** require an invitation to the creditors.

   c) Before sanctioning the reduction, the court shall satisfy itself that:

   ➢ The reduction will be fair considering the interest of all the classes of shareholders.
   ➢ The reduction will not be prejudicial to the interest of the creditors.
   ➢ The court may direct the company to add the words 'and reduced' at the end of the name of the company and publish explanation of the reduction. S 648(1)

6. **Registration: Under s 649** the company shall deliver to the registrar for registration:

   a) A copy of the order of the court and
   b) A copy of the minutes approved by the court.

Diagram 1: Methods of reduction of share capital

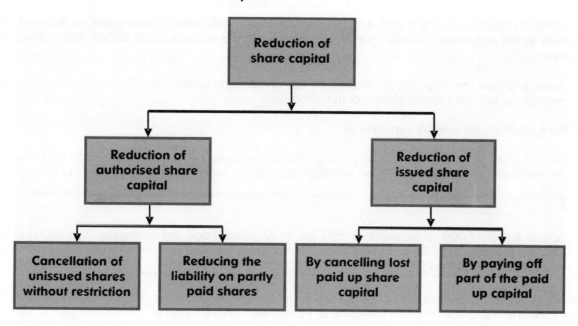

SYNOPSIS

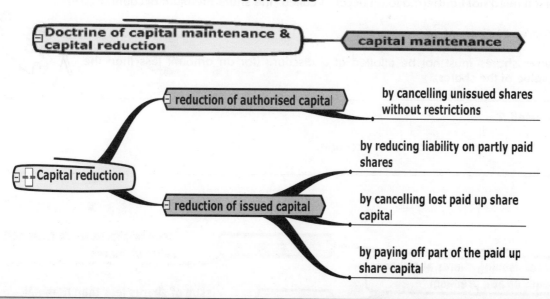

2. Examine the effect of issuing shares at either a discount, or at a premium

[Learning outcome b]

Share premium

The expression 'share premium' is used where the amount payable to take up the shares issued by a company is greater than the nominal / par value of the shares.

Example

A company may decide to issue shares having a nominal / par value each of £1 and may require payment of £1.50 per share. The share premium in this example is £0.50 per share.

Application of share premiums

1. If a company issues shares at a premium, whether for cash or otherwise, a **sum equal to the total amount or value of the premiums** on those shares shall be **transferred to an account called "the share premium account".**

2. The share premium account may be applied by the company in paying up unissued shares to be allotted to members as fully paid bonus shares, or in writing off:

    a) The company's preliminary expenses or

    b) The expenses of, or the commission paid or discount allowed on, any issue of shares or debentures of the company, or in providing for the premium payable on redemption of debentures of the company.

Example

Pasco Plc has issued 5,000 debentures at £50 each 20 years back. The company is now repaying the debentures at a premium of £10 each. In this case, the company can use its share premium account to pay off this premium of 5,000 x £10 = £50,000

---

3. Subject to this, the provisions of the Companies Act relating to the reduction of a company's share capital apply as if the share premium account were part of its paid up share capital.

Merger relief

➢ The relief applies where the issuing company has secured at least a 90 per cent equity capital in another company as consideration for the allotment of equity shares in the issuing company.

➢ If the equity shares in the issuing company allotted in accordance with the arrangement in consideration for the acquisition or cancellation of equity shares in the other company are issued at a premium, such premium need not transferred to an account called "the share premium account".

Issuing shares at discount

A company's shares must not be allotted at a discount (for an amount less than the nominal value of the shares).

Test Yourself 2

Write a short note on share premium accounts.

SYNOPSIS

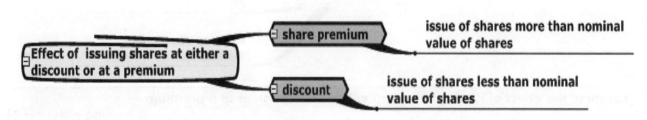

3. Explain the rules governing the distribution of dividends in both private and public companies
[Learning outcome c]

What is dividend?

> **Definition**
>
> The dividend is the stockholders' share of the profits left after the company sets aside funds to finance operations, expansion and modernisation.

A dividend is a portion of a company's profit distributed to shareholders. In other words, dividend is an investor's share of a company's profits.

The management of a company can do either of the following with operating profit:
➢ Declare a dividend and distribute a share of the profits to the shareholders.
➢ Keep the profit - reinvest the profit back into the company with the aim to further increase profit and stock value.

A company cannot justify reinvesting profit back into the company unless its keeps growing above the market norm. It will have to pay a dividend to keep shareholders engaged if the companies' growth slows and the stock becomes stagnant. When companies achieve a large market capitalisation, it is normal to see a slow down in growth. No matter how much money is reinvested back into the organisation, it is simply impossible to sustain an annual growth rate of 30-40% once the company has reached a certain size.

Microsoft offers a prime example of a slow down in growth and illustrates that it's impossible to be a high performing stock forever. Microsoft declared a dividend payment in January 2003. They simply had more money in the bank than new projects to invest in, so they had no choice but to share their profits with their shareholders in the form of a dividend.

The Companies Act 2006 contains provisions for the amount of a company's profits available for distribution. Some points to remember are:

a) A company is not bound to distribute its profits among its members unless the Articles of Association so provides.

b) Under the Articles of Association of most companies it is the **directors who normally recommend the amount of the dividend**, which is **subject to the approval of the company in a general meeting.**

Case Study

Scott v Scott (1943)

The company passed a resolution to pay dividends on ordinary shares, in its general meeting.

Court's decision: It was held that general meeting has no power to declare a dividend unless it is first recommended by the Board of Directors. The resolution was held ineffective.

c) The Articles usually provide that the **dividend shall not exceed the amount recommended by the directors** so that, while the **shareholders** cannot increase it, they **can reduce the amount of the dividend.**

d) Dividends are normally declared on the paid up amount of share capital of a company.

> **Example**
>
> A £10 fully paid up share will be entitled to double the dividend as a £10 share on which only £5 is paid.

e) The directors may even declare an interim dividend. An interim dividend is the dividend which is declared and distributed before the company's annual earnings have been calculated; these are often distributed quarterly.

f) A dividend is paid in cash. It may be paid by issue of additional shares or by cheque or by a warrant sent to the shareholder at his registered address through post, provided it is expressly stated in the articles.

g) A dividend is a debt only when it is declared and due for payment. A shareholder is not entitled to any dividend unless it is declared in accordance with the procedure laid down in company's articles.

3.1 Distribution of dividends

The companies Act provides that a company **whether public or private**, may not make a distribution except out of profits available for the purpose of distribution i.e. the distributable profits (s 830 (1))).

What are Distributable profits?

> **Definition**
>
> Distributable profits are **accumulated, realised profits**, so far as not previously utilised by distribution or capitalisation, **less accumulated realised losses**, so far as not previously written off in a reduction or reorganisation of capital duly made s 830

> **Tips**
>
> Accumulated distributable profits mean **profits brought forward from previous years after setting off any realised losses of previous years**. Realised loss **also includes depreciation**, debited against profits.

> **Tips**
>
> Realised profits and losses are those **treated as such in accordance with accounting principles, including accounting standards generally accepted** at the time the accounts are prepared. It does not include profits arising on revaluation of non current assets.

Test Yourself 3

Zen Ltd had a carried forward loss of £5,000 at the beginning of the year. During the year, it made trading profit of £10,000 and revalued its non current assets by £3,000. What are the company's distributable profits?

What are undistributable reserves?

According to s831), they include:
➢ The share premium account.
➢ The capital redemption reserve.
➢ The excess of accumulated unrealised profits not previously utilised by capitalisation over accumulated unrealised losses not previously written off in a reduction or reorganisation of capital.
➢ Any other reserve which the company is prohibited from distributing by any enactment or by its Articles.

3.2 Additional restriction on distribution of profits by public companies

A public company may only make a distribution of its distributable profits if at that time the amount of its net assets is not less than the aggregate of its called up capital and undistributable reserves, and if and to he extent that the distribution does not reduce net assets below that aggregate.

> **Tips**
>
> **Called up capital:** Is the **part of the issued capital which has been called up** or demanded by the company.

Example

The issued and paid up capital of a company is £500,000 and balance in share premium account is £200,000. In this case, if the company's net assets are £700,000 or less, then the company can not distribute any dividend. If the company's net assets are £1,000,000, then it can pay dividend to such extent that will bring down the net asset up to £700,000. i.e. the maximum dividend the company can pay is £300,000. Because the dividend is more than £300,000 it will bring the company's net asset below £700,000 and this is not allowed under the Company's Act 2006 s 831.

Along with the dividend, the above rule is applicable to every form of distribution of assets of the company to its members **except the distributions by way of:**

➢ an issue of fully or partly paid bonus shares.
➢ a redemption or purchase of the company's shares out of capital or out of unrealised profits.
➢ a distribution by a company to members on winding up. Distributions in cash or non cash assets are both covered.
➢ a reduction of share capital, whether by paying off paid up shares or extinguishing or reducing the liability on partly paid shares.

Tips

Bonus shares: These are the free shares of stock given to current shareholders, based upon the number of shares that a shareholder owns.

The consequences of payment of dividend out of capital

The consequences of payment of dividend out of capital are as follows:

1. The directors who knowingly paid dividends out of capital shall be held personally liable to make good the losses caused to the company.

Example

In Flitcroft's case, there was a breach of the rules for dividend distribution i.e. a dividend was paid out of the capital of the company. As the breach was by the directors, they were held jointly and severally liable to the company.

2. There is a provision in s847 Companies Act 2006 stating that shareholders knowingly receiving the dividend from capital shall be liable to repay any such money received.

Test Yourself 4

Explain undistributable profits.

Test Yourself 5

What are the main rules of dividend distribution?

SYNOPSIS

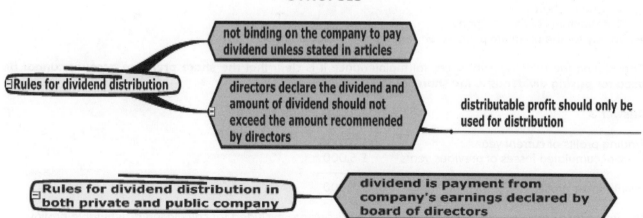

Answers to Test Yourself

Answer 1

Consistent with the principles of preservation and maintenance of capital, the law protects creditors by the following means:

1. The company may not reduce its share capital, **except in limited circumstances** with the **consent of the court** s.641 for e.g., where the company has huge accumulated losses which prevent it from having the distributable profits available to declare a dividend. In such case, the company may, with the consent of the court, reduce its share capital by way of writing off accumulated losses.

2. A company may not purchase its own shares s.658, except in certain limited circumstances, and in the case of private companies only. The reason for this is that in paying a third party for its own shares capital has been taken out of the company without the appropriate consents.

3. A public company may not give financial assistance in the purchase of its own shares s.678. This flows as a consequence of the rule against the purchase of company's own shares. Exceptions to this rule include a procedure to allow financial assistance in strictly limited circumstances where the directors of the company effectively guarantee the debts of the company for a period of 12 months. A private company is exempt from this provision.

4. The company may not pay dividends to shareholders unless there are adequate distributable profits. In the absence of such profits, payment of a dividend is effectively a reduction of capital and, therefore, a potential threat to the interests of creditors.

Answer 2

It is not uncommon for a company to require prospective subscribers to pay more than the nominal value of the shares they subscribe for. This is especially the case when the market value of the existing shares is trading at above the nominal value. In such circumstances the shares are said to be issued at a premium.

The premium is the value received over and above the nominal value of the shares.

S687 of the Companies Act 2006 provides that any such premium received must be placed into a share premium account. The premium obtained is regarded as equivalent to capital and, as such, there are limitations on how the fund can be used.

The share premium account can be used for the following purposes:

➢ to pay up bonus shares to be allotted as fully paid to members.
➢ to write off preliminary expenses of the company.
➢ to write off the expenses, commission or discount incurred in any:
  i. issue of shares or
  ii. debentures of the company.
➢ to pay for the premium payable on redemption of debentures.

Considering the rules relating to capital maintenance it is clear that **the share premium account cannot be used for paying dividends to the shareholders.**

Answer 3

Trading profits of current year	£10,000
Less: accumulated losses of previous years	£ 5,000
Distributable profits	£ 5,000

The unrealised profits on revaluation of non current assets are excluded for calculating distributable profits.

Answer 4

According to s831, it includes:
➢ The share premium account.
➢ The capital redemption reserve.
➢ The excess of accumulated unrealised profits not previously utilised by capitalisation over accumulated unrealised losses not previously written off in a reduction or reorganisation of capital.
➢ Any other reserve which the company is prohibited from distributing by any enactment or by its Articles.

Answer 5

The following are the main rules for dividend distribution:
a. It is not binding on the company to distribute profits if it is not stated in the Articles of Association of the company.
b. The Boards of Directors recommend the amount of dividend which requires the approval in the general meeting.
c. The amount of dividend should not increase the amount recommended by the directors. Shareholders can not increase the amount but they can reduce the amount.
d. Generally dividend is paid on the paid up value of the share capital of the company and interim dividend can also be paid.

Quick Quiz

State True or False

1. A limited company is permitted to cancel its unissued shares without any restriction.

2. A company can issue shares at discount.

3. A company can pay dividends to its shareholders out of the current year's surplus.

4. If a company issues shares at a premium, a sum equal to the aggregate amount or value of the premiums on those shares shall be transferred to an account called "the share premium account".

5. Shareholders can increase the amount of dividend.

Answers to Quick Quiz

1. **True,** provided in case of public company, the capital can not be reduced below £50000

2. **False,** a company is prohibited from issuing shares at discount.

3. **False, a company whether public or private, may not make a distribution except out of profits available for the purpose of distribution** i.e. the Distributable profits (s 830)).

4. **True.**

5. **False,** Shareholders can not increase the amount of dividend; they can reduce the amount of dividend.

Self Examination Questions

Question 1

State the possible reasons for reduction of share capital.

Question 2

How can a company utilise the balance in a share premium account?

Question 3

Briefly explain the restrictions on distribution of dividends by public company.

Answers to Self Examination Questions

Answer 1

The reasons for a reduction of share capital may include:

➤ To eliminate accumulated losses.
➤ To return surplus capital to shareholders where such capital is in surplus to the company's requirements for the foreseeable future.
➤ Where partly paid up shares have been issued and a company decides that it no longer has any use for the unpaid fraction of those shares, it can release the shareholders from their liability of paying the balance due on those shares by extinguishing the unpaid capital.
➤ To create a distributable reserve for purposes other than declaring a dividend, for example if a company wishes to buy back its own shares from shareholders which can only be done out of distributable profits.
➤ Simplifying a company's share structure by cancelling and extinguishing any deferred shares to which little or no rights are attached.

Answer 2

The share premium account can be used for the following purposes:
➤ to pay up bonus shares to be allotted as fully paid to its members.
➤ to write off preliminary expenses of the company.
➤ to write off the expenses, commission or discount incurred in any:
  i. issue of shares or
  ii. debentures of the company.
➤ to pay for the premium payable on redemption of debentures.

Answer 3

a) **A company whether public or private, may not make a distribution except out of profits available for distribution** i.e. the distributable profits.

b) A public company may only make a distribution of its distributable profits if at that time the amount of its net assets is not less than the aggregate of its called up capital and undistributable reserves, and if and to the extent that the distribution does not reduce net assets below that aggregate. For e.g. the issued and paid up capital of a company is £500,000 and balance in share premium account is £200,000.

In this case, if the company's net asset are £700,000 or less then the company can not distribute any dividend. If the company's net assets are £1,000,000, then it can pay dividend to such extent that will bring down the net asset up to £700,000. I.e. the maximum dividend the company can pay is £300,000. Because dividend more than £300,000 will bring the company's net asset below £700,000 and this is not allowed under the company's Act 2006 s.831.

F 1

SECTION F - MANAGEMENT, ADMINISTRATION AND REGULATION OF COMPANIES

COMPANY DIRECTORS

Get through intro

A company is an artificial entity created under the provisions of the Companies Act 2006. Having a separate and distinct legal identity in law, once incorporated, a company is capable of exercising all its functions like a natural person. However, being an artificial person it needs people to act on its behalf.

The shareholders are collectively the owners of the company. However, it is very inconvenient and impracticable for all of them to manage the company. Hence they elect their representatives to run the company on their behalf. These representatives of the shareholders are the company directors.

The company directors are the eyes and ears of the company through which the company functions.

The Companies Act places a number of responsibilities on the directors. It is very important to be fully acquainted with all the provisions relating to the directors.

After qualifying ACCA, you are very likely to be associated with company directors who are actively engaged in running a company.

This Study Guide is very important. Questions invariably covered in the examination paper are from this topic.

LEARNING OUTCOMES

a) Explain the role of directors in the operation of a company
b) Discuss the ways in which directors are appointed, can lose their office or be subject to a disqualification order
c) Distinguish between the powers of the board of directors, the managing director and individual directors to bind their company
d) Explain the duties that directors owe to their companies
e) Demonstrate an understanding of the way in which the statute law has attempted to control directors

Introduction

The responsibility of the management of a company lies with the Board of Directors. As well ensuring all business activities are thoroughly conducted, the BOD also has hands on approach and manages and oversees the day to day operation of the company.

The role of director is critical to any organisation. Directors should be equipped with the right skills, qualities and experience which are relevant to the companies business, i.e. law, marketing, finance or general management. Attention to detail and the commitment to dedicate themselves to the companies operations are crucial skills a director needs to possess. Teamed with integrity, energy, analytical skills, directness, the readiness to challenge and independence, directors are expected to work both individually and as part of a team.

1. Explain the role of directors in the operation of a company

[Learning outcome a]

Definition According to s.250 of the Companies Act 2006, **the term director 'includes any person occupying the position of director by whatever name called"**

This definition can also be found in s. 251of Insolvency Act 1986 and s.22 of the Company Directors Disqualification Act 1986, where it is extended to include shadow directors.

Tips **Shadow Director:** A "shadow" director is a person who is **not actually appointed** as a director but in accordance with whose directions or instructions the directors of the company are accustomed to act.

In Re, Forest of Dean Coal Mining Co, (1878) it was stated that "function is everything; the name matters nothing." So long as a person is duly appointed by the company to control the company's business and is authorised by the Articles to contract in the company's name and, on its behalf, he functions as a Director. The Articles of a company may, therefore, designate its Directors as governors, members of the governing council or, the board of management, or give them any other title. However, so far as the law is concerned, they are simply Directors.

The prime role of the director is to protect the interests of the company ahead of all other interests. This was demonstrated in the case of **Automatic Self - Cleaning Filter Syndicate Co Ltd v Cuninghame (1906),** where the court held that the directors could not act on a request of the shareholders, as they believed it was not in the best interests of the company.

➢ S260 CA 2006 introduces a new statutory procedure for a derivative action, which replaces the old common law rules and widens the circumstances in which a derivative action can be brought but the rule in Foss v Harbottle still survives after the CA 2006. The new procedure reflects the recommendations of the Law Commission that there should be a new derivative procedure with more modern, flexible and accessible criteria for determining whether a shareholder can pursue an action. The CA 2006 permits a derivative claim to be brought in respect of a cause of action arising from negligence, default, breach of duty or breach of trust by a director. It will not be necessary for the claimant to show that the wrongdoing directors control the majority of the shares. The inclusion of negligence in the legislation has given rise to fear that there may be a flood of litigation in respect of director's negligence, which was not permitted under common law.

However, the new procedure does encompass some safeguards, in that a member of a company who brings a derivative action must apply to the court for permission to pursue the claim and the court will take into account various factors before granting permission, such as:

➢ whether the company has decided not to pursue the claim – if so the court has to decide whether to override this decision. It may do so, for example, if the wrongdoers control the voting and clearly would not pursue a claim against them.

➢ the views of disinterested members.

➢ whether the claim would promote the success of the company – sometimes litigation is not in the best interests of the company as it could be more damaging to the company for it to be seen publicly to be in a state of litigation.

➢ whether there has been, or could be, authorisation or ratification of the act or omission giving rises to the claim.

➢ the good faith of the claimant.

This seems to be in line with the philosophy of the rule in Foss v Harbottle that a member should only be able to pursue a derivative claim because this is in the best interests of the company, not because this is for the benefit of the member personally.

Remedies

By s 996(1) CA 2006 the court may make such order as it thinks fit:
➢ authorise civil proceedings to be brought in the name of the company
➢ regulate the conduct of the affairs of the company for the future
➢ require the company to refrain from doing or continuing to do an act complained of
➢ require the company not to make any alterations to its articles without leave of the court
➢ order the purchase of any shares of any member of the company

The petitioner must specify the relief sought and it must be appropriate to the conduct of which the petition complains.

Directors are the persons who direct, control and regulate the functioning of the company. The role of directors in the operation of a company is as follows:
1. Directors as agents of a company
2. Directors as trustees of a company
3. Directors as managing partners of a company

1. Directors as agents of a company

As we have seen earlier, a company is a legal entity. Hence it acts through individuals i.e. directors. Therefore, the relationship between the company and directors is that of principal and agent. Therefore, where directors enter into any contract in relation to any company operation, it is the company which is bound by the contract and not the director in his individual capacity.

However, in some cases as outlined below the director will be personally liable to the third party for any contract entered into by him i.e.:

➢ Where he acts in his own name.
➢ Where he does not mention that he is signing the contract on behalf of the company.
➢ Where he exceeds his liability for example, where he borrows in excess of the limits imposed on him.
➢ Where the company's name is quoted incorrectly for example without adding the words "limited" or "PLC".

Where a director exceeds his power, the contract is still binding on the company but then the company can claim the damages from the director.

Tips

The directors are the agents of the company but not of the individual shareholder.

2. Directors as trustees of a company

Directors are regarded as the trustees of the company. They stand in a fiduciary position towards the company in respect of their powers and capital under their control. This is mainly because they are required to act in the interest of the company and not for their own personal interest. The directors are also regarded as trustees of the company's property as the administration of company's property are trusted to them. If the property is misused it would amount to breach of trust.

Example

Bright Plc decided to sell some of its machinery. Jackson, the director of the company purchased the machinery for his son's business. The price paid by Jackson to the company was much less than the market price of the machinery. Here, Jackson has breached his trust and will be liable to the company for breach of fiduciary duty.

3. Directors as managing partners of a company

A company is owned by the shareholders collectively. However the management of company is entrusted by them to their representatives i.e. directors. Therefore, in a way, directors are the managing partners whereas shareholders are the dormant partners of the company. I would not use this analogy with a partnership as they are completely different creatures. Suggest that there is a separation of ownership and control, the shareholders being the owners and the directors the controllers.

Directors are the representatives of the shareholders who are entrusted with managing the affairs and operations of the company for the benefits of all shareholders of the company.

Tips

Note: Do not confuse with partner of partnership firm, here it is given only to explain the nature of director's position.

Test Yourself 1

Directors are regarded as the agents of a company. State how the position of a director is different from that of an agent.

Test Yourself 2

Explain the position of director as trustee of the company.

Diagram 1: Role of director

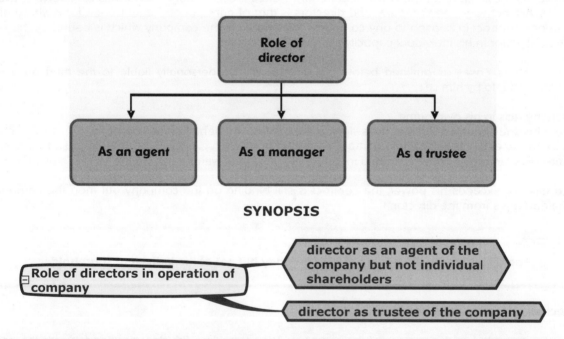

SYNOPSIS

Role of directors in operation of company

director as an agent of the company but not individual shareholders

director as trustee of the company

---

2. Discuss the ways in which directors are appointed, can lose their office or be subject to a disqualification order

[Learning outcome b]

Appointment of the first directors of the company

At the time of delivering various documents to the registrar for the incorporating of the company, Form No.10 is also required to be submitted. This form contains the particulars of the first directors and is signed by them to signify their consent to act as directors. On the formation of the company, those people become the first directors of the company.

Appointment of the subsequent directors of the company

The directors are usually appointed by election in general meeting by the shareholders. Casual vacancies in the office of directors are filled up by the Board of Directors co-opting someone to act as a director.

Shareholders are generally free to appoint any person as a director whom they believe will run the company well on their behalf. However there are **certain restrictions** on candidates to be appointed as directors, these are:

➢ The person must **not have been disqualified by a court from being a director:** if he is so disqualified he needs the court's permission to act as director for a particular company.

➢ The person **must not be an undischarged bankrupt:** if he is so, he needs the court's permission to act as director for a particular company.

➢ Sole corporate directors are abolished and all companies are required to have at least one actual person as a director.

➢ A new minimum age of 16 is set for directors. Existing under-age directors will cease to be directors.

➢ For a public limited company, **if his age is over 70** years, his appointment must be **approved at a general meeting** of the company.

The appointment of directors must also comply with the company's Articles of Association. They may include, for example:

➢ How many directors can be appointed
➢ How long they can serve
➢ What happens at the end of their term? For example, in many companies directors are required to retire after a set term - say three years. They can offer themselves for re-election at the shareholders' annual general meeting.
➢ The minimum number of shares (qualification shares) the proposed director needs to hold in the company.
➢ The time limit to acquire qualification shares after appointment as director and consequences of not acquiring them within prescribed time.

Removal of directors

A director can be removed from his position as a director in number of situations for the following reasons:

1. Under the provisions of the Companies Act

The procedure for dismissal of director is as follows:

➢ A company can remove a director by passing an **ordinary resolution** (s.168).

➢ The shareholders intending to propose the resolution for removal of a director must send a **special notice** (28 days) to the company.

➢ The shareholders proposing a resolution to remove a director, must hold
  ✓ either **1/20th voting** rights
  ✓ Or, represent 100 **members with an average of £100 paid up** on shares.

➢ A copy of the special notice is to be given to the director by the company.

➢ The director concerned should be given opportunity of being heard, he has the right to address the meeting at which the resolution for his removal is considered.

➢ The director may require that a memorandum of reasonable length be issued to members and the company must send that notice to every shareholder who is sent notice of the meeting.

➢ If the company receives these too late for them to be sent out to the shareholders, then the director is entitled to allow them to be read out at the meeting.

2. By disqualification

The **articles of company usually provide** for circumstances on happening of which the director is regarded as disqualified to act as the director of the company. Some of such circumstances may include **mental incapacity, bankruptcy, prolonged absence from board meeting** etc.

Example

The articles of Bright Ltd contain a provision whereby the company can remove a director from his position if he does not attend for 5 consecutive meetings of the BOD. Ted was unable to attend seven BOD meetings of Bright Ltd held during the last six months as he was dealing with financial problems in his own business. Here, the company may remove Ted from the position of director as he was not present for 5 consecutive meetings of the board.

---

3. By rotation

The model articles for a public company, under CA 2006, article 20, provide that at each Annual General Meeting, **one-third** (or the number nearest to one-third) **of the total number** of directors has to retire by rotation. The directors longest in service since their last appointment shall retire first. A managing director or director holding executive office is not subject to retirement by rotation and he will not be included in total number of directors for counting the one-third. The director retiring by rotation may be reappointed by the company in general meeting. A director shall be deemed to be reappointed unless the contrary is decided by the general meeting.

Tips

Remember, 1/3 of all directors must retire by rotation each year!

4. By retirement

A public company cannot have a director whose age is above 70 years. Hence directors of public companies are required to retire before or at the first AGM after their attaining the age of 70. However, this rule is not applicable if the **articles permit** the director to continue as such or if his continued appointment is **approved by the company in general meeting.**

5. By resignation of director

A director can be removed from his position if he resigns from the post of director.

6. By dissolution of a company

On dissolution of the company, the directors are automatically removed from their position.

Diagram 2: Removal of directors

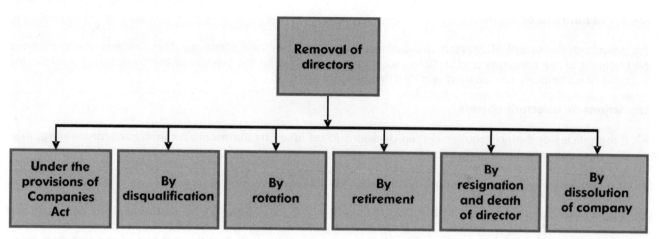

SYNOPSIS
Appointment and removal of directors

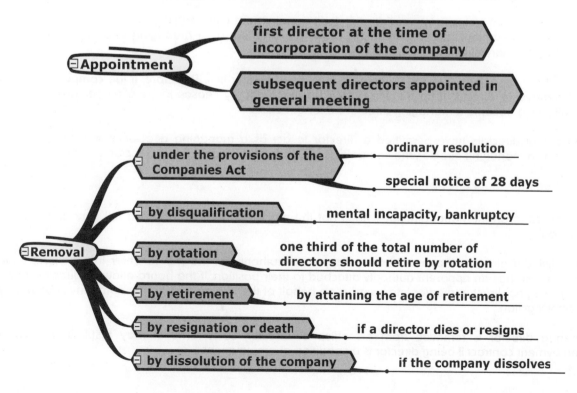

3. Distinguish between the powers of the board of directors, the managing director and individual directors to bind their company

[Learning outcome c]

Powers of board of directors

The powers of the board of directors are defined by the articles of the company. The directors are to manage the business of the company and, in doing so, they can exercise all the powers of the company. Therefore, the directors of a company can do anything that the company can do.

Restrictions on director's powers

➢ If the articles or the Act requires certain decisions to be taken by the **members in a general meeting,** then directors cannot take such decisions.

➢ The directors obviously cannot do anything which is illegal.

As long as the directors are acting in good faith and doing their best for the company, they can take any decisions and perform any actions. The company in a general meeting does not have the power to set aside the day-to-day actions of the directors, **provided it can be established that the actions of the directors were within the powers of the directors.**

Powers of managing director

If the company's Articles so provide, the board may appoint one or more directors as managing director.

The duties and authorities of a managing director are delegated to him by the board. However, in dealing with third parties, the managing director has **apparent authority** as agent to enter into business contracts on the company's behalf. Other directors do not enjoy the same authority as the managing director, even if they work full time.

Tips **Apparent authority:** This is explained in Study Guide D1 Agency. Apparent authority is the authority as it appears to others. In the case of a company, outsiders dealing with the company can reasonably believe that the MD has the right to perform a particular act on the company's behalf. Hence, even if that act was outside the powers of the MD, the company is bound to the outsider for such his acts.

In spite of his special status, a managing director's appointment can be terminated in the same way as for other directors or employees. On termination of his appointment as a managing director, he returns to the position of an ordinary director.

In order to be a managing director, a person has to be a director first. Therefore, if the company in a general meeting removes a director from his office, then he automatically ceases to be a managing director as his basic eligibility to become a managing director no longer exists.

If the board of directors have permitted a director to act as a managing director, when he is not actually appointed as a managing director, the company is bound by the actions of that director.

Powers of an individual director

The authorities of an individual director who is not the managing director and is a full time employee of the company are:

1. An individual director does not have an apparent authority as the MD to enter into general contracts. However, he has an apparent authority attached to their position. If the board allows a director other than the managing director to enter into contract on behalf of the company, then the company is bound by that director's action.

2. When a director is removed from his office of director, such removal may result in breach of his employment contract if being director is a condition of employment.

4. Explain the duties that directors owe to their companies

Directors' duties towards the company can be summarised as follows:

1. Reasonable skill and care

Duty to Exercise Reasonable Care, Skill and Diligence – s 174 CA 2006

Directors owe the duty to exercise reasonable care, skill and diligence. Exercised by a reasonably diligent person with:

a) the general knowledge, skill and experience that may reasonably be expected of a person carrying out the functions carried out by the director in relation to the company; and
b) the general knowledge, skill and experience that the director has."

This duty codifies the director's duty to exercise reasonable, care, skill and diligence, but once he has done so, the decision as to what constitutes the success of the company is one for his good faith and judgement. This corresponds to the present law and ensures that business decisions on, for example, strategy and tactics, are for the directors and not subject to decision by the courts, as long as the directors are acting in good faith.

Example

Derek and Vanessa are directors of companies Excellent Plc and Bright Plc respectively. Derek is employed as a manager of the company. His responsibilities as a director include reporting to the board on the finances of the company. He has no specific financial or accounting qualifications. Vanessa has been recruited to the board of Bright PLC as a finance director. She is a qualified accountant.

In considering the accounts of Excellent Plc, Derek would be expected to show the care, skill and diligence which a reasonable director without any professional knowledge of accounts might show. However, Vanessa has particular experience and knowledge in this area and would be expected to examine the accounts with the care, skill and diligence expected of someone with her particular accountancy skills and knowledge of company accounts.

2. s172 CA 2006 expresses the main duty of a director as follows:

A director of a company must act in the way he considers, in good faith, would be most likely to **promote the success of the company for the benefit of its members as a whole.**

In fulfilling the duty a director must (as far as reasonably practicable) have regard to:
a) the likely consequences of any decision in the long -term,
b) the interests of the company's employees,
c) the need to foster the company's business relationships with suppliers, customers and others,
d) the impact of the company's operations on the community and the environment,
e) the desirability of the company maintaining a reputation for high-standards of business conduct, and
f) the need to act fairly as between members of the company.

This duty requires directors, in certain circumstances, to consider or act in the interests of creditors of the company."

Statutory duties under Companies Act 2006:

a) Duty to act within powers
b) Duty to promote the success of the company
c) Duty to exercise independent judgement
d) Duty to exercise reasonable care, skill and diligence
e) Duty to avoid conflicts of interest
f) Duty not to accept benefits from third parties
g) Duty to declare interest in proposed transaction or arrangement

Section 5, statutory controls over directors duties

The director is expected not to take any unauthorised benefits of his position. He should not make any secret profit for himself and should duly disclose all the advantages given to him from being the company director. He should not exploit for his own to use the corporate opportunity.

Case Study — Director should not make unauthorised benefits.

Rolled Steel Products Ltd v British Steel Corporation (1985)

One of the directors of Rolled Steel Products was also part of Scottish Steel. Scottish Steel was in debt to British Steel Corporation. If British Steel Corporation would demand the debt and were to sue, then Scottish Steel would go out of business. Rolled Steel Products guaranteed the loan so that if Scottish Steel didn't pay, then it would pay the debts to British Steel Corporation.

Court's decision: The court held that the guarantee was void. Rolled Steel Products had no interest in Scottish Steel continuing trading, and it was only in the director's interest. The director has taken undue benefit of his position in Rolled Steel Products and therefore did not act in good faith

3. No undisclosed conflicts of interest

The director should avoid conflicts of his own interests with that of company's interests and must act in the best interest of the company.

Case Study — Directors should act in the interest of the company.

Howard Smith v Ampol Petroleum (1974)

Directors preferred one take-over bid as opposed to another, which was supported by the majority shareholding. In order to defeat the bid they disliked, the directors issued new shares, effectively reducing the existing majority to a minority holding in the company, incapable of blocking their preferred take-over bid.

Court's decision: It was held that this was clearly an abuse of the directors' powers and a breach of their duty to act in the interests of the company.

Section 177 CA 2006 requires that every director who is in any way, directly or indirectly, interested in a contract or arrangement shall disclose the nature of his interest. If the director fails to disclose his interest in any contract or proposed contract, he shall be liable to a fine. The declaration may be (but need not be) made:

a) At a meeting of directors
b) By notice to the directors in accordance with s 184 (notice in writing) or s 185 (general notice)

A director need not declare an interest if it cannot reasonably be regarded as giving rise to a conflict of interest, or to the extent that the other directors are already aware of it.

Confidentiality

The director should not pass on the company's confidential information to any third party which will cause losses or any harm to the company, either to its assets or reputation. The company's confidential information shall not be inappropriately disclosed or used for the personal gain or advantage of anyone other than the company.

Example

Build Well Ltd is a company engaged in the business of construction of roads and dams. The company filed a bid for a big project. The director of the company discloses this confidential information of bid amount to a competitor company, and the competitor company bid below the price quoted by Build Well Ltd. As a result the contract was assigned in favour of the competitor company. Therefore, the director has breached the duty of confidentiality.

4. To promote the success of the company

A director is expected to give his best to promote the success of the company.

Tips

Directors owe their duty to the company and not to individual shareholders.

5. Other duties

The duties of the directors, however, are not comprehensive.
The directors individually and collectively as Board of directors, owe various duties to the company. Some of them are as follows:

a) To disclose their interest, if any, in the transactions of the company.
b) To enter into contracts on behalf of the company.
c) To take decisions in relation to the day to day management of the company.
d) Hold such meetings from time to time as are necessary to manage the company.
e) Appoint sub-committees and to lay down written procedural guidelines for the sub-committees and their various panels appointed from time to time.
f) To attend board meetings and participate in management of company.
g) To convene general meeting according to the provisions of Companies Act.
h) To file various documents and returns and records with the registrar, as and when required.
i) To maintain proper accounts of the financial transactions of the company.
j) To maintain various registers and records at the registered office or such other place as allowed by the provisions of the act.

Diagram 3: Duties of directors

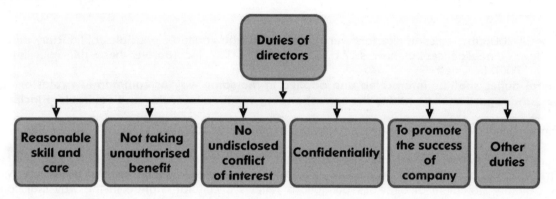

Test Yourself 4

Explain the fiduciary duties of directors towards the company.

SYNOPSIS

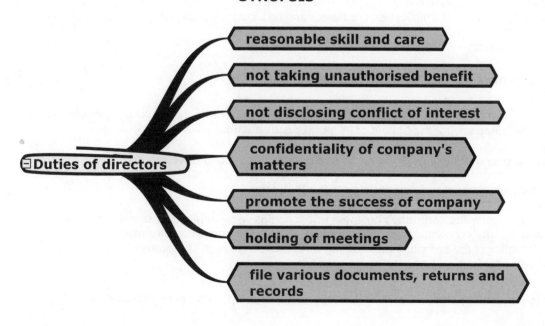

5. Demonstrate an understanding of the way in which the statute law, has attempted to control directors

[Learning outcome e]

One of the main characteristics of a company is that the **ownership and management of the company tend to be in different hands.**

The ordinary shareholders of a company are its owners. **The ordinary shareholders, by using their voting rights appoint the directors who manage the affairs of the company.**

Considering the immense trust placed on the directors of a company, and also the wide powers given to them, it becomes **necessary to have certain checks in place, so that they do not abuse or misuse the trust and powers vested in them.**

➢ Part 10 of the CA 2006 contains some of the most important provisions of the CA 2006, namely, a codification of directors' duties:

The Companies Act 2006 has transformed the law relating to directors' duties and has codified the fiduciary duties of directors.

Before the CA 2006 the duties of directors were governed by the equitable principles of fiduciary duty and the common law of negligence but now s.171-173 and s.175-177 incorporate these principles into statute. However, s. 170(4) provides:
'the general duties shall be interpreted and applied in the same way as common law rules or equitable principles, and regard shall be had to the corresponding common law rules and equitable principles'

Hence, earlier case law will still be relevant in interpreting the new codified duties.

The general duties of directors have been developed until now in case law but the CA 2006 now codifies these common law duties of directors in an attempt to make the rules more transparent and accessible. Moreover, the new statutory statement of director's obligations reflects a cultural change in the way that companies conduct their business and reflects what is known as the **'enlightened shareholder value'** model.

Traditionally UK company law has adhered to the **shareholder primacy** standard, which requires directors to discharge their fiduciary duties and make decisions in such as way as to maximise the interests of the shareholders ahead of any other interested stakeholders who might have claims against the company.

The **CA 2006 reflects the enlightened shareholder value model**, recognising that the central obligation of company law is to generate maximum value to shareholders, but equally to pay regard to the interests of other stakeholders, such as employees, creditors, suppliers, customers and the environment.

The duties of directors

➢ **Duty to promote the success of the company s 172**

A director of a company must act in the way he considers, in good faith, would be most likely **to promote the success of the company** for the benefit of its members as a whole.

In fulfilling the duty a director must (as far as reasonably practicable) have regard to:

a) the likely consequences of any decision in the long-term
b) the interests of the company's employees
c) the need to foster the company's business relationships with suppliers, customers and others
d) the impact of the company's operations on the community and the environment
e) the desirability of the company maintaining a reputation for high-standards of business conduct
f) the need to act fairly as between members of the company

➢ **Duty to act within powers,** s 171 – this section reflects the position in established case law.

➢ **Duty to exercise independent judgement,** s 173 – this provision makes it clear that a director who has been nominated to the board by a major shareholder must act in the best interests of the company he is serving rather than in the interests of the person who nominated him.

> **Duty to exercise reasonable care, skill and diligence,** s 174 – which means the care, skill and diligence that would be exercised by a reasonably diligent person with:

a) the general knowledge, skill and experience that may reasonably be expected of a person carrying out the functions carried out by the director in relation to the company, and

b) the general knowledge, skill and experience that the director has.

> **Duty to avoid conflicts of interest, s175**
> **Duty not to accept benefits from third parties, s176**
> **Duty to declare interest in proposed transactions-, s177**

Sections 175 – 177 Companies Act 2006 provide for certain **fiduciary duties** that must be adhered to by a director. A director must not:

a) make use of corporate opportunities (unless sanctioned by independent directors)
b) make a secret profit out of his position
c) compete with the company (unless sanctioned by independent directors)

Duty to Exercise Reasonable Care, Skill and Diligence – s174 CA 2006

Apart from the fiduciary duties owed by directors to a company, they also owe the duty to exercise reasonable care, skill and diligence. Exercised by a reasonably diligent person with:

a) the general knowledge, skill and experience that may reasonably be expected of a person carrying out the functions carried out by the director in relation to the company, and
b) the general knowledge, skill and experience that the director has."

This duty codifies the director's duty to exercise reasonable, care, skill and diligence, but once he has done so the decision as to what constitutes the success of the company is one for his good faith and judgement. This corresponds to the present law and ensures that business decisions on, for example, strategy and tactics, are for the directors and not subject to decision by the courts, as long as the directors are acting in good faith.

However, the difficulty with this is that the duty to act in good faith involves a subjective test and means, unless the courts employ objective considerations as a counterweight, as they have done in the past when assessing the good faith of a director, that the decisions of directors will be able to be challenged in few cases. Consequently, it is unclear, at present, how directors will be found liable for failing to have considered these factors, or for attaching insufficient weight to them. This is because directors appear to have complete discretion in so far as they only need to "have regard to" non-shareholder constituencies. Therefore directors will be held to have acted legitimately provided that they are acting in a way that they consider would most likely promote the success of the company for the benefit of the members. As long as a director can show that he did actually consider these statutory factors, even if he ultimately decided that they were less important than other factors, he will probably have discharged his duty. In any event, liability will only follow if the company can show it suffered a loss as a result of the directors' breach of duty, which, one might argue, will be a difficult thing to prove.

1. **Fiduciary duties are placed on directors.**

The directors are in fiduciary position in the company hence they have to act in a genuine manner keeping the best interest of the company in mind.

Duties of directors can be grouped into two types:

a) Duties of care and skill and
b) Fiduciary duties of loyalty and good faith which includes:
    > Duty not to take unauthorised benefits from his position as a director
    > Duty to avoid conflict of interest
    > Duty not to pass company's confidential information to third party
    > Duty to exercise their powers for a proper corporate purpose
    > Duty not to compete with the company

2. Companies Act prohibits a company from advancing loans to its directors or to the directors of its holding company.

In the absence of this section, it would become very easy for the directors to divert the flow of the funds of the company, in a way that would benefit them personally. Funds meant for the efficient running of the company, would be advanced as loans directly to the directors or indirectly in the form of loans to their relatives.

3. Important decisions, having serious and long term implications can be taken only by company at its general meeting.

Decisions have to be ratified at the general meetings; it helps to keep the directors in check. They cannot use their vast powers to take decisions which could prove to be beneficial for them but potentially harmful to the company. Such decisions would not get the requisite approval from the shareholders and hence the best interests of the company are always protected.

Some of the decisions that can be taken only by company at general meeting are:

➢ alteration to articles, memorandum and share capital.
➢ removal of director.
➢ decision to voluntarily wind up the company.

4. Declaration of their interest as required under of the Companies Act 2006.

This disclosure of interest must be to the full board of directors. It is not sufficient to disclose the interest merely to a fellow director or a committee of the directors.

This provision ensures that a director is not able to take undue advantage of his position in the company. The company is not forced to enter into transactions at uncompetitive rates with companies in which its directors have a vested interest. All transactions have to be on fair terms due to the fact that directors' interest is to be declared.

5. Power of general meeting to remove director.

Wide powers are given to the share holders to remove the directors from their position. Hence if the director's performance is not satisfactory, the shareholders can remove the director. This enforces the director to perform efficiently as otherwise they would be removed from their position.

SYNOPSIS

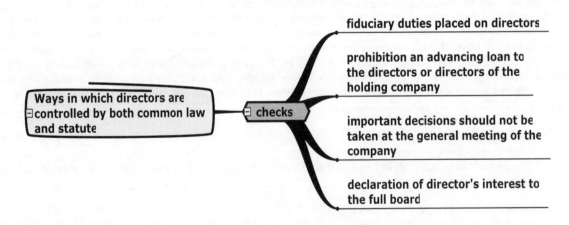

Answers to Test Yourself

Answer 1

Directors are not always considered to be the agents of a company. Their position is different than that of agents in the following respects:

➢ Notice to an agent amounts to notice to principal. But this is not the case with the director. Notice to director does not amount to notice to the company unless the director is entrusted with responsibility to receive such notice.

➢ If the director has personal knowledge in relation to certain issues it does not necessarily mean the company also has that knowledge.

For e.g., an advocate is appointed by the company to deal with legal matters of the company. The advocate was actually expelled by the association of advocates for two years. One of the directors was aware of the fact. When the company came to know the fact, the advocate was removed from the position. The advocate claimed that one of the directors was aware of the fact that he was not allowed to act as an advocate for next two years. Still the company appointed him which denotes the company's intention to avail his services in spite of his expulsion. So this can no more be a valid ground for his expulsion. But his claim is not sustainable because personal knowledge of director does not amount to knowledge of the company. Hence the company is justified in removing him after discovering the fact.

➢ An agent may enter into a contract in his own name but if a director enters into contract in his own name, he will be personally liable for the contract.

For example, a director of company 'Amway Ltd' enters into a contract without mentioning that he is acting for and on behalf of the company. Here, his principal i.e. 'Amway Ltd' is not liable for the contract. The director is **personally** liable for the Contract.

➢ An agent may not disclose the name of his principal but a director must disclose the name of his principal i.e. company on whose behalf, he is acting.

Answer 2

Directors occupy a fiduciary position in respect of the company of which they are directors. They are also to some extent trustees for the company.

First, they are the **trustees of the money and the property** of the company which comes under their remit or which is under their control.

Secondly, directors are in the position of trustees for their company as regards the **powers which they are authorised to exercise** on company's behalf.

Thirdly, a director's position partakes of a fiduciary character of trusteeship so that he is **precluded from allowing his personal interests to clash with the interests of the company**.

But the directors are **not trustees in the full sense of the word**. The **director is not the legal owner of the property he holds in tru**st for the company because the company itself is the legal owner. Another difference in the position of the trustee and the director is that a trustee contracts with the third party in his own name but **director contracts in the name of and behalf of the company**. Also, a trustee cannot be an employee of the trust. However, a **director can be an employee of the company.**

Answer 3

The total number of directors will not include Bob as he is appointed as managing director. Therefore total number of directors is four. One third of total number of directors is 1.333 i.e. 1.

Mr. Bob has served the longest but since he is Managing Director, the retirement by rotation is not applicable to him.

Mr. Clara has served the second longest so he shall retire first.

Answer 4

A fiduciary duty is a duty imposed on a person who is in a position of trust and confidence. A position of a fiduciary is similar to that of a trustee. The directors of the company are hence fiduciary and are delegated with some fiduciary duties which they have to perform for the company. They are:

1. To act in good faith and in the genuine interest of the company.

The directors are expected to act only in the genuine interests of their company. Secondly, directors when delegated duties are also endowed with some rights or authorities to carry out those duties. It is essential that this authority is used for the benefit of the organisation and not for personal benefits, or that this authority is not used improperly or unjustly.

For e.g., in **Howard Smith v Ampol Petroleum (1974)**, the directors preferred one take-over bid. However, the majority of shareholders supported another bid. In order to defeat the bid they disliked, the directors issued new shares. The issue of new shares effectively reduced the existing majority to a minority holding in the company. Therefore the shareholders became incapable of blocking their preferred take-over bid.

This was clearly an abuse of the directors' powers and a breach of their duty to act in a genuine manner in the best interests of the company. The directors used their authority unjustly by issuing new shares just to make a majority to reject the bid they did not like and to give preference to the bid of their choice.

2. To use their authority to meet the company's' objectives and interests.

The importance of this duty is that the directors should not perform in any way which will hamper the working of the company or go against the company.

For example, in board meetings, the director taking advantage of his influential position compels a person to use his vote favouring the decision of the director's interests and for this he enters into a contract with that person. This contract shows that the director has misused his powers.

3. To ensure their personal goals do not conflict with the interest of the company.

The directors should pledge loyalty and honesty towards the company and should not use his influential position for his personal interests. Rather he should keep the company's interest before his personal interests. The directors are expected to avoid such situations where they will be placed in a position of testing or choosing between personal and organisational goals. The directors have to disclose or take prior approval of the company, if he is using his position as the director of the company for his personal benefit.

In Regal (Hastings) v Gulliver (1942) the profits obtained on the sale of company's shares by directors in its subsidiary company were ordered to be returned to the company as they had taken advantage of their positions as directors of the company and made personal benefits thereby breaching the rule of their conduct in the interest of the company.

From this case you will know that the subsidiary company if purchases the shares of the parent company then it would not remain in its ownership but would gain a better position. The directors can do this only after declaring and getting the approval from the company.

Quick Quiz

State True or False.

a) Directors are the agents of the individual shareholders.

b) Directors owe their duty to the company and not to individual shareholders.

c) A public limited company can have one director.

d) Director has to perform his duties according to the company's norms but not according to the individual shareholder.

Answers to Quick Quiz

a) **False**, directors are the agents of the company but not of the individual shareholders.

b) **True.**

c) **False**, a public limited company must have at last two directors.

d) **True.**

Self Examination Questions

Question 1

In what circumstances, are directors of a company personally liable for their actions?

Question 2

Under what circumstances can a person be disqualified by a court from being a director?

Question 3

Can the board of directors delegate its powers to any one director?

Question 4

Who are the persons that are not eligible to be appointed as director of any company?

Answers to Self Examination Questions

Answer 1

The directors of a company incur a personal liability in the following circumstances:

➢ Where they contract in their own names.
➢ Where they use the company's name incorrectly, e.g., by omitting the word 'Limited' or "PLC".
➢ Where the contract is signed in such a way that it is not clear whether it is the principal (the company) or the agent who is signing.
➢ Where they exceed their authority, e.g. where they borrow in excess of the limits imposed upon them.

Answer 2

The court can disqualify certain categories of people from getting involved in the operations of the company. Under The Company Directors Disqualification Act (CDDA) 1986 there are three categories of conduct, which may, lead to disqualification by the court.

1. General misconduct in relation to companies

a) This kind of misconduct is in the case of promotion, formation, management or liquidation of a company or with the management of the company's property. **The court of summary jurisdiction can order a disqualification for a maximum period of five years and in other cases this period can be up to 15 years.**

b) The breach of companies legislation with respect of provisions which needs a return, account or other document to be filed with, or notice to be given to, the registrar. Here the court can order a **maximum disqualification for a period of five years.**

c) In case of fraud, in relation to the company's winding up, the court can order disqualification if, in the course of the closing down the affairs of the company, it comes to light that a person:
➢ has intentionally become a party to carry on the business of the company for indulging in fraudulent activities targeting the company's creditors or any other person; or
➢ has been guilty being an officer of the company for any fraud to the company or of shortfalls in his duty as an officer the court orders a maximum period of disqualification of 15 years.

2. Disqualified due to non eligibility

In the below mentioned case the persons involved are not eligible to be the directors of the company and thus are disqualified:

a) An undischarged bankrupt cannot be concerned in the management of any company without leave of the court.

b) A director can be disqualified if he is considered unfit to manage a company after investigation of a company under Company Directors Disqualification Act 1986 and the **maximum period of disqualification is 15 years.**

3. Other cases for disqualification

This category is for those:

a) Involved in fraudulent activities under s.213 of the Insolvency Act (IA) 1986 or if found guilty of wrongful trading under s.214 IA 1986 (s.10 of the CDDA 1986).

b) Have failed to pay the court administration order (s.12 of the CDDA 1986).

The court can pass a disqualification order under CDDA 1986, In case a person is found to be unfit as the director of an insolvent company, the court can make a disqualification order (s.6 of the **CDDA 1986**). A director who contravenes a disqualification order is liable to:

➢ imprisonment up to two years and / or a fine, on conviction on indictment, or
➢ imprisonment up to six months and / or a fine not exceeding the statutory maximum (s.13of the CDDA 1986).

Answer 3

The board can delegate its powers to a sole mandated person. Some of the powers that can be delegated are:

➢ to approve the annual budget and the company's business plan.
➢ to grant rental contracts or leases, to rent or lease, purchase, sell, pledge or charge any property, financial or other assets of the company including shares, quotas or bonds.
➢ to sell or acquire any business activity.
➢ to decide to associate the company with any other entity.
➢ to decide to issue bonds or to contract loans in the national or international financial markets and accept the supervision of the respective lending entities.
➢ to appoint third parties, individuals or corporate entities, to exercise offices (Including membership of Boards) in other companies.
➢ to decide that the company will give technical and financial assistance to subsidiary or related companies.

Answer 4

The following persons are not capable of being appointed as directors of any company:

➢ A person, found by a competent court, to be of unsound mind and the finding is in force.
➢ An undischarged bankrupt.
➢ A person, who has applied to be adjudged bankrupt.
➢ A person, who has been convicted by a Court of fraudulent trading.
➢ A person, who has not paid any call, in respect of shares of the company held by him, whether alone or jointly with others and, six months have elapsed from the last date, fixed for the payment of the call.
➢ A person, who has been disqualified by a Court, in pursuance of s.6 Insolvency Act 2006 Act, (which empowers the Court to restrain fraudulent persons from managing companies), and the order is in force, unless the leave of the Court has been obtained for his appointment.
➢ A Director, who has been removed from office by the Central Government, shall not be a Director of a company, for a period of five years from the date of order of removal.
➢ A person who has been convicted of an indictable offence relating to the promotion, formation or management of a company.
➢ A person under the age of 16

Note: A Private Company, which is not a subsidiary of a Public Company, may add to the above list of disqualifications.

SECTION F - MANAGEMENT, ADMINISTRATION AND REGULATION OF COMPANIES
OTHER COMPANY OFFICERS

Get through intro

This Study Guide deals with the procedure for appointing and the duties and powers of the company secretary and company auditors.

A qualified ACCA is eligible to be appointed as a secretary of a public limited company. After becoming ACCA qualified you may take up an appointment as a secretary of a company. Hence you need to be well-versed with the duties a secretary has in the company.

LEARNING OUTCOMES

a) Discuss the appointment procedure relating to, and the duties and powers of, a company secretary

b) Discuss the appointment procedure relating to, and the duties and powers of company auditors

Introduction

The role of company secretary continues to evolve. Constant changes and developments in the business world make this serious role more demanding. Assessing and analysing changes and investigating their wider business implications are an essential part of a company's secretary's job.

A company's reputation and image is one of its key assets. Keeping this asset untarnished is critical to sustaining long term growth. A large number of company law offences are punishable by fines or imprisonment, any violation of these regulations can and will ruin a company's reputation. The company secretary has to ensure that regulations are followed and complied with in full. They also need to ensure that their regulation knowledge is current and conduct risk assessments on any areas of potential risk.

Another key part of the company secretary's role is to operate a sound structure that caters for all levels of the organisation, from staff, to directors, to shareholders and investors.

1. Discuss the appointment procedure relating to, and the duties and powers of, a company secretary
[Learning outcome a]

Definition

A secretary is an officer of the company who is entrusted with the general administrative duties of the company.

Does a company secretary need any qualifications?

There is no provision in the Act which requires the secretary of a private limited company to have any specific qualifications, nor is it a requirement for a private company to appoint a secretary. Although any specific qualifications are not specified by the law for the company secretary of a private limited company, a secretary should be a well organised person as his basic responsibilities are to administer the statutory documents and records of the company and to ensure that Statutory Forms are filed promptly. N.B under CA 2006 it is not mandatory for a private company to have a secretary, but it may appoint one if it wishes, s270

However, s.271 Companies Act 2006 provides that the secretary of a **Public Limited Company must be an individual** whom the directors feel has the appropriate knowledge to carry out his/her role as the secretary. s. 273 CA 2006 imposes a duty on the directors of a pubic company to ensure that the company secretary is adequately qualified and experienced. Such as:

➢   a member of a body such as:

✓   the Institute of Chartered Accountants in England and Wales (ICAEW)
✓   the Institute of Chartered Accountants of Scotland(ICAS)
✓   the Institute of Chartered Accountants in Ireland(ICAI)
✓   the Chartered Association of Certified Accountants(ACCA)
✓   the Institute of Chartered Secretaries and Administrators(ICSA)
✓   the Chartered Institute of Management Accountants(CIMA)
✓   the Chartered Institute of Public Finance and Accountancy (CIPFA), or

➢   is someone who has been a secretary of a company for at least three out of the five years before the appointment as the current secretary, or

➢   is a barrister or solicitor, or

➢   is an individual whom the directors feel is capable of carrying out his role as a secretary because he / she holds, or has held, other similar position, or is a member of another body.

Position of a secretary in the company

Under s 1121(492) Companies Act 2006, a secretary is an officer of a company and as such may be criminally liable for any defaults committed by the company.

> **Example**
>
> Failure on the part of the secretary of a company to file within the allocated time any changes in the directors', secretary's details and the company's Annual Return is considered a default by the company. As the secretary is the officer of the company in charge of the submitting various records in time, he can be held responsible for the default.

The **secretary as agent of a company**

The role of the company secretary has developed over the years with the evolution of companies. Companies are required to handle many aspects in the day to day running and administration of their organisation. Appointing a mere subordinate to follow the instructions of the directors will not be helpful as he will not possess the powers of entering into a contract or to represent the company any where. The Court of Appeal, to overcome this hindrance, brought into existence the principle of apparent authority and gave a company secretary authority to enter into contracts and speak on behalf of the company for its normal running.

Case Study   Apparent authority to company secretary

Panorama Developments Guildford Ltd v Fidelis Furnishing Fabrics Ltd (1971)

Mr. Desmond was the secretary of Fidelis Furnishing Fabrics Ltd. He hired cars from Panorama Developments for bringing company's clients from London airport. He then had made false representation and misused the cars for his personal purpose. The bill presented by Car Hire Company was not paid and so the company claimed payment from Fidelis Furnishing Fabrics Ltd.

Court's decision: Fidelis Furnishing Fabrics Ltd was held liable to settle the bill as they had given apparent authority to Mr. Desmond to represent the company for the normal running of their company (the administration of the company). Hiring cars to receive guests of the company is in the normal function and which Mr. Desmond was authorised to do this. Mr. Desmond had not represented the company in its trade activities or any other administrative activity. Whether Mr. Desmond has used the car for his personal use or for company's use does not affect the third party.

The company should identify the company secretary as an important person and just giving him apparent authority and then not recognising this authority will not serve the purpose.

Can a director of company be the secretary of that company?

Even a director may be appointed as a secretary of a company. However, a sole director may not also be the secretary. That is if a company has only one director (which is possible in case of a private company) he cannot also be the secretary of that company.

Procedure for appointing company secretary

➢ Every public company **MUST** have a secretary.

➢ A public company must give particulars of the person who is to be the first secretary, s12 CA 2006.

➢ Subsequent secretaries are appointed in accordance with the provisions of articles of association of the company.

➢ A company can appoint two or more persons as joint secretaries.

Duties of company secretary

The secretary is an officer of the company under s.1121(2) of the Act; he is an officer responsible for the compliance of the company with various legal requirements under various acts as applicable to the company. He is entrusted with the overall responsibility of administration of the statutory documents and records of the company and ensuring that the statutory forms are filed promptly. He may be criminally liable for defaults committed by the company.

> **Example**
>
> A secretary may be held responsible for a failure by the company to file, in the time allowed, any change in the details of the company's directors and secretary, and the company's annual return.

The most common amongst his duties are:

1. Ensuring that statutory forms are filed promptly

A secretary is responsible for submitting the information and reports to the registrar by filling various forms. Submission of changes to registered address,, directors and secretaries or their particulars with the registrar within 14 days.

➢ Submitting the Annual Report .

2. Maintaining the statutory registers

These registers are:

➢ **The register of members** Companies Act mandates that every company shall keep a register of members containing the name, address and occupation of the members, the shares held by each member, the date at which each person's name was entered in the register and the date at which any person ceased to be a member.

➢ **The register of directors and secretaries** Every company must maintain this register which must contain details such as, the present and former forenames and surname, the service address, date of birth, nationality, and business occupation of the person appointed as director or secretary of the company.

➢ **The register of directors' interests** the main purpose of this Register is to provide information of any pecuniary interest or other material benefit which a director receives from the company.

➢ **The register of charges for Scottish companies):** Every company must maintain this register at its registered office which must contain the details of charges affecting the company property or undertaking giving the brief description of property charged, the amount of charge, the name of the person entitled to the charge etc.

➢ For public companies only, the **register of interests in shares.**

3. Sending a notice of meetings to members and auditors

A secretary is responsible for sending the auditor and members of the company, a **21 day** written **notice of the annual general meeting**. For a meeting which is neither an annual general meeting nor a meeting to pass a special resolution, 14 days written notice is sufficient. For an unlimited company, the period of written notice required is 7 days.

4. Sending the Registrar copies of resolutions and agreements

A secretary must send the Registrar copies of every resolution, for example special and extraordinary resolutions, within 15 days of them being passed.

5. Supplying a copy of the accounts

A secretary needs to send a copy of accounts to every member of the company, every debenture holder and every person who is entitled to receive notice of the general meetings or who have demanded them under of the Companies Act. The copies of accounts must send at least 21 days before any meeting at which they are to be laid

6. Keeping record of minutes of meeting

A secretary is responsible for keeping, or arranging for the keeping, of minutes of directors' meetings and general meetings.

> **Tips**
>
> **Minutes** are the record of the proceedings of the meeting

7. Ensuring the inspection of company records by members and others whom are entitled to do so

It is the secretary's duty to make available the necessary records to the members and others whom are entitled to inspect them.

Example

Members of the company and members of the public are entitled to a copy of the company's register of members, and members of the company are entitled to inspect the minutes of its general meetings and to have copies of these minutes. In such cases, when the copies are requested, it is the duty of the secretary to arrange for copies.

8. Custody and use of the company seal

Companies no longer need to have a company seal, but if they do, the secretary is usually responsible for its custody and use.

9. Special duty

The secretary may also have to make out a statement of the company's affairs if an administrative receiver or a provisional liquidator is appointed, or if a winding-up order is made under s.131 of the Insolvency Act 1986.)

Powers of company secretary

No specific powers are given to the secretary, but the Act allows them to sign the following re-registration applications:
➢ the re-registration of a limited company as unlimited
➢ the re-registration of an unlimited company as limited
➢ the re-registration of a public company as a private company and
➢ the re-registration of a private company as a public company

The secretary is also allowed to sign most of the forms prescribed under the Companies Act.

Test Yourself 1

What are the qualifications required for a company secretary of a public company ?

Diagram 1: Duties of company secretary

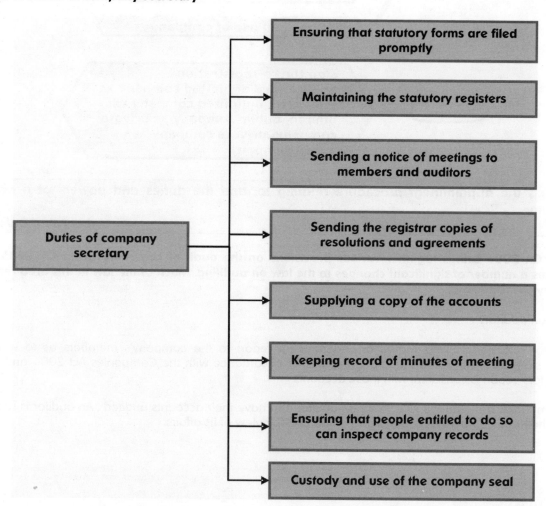

SYNOPSIS

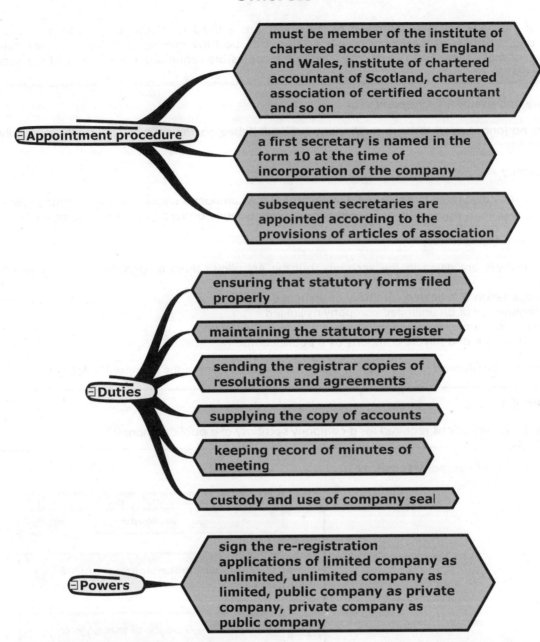

Appointment procedure
- must be member of the institute of chartered accountants in England and Wales, institute of chartered accountant of Scotland, chartered association of certified accountant and so on
- a first secretary is named in the form 10 at the time of incorporation of the company
- subsequent secretaries are appointed according to the provisions of articles of association

Duties
- ensuring that statutory forms filed properly
- maintaining the statutory register
- sending the registrar copies of resolutions and agreements
- supplying the copy of accounts
- keeping record of minutes of meeting
- custody and use of company seal

Powers
- sign the re-registration applications of limited company as unlimited, unlimited company as limited, public company as private company, private company as public company

2. Discuss the appointment procedure relating to, and the duties and powers of a company auditor

[Learning outcome b]

Part 16 CA 2006 brings together various provisions on the audit of companies from CA 1985. It also introduces a number of significant changes to the law on auditing. Much of the law in this area reflects EU Company Law Directives.

What is an auditor?

An auditor is a person who makes an independent report to the company's members as to whether its financial statements have been properly prepared in accordance with the Companies Act 2006 and whether the directors' report is consistent with those accounts.

Most companies are required to appoint an auditor and have their accounts audited. An auditor is required to report whether a company's accounts give a true and fair view of its affairs.

Who can be appointed as auditor?

1. Only a member of a recognised supervisory body is eligible to be appointed as an auditor.. The person to be appointed as the auditor is required to hold a professional accountancy qualification.
'Supervisory bodies' are established in the UK to control the eligibility of potential company auditors and the quality of their operation.. The recognised supervisory bodies are:

a) The Institute of Chartered Accountants in England and Wales,
b) The Institute of Chartered Accountants of Scotland,
c) The Institute of Chartered Accountants in Ireland,
d) The Chartered Association of Certified Accountants, and
e) The Association of Authorised Public Accountants.

The supervisory bodies mentioned above are also recognised as 'qualifying bodies', meaning that accountancy qualifications awarded by them are recognised professional qualifications for auditing purposes.

2. An auditor must be independent of the company, i.e. he should not be related to company in any capacity other than auditor. Therefore, a person cannot be appointed as an auditor if he is:

a) an officer or employee of the company

Example

Robert, an ACCA qualified person is employed with PNG Ltd as the chief accounts officer. As an employee of the company he cannot be appointed as the auditor of the company.

---

b) an officer or employee of an associated company, parent company or subsidiary company

---

Example

Robert, an ACCA qualified person is employed with PNG Ltd as the chief accounts officer. PNG Ltd is a subsidiary company of Powerful Ltd. Robert, being an employee of an associated company, cannot be appointed as the auditor of Powerful Ltd.

---

c) a partner or employee of such a person (i.e. officer or employee of company), or
d) a partnership of which such a person is a partner.

3. If a person has a current audit-practising certificate issued by a recognised supervisory body, then he may act as the company's auditor

The Companies Act does not contain any provision restricting a shareholder of a company or debtor or creditor of company or a close relative of any officer or employee of company to be appointed as an auditor. However, accepting an appointment as an auditor in such company is treated as professional misconduct by the regulations of the accountancy bodies of which they are member. Shareholders may agree a limitations of auditors' liability.

2.1. Procedure for appointing company auditor.

S485 applies to the appointment of auditors of private companies and ss 489 and 491 deal with appointment of auditors of a public company

➢ The first auditor of the company is **appointed by the Board of Directors.**

➢ The auditor appointed by the Board of Directors then **holds office until the end of the next general meeting at which the company's annual accounts are considered.**

Example

BBG Plc was incorporated on 10 June 20X5. The BOD appointed John as an auditor of the company on 15 June 20X5. The first annual general meeting of the company was held on 5 April 20X6. The auditor appointed by the BOD (i.e. John) on 15 June 20X5 will hold the office until the end of first general meeting held on 5 April 20X6.

➢ At the first meeting of the company, the accounts of the company are laid before the members. At that meeting the members of the company can re-appoint the auditor, or appoint a different auditor. Under s487 the auditor of a private company will automatically be re-appointed except in five cases: if he was appointed by the directors, if the company's articles require re-appointment, if the members have given notice to the company under s488, if there has been a resolution that the auditor should not be re-appointed, if the directors decide that they do not need auditors for the following year.

s. 489 provides that in the case of a public company an auditor must be appointed for each financial year, unless the directors reasonably resolve otherwise on the ground that audited accounts are unlikely to be required.

Example

As discussed in the above example, the shareholders of BBG Plc can either re-appoint John as the auditor or they can appoint another auditor in place of John.

➢ The auditor appointed at this meeting is to hold office from the end of that meeting until the end of the next meeting at which accounts are laid.

➢ Thereafter, every meeting at which accounts are laid before the members, the auditor is reappointed or new auditor is appointed in his place.

➢ Private companies can pass an **'elective resolution' not to lay accounts before the members in a general meeting.** If this is done, then the auditor has to be re-appointed, or a new auditor has to be appointed, at some other meeting of the company's members. The meeting for appointment or reappointment of auditors must be held **within 28 days** of the accounts being sent to the members.

Example

Peru Industries Plc has passed a resolution stating that the accounts of the company will not be laid before the members in general meeting. The company sent a copy of its accounts for the period ended on 31 March 20X5 to all members on 1 May 20X5. In this case, the company must hold the meeting to appoint or re-appoint auditor on or before 29 May 20X5.

➢ Private companies can also pass an **elective resolution dispensing with the need to appoint an auditor every year.** If that happens, the auditor already appointed remains in office without further formality until a resolution is passed to re-introduce the annual appointment or to remove him or her as the auditor.

 Tips **Elective resolution:** The primary purpose of elective resolutions is to simplify the running of the company in terms of the number of meetings and resolutions which it has to pass.

By passing such a resolution, time can be saved by not having to pass repetitive motions each year. It is only when a change is required that a new motion is required.

Removal of an auditor

➢ An auditor may be removed at any time by an ordinary resolution of the company .s510 CA 2006

➢ Any member proposing to remove an auditor should send a special notice to the company to that effect. A copy of such notice also needs to be sent to the concerned auditor, s 511 CA 2006

➢ Any auditor who is to be removed or not re-appointed is entitled to make written representations and require these to be circulated or have them read out at the meeting. S.511CA 2006

➢ An auditor may resign at any time by depositing notice in writing to the company's registered office, s516 CA 2006

➢ Notice of resignation must be accompanied by a statement of any circumstances that the auditor believes ought to be brought to the attention of members and creditors, or alternatively a statement that there are no such circumstances.

➢ The company is required to file a copy of the notice of resignation of auditor with the registrar of companies within 14 days.

> ➤ Where the auditor's resignation statement states that there are circumstances that should be brought to the attention of members, then he may require the company to call a meeting to allow an explanation of those circumstances to the members of the company.

2.2. Duties of company auditor

s. 498 CA 2006 deals with duties of an auditor. They can be summarised as:

1. Duty to make an audit report: It is duty of the auditor to report to the members:

> ➤ Whether the accounts of the company are prepared in accordance with the Companies Act.

> ➤ Whether they present a true and fair picture of the financial position of the company.

> ➤ Whether proper accounting records have been kept and proper records adequate for the purpose of his audit have been received from the companies' branches not visited by him.

> ➤ Whether the accounts prepared by the company are in agreement with the accounting records kept by the company.

> ➤ Whether all the information and explanations which where asked for were made available to the auditor.

> ➤ Whether the information provided in Director's report is in agreement with the accounts prepared by the company.

2. Duty to report whether the requirements of s 412 CA 2006 have been complied with.
S412 requires the company to properly disclose the payments and benefits made to directors. So it is the auditor's duty to verify whether all the payments and benefits accruing to directors from the company are properly disclosed in the accounts.

3. Duty to give reasons for qualifications.

An auditor has no power to change the accounts prepared by the company. However, where he is not satisfied with the treatment or disclosure of any item he may report the fact to the shareholders. Such comments of the auditor are called a qualification. An auditor should give proper reasons for all his qualifications.

Example

A company has included the fuel cost of a director's car in company's car and fuel expenses. But the auditor thinks that all the travelling was not related to the company's business hence the whole cost should not be charged to the company's profits. Some proportion of expenditure must be considered to be shown as benefits (to the director out of company).

At the general meeting, the report given by the auditor must be read out before the members and it must be kept open for inspection by members.

2.3. Powers of company auditor

The statutory rights are given by the Act to the auditors to enable them to discharge their function effectively. These powers:

1. Right to access records under s 499 CA 2006
An auditor of a company shall have a right to access at all times the books, accounts and vouchers of the company whether kept at the head office of the company or at any other place. The term 'books and records' include the financial, statutory, cost records, vouchers, documents, correspondence, agreements etc. The expression 'at all times' refers to the normal business hours on any working day.

2. Right to obtain information and explanation under s 499 CA 2006
An auditor is entitled to obtain information and explanations necessary for his audit from the officers of the company. If such explanation is not given by the officer or misleading information is given, a penalty in the form of imprisonment for a period of two years or fine or both can be imposed on the defaulting officers.

3. Right to receive the notice and attend the general meeting under s 502 CA 2006
All communications and notices relating to general meeting of a company are to be sent to the auditor whenever they are sent to the members of the company. The auditor has the right to attend the general meeting.

Tips

   (a)   Meetings of directors
       1) Meetings of Board of Directors
       2) Meeting of committee of directors
   (b)   Meeting of creditors of a company
       1) Meeting for the decisions of winding up of company
       2) Meeting for purpose other than winding up
   (c)   Meeting of members
       The meetings of members are of two types:
       1) General meeting
       2) Class meetings
       The general meeting is again of two types:
       1) Annual general meeting
       2) Extra-ordinary general meeting

4. Right to be heard at general meeting under s.502(2) CA 2006

The auditor has the right to attend any general meeting and speak on any matter which concerns him as an auditor.

5. Right to receive copy of written resolution under s.502 CA 2006

When any resolution is proposed to be made at meeting, a copy of the same must be sent to the auditor along with the notice of the meeting.

6. Right to require laying of accounts under s.498 CA 2006

Private companies can pass an **'elective resolution' not to lay accounts before the members in a general meeting.** In such case, the auditor is authorised to give written notice requiring that a general meeting be held for laying down the company's accounts before the members.

7. Right to receive notice of removal, s.511(2) CA 2006

When it is proposed to remove an auditor, the company shall give a notice to the auditor of his intended removal.

8. Right to make representation at meeting on removal, s.511(3) CA 2006

Where it is proposed to remove an auditor, the concerned auditor has right to make a representation and get it circulated to the members at the meeting.

Diagram 2: Duties of company auditor

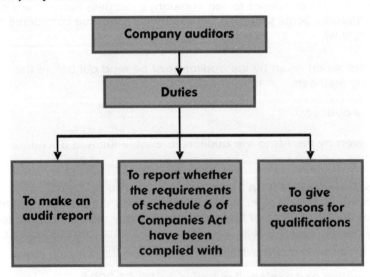

Diagram 3: Powers of company auditor

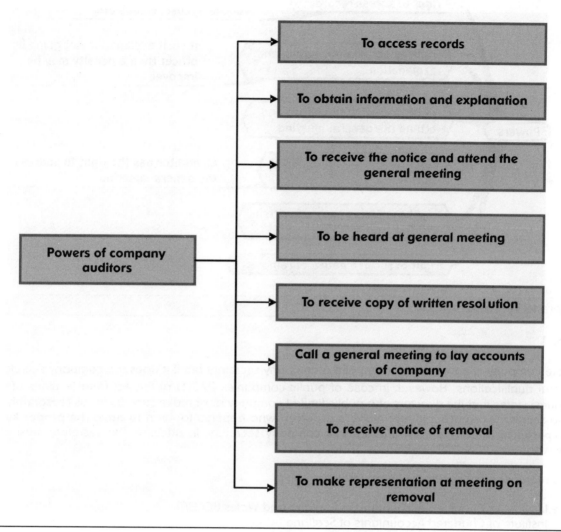

Test Yourself 2

Explain the term Auditor and state in brief the procedure for appointing an auditor.

Test Yourself 3

What are the duties of an auditor?

SYNOPSIS

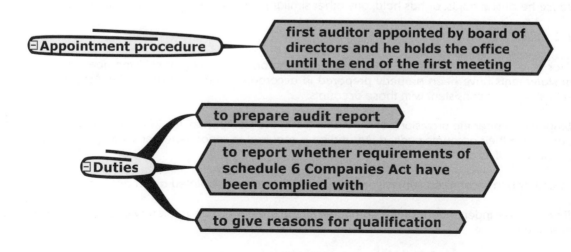

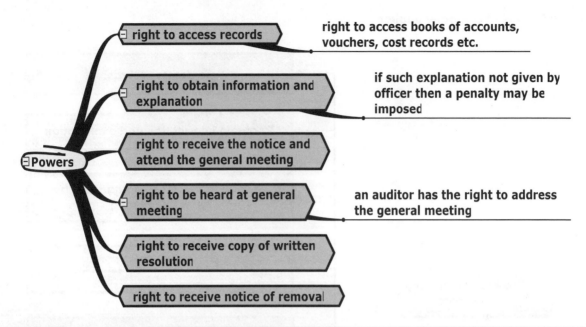

Answers to Test Yourself

Answer 1

A private company is not required to appoint a company secretary but if it does the company secretary needs no formal qualifications. However, in case of public companies 273(1) of the Act (qualifications of company secretaries) states that the directors of a public limited company must make sure, as far as reasonably possible, that the secretary, or each joint secretary, is a person who appears to them **to have the proper knowledge and experience** to carry out the functions of company secretary. In addition, the secretary must also be a person who:

a) is a member of any of the following institutes:

➤ The Institute of Chartered Accountants in England and Wales (ICAEW)
➤ The Institute of Chartered Accountants of Scotland (ICAS)
➤ The Institute of Chartered Accountants in Ireland (ICAI)
➤ The Chartered Association of Certified Accountants (ACCA)
➤ The Institute of Chartered Secretaries and Administrators (ICSA)
➤ The Chartered Institute of Management Accountants (CIMA)
➤ The Chartered Institute of Public Finance and Accountancy (CIPFA)

b) is someone who has been a secretary of a company for at least three out of the five years before the appointment as the current secretary, or

c) is a barrister or solicitor, or

d) is a person who appears to the directors to be capable of carrying out the functions of company secretary, because he or she holds, or has held, any other similar position or is a member of any other body.

Answer 2

An auditor is a person who makes an independent report to the company's members as to whether its financial statements have been properly prepared in accordance with the Companies Act 2006 and whether the directors' report is consistent with those accounts.

Most companies, under the provisions of Ch 2, Part 16 of the Companies Act 2006, are required to appoint an auditor and have their accounts audited. An auditor is required to report whether a company's accounts give a true and fair view of its affairs.

Only a member of a recognised supervisory body is eligible to be appointed as an auditor.

An auditor must be independent of the company, i.e. he should not be related with company in any capacity other than auditor.

Therefore, a person cannot be appointed as an auditor if he is:

➢ an officer or employee of the company.
➢ an officer or employee of an associated company, parent company or subsidiary company.
➢ a partner or employee of such a person (i.e. officer or employee of company) or
➢ a partnership of which such a person is a partner.

If a person has a current audit-practising certificate issued by a recognised supervisory body, then he may act as the company's auditor.

The procedure for the appointment of a company's auditor is as follows:

1. The Board of Directors of the company appoint the first auditor of the company. The auditor then holds the office until the end of the first meeting of the company at which the company's annual accounts are to be considered.

2. The company's accounts are laid in the next meeting. In that meeting, an auditor may be re-appointed or a new auditor may be appointed.

3. Thereafter, at every meeting at which accounts are laid before the members, the auditor is reappointed or a new auditor is appointed in his place.

4. Private companies can pass an **'elective resolution'** under to dispense with appointment of auditors annually.

Answer 3

Following are the duties of an auditor:

a) **Duty to make an audit report**

This is the main responsibility of an auditor. An auditor has to include in his report that all the accounts are maintained according to the provisions of the Companies Act, whether it shows the true and fair picture of the Company's financial position, and whether all accounting records are kept by the company.

b) **Duty to report whether the requirements of s. 412 Companies Act have been complied with**

s. 412 of the Companies Act states that payments and benefits to the directors are properly disclosed.

c) **Duty to give reasons for qualification**

If an auditor thinks that all the accounting records are not in accordance with the provisions of the Companies Act or disclosure is not proper, then he may qualify his audit report. It is his duty to give reasons for all the disqualifications included in his audit report.

Quick Quiz

1. State true or false

a) A company secretary is an officer the company.

b) A director of the company cannot be the secretary of the company.

c) A company can appoint more than one person as joint secretaries.

Answers to Quick Quiz

1.
a) **True.** Under s.1121 (2) of the Companies Act, a secretary is considered as an officer of the company.

b) **False,** a director of the company can be the secretary of the company but in case where there is only one director then the same person cannot be the secretary of the company.

c) **True.**

Self Examination Questions

Question 1

Briefly explain the duties of the company secretary.

Question 2

State any five rights of a company auditor?

Answers to Self Examination Questions

Answer 1

The company secretary has to perform various duties which are as follows:

a) **Ensuring that statutory forms are filed promptly:** A company secretary has to ensure that all the statutory forms which the company has to file, has been filed promptly.

b) **Maintaining the statutory registers:** A company secretary has to maintain the registers for members, directors, register of charges.

c) **Sending a notice of meetings to members and auditors:** A company secretary has to send a notice of the meetings to the members and auditors 21 days before the meeting.

d) **Supplying a copy of the accounts to the members of the company.**

e) **Keeping record of minutes of meeting.**

f) **Custody and use of the company seal is with the company secretary.**

Answer 2

The following are the rights of the company auditor:

1. **Right to access records under :s 499 CA 2006** A company auditor has the right to access the records of vouchers, financial and cost records at all the times whether they are kept at company's registered office or at any other place.

2. **Right to obtain information and explanation under : s 499 CA 206.** An auditor is entitled to receive information and explanation which he needs in performance of audit. Any defaulting officer is liable to a penalty in the form of imprisonment up to a period of two years or fine or both.

3. **Right to be heard at general meeting under s 502(1) CA 2006:** He has the right to attend the company's general meeting and speak on any matter which concerns him as an auditor.

4. **Right to receive copy of written resolution under .s 502(2) CA 2006.** A company auditor has the right to receive the copy of written resolution to be made at the proposed meeting.

5. **Right to receive notice of removal:** under s 514 CA 2006. A company auditor has the right to receive the notice of his intended removal from the position of auditor of company.

COMPANY MEETINGS AND RESOLUTIONS

Get through intro

This Study Guide deals with various provisions relating to company meetings. We know that a company is managed mainly by directors. However, shareholders, being the true owners of the company, must be given full information and their approval must be taken on important aspects and decisions of the company.

Hence a company requires convening a general meeting annually to give its members a fair chance to understand the position of company. Procedure to convene such a meeting and other meetings is specifically defined by the Companies Act 2006.

A thorough understanding of these procedures is necessary to decide, as an auditor, whether the company followed the procedures properly and what procedures are to be followed, as a company secretary.

A question from this topic is regularly asked in the exam paper. You are advised to study this topic with due attention.

LEARNING OUTCOMES

a) Distinguish between types of meetings: ordinary general meetings and annual general meeting meetings
b) Explain the procedure for calling such meetings
c) Detail the procedure for conducting company meetings
d) Distinguish between types of resolutions: ordinary, special, and written

Introduction

Most people are involved in meetings. Whether business meetings at work, meetings with our friends, or public meetings where we can influence the outcome.

Knowing how to manage a meeting is useful for business but can also be applied to any of the above situations.

Meetings are a crucial part of any companies operations. It's an opportunity for company members and directors to get together to discuss company matters. Debates and discussions usually form the basis for company meetings, with the final decision made according to the majority vote.

The changes in the law relating to meetings derive principally from the recommendations of the Company Law Review. Private companies will no longer be required to hold an AGM and to reflect the fact that private companies do not generally hold meetings, private companies can take decisions by written resolution. Such resolutions can be passed by e-mail. There are 2 things that a private company cannot do by written resolution:
➢ removal of a director
➢ removal of an auditor

1. Distinguish between types of meetings: ordinary general meetings and annual general meetings
[Learning outcome a]

Meaning

Meeting in simple words means getting together of two or more persons for discussing some issue of common interest. The word '**meeting' simply means the coming together of more than one person.**

The word 'meeting' when used in the context of a company duly registered under the Companies Act implies the coming together of two or more persons in accordance with the provisions of the Act and the Articles of Association of the company, for transacting some lawful business.

Why any meeting is convened?

As discussed earlier, a company is an artificial entity and so it cannot make any decisions nor can transact any business. It can do so only by passing resolutions at the various meetings. A resolution is the verdict or decision of the members of the company. Once a resolution is passed it becomes binding on the company as well as on all members and others persons dealing with it.

> **Example**
>
> When the dividend is approved by the company in general meeting, it becomes binding on the company to pay it to members and also members become entitled to receive the dividend.

Types of meetings

Meetings of directors
➢ Meetings of board of directors
➢ Meeting of committee of directors

Meeting of creditors of a company
➢ Meeting for the decisions of winding up of company
➢ Meeting for purpose other than winding up

Meeting of members
The meetings of members are basically of two types as under:
➢ General meeting
➢ Class meetings

General meeting is again of two types as:
1. Annual general meeting
2. General meeting

Diagram 1: Types of meetings

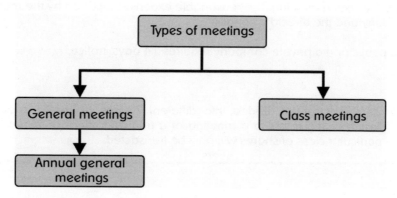

In this Study Guide, only meetings of members of the company are discussed as that is the only kind of meeting covered in the syllabus.

Abbreviations used in this Study Guide:

BOD – Board of Directors
AGM – Annual General Meeting
GM - General Meetings

General meeting: General meeting refers to meetings of members of the company. Although most of the decisions in the day to day management of the company are taken by the BOD, certain decisions can be taken only by the members of the company. These are reserved for members by the Act.

1. Annual general meeting (AGM)

Part 13 CA 2006 implements two general changes in relation to meetings:
➢ A private company no longer has to elect to dispense with the AGM; they will no longer be required to hold an AGM in the first place.
➢ Private companies can make decisions by written resolution without the need to hold a meeting.

Timing of AGM

S 336 CA 2006 deals with the AGM of public companies. Every public company must hold a general meeting as its annual general meeting in each period of 6 months beginning the day following its accounting reference date.

If a company fails to comply with s 336 then every officer in default is liable on conviction on indictment to a fine not exceeding the statutory maximum. Under the CA 1985, the AGM had to be held each year and not more than 15 months after the previous AGM; whereas under the CA 2006, a public company will now be required to hold an AGM within 6 months of its financial year end. This new requirement is intended to ensure that shareholders have a more timely opportunity to hold the directors of public companies to account.

a) The gap between **two AGMs must not be more than 15 months.**

Example

Grasim Textiles Plc held its AGM on 31 December 20X5. Then its next AGM must be held latest by 31 March 20X7.

---

b) If the company fails to hold an AGM within the prescribed time limits, both i.e. the company and the defaulting directors can be fined. S. 336(3)

Calling meetings

S.302 CA 2006 provides that the directors may call a general meeting.

S.303 CA2006 provides that members with 10% of the voting rights in a company may require the directors to call a general meeting. When the directors are required to call such a meeting they must send out a notice. This must be done within 21 days of the requisition for a meeting to be held not more than 28 days after the date of the notice convening the meeting.

As previously, if the directors fail to call the meeting then the requisitionists with more than half of the total voting rights may themselves call a meeting. The reasonable expenses incurred by the members must be reimbursed by the company and the directors penalised.

A general meeting of a public and a private company requires 14 days' notice.

2. Class meetings

A company may have its share capital divided into different classes of shares such as ordinary shares, preference shares etc. Class meeting refers to a meeting of a particular class of shares. In such meeting, the business relating to that particular class of shares will only be transacted.

Example

A class meeting of preference shareholders will be held if it is decided to make variation in any of the rights given to them.

Test Yourself 1

Peri Nitrates Plc was incorporated on 1 April 20X5. Explain the provisions of Companies Act regarding the time limit for holding AGM.

Test Yourself 2

Big Motors Plc holds its AGM on 15 June 20X4. State whether the provisions of the Companies Act are complied with if the next AGM of the company was held on-
1)   10 January 20X5
2)   20 November 20X5
3)   1 January 20X6

SYNOPSIS

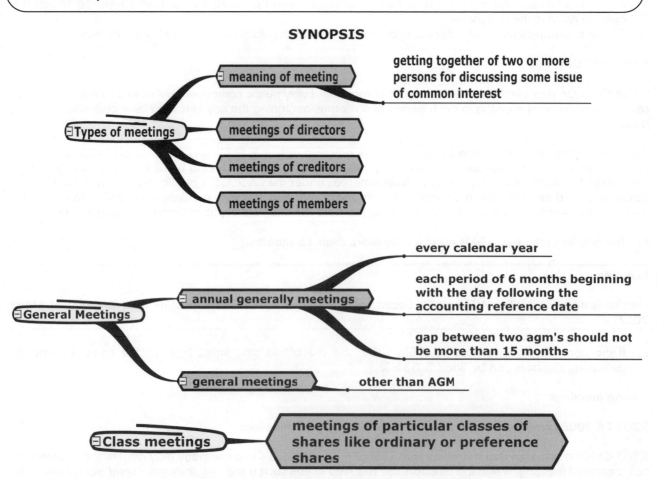

Types of meetings
- meaning of meeting — getting together of two or more persons for discussing some issue of common interest
- meetings of directors
- meetings of creditors
- meetings of members

General Meetings
- annual generally meetings
  - every calendar year
  - each period of 6 months beginning with the day following the accounting reference date
  - gap between two agm's should not be more than 15 months
- general meetings — other than AGM

Class meetings — meetings of particular classes of shares like ordinary or preference shares

2. Explain the procedure for calling such meetings

[Learning outcome b]

For any general meeting **to be valid** it must be:

1. Properly convened
2. Properly constituted
3. Properly conducted

2.1 When a meeting is said to be properly convened

The first requirement for a valid meeting is that it should be properly convened i.e.

➢ it should be **called by the authorised person** entitled to call the meeting
➢ **proper and adequate notice** must be given to all who are entitled to attend the meeting.

1. Who is authorised to call the meeting?

a) Board of Directors of the company

The directors are normally given the power in the Articles to convene a general meeting whenever they think fit. However, it is statutorily required to call an GM in certain circumstance.

Example

An **AGM must be convened** if the directors of a public company become aware of the fact the value of the company's net assets falls to 50% or less of its called up share capital. The directors must convene the meeting within 28 days from the day when the fact is known to a director and the meeting must be held within 56 days of such date.

---

b) Members

In certain circumstances, the members of the company are entitled to call a general meeting.

Example

The Managing Director of Alfa Ltd was found guilty of misuse of company funds during the internal audit of the company. In this event, as the matter is urgent and cannot be postponed till the next AGM, the members may requisite to call a GM to decide a plan of action to be taken against the Managing Director.

Requisition by the members

S 303 CA2006 provides that members with 10% of the voting rights in a company may require the directors to call a general meeting. When the directors are required to call such a meeting they must send out a notice within 21 days of the requisition for a meeting to be held not more than 28 days after the date of the notice convening the meeting.

As previously, if the directors fail to call the meeting, then the requisitionists with more than half of the total voting rights may themselves call a meeting. The reasonable expenses incurred by the members must be reimbursed by the company and the directors penalised.

If the directors do not convene a meeting within 21 days of the deposit of the requisition by the members, the members filing requisition and holding **more than half** of the total voting rights of all the requisitionists, may convene a meeting, which must be **held within three months of the deposit of the requisition** (s 303 CA 2006).

Example

Tetley Ltd has paid up share capital of £20,000. 50 members holding £7,000 of the capital filed a requisition with the company to convene an extraordinary general meeting. The requisition was filed on 1 January 20X5. In such case, the directors must convene the meeting on or before 21 January 20X5. In case the directors fail to convene such meeting, requisitionist members holding £3,500 capital among may convene a meeting themselves. Such meeting must be convened with 3 months of the deposit of the requisition, i.e. on or before 31 March 20X5.

Any reasonable expenses incurred by the requisitionists because of the directors' failure to convene a meeting are repayable by the company. A company may, however, recover such expenses from directors.

c) Requisition by resigning auditors

If a resigning auditor has made a statement that there are circumstances connected with their resignation which they feel should be brought to the attention of the members, they may request the directors to convene a general meeting. (s.519 CA 2006).

If the directors do not proceed to convene a meeting within 21 days after the deposit of the requisition then every director responsible for such failure is liable to a fine (s.517 CA 2006.

d) Requisition by the court

The Court has an inherent power to direct that meetings of the members or of a class of members shall be held, s306 CA 2006

The Court may on its own motion or on the application of a director or of any member entitled to attend and vote order that a meeting shall be convened.

2. Notice of meetings

S337 CA 2006 states that a notice calling an AGM of a public company must state that the meeting is the annual general meeting. The minimum period of notice is 21 days (s307) or longer if the articles so provide. An AGM can be called at shorter notice if all members of the company agree.

Members of a public company may require the company to give them notice of any resolution that may be moved at the meeting: s.338 (1).

Members holding at least 5% of the voting rights may require the company to circulate details of a resolution to all the members. So long as the request is received before the financial year end of the company, the members are not required to cover the costs of circulation. This is an entirely new provision.

The request may be in hard copy form or in electronic form and must:
➢ identify the resolution of which notice is to be given
➢ be authenticated by the persons making it
➢ be received by the company not later than 6 weeks before the AGM to which the request relates

i. The notice must **specify** that **it is a notice of an AGM.**

ii. The notice must state that a member is entitled to appoint a proxy to attend the meeting. A proxy is a person appointed by a member to attend the meeting and vote on his behalf.

iii. **21 days' notice** must be given (s.307). N.B. no longer clear days.

iv. An AGM can be called at shorter notice if all members agree, s307(2).

v. A notice must contain **information relating to date, time and place** of the meeting, s311 CA 2006.

vi. Whether the resolutions to be passed at the meeting are special resolution or ordinary resolution, must also be stated by the notice.

vii. The agenda of the meeting i.e. general nature of business to be transacted at the meeting must also be incorporated in the notice of the meeting.

An agenda is a list of meeting activities in the order in which they are to be taken up. Points on a typical agenda may include:

➢ Welcome / open meeting
➢ Support for absence
➢ Approve minutes of the previous meeting
➢ Matters arising from the previous meeting
➢ A list of specific points to be discussed – this section is where the bulk of the discussion in the meeting usually takes place.
➢ Any other business allowing a participant to raise another point for discussion.
➢ Arrange/announce details of next meeting

a) Notice of general meeting

All the provisions relating to notice of Annual General Meeting are applicable to a General Meeting. The length of notice for the convening of a GM depends upon the type of resolution being passed.

Length of notice of meeting to members by the company	
For AGM	Not less than 21 days unless all members agree to shorter notice
General meeting containing Special resolution	Not less than 14 days
Other general meeting	Not less than 14 days
When special notice given by member to company	Not less than 28 days

Where special notice is not required to be given, the members of a company may consent to the meeting being held at shorter notice than that specified above provided:
s.307(4) CA 2006 provides for shorter notice if agreed by the members.
The company's articles may provide for longer notice than specified in s.307.

What is a special notice?

i. This is a notice required to be given **by a member to the company** in respect of any resolution he intends to put before the meeting relating to:

For auditors

➢ appointment as auditor a person **other than a retiring auditor (s.515)**
➢ filling a **casual vacancy in the office of auditor** occurred due to death, resignation, bankruptcy of the auditor (s.515)
➢ **re-appointment of an auditor appointed by the director**s to fill a casual vacancy (s.515)
➢ **removal of an auditor before the expiration of his term** of office (s.511)
➢ **for directors**
➢ **removal** of a director (s.168)
➢ **appointment or re-appointment** of a director of a public company or a subsidiary of a public company who is over the **age limit of 70**

ii. Special notice of the resolution must be given to the company not less than **28 days or 6 weeks before the date** of the meeting at which it is to be moved.

Example

If a member wants to pass a resolution to appoint a new person instead of retiring auditor, in a meeting proposed to be held on 15 January 20X5 then he must give notice to company regarding his intention of proposing such resolution on or before 17 December 20X4.

---

iii. Where special notice has been received by the company it is required to give notice of the same to the members, if practicable, at the same time and in the same manner as it gives notice of the meeting.

iv. In addition, a copy of the special notice received to be sent to the person who is the subject of the proposed resolution.

Diagram 2: Principles for a valid meeting

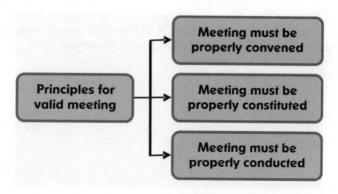

Test Yourself 3

Who are the various persons entitled to call a meeting?

SYNOPSIS
Procedure for calling such meetings

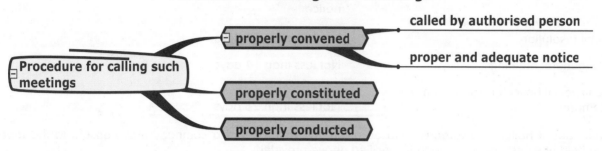

3. Detail the procedure for conducting company meetings

[Learning outcome c]

3.1 Meeting to be properly constituted

A meeting is said to be constituted properly if
➢ it is **chaired by proper person**
➢ proper **quorum was present**

1. Chairman

A chairman presides over and conducts the proceedings of a meeting. Any member of the company can act the chairman of the meeting

Duties of the chairman

a) Chairman has to ensure that all the provisions of the Companies Act 2006 and the Articles of Association of the company are complied with.
b) Chairman has to ensure proper order and discipline in the meeting and has power to adjourn i.e. to postpone the meeting.
c) He has to act bona fide in the best interest of the company.
d) He must preserve and maintain order in the meeting.
e) He must decide incidental questions arising for decision during the meeting
f) He must exercise his casting vote in the interests of the company.

Casting vote of chairman

➢ The chairman has a casting vote if so provided by articles
➢ In case of equality of votes, the chairman of the meeting shall have a second or casting vote.
➢ The chairman can use his casting vote in a different way in which he had exercised his first vote. He may decide not to use his casting vote at all.
➢ Casting vote can be used before declaration of result of voting and not afterwards.

2. Quorum

It is the minimum **number of persons** that have to be present for conducting the meeting. Unless the quorum is present, no business can be transacted at the meeting. CA 2006 s318 sets out rules on quorum for meetings in terms of the presence of one or two qualifying persons. A qualifying person is:
➢ an individual who is a member of the company
➢ a representative of a corporate member
➢ a proxy for a member

Can the presence of only one person constitute a quorum?

In the following circumstances, even one person constitutes a quorum:

a) In the case of a meeting of a particular class of shareholders and all the shares of that class are owned by the one member.

b) The mandatory rule for a company with only one member is that one qualifying person is a quorum, s.318 (1). The default rule for any other company is that two qualifying persons are a quorum. The default rule can be modified by a company's articles.

3. Proxy

A proxy is a person appointed by a member to attend the meeting and vote on his behalf. Proxy is an agent of the member appointing him.

a) A person to be appointed as proxy need not be a member of the company.

b) Proxy may vote at the meeting where voting is done by poll. But if the voting is done by show of hands, then the proxy cannot vote.

c) A member of a private company is entitled to appoint only one proxy. However, a member of a public company may appoint more than one person as proxy to attend and vote at the meeting on his behalf.

d) Proxy may speak in the meeting if the company is a private company. However in public company meeting the proxy does not have right to speak.

Meeting must be properly conducted

It means that the business at the meeting must be transacted validly and according to the provisions of the Act.

Business of an AGM

The AGM provides an opportunity for members to discuss the company's affairs. The following matters would normally be considered:
➢ Directors lay before the company the annual accounts and reports for the most recent financial year, thus making the AGM the accounts meeting (s437).
➢ The auditors' term of office ends so they must be reappointed or new auditors appointed.
➢ The directors' report must accompany the accounts. This will contain the directors' recommendation of the dividend to be paid to the shareholders.
➢ Some directors will retire at each AGM and will have to be re-elected or replaced.

Example

According to the Articles of a company, directors are delegated powers to raise a loan to the extent of £50,000. If directors feel that the company's business is increasing and it frequently requires raising a loan for more than £50,000 then they have to get this power approved by the members in a general meeting.

---

1. Allotment of shares i.e. if directors decide to raise capital by allotment of shares, the approval of shareholders in the general meeting is required.

2. If the company wants to enter into any contract for sale or purchase of a company's asset to directors then approval by the company in general needs to be obtained.

Example

A director of a company engaged in textile business wants to start a small textile mill. He wanted to buy one of the company's machines, which the company is going to replace. In that case, selling the machine to the director of the company, approval of members at the general meeting needs to be obtained.

Test Yourself 4

State the contents of the meeting or list out the business to be transacted at the meeting.

SYNOPSIS

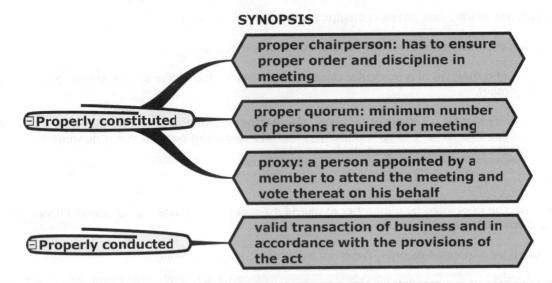

proper chairperson: has to ensure proper order and discipline in meeting

proper quorum: minimum number of persons required for meeting

Properly constituted

proxy: a person appointed by a member to attend the meeting and vote thereat on his behalf

Properly conducted

valid transaction of business and in accordance with the provisions of the act

---

4. Distinguish between types of resolutions: ordinary, special, and written

[Learning outcome d]

4.1 What is a resolution?

A resolution is an agreement or decision made by the directors or members (or a class of members) of a company. When a resolution is passed, the company is bound by it.

A proposed resolution is a motion. If the necessary majority is not obtained, then the proposed resolution fails.

4.2 Types of resolution

1. Ordinary resolutions

The ordinary resolutions are those which are passed by a **simple majority** of votes of members who are entitled to vote and present at a meeting, notice of which has been properly given. Voting may also be allowed by a proxy.

> **Example**
>
> In a general meeting of a company, if 500 members entitled to vote are present and on one resolution, 251 members cast their vote in favour of the resolution, then the resolution is said to be passed by simple majority.

Unless the Companies Act or the Articles of Association of a company contains provision for any other type of resolution, ordinary resolutions are required to be passed for all matters. The following **ordinary resolutions need to be filed at Companies House:**

a) a resolution to give, vary, revoke or renew an authority to the directors to allot shares
b) a resolution to give, vary, revoke or renew an authority to the company to make a market purchase of its own shares
c) a resolution to prevent or reverse a directors' resolution to allow title of shares to be evidenced or transferred without a written document
d) a resolution to authorise an increase of share capital. This type of resolution must be sent with Form 123 (notice of increase in nominal capital)

2. Special resolutions

These are the resolutions passed at a general meeting of which at least 14 days' notice specifying the intention to propose a resolution as a special resolution has been given. As similar to an extraordinary resolution, a special resolution requires a 75% majority.
It is required for important matters such as:

a) Alteration of Articles
b) Re-registration of a private company as a public company
c) Reduction of capital
d) Elective resolutions
e) Presenting petition by the company for an order for a compulsory winding up

When a resolution alters the Articles of Association of a company, a copy of the amended document must also be filed at Companies House.

Example

In a general meeting of a company, if 600 members entitled to vote are present then for passing a special resolution minimum 450 members (75%) must caste their vote in favor of the resolution.

Tips

Special resolution: requires a 75% majority. However, for special resolution, at least 14 days' notice specifying the intention to propose a resolution as a special resolution is required to be been given.

3. Written resolution

A written resolution is a resolution passed by the members or a class of members of a private company (s281). This procedure is not available for public companies. Unanimous consent is no longer required, but the normal majorities for resolutions apply, e.g. simple majority for an ordinary resolution and 75% for a special resolution. Instead of convening a general meeting, a written resolution is supplied to the members and their approval is taken by way of their signature on the resolution. The provisions of the Act in this regard are as follows:

a) A written resolution is not sufficient to remove a director or auditor before the end of their term of office.

b) Written resolution may be passed by a **private company only.**

c) To pass a written resolution, a meeting is not required and no prior notice is necessary. The company can circulate the resolution to the members and obtain their signature and get the resolution approved.

d) The date of a written resolution is the **date on which the last member signs.**

e) The signatures of each member do not need to be on a single document.

f) A copy of the proposed written resolution must be sent to the company's auditors at or before supplying it to the members for signature. A breach of this requirement would be a criminal offence but would not affect the validity of the resolution. This requirement does not apply to companies that do not have auditors.

g) Any other formalities specified by the company's articles of association are also need to be fulfilled in addition to the above stated statutory written resolution procedure.

Diagram 3: Types of resolution

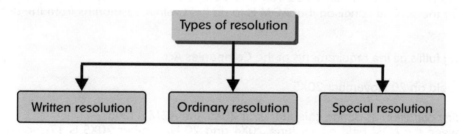

Test Yourself 5

What are the conditions specified by the Act for ordinary resolution and for special resolution?

SYNOPSIS

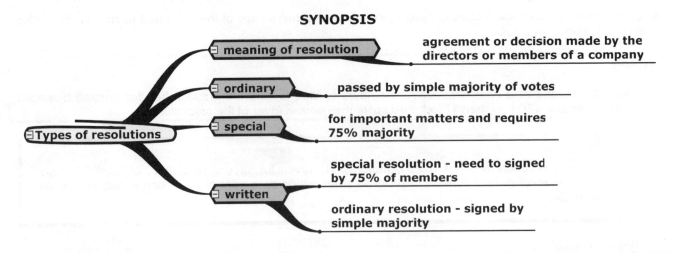

meaning of resolution	agreement or decision made by the directors or members of a company	
ordinary	passed by simple majority of votes	
special	for important matters and requires 75% majority	
written	special resolution - need to signed by 75% of members	
	ordinary resolution - signed by simple majority	

Types of resolutions

Answers to Test Yourself

Answer 1

Time period within which AGM is to be held.
Private companies no longer required to hold AGM.
Public companies must hold AGM each period of six months, beginning the day following its accounting reference date.
AGM is to be held in each calendar year.
AGM is to be held within 15 months from the date of last AGM

Hence, Peri Nitrate Plc must hold the AGM on or before 30 September 20X6. Also, an AGM will be necessary in every calendar year.

Answer 2

According to the provisions of Companies Act,

➢ AGM is to be held in each calendar year.
➢ AGM is to be held within 15 months from the date of last AMG.

Both these conditions are to be fulfilled simultaneously.

1. The meeting held on 10 January 20X5.

➢ It meets the first condition as during calendar year 2005, the AGM is held.
➢ The gap between the AGM held on 15.6.2004 and 10.1.2005 is 6 months and 25 days which is **less than 15 months**. So the second condition that AGM is to be held within 15 months from the date of last AMG is also fulfilled.

Hence the meeting fulfils all the requirements of the Companies Act.

2. The meeting held on 20 November 20X5.

➢ It meets the first condition as during calendar year 20X5, the AGM is held.
➢ The gap between the AGM held on 15 June 20X4 and 20 November 20X5 is 17 months and 5 days i.e. **more than 15 months**. So the second condition that AGM is to be held within 15 months from the date of last AMG is not fulfilled.

Hence the meeting does not fulfil all the requirements of the Companies Act.

3. The meeting held on 1 January 20X6.

➢ It does not meet the first condition as during calendar year 20X5, the AGM **is not held.**
➢ The gap between the AGM held on 15 June 20X4 and 10 January 20X6 is 18 months and 25 days i.e. more than 15 months. So the second condition that AGM is to be held within 15 months from the date of last AMG is also not fulfilled.

Hence the meeting does not fulfil all the requirements of the Companies Act.

Answer 3

Meetings may be convened in a number of ways by various people:

1. By the **directors** of the company under Model Article an AGM **must be convened** if the directors of a public company become aware of the fact the value of the company's net assets falls to 50% or less of its called up share capital.

2. By the **members using the power to requisition** a meeting. Members fulfilling following conditions have power to requisition a meeting.

a) Members holding at the date of the deposit of the requisition at least 10% of such paid-up capital as carry the right to vote at general meetings.

b) Where there is no share capital, members representing at least 10% of the total voting rights.

3. By the **auditor** of a company under, according to which a resigning auditor may require the directors to convene a meeting in order to explain the reason for the auditor's resignation.

4. **The Secretary of State** may under, on the application of any member, call a meeting of a company where it has failed to hold an AGM.

5. The **court** may order a meeting under s.371, where it is impracticable otherwise to call a meeting.

Answer 4

Following are some of the businesses to be transacted at the Annual General Meeting.

1. Consideration of the accounts, balance sheet, the report of Board of Directors and report of auditors. There may be circumstances where an Annual General Meeting must be held due to the requirements of s.366 but the accounts are not ready for presentation. In such circumstances, a company may find that at the AGM there is no business to be transacted.

2. Declaration of dividend: Normally a dividend is recommended by the BOD but it has to be declared by the company in AGM.

3. Appointment of directors in place of retiring directors: At every AGM, some directors retire by rotation and new directors are appointed in their place by way of election.

4. Re-appointment of auditor or appointment of new auditor: The appointment of auditor is till the conclusion of the next AGM. Hence, at every AGM, either the retiring auditor is reappointed or a new auditor appointed in his place.

5. Getting approval for extra powers than already delegated to Board of Directors. For e.g., according to the articles of company, directors are delegated powers to raise a loan to the extent of £50,000. If directors feel that the company's business is increasing and it frequently requires to raise loan for more than £50,000 then they have to get this powers approved by the members in general meeting.

6. Allotment of shares i.e. if directors decide to raise capital by allotment of shares, the approval of shareholders in the general meeting is required.

7. If the company wants to enter into any contract for sale or purchase of company's asset to directors then approval by the company in general is required to be obtained. For example, a director of a company engaged in the textile business wants to start a small textile mill. He wanted to buy one of the company's machines, which the company is going to replace. In that case, for selling the machine to the director of the company, approval of members in general meeting is required to be obtained.

Answer 5

Conditions for ordinary resolution:

1. The notice of the general meeting must be duly given.
2. The votes cast in favour of the resolution exceed the votes cast against the resolution.

Conditions for special resolution:

1. The notice of the general meeting must be duly given.
2. The intention to propose the resolution as special resolution has been duly specified in the notice of the meeting.
3. The votes cast in favour of the resolution are not less than 3 times (75%) the votes cast against the resolution.

Quick Quiz

State true or false

1. If the AGM held beyond the due date, all resolutions passed thereat are void.

2. A company's AGM was held in December 20X5 which was adjourned and held in January 20X6. No other AGM was held in 20X6. As there was this meeting held in January 20X6, the company had duly complied with the requirement of the Act that one AGM must be held every calendar month.

3. The legal representatives of the deceased members are also entitled to receive the notice of the AGM along with other members.

4. Casting vote for the chairman can be used only for passing an ordinary resolution and not a special resolution.

5. Only a member of the company can be appointed as a proxy by another member of the company.

Answers to Quick Quiz

1. **False,** even the AGM is held beyond the due date, all the resolutions passed at such AGM are valid, however, the company and every officer of the company who is in default is liable to pay penalty.

2. **False,** the adjourned meeting is merely an extension of the original meeting and not a fresh meeting. Therefore, adjourned AGM of last year cannot be said to be the AGM of current year. Thus, company failed to hold an AGM in 20X6.

3. **True,** because the legal representative is in the same position as of the member.

4. **True,** because a casting vote is applicable only in case of **equality of votes.** However, a special resolution requires 75% majority vote's caste in its favour hence even if the chairman uses his vote on special resolution it will be of no use as only a simple majority can be availed by a chairman's vote.

5. **False,** a proxy need not be a member of the company. The member of the company can even appoint an outsider as their proxy.

Self Examination Questions

Question 1

Explain the following in relation to the Companies Act:

(a) Annual general meeting
(b General meeting
(c) Class meeting

Question 2

Dewdrop Ltd issued a notice for holding of its AGM on 7 November 20X6. The notice was posted to the members on 16 October 20X6. Some members of the company allege that the company had not complied with the provisions of the Companies Act, 2006 with regard to period of notice and therefore the meeting was not validly called. Referring to the provisions of the Act, decide:

a) Whether the meeting has been validly called?
b) If there is a shortfall in the number of days by which the notice falls short of the statutory requirement, state by how many days does the notice fall short of the statutory requirement?
c) Can the shortfall, if any, be condoned?

Answers to Self Examination Questions

Answer 1

The ultimate control over a company's business lies with the members in a general meeting. Hence the Companies Act requires that meeting of members of the company must be held regularly.

Types of meetings of members

There are two types of meeting of members:

a) **The annual general meeting**

➢ Every company is required to hold an annual general meeting (AGM) every calendar year (s.366).
➢ The gap between two AGM must not exceed a maximum period of 15 months (s.366).
➢ If a company fails to hold an AGM then any member may apply to the Secretary of State to call a meeting in default (s.367).
➢ The business conducted at AGMs tends to be routine such as the re-election of directors, consideration of accounts and approval of dividends.
➢ According to the provisions of newly inserted s.366A, private are permitted, subject to approval by a unanimous vote, to dispense with the holding of annual general meetings.
➢ A private company may adopt the way of written resolution where the members have unanimously signed a written resolution setting out a particular course of action (s.381).

b) **The class meeting**

This refers to the meeting of a particular class of shareholder i.e. those who hold a type of share providing particular rights, such as preference shares. Where it is proposed to alter the rights attached to particular shares then it is necessary to acquire the approval of the holders of those particular shares to any such alteration. In order to achieve this approval, a meeting of those holding such shares has to be called to seek their approval of any proposed alteration (CA s.125–127).

Answer 2

The provisions of the Companies Act require that a general meeting can be called by giving at least 21 clear days notice in writing to all the members entitled to present and vote in the meeting. Date of issue of notice and date of meeting must be in addition to the said period of 21 days. Where a notice is sent by post, it is deemed to be served after 48 hours of posting. Thus, notice to be valid, it must be effectively dispatched **24 days before the date of the meeting.**

A **shorter notice may be held** valid if **consent** to short notice has been signed by all of the members entitled to attend and vote at the AGM.

In the given case, a general meeting is held on 7 November 20X6. The notice of this meeting is dispatched to the members on 16 October 20X6. After excluding the date of meeting (i.e. 7 November 20X6), date of dispatching the notice (i.e. 16 October 20X6.) and 2 days for service of the notice (i.e. 17/10/2006 and 18/10/2006), the remaining period is of 19 days (from 19 November 20X6 to 6 November 20X6).

Conclusion

➢ The meeting has not been validly called within 21 days' notice of the general meeting has not been given to the members.
➢ The shortfall in sending notice to the members is of 2 days.
➢ The shortfall can be condoned, if **consent** to short notice has been signed by all of the members entitled to attend and vote at the general meeting.

SECTION G - LEGAL IMPLICATIONS RELATING TO COMPANIES IN DIFFICULTY OR IN CRISIS

INSOLVENCY

Get through intro

This Study Guide deals with the methods of winding up of a company. Winding up means putting an end to the life of the company. Winding up can be either voluntary or compulsory. This study guide deals with the study of various ways of the voluntary winding up of the company and also on what grounds the compulsory winding up order will be given, and the procedure involved in winding the company . The position of liquidator will also be dealt with in this study guide, as will alternatives to winding up, such as administration orders.

As we have studied earlier, a company is a separate legal entity having a perpetual existence. A company comes into existence by the operation of law. Hence a company's existence can be brought to an end by following the procedure prescribed by law.

In your position as a company secretary or company auditor, you will have to play an important role in the liquidation process of the company. This process starts from the very beginning of deciding whether it is viable to wind up the company.

LEARNING OUTCOMES

a) Explain the meaning of and procedure involved in voluntary liquidation
b) Explain the meaning of and procedure involved in compulsory liquidation
c) Explain administration as an alternative to winding up

Introduction

> ### Case Study — Company Liquidations
>
> There were 3,439 liquidations in England and Wales in the first quarter of 2006 on a seasonally adjusted basis. This was an increase of 7.6% on the previous quarter and an increase of 17.0% on the same period a year ago.
>
> This was made up of 1,428 compulsory liquidations, an increase of 11.0% on the previous quarter and an increase of 29.5% on the corresponding quarter of the previous year, and 2,011 creditors' voluntary liquidations, an increase of 5.2% on the previous quarter and an increase of 9.5% on the corresponding quarter of the previous year.
>
> 0.7% of active companies went into liquidation in the twelve months ending Q1 2006, the same as the previous quarter and the same as the corresponding quarter of 2005.
>
> Statistics showing insolvencies in the first quarter 2006 where published on 5 May by the Insolvency Service.
>
>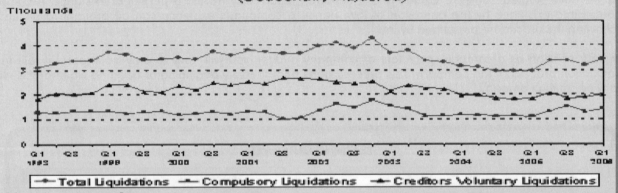
>
> **Number of Insolvencies in England and Wales (seasonally adjusted)**
>
> | | 2005 Q1r | 2005 Q2r | 2005 Q3r | 2005 Q4r | 2006 Q1p | % change Q1 2006 on: Q4 2005 | % change Q1 2006 on: Q1 2005 |
> |---|---|---|---|---|---|---|---|
> | **Company Liquidations** | 2,940 | 3,375 | 3,380 | 3,198 | 3,439 | 7.6 | 17.0 |
> | of which: **Compulsory** | 1,103 | 1,324 | 1,520 | 1,287 | 1,428 | 11.0 | 29.5 |
> | **Creditors Voluntary** | 1,837 | 2,052 | 1,860 | 1,911 | 2,011 | 5.2 | 9.5 |

(Source: http://www.insolvency.gov.uk/otherinformation/statistics/200604/index.htm)

1. Explain the meaning of and procedure involved in voluntary liquidation

[Learning outcome a]

You must have frequently come across two words: 'winding up', 'liquidation' and 'dissolution'. What is the difference between a winding up and dissolution?

Winding up and liquidation are synonyms, they carry the same meaning. Winding up or liquidation is the process of bringing to an end the life of a company. Winding up of a company **is the stage,** where by the company takes its last breath. It is a process by which the business of the company is wound up, and the company ceases to exist.

The difference between the winding up and dissolution can be summarised as follows:

➢ Winding up always precedes dissolution.

➢ In winding up, the assets are realised and liabilities are paid, but the corporate status of the company continues. Dissolution brings an end to the company's existence as a legal entity.

➢ The liquidator can represent the company in winding up proceedings. Once the order of dissolution is passed, the liquidator cannot represent the company.

➢ Creditors can prove their debts in the winding up proceedings but not after an order of dissolution has been made.

➢ Proceedings can be started against a company which is being wound up but not against a company which has been dissolved.

What is liquidation?

Liquidation is a legal process by which the affairs of a limited company are wound up. At the end of the process, the company ceases to exist. After the company is properly wound up the name of the company is removed from the register of companies at Companies House and the company is dissolved, which means it ceases to exist.

Types of liquidation

Liquidation can be either voluntary liquidation or compulsory liquidation.

Voluntary liquidation: When the members of the company decide to put an end to the life of the company it is called as voluntary liquidation. It is again of two types:

1. Members' voluntary liquidation

This is when the shareholders of a company decide to put the company into liquidation, and there are enough assets to pay all the debts of the company, i.e. the **company is solvent.**

> **Tips**
>
>
> **Solvent company:** A company is solvent if it is not insolvent. A company is insolvent if:
> i) it is unable to pay its debts
> ii) if its liabilities exceed its assets.

2. Creditors' voluntary liquidation

This is when the shareholders of a company decide to put the company into liquidation, but there are not enough assets to pay all the creditors, i.e. the **company is insolvent.**

Compulsory liquidation: When the court makes an order for the company to be wound up on the petition of an appropriate person, it is called as compulsory liquidation.

1.1 Voluntary liquidation

When a company may be wound up voluntarily-

1. On completion of duration of the company

When the period (if any) fixed for the duration of the company by the Articles expires, and the company at the general meeting has passed **an ordinary resolution** requiring it to be wound up voluntarily.

Example

Jimmy and Jerry are twin brothers. They incorporated a private limited company on 1January 1960 at the age of 20. They decided that when they turn 65 then they will close the company and retire from work. Hence they put a clause in the Articles of the company that the duration of the company will be up to 1 January 20X5. In that case, the company can be wound up voluntarily from 1January 20X5.

2. On occurrence of some event

If some event occurs, on the occurrence of which the articles provide that the company is to be dissolved, and the company at the general meeting has passed an **ordinary resolution** requiring it to be wound up voluntarily.

Example

Best builders Ltd is a company formed with the objective of constructing three flyovers in the city. The members of the company can decide to voluntarily wind up the company after the construction of flyovers is complete and project has ended.

---

3. On any other ground

If the company resolves by special resolution that it be wound up voluntarily. The **special resolution** may be passed on any grounds.

4. On liabilities exceeding its assets

If the liabilities of the company exceed its assets and by reason of its liabilities it is not feasible to continue its business, then the company may decide to wind up its operations by passing an **extra-ordinary resolution**

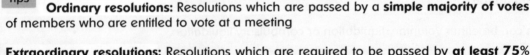

Tips

Ordinary resolutions: Resolutions which are passed by a **simple majority of votes** of members who are entitled to vote at a meeting

Extraordinary resolutions: Resolutions which are required to be passed by **at least 75% of the members** who vote on the motion, in person or by proxy at a general meeting. At least 14 days notice must be given.

Special resolutions: Resolutions passed at a general meeting of which at least 14 **days' notice** specifying the intention to propose a resolution as a special resolution has been given. Special resolution requires a 75% majority.

Member's voluntary liquidation
Procedure Involved:

1. Passing a resolution

When the members in the general meeting decide to liquidate the company, a resolution to that effect is required to be passed in the meeting. Where the winding up is due to the completion of the duration of the company or due to the occurrence of any event as specified in the articles, the resolution to be passed is an **ordinary resolution**. If the company has decided to be liquidated on any other ground, a **special resolution** is required to be passed in the general meeting.

Diagram 1: Resolutions

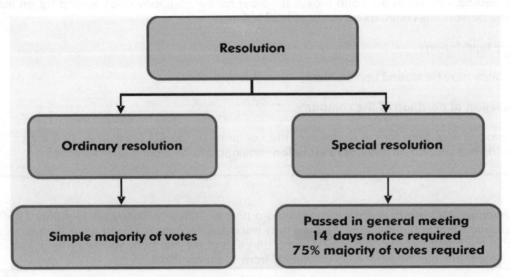

2. Advertisement of the notice of meeting: The advertisement in the meeting notice announcing that a resolution for voluntary winding up is to be passed

➤ The **London Gazette** and
➤ In **two newspapers** in the area where the company has its principal place of business.

3. Notice of resolution: When a company has passed a resolution for voluntary winding up, it shall:

➤ **Within 14 days** after the passing of the resolution, give notice of the resolution by advertisement in the Gazette.
➤ Within 15 days after the passing of the resolution, send a copy of the resolution to the registrar.

If any default is made in complying with this section, the company and every officer of it that is in default is liable to a fine and, to a daily default fine if the default continues.

Tips
Gazette: The Gazette is the official newspaper of record which contains various statutory notices and advertisements.

4. Commencement of voluntary liquidation: Voluntary winding up is deemed to commence at the **date of the passing of the resolution.**

5. Declaration of solvency

It refers to an undertaking from the directors that the company will be able to pay its debts in full, together with interest at the official rate within a period not exceeding 12 months from the commencement of the winding up procedure.

Important points in this regard:

➤ The declaration of solvency is **to be made by the directors**. If a company has more than two directors, the declaration of solvency is to be given by the **majority of the directors.**

➤ The declaration can be made **at a director's meeting.**

➤ **The declaration** has to be made on the basis of their enquiry into the affairs of the company, they   have formed an opinion that the **company will be able to pay its debts in full, together with interest at the official rate within a period not exceeding 12 months** from the commencement of the   winding   up,   as may be specified in the declaration.

➤ Such declaration has to be made within **the 5 weeks immediately preceding** the date of the passing of the resolution for winding up, or on that date but before the passing of the resolution.

➤ The declaration must include a **statement of the company's assets and liabilities** as at the latest feasible date before the making of the declaration.

➤ The declaration has to be delivered to the registrar for registration before the expiration of 15 days immediately following the date on which the resolution for winding up is passed. If it is not so delivered within the time prescribed, the company and every office in default is liable to a fine and, for continued contravention, to a daily default fine.

➤ Where the directors make a declaration of solvency but the company fails to pay its debts within 12 months of commencement of liquidation then it is presumed that the declaration was not made on reasonable grounds. The directors are held liable for committing a criminal offence.

6. Appointment of liquidator

At the general meeting where the resolution for winding up is passed, the members will also pass a resolution for appointment of liquidator. The liquidator is appointed to wind up the company's affairs.

➤ Within 14 days of being appointed, a liquidator must publish a notice of appointment in the Gazette and notify the Registrar.

➤ In case of voluntary liquidation, the liquidator must also give notice in a newspaper in the area where the company has its principal place of business.

➤ The liquidator must also send a statement of receipts and payments for the first 12 months of liquidation. After that, statements must be sent every 6 months until the winding up is complete.

The duties of a liquidator

➢ The liquidator has to take in his possession, all the company's assets and liabilities.
➢ He has to dispose of the company's assets and pay off all the liabilities.
➢ If anything is left over, the liquidator distributes it among the members of the company.
➢ The liquidator must hold a meeting of the company each year and provide details of his or her actions and dealings, and of the conduct of the winding up in the preceding year.
➢ As soon as the affairs of the company are fully wound up, the liquidator will make an account of the winding up and hold final meetings of the company and its creditors.
➢ He also has a duty to make a report to the Secretary of State, under the Company Directors Disqualification Act 1986, regarding the conduct of the company's director.
➢ In a creditors' voluntary liquidation, the liquidator has to hold annual creditors' meetings for the same purpose.

Tips

Remember

Notice of resolution for voluntary winding up	within 14 days of passing of resolution
Sending a copy of the resolution for winding up to the registrar	within 15 days after the passing of the resolution
Declaration of solvency by the directors	within **the 5 weeks immediately preceding** the date of the passing of the resolution for winding up, or on that date but before the passing of the resolution
Delivering the declaration to the registrar for registration	before the expiration of 15 days immediately following the date on which the resolution for winding up is passed
Publication of notice of appointment by liquidator	within 14 days of being appointed

---

7. Consequences of winding up

a) Effect on business and status of company

➢ On passing a resolution for a voluntary winding up, the company shall **cease to carry on its business**, except so far as may be required for the beneficial winding up of the business.

➢ However, the **corporate state and corporate powers** of the company, notwithstanding anything to the contrary in its articles, **continue until the company is dissolved.**

➢ Any **transfer of shares**, not being a transfer made to or with the sanction of the liquidator, and any **alteration in the status of the company's members**, made after the commencement of a voluntary winding up, **is void.**

Example

Star track Ltd passes a resolution for voluntary winding up on 13 March 2006. The company appointed a liquidator on 15 March 2006. One of the shareholders, Richard, transferred his 500 shares in the company to his friend on 19 April 2006. The sanction from the liquidator to transfer the shares was not obtained. Here, the transfer of shares is void. As the transfer is made after the commencement of winding up, obtaining sanction from the liquidator is necessary for the transfer being valid.

b) Cessation of the powers of the board

➤ The liquidator takes control of the company's affairs and almost all the powers of the directors cease.
➤ It is the duty of the company's directors that they must:
   ✓ provide information about the company's affairs to the liquidator and
   ✓ attend interviews with the liquidator as and when reasonably required,
   ✓ look after and hand over the company's assets to the liquidator,
   ✓ hand over all the books, records, bank statements, insurance policies and other papers relating to company's assets and liabilities.

c) Disposal of company's assets

➤ The liquidator sells all the company's assets, claims against contributories, and raises money on the security of company assets.
➤ Pays off the costs and expenses of the liquidation.
➤ Pays off the company's debts.
➤ Distributes any remaining money to the shareholders.

> **Tips**
>
> **Contributories:** A contributory includes every person who is liable to contribute to a company's assets in the event of its being wound up

8. Final meeting and dissolution

➤ After winding up the affairs of the company, the liquidator shall **prepare an account of winding up** of the company, showing how winding up of the company has been conducted and how the property of the company has been disposed off.

➤ As soon as the affairs of the company are fully wound up, the liquidator will **hold final meetings** of the company and its creditors.

➤ The notice of these meeting duly specifying the time, place and business to be conducted at the meeting must be published in the London Gazette at least one month before the meeting.

➤ At the meeting the liquidator shall present the accounts of the proceedings of winding up and give any explanations, if asked for by any member or creditor.

➤ Liquidation ends when the company is dissolved after the final meeting is held by the liquidator.

➤ Once the liquidation process has been completed the company will be dissolved and cease to exist.

➤ A copy of accounts and a return of holding of the meeting and their dates must be sent to the registrar of companies by the liquidator within one week after the date of meeting.

➤ The registrar will then register the account and return as to the meeting. **Three months after the registration,** the company is deemed to be dissolved.

➤ On liquidation, the company's name will be removed from the register of company names by the registrar.

SYNOPSIS

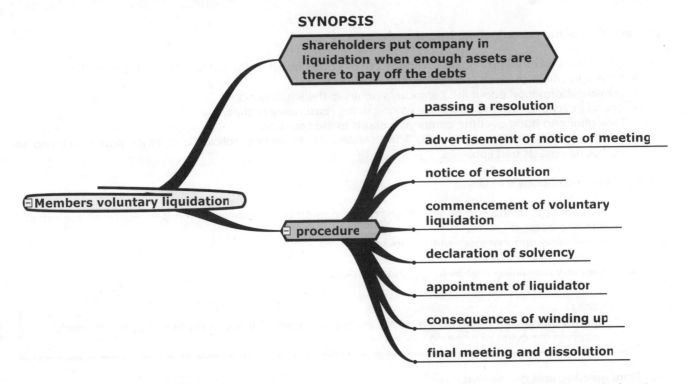

Members voluntary liquidation

shareholders put company in liquidation when enough assets are there to pay off the debts

procedure
- passing a resolution
- advertisement of notice of meeting
- notice of resolution
- commencement of voluntary liquidation
- declaration of solvency
- appointment of liquidator
- consequences of winding up
- final meeting and dissolution

Creditor's voluntary liquidation: When the Board of Directors of the company are unable to give a declaration of solvency i.e. the undertaking that the company will be able to pay its debts in full, together with interest at the official rate within a period not exceeding 12 months from the commencement of the winding up, then the liquidation is called creditor's voluntary liquidation.

The **additional procedure in case of creditor's voluntary winding up is:**

1. The company must call a meeting of its creditors within 14 days of the meeting of it's members where the extra-ordinary resolution to wind up the company was passed.
2. The notice of the meeting where the resolution for voluntary winding up is to be passed must be advertised in:
   ➢ The **London Gazette** and
   ➢ In **two newspapers** in the area where the company has its principal place of business.

3. A full statement of company's affairs along with **a list of creditors and estimated amount of liability** must be prepared by the Board of Directors and placed before the creditors in their meeting.

4. The liquidator will be nominated at the meeting of the members where the extra-ordinary resolution to wind up the company was passed and also at the creditor meeting. If the person appointed as the liquidator by the two meetings is different than the **person appointed after creditors meeting will be held appointed as liquidator.**

5. A **liquidation committee** may also be appointed by the creditors to work with the liquidator in the process of company liquidation. The committee consists of **representatives of creditors as well as members of the company.**

Case Study

Re Centrebind Ltd 1966

A general meeting of the company was arranged by the directors of the company. But they failed to make the statutory declaration regarding solvency of the company. They also did not convene the meeting of the creditors on the same day or the very next day. There was a penalty applicable for this (at present this is a maximum of £200). The liquidator appointed by the members of the company had already disposed off the assets of the company before the creditors could appoint the liquidator. It was argued by the liquidator of the creditor that the sale of the assets was at low price and hence was invalid.

Court's decision: It was held that when the liquidator appointed by the members made the sale of assets, he was in the office and hence it was a valid one under the normal power of sale.

6. Where the liquidation procedure continues for more than a year, the liquidator must hold a **meeting of the creditors each year** and provide details of his or her actions and dealings, and of the conduct of the winding up of the company in the preceding year.

7. As soon as the affairs of the company are fully wound up, the liquidator will make an **account of winding up** of the company and **hold final meetings** of members and creditors.

8. The **notice of this meeting** duly specifying the time, place and business to be conducted at the meeting must be published **in the London Gazette** at least **one month before the meeting.**

Diagram 2: Liquidation

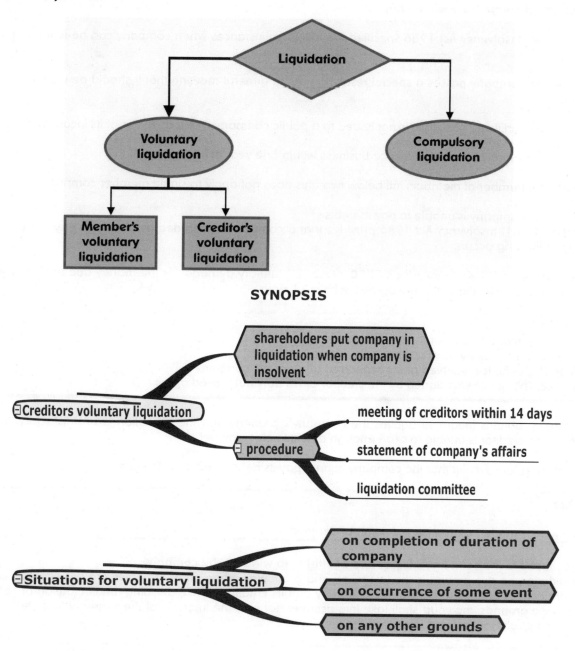

2. Explain the meaning of and procedure involved in compulsory liquidation
[Learning outcome b]

Compulsory winding up is a legal process by which a liquidator is appointed **by an order of the court to 'wind up' the affairs of a limited company.** The purpose of winding up a company is to ensure that all the company's affairs have been dealt with properly. At the end of the process the company ceases to exist.

Procedure of compulsory winding up of a company

1. Grounds of compulsory winding up

Section 122 of Insolvency Act 1986 specified the following instances when company can be wound up by the court.

a) Where the company passes a special resolution at the general meeting that it should be wound up by the court.

b) Where the certificate of trading is not issued to a public company within one year of its incorporation.

c) Where a company fails to commence business within one year of its incorporation.

d) Where the number of members fall below two (this does not apply to single member company).

e) Where the company is unable to pay its debts.
   Section 123(1) Insolvency Act 1986 provides that a company is regarded as unable to pay its debts if any of the following occurs:

➢ A creditor who is **owed more than £750,** serves a 'statutory demand' for the money due and it is not paid or secured, or a settlement is not agreed, **within 21 days.**

> Tips
>
> A demand is a statutory demand if-
> 1. It is made by serving a notice in writing
> 2. The notice is served at the registered office of the company
> 3. The notice was signed by the creditor or his duly authorised agent

➢ A creditor obtains judgment against the company's property and the execution is unsatisfactory. In other words the creditor is unable to seize enough assets to clear the debt.

➢ It is proved to the court that the company cannot pay its debts when they fall due.

> **Example**
>
> No payment is made in response to a letter of demand.

f) It is proved to the court that it **is just and equitable to wind up the company.**
   Liquidation on this ground is the last resort and is allowed when other remedies are not effective enough to protect the general interest of the company and its creditors. While deciding the liquidation of company on these grounds, the court shall take into account not only the interests of the shareholders and creditors but also public interest and interest of the employees.

> **Example**
>
> A company had two members both of them were the directors. The two directors always had disputes among them and failed to agree on any important matters. There was a complete deadlock in the management. This can be held as a just and equitable reason for winding up of a company.

2. Submitting winding up petition

Who may petition the court for winding up?

The following persons may petition the court for winding up a company-

a) **The company:** The Company itself may file a petition where it has passed a special resolution for compulsory winding up.

b) **The creditor:** A creditor can file the petition if the company is unable to pay its debts. A company is said to be unable to pay its debts if a creditor to whom the company owes an undisputed debt of at least £750 serves a statutory demand in that respect but the company neglects to pay. The creditor for this purpose also includes a secured creditor, a debenture holder and the trustee for the debenture holders.

c) **The official receiver:** An officer appointed by the court can also file a petition for compulsory liquidation of the company.

d) **The department of trade and industry, following an investigation**: If after investing the affairs of the company, the Department is satisfied that it is expedient to wind up the company, it may submit a petition to the court to wind up the company on just and equitable grounds.

e) **A contributory:**

    i   A contributory includes every person who is liable to contribute to company's assets in the event of its being wound up.

    ii   A contributory shall be entitled to present a petition for winding up a company, notwithstanding that he may be the holder of fully paid-up shares or partly paid up shares.

    iii A contributory can present the petition for winding up if-

    ➢ the shares were originally allotted to him or
    ➢ he has held his shares for **at least 6 months during the 18 months** immediately **preceding** the commencement of winding up or
    ➢ The shares have been passed to him through the death of a member.

3. Appointing receiver by the court

On the presentation of the compulsory winding up petition, the court will appoint the official receiver. He may require any of the following persons to prepare the statement of company's affairs:

➢ Present employees of the company.
➢ The employees of the company during one year preceding the date of winding up.
➢ Present and past officers of the company.
➢ Persons involved in the formation of the company up to one year preceding the date of winding up.

The company's statement of affairs must disclose-

➢ The details of company's assets and liabilities
➢ The list of creditors of the company along with addresses
➢ The details of charges (foxed or floating) held by the creditors on company's assets along with the dates of creating the charge.
➢ Any other details as required by the receiver

4. Appointment of liquidator

The official receiver will then call a meeting of company's members and creditors to appoint a liquidator in his place. At this meeting, the members and creditor may also set a committee of liquidation consisting representatives of members and shareholders to assist the liquidator in his work. If the liquidator appointed by the members and the creditors is not the same person, the person appointed by creditors will prevail. The liquidation committee must meet from time to time, the first meeting being held within three months of its constitution.

5. Effects of winding up order

➢ All actions for **recovery of debts against the company are stopped.**
➢ The company shall **cease to carry on its business,** except so far as may be required for its beneficial winding up of the business.
➢ The services of the employees of the company are terminated although the liquidator can re-employ them to help him in winding up.

6. Disposal of company's assets

➢ The liquidator then disposes of all the company's assets.
➢ Pays off the costs and expenses of the liquidation.
➢ Distributes any remaining money to the creditors.

7. Order of payment of company debts:
The assets of the company being wound up are applied in the following order-

a) Fixed charge holders
The payment to this category of creditor is made from the assets before any other payment is made. The receiver appointed by fixed charge holders sells the assets subject to charge. Any surplus after the debts of secured creditors is returned to the liquidator. However, if the security is insufficient to meet the full debt amount, then the creditors will prove for the balance outstanding debt as an unsecured creditor.

Example

The debts due to creditors were £10,000. However the asset subject to charge could recover only £8,000. Here, as the security was insufficient to meet the full debts, the secured creditors stand along with unsecured creditors for a balance of £2,000

---

b) Liquidation expenses
The liquidator's remuneration and the liquidation expenses rank next in order.

c) Preferential creditors
Preferential creditors rank equally among themselves. If the assets are insufficient to pay the whole amount due to preferential creditors then the payment is made proportionately.
N.B the class of preferential creditors has been reduced considerably by the Enterprise Act 2002.

d) Floating charge holders
The next in the order are the creditors who are secured by a floating charge over the assets of the company

e) Unsecured creditors:
Unsecured creditors rank equally among themselves. If the assets are insufficient to pay the whole amount due to unsecured creditors then the payment is made proportionately.

f) Member's dividend
Any dividend declared to members but which is still unpaid.

g) Member's capital
Any surplus, remaining after paying to all the above stated categories is distributed among the members of the company.

Tips

Fixed charge: A charge held over specific assets. The debtor cannot sell the assets without the consent of the secured creditor or repay the amount secured by the charge.

Floating charge: A charge held over general assets of a company. The assets may change (such as stock) and the company can use the assets without the consent of the secured creditor until the charge "crystallises" (becomes fixed).

---

8. Final meeting and dissolution

➢ After winding up the affairs of the company, the liquidator shall prepare an account of winding up, showing how the winding up procedure has been conducted and how the properties of the company has been disposed off.
➢ As soon as the affairs of the company are fully wound up, the liquidator will hold the final meetings of the company and its creditors
➢ The notice of these meeting duly specifying the time, place and business to be conducted at the meeting must be published in London Gazette at least one month before the meeting.
➢ At the meeting the liquidator shall present the accounts of the proceedings of winding up and give any explanation, if asked for by any member or creditor.
➢ A copy of accounts and a return of holding of the meeting and their dates must be sent to the registrar of companies by the liquidator within one week after the date of meeting.
➢ The registrar will then register the account and return as to the meeting. Three months after the registration, the company is deemed to be dissolved.

Test Yourself 1

What is the difference between voluntary liquidation and compulsory liquidation?

Diagram 3: Payments to creditors in compulsory liquidation

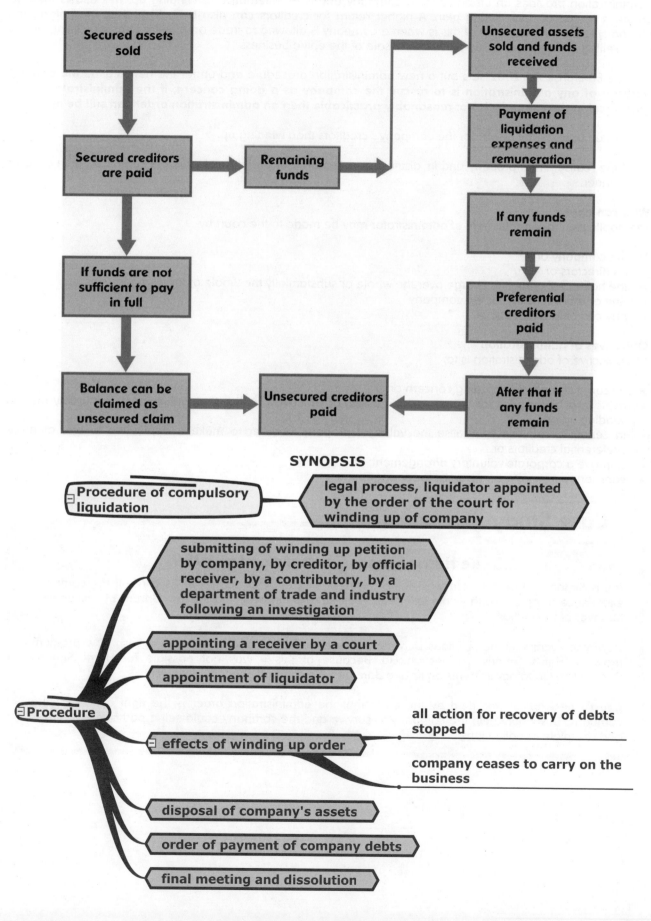

SYNOPSIS

Procedure of compulsory liquidation — legal process, liquidator appointed by the order of the court for winding up of company

Procedure
- submitting of winding up petition by company, by creditor, by official receiver, by a contributory, by a department of trade and industry following an investigation
- appointing a receiver by a court
- appointment of liquidator
- effects of winding up order
  - all action for recovery of debts stopped
  - company ceases to carry on the business
- disposal of company's assets
- order of payment of company debts
- final meeting and dissolution

3. Explain administration as an alternative to winding up

What is administration?

Administration provides an umbrella for a company and is an alternative to winding up. This allows them to create a rescue or restructuring plan. A higher return for creditors can also be achieved by maximising the company's value. An example of this is when a company is allowed to trade on a limited basis, by filling orders or by selling its assets or realising an efficient sale of the entire business.

NB. The Enterprise Act 2002 sets out a new administration procedure and under the new regime **the primary purpose of any administration is to rescue the company as a going concern, if the administrator thinks that rescuing the company is not reasonably practicable then an administration order can still be made:**

➢ If it can bring better results for the company's creditors than winding up.

➢ If the realisation of property and its distribution to secured or preferential creditors can be done in a better manner.

Who can apply?
The application for appointment of administrator may be made to the court by-

➢ the company or
➢ it's directors or
➢ the holders of a floating charge over the whole or substantially the whole of the company's assets
➢ one or more creditors of the company
➢ any combination of above

Objectives of administration
The objective of administration is to:

➢ rescue a company as a going concern or
➢ achieve a better price for the company's assets or otherwise realise their value more favourably than in winding up or
➢ in certain circumstances, realise the value of property in order to make a distribution to one or more preferential creditors or
➢ approve a corporate voluntary arrangement; or
➢ sanction (agree to) a compromise or arrangement

Case Study

Re Harris Simons Construction Ltd 1989

Harris Simons Constriction Ltd was doing business with another company. As a result the company experience a rapid growth within last three years and its turnover had increased from £1 million to a turnover of £27 **million.**

However, eventually the relations between them turned bitter and as a result a cash flow problem arose in Harris Simons Constriction Ltd. Because of this it was not possible for Harris Simons Constriction Ltd to pay its debts on its due date and the company became insolvent.

Court's decision: It was held by the court that the administration order is the right option for the company. This would help the company to survive and the company could sell a part of the business and complete its obligations.

Effect of administration

When a company enters administration:

➤ any pending winding-up petitions will be dismissed or suspended;
➤ there will be moratorium on insolvency and on other legal proceedings; the moratorium is the essential feature of the administration procedure and ensures that the company is given a breathing space in order to restructure its financial affairs
➤ if an administrative receiver has been appointed, he or she must vacate office;
➤ if a receiver of part of the company's property has been appointed, he or she must vacate office (if the administrator requires this).

3.1 Appointment of administrator by the court: Court can order an administrator in response to the application for administration by the person eligible to apply for the administration.

1. Once an administration application has been made to court :

a) It **cannot be withdrawn without the permission of the Court.**

b) The applicant has to **notify a person who is to be appointed** or is eligible to be appointed **as administrator.**

c) Once the application to the Court has been made, the Court can **make or dismiss the order sought, make an interim order, treat the application as a winding up petition,** or make any other order it may choose.

2. The Court can make an administration order only if it is satisfied that-

a) The company is, or is likely to become **unable to pay its debts,**

b) And that the **administration order is likely to achieve the statutory purpose of the administration.**

3. Once the application has been made, the applicant has a duty to notify anyone who has or who is entitled to appoint an administrator or an administrative receiver.

3.2 Appointment of the administrator by company or directors: the company itself or its directors can appoint the administrator without a **court order.**

However, there are certain restrictions on the power to appoint by the company itself or its directors without a Court Order. These are:

➤ The company or its directors have to show that the company is, or is likely to become **unable to pay its debts**
➤ The company has not been in administration, or subject to a moratorium in respect of a failed Creditors Voluntary Application in the previous twelve months
➤ A **winding up petition has not been presented** to the court
➤ The **company is not in liquidation** and
➤ **No administrator** or administrative receiver **has been appointed**

1. **Notice of intention to appoint an administrator:** Where a company or the directors of a company propose to make an appointment of an administrator, the following formalities must be fulfilled-

➤ **A minimum of five business days' written notice must be given** to anyone who is entitled to appoint an administrator or has appointed an administrator or administrative receiver.
➤ Notice must be given in the prescribed form.
➤ Notice must identify the administrator.
➤ Notice of Intention to appoint must be filed with the Court.
➤ The notice must be accompanied by a statutory declaration that -

✓ the company is or is likely to become unable to pay its debts,
✓ that the company is not in liquidation and other such additional information as prescribed.
✓ If the information provided in the statutory declaration is false then it is treated as an offence.

➤ During the period of five business days, floating charge holders may either agree with the appointment or appoint the administrator of their choice.
➤ If the floating charge holder agrees with the appointment, or does not reply, then Notice of Appointment must be filed with the Court within ten days of filing the Notice of Intention to Appoint.
➤ After that period is over, the right of the floating charge holder to appoint an administrator ceases.

2. Notice of appointment

➢ Where a company or the directors of a company appoint an administrator, Notice of Appointment must be filed with the Court.

➢ The Notice of Appointment must be in the prescribed form and must contain a statutory declaration by or on behalf of the person who makes the appointment that the person appointing is entitled to appoint, the appointment is in accordance with the provisions of the Companies Act and that the statements made and information given is accurate.

➢ The Notice must identify the administrator and state that in his opinion the purpose of the administration will be achieved.

➢ It is an offence to knowingly make a false statement in a statutory declaration.

3. Procedure following appointment

a) As soon as is reasonably practicable after his/her appointment, the administrator shall:

➢ send notice of his appointment to the company
➢ publish notice of his appointment in the prescribed manner
➢ obtain a list of creditors
➢ send notice of appointment to each creditor of whose claim and address he is aware

b) The administrator must send notice of his/her appointment to the registrar of **companies within seven days of the** administration order (if appointed by order).

c) As soon as reasonably practicable after the appointment of the administrator, the company shall provide a statement of affairs to the administrator.

d) The administrator shall **within twenty-eight days of** the company entering administration send a copy of his/her proposals to the registrar, creditors and members.

e) In case of creditors, the proposal must include the date of the creditors meeting which must be within six weeks of the date that the company entered into administration.

f) The appointment of the administrator **ends automatically after twelve months** from his appointment.

g) The administrator can apply to the Court for a specified extension or a six month extension can be agreed by consent.

3.3 Appointment of administrator by the holder of a floating charge

The creditors having a floating charge over the whole or substantially the whole of the company's assets can directly appoint an administrator of their own selection.

1. The preconditions to appointing an administrator without a court order are-

➢ the floating charge holder has given at least two business days written notice to any holders of qualifying floating charges with priority over the applicant's (i.e. in that they were created before or take precedence by way of an agreement), and

➢ the relevant floating charge is enforceable (i.e. the holder is entitled to call in the security), and
➢ the company is neither in liquidation nor has a provisional liquidator been appointed, and
➢ neither an administrator nor an administrative receiver is already in office.

2. Notice of appointment

➢ The floating charge holder then files a Notice of Appointment with the Court.

➢ They have to give two days notice to the other floating charge holders who have priority over their own floating charge. If those charge holders have any objection to the appointment of administrator by the floating charge holders then they may appoint their own administrator.

Example

Andrew holding 90% debentures has a floating charge over the assets of Big Plc. However, Brown is holding specific charge over the machinery of the company. Andrew wants to appoint Tony as an administrator, so he has to give two day's notice to Brown as he has priority over Andrew's floating charge. If Brown has any objection to the appointment of Tony as an administrator, then he can appoint an administrator of his choice.

> The notice must include a statutory declaration that :
>   ✓ The applicant holds a qualifying floating charge
>   ✓ The charge is enforceable, and
>   ✓ The appointment is in accordance with the Companies Act.

> An offence is committed by the applicant if in the declaration he makes a false statement, or one which he does not reasonably believe to be true.

> The Notice of Appointment should:
>   ✓ Identify the administrator
>   ✓ Contain a statement that he consents to the appointment
>   ✓ And a statement that the purpose of the administration is likely to be achieved.

> If a winding up order has been made, a qualifying floating charge holder cannot appoint the liquidator without a Court Order, but can, unlike the company itself or its directors; apply for administration through the court.

> If this application is successful, the winding up order will be discharged.

3. Once an administration application has been made-

> It cannot be withdrawn without the permission of the Court.
> The applicant has to notify a person who is to be appointed or is eligible to be appointed as administrator.
> Once the application to the Court has been made, the Court can make or dismiss the order sought, make an interim order, treat the application as a winding up petition, or make any other order it may choose.

3.4 Duties of the administrator

The administrator must:
> Notify the company, the creditors and the registrar of company and publicise his appointment
> Obtain a statement of company's affairs
> Arrange creditor's meeting
> Take company's property under his control
> Manage the company's affairs, business and property in accordance with approved proposals for achieving purposes of the administration
> Comply with court's directions
> Take reasonable care to obtain the best price for property disposed of
> Report on the conclusions of the administration

3.5 Powers of the administrator

An administrator's powers are very broad. They include:
> Powers to carry on the company's business

> Power to realise company's assets. **In Re T and D Industries Plc (1999)**, it was held by the High Court that an administrator is entitled to dispose of any of the assets of the company without obtaining the court's permission and also before the court approving the administrator's proposals for administration.

> The administrator displaces the company's board of directors from its management function and has the power to remove or appoint directors.

> Power to dispose off the property subject to floating charge without the consent of floating charge holders. However, the floating charge holders are entitled to be paid first from the proceeds.

> Power to make distribution to secured and preferential creditors without the permission of the court.

> Power to make distributions to unsecured creditors with the permission of the court.

3.6 Disadvantages of administration

The company: This is an expensive procedure as the day to day control of the affairs of the company is assumed by the Administrator's firm.

Directors: The directors lose control of the day to day running of the company and can often lose their jobs.

Creditors: The Administrator cannot bring actions for fraudulent or wrongful trading, although if the company proceeds into liquidation following the administration, actions can be brought at that time by the liquidator.

SYNOPSIS

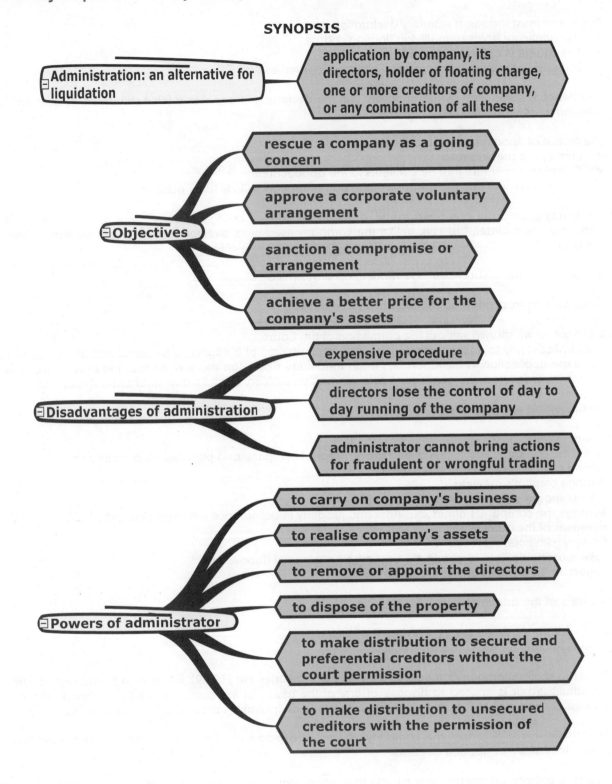

Administration: an alternative for liquidation
- application by company, its directors, holder of floating charge, one or more creditors of company, or any combination of all these

Objectives
- rescue a company as a going concern
- approve a corporate voluntary arrangement
- sanction a compromise or arrangement
- achieve a better price for the company's assets

Disadvantages of administration
- expensive procedure
- directors lose the control of day to day running of the company
- administrator cannot bring actions for fraudulent or wrongful trading

Powers of administrator
- to carry on company's business
- to realise company's assets
- to remove or appoint the directors
- to dispose of the property
- to make distribution to secured and preferential creditors without the court permission
- to make distribution to unsecured creditors with the permission of the court

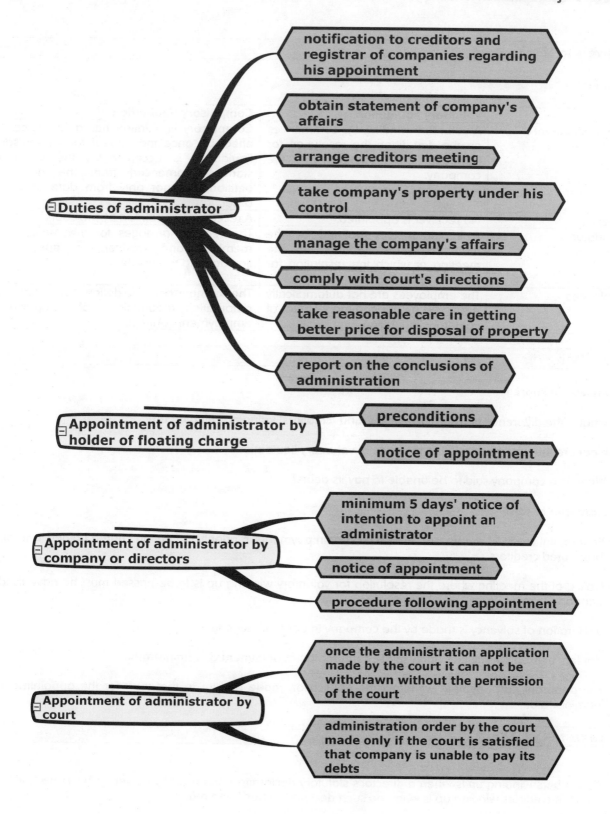

Answers to Test Yourself

Answer 1

	Voluntary liquidation	Compulsory liquidation
Commencement	A voluntary winding up commences on the day when the resolution for liquidation is passed by the company.	Compulsory liquidation has a retrospective effect i.e. once the appeal for compulsory liquidation is accepted by the Court; it stands commenced from the date of petition and not only from date of court order.
Receiver	No receiver is appointed.	A receiver is appointed by the court.
Liquidator	A liquidator is appointed by the members and creditors in the meeting at which the resolution for winding up is discussed.	The receiver arranges for the meeting of members and creditors to appoint a liquidator to replace him.
Employees	The employees are not automatically dismissed by the commencement of voluntary liquidation.	The compulsory liquidation has effect of automatic repudiation of employee's employment contract.

Quick Quiz

1. Answer in short

a) What is the difference between "members" and "creditors" voluntary winding up?

b) What are the provisions relating to notice of voluntary liquidation?

c) When is a company said to be unable to pay its debts?

2. State true or false

a) Preferential creditors are entitled to receive certain payments in priority to floating charge holders and other unsecured creditors.

b) Notice of the meeting where the resolution for voluntary winding up is to be passed must be advertised in London Gazette

c) Declaration of solvency is made by the company in general meeting.

d) Holders of fixed charge can apply to the court for the appointment of administrator.

e) The applicant can any time withdraw the application made by him to the court for the appointment of administrator.

Answers to Quick Quiz

1.
a) A members winding up is when a director's statutory declaration under s.89 Insolvency Act 1986 has been made. A creditors winding up is when no such declaration has been made.

b) Notice of the special resolution for voluntary winding-up of the company must be **published in the Gazette** within **14 days** of the general meeting. The company must also send a copy of the declaration and the special resolution to the Registrar within 15 days of the general meeting.

c) Section123 (1) Insolvency Act 1986 provides that a company is regarded as unable to pay its debts if any of the following occurs:

➢ A creditor, who is **owed more than £750,** serves a demand for the money due and it is not paid or secured, or a settlement is not agreed, **within 21 days.**

➢ A creditor obtains judgment against the company's property and the execution is unsatisfactory i.e. the creditor is unable to seize enough assets to clear the debt.

➢ It is proved to the court that the company cannot pay its debts when they fall due.

2.
a) **True**
b) **True**
c) **False,** it is made by directors at director's meeting.
d) **False,** the application for appointment of administrator may be made to the Court by:
   ➢ The company or
   ➢ It's directors or
   ➢ The **holders of a floating charge** over the whole or substantially the whole of the company's assets
   ➢ One or more creditors of the company
   ➢ Any combination of above
   The fixed charge holders are not covered in the above list.

e) **False,** once the administration application has been made to the court, it cannot be withdrawn without the permission of the court.

Self Examination Questions

Question 1

What is the order of payment of creditors in winding up?

Question 2

What are the possible disadvantages of administration?

Answers to Self Examination Questions

Answer 1

Winding up of the company means putting an end to the business of the company. Below is the order in which directors will be paid during winding up:

a) **Fixed charge holders**

The payment to this category of creditor is made from the assets before any other payment is made. The receiver appointed by fixed charge holders sells the assets subject to the charge. Any surplus after the debts of secured creditors is returned to the liquidator. However, if the security is insufficient to meet the full debt amount, then the creditors will prove for the balance outstanding debt as unsecured creditor. For example, the debts due to creditors were £10,000. However the asset subject to charge could recover only £8,000. Here, as the security was insufficient to meet the full debts, the secured creditors stand along with unsecured creditors for balance £2,000

b) **Liquidation expenses**

The liquidator's remuneration and the liquidation expenses rank next in order.

c) **Preferential creditors**

Preferential creditors rank equally among themselves. If the assets are insufficient to pay the whole amount due to preferential creditors then the payment is made proportionately.

d) **Floating charge holders**

The next in the order are the creditors who are secured by a floating charge over the assets of the company.

e) **Unsecured creditors**

Unsecured creditors rank equally among themselves. If the assets are insufficient to pay the whole amount due to unsecured creditors then the payment is made proportionately.

f) **Member's dividend**

Any dividend declared to members but which is still unpaid.

g) **Member's capital**

Any surplus, remaining after paying to all the above stated categories is distributed among the members of the company.

Answer 2

Disadvantages of administration

The company: This is an expensive procedure as the day to day control of the affairs of the company is assumed by the Administrator's firm.

Directors: The directors lose control of the day to day running of the company and can often lose their jobs.

Creditors: The Administrator cannot bring actions for fraudulent or wrongful trading, although if the company proceeds into liquidation following the administration, actions can be brought at that time by the liquidator.

CORPORATE GOVERNANCE

Get through intro

We have already examined in previous Study Guides, that the company is owned by the shareholders but managed by the board of directors. The ownership and management are separate. Those who are responsible for the day to day management of the company have to always give utmost priority to the interest of the shareholders. Governments and societies no longer just expect ethical behaviour from an organisation, they demand it. That is why the concept of corporate governance came into existence.

We are witnessing more and more organisations building in systems of corporate governance and corporate social responsibility into their frameworks. Having such systems in place ensures that an organisation has a strict set of policies and procedures that specify which types of decisions and actions are ethical and which are not.

It is very likely that any organisation you join will have a system of corporate governance in place. You will be expected to abide by the standards that these systems set whilst doing your job. Also if any organisation not following these system then you will require to guide those organisations and get these systems operated. Therefore it is crucial you understand what corporate governance is and how is it important.

This Study Guide will explain what corporate governance is all about. It will explain why it exists and what it hopes to accomplish. Lastly, this Study Guide will explain how and why organisations attempt to meet the needs of all their stakeholders.

LEARNING OUTCOMES

a) Explain the idea of corporate governance
b) Recognise the extra-legal codes of corporate governance
c) Identify and explain the legal regulation of corporate governance

Introduction

Some people will tell you that business and ethics cannot go hand in hand. In the short run, they may appear to be right as those businesses which follow their principles are disadvantaged while their competitors flourish. However, in the long run, stakeholders will learn to distinguish between ethical and unethical companies. Companies who maintain their values will survive and prosper whereas less scrupulous companies will flounder.

The goal of corporate governance is to maximise shareholder value in the long term, legally and ethically. In the process, every stakeholder i.e. the Company's customers, investors, employees, vendor-partners, the community and the government, must be treated fairly. Therefore, corporate governance reflects a Company's policies, culture and its relationship with its stakeholders, and its commitment to values.

1. Explain the idea of corporate governance

[Learning outcome a]

In case of sole traders, partnerships and private limited companies, ownership and control is usually shared by a small group of individuals. However in the case of public limited companies, the scenario changes and the concept of **separation between ownership and control** comes into effect. With these types of organisations, one set of individuals **own the business and another set run the business**. In these types of company organisations, those who **make all the decisions** for the company (e.g. which products or services to provide and how) are the Board of Directors (BOD).

> **Example**
>
> Citibank is a very large US multinational corporation. Its shareholders number in the hundreds of thousands and are spread across the globe. However, none of these owners are involved in the running of its business.

However, to implement the decisions of the BOD and to manage the operations of organisations, **teams of professional managers and executives** were brought in (individuals who have no ownership in the organisation but instead receive a salary from it). The **Board of Directors** oversee the overall strategy and running of the company. This means that all decisions and effective control of the company is in the hands of the managers and not the owners.(shareholders)

It is mainly because of this **separation that** a system of corporate governance has been introduced into organisations. **The main purpose of corporate governance is to align the interests of managers, executives and the board of directors with those of shareholders.**

What is corporate governance?

Corporate governance represents the set of policies and procedures that determine how an organisation is **directed, administered and controlled.** It sets the broad framework or parameters from which the organisation must operate. It provides the structure and process to ensure companies are managed in the interests of their owners.

Corporate governance sets out what an organisation is supposed to do thus providing a benchmark against which the future performance and actions of managers / executives can be measured and evaluated by shareholders.

Definition

The OECD (Organisation for Economic Co-operation and Development) defines corporate governance as "the system by which business corporations are directed and controlled".

There are various participants of corporate governance structure such as the board, managers, shareholders and other stakeholders (i.e. employees, customers, suppliers, government and society at large). The corporate governance structure specifies the allocation of rights and responsibilities among these different participants in the corporation and spells out the rules and procedures for making decisions on corporate affairs. By doing this, it also provides the structure through which the company objectives are set, and the means of attaining those objectives and monitoring performance.

Tips

Corporate governance is about promoting corporate fairness, transparency and accountability.

Example

Although the contents of corporate governance will vary from organisation to organisation, almost all will have the following components:

a) Accountability: Managers, executives and the board of directors are ultimately responsible to and must always act with the best interests of shareholders in mind.

b) Compliance: Managers, executives and the board of directors must always comply with all laws and regulations.

c) Transparency: Information on the financial performance and position of the organisation as well as any activities the organisation is engaged should always be available and known to shareholders.

d) Integrity: Managers, executives and the board of directors must always behave in an ethical manner. Their actions and decisions should represent not only what is legal but also what is morally right.

Parties to corporate governance

Parties involved in corporate governance include the **chief executive officer, the board of directors, management and shareholders and other stakeholders** which include suppliers, employees, creditors, customers, tax authorities and the community at large.

In corporations, the shareholder delegates the rights to make decisions to the manager to act in the company's best interests. This separation of ownership from control involves a loss of effective control by shareholders over managerial decisions. Partly as a result of this separation between the two parties, a system of corporate governance is implemented to assist in aligning the incentives of managers with those of shareholders. With the significant increase in equity holdings of investors, there has been an opportunity for a reversal of the separation of ownership and control and problems have occurred because ownership is not so separated.

A board of directors often plays a key role in corporate governance. It is their responsibility to endorse the organisation's strategy, develop directional policy, appoint, supervise and remunerate senior executives and to ensure accountability of the organisation to its owners and authorities.

All parties to corporate governance have an interest, whether direct or indirect, in the effective performance of the organisation. Directors, workers and management receive salaries, benefits and reputation, while shareholders receive capital return. Customers receive goods and services; suppliers receive compensation for their goods or services. In return these individuals provide value in the form of natural, human, social and other forms of capital.

A key factor in an individual's decision to contribute in an organisation (by investing) is that they will receive a fair share of the organisations returns. If some parties receive more than their fair return then the investors may choose to leave the organisation and the organisation will collapse.

Stakeholders and corporate governance

Corporate governance structures have traditionally been a private matter between shareholders and managers. But the Sarbanes-Oxley Act (SOA) in the United States has made structures governing the conduct of the corporation a matter of federal law. Corporate governance also extends to the stakeholders of an organisation. Stakeholders include employees, customers, suppliers, government and society at large. This tie in the concept of social responsibility with corporate governance. Social responsibility is also often referred to as the **conscience** of the organisation.

Contemporary organisations recognise that they do not exist in a vacuum. They realise that they cannot be successful without the support of their stakeholders. Therefore, they also have a responsibility to treat their stakeholders with a certain amount of care.

Examples of the types of responsibilities organisations have to their stakeholders include:

➢ to deal ethically with their suppliers and customers.
➢ to treat their employees fairly and maintain a healthy working environment.
➢ to be a good "corporate citizen" by paying all taxes and complying with all government legislation and
➢ to return some of their profits to society.

Diagram 1: Corporate governance

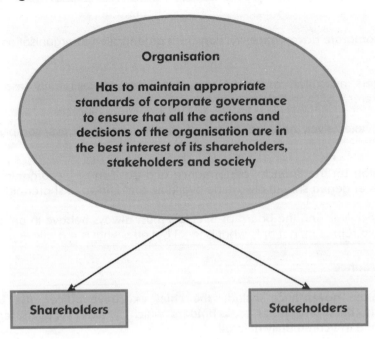

Objectives of governance

In the past few years, some high profile business frauds have been revealed such as Enron and World.Com. Therefore the public at large has lost its confidence in the reliability of financial statements as well as the integrity of management. As a result the need for corporate governance has increased to a great extent.

Due to globalisation and the separation of owners and managers, it is necessary to trust someone who is representing shareholders i.e. management. It is the duty of management to run the business in the interest of the shareholders. The shareholders should be ensured that the resources of the entity are best utilised and aimed at the achievement of the organisational objectives.

Because of the separation between the **ownership and control** of big entities, corporate governance has been introduced. It keeps a check on the working practices of those who are in control of the entity i.e. management. It sets the broad framework within which the entity must operate.

The main purpose of corporate governance is to align the interests of managers, executives and the board of directors with those charged with governance.

Objectives of governance mainly include

1. To protect the interest of the shareholders by aligning the interest of the board with the shareholders

The primary objective of corporate governance is to protect the interest of the shareholders. This requires running the business honestly and ethically.

Corporate governance aims at aligning the interest of the board of the entity with the interest of the shareholders.

2. To meet the organisational objectives by:

a) **Directing and controlling the organisation**

An organisation is a set of people chasing a certain objective. To meet these objectives the set of people should be lead by managers, who will give proper direction and control to all activities. Corporate governance entrusts various responsibilities on managers to supervise, control and direct the company. Corporate governance also provides certain rules and regulations for decision making to ensure that the person responsible for taking the decisions cannot manage/manipulate the financial statements. Governance provides assurance to the shareholders and management that the entity is chasing its objectives.

b) Ensuring effective internal control system

Those charged with governance are responsible for the adequacy and effectiveness of the internal control system. An effective internal control system provides reasonable assurance that organisation objectives are met.

Corporate governance requires the directors to design and implement an effective internal control system.

Example

International code requires that the board should review the need for the internal audit every year. Internal audit is a tool n the hands of the board to determine the adequacy and effectiveness of the internal control system over the period.

Test Yourself 1

Explain the responsibilities placed on organisations by a corporate governance structure to their stakeholders.

Test Yourself 2

What are the components of the corporate governance?

SYNOPSIS

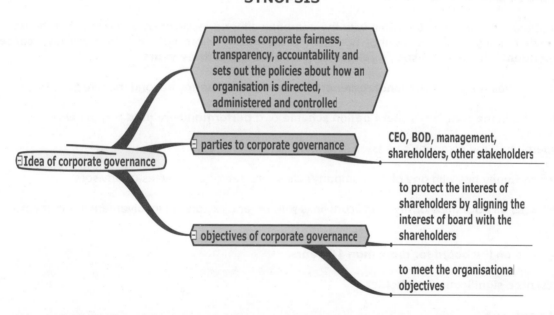

promotes corporate fairness, transparency, accountability and sets out the policies about how an organisation is directed, administered and controlled

Idea of corporate governance

parties to corporate governance — CEO, BOD, management, shareholders, other stakeholders

objectives of corporate governance — to protect the interest of shareholders by aligning the interest of board with the shareholders

to meet the organisational objectives

---

2. Recognise the extra-legal codes of corporate governance

[Learning outcome b]

The key source of corporate governance recommendations for UK listed companies is the combined code. The Listing Rules require annual reports to state how the company has applied the principles, where it has complied with the combined code and where it has not. The combined code consolidates the work of the Hampel report, the Cadbury report, the Greenbury report, the Higgs report and Smith report. It consists of principles of good governance, most of which have their own set of more detailed provisions which, in most cases, amplify the principles. The principles deal with the following areas:

2.1   Directors
2.2   Directors' remuneration
2.3   Accountability and audit
2.4   Relations with shareholders
2.5   Institutional investors

Discussion of these in turn:

2.1 Directors: This is again divided in six headings:

1. The board
2. Chairman and CEO
3. Board balance
4. Supply of information
5. Appointment of the board
6. Re-election

We need to understand certain terms before discussing the combined code requirements.

i. **What is an executive director:** An executive director is a director responsible for the administration of a company. He is primarily responsible to carry out the strategic plans and policies as established by the board of directors.

ii. **What is a non-executive director (NED):** A non-executive director is a director without day-to-day operational responsibility for the company.

iii. **What is an independent non-executive director:** The code states that a non-executive director will be 'considered independent when the board determines that the director is independent in character and judgement and there are **no relationships or circumstances** which could affect or appear to **affect the director's judgement'**.

Such relationships or circumstances would include cases where the non-executive director:

➢ is a former employee of the company or group – the NED will only be treated as independent **five years after the employment has ended.**

➢ has a material business relationship with the company either directly, or as a partner, shareholder, director or senior employee of a body that has such a material relationship – the NED will also **cease to be independent if he has had such a relationship within the last three years.**

➢ receives or has received **additional remuneration** from the company beyond the director's fee.

➢ participates in the company's **share option scheme** or a **performance-related pay scheme.**

➢ is a member of the company's **pension scheme.**

➢ has **close family ties** with any of the company's directors, senior employees or advisors.

➢ holds **cross-directorships** or has significant links with other directors via involvement in other companies or bodies.

➢ has served **on the board for more than 10 years.**

➢ represents a **significant shareholder.**

1. The board

Every listed company should be headed by an effective board which should lead and control the company.

Code provisions

➢ The board should meet regularly.

➢ A formal schedule of matters should be specifically reserved to the Board of Directors for its decision.

➢ The board should ensure that directors, especially non-executive directors, have access to independent professional advice at the company's expense where they judge it necessary to discharge their responsibilities as directors.

➢ All directors should have access to the advice and services of the company secretary, who is responsible to the board for ensuring that board procedures are complied with. Both the appointment and removal of the company secretary should be a matter for the board as a whole.

➢ All directors should bring an independent judgement to bear on issues of strategy, performance, resources, including key appointments, and standards of conduct.

> On the appointment of a person on the Board of a listed company for the first time, appropriate training should be given to him. Subsequently also the training should be given as and when necessary.

2. Chairman and CEO

The roles of chairman and chief executive officer involve two distinct tasks – running the board (chairman) and taking executive responsibility for running the company's business (CEO). The CEO is primarily responsible for executing strategic plans and adhering to policies as established by the board of directors. The CEO reports to the board of directors. In other words the chairman is responsible for making decision and the CEO is responsible for the implementation of those decisions. There should be a **clear division of responsibilities among these positions** at the head of the company which will **ensure a balance of power and authority.**

Code provisions

> The roles of chairman and CEO should not be exercised by the same individual. If a single person is to be appointed in these two posts of chairman and CEO then such decision should be publicly justified.

> The board should appoint one of the independent non-executive directors to be the senior independent director. The senior independent director should be available to shareholders if they have concerns which contact through the normal channels of chairman, chief executive or finance director has failed to resolve or for which contact through normal channel is inappropriate.

> The chairman, chief executive and senior independent director should be identified in the annual report.

3. Board balance

The number of executive and non-executive directors in the Board, including **independent non-executives,** should be properly balanced to ensure that no individual or small group of individuals can dominate the board's decisions.

Code provisions

> The board should include non-executive directors of sufficient talent and number for their views to carry significant weight in the board's decisions. **Non-executive directors should comprise not less than one third of the board.**

Tips

A **Non-executive director** is the director of a company who is not entrusted with day-to-day operational responsibility for the company, but brought in as an advisor

> The majority of non-executive directors should be independent of management and free from any business or other relationship which could materially interfere with the exercise of their independent judgement.

> Non-executive directors considered by the board to be independent in this sense should be identified in the annual report.

4. Supply of information

The board should from time to time be supplied with quality information to discharge its duties in an efficient manner.

Code provisions

> Management has an obligation to provide the board with appropriate and timely information. This does not mean that the Board has to rely only on the information provided by the management. The information provided by the management may not be enough in all circumstances and the directors should make further enquiries where necessary to take their decisions.

> The chairman should ensure that all directors are properly briefed on issues arising at board meetings.

5. Appointments to the board

There should be a formal and transparent procedure for the appointment of new directors to the board.

Code provisions

➢ Unless the board is small, a nomination committee should be established to make recommendations to the board on all new board appointments.

➢ A majority of the members of this committee should be non-executive directors, and the chairman should be either the chairman of the board or a non-executive director.

➢ The chairman and members of the nomination committee should be identified in the annual report.

6. Re-election

All directors should be required to submit themselves for re-election at regular intervals and at least every three years.

Code provisions

➢ All directors should be subject to election by shareholders at the first annual general meeting after their appointment, and to re-election thereafter at intervals of not more than three years.
➢ The names of directors submitted for election or re-election should be accompanied by sufficient biographical details and any other relevant information to enable shareholders to take an informed decision on their election.
➢ Non-executive directors should be appointed for specified terms subject to re-election and to Companies Acts provisions relating to the removal of a director.
➢ The board should set out to shareholders in the papers accompanying a resolution to elect a non-executive director why they believe an individual should be elected.
➢ The chairman should confirm to shareholders when proposing re-election that, following formal performance evaluation, the individual's performance continues to be effective and to demonstrate commitment to the role.
➢ Any term beyond six years (e.g. two three-year terms) for a non-executive director should be subject to particularly rigorous review, and should take into account the need for progressive refreshing of the board. Non-executive directors may serve longer than nine years (e.g. three three-year terms), subject to annual re-election.

2.2 Director's remuneration

1. The Level and make-up of remuneration

Levels of remuneration should be sufficient to attract and retain the directors needed to run the company successfully, but companies should avoid paying more than is necessary for this purpose. A proportion of executive directors' remuneration should be structured so as to link rewards to corporate and individual performance.

Code provisions

Remuneration policy

➢ The remuneration committee should provide remuneration packages designed to attract, retain and motivate executive directors of the quality required but should avoid paying more than is necessary for this purpose.
➢ The performance-related elements of remuneration should form a significant proportion of the total remuneration package for the executive directors and should be designed to align their interests with those of shareholders. They should also give these directors keen incentives to perform at the highest levels.

> **Example**
>
> Executive share options can be given as incentives.

➢ Executive share options should not be offered at a discount save as permitted by provisions of the Listing Rules.
➢ In designing schemes of performance related remuneration, remuneration committees should follow the provisions in Schedule A of this code.

Service contracts and compensation

➢ The remuneration committee should carefully consider what compensation commitments (including pension contributions and all other elements) their directors' terms of appointment would entail in the event of early termination. The aim should be to avoid rewarding poor performance.
➢ They should in particular consider the advantages of providing clearly in the initial contract for such compensation commitments except in the case of removal for misconduct.
➢ Notice or contract periods should be set at one year or less.
➢ If it is necessary to offer longer notice or contract periods to new directors recruited from outside, such periods should reduce after the initial period.

2. Procedure

Companies should establish a formal and transparent procedure for developing a policy entailing executive remuneration and for fixing the remuneration packages of individual directors. No director should be involved in deciding his or her own remuneration.

Code provisions

➢ To avoid potential conflicts of interest, board of directors should set up remuneration committees of independent non-executive directors to make recommendations to the board. This should be within the agreed terms of reference on the company's framework of executive remuneration and its cost. It will determine on their behalf specific remuneration packages for each of the executive directors, including pension rights and any compensation payments.

➢ Remuneration committees should **consist exclusively of non-executive** directors who **are independent of management** and free from any business or other relationship which could materially interfere with the exercise of their independent judgement.

➢ The members of the remuneration committee should be listed each year in the board's remuneration report to shareholders.

➢ The board itself or, where required by the Articles of Association, the shareholders should determine the remuneration of the non-executive directors, including members of the remuneration committee, within the limits set in the Articles of Association. Where permitted by the Articles, the board may however delegate this responsibility to a small sub-committee, which might include the chief executive officer.

➢ Remuneration committees should consult the chairman and / or chief executive officer about their proposals relating to the remuneration of other executive directors and have access to professional advice inside and outside the company.

➢ The chairman of the board should ensure that the company maintains contact with its principal shareholders about remuneration in the same way as it communicates other matters.

3. Disclosure

The Company's annual report should contain a statement of remuneration policy and details of the remuneration of each director.

Code provisions

➢ The board should report to the shareholders each year on remuneration. The report should form part of, or be annexed to, the company's annual report and accounts. It should be the main vehicle through which the company reports to shareholders on the directors' remuneration.

➢ The report should set out the company's policy relating to the executive directors' remuneration. It should draw attention to factors specific to the company.

➢ Shareholders should be invited specifically to approve an all new long term incentive schemes.

➢ The board's annual remuneration report to shareholders need not be a standard item on the agenda for the AGMs. But the board should consider each year whether the circumstances require the AGM to be invited to approve the policy set out in the report.

2.3 Relations with shareholders

1. Dialogue with institutional shareholders

Companies should be ready, where practicable, to enter into a dialogue with institutional shareholders based on mutual understanding of objectives.

2. Constructive use of the AGM

Boards should use the AGM to communicate with private investors and encourage their participation.

Code provisions

➢ Companies should count all proxy votes and, except where a poll is called, should indicate the level of proxies lodged on each resolution, the balance for and against the resolution, after it has been dealt with on a show of hands.
➢ Companies should propose a separate resolution at the AGM on each substantially separate issue, and should in particular propose a resolution at the AGM relating to the report and accounts.
➢ The chairman of the board should arrange for the chairmen of the audit, remuneration and nomination committees to be available to answer questions at the AGM.

➢ Companies should arrange for the Notice of the AGM and related papers to be sent to shareholders at least 20 working days before the meeting.

2.4 Accountability and audit

1. Financial reporting

The board should present a balanced and understandable assessment of the company's position and prospects.

Code provisions

➢ The directors should explain their responsibility for preparing the accounts, and there should be a statement by the auditors about their reporting responsibilities.
➢ The board's responsibility to present a balanced and understandable assessment extends to interim and other price-sensitive public reports and reports to regulators as well as to information required to be presented by statutory requirements.
➢ The directors should report that the business is a going concern, with supporting assumptions or qualifications as necessary.

2. Internal control

The board should maintain a safe and registered system of internal control to safeguard the shareholders' investment and the company's assets.

Code provisions

➢ The directors should, at least annually, conduct a review of the effectiveness of the group's system of internal control and should report to shareholders that they have done so. The review should cover all controls, including financial, operational and compliance controls as well as risk management.
➢ Companies which do not have an internal audit function should from time to time review the need to have one.

3. Audit committee and auditors

The board should establish formal and transparent arrangements for considering how they should apply financial reporting and internal control principles, and for how to maintain an appropriate relationship with the company's auditors.

Code provisions

➢ The board should establish an audit committee of **at least three directors, all non-executive**, with written terms of reference which deal clearly with its authority and duties.

➢ The members of the committee, a majority of whom should be independent non-executive directors, should be named in the report and accounts.

➢ The duties of the audit committee should include: keeping under review the scope and results of the audit, its cost effectiveness and the independence and objectivity of the auditors.

➢ Where the auditors also supply a substantial volume of non-audit services to the company, the committee should keep the nature and extent of such services under review, seeking to balance the maintenance of objectivity and its value for money.

2.5 Institutional investors

1. Shareholder voting: Institutional shareholders have a responsibility to make considered use of their votes.

Code provisions

➢ Institutional shareholders should endeavour to eliminate unnecessary variations in the criteria which applies to corporate governance and the performance of the companies in which they invest.

➢ Institutional shareholders should, on request, make available to their clients the information on the proportion of resolutions on which votes were cast and non-discretionary proxies lodged.

➢ Institutional shareholders should take steps to ensure that their voting intentions are being translated into practice.

2. Dialogue with companies

Institutional shareholders should be ready, where practicable, to enter into a dialogue with companies based on the mutual understanding of objectives.

3. Evaluation of governance disclosures

When evaluating companies' governance arrangements, particularly those relating to board structure and composition, institutional investors should give due weight to all relevant factors drawn to their attention.

Diagram 2: Codes of corporate governance

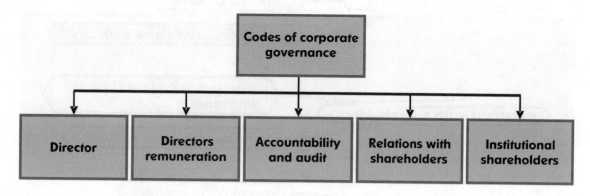

Test Yourself 3

What do the following terms mean: Executive director, Non-executive director and Independent non-executive director.

Test Yourself 4

Explain the provisions relating to the executive and non-executive directors in relation to corporate governance

SYNOPSIS

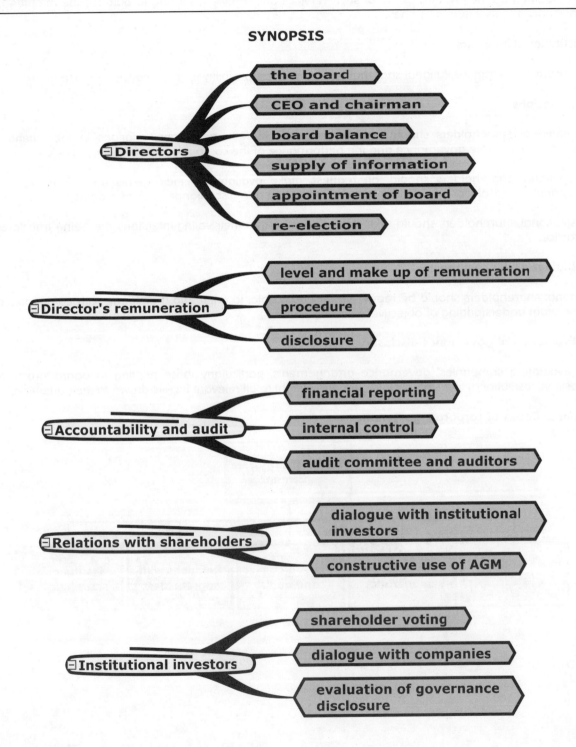

3. Identify and explain the legal regulation of corporate governance

[Learning outcome c]

Currently in the UK a legal regulation of corporate governance comparable with the combined code does not exist, apart from some aspects of the Companies Act. The new Companies Act 2006 includes some new provisions which agree with the Combined Code. Following are the important amendments made in this respect:

1. **Directors notice period:** The Companies Act 2006 requires a member's agreement where the directors notice period is more than two years. According to the Combined Code more than one year should be reduced to less or equal to one year.

2. **Removal of auditor or director:** To terminate the services of an auditor or a director a meeting of the shareholders is required.

3. **Listed Company's AGM:** The shareholders of a listed company should be given at least 21 days notice of its AGM , s307 CA 2006, unless all the member entitled to attend and vote at the meeting agree to shorter notice, s337(2

4. **Results of poll:** The listed companies can announce the results of a poll on their websites.
The Companies Act 2006 aims at defining the relations between directors, shareholders and auditors more precisely in order to provide more sound corporate governance in the following way:

1. It has ensured that only the articles of a company contain the company's constitution. It has also ensured to provide different model Articles for different types of company, eliminating as far as possible any kind of confusion.

2. The company directors should have attained the age of 16 at the time of his appointment as a director.

3. The company should have one natural person at least acting as a director.

4. Providing the directors with a code of their duties towards their companies.

5. Loans to directors' are revised and the rules for the same are more clearly stated.

6. A directors' service agreement is made available to the members.

7. It has more precisely and in more detail stated the definition of the person's who can be deemed to be connected to the director.

8. It also mentions the procedures a member should follow to take action on a director / former director of a company for the breach in his duties.

9. It also empowers the shareholders having only 5% holding in the company to demand an independent report on a poll vote and ask for the resignation report of the auditor to be put on the company's website.

10. The auditors are required to disclose the charges for the services provided other than audit.

11. It empowers the auditor of a listed company to report for his resignation.

Tips

The companies Act 2006 will be examined from June 2008.

SYNOPSIS

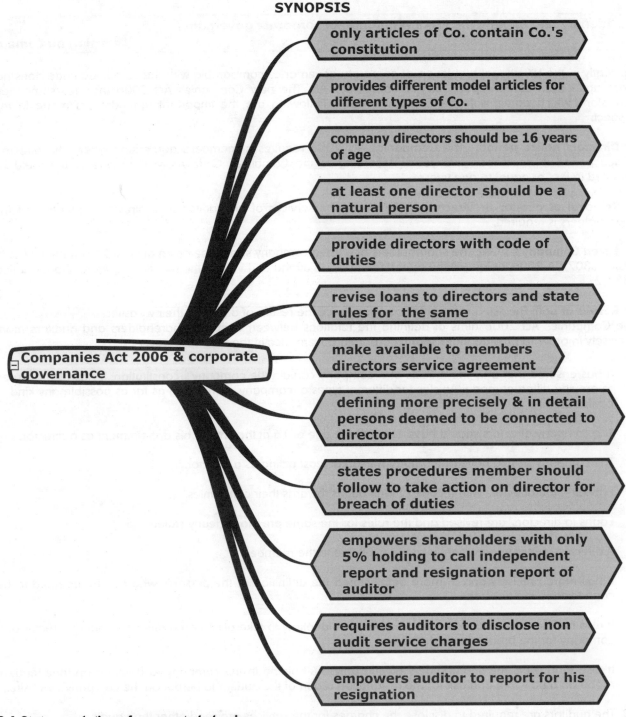

only articles of Co. contain Co.'s constitution

provides different model articles for different types of Co.

company directors should be 16 years of age

at least one director should be a natural person

provide directors with code of duties

revise loans to directors and state rules for the same

make available to members directors service agreement

defining more precisely & in detail persons deemed to be connected to director

states procedures member should follow to take action on director for breach of duties

empowers shareholders with only 5% holding to call independent report and resignation report of auditor

requires auditors to disclose non audit service charges

empowers auditor to report for his resignation

Companies Act 2006 & corporate governance

3.1 State regulation of corporate behaviour

Financial Services Authority (FSA): It is the agency which regulates the activities of the financial services industry, company markets and stock exchange of the UK. The FSA is a non government agency. It is a private company limited by guarantee. The guarantor is the HM Treasury and its finances are arranged by the financial services industry. The UK Government Treasury Department appoints the board of the FSA.

The regulation of the statute and corporate governance is affected by the FSA in the UK. To understand the working of the FSA in a better way, it is put in the following points:

1. It is an authorising body for the agency's carrying on regulated activities.
2. It regulates the activities of the exchange and clearing houses in UK
3. It approves the listing of the companies in UK
4. It makes rules, so is called a rule making body
5. It supervises
6. It has powers of enforcement

3.2 Objectives of FSA

1. maintain the reliability of the UK financial system
2. public awareness of the financial system
3. protecting the rights of consumers to an appropriate degree and creating consumer awareness towards their responsibility
4. control and reduce the scope to crime
5. supervising the rules followed by the listed companies

The FSA also plays an important role in investigating the companies involved in market abuse, insider dealing and money laundering.

3.3 Company investigations

The FSA has wide powers to investigate companies which it suspects of offences like:

1. Market abuse
2. Insider dealing
3. Money laundering
4. Misleading statements and practices
5. Breach of rules

The FSA has the power to investigate the companies with the Government's department of trade and industry that investigates liquidation of companies also.

> **Tips**
>
> Exam focus is more on the offences of insider dealing and money laundering.

SYNOPSIS

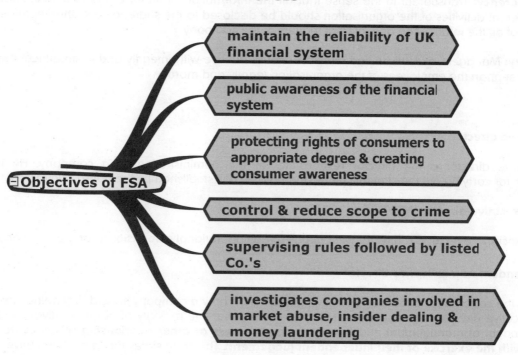

Answers to Test Yourself

Answer 1

Corporate governance also extends to the **stakeholders** of an organisation. Stakeholders include employees, customers, suppliers, government and society at large. These ties in the concept of social responsibility with corporate governance. Social responsibility is also often referred to as the **conscience** of the organisation. Contemporary organisations recognise that they do not exist in a vacuum. They realise that they cannot be successful without the support of their stakeholders. Therefore, they also have a responsibility to treat their stakeholders with a certain amount of care.

Examples of the types of responsibilities organisations have towards their stakeholders include:

➢ dealing ethically with their suppliers and customers.
➢ treating their employees fairly and maintain a healthy working environment.
➢ being a good "corporate citizen" by paying all taxes and complying with all government legislation.
➢ returning some of their profits to society.

Answer 2

Corporate governance is the system which helps investors to know the internal matters of the company. It protects the interest of the company.

The following are components of corporate governance:

➢ **Accountability:** Accountability means all the managers, directors, executives are responsible for the tasks of the organisation and they must align with the interest of shareholders.

➢ **Compliance:** Managers, executives and directors should comply with all laws and regulations

➢ **Transparency:** Transparent in the sense that all the information of financial performance, information on the different activities of the organisation should be disclosed to the shareholders. Shareholders should be aware of all the information and internal matters of the company.

➢ **Integrity:** Managers, executives and directors should behave with integrity and in an ethical manner. They should support the employees of the organisation legally and morally.

Answer 3

a) **Executive director**

The executive director is the director responsible for the administration of a company. He is primarily responsible for carrying out the strategic plans and policies as established by the board of directors.

b) **Non-executive director (NED)**

The non-executive director is a director without day-to-day operational responsibility for the company.

c) **Independent non-executive director**

At present, the code does not contain definitive guidance on how a company should determine whether or not a non-executive director is independent. It simply requires that 'the majority of non-executive directors should be independent of management and **free from any business or other relationship which could materially interfere with the exercise of their independent judgement'.** The code states that a non-executive director will be 'considered independent when the board determines that the director is independent in character and judgement and there are **no relationships or circumstances** which could affect or appear to **affect the director's judgement'.**

Such relationships or circumstances would include cases where the non-executive director:

➤ is a former employee of the company or group: the NED will only be treated as independent **five years after the employment has ended.**

➤ has a material business relationship with the company either directly, or as a partner, shareholder, director or senior employee of a body that has such a material relationship: the NED will also **cease to be independent if he has had such a relationship within the last three years.**

➤ receives or has received **additional remuneration** from the company beyond the director's fee.

➤ participates in the company's **share option scheme** or a **performance-related pay scheme.**

➤ is a member of the company's **pension scheme.**

➤ has **close family ties** with any of the company's directors, senior employees or advisors.

➤ holds **cross-directorships** or has significant links with other directors via involvement in other companies or bodies.

➤ has served **on the board for more than 10 years.**

➤ represents a **significant shareholder.**

➤ where the board has determined that the definition of independence is satisfied in relation to a NED, the board must provide a statement in its annual report that the NED is independent. Where circumstances or relationships exist that may affect the independence of a NED but the board still reaches a conclusion that the NED is independent, the board must provide an explanation in the annual report as to why it considers the NED to be independent.

Answer 4

The structure of the board of directors the combined code requires is:

➤ the board should include a **balance of executive and non-executive directors** (and in particular independent non-executive directors) such that no individual or small group of individuals can dominate the board's decision taking

➤ executive directors usually work on a full time basis for the company and may be employees of the company with specific contracts of employment.

   ✓ Companies Act (CA) 2006 requires that the terms of any such contract must be made available for inspection by the members.

   ✓ Companies Act (CA) 2006 renders void any such contract, which purports to be effective for a period of more than five years, unless it has been approved by a resolution of the company in a general meeting.

   ✓ In fact the Combined Code on Corporate Governance recommends that the maximum period for directors' employment contracts should be one year.

➤ non-executive directors do not usually have a full-time relationship with the company; they are not employees and only receive directors' fees.

➤ the role of the non-executive directors, at least in theory, is to bring outside experience and expertise to the board of directors. They are also expected to exert a measure of control over the executive directors and to ensure that the latter do not run in the company in their, rather than the company's, best interests.

➤ as part of their role as members of the board, non-executive directors should constructively challenge and help develop proposals on strategy of the company.

➤ non-executive directors should scrutinise the performance of the management in meeting agreed goals and objectives as well as should monitor the reporting of performance.

➤ they should satisfy themselves on the integrity of financial information and that financial controls and systems of risk management are robust and defensible.

> they are responsible for determining appropriate levels of remuneration of executive directors and have a prime role in appointing, and where necessary removing, executive directors, and in the succession planning.

> it is important to note that there is no distinction in law between executive and non-executive directors and the latter are subject to the same controls and potential liabilities as are the former.

Self Examination Questions

Question 1

What is corporate governance?

Question 2

Explain the provisions relating to board meetings in relation to corporate governance.

Question 3

Explain the provisions relating to board structure and accountability under the combined code of corporate governance.

Answers to Self Examination Questions

Answer 1

Corporate governance has succeeded in attracting a good deal of public interest because of its apparent importance for the economic health of corporations and society in general. However, the concept of corporate governance is poorly defined because it potentially covers a large number of distinct economic phenomenons. As a result different people have come up with different definitions that basically reflect their special interest in the field. It is hard to see that this 'disorder' will be any different in the future so the best way to define the concept is perhaps to list a few of the different definitions rather than just mentioning one definition.

Corporate governance is the system by which business corporations are directed and controlled. The corporate governance structure specifies the distribution of rights and responsibilities among different participants in the corporation, such as, the board, managers, shareholders and other stakeholders, and spells out the rules and procedures for making decisions on corporate affairs. By doing this, it also provides the structure through which the company objectives are set, and the means of attaining those objectives and monitoring performance.

Corporate governance is about promoting corporate fairness, transparency and accountability.

Answer 2

The provisions are outlined as under:

1. **Number of board meetings:** The Board should meet and conduct meetings regularly.

2. **Board agenda:** The Chairman, in consultation with the other board members and management, should establish the agenda for each Board meeting. Any director may request that an item be included on the agenda.

3. **Conduct of meetings:** Management presentations should be scheduled with a view to ensure that a substantial amount of time will be available for discussion and comments. Ample time should be scheduled to assure full discussion of important matters. Where feasible, board members should receive the agenda and supporting documentation in advance of board meetings in order to provide the Board members with an opportunity to prepare for the meetings. Any written material not available in advance should be provided to each member of the Board at the meeting.

4. **Executive sessions of independent directors:** Independent directors should meet in executive session regularly, at a time they determine to be necessary and appropriate. Shareholders or other interested persons who wish to communicate with the non-management directors may be allowed do so by contacting the Corporate Secretary.

5. **Regular attendance of non-directors at board meetings:** In general, the Chief Financial Officer and Presidents of the Company's principal business areas are expected to attend Board meetings. The Chairman may designate other individuals to attend Board meetings, as may be appropriate. It is expected that these individuals will make presentations, respond to questions by the directors, or provide counsel on specific matters within their respective areas of expertise.

6. **Board access to management and independent advisors:** Board members shall have complete and unfettered access to the Company's management. The Board expects that there will be frequent opportunities for directors to meet with the members of the management, Board and Committee meetings and in other formal or informal meetings.

7. **Outside advisors:** The Board and its committees shall have the ability, at any time, to retain independent outside financial, legal or other advisors.

Answer 3

The corporate codes have specified a range of governance mechanisms ostensibly designed to increase the accountability of senior managers to shareholders. They originated with the Report of Cadbury Committee followed by that of the Greenbury Committee on Executive Remuneration, and the Hampel Committee, after which the **combined code was produced.**

While the code is ostensibly voluntary, the **UK listing rules require companies,** as part of their annual report, **to disclose how they have complied with the code** or, if they have not done so, to **give reasons for this departure** hence the approach which has come to be known as **'comply or explain'.**

➤ The principal aspects of the code emphasise the importance of non-executive directors as a mechanism of supervision of executives, the non-executives make up at least **a third of the board.**

➤ It is required that the non-executive directors should be possessing sufficient experience, expertise and independence for their views to carry significant weight in the board's decisions.

➤ The roles of CEO and chairman of the board are separated to ensure **a balance of power and authority.**

➤ The code provides for automatic re-election of directors **at least every three years.**

➤ The code suggests the use of board sub-committees for nomination for directorship

➤ The major role has been specified for non-executive and independent directors in relation to the disclosure to shareholders of policy concerning remuneration (a 'significant element' of which should be performance-related) and of service contracts (for which there is a 'strong case' for a maximum duration of one year)

In this way, the combined code has established itself as a focal set of issues around which the governance practices of companies are measured.

Empirical research suggests that the structure of the boards of public companies and the way in which they operate have changed in response to the dissemination of the code compliance levels with the combined code are now high. For e.g., PIRC (1999) found that 87% of their sample of listed UK companies had separated the roles of Chairman and CEO, and 93% had non-executives comprising more than one-third of the board.

FRAUDULENT BEHAVIOUR

Get through intro

The actual value of a company's share is different from the nominal value of a share which is stated in the company's Memorandum. For e.g. a share which has a nominal value of £10 may be traded at a price of £100 in the stock exchange. As the company's profitability increases, the prices for its shares in the market also increase. The market value of shares fluctuates daily depending upon market conditions, company's profitability, major decisions taken by the company such as merger or takeovers, change in government policies, and competitor's actions..

An individual who can predict share price fluctuations can make huge profits or avoid losses by taking the decisions to purchase or sell shares. If an individual was in a position to have prior knowledge of how companies had performed before the information is published officially, then that individual could predict the effect of those transactions on the prices of the company's shares. For e.g., if an individual knows that a company is going to make a takeover bid, he can reasonably guess that the prices of the company's shares would go up. He can then make use of this advance knowledge by buying shares before price rise and then sell the shares later at a profit.

Such trading in shares is known as insider dealing which is discussed in detail in this Study Guide.

This Study Guide also discusses activities such as money laundering and wrongful and fraudulent trading and the consequences when directors or employees or members are considered to be guilty of these offences.

Whilst delivering your professional duties as a statutory auditor of companies, a working knowledge of all these provisions will enable you to identify if any fraudulent behaviour exists.

LEARNING OUTCOMES

a) Recognise the nature and legal control over insider dealing
b) Recognise the nature and legal control over money laundering
c) Discuss potential criminal activity in the operation, management and winding up of companies
d) Distinguish between fraudulent and wrongful trading

Introduction

> ## Case Study — Insider dealing
>
> ### Percival v Wright (1902)
>
> A member of the company (claimants) expressed willingness to the directors of the company for the sale of their shares at £12.50 each and asked the directors to find buyers for the shares. The directors themselves purchased the shares at that price. At the time of purchasing the shares, the directors knew that a third party was interested in buying the entire issued share capital at a price higher than £12.50. In fact nothing came of these negotiations. But the claimants demanded that as the directors had disclosed the possibility of resale of shares by them at a higher price, their sale of shares to the directors should be rescinded.
>
> **Court's decision:** The directors do not owe any duty to the individual shareholder. Hence they are not liable to disclose every fact to each shareholder.

In this Study Guide, we will try to understand this concept in more detail.

1. Recognise the nature and legal control over insider dealing

[Learning outcome a]

Rules on insider trading are included in Part V of the Criminal Justice Act 1993. Let us first discuss the meaning of some important terms frequently used in this Study Guide
The FSA and the High Court can impose civil penalties for insider dealing as market abuse.

1. Concept of Market Abuse:

Taking advantage of inside information. This is a fraud on other investors and will lower public confidence in the market. It may also be a breach of trust if a director uses information to gain from his position.

Control of market abuse is effected by:
- Penalising insider trading and market manipulation
- Requiring insiders to declare their trading
- Requiring companies to publish all information affecting the value of their publicly traded shares.

FSAMA 2000, s118 identifies 3 forms of insider trading as market abuse:
- Where an insider deals or attempts to deal in a qualifying investment or a related investment on the basis if inside information
- Where an insider discloses inside information to another person otherwise than in the proper course of the exercise of his employment

Where the behaviour of any person, not necessarily an insider, is based on information not generally available

2. Insider

Insider means any person who is or was connected with the Company or is deemed to have been connected with the Company, and who is reasonably expected to have access to **unpublished price sensitive information** in respect of securities of the Company or who has received or has had access to such unpublished price sensitive information.

Section 57 of Criminal Justice Act 1993 states that a person has information from insider source if:

➤ He is **primary insider** i.e. he has access to the price sensitive information by **virtue of his being the director, employee or shareholder of the issuer** of the securities.

Example

If John, an employee who worked for Company Bright Ltd learned about the takeover of Company Sunrise Ltd whilst performing his work duties.

➤ He has **acquired the insider information from the director, employee or shareholder of the issuer** of the securities.

Example

If John, an employee who worked for Company Bright Ltd, learned about the takeover of Company Sunrise Ltd whilst performing his work duties. He passes on this information to Alan, a friend of John.

---

3. **Price sensitive information**

The following shall be deemed to be price sensitive information

➤ Periodical financial results of the Company.
➤ Intended declaration of dividends (Interim and / or Final).
➤ Issue of Securities or Buy-back of Securities.
➤ Any major expansion plans or execution of new projects.
➤ Amalgamation, merger or takeover.
➤ Disposal of the whole or substantially the whole of the undertaking.
➤ Any significant changes in policies, plans or operations of the Company having material impact on the financials of the Company.

4. **Inside information:** Section 56 of Criminal Justice Act 1993 defines insider information as:

➤ **Which relates to particular security** or securities and not to securities generally

---

Example

A general statement by a director to one of his friends that the company is going to takeover some companies cannot be considered as insider information. However, information that a takeover bid would be made for a particular company say Moon Ltd, a bid amount of £50,000. As this information is very specific, it may be considered to be insider information

---

➤ **Which relates to a particular issuer** or issuers of securities and not to issuers of securities generally

---

Example

Kelly obtains information from an employee of Tiptop Ltd that Tiptop Ltd is going to declare an interim dividend immediately after the issue of 50,000 equity shares at face value of £50 each. As this information is related to a particular issuer, it is insider information.

➤ Which is **very specific or precise**
➤ Which is **not made public**
➤ Which is **likely to have significant effect on the price** of the securities

5. **Securities**

These are any financial instrument traded on a stock exchange, such as shares, bonds, debentures, warrants, futures and options.

Tips

Futures: These are a standardised, transferable, exchange-traded contract that requires a delivery of a commodity, bond, currency, or stock index, at a specified price, on a specified future date. Futures convey an obligation to buy. The exchange of assets occurs on the date specified in the contract

Options: The right, but not the obligation, to buy or sell a specific amount of a given stock, commodity, currency, or debt, at a specified price during a specified period of time

Abbreviations used in the Study Guide

CA 2006	:	Companies Act 2006
CA 2002	:	Crime Act 2002
CDDA 1986	:	Company Directors Disqualification Act 1986
IA 1986	:	Insolvency Act 1986
CJA 1993	:	Criminal Justice Act 1993

When is an insider guilty of insider dealing?

Section 52 of CJA1993 states that an individual who has information as an insider is guilty of insider dealing if:

a) He **deals in securities** that are price-effected securities on the basis of the information. In other words, if a person merely receives the information but does not deal in the price-effected securities on the basis of that information then he is not guilty of insider dealing.

b) He **encourages another person to deal in price-effected securities** in relation to the information, knowing or having reasonable cause to believe that the trading would take place.

Example

Kelly, a director of Ultra Ltd receives information that the company will be taken over by Aqua Ltd and that the shareholders will not benefit. Kelly insisted that her brother Kevin sold all his shares of Ultra Ltd immediately before the proposed takeover of the company by Aqua Ltd. Here, Kelly had encouraged Kevin to deal in price-sensitive securities hence she might be held guilty of insider trading.

---

c) He **discloses the information, other than in the proper performance of the function** of his employment, office or profession, to another person.

A person is said to be **dealing in securities** if:

➢ he **acquires or agrees to acquire** the securities whether as principal or an agent or
➢ **disposes or agrees to dispose of** the securities whether as principal or agent.

It is important to note that s.52 of CJA 1993 reads as **"an individual who has information as an insider** is guilty of insider dealing....." As the word 'individual' is used specifically hence only human person can be held liable for insider dealing. In other words, the **companies,** being legal person and not human person, **cannot be held guilty of insider dealing.**

A person has information as an insider if and only if:

a) **It is, and he knows** that it is, inside information, and
b) **He has it, and knows** that he has it, from an inside source.

When a person is not guilty of insider dealing?

An individual is not guilty of insider dealing by virtue of dealing in securities if he shows:

i. that he **did not at the time expect the dealing to result in a profit or avoidance of loss** attributable to the fact that the information in question was price-sensitive information in relation to the securities, or

---

Example

Peter, a director of Perfect Ltd, informed one of his friends, Alan that the MD of Perfect Ltd was soon going to leave the company and join another company. Alan on the basis of this information sold all his shares in Perfect Ltd. After the MD leaves the company, the value of Perfect Ltd shares fall down terribly in the market as the new MD appointed was not a person of good reputation. Thus Alan, by selling his shares avoided heavy losses. But he cannot be regarded as guilty of insider dealing because at the time of selling the shares, he did not expect that it could avoid heavy losses.

---

ii. that at the time he **believed on reasonable grounds** that the information had been **disclosed widely enough** to ensure that none of those taking part in the dealing would be prejudiced by not having the information, or

---

Example

Jimmy, an employee of Fine Liquor Ltd sold all his shares of Fine Liquor Ltd as he was given to understand that the company was closing down its business. A notification by a Government Department was published in the official Gazette that all the liquor companies in that particular where ordered to be closed with immediate effect. Here Jimmy cannot be regarded as guilty of insider dealing. This is because a notification was published in the official Gazette informing all of the closure of liquor companies. He therefore has reasonable grounds to believe that everybody knew about it.

---

iii. that he would have done what he did even if he had not had the information.

Prosecution and consequences

An individual guilty of insider dealing shall be liable

➤ On summary conviction, to a fine not exceeding the statutory maximum or **imprisonment up to a term not exceeding six months or to both**

➤ On conviction on indictment, to a **fine or imprisonment for a term not exceeding seven years or to both.**

➤ Additionally, under the CDDA 1986, any person found guilty of insider dealing may be disqualified from acting as a director of a company for **up to five years** if convicted summarily and **15 years** if convicted on indictment.

Proceedings for offences shall not be instituted in England and Wales except by or with **the consent of**

➤ The Secretary of State; or
➤ The Director of Public Prosecutions.

Other important points

➤ No contract shall be void or unenforceable by reason of contravention of s.52 of Criminal Justice Act 1993.
➤ Any provisions for civil compensation such as damages, restitution or recovery of profit are not provided in Criminal Justice Act 1993. However, if a director is held guilty of insider dealing then he breaches his fiduciary duty to the company hence he is liable to account to the company for any profits made by him.

Test Yourself 1

In January the board of directors of Big Plc decided to take over Small Plc. After the decision was taken, but before it was announced the following chain of events occurs:
i. Peter a director of Big Plc buys shares of the Small Plc
ii. Peter tells his friend Mike about the likelihood of the takeover and Mike buys shares in Small Plc
iii. At a party Peter, without actually telling her about the takeover, advises his sister Tina to buy shares in Small Plc and Tina does so.

Required:

Consider the legal position of Peter, Mike and Tina under the law relating to insider dealing.

SYNOPSIS

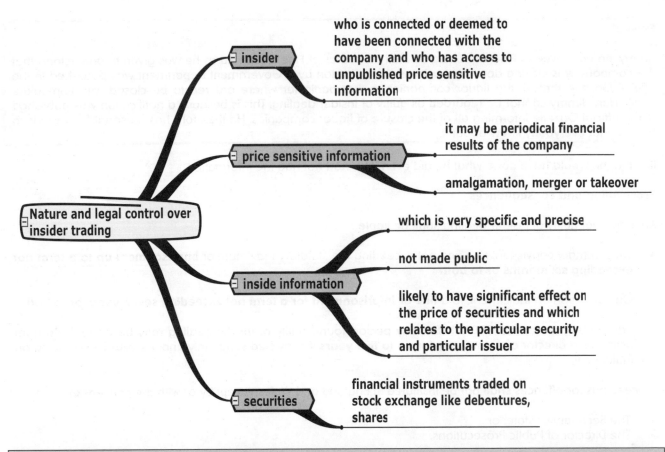

insider — who is connected or deemed to have been connected with the company and who has access to unpublished price sensitive information

price sensitive information — it may be periodical financial results of the company

amalgamation, merger or takeover

Nature and legal control over insider trading

inside information — which is very specific and precise

not made public

likely to have significant effect on the price of securities and which relates to the particular security and particular issuer

securities — financial instruments traded on stock exchange like debentures, shares

---

2. Recognise the nature and legal control over money laundering

[Learning outcome b]

Money laundering in simple terms means **'cleaning of money'**. Money laundering is the **process by which illegally obtained money is given the appearance of having originated from a legitimate source.**

Example

An individual comes into an antiques shop and offers to buy a piece of furniture for £12,000 in cash. This person may be a money launderer who then goes to another shop and sells the antique for say £9,000, being quite prepared to suffer the apparent loss. This time the criminal asks for a cheque that can then be paid innocently into a bank account, making the money look legitimate.

Money laundering allows maintaining control over the proceeds from illegal sources and ultimately provides a legitimate cover for illegal sources of income. The money laundering is regulated by the Proceeds of Crime Act 2002.

5.1 Money laundering process

Money laundering is not a single act but is in fact a process that is accomplished in three basic steps. The steps are

1. Placement

Placement refers to the physical disposal of the proceeds derived from illegal activity into an apparently legitimate business activity or property. The aims of the launderer are to remove the cash from the location of acquisition so as to avoid detection from the authorities and to then transform it into other asset forms; for e.g.: travellers cheques, postal orders, etc.

> **Example**
>
> Placement might be done by breaking up large amounts of cash into less conspicuous smaller sums that are then deposited directly into a bank account, or by purchasing a series of monetary instruments (cheques, money orders, etc.) that are then collected and deposited into accounts at another location.

2. Layering

Layering refers to the separation of illegitimate proceeds from their initial source by creating complex layers of financial transactions. This is done by repetitively transferring money from one business to another, from one place to another. Layering conceals the audit trail and provides inscrutability.

3. Integration

Integration refers to the re-injection of the laundered proceeds back into the economy in such a way that they re-enter the financial system as normal business funds.

> **Example**
>
> The launderer may choose to invest the funds into real estate, luxury assets, or business ventures.

There are also common factors regarding the wide range of methods used by money launderers when they attempt to launder their criminal proceeds. Three common factors identified in laundering operations are;

➢ The need to conceal the origin and true ownership of the proceeds
➢ The need to maintain control of the proceeds
➢ The need to change the form of the proceeds in order to shrink the huge volumes of proceeds generated by the initial criminal activity.

2.2. The offences

According to the provisions of Proceeds of Crime Act 2002, **laundering, failure to report and tipping off are criminal offences.**

1. **Laundering:** According to s.327 of this Act, a person commits an offence if he:

a) conceals criminal property
b) disguises criminal property
c) converts criminal property
d) transfers criminal property
e) removes criminal property from England and Wales or from Scotland or from Northern Ireland.

> **Example**
>
> Baker steels a precious jewel from a famous jewellery shop in London and gives it to his partner Laura to take that jewel to Dubai. Laura took the jewel to Dubai. As she has removed the criminal property from England, she has committed an offence under s 327 of Crime Act 2002.

 Tips

Disguise means to change somebody's appearance to avoid being recognised.

What is included in concealing: Concealing or disguising criminal property includes concealing or disguising its nature, source, location, disposition, movement or ownership or any rights with respect to it.

What is criminal property: According to S340 (3) of Proceeds of Crime Act 2002, the property is criminal property if:
i. It constitutes a person's benefit from criminal conduct or represents such a benefit
ii. The alleged offender knows or suspects that it constitutes or represents such a benefit.

> **Example**
>
> Rex kidnapped a child and demanded £50,000 as alimony. The parents of the child paid the money to Rex. This money is a criminal property as it is obtained from criminal conduct.

What is criminal conduct: According to S340 (2) of Proceeds of Crime Act 2002, the criminal conduct is one which:

i.   Constitutes an offence in any part of United Kingdom or

iii.   Would constitute an offence in any part of the United Kingdom if it occurred there.

A person commits an offence if he enters into or becomes concerned in an arrangement which he knows or suspects facilitates the acquisition, retention, use or control of criminal property by or on behalf of another person.

But a person does not commit such an offence if:

➢ He makes an authorised disclosure under s.338 and
➢ If the disclosure is made before he does the act and he has the appropriate consent
➢ He intended to make such a disclosure but had a reasonable excuse for not doing so.

Example

He intended to make a disclosure but before that he met an accident and went into coma for 2 months. This may constitute a reasonable excuse for not making the disclosure.

➢ The act he commits is done in carrying out a function he has relating to the enforcement of any provision of this Act or of any other enactment relating to criminal conduct or benefit from criminal conduct. Therefore police are exempt from the offence if they take possession of criminal property in the course of their official duties, and convert or transfer it pending further investigation.

2. **Failure to report:** According to s.330 of the Proceeds of Crime Act 2002, a person commits an offence **if each of the following conditions is satisfied:**

a) The first condition is that he:

➢ Knows or suspects, or
➢ Has reasonable grounds for knowing or suspecting that another person is engaged in money laundering

b) The second condition is that the information or other matter:

➢ On which his knowledge or suspicion is based, or
➢ Which gives reasonable grounds for such knowledge or suspicion came to him in the course of a business in the regulated sector

c) The third condition is that he does not make the required disclose as soon as is possible after the information comes to him.

What is required disclosure: The required disclosure is a disclosure of the information or other matter **to a nominated officer or a person authorised for the purposes of this Part by the Director General of the National Criminal Intelligence Service.**

3. **Tipping off**

The offence
A person commits an offence if

a) he knows or suspects that a disclosure falling within s.337 or 338 has been made, and
b) he makes a disclosure which is likely to prejudice any investigation which might be conducted following the disclosure within s.337 and 338.

But a person does not commit an offence if:

➢ he did not know or suspect that the disclosure was likely to be prejudicial

➢ the disclosure is made in carrying out a function he has relating to the enforcement of any provision of this Act or of any other enactment relating to criminal conduct or benefit from criminal conduct

➢ he is a professional legal adviser and the disclosure was:

✓ to (or to a representative of) a client of the professional legal adviser in connection with the giving by the adviser of legal advice to the client, or
✓ to any person in connection with legal proceedings or contemplated legal proceedings

Penalties

Section	Offence	Penalty
Section 327, 328 or 329	Money laundering	**On summary conviction,** imprisonment for a term not exceeding **six months** or ➢ to a **fine not exceeding the statutory maximum** or ➢ to both **On conviction on indictment** ➢ imprisonment for a term not exceeding **14 years** or ➢ to a fine or ➢ to both
Section 330, 331, 332 or 333	Failure to report and tipping off	**On summary conviction** ➢ imprisonment for a term not exceeding **six months** or ➢ to a **fine not exceeding the statutory maximum** or ➢ to both **On conviction on indictment** ➢ imprisonment for a term not exceeding **5 years** or ➢ to a fine or to both

Tips

Summary conviction: Summary conviction offences encompass the most minor offences in the Criminal Code. For e.g. harassing telephone calls.

Indictable offence: An indictable offence is more serious than a summary conviction offence. Conviction of an indictable offence exposes the offensor to greater penalties

Diagram 1: Money laundering

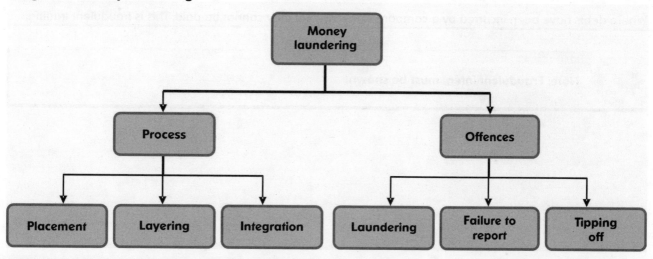

SYNOPSIS

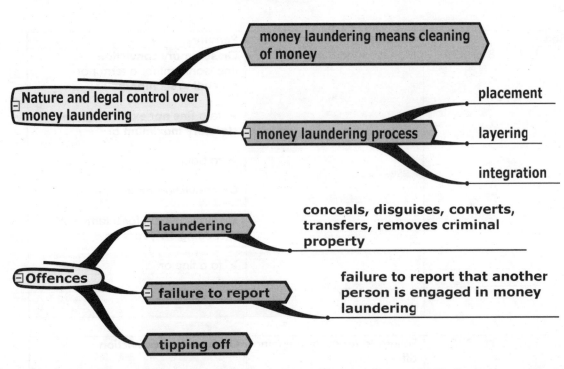

money laundering means cleaning of money

Nature and legal control over money laundering

money laundering process
- placement
- layering
- integration

Offences
- laundering — conceals, disguises, converts, transfers, removes criminal property
- failure to report — failure to report that another person is engaged in money laundering
- tipping off

---

3. Discuss potential criminal activity in the operation, management and winding up of companies

[Learning outcome c]

Directors may be held criminally liable under s.993 Companies Act 2006 if they are found guilty of fraudulent trading also criminal liability may be imposed if directors are found guilty of corporate manslaughter. However, successful prosecutions for corporate manslaughter are rare except in the case of small private companies which are effectively controlled by one director who can be regard as the alter ego of the company.

Liability of directors tends to be civil. Fraudulent trading is actionable both as a civil and a criminal offence. Other potential civil liability relates to wrongful trading and misfeasance proceedings. Sections 212, 213, 214, Insolvency Act 2006

---

4. Distinguish between fraudulent and wrongful trading

[Learning outcome d]

Fraudulent trading

According to s.213 of Insolvency Act 1986, fraudulent trading is where any **business of the company has been carried on with the intent to defraud creditors or for any fraudulent purpose.**

Example

Where debts have been incurred by a company knowing that they cannot be paid, This is fraudulent trading.

Tips

Note: Fraudulent intent must be shown.

Important points to note

➢ Where during the course of a winding-up it appears to the liquidator that fraudulent trading has occurred the liquidator may apply to the court for an order.

➢ Under the Insolvency Act 1986 **actions against directors** personally for fraudulent and wrongful trading may **only be brought by the liquidator of the insolvent company.** Prior to the Insolvency Act 1986 an individual creditor or contributory could bring an application for fraudulent trading. However, this was removed as it was thought it may encourage creditors to put improper pressure on directors to settle claims personally.

➢ Any person who was knowingly a party to fraud is to be made liable to make such contributions (if any) to the company's assets as the court thinks proper.

➢ Applications for orders in respect of fraudulent trading must be supported with the proof showing **intention to fraud.**

➢ Liability for wrongful trading under s.214 of the IA 1985 is restricted to persons who have been directors and shadow directors of the company.

Tips

Shadow director: A "shadow" director is a person who is not actually appointed as a director but in accordance with whose directions or instructions the directors of the company are accustomed to act.

➢ Where applications are brought for fraudulent trading it is usually because when the trading occurred, the company was not insolvent at that time (insolvency at the time of the trading is normally a requirement to establish wrongful trading, but not fraudulent trading.

Possible court orders

➢ Any person knowingly a party to the fraud may be made liable to contribute to the company's assets: Insolvency Act, 1986, s.213(2);

➢ Any person knowingly a party to the fraud may be convicted and imprisoned and / or fined: CA 2006, s.993;

➢ Any person knowingly a party to the fraud may be disqualified from being Director of any company by passing disqualification order up to 15 years: CDDA 1986, s.4.

Wrongful trading

According to s.214 of IA 1986, wrongful trading is where a **company has gone into insolvent liquidation** and it appears to the court that any person who has been a **director of the company knew or ought to have known** that this would occur and has **failed to take all reasonable steps to minimise the loss to the creditors.**

Example

Keeping a company in a situation where it is trading at a loss, thereby increasing the deficit to the creditors, rather than ceasing to trade or putting the company into liquidation, is clear failure to take such steps.

A director includes **any person occupying the position of director.**
The wrongful trading provisions in the law **also apply to a shadow director.**

Example

Where a UK company has local directors and a non-resident beneficial owner from whom those directors seek instructions as to how the company should be operated; the non-resident beneficial owner may also be liable under the wrongful trading provisions, even though he is not formally a director of the company.

However, a person is not deemed to be a shadow director by reason only that the directors act on advice given by him in his personal capacity.

> **Tips**
>
> Unlike fraudulent trading, wrongful trading needs no finding of 'intent to defraud'.

Wrongful trading is an action that can be taken only by a **company's liquidator**, once it has gone into insolvent liquidation. (This may be either a voluntary liquidation - known as Creditors Voluntary Liquidation, or compulsory liquidation).

Under the IA 1986 **actions against directors personally for fraudulent and wrongful trading may only be brought by the liquidator of the insolvent company. It is not available to the directors of a company whilst it continues in existence, or to other insolvency office-holders such as an administrator.**

> **Tips**
>
> A person may be held liable for wrongful trading under s.214 where:
>
> 1) The company has gone into insolvent liquidation
> 2) At some time before the commencement of the winding up of the company that person knew, or ought to have known, that there was no reasonable prospect that the company would avoid going into insolvent liquidation and
> 3) That the person was a director of the company at that time.

Possible court orders

The wrongful trading provisions under s.214 IA 1986 are **compensatory rather than punitive** and so, the amount which the directors can be called upon to contribute is the amount by which the company's assets were depleted as a result of the wrongful trading.

Director's liability is judged according to two standards as:

a) **Objective standards:** The objective standard is the minimum standard of care that all directors are required to exhibit. S214(4)provides that in determining the liability of directors the court will take into account the general knowledge, skill and experience that may reasonably be expected of a person carrying out the functions of a director.

b) **Subjective standard:** There is also a subjective element whereby the court will take into account the general knowledge, skill and experience that a director actually has.

Case Study — Wrongful trading

Re Produce Marketing Consortium Ltd (1989)

In this case, the liquidator of the company sought an order against the directors, as they had been found liable for wrongful trading they should contribute to the assets of the company. The liability argued in the case was owned jointly and severally by the directors and was a sum of £75,000 plus interest plus the cost of case.

Court's decisions: It was held that the amount to be contributed by the directors was to be assessed in the light of all circumstances of the case. The fact that the director's intention was not to commit any fraud cannot be a valid ground for giving a nominal or low figure of contribution.

The court may pass the following orders against the defaulting directors:

➢ Under wrongful trading legislation in the UK, if the company continues to trade whilst it is **insolvent** the directors of the company may become **personally liable** to contribute to the company's assets.

➢ The directors become personally liable to meet the deficit to unsecured creditors if the company's financial position is made worse by the directors continuing to trade instead of putting the company immediately into liquidation.

➢ Directors who continue to trade whilst insolvent may face disqualification under the Company Directors Disqualification Act 1986.

Defense

Directors may be able to avoid liability if they can show that they took every step to minimize the potential loss to creditors: s.214 (3) Insolvency Act 1986

Test Yourself 2

From the above discussion explain the difference between fraudulent and wrongful trading.

SYNOPSIS

Answers to Test Yourself

Answer 1

Section 52 of CJA 1993 states that an individual who has information as an insider is guilty of insider dealing if:

1. He **deals in securities** that are price-effected securities on the basis of the information.

2. He **encourages another person to deal in price-effected securities** in relation to the information, knowing or having reasonable cause to believe that the dealing would take place.

3. He **discloses the information, otherwise than in the proper performance of the function** of his employment, office or profession, to another person.

The CJA goes on to explain the meaning of some of the above terms as follows:

a) Dealing is defined in s.55 CJA according to which;

A person is said to be **dealing in securities** if:

i. he acquires or agrees to acquire the securities whether as principal or agent or
ii. **disposes or agrees to dispose of** the securities whether as principal or agent

b) Inside information is defined in s.56 as:

➢ relating to particular securities,
➢ being specific or precise,
➢ not having been made public and
➢ being likely to have a significant effect on the price of the securities

c) Section 57 states that a **person has information as an insider only if they know it is inside information and they have it from an inside source.** The section then goes on to consider what might be described as primary and secondary insiders.

The **primary insiders** cover those who get the inside information directly through either:

➢ Being a director, employee or shareholder of an issuer of securities; or
➢ Having access to the information by virtue of their employment, office or profession.

The **secondary insiders** include those who's source, either directly or indirectly, is a primary insider, as defined above.

Applying the general law to the problem scenario, one can conclude as follows:

1. Peter is an 'insider' as he receives inside information from his position as a director of Big Plc. The information fulfils the requirements for 'inside information' as it relates to;
   - particular securities i.e. the shares in Small Plc
   - is specific as it relates to takeover
   - has not been made public
   - and is likely to have a significant effect on the price of the securities.

   On that basis, Peter is clearly guilty of an offence under s.52 when he buys the shares in Small Plc.

2. When Peter tells his friend Mike about the likelihood of the take-over, he commits the second offence of disclosing information he has as an insider. Mike then becomes an insider himself and is guilty of dealing when he buys shares in Small Plc.

3. When Peter advises his sister Tina to buy shares in Small Plc, he commits the third offence under s.52 of encouraging another person to deal in price-affected securities in relation to inside information. Tina on the other hand has committed no offence for the reason that, although she has bought shares in Small Plc, she has not received any specific information and therefore cannot be guilty of dealing on the basis of such information.

   An individual guilty of insider dealing shall be liable
   a) on summary conviction, to a fine not exceeding the statutory maximum or **imprisonment up to a term not exceeding six months or to both**,
   b) on conviction on indictment, to a **fine or imprisonment for a term not exceeding seven years or to both.**

Answer 2

Distinction can be given as under:

Point of difference	Fraudulent trading	Wrongful trading
Who can be held liable?	**Any person** who was knowingly a party to the carrying on a business with intent to defraud creditors may be held liable for fraudulent trading under s.213 of the IA 1986.	Liability for wrongful trading under s.214 of the IA 1986 is **restricted to persons who have been directors and shadow directors** of the company.
Definition	According to s.213 of IA 1986, fraudulent trading is where any **business of the company has been carried on with intent to defraud creditors or for any fraudulent purpose.**	According to s.214 of IA 1986, wrongful trading is where a **company has gone into insolvent liquidation** and it appears to the court that any person who has been a **director of the company knew or ought to have known** that this would occur and **failed to take all reasonable steps to minimise the loss to the creditors.**
Fraudulent intent.	**Fraudulent intent must be shown.**	Unlike fraudulent trading, wrongful trading needs no finding of 'intent to defraud'.
Possible court order	<ul><li>Any person knowingly a party to the fraud may be made liable to contribute to the company's assets: Insolvency Act, 1986, s.213(2),</li><li>Any person knowingly a party to the fraud may be convicted and imprisoned and / or fined: CA 2006, s. 993,</li><li>Any person knowingly a party to the fraud may be disqualified from being Director of any company up to 15 years by passing disqualification order: CDDA 1986, s.4.</li></ul>	<ul><li>The directors of the company which continues to trade whilst it is insolvent may become personally liable to contribute to the company's assets.</li><li>The directors become personally liable to meet the deficit to unsecured creditors if the company's financial position is made worse by the directors continuing to trade instead of putting the company immediately into liquidation.</li></ul> Directors who continue to trade whilst insolvent may face disqualification under the CDDA 1986.

Quick Quiz

Sate true or false

1. A company cannot be held guilty of insider trading.

2. For adjudging a director of fraudulent trading, fraudulent intent must be shown.

3. Wrongful trading needs finding of 'intent to defraud'

4. Insider information is one which is likely to have a significant effect on the price of the securities.

Answers to Quick Quiz

1. **True**, because only an individual can be found criminally liable of insider trading and company is an artificial person so a   company cannot be held guilty of insider trading. However, under FSAMA 2000, which deals with civil liability, a company may be an insider

2. **True**.

3. **False,** Wrongful trading does not need findings of 'intent to defraud'.

4. **True**.

Self Examination Questions

Question 1

Explain wrongful trading.

Question 2

Greg and Nancy have founded a fruit business named Fresh Fruits Ltd. They have been the sole directors since its inception in 1995. The business had never earned enough profits to declare a dividend and was not successful. It has only managed to carry on transactions by using its £25,000 overdraft facility with the bank.

In January 20X2, Fresh Fruits Ltd made a large contract with the Apple futures market, and by June 20X2, it had lost £70,000 on the contract. Greg and Nancy disguised the loss and ignored the limit of the overdraft and delayed the payment on their outstanding contracts. They decided to enter into another contract to cover their losses but unfortunately that contract failed by September and the business lost another £45,000. In spite of this, both Greg and Nancy thought carelessly that they can recoup everything in the following summer's mango market. Again, in this contract they lost £25,000.

In October 20X3, Greg and Nancy applied to have Fresh Fruits Ltd wound up, owing debts of £95,000.
The realisable value of the Company's assets was £20,000.

Analyse from above situation, Greg and Nancy's liability for either fraudulent or wrongful trading under the Insolvency Act 1986 and state their potential liability to their various creditors.

Answers to Self Examination Questions

Answer 1

Wrongful trading occurs when the directors of a company have continued to trade a company past the point when they:

➢ knew, or ought to have concluded that there was no reasonable prospect of avoiding insolvent liquidation; and

➢ they did not take every step with a view to minimising the potential loss to the company's creditors.

The wrongful trading provisions also apply to a shadow director.

Under the IA 1986 **actions against directors for fraudulent and wrongful trading may only be brought only by the liquidator of the insolvent company.** It is not available to the directors of a company whilst it continues in existence, or to other insolvency office-holders such as an administrator.

Under wrongful trading legislation in the UK, the **court may pass the following orders against a director liable of fraudulent trading:**

> The court may hold the concerned directors **personally liable** to contribute to the company's assets.

> The directors become personally liable to meet the deficit to unsecured creditors if the company's financial position is made worse by the directors continuing to trade instead of putting the company immediately into liquidation.

> Directors who continue to trade whilst insolvent may face disqualification under the Company Directors Disqualification Act 1986.

Answer 2

Fraudulent trading

According to s.213 of Insolvency Act 1986, fraudulent trading is where any **business of the company has been carried on with intent to defraud creditors or for any fraudulent purpose.** It must have **intent** to **defraud the creditors.**

If there is any fraudulent trading a liquidator may apply to the court for an order.

Prior to the Insolvency Act, 1986 an individual creditor or contributory could bring an application for fraudulent trading, but this was removed because with this creditors may pressure the directors to settle their personal claims.

Wrongful trading

According to s. 214 of Insolvency Act 1986, wrongful trading is where a **company has gone into insolvent liquidation** and it appears to the court that any person who has been a **director of the company knew or ought to have known** that this would occur and **failed to take all reasonable steps to minimise the loss to the creditors.**

A director is any person holding the position of director and these provisions also applies to a shadow director. Wrongful trading does not need 'intent to fraud'.

Under UK legislation of wrongful trading, if the company continues to trade even if it is insolvent, then directors of the company may become personally liable to contribute to the company's assets and directors may be disqualified under the Company Directors Disqualification Act 1986 if they still continue the business in the insolvent stage.

In the above situation, it is not enough to state that Greg and Nancy have committed **fraudulent trading** as they seriously thought that they could trade in such a way to overcome their losses. They did disguise the debts of the company, but they did not do this to benefit themselves. There should be **intent to defraud** the creditors in case of fraudulent trading, but these two directors did not intentionally defraud the creditors for their benefit.

It is clear from above that Greg and Nancy are **liable for the wrongful trading** as they continued the business even though it was known to the directors that the business was in loss and they did not take any steps to minimise the company's loss. So Fresh Fruits Ltd suffered a greater loss than if the company had wound up at an earlier dare.

In reference to the above, the directors Greg and Nancy will be personally liable for any debt from the June, 20X2 as by that time it was reasonable clear that the company was in insolvent position. However, in **Re Produce Marketing Consortium Ltd 1989, it** was held that the amount to be contributed by the directors is to be assessed in the light of all circumstances of the case. Hence the amount to be contributed by the directors to the assets of the company will be decided taking into consideration the relevant circumstances.

In addition, the directors may also hold liable to be disqualified as the company directors under Company Directors Disqualification Act 1986.

A

Accumulated distributable profits – These are profits brought forward from previous years after setting off any realised losses of previous years. Realised loss also includes depreciation, debited against profits - E3.10

Agent – He is a person employed to do any act for another or to represent another in dealing with a third person, the person for whom such act is done, or who is so represented, is called the principal. - D1.2

Auctioneer – He is an agent who sells property goods at a public auction - D1.5

B

Bonus shares - These are the free shares of stock given to current shareholders, based upon the number of shares that a shareholder owns - E3.11

Breach - means breaking or violating a law, right, or duty, either by commission or omission - B3.7

Breach of contract - is an unjustified failure to fulfill the duties under the contractual terms when the performance is due. - B3.7

Broker – He is an agent who is employed by a principal to enter into contracts for sale or purchase on behalf of the principal - D1.4

C

Called up capital: - it is the part of the issued capital which has been called up or demanded by the company - E3.10

Charge – it is a right given to the creditor/lender to have a designated asset of the debtor appropriated to the discharge of the indebtedness, but not involving any transfer either of possession or ownership - E2.8

Commercial agent – He is a self-employed intermediary who has continuing authority in relation to the sale or purchase of goods - D1.5

Condition – it is a stipulation essential to the main purpose of the contract - B2.9

Corporate governance – It is the system by which business corporations are directed and controlled - H1.2

Crystallisation – It is the conversion of a floating charge into a fixed charge - E2.9

D

Debentures – It is an instrument under seal, evidencing a deed, the essence of it being the admission of indebtedness - E2.3

Deferred shares – These are the shares which are generally issued to company founders and on which dividends can not be paid until dividends have been distributed to all other classes of shareholders. - E3.5

Del credere agent – He is an agent who, for some extra commission, assures the principal that the other party will perform their contractual obligation - D1.4

Delegated legislation – it is the law made by executive authority acting under powers given to them by the primary legislation in order to implement and administer the requirements of various acts - A2.8

Director – It includes any person occupying the position of director by whatever name called - F1.2

Discharge of contract by agreement - When both parties agree to terminate the contract, this is called - B3.2

Discharge of contract by frustration - When a contract is terminated because it became impossible or illegal to perform the contract, this is called a - B3.3

Distributable profits – These are accumulated, realised profits, so far as not previously utilised by distribution or capitalisation, less accumulated realised losses, so far as not previously written off in a reduction or reorganisation of capital duly made s263 (3). - E3.10

Dividend – It is the stockholders' share of the profits left after the company sets aside funds to finance operations, expansion and modernisation - E3.9

Divisible contract - part performance of one party will lead to a partial liability for the other party - B3.4

E

Employee – He is an individual who has entered into or works under a contract of employment - C1.2

Employer – He is any person or organisation for whom an individual performs or has performed any service, of whatever nature, as an employee - C1.2

Entire contract - the contractual liability of one party does not begin until the other party has completed its performance of the contract - B3.4

Estate agent – He is an intermediary who is entrusted with the job of finding a buyer for the principal's property - D1.5

Expressed terms – These are explicitly agreed between the employee and employer. - C1.8

F

Factor – He is an agent who is entrusted with the possession and control of the goods to be sold by him for his principal - D1.4

Firm. - Persons who have entered into partnership with one another are collectively called - D2.2

Fixed charge –It is created on the specific asset i.e. asset is determined and defined at the time of creating the charge. - E2.8

Fixed charge: - A charge held over specific assets. - G1.12

Floating charge – It is a charge that does not affect the assets charged until some event 'crystallises' (fixes) the charge to a certain point in time - E2.8

Floating charge: - A charge held over general assets of a company - G1.13

Fraudulent trading –Where any business of the company has been carried on with the intent to defraud creditors or for any fraudulent purpose - H2.11

G

Gazette – It is the official newspaper of record which contains various statutory notices and advertisements. - G1.5

I

Implied term – it is one in which even though not expressed in words, they are part of the contract due to implication. - B2.6

Injunctions – These are court orders which prevent a party from carrying out a certain act. An injunction is an equitable measure which directs a party not to break its contract. - B3.22

Insider – He is a person who is or was connected with the Company or is deemed to have been connected with the Company, and who is reasonably expected to have access to unpublished price sensitive information in respect of securities of the Company or who has received or has had access to such unpublished price sensitive information. - H2.2

Integration – It is the re-injection of the laundered proceeds back into the economy in such a way that they re-enter the financial system as normal business funds - H2.6

L

Law – a rule or body of rules of conduct inherent in human nature and essential and binding upon human society. - A1.2

Law - the rules established by a governing authority to institute and maintain orderly co-existence - A1.2

Layering – it is the separation of illegitimate proceeds from their initial source by creating complex layers of financial transactions. This is done by repetitively transferring money from one business to another, from one place to another - H2.6

Limited partnership – it is a partnership formed by two or more persons / entities, one or more of whom are general partners and one or more of whom are limited partners - D2.3

Liquidated damages - when the parties to a contract agree to the payment of a certain sum as a fixed and agreed upon compensation for not doing certain things specifically mentioned in the agreement, the sum is called - B3.18

Liquidation – it is a legal process by which the affairs of a limited company are wound up - G1.3

M

Material breach - is any failure to perform that permits the other party to the contract to either compel performance, or collect damages because of the breach. - B3.8

Meeting – it means coming together of more than one person - F3.2

Minor breach - is a partial breach or an immaterial breach - B3.8

Minutes – They are the record of the proceedings of the meeting - F2.4

N

Novation – it means the substitution of a new contract for an old one; or the substitution of one party in a contract with another party - D4.4

O

Offer - is a definite promise to be bound by particular terms and it must be capable of acceptance - B1.15

P

Partners - persons who have entered into partnership with one another are individually called - D2.2

Partnership - the relation which subsists between persons carrying on a business in common with a view of profit. - D2.2

Placement – It is the physical disposal of the proceeds derived from illegal activity into an apparently legitimate business activity or property - H2.6

Precedent – i t is a legal case establishing a principle or rule which a court may need to adopt when deciding subsequent cases with similar issues or facts. - A2.2

Pre-incorporation contract – it is a contract purported to be made by a company or its agent at a time before the company has received its certificate of incorporation - D4.4

Prima facie - is used to describe the apparent nature of something at first glance. - B3.15

Promoter - a person who as principal, procures or aids in procuring the incorporation of a company - D4.2

Public company –it is a company in which the memorandum of the company states that it is a public company & has complied with the appropriate registration requirements .

Q

Quantum meruit – it is the amount one deserves or what the job is worth - B3.5

R

Realised profits and losses – These are treated as such in accordance with accounting principles, including accounting standards generally accepted at the time the accounts are prepared. It does not include profits arising on revaluation of non current assets - E3.10

Redundancy – It is simply dismissal from employment because the job or the worker has been deemed no longer necessary. - C2.7

Redundancy pay – It is the amount which is paid at the time of dismissal with reference to age, length of service, final remuneration - C2.11

Representation – it is a pre-contractual statement of fact made to induce another person to enter into a contract. - B2.2

Repudiate - means to reject or to disclaim - B3.10

Repudiatory breach of contract. - Where a party to a contract, either by words or by conduct, indicates that he does not intend to honour his contractual liability, - B3.10

Resolution – It is an agreement or decision made by the directors or members (or a class of members) of a company. When a resolution is passed, the company is bound by it. - F3.10

S

Salaried partner - A partner who has no right to participate in the profits and losses of the partnership and who is paid salary by the firm is - D2.8

Secretary - It is an officer of the company who is entrusted with the general administrative duties of the company. - F2.2

Shadow" director – It is a person who is not actually appointed as a director but in accordance with whose directions or instructions the directors of the company are accustomed to act. - F1.2

Standard partnership - is a contractual association of two or more persons or entities to operate a common enterprise and to share in the management and profits and losses of the stipulated business. - D2.2

T

Term. - Where the statement is of such major importance that the promisee would not have entered into the agreement without it will be construed as - B2.2

The limited liability partnership - is a form of partnership that differs from standard partnership and limited partnership in that all partners have a limited liability - D2.3

Tribunal – it is an assembly to conduct judicial business - A1.12

U

Unliquidated damages - If the provisions are considered to be a penalty by the court, it will set aside the so-called liquidated damages and will award damages in the normal way, -

Uunfair dismissal - When an employee is dismissed from the job and the employer doesn't have a valid reason for dismissing him / her or if an employer has not used proper or fair procedure to dismiss the employee. - C2.2

V

Valuable consideration- it may consist either in some right, interest, profit, or benefit accruing, to one party, or some forbearance and detriment, loss or responsibility given, suffered or undertaken by the other - B1.30

Voidable contracts – these are contracts which may be avoided, that is, set aside, by one of the parties. - B1.7

W

Warranty – it is stipulated collateral to the main purpose of the contract - B2.10

Wrongful trading - Where a company has gone into insolvent liquidation and it appears to the court that any person who has been a director of the company knew or ought to have known that this would occur and has failed to take all reasonable steps to minimise the loss to the creditors. - H2.11

E

F

G

H

I

J